JESUS' ATTITUDE TOWARDS THE LAW

Jesus' Attitude towards the Law

A Study of the Gospels

WILLIAM R. G. LOADER

WILLIAM B. EERDMANS PUBLISHING COMPANY
GRAND RAPIDS, MICHIGAN / CAMBRIDGE, U.K.

Originally published by Mohr Siebeck
© 1997 J. C. B. Mohr (Paul Siebeck), Tübingen

This edition © 2002 Wm. B. Eerdmans Publishing Co.

Wm. B. Eerdmans Publishing Co.
255 Jefferson Ave. S.E., Grand Rapids, Michigan 49503 /
P.O. Box 163, Cambridge CB3 9PU U.K.

Printed in the United States of America

07 06 05 04 03 02   7 6 5 4 3 2 1

ISBN 0-8028-4903-2

www.eerdmans.com

Preface

The present work has come into being over a number of years. In the jumps and starts of its career, fitted in amid teaching and semester breaks, it owes its origin substantially to two periods of study leave, taken in 1991 and 1995. For these I am especially grateful to my two employers, the Perth Theological Hall of the Uniting Church in Australia and Murdoch University. Their very adequate study leave provisions enabled me to travel to spend time poring over the volumes of the Theologicum of the Evangelische and Katholische Faculties of Tübingen University and taking advantage of borrowing rights from the University library. I am especially grateful to Professor Dr Martin Hengel and Professor Dr Hermann Lichtenberger, who as Directors welcomed me as guest of the Institut für Antikes Judentum und Hellenistische Religionsgeschichte in 1991 and 1995 respectively. The study leave grants and a Special Research Grant from Murdoch University enabled me also to purchase research resources and to spend uncluttered time in the intensity of reading and writing at home in Perth.

My thanks are also due to Professor Dr Martin Hengel, Professor Dr Otfried Hofius, as Editors, and to Herrn Georg Siebeck, as Manager of J. C. B. Mohr (Paul Siebeck), who resolved to publish the book in the distinguished series, *Wissenschaftliche Untersuchungen zum Neuen Testament*. Behind the scenes many people have helped with technical and other advice. My colleague, Revd Dr John Prendiville SJ, read the manuscript and made helpful comments on style and content. Shaughan Daniel gathered valuable research material. Moira Main helped key in data for the Indices.

Finally I should like to thank my parents-in-law in Esslingen, Eva Schwarz and the late Pfarrer Hans Schwarz, who provided me with warm hospitality during my research visits. To my wife, Gisela, gratitude beyond words for sustaining companionship and patience.

I dedicate this work to all who seek for peace and greater understanding among human communities, not least, among the sons and daughters of Abraham.

July 1997   William R. G. Loader
Perth, Western Australia

Table of Contents

Introduction

In the present study I am concerned with Jesus' attitude towards Torah as it is presented in the gospels. The aim is not to homogenise disparate material into a single picture, but to consider the various ways in which each individual gospel depicts this attitude. This aim belongs within a broader interest which includes the traditions which lie behind the gospels and, ultimately, what we can retrieve about the attitude of the historical Jesus himself. But these are not the subject of the present investigation. Its focus is on the gospels themselves. Each portrays, directly or indirectly, an image of Jesus' attitude towards Torah.

I have chosen to include within my consideration, not only the Gospels of Matthew, Mark, Luke and John, but also the hypothetical document Q, as reconstructed by the SBL International Q Project,[1] the Coptic Gospel of Thomas and fragments of Gospels or significant additional material relevant to the theme found in some Gospel manuscripts (notably Luke 6:5D and John 7:53 – 8:11). In this I assume that both Q and Mark were sources for Matthew and Luke.

In using the word, attitude, in this investigation, I am referring to an assessment of the tendencies reflected in the received material. This is far from a reconstruction of the inner attitude of the historical Jesus or of the mind of a tradition bearer or even that of an evangelist about such an attitude. Such inner thoughts are not available to the historian and difficult enough to assess even during someone's lifetime. This study must operate within the limitations which are inevitable for the historian. It will seek, therefore, to investigate only the attitude reflected in the preserved material. Nevertheless I shall assume some coherence between what an author writes and what the author intends and consequently I ask the reader's indulgence that, to avoid clumsy qualifications, I resort to the shorthand of speaking, for example, of Matthew's attitude or the attitude of Matthew's Jesus.

Torah may be defined as the Law of Moses, preserved in the Pentateuch.

---

[1] J. M. Robinson et al., "The International Q Project," *JBL* 109 (1990), pp. 499–501; 110 (1991), pp. 494–498; 111 (1992), pp. 500–508; 112 (1993), pp. 500–506; 113 (1994), pp. 495–500; 114 (1995), pp. 475–485.

Such a definition is however both too narrow and too broad.[2] We might also speak of Jesus' attitude towards his own culture and religion. Mostly the concern of our study is with the laws and provisions within the Pentateuch, seen as a whole. While there may be slight variations from gospel to gospel, the Law is commonly understood to be the Mosaic Law enshrined in the Pentateuch. That Law presents itself as the expression of God's will. It demands to be applied and to be obeyed and forms the basis of Jewish identity as the people of God.

Research over the past two decades has underlined the diversity of pre-70 Judaism.[3] This diversity relates, in particular, to attitudes of various groups towards Torah. It is no longer meaningful to speak simply of three or four parties, Sadducees, Pharisees, Essenes and Zealots, or to make sharp distinctions between Palestinian and Diaspora Judaism. Simplistic ideological portrayals of Judaism as a religion of self righteousness no longer stand. Nor is it possible to presume that later rabbinic writings necessarily reflect the Judaism of the first century or that its attributions necessarily reflect historical reality.

The diverse Judaisms were mostly united in commitment to Torah, but both in extent and in interpretation there was wide variety. Pentateuchal laws were central, but each group had both its additions and its interpretations, although often the difference between these was obscured. For instance, the author of 11QTemple will have seen himself as faithful to Torah, despite radical revisions and rewriting of the Pentateuchal laws. Any attempt to

---

[2] See the discussion in P. S. Alexander, "Jewish Law in the Time of Jesus: Towards a Clarification of the Problem," in *Law and Religion. Essays on the Place of the Law in Israel and Early Christianity*, edited by B. Lindars, (Cambridge: Clarke, 1988), pp. 44–58; K. Müller, "Gesetz und Gesetzeserfüllung im Frühjudentum," in *Das Gesetz im Neuen Testament*, edited by K. Kertelge, (Freiburg: Herder, 1986), pp. 11–27; K. Müller, "Beobachtungen zum Verhältnis von Tora und Halacha in frühjüdischen Quellen," in *Jesus und das jüdische Gesetz*, edited by I. Broer, (Stuttgart: Kohlhammer, 1992), pp. 105–134; P. Richardson and S. Westerholm, *Law in Religious Communities in the Roman Period. The Debate over Torah and Nomos in Post-Biblical Judaism and Early Christianity*, Studies in Christianity and Judaism 4, (Waterloo: Wilfred Laurier Univ. Pr., 1991).

[3] See the works listed in the previous note and also *Early Judaism and its Modern Interpreters*, edited by R. A. Kraft and G. W. E. Nickelsburg, (Atlanta: Scholars, 1986); E. P. Sanders, *Paul and Palestinian Judaism*, (London: SCM, 1977); *Jewish Law from Jesus to the Mishnah*, (London: SCM; Philadelphia: Trinity, 1990); *Judaism: Practice and Belief 63 BCE – 66CE*, (London: SCM; Philadelphia: Trinity, 1992); J. Neusner, *Judaism: The Evidence of the Mishnah*, (Chicago: Univ. of Chicago Pr., 1981); *Judaism in the Beginning of Christianity*, (London: SPCK, 1984); *Judaic Law from Jesus to the Mishnah. A Systematic Reply to Professor E. P. Sanders*, South Florida Studies in the History of Judaism 84, (Atlanta: Scholars, 1993); M. Hengel and R. Deines, "E. P. Sanders' 'Common Judaism', Jesus, and the Pharisees," *JTS* 46 (1995), pp. 1–70.

investigate the various images in the gospels of Jesus' attitude towards the Law must take this diversity into account. It will simply not do, for instance, to interpret the antitheses forbidding divorce and remarriage or oaths in Matthew's Sermon on the Mount as necessarily expressing an attitude of sovereignty over, let alone, rejection of Torah, when such champions of Torah interpretation as the writer of the Damascus Document and the Essenes could make similar claims.

The present research is timely in the light of these advances in our understanding of Judaism. It also comes at a time when New Testament scholarship has been revisiting the issue of the 'partings of the ways' with great vigour. The revised appreciation of Judaism has produced a plethora of new works on Paul, especially, on Paul and the Law. Beside these, there is a growing body of research focusing on the diversity within early Christianity of responses to Judaism and to Torah. The two are not identical; or, at least, that is one of the issues. Related is the attitude to and use of scriptures. This study, while taking into account the wider issues of relations between Christians (Jews and Gentiles) and Jews (other Jews), and of the use of scripture, focuses more narrowly on one particular aspect of the debate: how did people portray Jesus' attitude towards the Law?

The issue has been the subject of study from a variety of perspectives. Rather than review these contributions here, I shall deal with them directly in relation to the different gospels. A number of studies have emerged recently which investigate attitudes towards Torah in individual gospels. These include Sariola on Mark (1990);[4] Wilson (1983),[5] Klinghardt (1988)[6] and Salo (1991)[7] on Luke; Pancaro (1975)[8] and Kotila (1988)[9] on John. Apart from Barth's treatment (1960),[10] most treatments of the theme in Matthew

---

[4] H. Sariola, *Markus und das Gesetz. Eine redaktionsgeschichtliche Untersuchung*, Annales Academiae Scientiarum Fennicae Dissertationes Humanarum Litterarum, (Helsinki: Suomalainen Tiedeakatemia, 1990).

[5] S. G. Wilson, *Luke and the Law*, SNTSMS 50, (Cambridge: CUP, 1983).

[6] M. Klinghardt, *Gesetz und Volk Gottes. Das lukanische Verständnis des Gesetzes*, WUNT 32, (Tübingen: J. C. B. Mohr [Paul Siebeck], 1988).

[7] K. Salo, *Luke's Treatment of the Law. A Redaction-Critical Investigation*, Annales Academiae Scientiarum Fennicae Dissertationes Humanarum Litterarum 57, (Helsinki: Suomalainen Tiedeakatemia, 1991).

[8] S. Pancaro, *The Law in the Fourth Gospel. The Torah and the Gospel, Moses and Jesus, Judaism and Christianity according to John*, SuppNovT 42, (Leiden: Brill, 1975).

[9] M. Kotila, *Umstrittene Zeuge. Studien zur Stellung des Gesetzes in der johanneischen Theologiegeschichte*, Annales Academiae Scientiarum Fennicae Dissertationes Humanarum Litterarum 48, (Helsinki: Suomalainen Tiedeakatemia, 1988).

[10] G. Barth, "Das Gesetzesverständnis des Evangelisten Matthäus," in G. Bornkamm, G. Barth, H. J. Held, *Überlieferung und Auslegung im Matthäusevangelium* WMANT 1,

belong within wider studies; for instance, those of Overman (1990)[11] and Saldarini (1994).[12] On Q the major treatment is that of Kosch (1989)[13] and, apart from that, the articles by Tuckett (1988)[14] and Kloppenborg.[15] There are no major treatments of the theme in Thomas and other so-called non-canonical gospels.

Beside these studies are a number which consider the three synoptic gospels. These include the work of Berger (1972),[16] Hübner (1973),[17] Banks (1975)[18] and Vouga (1985).[19] Berger's massive work (631pp.) deals with Mark and Markan parallels, but covers only the great commandments;the encounter with the rich man; the confrontation over *corban* and over the commandment to honour parents; and divorce; but offers a rich resource of non biblical parallel material. Hübner's study is concerned with the development of the synoptic tradition and the extent to which in Matthew and Luke it shows signs of having been made to conform more to Torah. He limits his study to Matt 5:17–20; the Matthean antitheses; the sabbath controversies; and the purity controversy of Mark 7:1–23 and parallels. The study of Banks is more comprehensive in its treatment of the material, dividing it according to form: incidental sayings and actions; debates and controversies; and extended teaching. Banks's concern is with the historical

---

(Neukirchen-Vluyn: Neukirchener, 1960, 2nd edn, 1970), pp. 54–154; English: G. Barth, "Matthew's Understanding of the Law," in G. Bornkamm, G. Barth, H. J. Held, *Tradition and Interpretation in Matthew*, (London: SCM, 1963, 2nd edn., 1982), pp. 58–164.

[11] J. A. Overman, *Matthew's Gospel and Formative Judaism. The Social World of the Matthean Community*, (Minneapolis: Fortress, 1990).

[12] A. J. Saldarini, *Matthew's Christian-Jewish Community*, (Chicago: Univ. of Chicago Pr., 1994).

[13] D. Kosch, *Die eschatologische Tora des Menschensohnes: Untersuchungen zur Rezeption der Stellung Jesu zur Tora in Q*, NovTest et OrbAnt 12, (Göttingen: Vandenhoeck und Ruprecht, 1989).

[14] C. M. Tuckett, "Q, the Law and Judaism," in *Law and Religion. Essays on the Place of the Law in Israel and Early Christianity*, edited by B. Lindars, (Cambridge: Clarke, 1988), pp. 90–101.

[15] J. S. Kloppenborg, "Nomos and Ethos in Q," in *Christian Origins and Christian Beginnings In Honor of James M. Robinson*, edited by J. E. Goehring et al., (Sonoma: Polebridge, 1990), pp. 35–48.

16 K. Berger, *Die Gesetzesauslegung Jesu . Ihr historischer Hintergrund im Judentum und im Alten Testament. Teil I: Markus und Parallelen*, WMANT 40, (Neukirchen-Vluyn: Neukirchener, 1972).

[17] H. Hübner, *Das Gesetz in der synoptischen Tradition*, (Witten: Luther-Verlag, 1973; 2nd edn., Göttingen: Vandenhoeck und Ruprecht, 1986).

[18] R. Banks, *Jesus and the Law in the Synoptic Tradition*, SNTSMS 28, (Cambridge: CUP, 1975).

[19] F. Vouga, *Jésus et la Loi selon la Tradition synoptique*, (Genève: Labor et Fides, 1988).

Jesus and with arguing the dominant influence in the various traditions of the christological dimension, namely Jesus' independent authority. Vouga limits himself to six conflict stories (the two sabbath conflicts, and the episodes dealing with purity, divorce, the rich man, and the great commandments) and the antitheses of the Sermon on the Mount. In each he is concerned to reconstruct tradition and identify redaction, but also to relate such reconstruction to stages in the development of early Christian communities (the conservative Jerusalem church, Jewish Christian Hellenistic itinerant missionaries, Palestinian Jewish Christian missionaries; and the Palestinian Jewish Christian apocalyptic movement).

The procedure which I have followed in this book offers a significant alternative to the method followed by previous studies. I am convinced that it is not adequate to seek to identify the stance of a writing by dealing only with the more obvious passages where the Law comes into question. The way a writing portrays Jesus' attitude towards the Law is bound up with a number of other issues, not least, issues of authority and christology. It is also related to the way therelevant material functions within its narrative context. I shall, therefore, be considering each gospel sequentially; that is, I shall examine the way the issue of Jesus' attitude appears, disappears and reappears as the narrative unfolds. In doing so, some sections of the gospels will deserve closer attention than others because of their direct relation to the theme, but I shall treat them within the whole. By proceeding in this way I believe that the issues entailed in the work as a whole will become more visible.

In the sequential analysis I shall seek to keep in mind the hearers and the way the text might have worked for them. In this I will not assume that all such hearers were hearing the story of Jesus for the first time, although for some this may have been the case. Nor, however, will I presume that hearers possessed a comprehensive map of intricate structural allusions. Instead, it seems reasonable to me to assume that hearers were, by and large, people who believed in Jesus, and had a basic grasp of his story. I assume therefore that they would not have been overwhelmed by novelty. At the first hearing or at least at subsequent hearings, they would have sensed patterns such as inclusios among and within episodes, and would have picked up common themes within larger narrative contexts. Approaching the narrative as a whole and in larger sequences of episodes enables one to come to a closer understanding of both how hearers might have sensed the image of Jesus being portrayed and how the author might have intended to portray it.

In discussing hearers I have already alluded to the possibility that at times there may have been non believers among them. More complicated is the question whether the hearers were Jews or Gentiles. For instance, while Mark's explanations in 7:3–4 imply Gentiles in the audience, to what extent in relating the story of the woman with a flow of blood or Jesus' excursion to Gerasa, does he assume an appreciation of Jewish attitudes towards purity issues among his hearers? On this depends, in part, our picture of Mark's understanding of Jesus' attitude towards Torah. Such issues will be significant in evaluating each of the gospels.

In each chapter I shall first identify overall issues raised by previous research, proceed to a sequential analysis, and finally return to a conclusion which seeks to synthesise findings in relation to that particular gospel. The conclusions in relation to single writings will not be repeated again in the final chapter, except in brief overview. Rather there I shall interrelate these conclusions and raise issues which emerge for understanding the development of the tradition and the question of the attitude of the historical Jesus.

This work is deliberately an overview. It has not been possible to address the many individual issues of interpretation in detail, though I have sought to take all such issues into account in developing a picture of the whole. Inevitably the wide ranging character of the work has meant I have had to live with the frustration of knowing that there was always more to read, including pertinent studies which have appeared since completion of the substantial work on this manuscript early in 1996. My indebtedness both to scholars of Judaism and to New Testament specialists who have addressed these issues will be obvious, far beyond the acknowledgments in footnotes and detailed discussion.

I have approached the task primarily as a biblical exegete. My interest in the history of New Testament tradition goes back to my research on the christology of Hebrews in the early 1970s, which was subsequently published in 1981.[20] While there the interest in christology was paramount, the epistle is a window on one particular way in which an author grappled with revered biblical heritage, not least the Law and cultic Law in particular. As one who has for many years taught the exegesis of Romans, I have had an ongoing engagement with the intricacies of Paul's grappling with Torah. My teaching interests have directed me to Matthew and more recently to Mark. Christology was again the focus in my work on John.[21] What there began as a traditio-historical study became a study of the christology of the received

---

[20] W. R. G. Loader, *Sohn und Hoherpriester. Eine traditionsgeschichtliche Unter-suchung zur Christologie des Hebräerbriefes*, WMANT 53, (Neukirchen-Vluyn: Neukirchener, 1981).

[21] W. R. G. Loader, *The Christology of the Fourth Gospel. Structure and Issues*, BET 23, (Frankfurt: Peter Lang, 2nd edn, 1992).

text as I came to see the priority of listening to the text as received before proceeding to the equally legitimate issues of the history of tradition.

My concern in this work is with the way the gospels portray Jesus' attitude towards the Law. Beyond that , and so beyond the present investigation, my interest is also with the way the pre-gospel traditions portray Jesus' attitude. Not least, I am also concerned with the attitude of the historical Jesus himself. These concerns belong also to a broader interest in what happens to a religion and culture when it is exposed to other religious and cultural influences, especially in the tension between universal and particular values. I believe that there is much to be learned by observing this process within Judaism in its grappling with life in a Hellenising world, already from the third century BCE onward,[22] and in observing the emergence of the Christian movement in this context. Two millennia later many of us grapple with similar issues and observe an equally baffling array of responses.

---

[22] On this see M. Hengel, *Judaism and Hellenism*, 2 vols, (London: SCM; Philadelphia: Fortress, 1974); *The 'Hellenization' of Judaea in the First Century after Christ*, (London: SCM; Philadelphia: Trinity, 1990); J. J. Collins, *Between Athens and Jerusalem. Jewish Identity in the Hellenistic Diaspora*, (New York: Crossroad, 1984); S. Freyne, *Galilee, Jesus, and the Gospels: Literary Approaches and Historical Investigations*, (Philadelphia: Fortress, 1988); G. Delling, *Die Bewältigung der Diasporasituation durch das hellenistische Judentum*, (Göttingen: Vandenhoeck und Ruprecht, 1987); W. R. G. Loader, "Hellenism and the Abandonment of Particularism in Jesus and Paul," *Pacifica* 4 (1991), pp. 245–256.

Chapter 1

Jesus' Attitude towards the Law according to Mark

1.1 Recent Research

In 1972 Klaus Berger published his major work on Jesus' interpretation of the Law.[1] It preserves only part one of his dissertation and deals with a selection of Markan passages and their parallels: the great commandments (12:28–34), the rich man (10:17–22), the *corban* dispute (7:8–13) and divorce (10:2–12). He assembles a wealth of parallels from Jewish, Gentile and later Christian sources. His basic thesis is that the Markan material should be understood on the basis of a Hellenistic Jewish view of Torah which relativised or rejected cultic and ceremonial law. Its weakness is that the evidence for the latter is too slender and late (Pseudo-Clementine literature) to bear the weight of the thesis.[2] Berger is also overly rigid in distinguishing Palestinian and Hellenistic Judaism. But the book is a rich mine of resources and exegetical insight on individual issues. Its importance lies also in the questions it raises, in particular, about what kind of ethos made it possible for Mark to treat the Law the way he did.

Hans Hübner's work[3] appeared in 1973. He limits his focus to only certain central themes relevant to Mark: divorce (10:2–12), sabbath (2:23 – 3:6), and purity (7:1–23). He sees Mark's Jesus abrogating Torah in all three and argues that this is implied in the proclamation of the kingdom (pp.

---

[1] K. Berger, *Die Gesetzesauslegung Jesu. Ihr historischer Hintergrund im Judentum und im Alten Testament. Teil I: Markus und Parallelen*, WMANT 40, (Neukirchen-Vluyn: Neukirchener, 1972).

[2] See the criticism of the book in H. Hübner, "Mark vii 1–23 und das 'Jüdisch-Hellenistische' Gesetzesverständnis," *NTS* 22 (1976), pp. 319–345, esp. 325–345; W. G. Kümmel, "Ein Jahrzehnt Jesusforschung (1965–1975). III. Die Lehre Jesu (einschliesslich der Arbeiten über Einzeltexte)," *ThR NF* 41 (1976), pp. 295–363, esp. 334–337.

[3] H. Hübner, *Das Gesetz in der synoptischen Tradition*, (Göttingen: Vandenhoeck und Ruprecht, 2nd edn., 1986).

213–223). This comes through most strongly, he believes, in 7:15 ("There is nothing which entering a person from outside can defile a person, but the things that come from within a person are what defile a person"). It should also be assumed in 10:1–12 on divorce and possibly in 2:23–28 read in the light of these. Mark holds together scripture fulfilment, on the one hand, and abrogation of Torah, on the other (p. 224). Yet Hübner concludes on an uncertain note: "Mark does not think in the least way nomistically. Rather indications are to hand that he rejects the Law as such. Yet this claim cannot be made with final certainty" (my translation).[4]

Banks[5] focused primarily on the historical Jesus as reflected in the synoptic tradition, even though his discussion does note distinctive emphases of Mark. In his view Mark "is not primarily interested in the implications of Jesus' teaching for the Law or the oral tradition, but rather with its relevance and application to his Gentile audience" (pp. 248–249). This explains the universalising character of much of the Law material, which finds expression in a general concern for humanity (2:27; 3:5), in the focus on ethics rather than purity (7:15,19b), on a wider divorce prohibition (10:1–12) and on monotheism (12:28–34). It also explains Mark's emphasis on Jesus' ethical teaching and its negative implications for written and oral law.

Vouga[6] also focuses on the synoptic gospels and limits himself (in Mark) to six conflict stories: the two sabbath conflicts, and the episodes dealing with purity, divorce, the rich man, and the great commandments. In each he seeks both to offer an analysis of Mark and his tradition and to situate them in a historical construction of early church groups (the conservative Jerusalem church, Jewish Christian Hellenistic itinerant missionaries, Palestinian Jewish Christian missionaries; and the Palestinian Jewish Christian apocalyptic movement). Mark's account, written for Gentiles, stands under the influence of the Hellenists and itinerant radicalism (p. 321). The controversy stories no longer address issues of Law in Mark; they serve to demonstrate Jesus'

---

[4] "Markus denkt nicht im geringsten nomistisch. Eher sind Anzeichen dafür vorhanden, dass er das Gesetz also solches ablehnt. Doch kann diese Aussage nicht mit letzter Bestimmtheit gemacht werden" (p. 226). G. Dautzenberg, "Gesetzeskritik und Gesetzesgehorsam in der Jesustradition," in *Das Gesetz im Neuen Testament*, edited by K. Kertelge, (Freiburg: Herder, 1986), pp. 46–70, here: 54–55, bemoans these vague conclusions, arguing for the centrality of the attitude towards Torah preserved in 10:17–22 and 12:28–34 for Mark's thought (pp. 56–58). By his authority Jesus sets aside only certain laws (so: 2:28; 7:15).

[5] R. Banks, *Jesus and the Law in the Synoptic Tradition*, SNTSMS 28, (Cambridge: CUP, 1975).

[6] F. Vouga, *Jésus et la Loi selon la Tradition synoptique*, (Geneva: Labor et Fides, 1988).

authority and to expose the opposition (pp. 173, 321). Law is subordinated to christology and has become the instrument of unbelief. Otherwise Mark shows no interest in the Law as such; it belongs to the past; Mark is not interested in debates about its interpretation; nor are his hearers (pp. 173–175, 178). These observations raise important issues about the relative importance of the theme for Mark. Are the controversies now largely demonstrations of Jesus' ability to triumph over opposition or do they still deal with real issues for Mark and his community?

Neyrey's application of social science and anthropological perspectives to Mark's treatment of the law,[7] using the typology of M. Douglas,[8] provides an important basis for understanding purity issues both in the Judaism reflected in Mark and in Mark's own portrait of Jesus. Neyrey argues that Mark's narrative employs its own ideology of purity and establishes Jesus in those terms. In one sense to do so is to set Jesus in contrast to other purity systems. This does not however mean that where Mark portrays Jesus in such terms there is always a polemical edge over against the Jewish purity system. Purity language (whether moral or ritual) belongs to the language of religion. Neyrey (pp. 107–109) notes where Mark's Jesus crossed Jewish purity boundaries with regard to people: touching the leper (1:41), the corpse (5:41), being touched by the menstruating woman (5:24–28), calling a sinner to be an intimate (2:13–14), travelling extensively in Gentile territory (4:35–42; 7:31), having commerce with unclean people (7:24–30), having contact with the possessed, blind, lame, deaf (cf. Lev 21:16–24); with regard to bodily orifices or emissions: disregarding dietary restrictions (7:19c), sharing meals with unclean sinners (2:15), not washing hands before eating (7:2), using spittle (7:33; 8:23), showing no regard for purity issues at the feedings of the 5000 and 4000; with regard to time: unlawful action on the sabbath (2:23–28; 3;1–6); with regard to space: disrupting the temple system (11:15–17), critique of temple space (12:33), and critique of the temple (14:58; 15:29).

For Neyrey, Mark's Jesus and his followers have developed a new purity system where "purity rules are concentrated in the core law, the Ten Commandments, . . . purity concerns are focussed on the heart" and on guarding against uncleanness from within; for purity resides within, "in faith

---

[7] J. H. Neyrey, "The Idea of Purity in Mark's Gospel," *Semeia* 35 (1986), pp. 91–128; also "A Symbolic Approach to Mark 7," *Forum* 4 (1988), pp. 63–91. See also B. J. Malina, "A Conflict Approach to Mark 7," *Forum* 4 (1988), pp. 3–30; D. Rhoads, "Social Criticism: Crossing Boundaries," in *Mark and Method. New Approaches in Biblical Studies*, edited by J. C. Anderson and S. D. Moore, (Minneapolis: Fortress, 1992), pp. 135–161.

[8] M. Douglas, *Purity and Danger*, (London: Routledge and Kegan Paul, 1966); *Natural Symbols*, (New York: Vintage Books, 1973).

and right confession of Jesus . . . Purity rules are inclusive, allowing Gentiles and the unclean to enter God's kingdom" (p. 116). He contrasts the purity systems of mainstream Judaism and Jesus as reflecting differing core values: holiness in contrast with mercy; created order in contrast with free, unpredictable, covenant grace; a strong particularist system in contrast with a weaker, more inclusive, system; a defensive strategy in contrast with mission, mercy-as-election, inclusivity; a basis in Mosaic scriptural law in contrast with a basis in pre-Mosaic and prophetic sections of scripture (p. 118). Jesus is not anti-purity, but a limit breaker who establishes a new purity system based on the same scriptures, but from a different perspective (pp. 119–123).

Neyrey's is a useful description of the behaviours of Mark's Jesus which raised issues of conflict and of the characteristic emphases of the contrasting systems. It needs to be set beside the complex issue of authority, including, for instance, the differentiation between transgressing a boundary developed through interpretation of written Torah and one set by Torah itself and, above all, the interrelationship between the new authority of Jesus and that of scripture.

Sariola's is the only full monograph treatment of the theme in recent research.[9] He deals with the material thematically and in the following order: ritual purity (7:1–23), sabbath (2:23–28; 3:1–6), marriage (10:2–12), decalogue (10:17–27), the greatest commandment (12:28–34), and the temple (11:15–19). In each section he also appends discussion of related material in Mark. The focus is strongly redaction critical and entails detailed attempts to reconstruct the shape of source material. The consideration of Law issues moves then from discussion of the reconstructed sources to discussion of the final redaction. In discussing individual passages we shall have cause to interact with his particular findings.

In the synthesis of his results Sariola notes the absence not only of the word νόμος ("law") in Mark, but also of any systematic treatment of the theme by Mark, such as the relation between the Law and the Old Testament or the Law and the commandments (pp. 239, 248). The theme of Law is not central to Mark's theology. Rather Jesus is the authority for Mark, which relativises the authority of the Law. Jesus exercises authority in interpreting the Law, nullifying parts of it and going beyond its demands with demands of his own (pp. 249–250). Mark associates Jesus' response to the Law with

---

[9] H. Sariola, *Markus und das Gesetz. Eine redaktionsgeschichtliche Untersuchung*, Annales Academiae Scientarum Fennicae Dissertationes Humanarum Litterarum 56, (Helsinki: Suomalainen Tiedeakatemia, 1990).

his messiahship as Son of David (pp. 250–251). God's will at creation also functions as a criterion for Jesus' Torah interpretation; this shows itself in ,concern for human beings rather than in a casuistic concern for laws (pp. 251–252). Mark sets the will of God as outlined in the ethical commands of the decalogue and especially in the two greatest commandments in contrast to all else (pp. 252–255). Mark also sees Jesus making distinctions within the Law on the basis of sheer rationality and on the basis of the contrast between the internal, moral, and the external, ritual and cultic (pp. 255–261). On the basis of these criteria Mark sometimes has Jesus speak positively of the Law (the decalogue, the great commandments) and sometimes negatively (ritual purity, divorce, and for the most part, temple and sacrificial cult). Mostly Jesus is shown rejecting the ritual and valuing the moral, but the distinction is not absolute.

This is an excellent guide and a thorough analysis. It is particularly important in the questions it raises about the role of rationality in Mark's critique of the Law. My own treatment will differ in the area of methodology at some points. I do not share Sariola's confidence in being able to reconstruct the wording of sources. I shall also give greater weight to the narrative context of allusions to the Law in Mark than does Sariola. This lack was an almost inevitable result of his method of treating blocks of material according to content. It has meant, for instance, that the place of the Law in major sections like 6:7–8:26 and 11:1–13:37 does not come sufficiently to expression, despite a number of important observations which he makes about these contexts.

Discussion of the way Mark portrays Jesus' attitude towards the Law has focused rightly on the impact of Mark's christology. How has it affected his understanding of the authority of the Law? Does it imply abrogation in the sense that one authority replaces another? Does Mark understand Jesus to have retained only parts of the Law or, alternatively, abrogated only parts of the Law? Does Law matter at all to Mark? Is Mark's Gentile setting combined with his emphasis on Jesus' authority sufficient to explain Mark's stance? Or do other factors play a role, such as ideology, alternative views of the Law, as Berger suggested? These issues will be in the background as we survey the text.

As already indicated, I have chosen to avoid looking only at so-called relevant blocks of material, but will, instead, follow the Markan sequence. I believe that this will best enable us to sense the attitude implied in the text. I shall deal with the narrative in six main sections: (1.2) 1:1 – 3:6; (1.3) 3:7 – 6:6; (1.4) 6:7 – 8:26; (1.5) 8:27 – 10:52; (1.6) 11:1 – 13:37 and (1.7) 14:1 – 16:8. These divisions reflect natural breaks in the text, although often the joins are not unambiguous, since the author employs narrative transitions which might count either way, reflecting the nature of material prepared for oral presentation where shifts in narrative occur more easily with overlapping – to the frustration of those scholars who want to know where to draw lines!

1.2 Mark 1:1 – 3:6 in Review

1.2.1 Mark 1:1–45

At one level, the prologue to the gospel leaves the hearer in no doubt as to who Jesus is. He is the Christ, God's Son (1:1). What this means becomes clear as the narrative proceeds. Mark sets this claim immediately in the context of scripture fulfilment and Israel's hope (1:2–3), implicitly claiming continuity with Israel's tradition. Jesus' authority does not stand alone. In the same breath he sets Jesus in connection with John the Baptist, who also belongs in this tradition. The typology of the wilderness and of John's manner of life (1:4–6) establishes further links with the tradition. The flocking crowds affirm John's position.

Yet, like Jesus, John is not without controversy, as Mark will indicate (11:32). For within the context of a call to repentance, John performs a ritual act for forgiveness of sins. Mark does not bring the controversy to the surface of the text in the prologue. We are not able to derive from this account a deliberate rivalry with more established means of cleansing (cf. 2:5–10). Similarly Mark does not use Jesus' submission to such baptism (1:9–11) to portray an attitude towards the temple cult. Mark does not indicate a relationship between the rending of the heavens (1:10) and the rending of the temple curtain (15:38). The mention of John's arrest (1:14) establishes no link with potential conflict with the established cultus. Yet we know from 11:27–33 that Mark knows there is a problem about John's authority. The primary focus in the prologue, however, is continuity with God's action in the past and with promises of hope which are now being fulfilled in something new.

Accordingly, the prologue not only announces Jesus as Christ and Son of God, but depicts the heavens rent apart for God to affirm this sonship and equip this Son with the Spirit.[10] Jesus fulfils both scripture's and John's inspired prediction of the greater one to come (1:2–3,7–8). He will be the

---

[10] For the view that Mark intends an allusion in the splitting of the curtain (15:37–39) to the splitting open of heaven in the baptism scene (1:9–11; cf. 10:38–40), see S. Motyer,

one to baptise with the Spirit. What Mark has established is Jesus' authority and power. In this power Jesus is exalted above the enemy, Satan, and over the angels who serve him (1:12–13). Mark subtly portrays the beginning of a new age, possibly with echoes of a new Adam, possibly with echoes of Israel's exodus from Egypt through the sea (baptism) and being tested forty years in the wilderness, an allusion developed in the Q version of the story. The primary focus is, however, not echoes of the old (and, for our purpose, implications for understanding attitude towards the Law), but assertion of the new.

For the hearer it comes as no surprise that this Jesus proceeds to announce the time of fulfilment, the coming of God's reign (1:14–15). The impending future, already being made present in the person of the Son of God, demands the response of repentance. Jesus' first act is to call disciples (1:16–20), not primarily to offer a paradigm of repentance, but to engage them as participants in God's coming reign. The demands are striking – the abandonment of family, possessions and work. The radical demand helps to underline that here something radically new has begun. Mark shows no interest here in contrasting this new demand with that of Torah (for instance, in attitudes towards family and material blessings) nor in contrasting this new discipleship with that reflected among Jewish teachers of the day.[11] For Mark, the formation of the community is both part of the fulfilment and the means for fulfilment: from now on these Galileans are to fish for people. Now not only John and Jesus, but also his disciples have become part of the fulfilment and, at the same time, of something new.

"The Rending of the Veil: a Markan Pentecost," *NTS* 33 (1987), pp. 155–157; H. M. Jackson, "The Death of Jesus in Mark and the Miracle from the Cross," *NTS* 33 (1987), pp. 16–37, here: 23, 27, 31; E. S. Malbon, *Narrative Space and Mythic Meaning in Mark*, The Biblical Seminar 13, (Sheffield: JSOTPr., 1991), p 187 n. 93; D. Ulansey, "The Heavenly Veil Torn: Mark's Cosmic *Inclusio*," *JBL* 110 (1991), pp. 123–125; T. Shepherd, *Markan Sandwich Stories. Narration, Definition, and Function*, Andrews Univ Sem Doct Diss Ser 18, (Berrien Springs: Andrews Univ. Pr., 1993), pp. 225–226 n. 2. Common features also include: allusion to the giving of the Spirit, to Jesus as Son of God, and to Elijah. Ulansey adds that the outer veil of the temple depicted the heavens according to Josephus, *JW* 5.212-214, and so would more easily have recalled the tearing of the heavens at Jesus' baptism. First hearers would not find an allusion in 1:10 to the events of the crucifixion, but would regular hearers of the gospel? Is Mark already signalling the replacement of the temple by Jesus already in the prologue? Nothing else in the context suggests so.

[11] Cf. W. Grundmann, *Das Evangelium nach Markus,* (Berlin: Ev. Verlagsanstalt, 1977), pp. 55–56, who contrasts this with the pattern of discipleship found among rabbis and suggests that here Jesus takes the place of the Law. Cf. R. H. Gundry, *Mark. A Commentary on His Apology for the Cross*, (Grand Rapids: Eerdmans, 1993), p. 70, who rightly comments, "Jesus stands not merely in the place of the Law . . . but in the place of God."

Jesus' relation to Israel and its traditions returns more directly to view when Mark narrates the first public act of Jesus' ministry in 1:21–28. Jesus enters the synagogue on the sabbath day. At one level this would not be unexpected of any Jew of the time and Mark does not suggest otherwise. Mark's focus, however, is Jesus' authority. Jesus teaches. Mark adds: "They were astonished at his teaching; for he was teaching them as one having authority and not as the scribes" (1:22). Mark makes the point again at the end of the narrative: "And they were all so amazed that they discussed among themselves: 'What is this? A new teaching with authority. He commands even unclean spirits and they obey him!'" (1:27). The passage, 1:21–28, especially 1:27, is of programmatic significance for Mark's gospel.[12] Newness is a key theme. Depicting the first public event in Jesus' ministry, the passage illustrates Jesus' authority over the powers and in teaching as something new. It illustrates in action the claims of the prologue, but now with something of the other side of the coin: contrast with the teaching authorities of the time.

For the hearer there can be no question after the prologue where this authority comes from. This is the Son of God. The demon in the possessed man also recognised this reality and so addresses Jesus the Nazarene as "the holy one of God".[13] The unholy (the "unclean spirit") confronts the holy.[14] Yet this has not been systematised into a contrast between the holiness of Jesus and that maintained by the scribes and their temple. Mark has taken up an account of an exorcism by Jesus and given it exemplary character. The exorcism illustrates Jesus' authority over the powers. For Mark this is inseparable from his authority as a teacher. The exorcistic power confirms the legitimacy of the claim to teaching authority. This, in turn, confirms for the hearer what has already been disclosed in the prologue.

---

[12] So J. Kiilunen, *Die Vollmacht im Widerstreit. Untersuchungen zum Werdegang von Mk 2,1–3,6*, AASF Dissertationes Humanorum Litterarum 40, (Helsinki, 1985) pp. 22–23; E. K. Broadhead, *Teaching with Authority. Miracles and Christology in the Gospel of Mark*, JSNTS 74, (Sheffield: JSOTPr., 1992), p. 62; see also K. Scholtissek, *Die Vollmacht Jesu. Traditions und redaktionsgechichtliche Analyse zu einem Leitmotiv markinischer Christologie*, NTAbh NF 25, (Münster: Aschendorff, 1992), p. 137, who argues that Mark derives the statement about Jesus' authority from the Son of Man tradition in 2:10 and implicitly from Dan 7:14 LXX (pp. 126–127).

[13] On the play on words between Nazarene and "holy one" see Scholtissek, *Vollmacht*, pp. 109–110; but see also Gundry, *Mark*, p. 82 for a contrary view.

[14] Neyrey, "Idea of Purity," 105–106, points out that the effect of the scene is in part to identify Jesus in the context of purity values. He is in the right place, at the right time, with the right people, and the enemy of the unclean forces. Purity values are also strongly present in 1:1–13: John's unworthiness, the baptism, God's testimony, the temptations (pp. 106–107).

The common use by Mark of the adjective, "unclean", before "spirit", raises the question what this implies concerning Mark's understanding of "clean" and "unclean". Does it, for instance, imply that Mark was operating within a Jewish frame of reference where the categories of "clean" and "unclean" are defined by Torah and its further exposition? Or is it merely a metaphor for evil or a common expression[15] which need not evoke the connotations of an elaborate purity system? The interchangeability of "unclean spirit" and "demon" in Mark may suggest the latter. Mark's redrawn boundaries of purity, which we have yet to explore, also include territory in common with Judaism's understanding of purity; demonology forms part of this common ground. Assuming some coherence in his thought, his demons will be defined primarily in accordance with his purity system and not in accordance with Jewish purity system, especially where (or if) these differ. The extent to which Mark espouses a revised set of values for "clean" and "unclean" will arise regularly within the gospel.

The contrast with the scribes (1:22) already contains a hint of the conflicts which will follow. This is present not only in the specific contrast with the teaching of the scribes, but also in the designation of Jesus' teaching as "new" (1:27).[16] We have already noted the potential for conflict in the new movement, beginning with John's unusual practices, and that Mark was sensitive to the problem posed by both Jesus and John. He makes it explicit in the climax and conclusion of Jesus' ministry, where the first issue of conflict to arise is that of authority (11:27–12:12). There, Jesus replies by associating his authority with John's and then proceeds to his defence with a very pointed reworking of Isaiah's vineyard parable. Thinly disguised, Jesus appears there as the beloved son and predicts the foundation of a new building. The correspondence of motifs between 11:27 – 12:12 and 1:1–28 is striking (beloved son, John and Jesus, authority, a new building/community of faith). Perhaps alert hearers would catch the allusions and probably Mark intended them. But we cannot read back into the contrast in 1:22 the full weight of later allusions. Here we have mere hints of rivalry. While hearers would surely have known of the conflicts, at least, of Jesus' rejection and crucifixion, at the level of the narrative Mark's allusions here remain preparatory.

In the first of the five episodes which follow (1:29–45) Jesus emerges as healer of Simon's mother-in-law (1:29–31). Then in the evening he heals

---

[15] So F. Hauck, Art. "ἀκάθαρτος, ἀκαθαρσία," *TWNT* 3 (1938), pp. 430–432. Gundry, *Mark*, p. 91, argues that the choice of "demon" or "unclean spirits" depends on linguistic habit rather than finer distinctions.

[16] There is no indication here that Mark is thinking of the expectation that the Law will receive new interpretation in the messianic era. On this see Gundry, *Mark*, p. 85.

many who were sick or possessed (1:32–34). These events serve to confirm Jesus' power. Thus the note about suppressing the cries of the demons (1:34) recalls for the hearer the cry of the demon in 1:24, addressing Jesus as "the holy one of God". At the same time it reconfirms the message of the prologue: here is God's Son; supernatural powers recognise him.

Incidental to the story, yet consistent with the Jewish context, is the detail that it was in the evening after sunset, ie. after the end of the sabbath, that the crowds brought the sick to Jesus. Perhaps Mark was aware of its significance.[17] If so, he would have been aware that the exorcism and the healing of Simon's mother-in-law took place on the sabbath, and, in the light of the controversies about the sabbath healing in 3:1–6, had been potentially also a source of controversy.[18] If, as Sariola argues,[19] Mark would still have considered the evening healings to be taking place on the sabbath, since he operated with a Greco-Roman system of dividing days (cf. 11:11–12,19–20; 15:42), the problem would have been more acute. But Mark shows, here, no concern. Did his community no longer celebrate the sabbath? Or did it celebrate it in accordance with the liberal interpretation enshrined in 2:27–28? The practice of observing sabbath or not was no small matter. It had considerable social implications. We shall return to the issue when discussing 2:23–28 and 3:1–6 below.

1:35–38 recalls 1:16–20 in featuring the disciples, but also the prologue in mentioning Jesus' return to a desert place. We are ready for a new cycle of activity; that is precisely the import of Jesus' announcement to the disciples: "Let us go away from here to the villages around about, so that I may preach there, too. For it was for this purpose that I went out" (1:38). Mark is rounding off the narrative and bringing us back to 1:14–15, where Jesus first set out to preach.

As Mark has Jesus begin in 1:21–28 by entering a synagogue and performing an exorcism, so in 1:39–45 he has Jesus entering synagogues[20]

---

[17] Cf. D. A. Carson, "Jesus and the Sabbath in the Four Gospels," in *From Sabbath to Lord's Day: A Biblical, Historical, and Theological Investigation*, edited by D. A. Carson, (Grand Rapids: Zondervan, 1982), pp. 57–97, here p. 60, who suggests that Mark may imply criticism of the Pharisees that their regulations had kept people from access to Jesus. A possibility.

[18] So Vouga, *Loi*, p. 42.

[19] Sariola, *Markus*, pp. 112–115, who argues that the double reference to the evening having come in 1:32 is not unique in Mark (eg. 4:35; 6:47; 14:17; 15:42) and so should not be read as drawing attention to the ending of the sabbath. According to Sariola, Mark's ignoring the sabbath issues here shows that for his community the sabbath is no longer relevant.

[20] Sariola, *Markus*, p. 115, notes that Mark speaks of "their" synagogues and reads it

and casting out demons and then demonstrating his power through healing. As there, Mark noted that Jesus' fame spread a abroad (1:28), so here, the healed leper went out and spread the news about Jesus (1:45). Mark 1:39–45, therefore, recalls 1:21–28 and helps 1:21–45 form a structural unit. Loosely 1:21–45 exhibit a fivefold symmetrical pattern. 1:29–31 (the healing of Simon's mother-in-law) and 1:35–38 (Jesus praying) both involve the disciples; 1:32–34 (evening healings and exorcisms) forms the middle point and is summary both in form and in function within the narrative.

At the same time, however, 1:39–45 also introduces new elements.[21] From the synagogue congregation in 1:21–28 we move to the whole city pressing at his door in 1:32–34. The next day the press continues and Jesus goes beyond Capernaum (1:35–39) until finally the leper's disregard of Jesus' request brings crowds pursuing him even to the desert. One recalls the crowds flocking to John (1:5). Jesus' resolution, according to the Markan narrative, is not to stay there (what would be the point, crowds can still reach him?), but to reenter Capernaum and thus a new chapter begins (in substance, not just in the imposed structure). The healing of the leper is also a climax of Jesus' power to make people whole. To heal a leper is like raising the dead (cf. 2 Kgs 5:7).

More relevant for our theme is another major feature of 1:39–45 which links it to the unit 1:21–45, and especially 1:21–28: the return to the issue of Jesus' relation to established religious authority. It emerges at a number of points in the way Jesus responds to the leper. The reading, ὀργισθείς ("angered", 1:41)[22] would have made good sense to both Jew and Gentile of the time as a response of anger because the leper had broken established norms by making the ap-

---

as an indication of Mark's community having broken with synagogue Judaism. This may, but need not, be the case. Read in the context of the gospel as a whole, it doubtless is so.

[21] On 1:39–45 see also my treatment in W. R. G. Loader, "Challenged at the Boundaries: A Conservative Jesus in Mark's Tradition," *JSNT* 63 (1996), pp. 45–61.

[22] According to Codex Bezae and related texts (D ff[2] r[1]) Jesus' response was not initially compassion, but anger, already in 1:41. Commentators are divided about the original reading. Some see ὀργισθείς as the result of influence from ἐμβριμησάμενος. So H. Räisänen, *The "Messianic Secret" in Mark's Gospel*, (Edinburgh: T&T Clark, 1990), p. 145; D. Lührmann, *Das Markusevangelium*, HNT 3, (Tübingen: J. C. B. Mohr [Paul Siebeck], 1987), p. 54; L. W. Hurtado, *Mark*, New International Biblical Commentary, (Peabody: Hendricksen, 1989), p. 30; W. Schmithals, *Das Evangelium nach Markus. 2 Bde*, OekTNT 2/1, 2, (Gütersloh: Mohn, 1979), p. 143; Gundry, *Mark*, p. 95; B. M. Metzger, *A Textual Commentary on the Greek New Testament*, (Stuttgart: Deutsche Bibelgesellschaft; London: United Bible Societies, 2nd, edn., 1994), p. 65, noting that copyists have not changed the two other occurrences of anger in Mark at 3:5 and 10:14. Cf. J. D. Crossan, *The Historical Jesus. The Life of a Mediterranean Jewish Peasant*, (San Francisco: Harper, 1991), p. 323, who speculates that the original story had σπλαγχνισθείς and was changed

proach.[23] For Mark, Jesus, himself, was not in danger.[24] His anger would then be most naturally understood as anger at the man's blatant disregard of the norms of society.[25] This coheres with Jesus' stern instruction to the man to obey such

to anger because of the motive of touching and that then a later scribe added ἐμβριμησάμενος. Others point out that normally Matthew and Luke would have preserved an original σπλαγχνισθείς, suggesting that a scribe is more likely to have changed the reading from ὀργισθείς. So C. E. B. Cranfield, *The Gospel according to Saint Mark,* (Cambridge: CUP, 1963), p. 92; H. C. Cave, "The Leper: Mark 1.40–45," *NTS* 25 (1978–79), pp. 245–250, here: 247; C. R. Kazmierski, "Evangelist and Leper: A Socio-Cultural Study of Mark 1.40–45," *NTS* 38 (1992), pp. 37–50, here: 40 n. 5; R. A. Guelich, *Mark 1–8:26*, WordBibComm 34A, (Waco: Word, 1989), p. 72; J. Gnilka, *Das Evangelium nach Markus,* 2 vols, (Zürich/Neukirchen-Vluyn: Benziger/Neukirchener, 1978/79), I p. 93; E. Schweizer, *Das Evangelium nach Markus,* (Göttingen: Vandenhoeck und Ruprecht, 1968), p. 31; W. L. Lane, *The Gospel according to Mark*, (Grand Rapids: Eerdmans, 1974), p. 84; R. Pesch, *Das Markusevangelium,* HTKNT II/1.2, (Freiburg: Herder, 1977), I p. 141; M. D. Hooker, *A Commentary on the Gospel according to St Mark*, Blacks NTComm, (London: A&C Black, 1990), p. 79. Some dispute that there is any reference to anger in the pericope, suggesting that ἐμβριμησάμενος means "sternly charged". So Gundry, *Mark*, p. 96; Gnilka, *Markus I*, p. 193. J. Jeremias, *Neutestamentliche Theologie I. Die Verkündigung Jesu,* (Gütersloh: Mohn, 1971), p. 96 and E. F. F. Bishop, *Jesus of Palestine*, (London: Lutterworth. 1955), p. 89, suggest the word implies silencing. H. C. Kee, "Aretalogy and the Gospel," *JBL* 92 (1973), pp. 402–422, argues for the meaning, "growl" (p. 418). This is certainly possible, although this is not the way Mark usually employs the word (Mark 7:34; 9:19,23; cf. John 11:33,38). There are strong grounds for finding one if not two references to anger.

[23] On Jewish Law in relation to leprosy see Lev 13–14; also 11QT 45:16,18; 48:14–15,17 – 49:4; 1QSa 2:3–4; 4QMMT 67–75; Jos *Ant* 3:261–264 and *mNega'im*. While Kazmierski, "Evangelist and Leper," pp. 43–44, points to a certain leniency in relation to lepers, illustrated, for instance, by the anecdote of encounter of Jesus with lepers in a village in Luke 17:1–2, most agree that this would be recognised as an act contrary to Jewish law (so Hooker, *Mark*, p. 77; and cf. Lev 5:3; 13:1–46; Nu 5:2; Justin *Apol* I 31 §281), even though, as Gundry, *Mark*, p. 95, rightly notes, Mark makes nothing of it. Cf. Cave, "The Leper," p. 249, who suggests Jesus' anger is against the lax Galileans for approaching him for a priestly declaration. Mostly this is understood in terms of purity; would the ancient world have distinguished such contamination from the health danger? On leprosy (probably Hansen's disease – Gundry, *Mark*, p. 101) as a social issue in the ancient world see Kazmierski, "Evangelist and Leper," p. 41 and J. J. Pilch, "Biblical Leprosy and Symbolism," *BibThBull* 11 (1981), pp. 108–113.

[24] Rightly Grundmann, *Markus*, p. 68, suggesting Mark has abandoned such categories; cf. also Hooker, *Mark*, p. 80 and Gundry, *Mark*, p. 74.

[25] Cf. Schweizer, *Markus*, p. 31; Hooker, *Mark*, pp. 80–81; K. Kertelge, *Die Wunder Jesu im Markusevangelium. Eine redaktionsgeschichtliche Untersuchung*, (Munich: Kösel, 1970), p. 67; Sariola, *Markus*, p. 66 n. 86, who suggest that Jesus is angry at demonic influence. Cranfield, *Mark*, p. 92; Gnilka, *Markus*, p. 93; Grundmann, *Markus*, p. 68; Guelich, *Mark*, p. 74; Lane, *Mark*, p. 86; Schweizer, *Markus*, p. 31, who suggest (also) that Jesus is angry at the distortion of creation. Other suggestions include anger at miracle mongering, or at the temple system – so C. Myers, *Binding the strong man: a political reading of Mark's story of Jesus*, (Maryknoll, N.Y. : Orbis Books, 1988), or that Jesus is

laws and show himself to the priest.[26] Even if we read, σπλαγχνισθείς ("moved with compassion"), some disturbance on Jesus' part is not to be denied. The leper is no angel and, one could almost say, true to characterisation of lepers (eg. nine of the ten lepers in Luke 17:11–18), continues an independent course.[27]

The passage raises a number of other questions regarding the image it portrays of Jesus' attitude towards the Law. Was Jesus' word of healing, καθαρίσθητι, the equivalent of a priestly declaration about the man's impurity[28] or just a word of healing? Was Jesus' instruction genuine instruction that he should act in accordance with the provisions concerning leprosy[29] or, in the light of εἰς μαρτύριον αὐτοῖς, just a ploy to bear evangelical witness to the priests,[30] perhaps, even, as some have suggested,

---

showing typical agitation of the miracle worker; so Pesch, *Markusevangelium I*, p. 144; G. Theissen, *The Miracle Stories of the Early Christian Tradition*, (Edinburgh: T&T Clark, 1983), pp. 57–58; Gnilka, *Markus I*, p. 93. Cf. also M. Wojciechowski, "The Touching of the Leper (Mark 1,40–45) as a Historical and Symbolic Act of Jesus," *BibZ* 33 (1989), pp. 114–119, who suggests that Jesus may be expressing a state of anger within himself (p. 116). For other suggestions and guesses see Cave, "The Leper," p. 247.

[26] To reject this observation on the grounds that Jesus would not then have touched the man (so, for instance, Guelich, *Mark*, p. 74) misses the crucial point and presumes that Jesus could not have had both reactions, one of anger and yet a willingness to cross the boundary, just as he did with the Syrophoenician woman in 7:24–30.

[27] Note that Mark portrays the man as disobedient to Jesus' instruction about silence. So Räisänen, *Messianic Secret*, p. 148; Schmithals, *Markus*, p. 136; H. Waetjen, *A Reordering of Power. A Socio-political Reading of Mark*, (Philadelphia: Fortress, 1989), p. 85; Hurtado, *Mark*, pp. 31, 34; Lane, *Mark*, p. 88. Others understand Mark as excusing the action as positive exuberance (Pesch, *Markusevangelium I*, p. 146; Guelich, *Mark*, p. 97; Gundry, *Mark*, p. 79). Opinions also vary about the nature of the command to silence. Was it until the man had seen the priest? So Gundry, *Mark*, p. 97; Schmithals, *Markus*, p. 137; J. Ernst, *Das Evangelium nach Markus*, RNT, (Regensburg: Pustet, 1981), pp. 176–177; Räisänen, *Messianic Secret*, p. 147; or originally so? – so G. Theissen, *Lokalkolorit und Zeitgeschichte in den Evangelien*, NTOA 8, (Freiburg, Schweiz/Göttingen: Universitätsverlag/Vandenhoeck und Ruprecht, 1989), p. 107; or related only to the manner of the healing? – so Grundmann, *Markus*, p. 67; or was the silence to be permanent? – so Theissen, *Lokalkolorit*, p. 107; or at least as an open secret? – so Kazmierski, "Evangelist and Leper," p. 47.

[28] So Broadhead, *Teaching*, p. 74; similarly Hooker, *Mark*, p. 80; Guelich, *Mark*, p. 75; earlier H. J. Holtzmann, *Die Synoptiker*, HCNT 1/1, (Tübingen: J. C. B. Mohr, 3rd edn., 1901), and Grundmann, *Markus*, p. 69: as messianic high priest. For further criticism of this view see Gnilka, *Markus I*, p. 90; Lane, *Mark*, p. 87; Gundry, *Mark,* pp. 96, 107.

[29] So Gnilka, *Markus I*, pp. 91, 94; Hooker, *Mark*, p. 82; Lührmann, *Markusevangelium*, p. 55; Pesch, *Markusevangelium I*, p. 146. The phrase governs the action seen as a whole (showing and offering) and should not be restricted to what immediately precedes, namely, the offering.

[30] Cf. Guelich, *Mark*, pp. 77, 79, who says that it was to show the priests that Jesus really did keep the Law and that it was not passé for him, though Mark has little interest in the Law. Grundmann, *Markus*, pp. 69–70, also includes concern to show them that the

to confront them?[31] Does Mark mean us to sense the issue of potential contamination in Jesus' touching the leper and so present Jesus as reversing the direction, as the holy one, making the unclean well by his power?[32] This, in turn, relates to the question, to what extent Jesus' anger and sternness were a response to his concern about transgression of Torah in particular[33] and so indicative of Mark's view of Jesus' attitude towards the Law?

The meaning of καθαρίσθητι and point of Jesus' instruction are closely connected. Nothing indicates that Jesus' instruction is a mere ploy, to confront the priests as part of an ongoing confrontation, as some have understood the words, εἰς μαρτύριον αὐτοῖς. This presupposes a level of confrontation for which the narrative has not prepared the hearer. Hints of potential tension with scribes in 1:22 are not sufficient to bear the weight of such an interpretation.

This means that it is most unlikely that with καθαρίσθητι Mark intends to portray Jesus as making a priestly declaration of cleanness and thus usurping priestly authority Some might see him implicitly doing so in the episode which immediately follows through declaring sins forgiven; but this, as we shall see shortly, is based on a misunderstanding. In employing the

---

kingdom has come. Gundry, *Mark*, p. 97, argues that it is to show the crowds, not the priests. Crossan, *Historical Jesus*, pp. 321–323, argues that PapEgerton 2 preserves an account of the story independent of the gospels, arguing from it that in Markan tradition the sending of the leper to the temple was introduced out of sensitivity to the act of touching. The original story had portrayed Jesus as declaring the man clean. Mark then added "against them" turning the sending into an act of confrontation. Cf. Kazmierski, "Evangelist and Leper," p. 48, who sees it as an act of sarcasm and confrontation by Jesus the limit breaker (also pp. 45–46).

[31] So E. K. Broadhead, "Mark 1,44: The Witness of the Leper," *ZNW* 83 (1992), pp. 257–265, here: 260–263; also in his *Teaching*, pp. 73–74, 77; "Christology as Polemic and Apologetic: The Priestly Portrait of Jesus in the Gospel of Mark," *JSNT* 47 (1992), pp. 21–34, esp. 24–25. Similarly Kiilunen, *Vollmacht*, p. 33 n. 17; Banks, *Law*, p. 103. Sariola, *Markus*, pp. 67–68, argues that Mark understood it as evidence against the Jews, but Mark's tradition had understood it positively. Cf. Myers, *Binding the Strong Man*, p. 153, who argues that the witness is against them because they had declared him unclean.

[32] Gundry, *Mark*, p. 95. M. J. Borg, *Conflict, Holiness and Politics in the Teachings of Jesus*, Studies in the Bible and Early Christianity 5, (New York: Edwin Mellen, 1984), p. 135, argues that the story shows Jesus as being an active transmitter of holiness rather than a passive recipient of contamination; similarly Neyrey, "The Idea of Purity," pp. 112–113 and 124, speaks of Jesus as a limit breaker who establishes a different system of purity (p. 113); similarly Wojciechowski, "Touching of the Leper," pp. 118–119.

[33] So B. H. Branscomb, *The Gospel of Mark*, Moffat NT Comm, (London: Hodder & Stoughton, 1941), p. 38; Albright in: C. S. Mann, *Mark*, AnchBibComm 27, (New York: Doubleday, 1986), p. 219.

word, καθαρίσθητι, Mark indicates both the healing and the effect. The effect must still be formally certified in accordance with the provisions of Torah and the man declared clean so that he can reenter the community. This action which Jesus enjoins would, for Mark, more than likely draw attention to Jesus as the healer and place him firmly on the agenda of the authorities. But it should be seen primarily as an injunction to obey a Torah provision. One may even suggest that such detail is relatively incidental, since Mark's primary concern lies elsewhere.[34] Such conformity to Torah was as natural as Jesus' attendance in the synagogue on the sabbath day. However, the effect of this detail is certainly to have Jesus enter the series of episodes of controversies as one who is known to keep Torah, not flout it. This will have implications for the way Mark's Jesus appears within these episodes.[35]

There is little doubt that the episode entails purity issues. We meet here a problem which will recur throughout Mark. Mark rarely comments on the purity issues. Was he aware of them, but chose not to mention them because such categories were no longer relevant for him and many of his readers? Or are we to assume that Mark operated within a Jewish frame of reference and that he sees Jesus as having the power to counter the effects of "uncleanness" as "the holy one"? Mark's chief interest is in the mighty power of Jesus to heal. His power enables him to touch the leper and make him whole.

Within a Jewish frame of reference concerning purity Jesus' action and word of healing raise a number of issues. The leper was indeed "unclean" and touching a leper would have rendered Jesus unclean until the evening.[36] It would then have prevented Jesus' entering the city that day, at least from the kind of public contact which such entry would entail. Was Jesus' silencing the leper originally designed to prevent it becoming known that Jesus was thus unclean? But this would entail a deliberate circumvention of the purity

---

[34] Cf. Gundry, *Mark*, p. 103.

[35] So D. E. Nineham, *The Gospel of St Mark*, (Harmondsworth: Penguin, 1963), p. 87; Kiilunen, *Vollmacht*, pp. 33–34; Sariola, *Markus*, p. 69; H.-W. Kuhn, *Ältere Sammlungen in Markusevangelium*, SUNT 8, (Göttingen: Vandenhoeck und Ruprecht, 1971), p. 219, who also points to the similar role of 12:28–34 in showing Jesus' attitude towards the Law (p. 304). Note also the observation of R. P. Booth, *Jesus and the Laws of Purity. Tradition History and Legal History in Mark 7*, JSNTS 13, (Sheffield: JSOTPr, 1986), p. 31, that Mark also uses the allusion to Jesus' tassel, κρασπέδον (6:56), immediately prior to the conflict over purity in 7:1–23, as a way of asserting Jesus' adherence to Torah.

[36] For Jesus' act of touching the leper as contrary to the Law see Hurtado, *Mark*, p. 30; Lane, *Mark*, p. 87; Lührmann, *Markusevangelium*, p. 54; Kazmierski, "Evangelist and Leper," p. 47. Some note that the result of touching the man would render Jesus unable to

law by Jesus (while in the same breath ensuring another of its requirements be fulfilled) and might have been unrealistic had people of the city noticed the man. Mark, however, appears to see the matters differently. For Mark, it is Jesus' popularity which prevents Jesus' being able to enter the city. He says nothing about Jesus being rendered "unclean".

There are grounds elsewhere in Mark (see especially the discussion below of Mark 5–8) for claiming that Mark was aware of the Jewish frame of reference, but that he did not operate within it. It would therefore be wrong to interpret Mark's understanding of the episode from within a Jewish frame of reference, and so portray Jesus as a new factor, so to speak, within the value system, who was able to handle its issues more effectively, but still on its terms. Mark may have intended to assure us that by his power Jesus has reversed the direction of impurity: his own holiness had reached out and made the man pure; but this is not said. The fact that this episode shows Mark is aware of the required provisions about leprosy and has Jesus enjoin that they be fulfilled is no proof that Mark still adhered to the total Jewish system of purity. It is more likely that Mark's new value system has overlaps with the Jewish frame of reference and these include the understanding of lepers as "unclean", a stance not difficult to understand within the broader non Jewish value systems of the day, given the widely felt concern about lepers in ancient society.[37] Flouting these values by crashing forbidden barriers would anger Mark, as it angers Mark's Jesus, and Mark obviously includes in his value system the need for official acts which enable reintegration of the leper within society.[38]

Jesus' word of healing, καθαρίσθητι, must also be understood within this frame of reference, and not as an implicit reaffirmation of Jewish purity laws in general. The healing makes it possible for the man to be declared clean, to reenter society. Mark's silence, otherwise, on matters of Jewish purity laws is understandable on the basis that he does not presuppose such values. This explains his silence here about the possible consequences of touching a leper, as it does elsewhere, for instance, when Jesus is touched by the woman with the issue of blood and when he touches the corpse of the young girl in chapter 5. In that silence we can only speculate that Mark and

---

enter populated areas (so 1:45), but that would have lasted only a day and is unlikely to have been the kind of thing one would recited in an anecdote. So Kazmierski, "Evangelist and Leper," p. 50, against B. Malina, *The New Testament World. Insights from Cultural Anthropology*, (Atlanta: Jn Knox, 1981), pp. 124–125, and Myers, *Binding*, p. 154.

[37] On this see Kazmierski, "Evangelist and Leper," p. 41 and Pilch, "Biblical Leprosy."

[38] The alternative is to posit that Mark uses in 1:44 a tradition which runs contrary to his own view, as does Sariola, *Markus*, p. 73.

at least some of his hearers would have been aware of the issues and how they would have understood them.[39]

Nevertheless, in relation to Jesus' attitude towards the Law in Mark, the effect of the narrative, 1:39–45, is to portray Jesus, the one who teaches with greater authority than the scribes, as one who encourages a leper to fulfil the Law relating to leprosy and is angry when it is disregarded. The response of Jesus and his injunction to the man leave the impression that Jesus upholds Torah. This is certainly so, although the situation is much more complicated, as we have seen. It does, in any case, enable the hearer to move into the controversies which follow with this positive impression to the fore. Jesus was not one who was bent on flouting revered tradition. These aspects are however subordinate to Mark's major emphasis which is to illustrate Jesus' power and underline its impact. The episode functions as an important transition to the five controversy stories which follow.[40]

In summary, the prologue (1:1–15) presents Jesus as God's Son, anointed by the Spirit, come in fulfilment of the scriptures, to announce the good news of the kingdom. The focus is Jesus' authority and continuity with scripture. Potential conflicts related to the Law of which we know Mark is

---

[39] Cf. Sariola, *Markus*, pp. 241–244, who highlights two possible explanations concerning the implicit character of much of the Markan material relating to the Law: Mark was a Gentile often ignorant of finer points of the Law; or he belonged to a community which has long since left Law issues behind.

[40] On the tradition reflected in Mark 1:40–45, see my,"Challenged at the Boundaries," pp. 51-58. Mark's interest in portraying Jesus' action and subsequent injunction is primarily to highlight Jesus' power. This was doubtless also the focus in the pre-Markan tradition. Mark would have understood Jesus' reaction primarily as a response to the man's crashing appropriate boundaries, which he and his Gentile and Jewish hearers would have respected. In a more directly Jewish context one might suspect that Jesus' response would have been interpreted more directly in terms of the man's transgression of Torah. Whether in addition at that stage the tradition reported that because he had touched the leper (or it had become known that he had), Jesus was not able to enter the centres of population (until the evening) is uncertain. The anecdote may well reflect an event in the life of Jesus. It would show him responding with anger at the leper's approach, yet willing to touch the leper to heal him. Apart from the issues of the historical credibility of such a healing, the story presents us with a believable tradition about Jesus. It pictures Jesus as a conservative Jew concerned at the leper's approach and asking that he fulfil Torah requirements after the healing. Yet it is a Jesus who, confronted with such a boundary violation, himself responds to the man and crosses the boundary to do so by touching him. Probably Jesus would have been seen as someone with charismatic power which enabled him to do so without contamination (as Elijah and Elisha. So Banks, *Law*, p. 105). Other traditions about Jesus' initial reluctance at purity boundaries include the encounter with the Syrophoenician women (7:24–30), the healing of the woman with the flow of blood (5:23–34) and from Q, the healing of the centurion's servant. These reflect a Torah observant Jesus concerned about boundaries.

aware remain below the surface. The call of the disciples shows both the radical nature of this new beginning and its inclusion of a community. Heading the five units of material which follow is a narrative emphasising Jesus' new authority in contrast to that of the scribes and closing it is a narrative which effectively links that authority with a positive attitude towards Torah. Both the first and last of the five units show Mark's interest in Jesus in relation to religious authorities. Within the section as a whole many issues of Law are left unaddressed (John's baptism, Jesus' call to loyalty above family and material blessings, exorcism and healings on the sabbath, touching a leper). The encounter with the leper portrays Jesus as upholding the Law, but we should be careful not to read this particular instance as evidence that Mark espouses Jewish purity Law in general or the Law as a whole. At least by Mark 7 we see that this is not so. Mark is exploiting the overlap between Jewish Law and his own purity system which remains concerned about the dangers of leprosy and accepts rites of reintegration.

We approach 2:1 – 3:6 with an image of Jesus as the Son of God who has authority greater than that of the scribes, but upholds the provisions of the Law. In Jesus God has undertaken something new. The new inevitably raises questions about the relation with the old. This issue, implicit in the prologue, and hinted at in the contrast with the scribes, comes to the surface in 2:1 – 3:6.

1.2.2 Mark 2:1 – 3:6

The composition of 2:1 – 3:6 reflects the five fold structure already found in 1:21–45, but with much more extensive patterns of symmetry, as Joanna Dewey has shown.[41] 2:1–12 is a narrative of the healing of a paralysed man and includes a controversy dialogue; 3:1–6 is also a narrative of healing (of a man with a withered right hand), including controversy dialogue. Both 2:13–17, Jesus' eating with toll collectors and sinners, and 2:23–28, the plucking and eating of grain on the sabbath, concern controversy over food. At the centre of the symmetrical pattern, set immediately between the two narratives concerning food, is the controversy about fasting in which Jesus declares that in him something new has come in contrast to the old (2:18–22). The five fold pattern is broken thematically by the narrative of the call of Levi in 2:13–14, which, however, forms an important cross reference to the call of the disciples in 1:16–20.

---

[41] J. Dewey, *Markan Public Debate: Literary Technique, Concentric Structure, and Theology in Mark 2:1 – 3:6*, (Chico: Scholars, 1980); see also the discussion in Kiilunen, *Vollmacht*, pp. 73–78.

The pattern developed by Mark reveals major Markan concerns which pertain to Jesus' authority. These are especially evident in what Mark places at the head of the section and in what lies at its centre. At the head of the group of five narratives with which Mark began the account of Jesus' public ministry in 1:21–45, he had the people contrast Jesus' authority with that of the scribes (1:22) and affirm that in Jesus there is "a new teaching with authority" (1:27). At the head of the second group of five narratives we find the same theme. Over against the complaining scribes Jesus asserts of himself: "The Son of Man has authority on earth to forgive sins" (2:10). Here, as in 1:21–28, Jesus' authority is confirmed by the miraculous: "That you may know that the Son of Man has authority on earth to forgive sins, he said to the paralysed man, 'I tell you, rise, take up your pallet and go to your home.' And he arose and immediately taking up his pallet went out before them all" (2:10–11). Similarly, at the conclusion of the controversy over the disciples' plucking grain on the sabbath Jesus also makes a similar claim to authority: "The Son of Man is lord also of the sabbath" (2:28).

Correspondingly, the central of the five narratives portrays Jesus as one with authority of a special kind. Jesus is the bridegroom, a familiar eschatological image (2:19; cf. John 3:29; Matt 22:1–14; Rev 19:9; Isa 61:10; 62:5; 4Q434 f. 1,1:6). This echoes the prologue's announcement that the eschatological promise is being fulfilled in Jesus. More striking is the way Mark takes up the theme of 1:27 (a new teaching with authority; cf. also 1:22) in 2:21–22. The new patch and the new wine are set in contrast with the old. These verses are both a commentary on the surrounding controversies and conversely depend on them for their interpretation.

The sense of an incompatible conflict of authority is already present in 2:1–12 where the scribes charge Jesus with blasphemy. The charge of blasphemy will also be levelled against Jesus in Mark's account of the Jewish trial (14:63–64). Mark is already setting the scene for the final showdown. In the corresponding fifth narrative the Pharisees respond to Jesus' healing on the sabbath by consorting with the Herodians to plot Jesus' death (3:6). His death is also foreshadowed in the image of the departure of the bridegroom in 2:19–20.

2:1 – 3:6 continues, therefore, Mark's emphasis on Jesus' new authority in contrast to that of the scribes and already indicates that the contrast means conflict and will lead to Jesus' death. Read in the light of what precedes, the authority of the Son of Man is the authority of the one hailed as God's Son and as the promised one. There are two elements here: Jesus' authority is rooted in his being the Son of God anointed by the Spirit and he is the promised one who brings the new; in broadest terms, the christological and the eschatological. The narrative of Levi's call in 2:13–14 cements the link with the christology of the prologue since it echoes in substance and language the call of the first disciples in 1:16–20. Similarly, Jesus words in 2:17, "I have not come to call the righteous, but sinners," also reflects Jesus' sense of authority and the authorisation reflected in the prologue.

A third element which emerged from the preceding section is the question of Jesus' authority in relation to the Law. We saw in 1:39–45 that Jesus seeks to have the leper fulfil the Levitical requirements for lepers concerning reentry into the community. This presentation of Jesus as Torah observant casts a significant light on the controversies which follow and on the contrast between old and new. In these is Mark portraying Jesus as opposing Torah, opposing certain interpretations of Torah or superseding Torah? Are the old garment, the old wineskins, the time before the wedding (2:18–22), representative of the scribes and their interpretations or of the Torah itself? The answer may be a combination of these alternatives. In the following I shall focus in particular on the causes of offence and Jesus' response.

In 2:1–12 the cause of offence is the declaration of forgiveness. Mark portrays the accusation as blasphemy. It is a paramount Law issue, but, for Mark, the accusation is manifestly false because it fails to recognise Jesus' authorisation and therefore misconstrues his action as a claim to independent authority. The scribes complained that Jesus' declaration of forgiveness of sins to the paralysed man amounted to blasphemy because it usurped God's role. The issue for them was not that he had no authority, whereas others did, even though this will have played a role in Mark's tradition (On this see the discussion of the passage in the excurse below). It was blasphemy; usurping God's role. As noted above, the same charge of blasphemy reappears in Mark's account of the Jewish trial of Jesus. According to both accounts the charge of blasphemy is false. The answer to the charge is similar: Jesus is the eschatological Son of Man (14:62); as Son of Man Jesus has God's authority (2:10). As the Son of Man he is properly authorised to act on God's behalf. He is not claiming to act as God or independently of God.

The words, "Your sins are forgiven," would normally be understood as a divine passive.[42] That this is the case also in this context is evident from the language of authorisation which follows. The effect of Mark's Son of Man christology is to refute any charges that Jesus replaces God or is a second god. In this sense the present narrative offers a picture of scribes arguing that Jesus is claiming to act as God, much as does Jesus' opposition according

---

[42] So Sanders, *Jewish Law*, pp. 62–63.

to the fourth gospel (5:19–20; 10:22–39; 19:7).[43] There, too, the defence uses the language of authorisation and commissioning, although the christology is fundamentally different, since John assumes an envoy model which entails full pre-existence. The charge here, as in the Jewish trial in the Markan passion narrative (14:61), probably reflects the kinds of accusations which were directed at Christians about their christology in the Markan context.

Integrated within 2:1–12 is a subordinate argument. Jesus' initial response to the scribes' complaint is the remark: "Which is easier: to say to the paralytic, 'Your sins are forgiven,' or to say 'Rise and take up your pallet and walk'?" (2:9). At one level, the level of sheer physicality, it is much harder to ask a paralytic to walk than to pronounce forgiveness of sins, because it entails a miracle! At another level, the level of what is permissible (or perceived to be) under Torah, it is more difficult to declare forgiveness! This is a riddle, a *mashal*. The riddle has the effect of relativising the problem of declaring forgiveness and of placing it on the same level as healing. There are two aspects here. Firstly, both healing and declaration of forgiveness are a response to human need and, secondly, both are God's actions.[44] The effect of Jesus' *mashal* is to ridicule any distinction between the two by displaying both as God's response to human need. The implication of the first aspect is that a person should feel as much authorised to do the one as to do the other. But Mark's primary concern is warding off the accusation of blasphemy and thus with the second aspect: to charge a person for blasphemy in one case and not in the other is meaningless.[45]

2:10, then, states the underlying assumption of the narrative: "That you may know that the Son of Man has authority on earth to forgive sins." Jesus is not blaspheming, setting himself up beside or in place of God. If he is

---

[43] See W. Loader, *The Christology of the Fourth Gospel. Structure and Issues*, BBET 23, (Frankfurt: Lang, 2nd edn., 1992), pp. 160–165.

[44] O. Hofius, "Vergebungszuspruch und Vollmachtsfrage. Mk 2,1–12 und das Problem priesterlicher Absolution im antiken Judentum," in *"Wenn nicht jetzt, wann dann?": Aufsätze für Hans-Joachim Kraus zum 65. Geburtstag*, edited by H.-G. Geyer, (Neukirchen-Vluyn: Neukirchener Verlag, 1983), pp. 115–127, draws attention to the conjunction of healing and forgiveness in Ps 103:3 "who forgives all your sins and heals all your diseases" (pp. 126–127). On the link between sickness and sin in Judaism, see also Broer, "Jesus und das Gesetz," p. 81.

[45] The observation of U. Luck, "Was wiegt leichter? Zu Mk 2,8," in *Vom Urchristentum zu Jesus. Für Joachim Gnilka*, edited by H. Frankemölle und K. Kertelge, (Freiburg: Herder, 1989), pp. 103–108, here: 106–108, that Jesus' contrast is not between word and action, but between two things he might say, and that the issue was which would be the more blasphemous, draws attention to the fact that in both the issue of exercising divine authority is at stake.

not, then there arises the issue: he must be doing it on God's behalf. Is he authorised to do so? This will be a question with which Jesus will be confronted in Jerusalem (11:28) where it is linked with John's authorisation. In 2:1–12 the questions which, the narrator informs us, are raised in the minds of the scribes are not focused on the issue of authorisation; the scribes appear to have ruled out any possibility of legitimacy. They are not, therefore, criticising Jesus for usurping the rights of, for instance, the priests to declare forgiveness; their charge is: Jesus is usurping God's rights. Mark, however, refutes the blasphemy charge precisely because it fails to contemplate legitimacy. For Mark the legitimacy issue is clear cut: "The Son of Man has authority on earth to forgive sins." By this Mark doubtless means: as Son of Man, Jesus has such authority. Whatever other associations the term, "Son of Man", may have had for Mark's hearers, it is to be heard in the context of the preceding narrative for first hearers and for others in terms of the gospel as a whole: a designation which encompasses Jesus' dignity. Charges that Jesus is acting contrary to Torah are groundless.

2:13–14, the call of Levi, recalls Jesus' act of authority in calling the disciples in 1:16–20. It connects the Jesus of the controversies strongly with the disciples and so with the Christian community, so that his story becomes all the more applicable to their story. This is reinforced where controversy focuses on activities of the disciples, themselves, for which Jesus is held responsible, or on issues they must face about him. 2:13–14 also sets the scene for what follows in 2:15–17. There the offence is eating with toll collectors and sinners, in Levi's house.[46] The issue is unholy company, understood primarily in moral terms.[47] Jesus does not dispute the moral status of the company, instead he disputes the need to remain separate from such people. The Law issue is of a general character: the admonition not to keep company with sinners (eg. Psalm 1:1). However, there may also be purity issues entailed in the offence. Mixing with such company shows lack of care on the part of Mark's Jesus about avoidable contamination through such encounters (eating untithed food, contracting uncleanness from garments and implements of unclean people).[48] While this may be implied, it is not

---

[46] So Lührmann, *Markusevangelium*, p. 59. Perhaps it would have been even more serious if Jesus had invited these people into his house. On the other hand, potential purity issues (eg. use of untithed food and other breaches of purity laws) would have been more likely to have been seen as an additional danger elsewhere.

[47] So S. Westerholm, *Jesus and Scribal Authority*, Coniectanea Biblica NT Ser 10, (Lund: Gleerup, 1978), p. 70; E. P. Sanders, *Jesus and Judaism*, (London: SCM, 1985), p. 178.

[48] So Westerholm, *Scribal Authority*, pp. 70–71; Booth, *Purity*, p. 110; J. D. G. Dunn, *The Partings of the Ways. Between Christianity and Judaism and their Significance for*

directly addressed in Mark's story. The issue is unlikely to have been food
that was not *kosher*. That became a concern in the early days of Christianity
about eating with Gentiles; nothing suggests Gentiles here; nor is any mention
made of "unclean" food.[49]

In response to the accusation, Jesus makes a twofold answer: "It is not
the well who have need of a doctor, but rather the sick. I came not to call the
righteous but sinners" (2:17). The first half is a *mashal*, a riddle. It argues
that Jesus is like a doctor and the toll collectors and sinners are like his
patients. It is an argument based on the priority of responding to people's
need. The second part is a christological statement about Jesus' commission
and authorisation and justifies Jesus' action on that christological basis. There
is a similarity in thought and structure to Jesus' response in 2:1–12: a *mashal*,
justifying behaviour in relation to human need, plus a christological statement
of authorisation. In the broadest sense, here, as there, the first argument
appeals at most to basic principles of care present in the Law; the second
argument is not related to the Law at all. Again Mark has shown that charges
that Jesus acts contrary to Torah are without foundation.

In 2:18–22 the question is about fasting. Not to fast is not an offence
(except on the Day of Atonement, which is not in focus here).[50] The issue is
a religious practice which some imposed on themselves (and expected of the
truly pious) in order to help them keep the Law.[51] Again the first response is

---

the *Character of Christianity*, (London: SCM, 1991), pp. 102–113; Sariola, *Markus*, pp.
65–66, who points out that the juxtaposition of 13–14 with 15–17 establishes the nature of
the problem, that the purity of the food could not be guaranteed. On concern in Mishnaic
Law about the uncleanness of toll collectors for Haberim see *mToh* 7:1–6; 8:1–6; cf. also
mBaba Kamma 10:1. Generally on Haberim avoiding table fellowship with the unclean or
those who may be suspected of not paying proper tithes see *mDemai* 2:2–3; 4:2,6; or of
their not washing hands or having unclean clothes: *mHag* 2:5,7. On avoiding contact with
the wicked, cf. *mAboth* 1:7.

[49] So Kiilunen, *Vollmacht*, p. 152; J. D. G. Dunn, "Mark 2:1 – 3:6: A Bridge between
Jesus and Paul on the Question of the Law," in *Jesus, Paul and the Law. Studies in Mark
and Galatians*, (London: SPCK, 1990), pp. 10–36, here: 19–20, who nevertheless notes
that the anecdote would have been of use in such disputes.

[50] On fasting see E. P. Sanders, *Jewish Law from Jesus to the Mishnah*, (London:
SCM, 1990), pp. 81–83.

[51] On the issue of whether for Mark the passage is commending the practice of Christian
fasting (cf. Did 8:1), see Kiilunen, *Vollmacht*, 163–195, esp. 193–194, who suggests that
the issue is not justification of fasting itself, but of the reasons for fasting, as opposed to
the reasons why the Baptists and the Pharisees fasted. Christians fasted because of the
absence of Jesus, not for ascetic reasons, nor because of sadness. Mark's primary interest
is not fasting as such but the hint of Jesus' coming passion. Note also R. A. Wild, "The
Encounter between Pharisaic and Christian Judaism: Some Early Gospel Evidence," *NovT*
27 (1985), pp. 105–124, who thinks that the Pharisees' question reveals the assumption

also in the form of an image as a *mashal*: "The children of the bridal chamber cannot fast while the bridegroom is with them" (2:19a). The new happening justifies departure from previous practices. 2:19b–20 supplements the argument with further explanation about the future departure of the bridegroom. "On that day" may also function within Mark's narrative to draw attention to the consequences of Jesus' conflicts, his execution (cf. already the blasphemy charge in 2:6 and the plotting in 3:6). The argument in 2:19a, which responds to the immediate issue, is implicitly eschatological and christological. For Mark, with Jesus the new has come and Jesus is the bridegroom. What at one stage was most likely a proverbial *mashal* about change is in Mark a christological statement.

The conflictual implications, which derive from the fact that Jesus' authority challenges previous authority, come to the fore in the images of the patch and the wine. They function strategically for Mark as a commentary on the nature of Jesus' conflict within these passages. Torn garments and ruptured wineskins are images of destruction and loss. In the light of the preceding context the previous authority being challenged is not the Torah, but its body of interpreters, represented by the scribes and Pharisees.[52] To follow their way would be to cause destruction and loss of the old. According to the imagery, the issue is not that one should discard old garments and old wine and use only the new. On the other hand, the image implies the new is better and this fits the broader context where newness has been a theme. The issue is what happens when the old and new are inappropriately related. The scribes are trying to confine Jesus within the old, failing to realise that in him the new has come. Thus "new" is legitimising difference, while not denying continuity. The old must include Torah.

Yet the "new" would not be new if it were just offering alternative (albeit new) interpretations of the old. The imagery suggests that with Jesus new cloth and new wine has come. Here is both continuity and discontinuity. Yet the primary focus is "the irresistibility of Jesus' new teaching".[53] As the centrepiece within the five fold structure of 2:1 – 3:6, 2:18–22 reinforces the theme of the new and raises acutely the issue of the nature of this

---

that Jesus and his group belong together with the Pharisees (p. 116). This is more relevant for Mark's tradition than for Mark.

[52] Pesch, *Markusevangelium I*, p. 177, speaks of the contrast as between Jewish and Christian practice; similarly Gnilka, *Markus I*, p. 116, in relation to fasting practice. But this is too narrow; it fails to take into account the central role of the contrast within 2:1 – 3:6 as a whole.

[53] So Gundry, *Mark*, p. 134.

continuity and discontinuity, especially as it affects our understanding of Jesus' attitude towards the Law in Mark.

The two sabbath controversies are about right behaviour on the sabbath, ie., the application of sabbath law.[54] Disciples, in the first, 2:23–28, were working on the sabbath according to the interpretation of sabbath law by Mark's Pharisees, plucking grain (cf. Exod 34:21). In the face of available evidence Mark's image of the Pharisees is an extreme stereotype (much as his claims about Pharisees and all Jews in 7:3–4). I shall return to this in the excurse below in the context of looking at pre-Markan tradition and especially possible historical roots of the anecdote. There is no indication that other Law issues played a role, such as going beyond a sabbath's limit,[55] making a path on the sabbath,[56] or stealing.[57]

2:23–28 contains more than one argument. In 2:28 we have Jesus' claim to authority over the sabbath as Son of Man. But, reflecting the pattern already noted in the first two episodes, a *mashal* like saying precedes the christological statement: "Human beings were not made for the sabbath, but the sabbath for human beings" (2:27). It has the force of an argument about interpretation of Torah on the basis of what God intended in creation. Before it is a further argument of a different kind. It appeals to scriptural precedent, to the priority of human need over other Torah rules, and is, perhaps, implicitly already christological.

The arguments function as a whole. The argument from precedent takes

---

[54] On sabbath law see Sanders, *Jewish Law*, pp. 6–19. On concern with sabbath law see Jub 2:17–33; 50; 4Q265 f. 2 I (among other things, forbidding rescuing an animal, but allowing rescuing a human being on the sabbath); Jos *Ap* 2:282 (claiming that keeping the sabbath had spread to other peoples); *JW* 2:517; *Ant* 12:274–277; 13:64 (concerning taking up arms in defence on the sabbath; similarly 1 Macc 2:40; *JW* 2:147 (about strict observance by the Essenes); Philo *De Vit Mos* 2:213–220; *De Spec Leg* 2:56–78, 249–251; *De Migr Abr* 90–91; *mShabb* 7:2 for Mishnaic law defining work on the sabbath; for the notion of another concern overriding the sabbath in Mishnaic law see *mShabb* 18:3 (about child birth); 19:2–3 (about circumcision; similarly *mNed* 3:11); *mMen* 11:3 (about baking cakes for the high priest). Note also the "general rule" attributed to Akiba in *mShabb* 19:1, "Any act of work that can be done on the eve of Sabbath does not override the Sabbath, but what cannot be done on the even of the Sabbath overrides the Sabbath" (also *mPes* 6:2; *mMen* 11:3). On the death penalty for wilful profaning of the sabbath: *mSanh* 7:8, as Nu 15:32–36.

[55] So rightly Schweizer, *Markus*, p. 34; Banks, *Law*, p. 114;

[56] On this, see the discussion in F. Neirynck, "Jesus and the Sabbath. Some observations on Mk II,27," in *Jésus aux origines de la christologie*, BEThL 40, edited by J. Dupont, (Leuven, 1975), pp. 227–27, here: 254–258; Cf. Hooker, *Mark*, p. 102.

[57] Cf. Kiilunen, *Vollmacht*, p. 210, with reference to Deut 23:25–26. He suggests that the issue was not transgression of sabbath law, but of the law, theft, on the sabbath. On this see Sariola, *Markus*, p. 98.

the form of a confrontation: "Have you not read?" (2:25a). This sets Jesus' expertise as interpreter against that of the Pharisees as interpreters. It continues Mark's theme of conflict between Jesus and the Pharisees. The primary focus in this argument from precedent is that as the need of David's men justified setting aside what was normally forbidden, so the need of the disciples justifies setting sabbath law aside. That is how the argument works within the narrative dialogue. For Mark and Mark's hearers, another allusion may be present: appeal to David by the one who is Messiah, Son of David (greater than David – so 12:35–38!).[58] For Mark and Mark's hearers this christological argument receives fuller expression in 2:28: "The Son of Man is Lord also of the sabbath". Within the dialogue of the narrative, 2:27 is supporting argument: the sabbath was created for the sake of people.[59] This additionally justifies taking into account human need in applying sabbath law.

Jesus is not advocating abandoning sabbath law as such.[60] That would not make sense within the narrative. The argument is not: David broke the law, therefore so can I;[61] but need justified David's breaking a law; ie. another

---

[58] So Sariola, *Markus*, p. 104; F. W. Beare, "The sabbath was made for man?" *JBL* 79 (1960), pp. 130–136, here: 134; M. Hengel, "Jesus und die Tora," *Theol. Beitr* 9 (1978), pp. 152–172, here: 166; see also his "Jesus, der Messias Israels. Zum Streit über das 'messianische Sendungsbewusstsein' Jesu," in *Messiah and Christos: studies in the Jewish Origins of Christianity, presented to David Flusser on the occasion of his seventy-fifth birthday*, Texte und Studien zum antiken Judentum 32, edited by I. Gruenwald (Tübingen: J. C. B. Mohr [Paul Siebeck], 1992), pp. 155–176, where he argues that the sense of messiahship and fulfilment are the key to understanding Jesus' teaching and actions.

[59] On the parallel statement, "The sabbath is delivered to you, not you to the sabbath," in *Mekh Ex* 14.14; *b*Yom85b, see Banks, *Law*, 119, who rightly identifies Mark's version as more sweeping. Similarly H. Braun, *Spätjüdisch-häretischer und frühchristlicher Radikalismus. Jesus von Nazareth und die essenische Qumransekte II: Synoptiker*, BHTh 24, (Tübingen: J. C. B. Mohr [Paul Siebeck], 2nd edn., 1969), p. 70 n. 2. See also H. Weiss, "The Sabbath in the Synoptic Gospels," *JSNT* 38 (1990), pp. 13–27, here: 21, who notes also the problem of the late dating of the source.

[60] Against W. Rordorf, *Sunday: The History of the Day of Rest and Worship in the Earliest Centuries of the Christian Church*, (London: SCM, 1968), pp. 62–63; Schweizer, *Markus*, p. 40; Banks, *Law*, p. 119; G. Dautzenberg, "Frühes Christentum - Gilt die Tora weiterhin? Hellenistische Mission, Paulus und das Markusevangelium," *Orientierung* 55 (1991), pp. 243–246, here: 245. Dautzenberg assumes that on their own 25–26 and 27 do assume the validity of sabbath law, but that Mark assumes that the sabbath is abolished. Neyrey, "Symbolic Approach," p. 81, suggests that in 2:21–28 and 3:4 the issue is not respect of the basic maps but where to draw the lines. But Jesus and the Christians do reject strict lines on the map of meals and put themselves "clearly in discontinuity with the established traditions" (p. 81). Neyrey's categories do not however allow him the distinction between scripture and tradition and here is where major conflict arises.

[61] Against Westerholm, *Scribal Authority*, p. 98, who nevertheless rightly points out

principle of Torah overrode the law that only priests should eat showbread. There is nothing either in the citation of the precedent or its use which suggests that in both David's case and the case of Jesus the actions were legitimised because of a claim to priesthood.[62] Nor in 2:27 is an appeal being made to a new eschatological sabbath come in Jesus.[63] Nothing of that appears in the text. At most, as we have noted, there is for Mark and his hearers an implied hint in 2:25–26 of Jesus as the Messiah, which connects with 2:28. Nor should 2:27 be read in a narrow christological sense, as if it intended: the sabbath was made for the Son of Man, on the assumption that Mark and his hearers would be alert to a possible play on words. This denies the strong emphasis on response to human need in what precedes and in the following sabbath episode, not to speak, of the first two episodes in the series.

The words of 2:28, "So the Son of Man is Lord also of the sabbath", are not, in a narrow sense, the conclusion drawn from 2:27, but the conclusion of the anecdote and of Jesus' arguments within it as a whole. It also goes beyond the argument from precedent (25–26) and the argument from principle (27) in that it asserts Jesus' authority to interpret sabbath law. The word, καὶ ("also"), points back to 2:10: "The Son of Man has authority on earth to forgive sins." Jesus is the ultimate authority, yet Jesus is also an authority who takes the trouble to justify his (his disciples') behaviour using scriptural arguments. The anecdote is more, therefore, than an example of Jesus outwitting his opponents, as Vouga suggests.[64] The issue of Law is still present. The Lord of the sabbath upholds sabbath law and justifies appropriate behaviour with argument.

In the following episode the Pharisees (of whom we do not hear until 3:6, but who are presumed after 2:23–28) suspect an act of healing on the sabbath,

---

that the argument does not function well within Jewish casuistry. He adds: "The argument is rather that David's action, though contrary to the letter of the law, is countenanced by scripture; it thus cannot be the intention of the divine lawgiver that the terms of torah be interpreted rigidly and every deviation from such an interpretation condemned." This is Christian halakah.

[62] As suggested by, for instance, J. Roloff, *Das Kerygma und der irdische Jesus. Historische Motive in den Jesus-Erzählungen der Evangelien*, (Göttingen: Vandenhoeck und Ruprecht, 1970), pp. 71–72; Broadhead, "Christology," p. 28; against this Westerholm, *Scribal Authority*, p. 98. Nor is there any indication in the text of Jesus assuming priestly authority in 3:1–6 (against Broadhead, p. 28).

[63] There does not appear to be a reference to sabbath in an eschatological sense. Cf. J. M. Robinson, *The Problem of History in Mark*, SBT 21, (London: SCM, 1957), p. 47; Carson, "Sabbath," p. 65.

[64] Cf. Vouga, *Loi*, pp. 173–174. See also R. Parrott, "Conflict and Rhetoric in Mark 2:23–28," *Semeia* 64 (1993), pp. 117–138, who discusses the rhetoric of 2:23–28 in detail.

which they (according to Mark) would interpret as breaking the sabbath (3:1–6). Again we appear to be dealing with an extremist stereotype of the Pharisees, which may have its roots in history (see the discussion of the anecdote in the excurse below). Mark's agenda is polemical. He has Jesus refute their sabbath interpretation as indicative of hardness of heart, a heavily loaded expression in Israel's tradition. He does so in the form of a *mashal*: "Is it lawful on the sabbath to do good or to do harm, to save life or to kill?" (3:4). Again we meet a pithy saying such as we found in the other controversies. The first half of the response, "to do good or to do harm (or evil)", is as radical as 2:27. It responds to the issue of Law interpretation by enunciating a principle in the form of an absurd alternative. At one level, of course, no one should choose to do evil on the sabbath or at any other time; of course, one should do good! Yet it is at this point that the issue arises: assuming one should always only do good, which activities are appropriate on the sabbath and which, not? Doing good in this context is more specific; it means doing good to people and applies here to healing. The next set of alternatives, saving life or killing, relates the saying more directly to the prospective healing, but also prepares for the irony of the plot of death in 3:6.

In reality, Mark's Jesus is ignoring the issue of what constitutes work on the sabbath and what could be left for another day. There is no indication the man's life was in danger. Instead the effect of Jesus' response is to shift the ground of the discussion about sabbath law on the basis of the principle enunciated in 2:27. Helping people in need is justified on the sabbath, whether giving the hungry food or making the sick well, because the sabbath was made for people. This leaves a lot of loose ends and hardly addresses issues of how such an axiom for sabbath law might work out in practice. For Mark the issue is one of orientation (the priority of compassion for need) and ultimately one of authority: Jesus is Lord also of the sabbath (2:28). This christological statement functions for both anecdotes. Some have suggested that when Jesus goes on to heal the man by word alone, Mark is deliberately portraying Jesus as choosing an alternative to a healing act in order to remain within the sabbath law, but this would entail Mark contradicting his own argument, according to which he has already justified acts of healing on the sabbath in principle.[65]

3:1–6 belongs closely with 2:23–28 in portraying Jesus as the Lord of the sabbath who interprets sabbath law in accordance with the radical principle that response to human need has highest priority. Jesus' response is set in

---

[65] Against Gundry, *Mark*, p. 152; Sanders, *Jewish Law*, p. 21. Cf. also G. Vermes, *The*

contrast with the "hardness of heart" of his opponents, a laden expression in decrying Israel's unfaithfulness in the Old Testament. For Mark and his hearers, the second alternative, "to save life or to kill", goes beyond the immediate argument. It functions with "to do evil" as an allusion to the Pharisees' plot (on the sabbath!) to kill Jesus (3:6). The effect is to range the Pharisees not on the side of the Law, but on the side of those who transgress it. By contrast, Mark portrays Jesus as having new authority and as offering right interpretation of the Law.

On Mark's understanding, then, in none of the five instances does Jesus act contrary to Torah. In the first he is falsely accused of blasphemy. Mark does not address the issue of the legitimacy of Jesus' role according to the Law, nor do his scribes. He has Jesus argue the legitimacy of his action, but ultimately Jesus' legitimacy derives from his status as Son of Man (2:10). The same is true in 2:23–28 (and by association, 3:1–6), and, though expressed differently, also in 2:15–17 and 2:18–22. Mark has already grounded this authority of Jesus in the prologue, and in the following episodes of chapter 1, as derived from God and something new. For Mark, then, Jesus stands beside Torah as someone with new authority. 1:40–45 portrayed him on the side of Torah; 3:1–6 portrays his opponents as transgressors of Torah.

Does he simply bring a more authoritative interpretation of Torah over against that of the scribes, or is there more to it? Both in 2:10 and (linked with it) in 2:28 Mark has Jesus move beyond argument for interpretation of Torah to statements of divine authority which stand independently of Torah. In 2:10 he is adding himself as an instance authorised to declare forgiveness beyond and apart from (though not in contravention of) what is foreseen in the Law. Within their Markan context the images of the wedding (2:19a), the garment and wine (2:21–22), suggest the "new" is an authoritative departure from the old. Yet it is probably not pressing the images too far to note that they at least indicate some sense of continuity.[66] Certainly with the wedding this is so; the difference is between hope and fulfilment. And, at least, with the garments and the wine there is a continuity of function. For the latter

---

Religion of Jesus the Jew (Minneapolis: Fortress, 1993), p. 23, who writes of the controversy as "a storm in a tea-cup since none of the Sabbath cures of Jesus entailed 'work'".

He rightly points out that the appropriate description of the episode in Mark is not a debate but a fight showing Jesus as victorious (p. 133).

[66] So also Dunn, "Mark 2.1 – 3.6," pp. 20–21; Gundry, *Mark*, p. 134.

images, however, incompatibility is to the fore. The authority of Jesus is something new, not simply to be assimilated within the existing Torah system. This coheres with the image of Jesus' authority presented in the opening scenes of the gospel, where Jesus is acknowledged as God's Son, declares God's rule, commands discipleship and teaches and exorcises with incomparable authority.

Mark seems, therefore, to see Jesus as one who, in coming with eschatological authority, effectively replaces the authority of Torah as the absolute court of appeal. I emphasise: as the absolute court of appeal. For there is no indication that Mark intends a total replacement or abrogation. In the light of what follows in the gospel we see that Mark's Jesus does discard major portions of the Law (food laws, purity laws, the cultic system), but this is not the focus in 2:1 – 3:6. The new authority vested in Jesus is reflected in the fact that in these episodes Mark's arguments are primarily christological and eschatological. The conflict is between Jesus, the new authority, who exercises that authority also to interpret Torah and the stereotyped scribal and Pharisaic interpreters. The liberal interpretation of Law reflects a hierarchy of values which leaves one wondering, for instance in 3:1–6, what might still remain of sabbath observance. Yet in these chapters the defence is primarily authoritative defence of Torah observance and, we may assume, indicative of this level of Lay observance in Mark's community.

There is a remarkable similarity of substance and style of argument used to justify Jesus' behaviour in relation to the Law in all five controversy stories. Each contains a pithy *mashal*-like response designed to disarm the criticism of Jesus' attitude towards the Law and justify his own or his disciples' behaviour. Yet, with the exception of the final episode, beside these pithy sayings are arguments of a different kind, based on Jesus' claim to authority. In each they form the climax and carry the primary weight.

1.2.2.1 Excursus: Behind Mark 2:1 – 3:6.
Tradition and the Historical Jesus

1.2.2.1.1. Tradition

The extent to which the five narratives in 2:1 – 3:6 existed already as a collection before Mark, perhaps also including other anecdotes, has been subject of considerable debate.[67] It seems to me that a strong case can be made for Mark's redactional hand in setting the stories together as a group of five, composed on a symmetrical pattern, introduced by one focusing on Jesus' authority and concluding with the hint of Jesus' execution.

There are strong grounds for seeing Mark's hand in the presence of the sayings which stress Jesus' authority over the law. These include the introduction of the Son of Man sayings in 2:10; 2:28; and of the logia about the new patches and the new wine in 2:21–22. 2:17b and 3:4b ("to save life or to kill") may also reflect Markan expansions. Mark has probably introduced the account of the call of Levi in 2:13–14, expanded the saying about the bridegroom in 2:19b–20, and developed the hints of the passion narrative both through 3:6 and through the accusation of blasphemy in 2:7. On the other hand, the remarkable homogeneity of argument about the Law in all five controversy accounts would support the view that all five may have been linked together before Mark.

The narrative in 2:1–12 includes both a healing and a controversy. It has often been pointed out that the conclusion of the narrative appears to reflect no knowledge of the controversy. It says: "All were astonished and glorified God, saying, 'We have never seen anything like this before!'" (2:12). Thus Bultmann saw it as the ending of what was originally simply a healing story into which at some stage a controversy had been inserted.[68] I would argue that this would have had to have happened before Mark, because of the different levels of argument in 2:5b–10. If the controversy had been inserted secondarily into a miracle story, we could then argue that the controversy is a secondary creation or that it reflects a tradition which existed independently. If it had existed independently, it has lost its original setting, assuming that there were a group of scribes who were reacting to Jesus'

---

[67] See the extensive discussion in Kiilunen, *Vollmacht*, pp. 263–266, who rejects the theory of a written collection, but nevertheless contemplates an association of stories used over a long period by the author of the gospel. See also the review of research in Scholtissek, *Vollmacht*, pp. 137–147.

[68] So R. Bultmann, *The History of the Synoptic Tradition*, (Oxford: Blackwell, 1963), p. 15.

declaration of forgiveness to someone. It is more likely that the story never existed without its controversy. The usual objection arising from 2:12 is not strong and depends on an arithmetical insistence that the "all" must be all inclusive (ie. include the scribes).

In 2:1–12 I would see a pre-Markan tradition existing possibly without 2:10 and probably the "blasphemy" accusation of 2:7. I assume then a healing narrative in which Jesus is recorded as declaring forgiveness of sins.[69] The issue of blasphemy most likely reflects a Markan addition which links the passage with the trial narrative. Probably in the pre-Markan tradition the issue was not: why do you act like God, but why do you do something for which you are not authorised, but others are (or think they are)?[70] This

---

[69] Cf. Kiilunen, *Vollmacht*, who also believes 2:10 is secondary over against 2:9 (p. 109). I am less confident than he is in assuming it is a Markan creation on the basis of Dan 4:17, 27, 31 (p. 120). Scholtissek, *Vollmacht*, pp. 154–156, sees 6–10 as a Markan addition, resulting in a typical Markan sandwich construction. Such reconstructions do not take sufficiently into account the problem posed by the tension between the blasphemy accusation and the declaration of forgiveness.

[70] Cf. Hofius, "Vergebungszuspruch," shows that there is no evidence that priests or high priests had exclusive authority to forgive sins; similarly Sanders, *Jewish Law*, p. 62: "it is possible that forgiveness was understood rather than pronounced." On the other hand Hofius acknowledges that Ps 130:5 which speaks of waiting for Yahweh's word of forgiveness could imply that a priest would express it, but only with a delegated authority (p. 126). In 2:5b, he claims, this is not the case and cites 2:10 as evidence. But this is surely a misunderstanding. The reference to authority in 2:10 also implies authorisation. This is even the case in the fourth gospel with its much more developed christology. As Hofius's priest behind Ps 130:5 would have expressed God's forgiveness, an effective word, so Jesus expresses God's forgiveness as an effective word (hence also the passive). Sanders concludes, p. 63: "the best case that can be made for connecting Jesus' statement 'your sins are forgiven' with blasphemy is presumption – not the presumption of forgiving sins in place of God (the text does not say that), nor the presumption of discussing forgiveness even though not accredited (the priesthood did not exercise that kind of control). One might find blasphemous presumption in Jesus' saying that God forgave a man who was not known to have confessed and made restitution." Cf. W. Weiss, *"Eine neue Lehre mit Vollmacht." Die Streit- und Schulgespräche des Markusevangeliums*, BZNW 52, (Berlin: de Gruyter, 1989), p. 137. Dunn, *Partings*. p. 46, argues that the issue is that Jesus "usurped the role of God which God had assigned to priest and cult". Cf. also Gundry, *Markus*, p. 116, who cites 4QprNab according to which a Jewish diviner forgives Nabonidus but hastens to add that he give glory to God. I. Broer, "Jesus und das Gesetz. Anmerkungen zur Geschichte des Problems und zur Frage der Sündenvergebung durch den historischen Jesus," in *Jesus und das jüdische Gesetz*, edited by I. Broer, (Stuttgart: Kohlhammer, 1992), pp. 61–104, here: 82–98, offers a thorough discussion of the issue of forgiveness of sins in Judaism and comes to the conclusion that forgiveness was by no means limited to the sacrificial cult, but formed part of the understanding of repentance and conversion. This makes it likely that, as in the case of the sabbath and hand washing controversies, that the objectors are representative of a group which wanted to limit such authority. The same concern was present with John the Baptist, further evidence for such thinking. Therefore

makes better sense of the answer in 2:9, which fits better as a response to the accusation that Jesus acts without authorisation, than it does to the accusation of blasphemy. The response is a *mashal*, a riddle. We noted the two levels at which it functions: at the level of ability, it is harder to heal than to pronounce forgiveness; at the level of legality, the declaration of forgiveness is more difficult, because it exercises an authority, which in the mind of certain Jews, would lie beyond Jesus' competence.[71]

The issue was traditional and had also been there with John the Baptist. Jesus' clever answer, according to the tradition, is effectively an appeal to the overriding priority of compassion for human need which warrants a declaration of God's forgiveness at the point of suffering. Jesus is not portrayed as quoting one part of Torah against another, but as challenging scribes who want to make a distinction between a word of healing and a statement entailing a claim to legal authorisation. Jesus refuses to recognise such a distinction. The choice in the tradition is not between human need and God's Law. For God's Law is about compassion for human need and Jesus appears willing to sit lightly to specific institutional provisions for dispensing divine compassion in the light of immediate need (2:9). Interestingly, 2:10 continues to reflect the issue of authorisation and may possibly have been part of the same tradition. Alternatively, it has been brought into the tradition by Mark to deal with the charge of blasphemy which seems to be Mark's major concern to expose as false.

I agree with many that Mark has inserted the call of Levi in 2:13–14.[72] It recalls 1:16–20 and the associated christology which precedes. Probably 2:15–17 once stood on it own. The complaint is about Jesus' eating with toll collectors and sinners. As we have seen, for Mark the focus is primarily moral, that is, about Jesus in bad company, contrary to the injunctions of scripture and the Law in general. In addition, there may also have been purity issues involved. Without 2:13–14, the anecdote does not give any clear indication where the meal would have taken place. If it had been in Jesus' own house, the issue would be connected with why he invited such people into his house. Apart from the moral, the purity issues would have

---

Broer's conclusion, that Mark 2:1–12 must derive from a community proclaiming forgiveness solely on the basis of Jesus' atoning death, is unnecessary. On forgiveness through prayer see 1 En 13; SibOr 4:165, linked with lustration and echoing John's baptism; cf. also Sir 3:30; 1QS 5:6; 8:1–4.

[71] Against the view that only priests could forgive see the previous note. This counts, in turn, against the view of Broadhead, "Christology," pp. 26–27, that Mark intends a priestly claim on Jesus' part.

[72] See, for instance, Kiilunen, *Vollmacht*, pp. 127–136; Weiss, *Vollmacht*, p. 85.

pertained to the inviting of people who were unclean, but presumably not to the danger of untithed or inappropriately prepared foods, which would have arisen when eating in their houses. Whatever the case, in the view of the complainants Jesus ought not to be eating with such people.

The tradition preserves Jesus' response in two parts in 2:17, "It is not the well who have need of a doctor, but rather the sick. I came not to call the righteous but sinners." The words, "I have not come to call righteous but sinners" (2:17b), may well reflect a secondary expansion over against 2:17a.[73] They are making a christological statement. 2:17a ("It is not the well who have need of a doctor, but rather the sick") is different. It has the character of a *mashal* and uses imagery attested in Hellenistic literature.[74] With this proverbial aphorism Jesus justifies his behaviour. It is an appeal to response to human need as overriding concerns about bad company (and possibly purity). Probably at some stage the anecdote ended here.[75] As in 2:1–12 it now stands beside another which argues from Jesus' authority.

The contrast, well-sick, seems best suited to the context of a complaint concerned with moral company rather than with purity issues, although both

---

[73] Are the "righteous" really the self-righteous? This reading might make best sense in the later Christian communities. On the lips of Jesus it might have reflected a preference for reaching out to sinners and an implicit acknowledgment that among his Jewish contemporaries were also many who were genuinely righteous. Cf. also Gundry, *Mark*, pp. 129–130, who takes it in a non exclusive sense. That it is a secondary expansion of 2:17a: Koch, D.-A. "Jesu Tischgemeinschaft mit Zöllnern und Sündern. Erwägungen zur Entstehungs von Mk 2.13–17," in *Jesu Rede von Gott und ihre Nachgeschichte im frühen Christentum. Beiträge zur Verkündigung Jesu und zum Kerygma der Kirche. FS für Willi Marxsen*, edited by D.-A. Koch et al., (Gütersloh: Mohn, 1989), pp. 57–73, here: 69.

[74] On the Hellenistic parallels to this saying see Weiss, *Vollmacht*, p. 90; F. G. Downing, *Christ and the Cynics. Jesus and other Radical Preachers in First-Century Tradition*, JSOT Manuals 4, (Sheffield: JSOTPr., 1988), pp. 122–123; see also B. L. Mack, *A Myth of Innocence. Mark and Christian Origins*, (Philadelphia: Fortress, 1988), pp. 187–188.

[75] So Kiilunen, *Vollmacht*, pp. 159–160; A. Hultgren, *Jesus and his Adversaries. The Form and Function of the Conflict Stories in the Synoptic Gospels*, (Minneapolis: Augsburg, 1979), pp. 109–110, believes that the scene was generated on the basis of the saying. This reflects a common understanding of the creation of *chreiai*, reaching back to Bultmann, *Synoptic Tradition*, pp. 18; see also the more discussion in Weiss, *Vollmacht*, pp. 268–279, who distinguishes three stages: the isolated logion (as wisdom argument), the development of an accusation to which the logion responds, and the development of the scene. See also R. Tannehill, "Types and Functions of Apophthegms in the Synoptic Gospels," *ANRW* II.25.2 (1984), pp. 1792–1829. See also Koch, "Tischgemeinschaft," pp. 64–68, who argues that Bultmann's theory does not adequately explain 2:15–17. Koch sees the anecdote having a Palestinian origin, but then being used in Hellenistic Jewish communities where it would have relevance for the issue of mixed table fellowship and finally in Mark's Gentile communities where, with the introduction, 2:24, it appealed to Jesus' authoritative action (pp. 70–73).

may be implied in the anecdote. Either way, it is striking that the aphorism assumes the applicability of the category sick to the toll collectors and sinners and so indirectly attests some common value system between Jesus and his questioners, which will have been based in Torah.

2:18–19a present an anecdote of similar form.[76] Probably Mark has introduced the reference to the disciples of the Pharisees beside the disciples of John the Baptist, making it more of a whole with the anecdotes which precede and follow, if this had not already occurred in a prior Markan collection of the anecdotes. The anecdote relates Jesus' response to the question about fasting: "The children of the bridal chamber cannot fast while the bridegroom is with them." This pithy response uses wedding imagery to justify Jesus' difference from John by implying that the longed for wedding time has come.[77] It need not in itself be claiming that Jesus is the bridegroom. It does however presuppose a claim that with his ministry a new age has arrived.[78] It very easily lent itself to being interpreted directly in a christological manner and this is evident in the expansion of the saying to include a reference to Jesus himself as the bridegroom, then to his death and to subsequent fasting.[79]

The sayings about cloth and wine relate more directly to 2:19a, the theme of the new, and appear to be logia which either Mark or premarkan tradition had secondarily attached to the anecdote. Perhaps they were attached to 2:19a before its christological expansion in 2:19b–20.[80] In themselves they highlight a contrast between the new and the old, reflecting in all likelihood a claim of eschatological significance for Jesus' ministry. If they were attached to this anecdote before it included a reference to the Pharisees, which seems likely, then the contrast is primarily between John the Baptist and Jesus and their widely attested divergence, which was all the more striking

---

[76] So Pesch, *Markusevangelium I*, p. 174; M. Waibel, "Die Auseinandersetzung mit der Fasten und Sabbatpraxis Jesu in urchristlichen Gemeinden," in *Zur Geschichte des Urchristentums*, QD 87, edited by G. Dautzenberg, H. Merklein, K. Müller, (Freiburg: Herder, 1979), pp. 71–76.

[77] Similarly Weiss, *Vollmacht*, p. 100.

[78] Cf. John 3:29–30 for possible further evidence of the wedding motif in tradition about Jesus and John.

[79] So Kuhn, *Sammlungen*, pp. 68–71, who argues that the difference between "day" and "days" reflects the fact that before Mark a community wanted to draw attention to its particular day of fasting on Friday and its relation to the death of Jesus (cf. Did 8:1); Waibel, "Auseinandersetzung," p. 67.

[80] So Pesch, *Markusevangelium I*, p. 117; Waibel, "Auseinandersetzung," pp. 76–78. Cf. Bultmann, *Synoptic Tradition*, p. 19; Grundmann, *Markus*, p. 66.

because of their historical association. This contrast depended strongly on differing understandings of eschatology, and, especially on Jesus' announcement of the breaking in of the reign of God. They would then not have related to the issue of Torah or Torah interpretation, as they do in Mark. In isolation these two sayings probably belonged within an eschatological setting. As isolated logia (as they now occur in Thomas 47) they would have been open to a variety of interpretations.[81]

The passage, 2:23–28, currently includes at least three kinds of argument, as we have seen. 2:28 ("The Son of Man is lord also of the sabbath") represents an appeal to Jesus' superior authority in line with 2:10 (hence the "also") and with the major arguments in the first three anecdotes and probably derives from Mark 2:27 ("The sabbath was made for people; not people for the sabbath") argues on a different basis and corresponds to what we believe to be the response of Jesus in the other anecdotes: a short pithy saying. It is likely also to have formed Jesus' response in the earliest form of the tradition behind this Markan episode.[82] It legitimises Jesus' (ie. his disciples')

---

[81] See Weiss, *Vollmacht*, p. 105, for the view that they were originally independent logia.

[82] So Luz, U. in: R. Smend and U. Luz, *Gesetz*, Kohlhammer Taschenbücher – Biblische Konfrontationen 1015, (Stuttgart: Kohlhammer, 1981), p. 59; Berger, *Gesetzesauslegung*, pp. 29, 197–198, 584; Hultgren, *Adversaries*, p. 114; Schweizer, *Markus*, p. 35; Waibel, "Auseinandersetzung," p. 88; Lührmann, *Markusevangelium*, p. 64; Weiss, *Vollmacht*, pp. 42–45; Scholtissek, *Vollmacht*, pp. 173–177; Parrott, "Conflict," p. 127, who discusses the subsequent rhetorical elaboration in dialogue with Robbins, pp. 124–131; cf. esp. B. L. Mack, and V. K. Robbins, *Patterns of Persuasion in the Gospels*, (Sonoma: Polebridge, 1989), pp. 107–141. Cf. Sariola, *Markus*, p. 87, who argues for the position taken by Bultmann, *Synoptic Tradition*, pp. 16, that 25b–26 forms the original answer. Similarly Lane, *Mark*, pp 118–119; Pesch, *Markusevangelium I*, p. 178; Gnilka, *Markus I*, p. 120; Kiilunen, *Vollmacht*, pp. 203, 217. Hübner, *Gesetz*, pp. 120–121, argues for 27–28 belonging originally together on the basis that "son of man" originally meant human being; similarly, Roloff, *Kerygma*, pp. 58–62; cf. also Bultmann, *Synoptic Tradition*, pp. 16–17. On this see also Dunn, "Mark 2.1 – 3.6," p. 26; G. Vermes, *Jesus the Jew*, (London: Collins, 1973), pp. 180–181. Vouga, *Loi*, pp. 41, 170, argues that the original tradition included 2:23–26 and 28, but that the addition of 2:27 changed the focus from an absolute christological claim to an argument about sabbath interpretation. See also his "Die Entwicklungsgeschichte der jesuanischen Chrien und didaktischen Dialoge des Markusevangeliums," in *Jesu Rede von Gott und ihre Nachgeschichte im frühen Christentum. Beiträge zur Verkündigung Jesu und zum Kerygma der Kirche. FS für Willi Marxsen*, edited by D.-A. Koch et al., (Gütersloh: Mohn, 1989), pp. 45–56, here: 46–47. Those who argue for 25b–26 being the original response in the tradition emphasise similarities in vocabulary with 23–24, on the assumption that such similarity indicates common origin, a hazardous argument. Arguments for the originality of 2:27 also have a tentative quality. They include formal similarity to other anecdotes in which a pithy saying forms the original responses and to which scriptural argument is secondarily added. These are, however, cumulatively significant. For a detailed review of research prior to the mid

behaviour towards the Law on the basis of a different interpretation of sabbath law from those who accuse his disciples. The additional argument in 2:25–26 is one of precedent and probably reflects a secondary support of what lies in 2:27, but it is different in kind.[83] It throws the emphasis on human need ("when he was in need and was hungry along with his companions" 2:26) and, perhaps, in addition, on the person of Jesus and the person of David as authorities, the David messianic connection.[84]

The anecdote, without 25–26, does not suggest the disciples were hungry.[85] In it, therefore, 2:27 was not an argument justifying response to human need on the sabbath,[86] but a protest against unnecessary strictness in sabbath law, arguing that sabbath should be interpreted on the basis that it is a gift rather than a demand.[87] It does not represent an argument so much as a challenge to think differently, formulated as a neat pithy response. It reflects thus the kind of approach found in 2:9.

In the fifth narrative Mark is probably also using traditional material. Here we find a similar kind of argument. "Is it lawful on the sabbath to do

---

1970s see the report of Neirynck, "Jesus and the Sabbath." For the view that 2:27–28 formed the pre-Markan tradition answer, with 28 understood christologically, and that Mark added 25–26, see Waibel, "Auseinandersetzung," pp. 83–86. Cf. Beare, "Sabbath," who argues that 2:27–28 form the nucleus of the tradition, originally were words of the primitive community in conflict with the Pharisees and both referring to Jesus as Son of Man. Around this formed the scene and then the supplement referring to David on the basis of royal messianic precedent. But how credible is such a claim that 2:27 would be making for Jesus, and in particular, does it really make sense of 27b?

[83] Treating 2:25–26 independently of 2:27 leads Kiilunen, *Vollmacht*, p. 210, to argue that the dispute is not about breaking sabbath law, but breaking a law on the sabbath, because the David episode has nothing to do with the sabbath. This must run the gauntlet of arguing that both Matthew and Luke have got it wrong. See the discussion in Sariola, *Markus*, p. 98. Roloff, *Kerygma*, pp. 71–72, suggests that the point is that as priestly rights are claimed for David and his men, so they are to be claimed for itinerant missionaries. Similarly Broadhead, "Priestly Portrait," p. 28. No such priestly claim (and implied commitment to the system of thought which undergirds it in Torah) is to be found elsewhere in Mark or his tradition..

[84] So Sariola, *Markus*, p. 104.

[85] Dunn, "Mark 2.1 – 3.6," pp. 22–23, notes the lack of proportion which the argument about hunger introduces, rightly underlining that the original focus is freedom on the sabbath, not response to need. In my view 25–26 has entered the pericope, just as did the scriptural argument in 10:6–8, to offer scriptural argument to support what had originally been a provocative pithy response (10:9).

[86] Cf. Borg, *Conflict*, p. 156, who argues that "man" in 2:27 originally meant Israel; the disciples were on a mission to Israel!

[87] Gundry, *Mark*, p. 142, argues that even in Mark, 2:27 should not be understood as arguing that the disciples were in need.

good or to do harm?" (3:4). It is similar to 2:27 in laying down a challenge to think differently about the sabbath through provocative generalisation.[88] It is debatable whether the additional words, "to save life or to kill?" belonged to the premarkan tradition.[89] While they reflect the same style of confrontation and may be already a pre-Markan expansion, they are probably a Markan expansion.[90] By this expansion Mark establishes the irony with which he then ends the anecdote, and the series of anecdotes, in 3:6: the resolution of the Herodians and Pharisees to plan to kill Jesus.[91] The theme of hardness of heart and the plot to kill Jesus play a major role in the development of the gospel story as a whole.

Each of the five traditional anecdotes reflects similar style and context. In response to a question or objection relating to behaviour, Jesus issues a pithy *mashal*-like saying (2:9,17a,19a,27; 3:4a; cf. similarly 7:15; 10:9; 12:17).[92]

> What is easier: to say to the paralytic, "Your sins are forgiven," or to say, "Arise, take up your pallet and walk"?(2:9)
>
> It is not the well who have need of a doctor, but rather the sick. (2:17a)
>
> The children of the bridal chamber cannot fast while the bridegroom is with them. (2:19a)
>
> The sabbath was made for people; not people for the sabbath. (2:27)
>
> Is it lawful on the sabbath to do good or to do harm? (3:4)

---

[88] So Westerholm, *Scribal Authority*, p. 100, who notes that the issue is not application of halakah, but its moral propriety.

[89] Cf. Borg, *Conflict*, pp. 156–162, who argues that there is an allusion here to the decision reported in 1 Macc 2:29–41 to allow armed resistance on the sabbath. "Kill" is stronger than that. So Gundry, *Mark*, p. 153. On echoes of the withering and restoration of Jereboam's hand (1 Kgs 13:4–6), see J. Sauer, "Traditionsgechichtliche Überlegungen zu Mk 3:1–6," *ZNW* 73 (1982), pp. 183–203; cf. also S. H. Smith, "Mark 3,1–6: Form, Redaction and Community Function," *Biblica* 75 (1994), pp. 153–174, here: 155 n. 6, 154–165, who argues for a possible link with the Exodus so that Jesus is pictured as both stretching out the hand, like Yahweh (cf. 1:41) and enabling others to do the same, as here. The man represents Mark's faction against critical Christians denying that Jesus' freedom over the sabbath allows that also for them (pp. 169–174). This is too speculative.

[90] So Vouga, *Loi*, p. 56; Sariola, *Markus*, 94

[91] For the view that Mark has added 3:6 see Kiilunen, *Vollmacht*, p. 233; Weiss, *Vollmacht*, p. 110; Smith, "Mark 3,1–6," pp. 160–164; Sariola, *Markus*, p. 94, who notes, in particular, the link made by Mark between 3:6 and the life-death addition in 3:4 (p. 108).

[92] These need not have originally circulated in isolation. Some require their context. Hultgren, *Adversaries*, pp. 81, 82 makes this case for 2:19a; 3:4a. But it must also be the case for 2:9. On *mashalim* among Jesus' sayings see Bultmann, *Synoptic Tradition*, pp. 81–82; also P. Sellew, "Aphorisms in Mark: A Stratigraphic Analysis," *Forum* 8 (1–2, 1992), pp. 141–160.

All five are antithetical in structure (2:19a, indirectly). The question about fasting focused originally on the different practices of Jesus and John in relation to fasting. In the other four the concern is application of Torah. In each Jesus responds to criticism on the basis of the Law with a brief aphorism which effectively challenges the hearers to think differently about Torah. The aphorisms are almost mischievous – at least, viewed from the perspective of Jesus' opponents, because they do not deal directly with the issue at hand. The four dealing with Torah imply that human life takes precedence in application of Torah and thus seek to frustrate Torah interpretation which seeks to define limits of human behaviour on the basis of the authority of the Law's formulations. The wisdom style of the aphorisms appeals to principles and attitudes, on the basis of which the anecdote assumes the behaviour can be justified. Originally they will have stood alone as the "punchlines" of their stories.

In at least two cases (2:19b–20; 2:25–26; possibly 3:4b) there are signs that already before Mark these pithy sayings have been supplemented by argument. In addition, it appears likely that each has been further supplemented, probably by Mark, by directly christological statements which appeal to Jesus' authority, which now supersedes the Law as the final court of authority (2:10; 2:17b; 2:19b–20,21–22; 2:28; 3:4b,6).

1.2.2.1.2 The Historical Jesus

Within 2:1 – 3:6 we have argued that four pre-Markan traditions display a distinctive attitude of Jesus towards the Law and one in which the contrast in practice between Jesus and John is addressed. They are anecdotes about Jesus in which this distinctive attitude will have been the punchline. In this section I want to explore the possibility that they may represent historical recollection of Jesus' own attitudes. This entails examining each story for its credibility, given what we know of Jesus and the Jews.

How does the tradition of 2:1–12 (as outlined above, assuming 2:10 and the accusation of blasphemy as secondary expansion) stand up if we were to see in it a recollection from the ministry of Jesus? At present it speaks of a crowd; this is the apparent motivation for the friends' letting the man through the roof. Even though crowding Jesus is a strong Markan motif, this element of the story is probably integral since it best explains their action of coming in through the roof. If we stay with the crowd, we have the problem of where the scribes must have been. Galilean houses were not all that large. We must assume they would have been in earshot of Jesus' words. Were they inside or outside? Perhaps the roof escapade is a legendary touch to

highlight Jesus' popularity. Notwithstanding these reflections, it is not difficult to imagine that an actual event lies behind the anecdote, assuming we
consider the healing, itself, as credible.

More important for our purposes is to ask whether the controversy is credible. Might scribes have objected to Jesus' declaration of forgiveness? Might
Jesus have made such a declaration? With the latter I see no difficulty, given
the popular link understood to exist between sin and sickness (here, paraly-
sis). Given Jesus' understanding of his ministry as announcing what God
intended, however that be formulated (kingdom of God), and as expressing
an inclusive understanding of God's favour to the needy in Israel, it is, to my
mind, quite thinkable that he would express that in terms of God's forgiveness of sins. In this he stood close to John. Although the story might later
be read christologically or in the light of the cross as the activity of Jesus the
saviour from sins, in its earliest form it doubtless belongs within the framework of Jesus' claim to announce and express God's will. Hence the equation, here, of healing and forgiveness. Both are therapeutic acts done in the
name of God.

Might scribes really have objected to this? We must assume that their
objection was grounded in their understanding of Torah. What was the problem with announcing forgiveness? It would not have been the blasphemy of
acting as God, as Mark suggests. People announced forgiveness, God's forgiveness. The issue was who was authorised to do so. The assumption is
probably that this was the preserve of the cult, but there is no clear basis for
this in Law, even though the Law was the authority for the cult. It was the
system given by God in the Torah. By what authority was Jesus making
such declarations? This seems to have been similar to the difficulty which
the scribes had with John the Baptist who also effectively offered forgiveness of sins. The problem arose in part because no formal limitations existed in the Law, yet the Law clearly sanctioned some authorities. John's
activity was somewhat maverick, yet not outside the Law. The historical
issue is reflected in Mark 11:27–33.

Jesus may have claimed authorisation for himself as a special case, and,
as we have seen, perhaps 2:10 reflects originally such a claim. But the answer Jesus gives the scribes argues for the possibility of making forgiveness
as freely available as healing itself. The effect is to break the *de facto* monopoly of formal channels in the interests of human need, but that is already
pushing forward to the implications of Jesus' actions which may be beyond
what he intended. In the story he does declare such forgiveness and justifies
it primarily on the basis of response to human need overriding the concerns
of the scribes about matters of authorisation. It is not a little unlike the

controversy which might erupt in many ecclesiastical circles if a lay person saw it appropriate in the face of an urgent human need to offer the elements of the eucharist, or, indeed, in many traditions to declare forgiveness of sins! Yet what made it different was that we know of no such formal stipulations in surviving tradition and there probably were none, making it hard to "nail" either Jesus or John for wrongdoing.

Behind 2:15–17 lies in all probability an anecdote about Jesus' conflict with "the scribes of the Pharisees" about Jesus' eating with toll collectors and sinners with its high point in Jesus' reply: "The well are not those needing a doctor, but the sick." How might we imagine an historical context for such a tradition? Jesus is reclining for a meal, the typical Hellenistic posture apparently now part of acceptable Galilean behaviour, and does so in the company of "many toll collectors and sinners"; "they were following" Jesus (2:15). "Following" need mean no more than that they were interested in what Jesus had to say. Scribes of the Pharisees apparently observe the common meal and speak about it to the disciples. We have to assume a place sufficiently large for many toll collectors and sinners, Jesus, the disciples, and scribes of the Pharisees all to be present. Jesus must have had a large house! Alternatively, he may be sharing a meal at the home of a toll collector (or sinner) who is wealthy and (therefore) has such space. It needs to be a situation where Pharisees might either observe what was happening from outside or themselves be present among the guests. The latter is less cumbersome, but more problematic; for then they should ask themselves their own question! The former is more likely and reflects a common near eastern custom for people to stand observing feasts.[93]

Now whether we should envisage this as an actual event or as an anecdotal reconstruction, it needs to have some internal coherence or some verisimilitude. Perhaps, in its present form it is more of a construction which has to assume rather too many people fitting into a normal Galilean house and this is the story teller's licence. Perhaps the kind of conflict here envisaged occurred after the event. We cannot know. For our purposes, nothing so far makes such an event or the conflict over it inherently unlikely.

In discussing the tradition we noted that the conflict might be moral only (more serious if Jesus is host), but could also include associated purity concerns (especially if Jesus is guest).[94] The same concerns appear to be re-

---

[93] So Gundry, *Mark*, p. 129, with reference to Luke 7:37; *bTaan* 23ab and K. E. Bailey, *Through Peasant Eyes*, (Grand Rapids: Eerdmans, 1980), pp. 4–5. Cf. Bultmann, *Synoptic Tradition*, p. 18.

[94] On the extent to which such purity concerns mattered to Pharisees of the time see

flected in the Q narrative, Luke 7:31–35. Biblical injunctions against keeping the company of immoral people are common and while it was inevitable
that pious Jews had, on occasion, to be present at meals with Jewish sinners
and even Gentiles, the problem with Jesus seems to have been that he had no
scruples about letting this be a regular feature of his activity. That is already
going beyond the evidence of this particular passage, but it makes best sense
of the conflict here. Such a conflict is credible in the setting of Jesus' ministry. It is not primarily about purity laws, but about the flouting of a moral
injunction. Jesus justifies the extent of his non observance of this injunction
not by disputing that they were sinners, but by appealing to the needs of the
people concerned.[95]

The first Christians would continue to face such issues both in its Jewish
context, where Jesus' own response becomes exemplary precedent and in
the wider Gentile context, where the story might be used beside other arguments to justify mixing with and eating with Gentiles. The story, in itself,
does not solve that problem. A Peter who was present here and fully awake
would not necessarily see eating with Gentiles in the same light, as more
than one later tradition confirms (Gal 2:11–14; Acts 10). In the matter of
keeping bad company degrees of flexibility were possible, which did not
exist in the matter of purity laws.

2:18–19a preserves an anecdote related to differences between John the
Baptist and Jesus. It is interesting to note that the preceding anecdote also
focuses on a difference in practice between Jesus and John. Here the contrast is between the disciples of each. That need not imply that the issues
arose only after the death of John or of both Jesus and John. Jesus' reply,
"The children of the bridal chamber cannot fast as long as the bridegroom is
with them", coheres with what we know otherwise of the contrast between
the two as recorded in early tradition: John was ascetic; Jesus ate and drank
freely (see esp Q 7:31–35).[96] We should probably not see in the image of

---

the ongoing debate between Sanders and Neusner. J. Neusner, *A History of the Mishnaic
Law of Purities*, 22 vols, (Leiden: Brill, 1974–77); *Judaism: The Evidence of the Mishnah*,
(Chicago: Univ. of Chicago Pr., 1981); Sanders, *Jewish Law*, pp. 152–254; J. Neusner,
Judaic Law from Jesus to the Mishnah. A Systematic Reply to Professor E. P. Sanders,
South Florida Studies in the History of Judaism 84, (Atlanta: Scholars, 1993).

[95] See also Borg, *Conflict*, pp. 82–86, who sets Jesus' behaviour in contrast to a strategy
of withdrawal and protection of purity boundaries. Jesus' eating with toll collectors and
sinners was not only an expression of acceptance and forgiveness, but also a programmatic
statement about Israel's identity, an alternative vision of holiness (pp. 93–95).

[96] Cf. Mack, *Myth of Innocence*, p. 188, who sees in the saying "a bit of Cynic
impertinence".

the bridegroom an image of Jesus himself. The focus is on hope and expectation. With Jesus the time of fulfilment has come; the kingdom of God is at hand.

Strictly speaking there is no issue of Torah, here. There is rather an issue of contrast between Jesus and his group and John and his. Nevertheless the question might be raised by any who saw fasting as appropriate, why Jesus did not follow such practices. His eating and drinking would be seen as controversial. This allows Mark to introduce Pharisees into the story. Jesus' response coheres with the responses in the other anecdotes to the extent that he emphasises gift and generosity rather than command.

In discussing the logia about the patch and the wine, I identified that, detached from the anecdote about John and John, they were capable of a range of interpretation. I believe that to set them within the ministry of Jesus they should be understood within the framework of Jesus' eschatological expectation and not as unrelated wise observations which might apply to life in general. Within the eschatological framework they do express tension between the old and the new and whoever placed them in the anecdote probably reflected their orientation. Their original reference on the lips of Jesus may have been to more than just himself and John. It might have included a reference more generally to God's new initiative and the challenge it was bringing. Potentially the sayings might have related directly to Jesus' understanding of Torah and its application, but about that we can only speculate. They certainly need not imply abrogation or the like, while, conversely, they certainly imply an element of discontinuity and incompatibility.

In 2:23–28 we are asked to imagine a scene where Jesus and the disciples are wandering through stands of grain on the sabbath (not making a path), the disciples pluck the grain and the Pharisees accuse them of breaking sabbath law.[97] In itself the scene is credible.[98] It is not uncommon for teach-

---

[97] See the discussion of prevailing attitudes towards the sabbath law in Sanders, *Jewish Law*, pp. 6–19.

[98] An objection to its credibility, repeated (I think uncritically) across generations of scholars, is the unlikely presence of the Pharisees, trailing the disciples. So, for instance, Beare, "Sabbath," p. 133; Hultgren, *Adversaries*, p. 112: Weiss, "Sabbath," p. 21; Sanders, *Jewish Law*, p. 1; cf. Waibel, "Auseinandersetzung," p. 89, who suggests it reflects the itinerant ministry of Jesus and the disciples. Similarly Borg, *Conflict*, pp. 152–154, who also speaks of the urgency of the disciples' mission. Walking in a field need not imply more than walking in a field! Cf. also Dunn, *Partings*, p. 100

ers to be asked to justify the actions of their disciples.[99] Nothing implies the stands of grain were a long distance from areas where Pharisees might be found on a sabbath. People pluck grain and rub it as the simplest way of releasing the seed itself so that one can eat it. I have done it often enough myself; both with ripe grain and with grain still green, when it is still soft and, to my taste, very palatable. The anecdote rightly assumes a desire on the disciples to eat, but not that they are hungry.

Our discussion of the tradition suggested that in the original anecdote the response of Jesus was the aphorism: "The sabbath was made for people, not people for the sabbath" (2:27). Jesus' response in 2:27 is not an appeal to compassion for the hungry, but simply an argument seeking to put the case that sabbath law is there for human good, including the human enjoyment of plucking and leisurely eating from standing grain. It has the effect of countering an approach to sabbath law where the focus seems to be on the Law for its own sake, irrespective of human beings.

But what is the Pharisees' objection? Is it plausible or are they being set up as unreal stereotypes, either as mere foils for making Jesus look particularly wise or, more cruelly, as symbols of a rather nasty polemic against Jewish opponents of the early Christian communities? There seems to me little doubt that the story has been made to function in these ways. But might it nevertheless reflect a genuine historical conflict of Jesus with the Pharisees? There is no law or law interpretation known to us which Jesus' disciples would be contravening. If the incident has an historical base, we are probably best to assume a rather extreme group who would have seen the disciples' behaviour as contravening their own very strict interpretation of sabbath law. They would have classified the disciples' activity as work. As has rightly been noted, most Jews of the time would have disagreed and seen the issue as trifling.[100] I consider it possible, however, that such an event may have occurred and have given rise to the anecdote.[101]

---

[99] So D. Daube, "Responsibilities of Master and Disciples in the Gospels," *NTS* 19 (1972–73), pp. 1–16, here: 4–8.

[100] So Sanders, *Jewish Law*, pp. 22–23. He is concerned to show that differences on sabbath interpretation were tolerated, ie. not sufficient to want to put Jesus to death. While this may be so, there seems to be no reason to deny the credibility of the dispute itself. Sanders's discussion is limited because he assumes the disciples plucked grain because they were hungry (pp. 20–23).

[101] So Waibel, "Auseinandersetzung," pp. 88–91; against Sanders, *Jesus and Judaism*, p. 88, who argues that such a conflict would not have arisen in a Palestinian milieu. But surely how to keep the sabbath fits well in such a context, whereas issues of whether to, at all, does not. Cf. also Dautzenberg, "Eigenart," p. 162.

It is, of course, one of a number which are concerned with conflict over sabbath law interpretation. Another follows in 3:1–6. Might Pharisees really have objected to such an act? From extant discussion we see that the matter was a grey area where opinions might differ. Probably only the most rigorous extremists would object.[102] Others might point out that Jesus is being somewhat careless in his observance, on the assumption that it would have been just as easy for Jesus to have respected sabbath law and performed the cure on the following day (the synagogue leader's advice in Luke 13:10–17!). It was not as though this really was a matter of life and death for the man or that it was possible to do good to him only then.

Given that the conflict may have been with extremists, like those of 2:23, nothing in the scene 3:1–5 is incredible as a report from Jesus' times. Jesus heals a man with a withered hand on the sabbath. At most the miraculous healing presents a problem of historical credibility. The event occasions conflict. As already noted the anecdote has been reworked so that it forms a climax of the controversy stories, highlighting the Pharisees hardened opposition and resolve (on the sabbath) to kill. The motif of people watching to see what Jesus will do may be original or may be legendary accretion of the storyteller to heighten the drama.

In the tradition Jesus' response was probably confined to the words: "Is it lawful on the sabbath to do good or to do harm?" (3:4). This is a provocative confrontation which functions similarly to the alternative in 2:9. It calls into question the interpretation of sabbath law which measured rectitude in accordance with strict adherence to the letter. In its place it puts divine compassion for human need as the major or sole criterion.

In conclusion, a reasonable case can be made for some historical witness being preserved behind all five anecdotes. In three, issues of concern directly or indirectly related to John the Baptist are preserved (2:1–12; 2:15–17; 2:18–22). We have five anecdotes, similar in form, but, more important, containing clever sayings of coherent style, which probably reflect the same

---

102 See the discussion in Sanders, *Jewish Law*, pp. 6–23, esp. pp. 20–23, who is concerned to discuss historical probability and, at most, entertains the possibility of extremist objections. See also Vermes, *Religion of Jesus the Jew*, pp. 22–24, who cites the Tannaitic midrash, *Mekhilta de Rabbi Ishmael* (ed. Lauterbach III, 197–199) and *bYoma* 85b, referring to Akiba, and *mYoma* 8:6, as illustrating the principle that danger to life overrode the sabbath. "Generally speaking, Sabbath observance in the second century, and probably also in the first, was subservient to the essential well-being of a Jew" (p. 24).

genius (2:9; 2:17a; 2:19a; 2:27; 3:4a).[103] This may be the work of an early bearer of the tradition; it may be the work of Jesus. Of these 2:9 requires an anecdotal setting. Of the others, all but 2:27 probably also were transmitted within their anecdotal setting, and possibly also 2:27. The logia of the patch and the wine, 2:21 and 2:22, are probably secondary to their present setting and may well derive from Jesus and have circulated independently. Otherwise, despite the likely expansions, both in narrative detail and in words attributed to Jesus, there seems to be a good case for treating both the conflict settings and the saying responses as reflecting events and attitudes which may originate within the ministry of the historical Jesus.

Four portray Jesus as confronting criticism in relation to his and his disciples' behaviour as inappropriate or contrary to Law. In the fifth, the anecdote concerning fasting and in its associated logia, he justifies his differences from John by implying a new age of hope had superseded a time of expectation which justified a sharp difference in lifestyle. In the four dealing with Torah, in each case the accusation appears to come from an extremist position. In each case Jesus confronts the questioners with an alternative way of interpreting Torah which focuses on response to human need and on Torah as gift. The responses justify actions on the basis of a common broad stance embodied in an aphorism, but avoid engaging in detailed argument on the opponents' terms. The responses are both general and, in manner, somewhat 'off hand'. One could imagine a more moderate scribe wanting to sit Jesus down and ask: "This is all very well. But how do your principles work out in practice? What kind of work would you envisage as not allowed on the sabbath?" The Jesus of these traditions appears determined to remain

---

[103] Vouga, "Die Entwicklungsgeschichte der jesuanischen Chrien und didaktischen Dialoge des Markusevangeliums," in: (ed.), *Jesu Rede von Gott und ihre Nachgeschichte im frühen Christentum. Beiträge zur Verkündigung Jesu und zum Kerygma der Kirche. FS für Willi Marxsen*, edited by D.-A. Koch, et al., (Gütersloh: Mohn, 1989), pp. 45–56, raises the issue whether the *chreia* form was characteristic of a particular strand of Christianity. He identifies behind 2:15–28, 7:1–23; 10:1–9; and 12:35–37 didactic dialogues produced in a liberal Christian community to reinforce views of hearers over against other Christian groups (identified with Paul's opponents in Gal 2:11–14 and represented in the anecdotes as Pharisees). They assume a christology where a statement of Jesus is an argument in itself. He also suggests that Mark had access to paradox chreiae (3:1–6; 11:27–33; 12:13–17), which did not argue christologically, nor offer teaching, but presented Jesus baffling his opponents in a way comparable to Cynic anecdotes. See also the discussion of the pronouncement stories as *chreiai* in Mack, *A Myth of Innocence*, pp. 173–205. He draws attention to the striking parallels between many of Jesus' aphorisms and Cynic parallels. He assumes creation of *chreiai* in the context of Christian community, but also using memory of Jesus as being Cynic-like in his provocative behaviour. This belongs in turn to the continuing debate about the appropriate use of Cynic parallels within the reconstruction of early Christianity, which lies behind the scope of this study.

aloof from such issues. He is operating outside the circles which have responsibility for defining Law in society.

1.2.3 Conclusion

In 1:1 – 3:6 Mark sets the scene for what follows in his gospel. The primary focus is Jesus' authority. The prologue establishes Jesus' authority as Christ and Son of God. As such he receives the Spirit. This authority finds expression in Jesus' proclamation of the kingdom and in his summoning disciples. It also features in an inclusion in 1:21–28 by which Jesus associates Jesus' power to exorcise and his teaching authority. The five linked anecdotes in 2:1 – 3:6 continue the theme of Jesus' authority. It is an authority of final appeal beyond Torah and finds expression, in particular, in association with the Son of Man, who has authority on earth to forgive sins and who is Lord of the sabbath. His is therefore the supreme authority under God. Mark portrays Jesus' coming with such authority as the fulfilment of biblical hope. It is something new and as such, stands both in continuity and in contrast with what has gone before. The structure of Mark's narrative gives central prominence to the sayings about the patch and about wine which bear this message. Associated is also the eschatological image of the wedding.

Throughout the narrative there is evidence of this tension of continuity and discontinuity. Implicit already in the prologue in the appearance of John and then Jesus, it comes directly to expression where the people contrast the new teaching with authority with that of the scribes (1:22). Mark is not portraying the new as a total replacement of the old. He still has Jesus concerned that the leper obeys Torah provisions. He can still have Jesus confront one manner of Torah interpretation with his own. Torah still has a place, but it is ultimately subordinate to the new authority. Sometimes, aside from controversy, it disappears from view. At some points where issues of Law might arise, such as in Jesus' touching the leper, or healing and exorcising on the sabbath, Mark is silent. Even Jesus' sending the leper to observe the Law's provisions appears in Mark incidental and probably more to be understood in terms of a rite of social reintegration. When the Law becomes an issue, Mark emphasises continuity, but in such a way that the God of the Law has now instituted Jesus as the supreme authority both for interpreting Law and also for declaring it.

1.3 Mark 3:7 – 6:6 in Review

1.3.1 Mark 3:7 – 6:6

3:7–12 highlights Jesus' popularity, now reaching far beyond Galilee, and indicates, in summary, that Jesus continued in the same activities of healing and exorcism reported already in 1:21–45. The effect is to return to the thread of 1:45 and recall the activities typical of Jesus' ministry according to Mark. Thus in 3:11 the demons similarly recognise Jesus, addressing him here explicitly as "Son of God" (cf. 1:1:24,34). This brief passage, 3:7–12, serves therefore both as a summary and, like 1:21–45, as a reaffirmation of the christology explicit in the prologue. It is followed in 3:13–19, as is the prologue (cf. 1:16–20), by attention to the disciples, who are to share Jesus' preaching and exorcist activity. They are to share Jesus' authority to preach and cast out demons (3:15). That they are twelve will not be lost on Mark who uses the numerical image for Israel symbolically in 5:21–43; 6:30–44; and 8:18–20. Like Jesus, his group of disciples is a sign that the time of Israel's prophetic hope is being fulfilled.[104]

In the section 3:20–35 two negative responses to Jesus are illustrated. His family fail to understand his mission, but, more deliberately, scribes allege that his exorcist powers derive from Beelzebul. These scribes are from Jerusalem. This is more than a geographical reference; Jerusalem is the centre of the religious establishment, focused in the temple. The scribes cannot dispute Jesus' exorcisms occurred; they explain them differently. Thus they seek to remove any claim on Jesus' part to exercise authority from God, which would make him a challenge to their authority. This is similar to themanner of their argumentation (in thought, at least) in 2:7 where they discount the possibility of Jesus' being authorised and go straight to the assumption that he blasphemes, is usurping God's role. The authority theme is still very much to the fore.

Jesus' response is first to make nonsense of their suggestion and then to highlight the need to bind Satan and the power he exercises. Finally Mark has Jesus declare a new law concerning unforgivable sin (2:28–29), blasphemy against the Spirit with which his ministry is baptising people in fulfilment of John's announcement in 1:8. Rejecting Jesus is blaspheming against the Spirit. Not only has Jesus claimed authority to forgive sins (2:10); he now claims authority to declare what is unforgivable! Again power to

---

[104] In the list the description of Judas reminds us that Mark assumes that many hearers are already well acquainted with the story of Jesus.

exorcise and authority to teach and declare are linked, as already in 1:21–28. There is no direct reference to Torah in the passage, although the scribes' accusation is a charge of breaking the Law. On the one hand, Jesus rejects the charge; he is not acting against God's Law; on the other hand, he declares law, illustrating, as in 2:1 – 3:6, that he possesses an authority which goes beyond Torah.

The surrounding story of concern among Jesus' family (3:20–21,31–35) becomes the setting for a further new declaration. Jesus sets belonging with those who do God's will above the demands of family (3:34–35). In the context, God's will must mean more than Torah faithfulness; it must include also adherence to God's will as expounded both in Jesus' interpretation of Torah and in his own declarations. A similar challenge is implied already in the call of the disciples to follow him (1:16–20; 2:13–14). Here the challenge is not to follow; it is to do God's will; but this also implies adherence to Jesus' way of presenting God's will. The challenge to family loyalty, which is well grounded in the Law, not least in the command to honour parents, need not in itself be seen as disregard of the Law. That Jesus' call might take priority over family priorities need be no more anti-Law than the call to prophets of old to do the same.

The parables in 4:1–34 continue the theme of response to Jesus, with the focus now more on his teaching and preaching and on degrees of its acceptance. Response to the will of God and so belonging to those 'inside', the true family of Jesus, is the underlying theme throughout. At the same time the parables proclaim the hope of the kingdom, the new and final divine initiative. They are therefore also an implicit claim to an authority which is not necessarily in conflict with Torah, but is beyond it.[105]

Up to this point in the gospel Mark has still not said what Jesus taught, aside from the announcement of the kingdom of God. Teaching is incidental in the controversy anecdotes (2:1–3:6) and also in the response to the charges of the Jerusalem scribes (3:22–29). Mark portrays the parables as teaching, but, for the most part, they are more teaching about response to teaching. They tell the story of response to Jesus.[106] The declarations about

---

[105] Against the suggestion of B. B. Scott, *Hear Then the Parable*, (Minneapolis: Fortress, 1989), pp. 380–387, that Mark is concerned about avoiding the impression that Jesus transgresses the Law concerning mixing plants in the parable of the mustard seed and so substitutes soil for garden, see Gundry, *Mark*, p. 232.

[106] On the role of the parable of the sower within Mark see M. A. Tolbert, *Sowing the Gospel. Mark's World in Literary Historical Perspective*, (Minneapolis: Fortress, 1989), pp. 127–131, 148–164, though she presses detail too hard, for instance, in finding an allusion to Peter in the allusion to stony ground.

future manifestation of the hidden and about judgement according to measure (4:21–25) appear now in Mark to focus on the degrees of response to the
message and to relate to the theme of hardening. So far Jesus appears himself to be the message; that is, the call is to believe him. This reinforces the
centrality of Jesus' authority for Mark as an authority both beside and beyond the Torah. To this point the concentration of the message on Jesus
himself recalls the similar thought structure in John's gospel.

Mark's Jesus displays this power and authority dramatically in the stilling
of the storm (4:35–41), effectively an exorcism and thus another example of
Mark's pattern of linking teaching authority and exorcism. Typological allusion also cements continuity with the old. It is the God of the scriptures
and of Israel's history who has made this possible. Thus in 4:35–41 Jesus
acts like Yahweh in stilling the storm. He has been given authority over the
deep. By having Jesus chide the disciples Mark challenges the hearers to
grasp this message. This is the first of four extraordinary narratives in which
Jesus' miraculous power and authority are highlighted. The miracles function, therefore, as did the miracles in Mark 1. We even have another instance of demons confessing his sonship (5:7). But the miracles are on a
larger scale and contain important symbolic allusions.

In 5:1–20 Mark reports Jesus' arrival in the region of the Gerasenes, Gentile territory. Confronting Jesus is a man with an unclean spirit, who was
living among the tombs. Mark points out the man's superhuman powers.
The exchange recalls for the hearer Jesus' first exorcism in the synagogue
and subsequent acknowledgments of Jesus' sonship by demons. Mark depicts the scene in considerable detail . Finally, the demons, calling themselves, "legion," trick themselves into believing they had negotiated an escape and descend in a herd of pigs into the sea. Mark wants the hearers to
share in the victory and its humour. Jesus is victorious over the powers.
The demoniac now acclaims Jesus in the Decapolis.

Such is the detail in the surface of the text and such is its primary import.
Jesus' authority is paramount. In addition, it is important that the exorcism
took place where it did: in Gentile land. Thus Mark draws attention to the
expansion of the gospel to the Decapolis in the final verses of the episode.
More difficult for our study is the evaluation of what is not said explicitly.
Does Mark assume the notion that Gentile land is unclean and so understand
Jesus' action as an exorcism of Gentile land? Does Mark share the view that
the man's presence among tombs at night would render him unclean? Are
pigs still unclean animals for Mark? Does Mark intend a link between the
demons, described as "legion" and Roman legions and share the view that
they pollute the land? One might add, does Mark understand that on return

to Jewish territory Jesus would have gone through a rite of purification because of uncleanness contracted in the Gentile land?

It is important to notice, on the one hand, that the anecdote bristles with Law issues, and , on the other, that Mark does not display any particular interest in them. It is the man's power, not his uncleanness that is the focus of attention. Similarly it is the extension into Gentile territory, not the Gentile territory as unclean, that is Mark's focus. In 5:21–43 Mark neatly balances this miracle in Gentile land with twin miracles in Jewish land, as we shall see.

On the other hand, it is likely that Mark would have known of Jewish attitudes towards Jewish territory, pigs and cemeteries. Later he is prepared to report Jesus' initial reluctance to engage the request of a Gentile woman and Jesus' disparaging description of Gentiles as dogs, only to show that Jesus crosses that boundary (7:24–30). Mark is aware of such values, but it is unlikely that Mark shares them. The same is probably true of Gentile land and pigs, here. We might, however, assume a more widely based concern about cemeteries, which Mark and his hearers with pagan cultural background would also share, just as they would have had concerns about lepers. The reference to demons as "legion" certainly implies some association, at least at the symbolic level, between Roman legions and the realm of evil; but beyond that is speculation (eg. motives of a covert revolutionary declaration). Nothing elsewhere in the gospel suggests Mark espouses a notion of pollution which would see legions as a source of defilement. Doubtless many of these concerns played a major role in the pre-Markan stages of the tradition, especially in a Jewish setting, but they are not Mark's concern. This, in turn, tells us something about his relation to Jewish cultural values and the Law in general.[107]   Mark looks back on them, but no longer shares

---

[107] Turning to 5:1–20 as tradition, we have already noted a range of issues which are likely to have been of importance in any pre-Markan which assumed a Jewish audience. These include Gentile territory, the cemetery, the pigs, and the image of legion. The location at Gerasa is problematic, because of its distance from the sea. The most probable explanation is either that the name has entered the story secondarily at the hands of someone unaware of the geographical problem or that it belonged originally to the story, but that the apparent link with the sea of Galilee had been a secondary development. Mark apparently senses no difficulty.

The elaboration of the man's state in 5:3–5 appears to have been formulated on the basis of Isa 65:4 LXX. In the same context we also find reference to pigs. Perhaps an earlier story of an exorcism in Gerasa or some other unknown place has been elaborated under the influence of Isa 65 to include now both more reference to the man's plight and the motif of the pigs and their drowning in the sea. Assuming the anecdote existed at some stage in a Jewish environment many features would have been telling. Here is Gentile land, which is unclean, confirmed by the presence of the pigs. The land is not only unthem. He notes them only inasmuch as they pertain to the triumph of the gospel.

Mark juxtaposes the triumph of Jesus in Gentile territory in 5:1–20 with the account of two divine miracles in Jewish territory in 5:21–43. Both are stamped with the symbol 12, representative of Israel: the woman has had an issue of blood for 12 years; the girl raised from the dead is 12 years old.[108] The daughter's father, Jairus, is significantly a leader of the synagogue. Jesus exercises his divinely given power and authority both in Gentile land and in Israel. That is Mark's concern, not purification of the former, since such purity categories have no validity for him. Similarly, only God's power can raise the dead, as it did in the days of Elijah and Elisha. It is the power and authority of Yahweh himself, the one who raises the dead, which Mark will have his hearers identify in Jesus. Jesus' power miraculously cures a woman who had suffered for years and expended a fortune on doctors. By the same power he raises the dead 12 year old to life.

As with 5:1–20, the two stories woven together in 5:21–43 raise many issues of Law, but in the surface text Mark pays them no attention.[109] His

---

clean; it abounds with unclean spirits and probably the image, legion, indicates a strong sense that the Romans are connected with such spirits. The story celebrates the defeat of these powers. It works so well as a Jewish story.

Assuming it is Christian Jewish story, it appears to have been composed in a community in which Jewish purity values relating to Gentile land, cemeteries, pigs, and Romans were still operative. It would therefore reflect an image of Jesus as sharing these values. A further possibility is that the story functioned, or came to function, in relation to Gentile mission, in which case the herdsman's witness becomes important. It might then have been used to indicate that Jesus effectively exorcised Gentile land, making such mission possible. It would still, however, be operating with strongly Jewish assumptions (namely, that Gentile land was otherwise unclean). The pre-Markan tradition behind 5:1–20 preserves an image of Jesus which assumes he lives by Torah and that he shares the value of the Jewish community in relation to Gentile uncleanness. In such an isolated anecdote there would have been no need to address Jesus' subsequent purification upon returning from Gentile land. It would have been assumed.

[108] See also the symbolic discussion in Waetjen, *Reordering of Power*, p. 122, D. O. Via, *The Ethics of Mark's Gospel – In the Middle of Time*, (Philadelphia: Fortress, 1985), pp. 110–111 and Myers, *Binding the Strong Man*, pp. 200–201.

[109] So rightly, Sariola, *Markus*, p. 71: "Das Gesetzesproblem ist in dieser Erzählung ganz und gar umgangen worden." So also S. Freyne, *Galilee, Jesus, and the Gospels: Literary Approaches and Historical Investigations*, (Philadelphia: Fortress, 1988), p. 49; Gundry, *Mark*, p. 288 who points that the focus is on her affliction not on contamination, noting that Mark makes nothing of her uncleanness (p. 269), but rather is emphasising Jesus' supernatural power (p. 270). Similarly Lührmann, *Markusevangelium*, p. 104. Contrast Guelich, *Mark*, p. 296, who maintains that the purity issue is central here; similarly Hooker, *Mark*, p. 148.

focus is elsewhere: miraculous power, typological continuity with the acts of Yahweh, and with regard to the human condition: an apparently incurable plight of illness, and death. Mark does not address the purity issues. They include the following. Jesus had returned from a Gentile land and after undergoing purification would still remain unclean until evening. Was Jairus aware of this, especially in inviting Jesus to his home? More acutely, Jairus would have seen that Jesus had been touched by a woman who was unclean and therefore been rendered unclean (Lev 15:25–27; cf. 15:19–24).[110] The woman would have suffered also because the constant flow of blood would have rendered her constantly unclean and so excluded her from normal social relations. She would therefore have been transgressing Torah in deliberately setting out to touch Jesus.[111] Did Mark's Jesus realise this danger? In entering the house where the corpse lay Jesus would have been rendered unclean (Nu 19:11–22), along with the three disciples.[112] Similarly, in touching the corpse of the child, Jesus would be rendered unclean (Nu 19:11). He would also have been bringing pollution into the house, the house of a synagogue leader! This passage therefore also bristles with issues of purity. It is all the more striking that Mark shows so little interest. Would he have been aware, nevertheless, of some or all of these issues? Would he have shared such values?

The intercalation of the two stories appears to have linked the stories on the basis that both depict Jesus bringing the women from death to life, one, literally, the other, symbolically. The latter 'resurrection' rests on assumptions about purity laws in relation to women with a flow of blood. They would have applied in some sense both in a Jewish and Gentile milieu. The language used to describe the woman's plight reflects the language of the Law (ῥύσει αἵματος, 5:25; cf. Lev 15:19 LXX, ἡ πηγὴ τοῦ αἵματος, 5:29; cf. Lev 12:7 LXX).[113] It is likely that the Mark who had some grasp

---

[110] See M. J. Selvidge, "Mark 5:25–34 and Leviticus 15:19–20," *JBL* 103 (1984), pp. 619–623, here: 619–620, on the background and the strict practices of the time, referring to Jos *Ant* 13.9.5; *JW* 5:227; *ContAp* 2.8; Ps-Philo 7; Philo *SpecLeg* 3:132–133; 1QSa 2:3–4; CD 4:12–5:17; see also her *Woman, Cult, and Miracle Recital. A Redactional Critical Investigation on Mark 5:24–34*, (Lewisburg: Bucknell Univ. Pr., 1990), pp. 47–63; Trummer, P. "Zwischen Gesetz und Freiheit. Überlegungen zu einer Antinomie bei Jesus und Paulus" in *Jesus und das jüdische Gesetz*, edited by I. Broer, (Stuttgart: Kohlhammer, 1992), pp. 37–60, 54–55.

[111] So Sariola, *Markus*, p. 70.

[112] But note that Mark has Jesus declare her not yet dead, but sleeping (5:41), which would alleviate the purity issue.

[113] So Pesch, *Markusevangelium I*, pp. 301, 303; Gundry, *Mark*, p. 280; cf. Sariola, *Markus*, p. 71, who questions this, at least in relation to ἡ πηγὴ τοῦ αἵματος.

of Jewish Law, as 7:3–4 shows, also knew about Jewish purity laws with regard to such situations. That he found no need to explain these here to his hearers is probably best explained by the fact that some foreboding in relation to menstruant women was probably also present among the cultures to which Mark's hearers belonged, though less severe.[114] This fact may also be sufficient to explain why Mark might have effected the intercalation.[115] It would also account for the apparent disregard for the consequences in terms of Jewish Law.

Apart from this possibility, we find no interest in Mark in the other purity issues mentioned.[116] It is even probable that for Mark menstruants were no longer considered unclean and that for him the issue is only the healing, not removing for the woman a hurdle which for Mark no longer had validity. Mark may have been aware of the way Jewish purity concerns would have had a bearing on various aspects of the story, but his silence is best interpreted on the basis that for him such requirements no longer matter. Theoretically it could mean that he acknowledges them and chooses to say nothing; but it is much more likely that it means that he no longer acknowledges their applicability. Ultimately, Mark's silences also imply that for him Jesus also gave such provisions no regard.

The conclusion is then inevitable: the Jesus of Mark no longer operates on the assumption that clean-unclean boundaries which the passage raises have validity. This coheres with the attitude Mark expresses and has Jesus express in 7:1–23. Such were externals which cannot touch what matters, the inner person. At the same time, at no point does he depict Jesus as deliberately or even indirectly acting contrary to Torah. The issue is not present. At most one could argue that Mark is quite deliberately setting up a contrast between the way Jesus treated women and the exclusion which Leviticus requires.[117] Mark does not make this implicit, though this is the

---

[114] On attitudes to menstruation in the Hellenistic world see Selvidge, *Woman, Cult, and Miracle Recital*, pp. 71–74, who notes some foreboding and distancing in relation to menstruating women, but nothing as severe as in Jewish Law, so that women's participation in cultic activities seems not to have been affected. See also Pesch, *Markusevangelium I*, p. 304.

[115] For the view that Mark effected the intercalation, see Hooker, *Mark*, p. 147; Pesch, *Markusevangelium I*, p. 313; Hurtado, *Mark*, p. 86; cf. Guelich, *Mark*, pp. 292–293; Grundmann, *Markus*, p. 148; Gundry, *Mark*, pp. 286, 297, who argues that for Mark the woman suffered from an affliction, not from impurity (p. 288). This is certainly possible, although Mark may well have been aware of its social implications. Cf. the possibility that the name Jairus also plays a role: so Pesch, *Markusevangelium I*, p. 300; Gundry, *Mark*, p. 267.

[116] So Westerholm, *Scribal Authority*, p. 68; Gundry, *Mark*, p. 288.

[117] So Selvidge, *Woman, Cult, and Miracle Recital*, pp. 86–91.

effect of the way he tells the story. This makes it all the more interesting to contemplate the way the stories will have been understood in pre-Markan tradition, especially in contexts where such provisions of the Law were still assumed to have validity.[118]

The focus in the story for Mark, however, is Jesus' extraordinary power, which is so great that it can even be accessed involuntarily by the daring

---

[118] With regard to the pre-Markan tradition in 5:21–43, we have the many purity issues it raises. Someone with sensitivity to the consequences for the woman of her unclean state composed the intercalation. As we have seen, this might have been Mark. It could easily have been a pre-Markan editor operating from Jewish assumptions. The former is more likely, since the intercalation has created more problems. An unclean Jesus is still being taken by a synagogue leader into his house! I assume therefore that Mark is responsible for the intercalation, or that if it had been pre-Markan, it was performed by someone for whom the subsequent purity issues were either not seen or not acknowledged.

As far as the individual stories are concerned, Jesus' return from Gentile land is a purity issue only if we assume the Markan literary context. Without it the story of Jairus' daughter is much less problematic. There remains Jesus' entry into a house deemed unclean because it houses a corpse. Jesus' touching the girl to raise her to life is a potential problem. It is similar to the touching of the leper. As there, it may assume a subsequent purification by Jesus or that his charismatic power prevents his being contaminated. On the other hand, Jesus declares the girl not dead, but sleeping (5:39), which removes the purity issue. The story offers us little in regard to an image of Jesus and Torah.

With the woman with the flow of blood the matter is different. For Mark the issue seems to be the distress of her illness and it incurability at the hands of the doctors, probably with an awareness of the way such bleeding would prevent social intercourse. All the focus falls on Jesus' power, which works even when the woman just touches Jesus' garment. It is like magic. Yet Mark also ensures we note her action as one of faith and the disciples' rudeness as failure to believe.

While Mark shows little or no interest in the purity issues, the story told in a Jewish environment would have great dramatic intensity. The woman, like the leper, breaks across the boundaries set by Torah. Jesus' responds in anger, or so it seems. For Mark the issue is that power has been tapped anonymously. This fits Mark's focus on Jesus' power. Perhaps this element was already traditional and Mark seeks to correct an overly mechanical understanding by introducing the word about faith. At an earlier stage of the tradition it is likely that Jesus' response was not related to the accessing of power, but to being touched by someone who was unclean. In a Jewish environment the effect of Jesus' healing the woman would have been that she could resume normal relations in the community. In this sense it is similar to the story of the leper. The issue of Jesus' being rendered unclean would have lain outside the purview of the story and resolved either on the assumption that such would follow or that his charismatic power isolated him from the effects of uncleanness.

Understood with a strongly Jewish context the story celebrates Jesus' power to heal a woman in a constantly unclean state and thus to enable her to be restored to the community. With regard to the image it would preserve of Jesus' attitude towards Torah, little can be said. It doubtless assumed full conformity and that Jesus would have been aware of the resultant benefit for the woman. If Jesus' initial reaction had been not in response to power transfer, but to being touched by an unclean woman, then the story would preserve touch of Jesus' garments by a woman in need. Mark also dramatises again the disciples' failure to grasp who Jesus is, as he had in the stilling of the storm. Jesus, finding the woman, rewards her faith and declares her whole. In the raising of the girl the focus is similarly Jesus' power, not issues of Law.

6:1–6 offers us another instance of Jesus in a synagogue (cf. 1:21–28; 3:1–6), this time his home one. People admire him for both his wisdom and his miraculous power. In this sense it recalls 1:21–28. It is placed appropriately for Mark's hearers who, after the majestic miracles of 4:35 – 5:43, are more than ready to answer the people's question: "Where does this man get this from? And what is this wisdom given to him? And miracles like this which have been done by his hand?" They were 'flies on the wall' in 1:21–28 and already noted the acclamation of the new authority. They heard the prologue. They know that God has given this authority and power. They have heard Jesus' wisdom in responding to confrontation and reflecting on responses to the message of the kingdom. But the home crowd rejects its prophet. In this way the scene recalls the response of Jesus' family in 3:20–21,31–35. Jesus' own response links the two events. The prophet is without honour "in his own country, his kin and his family". Jesus' self reference as prophet also maintains implicitly the claim of continuity with Israel's tradition. As in 3:20–21,31–35, the implied challenge to family authority, highly valued in the Law, is not in itself a challenge to the Law.

The episode, while not directly addressing the issue of Jesus and Torah, nevertheless continues the theme of Jesus' authority and the conflict it evokes. By contrast, in 6:7–13 Jesus' own disciples, appointed in 3:13–19, receive their commission to go out to preach and to do exorcisms and healings. Like the summaries of Jesus' ministry in 1:14–15 and 3:7–12 and the focus on the disciples in 1:16–20 and 3:13–19, 6:6b and 6:7–13 seems to indicate a transition to a new section in Mark.

1.3.2 Conclusion

Mark continues to emphasise Jesus' authority and power as Son of God throughout 3:7 – 6:6. His fame reaches far and wide. He authorises his disciples, in turn, to preach and perform exorcisms. The section includes

---

an image of Jesus as one who shared Torah values in this regard and sensed either danger or, at least, the inappropriateness of the woman's action. His reaction here would then parallel his reaction to the Syrophoenician woman, and, perhaps, the leper, and indicate an image of Jesus as fundamentally conservative on such boundary issues, yet willing to cross them, but this is far from certain.

the amazing miracles of the storm stilling, the exorcism of demons at Gerasa, and the restorations to life, literal and symbolic, of two women. Beside the theme of Jesus' power, Mark focuses on response to Jesus' message. Jesus refutes the Jerusalem scribes' allegation and counters with declarations which stand as law, beside and beyond Torah. Similarly in response to the claims of family priority, Jesus declares the priority of a new allegiance to God, and implicitly to himself and his interpretation of God's will, but not at the expense of Torah. Consistent with this is his focus on appropriate response to the gospel in the parables, which effectively reinforces his ultimate authority. Implicitly, then, Jesus continues the claim to be an authority beside and beyond Torah.

In potential purity issues relating to the exorcism at Gerasa and the healings of the women Mark shows no interest. Mark does not appear to operate within a value system which sees Gentile land or pigs as unclean. He celebrates Jesus' triumphant power in the land of the Gentiles, matching it then by Jesus' exercise of Yahweh's power to raise the dead in the land of Israel. Mark was probably aware of the purity issues in these stories, but they were no longer his concern. At most in the intercalation of the two 'resurrections', Mark shows awareness that healing of the menstruant implied her restoration, but, even then, as with the leper, Mark may not be committed to a particular Jewish understanding of the issue. Mark shows no concern with the many purity issues raised both by the intercalation and by the sequence of his narrative. We may assume that Mark, and in Mark's eyes, Jesus, did not espouse such views. In this sense Mark assumes Jesus acted in disregard of such requirements of Torah. He was not anti-Torah, but, nevertheless, not Torah observant in the usual sense.

1.4 Mark 6:7 – 8:26 in Review

1.4.1 Mark 6:7 – 8:26 – structural overview

We have noted that the account of Jesus' appearance before his home synagogue, 6:1–6, recalls the encounter between Jesus and his own in 3:20–21,30–35. Its sequel, the sending of the disciples in 6:7–13, recalls their appointment in 3:13–19. The sending belongs closely with Jesus' visit to the synagogue, but also closely with what follows, namely, the account of the killing of John the Baptist, 6:17–29. Mark appears to juxtapose Jesus, the disciples and John, to highlight the dangers which will face the disciples. He will return to the theme of the disciples' need to suffer in 8:34–38. The immediate sequel to the sending is the account of Herod's questioning about who Jesus might be (6:14–16). This finds a correspondence in 8:27–31, where Jesus' elicits similar responses from the disciples.

However one might formally divide the verses at the beginning and at the end, it is clear that 6:7 – 8:26 is the main part of a major new section in Mark's gospel. This is evident also from its internal macrostructure which plays an important role in relation to the issue of Jesus and the Law. I want, therefore to begin by identifying this structure and its significance.

> In broad outline the section begins with
>   the sending of the disciples (6:7–13);
>   the questioning of Herod about Jesus' identity (6:14–16);
>   the flashback account of John's death (6:17–29).

> The return of the disciples makes a transition to
>   the account of the feeding of the five thousand (6:30–44);
>   which is followed by Jesus' walking on the water (6:45–52);
>   and a summary account of Jesus' healing (6:53–65).

> The controversy passage concerning Law follows in 7:1–23 in three parts:
>   controversy over washing (7:1–5);
>   tradition and abuse of the Law (7:6–15);
>   and exposition for the disciples (7:17–23)

> Immediately after this are narratives set in Gentile territory:
>   the encounter with the Syrophoenician woman and the healing of her
>   daughter from a distance (7:24–30);
>   the healing of the deaf and dumb man in the Decapolis region (7:31–
>   37);
>   and the feeding of the four thousand (8:1–10).

> Returning to Jewish territory,
>   Jesus refuses the Pharisees' request for a sign (8:11–13);
>   contrasts his teaching with that of the Pharisees and Herodians and
>   interprets the feedings (8:14–21);
>   and heals the blind man at Bethsaida (8:22–26).

8:11–21 is of particular significance for understanding the two feeding stories, but also the section as whole.[119] At first, in 8:11–13, Mark shows Jesus refusing to give a sign to "this generation". The irony is hardly to be

---

[119] See the discussion in G. Sellin, "Einige symbolische und esoterische Züge im Markus-Evangelium," in *Jesu Rede von Gott und ihre Nachgeschichte im frühen Christentum. Beiträge zur Verkündigung Jesu und zum Kerygma der Kirche. FS für Willi Marxsen*, edited by D.-A. Koch et al., (Gütersloh: Mohn, 1989), pp. 74–90, here: 80–84.

missed; as if the miraculous feedings were not sign enough! Then 8:14–21 makes use of the signs for the disciples. In 8:19–21 Jesus asks the disciples to notice the number of baskets in the two feeding miracles (12 and 7) and to see in this an important insight which supports Jesus' contrast between his own teaching and the leaven of the Pharisees and Herod. The reference to the latter recalls 3:6 which tells of the Pharisees and Herodians wanting to destroy Jesus. Mark is underlining the conflict which emerged from 2:1 – 3:6.

What do the numerical clues mean? As already in the narrative of the two women in 5:21–43, the figure 12 evokes Israel. Within the feeding of the 5000 it recurs. But in addition, in contrast to the feeding of 4000, we find also other significant motifs associated with Israel. The people are described as being like sheep without a shepherd, an image of Israel drawn from the description of Israel in Nu 27:17. Jesus has the crowds sit down in 100s and 50s, echoing the marshalling of Israel in the wilderness (Ex 18:25; Nu 31:14). The passage also shares with the other feeding the imagery of the wilderness which would have recalled Israel's manna in the wilderness. In addition, the feeding of the 5000 takes place in Jewish territory.

By contrast, the specifically Israelite imagery is absent in the feeding of the 4000. It takes place in Gentile territory and the people come "from afar", possibly also an allusion to Gentiles. The number of baskets of left over scraps is 7, not 12. 7, like 70, was a common enough symbol of the world of the nations.[120] It is evident that Mark wants us to see the two feedings as representing God's action through Jesus in regard to Israel and to the Gentiles.[121]

As in Mark 5, so here, we have juxtaposed the activities of Jesus in Jewish and Gentile territory. This extends also to the episodes which are associated with these feedings, especially in what follows, in the case of the first feeding, and what precedes, in the case of the second. Thus Jesus feeds 5000, walks on water and exercises a ministry of healing in Jewish territory (6:30–56). And in Gentile territory he heals the Syrophoenician woman's daughter, a deaf and dumb man, and feeds 4000 (7:24 – 8:10). Between

---

[120] It is less evident, though not impossible, that Mark might have seen already in the figures 5000 and 4000 some symbolic reference to the people of Torah (5 books; also 5 loaves?) and the people of the four winds or corners of the earth (and also 7 loaves?).

[121] So also Sellin, "Symbolische und esoterische Züge," pp. 82–83. He also notes "from afar" in 8:3 as symbolic of the Gentiles. This makes it a little strange that he refuses to recognise the role of the symbolic numbers when they occur in 8:19–21 (p. 81). Cf. Gundry, *Mark*, pp. 396–397, who dismisses all such symbolic allusions and at most recognises a pre-Markan interest in the Gentile mission in relation to the feedings.

these two complexes is 7:1–23, Jesus' teaching about purity. On either side of this narrative two sets of three narratives are contrasted.

The position of 7:1–23 between these complexes is significant, for 8:14–21 draws attention to the feedings in the context of discussion of rival teaching. This recalls for the hearer the major conflict with the Pharisees over teaching in 7:1–23. The issue at stake in the conflict relates to food laws and purity, an issue particularly relevant for relations between Jews and Gentiles. The encounter with the Syrophoenician woman, which follows immediately in 7:24–30, dramatises the issue. In the light of these considerations we can see that Mark has composed the complex, 6:7 – 8:26, and around the two feedings, with the teaching on purity as the centrepiece, to celebrate the inclusion of both Jew and Gentile in the kingdom.[122]

In addition, while doing so, Mark has employed food imagery for teaching. This is explicit in 8:14–21 and implicit in the feedings. The bread motif also reappears in the account of Jesus' walking on the water, where the disciples are criticised for not having understood about the bread (6:52). The bread motif reappears directly at the beginning of the controversy which forms the centrepiece (7:1–23): the disciples had not washed their hands before eating bread. It reappears in the following episode with the Syrophoenician woman, where the issue is whether children and the dogs may eat the bread (7:27–28). Finally it forms the introduction to the key interpretative narrative in 8:14–21, which begins with the disciples' anguish that they had not brought bread. In addition, as well as alluding to the earlier conflicts of 2:1 – 3:6, and 3:6, in particular, by the reference to the leaven of the Herodians Mark reminds the hearer of that other feast: Herod's birthday celebration, the occasion of John's beheading,[123] a kind of black eucharist. Before the feeding of the 5000 Mark also mentions that the disciples had been so busy they had not had time to eat (6:31; cf. also 3:20).

I have included 8:22–26, the healing of the blind man at Bethsaida, in the section because Mark uses it both positively as a miracle and negatively as symbol of the disciples' blindness, just as he does with the healing of blind Bartimaeus in 10:45–52. 8:22–26 also recalls 7:31–37, the healing of the deaf and dumb man. Together both stories symbolically provide a foil for

---

[122] Similarly Luz, *Gesetz*, p. 118; Sariola, *Markus*, pp. 62–63; T. R. Schmeller, "Jesus im Umland Galiläias. Zu den markinischen Berichten vom Aufenthalt Jesu in den Gebieten von Tyros, Caesarea Philippi und der Dekapolis," *BibZ* 38 (1994), pp. 44–66, here: 53; Gnilka, *Markus I*, pp. 290–293.

[123] R. M. Fowler, *Loaves and Fishes. The Function of the Feeding Stories in the Gospel of Mark*, SBLDS 54, (Chico: Scholars, 1981), pp. 85–86, argues that Mark deliberately juxtaposes the banquet of Herod and the banquet of Jesus in 6:14–29 and 6:30–44.

the disciples who fail to hear and understand the teaching of Jesus. Perhaps Mark would have been aware that Bethsaida was also Gentile territory, adding bite to the contrast. The beginning of the next major section in Mark, the question about Jesus' identity (8:27–31), echoing Herod's questions in 6:14–16, provides a further instance of Jesus' activity (the climactic confession of Peter!) in Gentile territory (Caesarea Philippi).[124]

The focus of the section lies primarily in the feedings and their link with Jesus' teaching about purity. It is of major importance for discussing Jesus' attitude towards the Law in Mark. Mark's striking composition is celebrating the inclusion of both Jews and Gentiles in the kingdom and doing so in contrast to teaching which, in Mark's mind, would render such inclusion impossible. This, then, forms the background for examining the section in greater detail.

1.4.2 Mark 6:7 – 6:56

As already noted, 6:7–13 returns to the theme of the disciples. The twelve, chosen in 3:13–19 to be sent with authority, are now sent out and given authority to cast out unclean spirits, to preach and to heal. As already intimated in 1:16–20, they also belong to the new phenomenon of God's action in the world. The mention of John the Baptist in 6:14–29 also reminds us of the beginning of the gospel. Mark's account of popular assessments of who Jesus might be (6:14–16) adds to the drama, since the hearers have known Jesus' identity since the prologue. There they had heard of John's arrest (1:14). Here Mark gives the details. In 6:18 he mentions that John had declared Herod's new marriage illegal. We may assume that Mark shares John's assessment: Herod acted contrary to God's Law by marrying his sister-in-law (Lev 18:16; 20:21). The detail is incidental. As we have seen, Mark seems to report the gruesome story here chiefly to prefigure what awaits Jesus and the disciples and, probably, to use this feast as a contrast to the feedings which follow.

As noted above, the feeding of the five thousand (6:30–45) is replete with symbolism of Israel. Mark shows no sign of sensing potential issues of purity at the feeding, although all 5000 would have fallen foul of Mark's Pharisees of 7:1 and there were surely plenty of sinners and perhaps a few toll collectors in the crowd! In conformity with Jewish practice Jesus gives thanks for the bread. The incidental inclusion of this detail and the inciden-

---

124 Cf. Schmeller, "Jesus," pp. 54–55, who speculates that this may reflect Mark's locality. See also Theissen, *Lokalkolorit*, p. 250.

tal omission of purity issues symbolise the level of Mark's interest. It is not Law observance as such, but Christ who matters; and the Law, only inasmuch as it is upheld or abrogated by him.

The primary focus is on Jesus' power to provide. For Mark, miracle and symbol are complementary, like exorcism and teaching authority. Jesus provides bread in abundance for Israel. The eschatological imagery of the feast undergirds the symbolic claim. Similarly Jesus' power to walk upon the water (6:45–52) celebrates his power over the forces of the deep and recalls his stilling of the storm. Mark notes that the disciples should have perceived the connection between the provision of loaves and the miracle on the water (6:52). Jesus is acting with God's own power to provide and to walk the deep. Beside this, they should have seen the symbolic allusion to Israel's past in the miraculous provision of loaves in the desert, corresponding to manna in the desert, and thus probably should have seen the crossing of the sea as an echo of the miraculous crossing of the Red Sea.

The party having set out for Bethsaida, arrives in Gennesaret. The changed location would alert hearers who knew that Bethsaida was technically in Gentile land, that that goal had not been reached.[125] Crowds flock to Jesus at Gennesaret and he in turn visits all the towns and cities of the region. Mark notes the healings and the requests to touch the hem of Jesus' garment (6:56), a motif which recalls the daring act of the menstruant woman (5:25–34). By recalling this episode, which Mark had used to highlight Jesus' mighty works in Israel after his mighty work in the Gentile Gerasa region, Mark may well intend the hearers to sense that this summary of activities in 6:53–56 reports Jesus deeds in Israel. The feeding of the five thousand had already given emphasis specifically to Israel symbolism.

Κράσπεδον probably alludes to Jesus' wearing of the *tefillim* and should be translated "tassel". The detail may be incidental, although Booth may be right in suggesting that its presence functions in a similar way here, before the controversy episode, 7:1–23, as does 1:40–45, the cleansing of the leper, before the controversies in 2:1 – 3:6. That function is to strengthen the impression that Jesus is respectful of the Law.[126] This would be another pointer to Mark's knowledge of Jewish Law and his strategic use of it in his composition.

---

[125] See Malbon, *Narrative Space*, pp. 28–29, who argues that the failure to reach the goal until after the teaching of Jesus about ritual purity and his own travel and action in Gentile territory is symbolic.

[126] Booth, *Purity*, p. 31.

1.4.3 Mark 7:1–23

The transition to 7:1–23 is stark and perhaps deliberately so. It is as provider and healer of Israel, that Jesus is now confronted by a second delegation from Jerusalem, from the centre of Jewish authority.[127] In 3:22 the scribes from Jerusalem alleged Jesus' collusion with Beelzebul. Here Pharisees and scribes raise with Jesus why the disciples are eating the loaves with unwashed hands and so disregarding the tradition of the elders. The allusion to loaves also links the episode with the broader context, for in the light of what precedes, we are probably correct to assume that Mark intends a reference to the miraculous abundance of loaves, the new manna, which they scarcely understood.[128] If Mark intends in this reference to loaves also a symbolic allusion to Jesus' teaching, as also the later commentary in 8:14–21 suggests, then the irony is remarkable: here is eschatological abundance; in contrast, the Pharisees and scribes are worried about purified hands!

While the broader context demands that we should bear such allusions in mind, it is clear that Mark means to narrate a dispute about actual handwashing. For him, it is closely related to the intake of food and the categories of clean and unclean food, which underlie the barrier between Jew and Gentile. In Mark's community these barriers have fallen.

In outline, 7:1–5 narrates the objection of the Pharisees and scribes and furnishes the hearer with a generalising editorial comment about purifications. Mark portrays Jesus' first response in 7:6–13. Jesus attacks hypocrisy and cites as evidence a Jewish tradition which was being used in contravention of the decalogue commandment to honour parents. 7:14–15 contains a statement of principle about the inner rather than the outer defiling a person. 7:17–23 narrates a private conversation between Jesus and his disciples in which he explains the meaning of this principle and into which Mark inserts a summary of its significance: Jesus declared all foods clean (7:19c). Within 7:1–23, the comments in 7:3–4 and 19c stand out as editorial explanations.

The thrust of Mark's narrative is to be found in its generalising application, both negatively and positively. Negatively, the explanation in 7:3–4 associates handwashing before eating with a wide range of other activities deemed to be characteristic of "all Jews": bathing before eating when they return from the market and washing of cups and of other utensils including beds.[129] Other extant evidence suggests that only extremists held to such

---

127 Possibly reflecting implied anti-temple critique on the part of Mark. So Sariola, *Markus*, pp. 60, 232.

128 So Gundry, *Mark*, p. 348.

129 On πυγμῇ see M. Hengel, "Mc 7,3 πυγμῇ: Die Geschichte einer exegetischen Aporie und der Versuch ihrer Lösung," *ZNW* 60 (1969), pp. 182–198.

scruples about handwashing.[130]   Mark, however, assumes the practice was general and had earlier in 2:1 – 3:6 pictured Pharisees as espousing extremist positions. By his elaboration Mark is probably holding such practices up to ridicule.[131]   These scruples belong to "the tradition of the elders" (7:3).

The Pharisees and scribes level their accusation not directly against Jesus, but against the disciples. As in 2:23–28, this need not imply that the story originated in the early church, since it was common practice to hold teachers responsible for the practices of their disciples. On the other hand, it may indicate this and, certainly for Mark, it relates to an issue concerning what believers may or may not do. They are acting contrary to "the tradition of the elders", which, for Mark, is not authoritative teaching, but belongs to and is concerned with mere externals.

The narrative then continues in 7:6–7 by having Jesus address the Pharisees and scribes as hypocrites and cite Isa 29:13 LXX as evidence. "This people honours me with their lips, but their heart is far from me. In vain do they worship me, teaching the commandments of human beings as their teachings." He uses it to contrast lip and heart and to attack mere human teachings (equated by Mark with the tradition of the elders; 7:8). The implicit contrast between mere externals and the internal in 7:3–4 now becomes one of external behaviour of the lips not matching the heart.[132]   The teachings are portrayed as enabling this to happen. Thus the tradition of the elders, which, according to 7:3–4, stipulates external washings, also cements, according to 7:9–12, a more serious division between religion of the heart and actual behaviour, between honouring parents and immorally robbing them of support through abuse of the *corban* system. 7:13b generalises here too:

---

[130] See the discussion in Sanders, *Jewish Law*, pp. 30–31, 39–40, 160–163, 228–231, 258–271, esp. 260–263, who argues that there is no evidence that Pharisees washed hands before eating ordinary food.   Booth, *Purity*, pp. 189–203, argues that the practice had developed as supererogatory observance among *haberim*, so that the Markan tradition reflects a dispute with *haberim*. See also Deines, *Steingefässe*, pp. 267–275, who argues that Sanders arrives at his conclusion by following Neusner's methodology of excluding anonymous mishnaic traditions such *mYad* 1; 2; *mHag* 2:5, which he believes should be taken into account. He also disputes Sanders's assumption that Pharisees did not seek to impose their views on others. The present passage reflects then an established practice among certain Pharisees; their influence is also evident in the presence of the stone jars in John 2:6. For a defence of Mark's generalisation, see Gundry, *Mark*, pp. 358–360.

[131] Sariola, *Markus*, p. 51, notes the sarcastic tone of both 3–4 and 18d–19b.

[132] On the rhetorical strategy of Mark in portraying Jesus as one, who has crossed a boundary in allowing disciples to eat with unwashed hands, yet avoids setting himself outside the system, so attacks it from within, see G. Salyer, "Rhetoric, Purity, and Play: Aspects of Mark 7:1–23," *Semeia* 64 (1993), pp. 139–170, here: 161–162.

"You do many such things like this!" This generalisation may emanate from the same editorial hand which inserted 7:3–4 and 7:19c, that of Mark.

As a complex, 7:6–13 is making a point only indirectly related to the concerns of the controversy. It applies a commandment and warning about honouring parents to what is really an abuse of another law, *corban*. The abuse is made possible by a loophole in the way it was being applied by the interpreters of the Law. What is more, the context, here, suggests that the interpreters deliberately encouraged such abuse. Therein is the hypocrisy. The argument is not against a Law, not even a playing off of one part of the Law against another, but against an interpretation which deliberately seeks to circumvent the Law. The same abuse is also acknowledged by later Jewish teachers.[133] Here, however, Mark's Jesus attributes this corruption generally to scribes and Pharisees through the generalising statements in 7:8 ("Abandoning the commandment of God you hold to human tradition") and 7:13 ("Disregarding the word of God by your tradition which you have passed on; and you do many other things like this"), in much the same way as he attributes hypocrisy to them in 12:38–40. These generalising comments frame the tradition and set it in perspective.

When, later, in 8:15 Mark has Jesus warn against the leaven of the scribes and Pharisees, he doubtless has such abuses in mind, but the primary focus is what prevents access for Gentiles, namely the issue of purity and food laws represented in 7:1–5 and 14–23. In 7:6–13 Mark appears, then, to have employed an earlier controversy over abuse of *corban* (preserved in part in 7:9–13a) as a typical example of the hypocrisy of scribes and Pharisees and to have added to it the introduction in 7:6–8 and the generalisation in 7:13b.[134] Mark places it within the narrative so as to discredit not only the views of

---

[133] So T. W. Manson, *The Teaching of Jesus*, (Cambridge: CUP, 2nd edn, 1955), pp. 315–319, with reference to *mNed* 3:2; 9:1. But see the discussion in Gundry, *Mark*, p. 363; Westerholm, *Scribal Authority*, pp. 76–78, who concludes that earlier Pharisaic teachers did not free people from vows even in such a case of conflict with parents' interests. See also the discussion in Sanders, *Jewish Law*, pp. 51–57, who points also to Philo's stance in *Hyp* 7:3–5, which is similar to the position being attacked here.

[134] I see this as more likely than that 7:6–13 belonged already with 7:1–2,5 before it came to Mark. For the view that 7:6–8 already formed part of the tradition, see Bultmann, *Synoptic Tradition*, p.17; C. E. Carlston, "'The Things that defile' (Mark vii. 14) and the Law in Matthew and Mark," *NTS* 15 (1968), pp. 75–96, here: 91; Schweizer, *Markus*, pp. 77–78; Gnilka, *Markus I*, pp. 267–269. For the view that 7:9–13 already formed part of the tradition: Hübner, *Gesetz*, pp. 142–146, 164–165, who sees the original conflict anecdote as 7:10a,11,12,13a; Westerholm, *Scribal Authority*, pp. 80, 82; Luz, *Gesetz*, p. 118; similarly Sariola, *Markus*, p. 49, who, however, attributes 11d,12 (the reference to the decalogue commandment) to Markan redaction.

the scribes and Pharisees (7:1–5, esp. 3–4), but also their integrity. Mark seems no longer as interested in the argument as such as he is in asserting Jesus' authority and undermining the authority of those who oppose him.

Thus far two kinds of attack have been made on the tradition of the elders: it concerns itself with irrelevant externals and it encourages people to justify disobedience towards the commandments, and thus hypocrisy. Mark's narrative assumes a strong commitment to the decalogue command to honour parents. 7:14–15 returns to the contrast: external - internal of 7:3–4: "There is nothing outside of a person which entering him defiles him, but the things coming out of a person are what defile the person." The present narrative invites us to listen to an explanation of its meaning in the verses which follow. We turn first to this explanation.

Within the Markan narrative, 7:14–15 and 17–23 follow a pattern familiar from elsewhere in Mark of having Jesus say something to the crowd, a parable, which he then explains to an inside circle of the disciples. The pattern receives its ideological grounding in 4:11–12 (which is then illustrated by the explanation of the parable of the sower in 4:13–20). This is a feature of Markan narrative (cf. 4:10; 9:28; 10:10). Again Mark upbraids the disciples for lack of understanding (7:18; cf. 6:52) and so forges another link within his wider composition and ultimately with 8:14–21. 7:18b–19 argues that the external intake cannot affect the heart, because it reaches only the stomach and then passes into the toilet. The tone is ridiculing. The heart - stomach/toilet contrast corresponds to the internal - external. This makes it clear that Mark will have understood the contrast in 7:15 as absolute.[135]

---

[135] So Luz, *Gesetz*, p. 118; Sariola, *Markus*, p. 54. On the other hand, in its earliest form it was probably an inclusive antithesis. This puts it in line with prophetic cult critique and makes better sense of the apparent absence of a word of Jesus in the early tradition which could have helped the church deal with the food issue. So E. Klostermann, *Das Markusevangelium*, HNT 3, (Tübingen: J. C. B. Mohr [Paul Siebeck], 1950), p. 79; Carlston, "Things that defile," p. 95; Luz, *Gesetz*, pp. 60–61; Borg, *Conflict*, pp. 96–97; Sanders, *Jewish Law*, p. 28; W. D. Davies, and D. C. Allison, *A Critical and Exegetical Commentary on the Gospel according to Saint Matthew*, Vol II, VIII–XVIII, (Edinburgh: T&T Clark, 1991), pp. 527–531. Hübner's suggestion, *Gesetz*, pp. 170–174, that early Christian preoccupation with affirming Jesus' messiahship led to such logia being overlooked, is not convincing. Equally unconvincing is Gundry, *Mark*, p. 370, who cites the possibility that the saying was known only to some and should be seen as similar to the anecdotes about eating with toll collectors and sinners in relation to fellowship with Gentiles. The latter is not an adequate parallel; sinners are not the same as Gentiles. Gundry's view that 7:15 was in any case ambiguous is especially difficult in the light of his espousal of the tradition that Peter stands behind Mark.

Cf. also J. W. Taeger, "Der grundsätzliche oder ungrundsätzliche Unterschied. Anmerkungen zur gegenwärtigen Debatte um das Gesetzesverständnis Jesu," in *Jesus und*

This *mashal* like response of Jesus in 7:15 is similar in character to those we found in the anecdotes of 2:1 – 3:6.[136] It probably formed the original response in a controversy anecdote about hand washing,[137] preserved behind 7:2,5 and was inclusive rhetoric.[138] 7:15 would have originally responded to the issue of the alleged pollution which is supposed by his complainants to occur when people ate food with unwashed, ie. ritually unclean, hands.[139] The assumption is that the unwashed hands render the food im-

---

das jüdische Gesetz, edited by I. Broer, (Stuttgart: Kohlhammer, 1992), pp. 13–36, here: 28–29, who considers that Rom 14:14,20 may reflect influence of the logion. Similarly Luz, *Gesetz*, p. 60. Against this Dautzenberg, "Gesetzeskritik," pp. 48–49. Cf. also Berger, *Gesetzesauslegung*, p. 507, who argues the logion must have arisen in a Hellenistic Jewish context, because, on his theory, it was there that the prophetic tradition of cult criticism was fostered. On this see the critique in Booth, *Purity*, pp. 72, 84–97; Gundry, *Mark*, pp. 366–367, who emphasises that Jewish parallels offer examples of relative weighting, not absolute antithesis between ethics and cult.

[136] The parallel structure to those anecdotes and the fact that here as there Jesus appears to be dealing with extremists, may well indicate a similar context at some stage of transmission. Perhaps originally, like the sayings in those anecdotes, the logion of 7:15 was directed to the complainants.

[137] So also Berger, *Gesetzesauslegung*, pp. 463–464; J. Lambrecht, "Jesus and the Law. An Investigation of Mk 7,1–23," *EThL* 53 (1977), pp. 24–82, here: 56, 66; Booth, *Purity*, pp. 62–67, 74; Mack, *Myth of Innocence*, p. 189; Weiss, *Vollmacht*, pp. 66–67; Vouga, *Loi*, p. 70; Taeger, "Unterschied," p. 24; Salyer, "Rhetoric," p. 142, who goes on to discuss the subsequent elaborations in the light of ancient rhetorical theory (pp. 142–146). Sariola, *Markus*, p. 30, objects that on this assumption it is hard to see why Mark has added the less logical material between 7:5 and 7:15. The answer surely lies in Mark's broader polemical purpose. Sariola suggests Mark has used two traditional sources, 7:3b–4c,5b–6a,9b–11c,11e,13ab and 15 already expanded before Mark by 18b–19b, 20 (p. 49). Gundry, *Mark*, pp. 368–369, points to the shift between 5 and 15, noting that one concerns eating with unwashed hands, the other with food which defiles, addressed to the crowd (so already Bultmann, *Synoptic Tradition*, p.17). The addressees are not a problem, if the change is seen as Markan editing. The transition from one aspect of purity to another need not be problematic. The assumption is that defilement of hands also affects food and so affects people – an extreme standpoint.

[138] So Westerholm, *Scribal Authority*, pp. 83–84; Luz, *Gesetz*, pp. 61, 118; Gnilka, *Markus I*, p. 280; Booth, *Purity*, pp. 69, 104–107; J. D. G. Dunn, "Jesus and Ritual Purity: A Study of the Tradition-History of Mark 7:15," in *Jesus, Paul and the Law. Studies in Mark and Galatians,* (London: SPCK, 1990), pp. 37–60, here: 58; Weiss, *Vollmacht*, p. 70; B. Lindars, "All foods clean: thoughts on Jesus and the law," in *Law and Religion. Essays on the Place of the Law in Israel and Early Christianity*, edited by B. Lindars, (Cambridge: Clarke, 1988), pp. 61–71, here: 71, who speaks of a "language event". For the contrary view: Gundry, *Mark*, p. 365; Taeger, "Unterschied," pp. 26–28; J. Riches, *Jesus and the Transformation of Judaism*, (New York: Seabury, 1980), pp. 136–138, who likens it to Jesus' rejection of pollution by adultery.

[139] Probably the saying was originally deliberately playful and ambiguous. It is a riddle or *mashal*, like a parable. At one level it functions as an argument, literally, that bodily emissions are a greater purity issue than eating contaminated food, which, with

pure, hence the words, ἔξωθεν . . . εἰσπορευόμενον εἰς αὐτόν.[140]   It is, however, by no means clear that unwashed hands would have rendered food eaten with unwashed hands unclean.[141]   It would be coming from an extremist position. On the other hand, it is possible that the saying may be a typically generalising response, such as we find in the anecdotes of 2:1 – 3:6. In other words, the reference to what is outside entering someone may only obliquely respond to the accusation and intend to make a wider statement of principle. In any case, the statement, whatever form it took, doubtless gave expression to an inclusive contrast, such as we find in Hosea 6:6 and elsewhere. "I desire mercy and not sacrifice" meant not an attack on sacrifice, but a setting of priorities. I desire mercy more than sacrifices.

It is clear that Mark takes the saying as a statement of principle in a broad sense and understands the contrast exclusively. His concern is, in any case, food laws in general. Thus in the explanation which follows the focus is not food contaminated through unwashed hands, but food itself. The explanation, probably already pre-Markan,[142] had shifted the focus from food contaminated by unwashed hands to food itself. In 7:19c the focus remains on unclean food. The logion, 7:15, and its exposition in 7:17–23, and reflecting a spirit of disparagement already present in 7:3–4, are central to Mark's

---

regard to the written law, was indeed the case. So Schmithals, *Markus*, p. 343; but cf. the critical discussion in Booth, *Purity*, pp. 208–209, Gundry, *Mark*, p. 366. On the motif of defecation in Hellenistic writing see Downing, *Christ and the Cynics*, pp. 129–130. Josephus, *JW* 2.149, reports that the Essenes washed themselves after defecation as people defiled (καθάπερ μεμιασμένος). Such attitudes may also have been reflected in the original aphorism.

[140] Following W. Paschen, *Rein und Unrein. Untersuchungen zur biblischen Wortgeschichte*, StANT 24, (Munich: Kösel, 1970), pp. 173–174, Booth, *Purity*, p. 68, argues that the original form of the saying was without εἰσπορευόμενον εἰς αὐτόν and read only ἔξω. Similarly Vouga, *Loi*, p. 72; Dunn, "Ritual Purity," pp. 42–44, 59, who argues that Matthew preserves the earlier form of the saying, reflected also in Thom 14 and behind 7:17–19b; Hübner, *Gesetz*, p. 167 (that earlier form of the saying is behind 7:18,20); B. Lindars, "'All foods clean': thoughts on Jesus and the law," in *Law and Religion. Essays on the Place of the Law in Israel and Early Christianity*, edited by B. Lindars, (Cambridge: Clarke, 1988), pp. 61–71, here 62–62. On this see Weiss, *Vollmacht*, pp. 68–72; Sariola, *Markus*, p. 40 n. 117; Gundry, *Mark*, pp. 364–366.

[141] See the discussion in Booth, *Purity*, pp. 155–203, who concludes, that nothing in the restrictive tradition indicated that ordinary food is contaminated by eating it with unwashed hands, since food could only suffer first or second degree impurity and that contamination from unwashed hands could only be at third degree. Nevertheless he argues that the practice alluded to here is one of supererogation to be ascribed to *haberim*. Cf. also Hübner, *Gesetz*, pp. 180–183.

[142] Similarly Sariola, *Markus*, p. 49, who suggests 15 had already been expanded before Mark by 18b–19b,20. The expansions reflect Gentile focus where concern would have been primarily foods, designated unclean, or unclean because offered to idols, an

concerns. They opened the way for acceptance of Gentiles who had been shunned above all because of their eating of unclean food. Accordingly the final four words of 7:19 generalise this to conclude that all foods are clean.[143] As narrator Mark is drawing the conclusion that the effect of Jesus' argument is to make an authoritative pronouncement which Mark will have known was contrary to the Law. This is the major emphasis and so is included at this point in the narrative. What follows in 7:20 states the obverse of 7:18–19. What defiles is immorality proceeding from within. The elaboration in 7:22–23 includes a list covering only moral sins. It is probably only of secondary interest to Mark that some of the list corresponds to the decalogue list.[144]

The words, καθαρίζων πάντα τὰ βρώματα ("making/declaring all foods clean", 7:19c) should not be treated in isolation from their narrative context within 7:1–23 and within the broader context, 6:7 – 8:26. Some later manuscripts have replaced καθαρίζων by καθαρίζον.[145] On this reading there would be a play on purification and getting rid of excrement. Such a reading or even an interpretation of καθαρίζων in this direction, were it possible,[146] would not, however, remove the fact that the effect of the surrounding context is to call both food laws and ritual washing into question. 7:19c is drawing a correct conclusion from the context. It coheres with Mark's disparagement of attention to such externals in 7:3–4. It also coheres with Mark's narrative strategy, especially in 6:7 – 8:26 of celebrating the inclusion of Jew and Gentile in the kingdom, for which, we know, food and purity laws were a barrier.

Thus Mark's interest is above all in discounting the significance of the food laws. In abandoning them the way is set free for the kind of Gentile Christianity to which Mark obviously belongs. These had been a stumbling block in the way of inclusion of Gentiles on equal terms with Jews. Mark has Jesus give authoritative teaching which justifies the abandonment of such scruples. Preoccupation with such externals is irrelevant and those

---

issue in the context of mission, which is reflected also in the context of the logion in Thomas. So Dunn, "Ritual Purity," p. 47. Gundry, *Mark*, p. 367, explains the awkward syntax of 19c on the basis that Mark has added it to traditional material.

[143] If in our context 7:17–23 were totally Markan, 7:19c would form part of this composition. It seems to me more likely that at least the substance of the explanation, if not its structure, is pre-Markan.

[144] So Sariola, *Markus*, p. 60; similarly, Booth, *Purity*, p. 33.

[145] See Metzger, *Textual Commentary*, p. 81.

[146] Against a reference to ἀφεδρῶνα see Banks, *Law*, p. 144; cf. Malina, "Mark 7," pp. 22–25; G. Vermes, *Jesus the Jew. A Historian's reading of the Gospels*, (London: Collins, 1973), p. 29, who argues that Mark has deliberately modified for his own purposes part of the original saying of Jesus which alluded to the function of the latrine "where

who focus on them are in any case also hypocritical, because they fail to keep the commandments. 7:6–13 and the list of virtues in 7:21–23 indicate that Jesus champions such commandments; but for Mark Jesus has a new teaching with authority which dispenses with laws concerning unclean foods and ritual impurity related to externals such as hand washing, cups, plates and beds. The approach is consistent with the image we found of Jesus in 2:1 – 3:6: Jesus is the ultimate authority beside and beyond Torah. Yet here, for the first time, we see the ultimate implications of this claim to authority: it may include permanently setting aside specific Torah provisions and demeaning them as worthless!

Did Mark still think that it was only *halakah* which Jesus attacked? Was he ignorant that the food laws were part of the written law? Sariola suggests that Mark may have left it open for Gentile readers to assume that only oral tradition was being attacked and may himself not have known.[147] But Mark's apparent knowledge of both the laws and the stories of Israel make this unlikely.[148]

In the light of the controversy section 2:1 – 3:6, we should assume also here that Mark is presenting Jesus as the ultimate authority beside and beyond Torah.[149] Nevertheless, in 7:1–23, it is interesting that this is not made explicit, as there. We might expect something like: "For the Son of Man has authority to declare God's will." Instead the point is made by argument. The argument is based on a value system which understands external ritual acts to be merely human religious tradition and therefore disparages suggestions that either contact with material things or consumption of food can have relevance for genuine purity. Thus 7:17–23 argues on a similar basis to what is implied in the explanation in 7:3–4, namely a contrast between inner and outer, internal and external. The element of ridicule is undeniable in both: fancy being concerned with washings cups and plates and beds! Fancy having purity concerns about food which can only enter the stomach and finally ends up in the toilet![150]   By contrast, what matters is ethics.

---

all food is cleansed away". This would reflect a pun between דּוּכָא ("the place") and דְּכָא ("be clean").

[147] Sariola, *Markus*, pp. 56–57.

[148] Vouga, *Loi*, p. 175, notes that Mark shows no signs of embarrassment at Jesus' words, since the debate with Judaism is well behind him. Banks's suggestion, *Law*, p. 145, that Mark intends a reference only to food offered to idols is too limiting. This was not the only food issue at stake in relations among Jews and Gentiles which will have interested Mark.

[149] So Gundry, *Mark*, p. 356, who writes: "Now Jesus himself is nullifying God's Word with regard to food. But it is the prerogative of Jesus as God's Son to change the Law."

[150] Mack, *Myth of Innocence*, p. 189, cites the saying as typical earthy Cynic humour.

Here human behaviour is seen as springing from human attitudes. Purity has been redefined to exclude ritual and cultic impurity; it is about morality. Mark sums up the message of the passage in the gloss at 7:19c: Jesus was declaring all foods clean.

In this way Mark aligns Jesus to a particular ideological stance with regard to the value of the external and the ritual. Our analysis will show that this stance informs his understanding of Jesus' attitude towards the Law also with regard to the temple. The effect of this ideological stance is to call much of the Law into question. At the same time our analysis of 2:1 – 3:6 showed that Mark usually subordinates argumentation to the assertion of Jesus' authority. In 7:1–23 the authority is certainly assumed. As far finding expression, it surfaces at most in 7:19c. For in 7:19c Mark's focus is probably more on Jesus' acting in authority, "declaring all foods clean", ie. an argument based on Jesus' authority, rather than just on summarising rational argument.[151]

The abandonment of these "human traditions" and of Levitical food laws sets Jesus' teaching directly in conflict with that of the scribes and Pharisees. Mark sets this in its wider context by seeing Jesus' teaching as removing the barriers for accepting Gentiles on equal terms. In effect, by his placement of 7:1–23, he makes it into the justification for celebrating the inclusion of both Jews and Gentiles in the kingdom. They, too, share the healing and the feasting of the kingdom, as the following context will demonstrate.

1.4.4 Mark 7:24 – 8:26

On the other side of the centrepiece of Mark's composition, the teaching about purity, we immediately find Jesus journeying into Gentile territory.

---

[151] It seems likely then that there has been a development behind 7:1–23 which included at an early stage an anecdote, not unlike those we find in 2:1 – 3:6, in which 7:15 formed the climax and related to the issue of hand washing. It would share with many of them the characteristic that it represents conflict with what we know to have been a position held only by an extreme group of Jews. The earlier anecdote has been expanded with an explanation in 7:18–23 which focuses more on the food laws and establishes a major contrast between cultic law and ethical law based on inward attitudes. The same attitude of cult critique appears in the explanations for Gentiles in 7:3–4. Into the narrative Mark has inserted an older tradition about Law interpretation (7:9–13a), framed by 9 and 13b and introduced by 6–8, in such a way as to discredit the integrity of Jesus' opponents. It may well have been added at the same stage as 7:3–4 and as 7:19c. Such passages are nearest to Mark's concern to underline Jesus' authority while discrediting his opponents' integrity and to report Jesus' authorisation of the current acceptance of Gentiles into the family of faith, the primary focus of 7:1–23 in the wider context.

Entering Gentile land is not a purity issue for Mark, as we saw in considering 5:1–43. His interest is the Gentile person. Mark's familiar theme of Jesus' finding no escape from the crowds introduces the encounter between Jesus and a Syrophoenician woman (7:24–30).[152] Mark presents her as breaching Jesus' isolation with a desperate request concerning her demon possessed daughter. The situation is full of tension when Jesus reacts negatively; "Let the children be fed first; for it is not right to take the children's food and throw it to the dogs."

The imagery is stark and simple. Israel, the people of God, are God's children; Gentiles are the dogs.[153] Nothing indicates that Mark means us to see here a playful Jesus talking of household puppies,[154] or making a deliberately provocative statement, tongue in cheek.[155] On the contrary, Mark takes the issues seriously, as does, Matthew, later, who provides a salvation historical explanation (Mt 15:23!). Within the broader context, Mark is alluding to the issue of inclusion of both Jew and Gentile among those who may receive the food of the kingdom. Jesus voices the exclusive position, modified only by "first". This allows the possibility that Gentiles may in

---

[152] See also my treatment in "Challenged at the Boundaries," pp. 45-51.

[153] Cf. the interpretation revived by Gundry, *Mark*, pp. 73-374, 377, that the contrast is not between Israel and the Gentiles but between the disciples' need for teaching and the need for exorcism. The disciples are the children; the dogs are those in need of exorcism. Jesus is primarily seeking privacy, argues Gundry, and draws attention to the similar situation in 9:30-31 where Jesus wants to be incognito; Jesus enters a house and teaches the disciples, a common pattern in Mark. Similarly Räisänen, *Messianic Secret*, p. 26; and Grundmann, *Markus*, p. 199, who suggests that in Mark's tradition the contrast was between the disciples and the woman, but that this is no longer the case in Mark. Yet there is mention neither of teaching nor of disciples in this passage. So rightly Guelich, *Mark*, p. 384, Gnilka, *Markus I*, p. 294.

[154] Cf. Lane, *Mark*, p. 262; similarly, M. Fander, *Die Stellung der Frau im Markusevangelium unter besonderer Berücksichtigung kultur- und religionsgeschichtlicher Hintergründe*, (Altenberge: Telos, 1990), pp. 460-461. The response of T. A. Burkill, "Historical Development of the Story of the Syro-phoenician Woman," *NovT* 9 (1967), pp. 161-177, here: 172, to such interpretation is noteworthy: "We may safely assume that any intelligent Hellenistic woman, addressed in such terms by a barbarian, would have immediately reacted by slapping the man's face. And, as in English, so in other languages, to call a woman "a little bitch" is no less abusive than to call her 'a bitch' without qualification." While "bitch" is a gender specific term of abuse, the point is taken: κύνες was a common term of abuse or at least deprecatory, and probably also κυνάρια. On this see the discussion in S. Pedersen, Art. "κύων," *EWNT II*, pp. 821-823. Cf. Pesch, *Markusevangelium II*, p. 390; Guelich, *Mark*, p. 386; Gundry, *Mark*, pp. 375, 381; P. Pokorny, "From a Puppy to a Child: Problems of Contemporary Biblical Exegesis Demonstrated from Mark 7.24-30/Matt 15.21-28," *NTS* 41 (1995), pp. 321-337, here: 324-325.

[155] So rightly, Gundry, *Mark*, p. 373, who dismisses the suggestion that Jesus is deliberately joking or the like or that we should see Jesus' reply as testing the woman's faith

future become recipients. The woman is too desperate to dispute the disparaging imagery. Instead she argues for simultaneous access; while the children eat, the dogs take the crumbs that fall from the table. Jesus relents; acknowledging her argument, he declares the daughter free of the demon.

Jesus' response symbolises the inclusiveness of Jews and Gentiles in the feast of the kingdom. The main point of 7:1–23, and of the broader context, finds here its symbolic fulfilment. This achievement at the symbolic level is not without some remaining problems. They include the issue whether Mark means the unequal status implied in the images (children and dogs) to persist so that the only change was one of timing.[156] This would seem unlikely. The "first" in Jesus' initial response makes sense against the background of salvation history.[157] Its effect, at a literal level, amounts to rejection of the woman's request. But challenged, Mark's Jesus abandons his initial stance

---

with a deliberately racist remark. Against Schmithals, *Markus*, pp. 354–355; Lane, *Mark*, p. 263; cf. E. Haenchen, *Der Weg Jesu. Eine Erklärung des Markusevangeliums und der kanonischen Parallelen*, STÖ II,6, (Berlin, 2nd edn, 1968), who with reference to the menstruant woman who drew on his power, speculates that Jesus was fearing loss of power (p. 274) and Theissen, *Lokalkolorit*, p. 169, who dismisses the suggestion of J. Weiss, *Die drei ältesten Evangelien*, SNT 2, (Göttingen, 1906), p. 128, that Jesus is speaking perhaps out of frustration at failure of Jews to respond to his message; cf. J. D. M. Derrett, "Law in the New Testament: The Syro-Phoenician Woman and the Centurion of Capernaum," *NovT* 15(1973), pp. 161–186, here: 169, who speaks of Jesus being in a quandary. The shocking character of the statement is reflected in the following descriptions: "racist" – so Waetjen, *Reordering of Power.*, p. 134; "unseemly, demeaning" – so B. van Iersel, *Reading Mark*, (Edinburgh: T&T Clark, 1989), p. 102; "fierce Jewish privilege" – so C. Bryan, *A Preface to Mark. Notes on the Gospel in its Literary and Cultural Settings*, (Oxford: OUP, 1993), p. 97.

156 The woman is prepared to stomach the abusive appellation for the sake of her daughter and pleads that her lower status in the order of things should not prevent her receiving what she needs. So Z. Kato, *Die Völkermission im Markusevangelium. Eine redaktionsgeschichtliche Untersuchung*, EHS.T 252, (Frankfurt: Peter Lang, 1986), p. 88; Guelich, *Mark*, pp. 387–388; Schmithals, *Markus*, pp. 354–355. The passage deals with the inclusion of Gentiles by clearing maintaining Israel's priority, as Paul does in Rom 1:17; so Burkill, "Historical Development," p. 169; Gnilka, *Markus I*, p. 290; Lührmann, *Markusevangelium*, p. 131, who makes the point however that Jesus' initial response assumes an exclusive understanding of priority in contrast to Paul's use. See also Waetjen, *Reordering of Power*, p. 134; Burkill, "Historical Development," pp. 162, 164; van Iersel, *Mark*, p. 103, who sees the status issue reflected in the difference between the numbers, 5000 and 4000.

157 So Guelich, *Mark*, p. 387; Gundry, *Mark*, p. 378. At the level of the literal story, telling the woman she must wait until after the people of Israel have been fed is nothing less than rejection of the woman's immediate need. Being told to wait until first the Jews have heard the gospel is beside the point for a mother facing her daughter's demon possession.

and so sets the precedent for inclusion of Gentiles in the blessings of the gospel. This extraordinary story of a heroic persistent Gentile woman serves Mark's broader purpose.[158]   It does so at the cost of contrasting two attitudes of Jesus. Mark can apparently live with this. It may have its parallel in Jesus' response in other boundary situations (1:40–41; 5:28–30): anger, yet willingness to respond to the leper and to the menstruant woman.[159]

The passage exhibits a number of features in relation to Mark's image of Jesus' attitude towards the Law. The first is Jesus' Jewishness. He had already pictured a Jesus wearing tassels (6:56). Here he portrays a Jesus reluctant to respond to a Gentile and making this plain in very disparaging terms. It coheres with this image that the healing takes place at a distance. Jesus does not enter a Gentile house. Perhaps Mark was aware of this as an issue, perhaps not. Yet Mark tells the story because of the opposite tendency, namely as a story symbolising inclusion of Gentiles. Mark's interest is what Jesus ended up doing. Mark uses the story to illustrate inclusiveness and so support the import of both 7:1–23 and the argument he is putting in the broader composition of his narrative, 6:30 – 8:22. It is an extraordinary story, told to illustrate the new openness, and obviously not sensed by Mark as told at Jesus' cost.

In 7:31–37 Mark celebrates a further healing in Gentile territory. The deaf and dumb person is made to hear and to speak. Jesus' actions as miracle worker reinforce the sense of struggle, but also his authority and power. The miracles here and in Jewish territory in 6:53–56 may well intend an allusion to Jesus as fulfilling both for Jew and Gentile eschatological expectations associated with Israel (cf. Isa 35:5; 61:1–2; 4Q521).

The account of the feeding of the four thousand (8:1–9) cannot but recall the feeding of the five thousand. It is therefore all the more notable that the disciples respond to the people's plight, drawn to their attention by Jesus, with astonishing density. Already in the account of the Jesus' walking on the water Mark notes their failure to understand about the loaves (6:52). There Mark alluded both to the literal miracle and to its typological allusion

---

[158] She wins Jesus over. A stance which demanded the woman wait is replaced by one which has room for her need. So Guelich, *Mark*, p. 387, who notes the change from one perspective which would have her wait to another where she is fed simultaneously; similarly Fander, *Stellung der Frau*, p. 74. Lane, *Mark*, p. 261, asks whether the woman should really be seen as understanding such subtleties of salvation history, but that confuses the story itself with its symbolic function in the narrative.

[159] Cf. also the Q account of the healing of the centurion's servant discussed below in the relevant chapter, where the best reading is probably also an initial reluctance on purity grounds.

to Yahweh's actions during the Exodus. Here the focus is at first literal. The imagery of feeding is, however, a continuing symbol throughout the broader composition. This feeding symbolises the availability of the food of the kingdom for the Gentiles. Accordingly, unlike the previous feeding, specifically Israelite allusions (sheep without a shepherd, seating in 100s and 50s, 12 baskets) are missing. Only the Exodus imagery remains. The people come "from afar". They are Gentiles in Gentile territory. Now 7 baskets are collected (and 7 loaves broken), symbolic of the nations of the world. Perhaps also by alluding to three days' wait, Mark is alluding to the historical reality that mission to the Gentiles came about after Jesus' resurrection. As with the feeding of the five thousand, so here issues of purity do not surface. Here they would be even more acute for some: eating with Gentiles!

Jesus returns in 8:10 to Jewish territory. Again, Mark is not interested in the related purity issue. Back in Jewish territory the Pharisees return to question Jesus (8:11–14). The effect is to recall for the reader the major discussion of purity in 7:1–23. Mark is winding up this great compositional structure and bringing it to its conclusion. The request for a sign is splendid irony in the light of all that has gone before, almost Johannine in its playfulness (cf. John 6:30). The same playful irony continues when the disciples again reveal their dense understanding by worrying about bread (8:14). Mark has been dropping loud hints all along the way! He transcends their concern by moving directly to the symbolic: he contrasts the nourishment he brings with that of the Pharisees and Herodians (8:15). The Pharisees' teaching excludes. As for the Herodians, they have already been identified by Mark as their companions in plotting Jesus' death. Herod's party was the scene of John's murder. Mark's Jesus chides the disciples for failing to understand the symbolic allusions concerning the true teaching which includes, and the false teaching which excludes (8:17–18). He offers one last set of clues: the numerical symbols in the baskets of leftovers after the feedings (8:19–20). He then concludes: "Do you not yet understand?" (8:21). Mark is addressing the hearer under the guise of the disciples. At stake is Jesus' new teaching which sets aside part of the Law for the sake of inclusion of the Gentiles.

The issue of understanding continues in 8:22–26, the healing of the blind man at Bethsaida. Bethsaida had been the original destination of the journey upon which the disciples embarked after the feeding of the five thousand (6:45). Possibly Mark intends the hearer to interpret the arrival also symbolically. The disciples have in that sense 'arrived'; they can now enter Gentile territory because they understand Jesus' teaching and he has demonstrated the lowering of the barriers. But it took a long time getting there!

Yet the story also stands in contrast symbolically with the disciples' blindness. Perhaps Mark intends some value to be attached to the two stage healing of the man, but this is far from certain. As a miracle, beside the healing
of the deaf and dumb man, it also shows both Gentiles and Jews enjoying
blessings announced to Israel in Isaiah 35:5. Jesus' messiahship becomes
the agenda in what immediately follows as Mark brings us back to where the
larger composition began, with questions about who Jesus is and about the
suffering of John, Jesus and the disciples. It may be significant that this
takes place again in Gentile territory: Caesarea Philippi.

1.4.5 Conclusions

Within 6:7 - 8:26 Mark has composed a unit of material through which he
celebrates the inclusion of both Jews and Gentiles in the feast of the kingdom. It is a remarkable composition and at its heart addresses an issue of
Law. The feedings and associated miracles function at a number of levels.
They are signs of eschatological blessing. Many recall acts of Yahweh in
Israel's history. Implicit is the claim to continuity and divine authority. In
addition, these signs of God's blessing take place both in Jewish and in Gentile territory, ie. among both Jews and Gentiles. Mark had already shown
this in the juxtaposition of 5:1–20, the healing of the Gerasene demoniac, in
Gentile territory, and 5:21–43, the healing of the women of Israel. But here
Mark goes much further: a miraculous feeding takes place in each location.
The motifs in the feeding of the 5000 and the numerical symbolism of the
baskets reinforce the message that the blessing of the gospel is for both. In
addition, even the itinerary may carry symbolic significance: only after Jesus' teaching and deeds can the disciples reach their original goal: Bethsaida
in Gentile land; and in Gentile land Peter makes his great confession.

The imagery of food, most obvious in the feedings, serves a symbolic
function throughout. Mark helps the hearer appreciate the symbolism when
he contrasts the teaching of Jesus with the leaven of the Pharisees and Herod.
Central to this teaching is Jesus' declaration about food and purity laws.
This is also central to the structure of the composition and to its message of
inclusion. For Mark is not just referring to Jesus' teaching in general terms;
he is referring in particular to his teaching which removes purity barriers
and frees the way for the inclusion of Gentiles. It is altogether an extraordinary composition.

At its heart is 7:1–23. The one who is Son of God in power and authority,
whose deeds echo Yahweh's deeds of old and fulfil eschatological expectation, confronts the Pharisees and scribes from Jerusalem. In other words,

Mark carries the theme of Jesus' divine authority into 7:1–23. By this same authority Mark's Jesus declares all food clean. Yet there is more here than setting one authority against another. The encounter also entails argument from Torah (about honouring parents and, implicitly, in the confrontation of hypocrisy). Most significant of all, for our study, is the particular value system which Mark's Jesus employs at the heart of his argumentation. This value system understands external ritual acts to be mere human religious tradition and on that basis disparages suggestions that either contact with material things or consumption of food can have relevance for genuine purity. It means that Mark sees Jesus as not so much abrogating certain parts of the Law, which would assume they once had validity, but declaring that they never could have had validity, because they concerned only the external. We shall see that the same value system also informs Mark's attitude towards the temple.

The effect of both the argument and of Jesus' declaration, according to Mark, is to declare all foods clean, thus to remove the barriers to open inclusion of Jew and Gentile together in the Christian community. The implied argument does a lot more than this. It disparages purity law altogether. Mark cements this reality by appending the anecdote of the encounter with the Syrophoenician woman, which preserves an outcome paradigmatic for the church's mission. The narrative is a paradigm of movement from reluctance and Gentile disparagement to willingness to cross such boundaries. Mark has included both aspects, probably tolerating the former in the light of the new outcome. There may be vestiges of salvation history in the passage, such as we have in Rom 1:17, "to Jew, first, and also to Greek", but for Mark the emphasis lies on the fact that now both Jew and Gentile share the blessings of salvation. The openness rests not on a change of Law, but the exposure of the invalid basis of the distinctions of the Law which were seen to exclude Gentiles.

Despite the radical argumentation employed in 7:1–23, there is no indication that Mark intended a thoroughgoing denial of the validity of all externals. Mark's Jesus apparently wears tassels (and Mark may well have deliberately exploited the fact); he breaks bread like a Jew; he was initially disparaging towards a Gentile woman, although that changed; he is assumed to have shared John's concern about Herod's breach of marriage kinship laws. Mark may be more interested in Jesus' authority than in the nature of his argumentation. On the other hand, the dualism implied in the disparagement of the external has a central role and must be taken into account in assessing Mark's attitude as a whole.

1.5 Mark 8:27 – 10:52 in Review

1.5.1 Mark 8:27 – 10:52

To divide Mark at this point is to some degree artificial, since 8:27–30 relate closely to what precedes. They form an *inclusio* with 6:14–17, where, as background to Herod's question about Jesus' identity, Mark notes a similar range of popular responses. Peter's confession also forms a climax and cannot be understood in isolation from the preceding narrative of Jesus' deeds and words. On the other hand, 8:27–30 also relates strongly to what follows, particularly to the misunderstanding by Peter which follows his confession, but also to the transfiguration where the figures of Elijah and Moses appear. Once again we have to do with overlapping hinge-pericopes rather than with sharp textual divisions.

From 8:27 on there is a much stronger emphasis on Jesus and the disciples and the road of suffering which lies ahead for him and them. Jesus is the Christ. He is also the Christ who will suffer. Jesus' rejection at Nazareth (6:1–6), juxtaposed to the disciples' commissioning (6:7–13) and the account of John the Baptist's fate (6:14–29), had already signalled the theme. In 8:27–30 and 8:31–38 it returns. Within Mark's narrative as a whole, Jesus' reference to himself as Son of Man in the context of the prospect of suffering is not totally unexpected. It had last occurred on his lips amid controversy, the outcome of which was the plan by the Pharisees and Herodians to kill him (2:10,28). That conflict, sharpened further by conflict with the two Jerusalem delegations (3:22–30 and 7:1–23), comes to expression in the so-called first passion prediction (8:31). In an extraordinary exchange, Jesus rebukes Peter, spokesperson of the disciples, as "Satan", because his focus is not God's, but human concerns (8:32–33). Jesus is also setting the pattern for his reluctant disciples to follow (8:32–37). Faithful following of Jesus becomes the criterion for the judgement day (8:38). The ultimate criterion is not the Law, but faithfulness to Jesus and his teachings. For Mark the ultimate authority under God is Jesus. That goes beyond Torah.

9:1 reaffirms the hope of the kingdom, the central message of Jesus, projecting the attention of the hearer to the future, but also recalling the summary of Jesus' preaching: "The time is fulfilled; the kingdom of God is at hand" (1:15). Within the narrative as a whole, the predictions of 8:38 and 9:1 and the proleptic fulfilment of the latter in the transfiguration account (9:2–13) are a new beginning. Thus the themes of the prologue recur: the threat of judgement, the promise of the kingdom, the fulfilment of scripture, the heavenly announcement concerning Jesus as God's Son, and the place of John the Baptist in the eschatological plan. Mark uses the transfiguration story as a foretaste of the future fulfilment of the kingdom. Mark's interest in Elijah's eschatological role (cf. 15:35) explains his prominence and finds expression in the conversation which follows (9:11–13). There we see that Mark probably intends both a future and a present reference in the transfiguration story. It both foreshadows and discloses. The select disciples are allowed to see what all will see when the kingdom comes with power, but what they see is also a present reality.

As part of present reality, in the narrative perspective, the presence of Elijah and Moses portrays a sense of continuity and also fulfilment, echoing the hope with which the gospel began. Despite Jesus' radical new authority, Mark is concerned with continuity. Mark may well also intend a more general symbolic allusion by Moses and Elijah to the Law and the Prophets, though in my view this is at most incidental, since we find no indication in the context of Mark developing such a distinction.

Mark depicts the disciples' response to this scene as incompetent and worthless. They want to erect tents, perhaps, shrines of honour. For Mark, such behaviour misses the point. He would probably have grouped it with the activities described in 7:3–4, as having only to do with outward matters, and with the temple "made with hands", which appears later (14:58). The disciples must grasp the new. Beside continuity and fulfilment is the contrast: Jesus is the Son of God. Mark leaves us in no doubt about Jesus' greater and final authority; the divine voice exhorts: "Listen to him!" This is probably an allusion to Deut 18:15–18. In announcing the coming prophet, Moses uses the same words. The scene symbolises Mark's understanding of Jesus' relation to Torah: fulfilment of hope; yet greater authority. In the brief dialogue which follows (9:11–13) Mark shows that he closely associates John and Jesus, both as bringing the time of fulfilment and as suffering rejection by the current generation.

8:27 – 9:13 forms, thus, a unit of great significance in which Mark returns to affirm central themes with which the gospel began. At the same time he is moving the narrative focus to the disciples. Throughout 8:27 – 10:52 Mark three times repeats Jesus' prediction that as Son of Man he will suffer rejection at the hands of the Jewish authorities and subsequently rise from the dead (8:31; 9:33; 10:33–34). Each time Mark sets this prediction in contrast to failure on the part of the disciples to grasp what this way of suffering means. At the same time this section contains much instruction for the disciples as a community. Here, in the broadest sense, are elements of Mark's understanding of Jesus' 'community rule'.

Mark has Jesus and the three disciples return to find the remaining disciples grappling with failure (9:14–27). The distraught father of the possessed child pleads with Jesus, "If you can, help us by having compassion on us!" (9:22). Jesus responds: "With regard to your 'If you can', everything is possible for the one who believes" (9:23). The issue has been the inability of the disciples to effect the healing. Mark then repeats the compositional pattern already found in 7:1–23 and first in 4:1–19; he gives instruction to the disciples alone: "This kind cannot come out by anything except prayer" (9:29). The effect of the passage is not to exclude the disciples from such activity, but to demand that they become a praying community. Mark's Jesus will return to the theme of the praying community in 11:22–24, where Jesus urges his disciples to have faith, to believe that by prayer they may move mountains. There the praying community is to become the new temple. Already here, therefore, Mark is preparing for that theme.

9:30–32 includes Jesus' second announcement of his impending execution and subsequent resurrection. The section which it begins runs to 10:31. Its focus is on the attitude and behaviour required of disciples. They are not to seek to be the greatest (9:33–37), not to be exclusive towards others who operate in the name of Jesus (9:38–40) and to be supportive and not destructive towards fellow Christians (9:41–50). To this point there is no direct implication concerning Jesus' attitude towards Torah, except in the broadest sense of caring for others.[160] But even here, where Jesus develops the ethic of service in contrast to human obsession with power, the primary model is not the teachings of the Law, but Jesus himself. Reference to Torah does, however appear in what follows, the anecdotes relating to divorce (10:2–12), children (10:13–15), and riches (10:16–31).

10:2–12 presents a typical teaching anecdote. Pharisees make an inquiry and in response Jesus elicits their Torah interpretation, based on divorce law in Deuteronomy 24.[161] The form of Jesus' question, which emphasises Moses as giving commandments ("What did Moses permit/command you?"), need not imply they are of lesser authority.[162] But, combined with the "you", it

---

[160] Gundry, *Mark*, p. 514, takes Jesus' words about self-mutilations literally and therefore contests that Jesus is flouting Jewish Law here. This is typical of Gundry's insensitivity to symbolism in Mark (eg. 8:14–21). By contrast Dautzenberg, "Gesetzeskritik," p. 56, argues, probably, rightly, that Mark would have understood the 'offences' in 9:43,45,47, in the light of the commandments. On the common use of cutting off limbs as a metaphor for seriousness in both Hellenistic and rabbinic literature, see H. D. Betz, *The Sermon on the Mount*, Hermeneia, (Minneapolis: Fortress, 1995), pp. 238–239.

[161] Gundry, *Mark*, pp. 537–538, emphasises, over against Sanders, *Jesus and Judaism*, pp. 256–257, that Jesus treats divorce not as permission, but as a command. But the command relates to what one should do when divorcing, not divorce itself.

[162] So rightly, Banks, *Law*, p. 149.

probably does imply distance between Jesus' teaching and the instruction Moses gave. Mark sets Jesus in contrast to the Pharisees, and, to some extent, to the Pharisees and their fellow Jews. On the other hand, if distancing is present, it is not directly from Moses. On the contrary, Mark portrays Jesus as being on side with Moses and as understanding that Moses' instruction was a concession because of their hard heartedness[163] or perhaps to evoke it (a motif Mark employs already in 4:11–12).[164] There is ambiguity concerning what Moses was doing. Was he commanding or permitting, as Mark's Jesus supposes? ἐπιτρέπω may mean either. The overall effect is to give a lower ranking to Moses' divorce provision.

Jesus appeals to the Genesis creation narratives to argue that people should not separate what God has joined together as one flesh. This is more than citing one scripture against another. It is an appeal to origins and reflects a theology and ideology: God's original purpose has priority. It finds a parallel in CD 4:21, which similarly cites Gen 1:27 as an argument against taking a second wife while the first is still alive. There are two kinds of argument in 10:2–9: one, on the basis of the scripture passages, the other, through the *mashal*, "What God has joined together let no human being separate." The scripture provides the ground for the declaration of the *mashal*, which Mark clearly understands as a statement of law by Jesus for his community.[165]

---

[163] Cf. Berger, *Gesetzesauslegung*, pp. 538, 556–557,who builds a major part of his thesis on the assumption that there existed within Hellenistic Judaism the understanding, attested first in the Pseudo-Clementine literature *Rec I* 35–37, that the cultic legislation was second rate and dispensable. See also K. Berger, "Hartherzigkeit und Gottes Gesetz. Die Vorgeschichte des antijüdischen Vorwurfs in Mc 10:5," *ZNW* 61 (1970), pp. 1–47. For critique see Sariola, *Markus*, p. 139 n. 15; Gundry, *Mark*, p. 538. In relation to his discussion of Acts 7, M. Klinghardt, *Gesetz und Volk Gottes. Das lukanische Verständnis des Gesetzes*, WUNT 32, (Tübingen: J. C. B. Mohr [Paul Siebeck], 1988), pp. 288–305, repeats Berger's claim and draws attention also to Strabo XVI 2, 35–39. He draws attention to the likelihood that Strabo uses a Hellenistic Jewish text as his source. It, too, contrasts an original Mosaic dispensation with other laws which it classifies as belonging to 'superstition' (food, circumcision, excision, and other like regulations). There are, however, significant differences between this text and Mark 10, despite the formal similarity of a contrast between an earlier and later law. The Strabo text contrasts temple cult with food and circumcision laws. Berger's Pseudo-Clementine text is also different; there the sacrificial cult is the later invention. See also the recent study by F. S. Jones, *An Ancient Jewish Christian Source on the History of Christianity. Pseudo-Clementine* Recognitions *1.27–71*, Texts and Translations 37, Christian Apocrypha Series 2, (Atlanta: Scholars, 1995), which came into my hands too late for incorporation into this study. Jones argues for an early Christian source for the passage cited by Berger.

[164] So Sariola, *Markus*, p. 140; Gundry, *Mark*, p. 538.

[165] The response by Jesus to such questions with a *mashal* is characteristic of the traditions we have identified behind 2:1 – 3:6 and 7:1–23. Probably this anecdote also

Following the familiar structural pattern, Mark has Jesus give further explanation to the disciples in private. In it Jesus declares that anyone divorcing a spouse and remarrying commits adultery.[166] Mark clearly places great
value on the ethic preserved in the commandment, "You shall not commit
adultery."[167] For Mark's community, in a society, where, unlike in Jewish
Law, women may divorce as well as men, and women as well as men may be
wronged (10:11, ἐπ' αὐτήν, "against her", cf. Deut 22:13–29), divorce and
remarriage are clearly forbidden for both. The declaration rests on two foundations: Jesus' own authority and the argument from scripture which gives
priority to God's purpose in creation. Altogether, Jesus' stricter attitude need

---

once contained the single response: "What God has joined together, let not a human being
separate" (10:9). When we consider the saying in isolation, its *mashal* character becomes
more evident. It is a riddle. It must be true; yet it throws into confusion the discussion
about what justifies divorce. It confronts such discussions with a principle about what
God has done. Cf. Bultmann, *Synoptic Tradition*, p. 74, who sees it as an originally isolated logion; similarly Hultgren, *Jesus and his Adversaries*, p. 120; Berger,
Gesetzesauslegung, p. 536; Weiss, *Vollmacht*, p. 191. The response, however, is not a
prescriptive argument, but a provocative *mashal* and should not immediately be interpreted as evidence of Jesus' adopting a stance within the argument. It is as practical and
impractical as Jesus' statements about the sabbath. The level at which the arguments from
scripture were introduced reflect more directly a prescriptive response and participate in .
the argument. However as soon as the anecdote came to imply distance, through the introduction of Jesus' counter question, we are probably seeing an image which understands
Jesus as standing independently of Moses and Judaism, closer to what has been emerging
thus far as Mark's own position.

[166] On the background of this and related variants, Luke 16:18; Matt 5:32; Matt 19:9;
1 Cor 7:10–11, see the recent discussion in J. L. Nolland, "The Gospel Prohibition of
Divorce: Tradition History and Meaning," *JSNT* 58 (1995), pp. 19–35, who concludes that
behind these is a single form which lacked the exception clause, included the man's remarriage as an essential part of what was being criticised and contained a formula about marrying a divorced woman. It attacked the use of the societal divorce provision to abandon
one wife for another with the innovative claim that such action amounts to adultery by the
man. The saying was an application of the maxim preserved in Mark 10:9, "What God has
joined let no human being separate." On the wider Jewish background, including the more
restrictive attitude towards divorce in Mal 2:14–16 ("'I hate divorce,' says the Lord" –
2:16a) and CD 4:21; 11QTemple 57:17–19 and the reported differences among the Pharisees between Shammai and Hillel, see also Sanders, *Jesus and Judaism*, pp. 256–260;
Jewish Law, p. 5; J. A. Fitzmyer, "The Matthean Divorce-Texts and Some New Palestinian
Evidence," in *To Advance the Gospel*, (New York: Crossroad, 1981), pp. 79–111; P. Sigal,
The Halakah of Jesus of Nazareth according to the Gospel of Matthew, (Lanham: Univ of
America Pr., 1986), pp. 83–118; Gundry, *Mark*, p. 537. Cf. also Berger, *Gesetzesauslegung*,
pp. 563–566, who argues that the greater strictness concerning divorce and remarriage of
a divorcee derives from the expansion of laws applied to high priests to the laity in certain
religious movements of the time. This is far from Mark's perspective.

[167] So Sariola, *Markus*, p. 143.

not have been seen as defying Mosaic Law.[168]   On the other hand, this may not have been an issue for Mark, who was clearly prepared to countenance Jesus deleting or revising Law on his own authority.

10:13–16 includes a tradition about Jesus welcoming children and carries within it a demand that all enter the kingdom with the faith of a child. Here, too, Jesus declares his own Torah. 10:17–22 is an anecdote about a seeker after eternal life. Jesus' response is thoroughly Jewish. He even challenges the man for calling him "good"; for he wants him to be in no doubt about the highest priority: love for God. Jesus' words, "No one is good but one, God," (10:18) echo the *Shema*: "Hear, O Israel. The Lord our God is one; and you shall love the Lord your God . . ." The echo is probably deliberate. It will reappear in the related passage, 12:28–34. But beyond that, Jesus cites fulfilment of the commandments as the requirement for receiving eternal life. They are cited in a form expanded by "Do not defraud", without "Do not covet", and generally following the order of the Septuagint translation.[169] Without question the narrative portrays these as the requirements.[170] Jesus loves the man for keeping them.[171]   In addition, however, Mark has Jesus lay upon the man the demand that he sell all, give to the poor and follow Jesus.[172]

Nothing in the text indicates that the problem is insincerity. Jesus does not doubt the man's word. On the contrary he loves him. Nor is there insincerity on Jesus' part, as though the instruction that he keep the commandments was not a real answer. When Jesus is shown adding a requirement, he

---

[168] So Sanders, *Jesus and Judaism*, pp. 256–257; Betz, *Sermon on the Mount*, pp. 255–256.

[169] A further exception is the placement of the command to honour parents, which comes from the first table. The list is not a direct quotation, but an assembly of ethical commands, drawn mostly from the second table of the decalogue, as popularly used. On this see Berger, *Gesetzesauslegung*, p. 390, who argues that they should not be seen primarily as a decalogue list but as a list of social mores. Similarly, Sariola, *Markus*, p. 172. He points to Sir 4:1 as the background for the presence of μὴ ἀποστερήσῃς here (pp. 156–157). Gundry, *Mark*, p. 553, argues that the change of order is deliberate: "honouring father and mother", the final commandment of the first table, is appended to the list because of the implications of the above for relationships; not defrauding is a substitute for not coveting which more easily allows the man to claim fulfilment of all, whereas the anecdote will expose that it is precisely coveting that is at the root of the man's problem. This may be oversubtle. Against it is Mark's comment that Jesus responded with approval, hardly appropriate if Jesus was simply setting him up by manipulating the list.

[170] So Dautzenberg, "Gesetzeskritik," p. 56.

[171] So Sariola, *Markus*, p. 176.

[172] Gundry, *Mark*, p. 554, seeks to avoid the implication that keeping the commandments is also a requirement, by interpreting the statement, "One thing is lacking," along the lines that only one thing is necessary. This forces the text.

is not drawing attention to the command, not to covet, which has not appeared in the summary.[173] The issue was not quantity but quality. Mark will have seen Jesus' demand as doing two things. It exposes the inadequacy of the man's obedience and it calls him to follow Jesus. The call to abandon possessions and give to the poor relates to the act of abandoning home and possessions in discipleship. At the same time it is probably also seen as exposing an aspect that was lacking in the man's obedience. What is missing is therefore not so much obedience to an additional instruction beyond keeping the commandments, but an attitude which needs to be there in keeping the commandments and which is also inseparable from radical obedience to Jesus. Both belong together. This is consistent with the tendency in Mark to set up Jesus as the authority to be followed. Here the following is not, therefore, against, or instead of, the commandments as outlined. They are affirmed, just as they represent the obverse side of the values listed as making people impure in 7:22–23. These commandments remain central for Mark. Understood in the context of Jesus' authority, they are, indeed, the way to eternal life. The anecdote illustrates thus both the sense of continuity and the radically new. In this Mark's primary concern is the authority of Jesus, but it is an authority that lays claim to a core of Torah.

Selling all is reminiscent of the call to abandonment of possessions and security implied in other calls to discipleship in 1:16–20 and 2:13–14 and in the instructions to disciples in 6:1–6. In addition, here, the benefits are to be for the poor. Primarily, the command is to follow Jesus. We see, however, through this conjunction of additional commands an implicit statement about Jesus' values, which cohere with the injunctions already expressed in this section.[174] The absolute claim of Jesus in this way always had the potential to bring people into conflict with other commands enjoined in the Torah, but this does not surface. Instead Mark portrays Jesus as demanding compliance with the Torah commandments cited and with the rest, by implication, only in general terms. The passage does not explore what this rest would include; from Mark 7 we know that it would not include food and purity laws.

The passage which follows portrays the consternation which such an approach towards riches presents for the disciples. Within it we see some of the solutions which Mark saw as offering comfort to the community of his

---

[173] Cf. the version of the encounter in Gosp Naz fr. 16, discussed below, according to which lack of response to fellow Jews in need is the heart of the problem.

[174] For the notion that giving to the poor is an expression of the second greatest command, see Sariola, *Markus*, pp. 175, 205–206.

day. The demands of radical poverty are so great. "Who, then, can be saved?" the disciples ask. Jesus replies: "With human beings it is impossible, but not with God. For all things are possible with God" (10:26–27). A certain tension exists within the narrative between the demand to keep the commandments, give up all, give to the poor and follow Jesus, on the one hand, and the promise here, on the other hand, that ultimately only God's grace can do the impossible. Yet Mark holds both: the believer's total commitment and God's total commitment. Faith and obedience do not earn eternal life as a reward, but they are implied in response to the gospel. With this promise Mark's narrative recalls the words of 9:29: the promise of what is the possible with God for the Christian community. At no point in the discussion does Mark indicate potential conflicts for the disciples arising from the call to poverty and abandonment of family, on the one hand, and the demands of Torah relating to family life and security, on the other .

The third section, 10:32 – 10:45, begins, as did the first two, with Jesus' prediction of his death and resurrection (10:32–34). James and John express, by contrast, their ambition to be the greatest (10:35–40). Jesus returns to the theme of humility and leadership with which the section began and, consistent with the emphasis in 8:31–37, teaches by example (10:41–45). As Son of Man, the one to be killed, Jesus came to serve and to give his life as a ransom for many. The saying points onward to the words of Jesus at the last supper (14:24). Mark leaves them in their simplicity; he adds no commentary on possible implications for understanding sacrifice or temple.[175]

The section ends with the healing of blind Bartimaeus. Jesus' final words: "Go, your faith has saved you" (10:52) are another way of expressing the theme of faith in what is possible with God. At the same time, the healing of Bartimaeus forms a link with the healing of the blind man at Bethsaida (8:22–26) to build a framework of healing for the entire threefold section, 8:23 – 10:52.[176] The blind men see; the disciples, by contrast, are preoccupied with anxiety about themselves and remain blind. The healings show what is possible with faith in God. It is this theme of the community of faith as one

---

[175] See also the discussion in Gundry, *Mark*, pp. 590–593, who denies an allusion here to Isa 53. "Vicarious atonement may stand in the wings of Mark 10:45, but it does not come on stage" (p. 591). We might add: much less does Mark develop an attack on sacrificial law from this base.

[176] The fact that the first of these takes place in Gentile territory, Bethsaida, and the second in Jewish territory, Jericho, means that faith among both Gentiles and Jews is being contrasted with that of the disciples. We have no way of determining whether Mark intended such a subtlety.

of people believing that God can do the impossible which forms a significant link with what follows, above all, with the theme of 11:15–17 and its
immediate context. The messianic cry, "Son of David," recalls Peter's confession, "You are the Christ," at the same time it will have its echo in the
scene which immediately follows: Jesus' entry into Jerusalem. It will also
help prepare the hearer for the theme of Jesus as the Christ and Son of God
in the chapters to follow.

1.5.2 Conclusion

In 8:27 – 10:52 the passages of primary relevance for considering Mark's
understanding of Jesus' attitude towards Torah are found in a teaching section focused on instruction for the disciples and the community of faith.
Before that, Mark highlights the confession of Jesus as Messiah and through
the transfiguration interprets this within the context of hope and fulfilment,
recalling also the special role of John the Baptist as Elijah. These are broad
perspectives which recall the beginning of the gospel. As there, they preserve both the sense of continuity and the qualitative difference of the new.
These continue to form the background for Mark's understanding of Jesus'
attitude towards Torah.

At the same time in this section Mark begins to focus directly on Jesus'
fate and links this paradigmatically to the path of discipleship. The disciples hear Jesus' three predictions, but do not understand their implications.
They fail to understand the model of discipleship and leadership which Jesus enjoins and models. Mark's Jesus rebukes Peter before the disciples for
setting his focus at the wrong level, not on the things of God but on those of
human beings. Peter remains at this level in wanting to construct tents for
Jesus, Moses and Elijah. The dualistic value system which disparages the
merely human and external, evident in 7:1–23, again shines through. By
contrast, Mark depicts Jesus as envisaging that the disciples might become a
community of faith and prayer where the impossible would become possible, a theme which comes to fuller expression in the remaining sections of
the gospel, where such a community will be set in contrast to the temple.

Within this overall framework Mark also includes Jesus' instructions to
the community about marriage, children, and wealth. Mark's version of the
marriage traditions highlights the distinctiveness of Jesus over against the
Pharisees and Judaism generally (the address, "you") and clearly relativises
the divorce law of Moses. There are prior values. These are what God
originally willed in creation and in the command not to commit adultery.
Mark portrays Jesus as absolutely committed to this commandment and this

understanding of God's intention for marriage. In that sense Jesus is pictured both as Torah faithful and as one who interprets Torah on the basis of these fundamentals. On the other hand, Mark also portrays Jesus as using such principles to argue against a Torah provision. As we saw, in discussing 7:1–23, Mark is content to portray Jesus as dismissing some Torah provisions. He would probably understand Jesus' attitude in this passage in the same light. This gains additional support from the way Mark has Jesus frame his counter question, "What did Moses permit you?" (10:30).

Mark's commitment to the commandments of the decalogue is also evident in 10:17–22. The ones cited apply to interpersonal relations. Those of the earlier part of the decalogue, up to the sabbath commandment, are also presupposed as valid, but on the basis of Jesus' interpretation (cf. also 12:28–34). Missing is the commandment about coveting, but this is probably not deliberate. It is more than compensated for by the positive injunctions about wealth and giving to the poor. 10:17–22 displays a Jesus committed to the commandments of the decalogue. The challenge to sell possessions and give to the poor both exposes the inadequacy of the man's obedience and forms part of the call to follow Jesus. Keeping these commandments and following Jesus become inseparable, but the primary authority is Jesus. The attitude towards wealth implied in the anecdote underlies the passage which follows and is paradigmatic for Jesus' attitude in Mark, not least in the chapters which follow.

1.6 Mark 11:1 – 13:37 in Review

1.6.1 Mark 11:1 – 13:37

Mark 11:1–10 narrates Jesus' entry into Jerusalem. As in the preparation for the Passover meal in 14:12–16, the disciples prepare the entry according to Jesus' instructions. For Mark this underlines Jesus' miraculous foreknowledge. But 11:1–10 stresses above all Jesus' welcome in royal messianic terms. What Bartimaeus voiced in his cry of faith, "Son of David, have mercy on me!" (10:47), the crowd now echoes: 'Blessed is the coming kingdom of our father, David' (11:10). The theme of Jesus as Messiah King will become central to the passion narrative. Already within 11:1 – 13:37 messiahship plays a significant role. Jesus rides into Jerusalem as predicted in Zech 9:9 of Israel's king. It also returns to focus when after the questioning by others Jesus himself grasps the initiative and redefines the royal messianic hope (12:35–37). Jesus is not only Son of David; he is David's Lord.

In 11:11 Mark has Jesus immediately enter the temple and look around at everything. Matthew and Luke merge this with Jesus' entry to purge the temple, but by portraying this as a separate act, and as the first after Jesus' entry into Jerusalem, Mark achieves central significance for the temple in what follows.[177] He also reflects accurately the centrality of the temple within Jerusalem. The climax is less Jesus' entry into Jerusalem than his entry into the temple. The temple becomes not only the site but, itself, the centre of controversy. Mark's seeming casual reference to Jesus' looking around at everything in fact prepares for what will be Jesus' confrontation. It will also receive a significant echo in the disciples' looking around in wonder at the temple buildings as they leave it in 13:1–2. Mark is crafting the narrative to prepare for what is to come; the prediction of the temple's destruction and its replacement by one not made with hands.

11:12 begins a new day. First Jesus curses a fig tree because it does not bear fruit (11:12–14). There immediately follows the account of the so-called cleansing of the temple in Mark (11:15–17). This brief account assumes great significance in Mark's narrative, but must be read in the light of the narrative as a whole. I shall, therefore, return to it in detail after consideration of its context. Already in 11:18 Mark signals the central significance of this act for Jesus' execution by noting that the chief priests and scribes sought in response to destroy him. The narrative of Jesus' departure from Jerusalem (11:19) and the discovery by Peter of the shrivelled fig tree[178]

---

[177] Cf. Sariola, *Markus*, p. 212, who describes 11:11 as without importance except as preparation for 11:15–17.

[178] On the symbolic use of the cursing of the fig tree in Mark, see W. R. Telford, *The Barren Temple and the Withered Tree. A redaction-critical analysis of the Cursing of the Fig-Tree pericope in Mark's Gospel and its relation to the Cleansing of the Temple tradition*, JSNTS 1, (Sheffield: JSOTPr, 1980), pp. 39–68; on the diverse use of the image in O. T. and Jewish literature: pp. 128–204. The fig tree represents the temple and its leadership. So also Shepherd, *Sandwich Stories*, p. 217 n. 2. Cf. B. von Kienle, "Markus 11,12–14.20–25. Der verdorrte Feigenbaum," *BibNotiz* 57 (1991), pp. 17–25, who argues that the fig tree stands for those people in the crowd who failed to support Jesus. She argues that not all responses in Jerusalem were negative; that Mark should not be assumed to have known of the fate of the temple; that the image of the fig tree was ambiguous. The weight of evidence in the wider context of conflict with Israel and its leaders counts against this.

Gundry, *Mark*, pp. 672–678, argues against a symbolic interpretation of the cursing of the fig tree. His argument, that an audience needing the explanation of 7:2–4 would not appreciate the symbolic allusions, makes unjustified assumptions about a homogenous audience. Symbolic allusions to Old Testament lore are found throughout Mark (eg. the transfiguration). Then Gundry demands that correspondences match precisely (an argument he commonly uses against typological allusion: see for instance, pp. 246; 329–334, 342–343, 430–401, 408–410, 475–478; and the programmatic statement p.1!); but he as-

(11:20–21) have the effect of interpreting the so-called cleansing as a symbolic act of judgement against the temple and the Jewish leadership it houses. It does not bear fruit.[179]

By contrast, in 11:22–25 Jesus goes on to speak of the power of faith to move mountains,[180] to promise answered prayer and to urge prayer that comes from a forgiving heart. At first reading we might consider the words of Jesus about prayer out of place in the context, until we realise that Mark is picking up Jesus' words in the temple episode: "My house shall be called a house of prayer for all nations" (11:17). The temple, in Mark's view, has been replaced by the praying community of faith.[181] We should also note that the issue of prayer and the impossible featured in the preceding division in Mark (9:28–29; 10:26–27; cf. also 10:52). In the division before that (6:7 – 8:26) Mark had been concerned to emphasise the openness of this community to include Gentiles. Jesus' words in the temple effectively reaffirm this: there is now a new "house of prayer for all nations".

11:27 begins a new section which presents Jesus teaching in the temple. The passage, 11:27 –12:12, is of major importance for the Markan gospel as

---

sumes they will appreciate the "I am" allusion in 6:50 (p. 337). This fails to appreciate the character of the allusive (already within the Old Testament itself; cf. Exodus typology used in prophecy of return of the exiles). The possibility that Jesus sought an early form of the fruit, not ripe fruit, does not destroy the imagery: the issue is fruit at all. Gundry's argument that stopping the traffic does not match the imagery of judgement which the fig tree episode presupposes ignores the association of Jesus' action with his words, which are a verdict of judgement, implying a coming execution of judgement. See also the discussion of symbolism in Mark in Sellin, "Symbolische und esoterische Züge".

[179] So Cranfield, *Mark*, pp. 356–357; Lane, *Mark*, p. 400; H. Giesen, "Der verdorrte Feigenbaum – Eine symbolische Aussage? Zu Mk 11,12–14.20f," *BZ* 20 (1976), pp. 95–111; C. A. Evans, "Jesus' action in the temple: Cleansing or Portent of destruction?" *CBQ* 51 (1989), pp. 237–270, here: 239. D. E. Oakman, "Cursing Fig Trees and Robbers' Dens: Pronouncement Stories Within Social-Systemic Perspective. Mark 11:12–25 and Parallels," *Semeia* 64 (1993), pp. 253–274, here: 257–263, esp. 261, raises the possibility that the fig tree had been left to go to wood by intention or neglect because of the ruling elite, reflecting a shift in agricultural priorities. Jesus would be cursing the system, not just the tree. He believes this also explains Mark's comment that it was not the season for figs. The point was that normally some figs would be found on the tree out of season at this time of the year. This all assumes historicity of the event itself, which is open to question.

[180] For the view that Jesus is alluding to the temple mount and so speaking of its destruction, see Telford, *Barren Temple*, pp. 58–59, 119; M. D. Hooker, "Traditions about the Temple in the Sayings of Jesus," *BJRL* 70 (1988), pp. 7–19, here: 8; C. Marshall, *Faith as a Theme in Mark's Narrative*, SNTSMS 64, (Cambridge: CUP, 1989), pp. 168–169.

[181] So rightly, D. Juel, *Messiah and Temple. The Trial of Jesus in the Gospel of Mark*, SBLDS 31, (Missoula: Scholars, 1977), pp. 135–136.

a whole. The question, "By what authority do you do these things or who gave you authority to do these things?" (11:28) will have reference to Jesus' action in the temple,[182] but probably also to Jesus' ministry as a whole. The narrative of the dispute returns to the central theme of the first major division (1:1 – 3:6): Jesus' authority. Here as there Jesus' authority is linked with that of John the Baptist.[183] John, too, exercised an unorthodox authority. Echoes of the prologue continue in 12:1–12: the image of sending the "beloved Son". In the parable Jesus continues his response by effectively telling the story of salvation history and of his ministry as its climax.[184] The parable (1–9) assumes the image of Israel as God's vineyard and the refusal of its keepers to produce the harvest. The sending of the servants and then the son represents God's sending of the prophets and John and their rejection, and finally God's sending of the beloved Son and his execution. In response the vineyard owner will come and kill the keepers and transfer the vineyard to others. This signals judgement and change of leadership. Finally, in 12:10–11, Mark's Jesus confronts his questioners with the words of Ps 118:22, "The stone which the builders rejected, this has become the head of the corner; this is the Lord's doing and it is marvellous in our eyes." It is a prediction of his vindication by resurrection under the image of the discarded stone which now forms a new foundation.

The parable sets out allegorically what Jesus had predicted in the Son of Man sayings of 8:31; 9:31; 10:33. In telling the story, Mark's Jesus confronts Israel's leaders with a new version of Isaiah's fruitless vineyard (Isa 5:1–7). The new twist in use of the imagery is that the problem is not the vineyard itself, but its keepers. Accordingly, the vineyard is not made desolate; rather the tenants put in charge of it are to be destroyed and it will be given to the charge of others. For Mark this should not be understood as a replacement of Jews by Gentiles, but rather as a replacement of religious authorities. It is part of Jesus' response to the question about authority. The vineyard stands for Israel, but more especially for its religious heritage. The religious heritage that was Israel's is no longer to be entrusted to the Jewish authorities. It is to be entrusted to the leaders of the Christian community, the community of both Jewish and Gentile believers (12:9). They will now tend it (including Torah) in accordance with the will of God's Son. They are

---

[182] So Evans, "Cleansing or Portent," p. 244; cf. Hultgren, *Adversaries*, p. 71, who suggests that Mark would not have made a link between the authority to do "these things" and the temple.

[183] On this see Tolbert, *Sowing the Gospel*, p. 234.

[184] On the major role of 12:1–12 in the narrative of Mark see Tolbert, *Sowing the Gospel*, pp. 234–239.

to replace the role which the temple authorities had in relation to Israel and its religious tradition.

Mark's narrative goes further: the rejected Son has become the corner-stone[185] of a new building. Within the broader context Mark will make much of the replacement of the old temple by a new. This has already been in view in the temple scene which directly gave rise to the scribes' question about Jesus' authority. It is therefore most probable that Mark intends that we should think of Jesus as being the foundation of a new temple.[186] It is one not made with hands (14:58). It will fulfil the role of being a house of prayer for all nations (cf. 11:17). The loss of tenancy of the vineyard and the establishment of the new temple imply judgement on the authorities be-cause they have rejected Jesus and the prophets. Correspondingly, in 12:12 Mark portrays the chief priests and the scribes and the elders as having the same kind of hostile reaction as they had to Jesus' temple demonstration in 11:18.[187] Mark states explicitly: they perceived (rightly) that the parable was directed against them as leaders. Jesus is making a claim to authority for himself and his own which rivals theirs. There is a new temple, a new source of authority: Jesus and his community.

The second incident has the Pharisees and Herodians test Jesus' loyalty to Caesar with a question about taxation (12:13–17).[188] The move has been from Jesus' personal authority, related in particular to his confrontation of the temple and temple authorities, to the political, a foreshadowing of a similar process in the movement from the Jewish to the Roman trial of Jesus. Jesus is innocent of the political charge. Jesus' response to the question is in the typical *mashal* form we have found in anecdotes elsewhere (2:9; 2:17; 2:19a;

---

[185] κεφαλὴ γωνίας could mean either the cornerstone laid first for the foundation of a building or the capstone. The context favours the former meaning. Here is a new begin-ning.

[186] So Evans, "Cleansing or Portent," p. 240; Hooker, "Traditions about the Temple," p. 9; J. Marcus, *The Way of the Lord. Christological Exegesis of the Old Testament in the Gospel of Mark*, (Louisville: Jn Knox/Westminster, 1992), pp. 119–129.

[187] Shepherd, *Sandwich Stories*, pp. 224–225 n. 3, makes the interesting observation that Mark 11:12–25 and 12:1–12 exhibit significant parallels: In the former: (i) Jesus seeks figs, (ii) gets none, (iii) it is not time for figs; (iv) he casts out the traders, (v) rulers plot to destroy Jesus, (vi) Jesus' temple action. In the latter: (i) the owner seeks fruit, (ii) gets none, (ii) at the appointed time, (iv) they cast out the dead son, (v) the Lord will destroy the farmers, (vi) the rejected stone becomes head of the corner. To this one might add for both: (vii) the authorities seek to destroy/arrest Jesus.

[188] Note Gundry, *Mark*, pp. 693–694, who suggests that the phrasing of the question flatters Jesus as a scrupulous Jew who eschews not only favouritism but also looking di-rectly at facial images on coins; Jesus then contradicts the flattery by asking for a coin that he may look at it. Maybe.

2:27; 3:4a; 7:15; 10:9). The issue is interpretation of the implications of
Torah concerning images; Jesus' response does not favour the extremists.
But his injunction to give to God may be affirming tithing. 12:18–27 narrates the controversy with Sadducees over resurrection in which Jesus rebukes them for disbelief, arguing on the assumption that "I am the God of
Abraham, Isaac and Jacob" implies these are still living. This aligns him
with Pharisees on the issue. Perhaps the sequence to the resurrection theme
continues to foreshadow the passion narrative.

Finally, the controversies end when one of the scribes asks Jesus about
the most important commandment.[189] The response of Mark's Jesus goes
significantly beyond the request. It gives two greatest commandments, loving God and loving one's neighbour, citing Deut 6:4–5 and Lev 19:18,[190]
and offers the first in an expanded form which emphasises the Markan theme
of understanding.[191] The scribe agrees with Jesus' answer, repeats it, and
adds that these commandments "are more important than all burnt offerings
and sacrifices" (12:33), echoing a common theme, an inclusive antithesis,
found already in the prophets (Hos 6:6; 1 Sam 15:22).[192] Jesus affirms the
scribe's response and adds that he is not far from the kingdom of God (he is
still not there!).

The explicit prioritising of these over against other commandments is
significant.[193] The contrast here is with sacrifices. Most Jews would have
explicated love of God in such a way as to include the cult, so that a contrast

[189] For recent discussion see K. Kertelge, "Das Doppelgebot der Liebe im
Markusevangelium," *TrierTheolZeit* 103 (1994), pp. 38–55.

[190] This is not without parallel in substance, even though it is rare in form to link
specifically these commandments in this way. Berger, *Gesetzesauslegung*, pp. 142–176,
notes that these two Old Testament passages are nowhere linked before Mark and argues
that the linking of the two ideas, love for God and for neighbour, derives from a common
Hellenistic theme which influenced Hellenistic Judaism. But see TIss 5:2, "Love the Lord
and your neighbour," which belongs within a wealth of Jewish ethical teaching emphasising love in the Testaments of the Twelve Patriarchs (cf. also TIss 7:6; TZeb 5:1; 7:1–4;
8:1; TBen 3:1–6; 4:1–3). While at points Christian interpolation is evident, it will not
account for the bulk of such ethical material, if any of it, and appears to be confined mostly
to christological references.

[191] Berger, *Gesetzesauslegung*, pp. 196–197, suggests that the emphasis on knowledge may reflect the influence of Hosea 6:6 ("I desire mercy and not sacrifice, the knowledge of God rather than burnt offerings"), which appears to lie behind the passage as a
whole.

[192] Cf. also Isa 1:11–17; Ps 40:6–8; 50:7–15; 51:16–17; Prov 21:3; 16:7. Possibly
Mark's formulation is influenced by Isa 56:7, which also refers to "burnt offerings and
sacrifices", a part of which Jesus cited according to 11:17 at the expulsion of the money
changers.

[193] For the practice of weighting commands of God variously in Judaism, see *mAboth*
2:1; 4:2; *mHullin* 12:5; cf. also Matt 23:23; 5:19.

between a summary of all laws with some of the same laws would make little sense. The two commandments are therefore not, strictly speaking, a summary of the Torah at all. For the spirit of the anecdote is to contrast not a summary with part of what is summarised, but these two commandments as attitude (which, of course leads to behaviour) with actions, and in particular, with cultic actions. It is therefore not even a contrast between attitude and behaviour, but between attitude and ethical behaviour, on the one hand, and cultic activity on the other.[194]

It is a matter of prioritising. But for Mark it is more than prioritising. For him the scribe mouths an important truth which justifies the abandonment of the temple as a sacrificial system. To that degree the man has understanding. His words have the effect of catching up the important theme of the temple; Mark will have understood the antithesis exclusively, as the wider context has shows; the scribe will have meant it inclusively (he still has a way to go!). For according to Mark's value system, the temple, like its laws governing externals, belongs in the earthly realm of things made by human hands (cf. 7:15–23; 8:33; 14:58).

The scribe is not far from the kingdom of God;[195] the next step is to

---

[194] This contrast has its roots in part in the Old Testament itself, as noted above. It probably also reflects the processes of inter cultural encounter which had the effect of relativising particularist values and strengthening others which were seen to be universal. Inevitably this process took place in the context of the encounter of Judaism with Hellenism and many parallels derive from this milieu. Berger, *Gesetzesauslegung*, pp. 168–170, suggests that the conjunction of the two commandments in the traditional anecdote comes not primarily from scripture study, but from Hellenistic summaries which emphasised εὐσέβεια and δικαιοσύνη, mediated through Hellenistic Judaism. But at the same time the prophetic and wisdom strands doubtless played a role.

[195] The anecdote about the scribe who asks about the greatest commandment may well have been accessible to Matthew and Luke in a second form. The agreements between Matthew and Luke are sufficiently strong to support such a proposal. So Kertelge, "Doppelgebot," pp. 42–44. For the contrary view: Kiilunen, J. *Das Doppelgebot der Liebe in synoptischer Sicht. Ein redaktionskritischer Versuch über Mk 12,28–34 und die Parallelen*, AASFB 250, (Helsinki: Suomalainen Tiedeakatemia, 1989). See also J. Lambrecht, "The Great Commandments Pericope and Q." in *The Gospel behind the Gospels. Current Studies on Q*, edited by R. A. Piper, (Leiden: Brill, 1995), pp. 73–96. Vouga, *Loi*, pp. 141–145, suggests that an original Aramaic *chreia* stemming from Palestinian apocalyptic Christian circles has been given a polemical focus in the translated version in Q which underlies Matthew and Luke and came to Mark in a version adapted to a Hellenistic Gentile environment. Hence the focus on "one God" and use of Stoic terminology, but also the influence of Hellenistic Jewish criticism of the cult system. Mark took what was an apologetic text (in relation to Hellenistic Judaism) and transformed it so that "not far from the kingdom" moves from being a positive comment (in line with Wisd 6:17–20) according to Berger, *Gesetzesauslegung*, pp. 185–186) to being a negative one. Mark reasserts christology.

acknowledge Jesus' authority, in effect, to see Jesus as the basis of a new temple, a new worshipping community which replaces the old. Mark has appropriately placed the anecdote in the court of the temple.[196] It also rounds off the series of questions put to Jesus. They began with hints of the new, including the new temple (11:27 – 12:12); they conclude the same way.

In 12:35–37 Jesus, himself, now takes the initiative. He asks a question. It is about messiahship. Within the narrative this has the effect of picking up the earlier theme of Jesus as Son of David (10:47; 11:10) and expanding it. It is striking that the sequence we have already noted appears to continue here: we have moved from Jewish trial issues, to the Roman trial, to resurrection, to the end of the old temple, and now go on with the interpretation of Ps 110:1. This goes beyond what Mark's passion narrative records, but reflects its christology.[197] Mark wants his readers to know that Christ the Messiah is more than Son of David. He is the exalted Lord. Perhaps Mark also has in mind the universal dimension which this entails, which is otherwise missing in Israel's hope for a Son of David. The motif, Son of David, which is both affirmed and transcended, may also relate to the temple motif, since, traditionally, not only David's son, Solomon (2 Sam 7:13), but also the royal messiah was expected to build or rebuild the temple.[198] Mark juxtaposes the temple motif with Jesus' messiahship also in 11:1–10 and 11:12–25; 14:58 and 14:61; 15:29 and 32. Mark may well have seen Jesus' establishment of the new temple as a work of Jesus in his role as Messiah.

In 12:38–40 Mark returns to the issues of Jewish leadership. For Mark, leadership is centred on the temple. The scribes come down from Jerusalem (3:22; 7:1). Some in Galilee had already written Jesus off as a blasphemer (2:6–7). Some were Pharisees (2:16). Mark has linked them with the Phari-

---

[196] So D.-A. Koch, "Inhaltliche Gliederung und geographischer Aufriss im Markusevangelium," *NTS* 29 (1983), pp. 145–166, here: 157; Sariola, *Markus,* pp. 200–201.

[197] Mark's sequence is quite possibly influenced by the widespread tradition linking death, resurrection and Ps 110:1. See W. R. G. Loader, "Christ at the Right Hand – Ps. cx.1 in the New Testament," *NTS* 24 (1978/79), pp. 199–217.

[198] On the link between messiahship and the hope for a new temple see Juel, *Messiah and Temple,* pp. 169–179. There he notes that 4QFlor reserves the building of the eschatological temple for God, despite its use of 2 Sam 7 where David's Son would build the temple. Nevertheless the use of 2 Sam 7, which links together the promise of royal Davidic lineage with the hope of the temple, is at least suggestive. Herod's rebuilding the temple may also reflect a claim to fulfil such aspirations. The evidence Juel cites otherwise for the messiah building the temple is from the targums (pp. 182–200). See also J. J. Collins, *The Sceptre and the Star. The Messiahs of the Dead Sea Scrolls and Other Ancient Literature,* (New York: Doubleday, 1995), pp. 106–109; and Gundry, *Mark,* pp. 898–900, who argues that no pre-Markan evidence exists for the link.

sees who take offence at Jesus' attitude towards the sabbath and plot with the Herodians for his downfall (2:24; 3:6). They belong to the temple system and its echelons of leadership. For their abuses the temple will be destroyed (11:11–25). With the chief priests, the scribes take offence at his action in the temple (11:18). In the temple, together with the chief priests and elders of the people, they question Jesus' authority (11:27) and feel stung by Jesus' response (12:12). With the chief priests, they will plot his arrest and execution, just as he had predicted (14:1; cf. 8:31; 9:31; 10:33). In reaching the climax of his portrayal of Jesus' public ministry Mark is careful to identify the grounds for the overthrow of the old system. This is the function of 12:38–40. Here Mark has Jesus warn the people against scribal hypocrisy and exploitation. We have already seen Jesus attack their hypocrisy in 7:6–13. Here he speaks of their activities in market places, synagogues and feasts, their exploitation of widows and pretentious prayers. We have not left the temple theme, for these are seen as retainers of the temple authorities, the scribes from Jerusalem. In the closing words Jesus reiterates the sentence of judgement already made in the interpretation of the vineyard parable and in Jesus' action in the temple.

As the counterpiece to the warnings about the scribes and their abuses Mark sets the account of the widow who gave all she had (12:41–44). She represents true piety. She also represents the helpless victims of the temple system and its scribes, to which Mark has just alluded (12:40). Mark holds out no hope for a reformed temple and so is not here urging devotion to the temple.[199] Rather, by inserting the passage here Mark adds another justification for the judgement which is to come, announced already in 12:40, but made specific in Mark 13: the destruction of the temple. For Mark, its replacement by a community that lives by the twofold law of love for God and neighbour will bring justice to the widow and it is now in the setting of the new temple that the widow's exemplary behaviour will have its application.

Thus Mark 13 belongs closely with what precedes. Its vision extends beyond the destruction of the temple, but Mark offers his readers evidence of Jesus' foreknowledge of the events emerging in his own time, when God's final judgement on the temple is being carried out. For Mark, the temple's validity had long since ceased. The debacle of 70 CE is but God's suspended judgement. In 11:11 Mark has Jesus enter the temple and look around; now he has the disciples look around (13:1). The intervening actions and

---

199 Sariola, *Markus*, pp. 232–233, rightly notes that the attitude towards the temple is positive in this episode; similarly, Gundry, *Mark*, p. 731.

words have made it clear that Jesus announces God's judgement on the temple and what it represents. While the issue of Law does not directly surface in the chapter; its tone is critical of the cult.[200] It is a fig tree which has not borne fruit (11:12–14,20–21). It has not been a house of prayer for all nations, but a den of brigands (11:17; Mark's readers would doubtless see contemporary events in these words). It will be replaced by a community of prayer and faith (11:22–25). Its leaders refuse to accept Jesus' authority (11:27 – 12:12). They refuse to offer the fruit of a true vineyard and want to kill God's beloved son. Instead he is the cornerstone of a new community. Some seek political charges against him (12:13–17). Some refuse belief in resurrection (12:18–27). Some are near in perceiving the temple system as dispensable, but still fail to recognise Jesus for who he is (12:28–34). He is greater than Jewish expectations of the Messiah (12:35–37). The scribes court judgement by their hypocrisy (12:38–40) and the plight of the pious widow cries out for justice (12:41–44). Therefore judgement will come. The temple theme continues in the passion narrative, as we shall see, especially in the trial and crucifixion.

The theme of the temple is an important focus in Mark's composition of 11:1 – 13:37. In it Mark develops the theme that the temple stands under God's judgement and has been replaced by the community of prayer and faith.[201] Effectively this implies an extension of the abrogation of the Law, noted by Mark in 7:19c. To replace the temple by a community is to replace substantial sections of Torah. Unlike the pious at Qumran, Mark does not use the temple imagery to describe a community without the temple in the hope of an eschatological temple.[202] For Mark, the old has been replaced by the new and the new is the community of faith, "made without hands", as he later describes it (14:58). This makes sense not only of the juxtaposition of the cursing of the fig tree and of Jesus' action in the temple with the words about the community of prayer. It also makes sense of the allusion to the new building of which the beloved son will become the cornerstone. For

---

[200] So Sariola, *Markus*, p. 226.

[201] Juel, *Messiah and Temple*, pp. 169, 208–209. R. E. Brown, *The Death of the Messiah. From Gethsemane to the Grave. A Commentary on the Passion Narratives of the Four Gospels*, 2 Vols, (New York: Doubleday, 1994), p. 456, suggests that Mark envisages a development in Jesus' attitude towards the temple, which becomes progressively more judgemental. For instance, only after finding no fruit does he curse the fig tree, but the evidence is slim. Already Jesus' action and words in the temple both name the ground and express the judgement.

[202] Cf. 4QFlor I, which speaks of the eschatological sanctuary, the polluted sanctuary, and the sanctuary of human beings.

Mark, sacrifices and burnt offerings are contrasted with love for God and love for neighbour in a manner which denies them any longer a relevant place in love for God. For Mark preoccupation with externals, with what is made with hands, with sacrifices and the like, is worthless. In addition we have seen that he attributes to the practitioners of such religion a propensity for hypocrisy and exploitation. The widow becomes a foil for Mark's depiction of the grounds for this judgement: injustice and exploitation. Mark 13 presages the events surrounding the temple's destruction, as will later the reported prediction of the temple's destruction and its symbolic fulfilment in the splitting of the curtain of the temple at Jesus' death.

On the positive side, Mark highlights the promise of a new temple, of a community of praying faith, a temple not made with hands, to be raised in three days, built around Jesus as cornerstone. The sequence of episodes corresponds to the sequence of the passion and its sequel. From accusations about the temple and about authority, corresponding to the Jewish trial, we move to issues of potential political revolution corresponding to the Roman trial, to resurrection corresponding to Jesus' resurrection, to the greatest commandment corresponding to the new community of faith, to Ps 110:1 corresponding to the exaltation of Christ the lord of the community. The new messiah, Son of David and David's Lord, will found a new temple, a new house of God. The vineyard, Israel's religious heritage, has been taken from its leaders and entrusted to a new community.

1.6.2 Mark 11:15–17 in the context of 11:1 – 13:37

Our consideration of 11:1 – 13:37 has shown the major significance which the temple theme has within it. 11:15–17 must, therefore, be understood within that context. From the context, not least, from Mark's intercalation of the anecdote within the story of the cursing of the fig tree,[203] we see that, whatever other aspects may be present, Mark treats the scene as an expression of God's judgement against the temple and the temple authorities.[204] Expelling those who bought and sold and overturning the tables of the moneychangers and the tables of those selling doves probably represents a symbolic act of judgement for Mark.[205] Jesus' words, "'My house shall be

---

[203] So Sariola, *Markus*, p. 216.

[204] So Hooker, "Traditions about the Temple," p. 7.

[205] Failure to acknowledge the significance of the symbolism of the intercalation leads Gundry, *Mark*, p. 639, for instance, to speak of Jesus' action as a 'cleansing' of the temple. That, too, would have had to have been only symbolic and would make little sense in the light of Mark's value system. See also Shepherd, *Sandwich Stories*, p. 219. It is

called a house of prayer for all nations,' but you have made it 'a den of brigands'," quotes Isa 56:7 and Jer 7:11. It is a statement giving grounds for God's condemnation. It condemns what the temple has become. For Mark's readers, λῃστῶν would probably evoke awareness of what had been going on in 66–70 CE, where many would have said the temple was in the hands of brigands. But, respecting Mark's sense of history here, we must assume he would also have intended a reference to the state of the temple in Jesus' time. Elsewhere Mark has Jesus attack temple servants, scribes and the like, as hypocrites and exploiters. It is likely that with the word, λῃστῶν, he is imputing the same here.[206]

If Mark sees in Jesus' words an expression of judgement on the temple because of such practices, he probably saw Jesus' action in the same light. But in this action Jesus is at the same time attacking certain activities. This raises a number of issues. What was it in these activities to which he objected? Did he object only to these activities? Or are they representative of broader issues and if so, how? The activities are: exchanging money, selling doves, and carrying things through the temple. The direct action relates to the money changers and sellers of doves. Both were a required service industry. People needed to contribute to the temple in appropriate coinage and doves were required for some sacrifices.

Why then attack the dealers? Because they swindle?[207] Taking λῃστῶν as a reference to stealing provides support for this view. But to limit it in this way in Mark's narrative denies the broader issues. The broader context shows that Mark does not have Jesus predict the temple's destruction solely on the grounds that these dealers swindle, if he believes they did. Therefore reading λῃστῶν in this way is to miss Mark's concern.

A further alternative is that Mark was concerned about the space taken up by such activities, including people carrying things through the outer courts. Removing the clutter would make more room for the place to be a house of

---

strange that, having affirmed the anti-temple stance in the context, Evans, "Cleansing or Portent," p. 241, denies its presence within the pericope 11:15–17 ("a protest in dishonesty"). He is arguing primarily against the view of Sanders, *Jesus and Judaism*, pp. 61–76, that Jesus' original action was predicting destruction and that the evangelists imposed the moral meaning of cleansing.

[206] Borg, *Conflict*, p. 174, argues against this on the grounds that through the LXX, apocrypha, New Testament and Josephus, λῃστής consistently meant one who killed and destroyed while plundering and argues that an allusion to the temple's political role in resistance is intended. But the meaning, at least in Jer 7:11, must be informed by 7:6, which speaks of oppressing aliens, orphans and widows, as well as shedding blood. See Gundry, *Mark*, pp. 644–645.

[207] So Gundry, *Mark*, pp. 644–645.

prayer for all peoples, especially Gentiles who were permitted only in the outer court.[208] It is possible to combine this with the concern about corrupt practices: these people not only clutter the space; they do so with corrupt practices. It is also difficult to imagine Mark picturing Jesus as concerned about stricter controls to preserve the sanctity of the temple or about people using the Gentile outer court as a short cut,[209] although we should note that Mark has no hesitation in having Jesus speak of the temple in the words of the quotation as God's house.

The major problem with each of these interpretations is that they assume Mark's Jesus wants to retain the temple, that he is basically concerned with reform. That is not Mark's belief, as we have shown. Mark is not interested in cleansing the Jerusalem temple; it is too late for that and, in any case, it is only a temple "made with hands".[210]

From the wider context we know that the grounds for God's judgement on the temple were much broader than concerns about money changers, dove sellers and people carrying things through the temple. They had to do with the abuses by temple personnel and their retainers, the scribes.[211] Mark sees the whole system as corrupt and riddled with hypocrisy and considers it to be a system preoccupied with the externals and not with what matters: prayer and openness to all peoples. As we have seen, Mark's cult critique is not only morally based; it also assumes an ideological stance which disparages focus on externals. Even the selective use of Isa 56:7, citing only the reference to prayer and not the reference to sacrifices, reflects this critique.[212]

Interpreting Mark's view of the temple episode in the light of the wider context does not, however, rule out the possibility that Mark would have intended that we see the dealers acting corruptly; but, if so, they would be doing so as part of a larger whole. This is preferable to the view which sees

---

[208] Cf. Borg, *Conflict*, p. 175, who points out the description of the outer court as 'the Gentile court' is "modern, unknown in antiquity".

[209] Cf. Evans, "Cleansing or Portent," p. 248.

[210] Cf. Evans, "Cleansing or Portent," pp. 248–256, who argues for temple critique and temple reform. The passages which he cites are nearly all associated with the threat of judgement, at least, by implication. His evidence of anti temple establishment sentiments in literature of the time is strong (pp. 256–264). See also his "Jesus' action in the temple and evidence of corruption in the first century temple," *SBLSemPapers* 1989, pp. 522–538. In "Predictions of the Destruction of the Herodian Temple in the Pseudepigrapha, Qumran Scrolls, and Related Texts," *JournStudPseud* 10 (1992), 89–147, he expands his review of relevant background material to include greater detail.

[211] So H. Anderson, *The Gospel of Mark*, (London:Oliphants, 1976), p. 266; see also Evans, "Cleansing or Portent," pp. 243–248.

[212] Sariola, *Markus*, p. 218, interprets this as directly the work of Mark, which strengthens the case for Markan cult critique even more.

Jesus' attack having nothing to do with moral concerns and primarily as trying to interrupt the system and so, symbolically, call it to halt, as a portent of its coming destruction.[213] The problem with this view is that it fails to give adequate weight to λῃστῶν and to the fact that such destruction would be interpreted theologically as judgement. Therefore a combination of these insights seems most adequately to reflect Mark's position.

Accordingly, Mark understood Jesus' action as both a symbolic gesture of judgement against the temple and one in which some manifestations of the corrupt system were attacked. Mark would be condemning the dealers not so much on grounds of their morality in individual transactions, which he may or may not have envisaged, but because they are part of a corrupt system. In addition, that system dealt with matters that are irrelevant to the life of faith. They have to do with externals. Already in Mark 7, Mark had linked preoccupation with externals with abuse and corruption. Both aspects are probably present here. Mark would also see the corrupt system as having led to the situation in his own day when the temple is held by brigands. The vision of the temple as a "house of prayer for all nations" had failed in Jerusalem. Mark may also have noted the effects of that clutter and business in the outer court; but, for him, that vision was to find its fulfilment in the Christian community. Jesus has brought a new temple, a new community of faith and prayer for all nations.[214]

1.6.2.1 Excursus: Behind Mark 11:15–17 and John 2:14–16

In discussing Mark 11:15–17 in isolation from its Markan context we noted a variety of interpretations which may be brought to the passage. Some of these may apply less to Mark and more to the way the passage will have been understood before Mark. The situation is further complicated by the existence of a further account of the same episode in John 2:14–16 which appears to be independent of Mark. Is it possible to reconstruct anything of the prehistory of the tradition in 11:15–17 before Mark? Maybe we can do no more than indicate possibilities.

---

[213] This is substantially the stance taken by Sanders, *Jesus and Judaism*, pp. 61–71, who sees the symbolic attempt to halt the temple as a portent of its coming destruction with a view to its future restoration, but his focus is not Mark but the Jesus of history.

[214] Cf. Sariola, *Markus*, p. 219, who denies any allusion on Mark's part to an eschatological or spiritual temple and sees the reference to a "house of prayer for all nations" as only a failed ideal. Gundry also argues against the idea of the Christian community as a new temple (pp. 901–902). See also the criticism in Sariola, *Markus*, pp. 219–220, against Schweizer, *Markus*, p. 128, who interprets Mark's concern here as abolition of the Law and vindication of the Gentile mission.

Within the Markan context the focus seems to be on Jesus' words and deeds as expressing judgement on what the temple had become in Jesus' day (and in a more nuanced political sense, also in Mark's day). It ought to have been a place of prayer open to all nations; it has failed to be this and represented instead a corrupt system to be replaced by Jesus and his community. For Mark, "place of prayer" seems to imply also that the temple as it existed was "made with hands" and its cultic provisions belong at the level of irrelevant external concerns.

Viewed apart from its Markan context, the passage appears to relate Jesus' action closely to his double citation of scripture. While the action of Jesus has its parallel in the independent Johannine account, the words are without parallel there and doubtless reflect a secondary attempt to interpret the significance of Jesus' deed.[215] They appear to combine two things: (a) criticism of the practices of the money changers and pigeon sellers as in some way related to the temple being a den of ληστῶν and (b) criticism of their presence in the Gentile court.[216] They may also imply some criticism of the temple as such in the words, "My house shall be called a house of prayer", though probably not in the radical way Mark appears to understand them. Possibly ληστῶν had always alluded to political intrigue in the temple.[217]

Had the person introducing the quotations taken into account the context of Is 56:7 and Jer 7:11, he would have been bemoaning that Gentiles were being prevented from participating fully in the cult and have been attacking

---

[215] I am holding open the possibility that the combined scripture citation is pre-Markan. For the view that it is the work of Mark, see Sariola, *Markus*, p. 215. For the view that the scripture citations are original and have been replaced in John, see R. J. Bauckham, "Jesus' demonstration in the temple," in *Law and Religion. Essays on the Place of the Law in Israel and Early Christianity*, edited by B. Lindars, (Cambridge: Clarke, 1988), pp. 72–89, here: 81–83. He argues that originally Jesus was protesting against exploitation by the temple authorities for their gain, an attitude he also detects in Jesus' response to the temple tax. He believes that Jesus is probably also expressing an act of God's judgement on the temple because of the abuses of the authorities (p. 85). By Gentiles Jesus would have meant proselytes (p. 86). The citation functions similarly to 2:27 as a challenge on the basis of what God intended the temple to be (p. 86).

[216] Cf. Borg, *Conflict*, pp. 163–299, who argues that the concerns of the anecdote cannot be with corruption, commerce, or access to the Gentile court, "but are directed rather at the quest for separation expressed in the Temple ideology which excluded Gentiles generally" (p. 175). Jesus attacks the money changing and the sale of animals, because both were designed to uphold the distinction between sacred and profane and symbolised the quest for resistance to the nations through separation, for which it would reap the reward of judgement (p. 176). Jesus' action was a prophetic act.

[217] So Borg, *Conflict*, pp. 171–177.

corruption in the priesthood which gave a false sense of security concerning the temple. The implication of the latter is that the temple faces destruction, as it did in Jeremiah's day. The use of the former has less to do with hope for Gentile participation in the sacrificial cultus than it does with the desirability of having Gentiles become one in worship with the people of God. Clearing the Gentile court of the merchants has to do with clearing it from corruption and so symbolically clearing it for Gentiles. Such a retelling of the story fits well in a period when the Gentile mission is well under way and the temple and its representatives stand under judgement. In itself the reference to Gentiles need not of itself imply Gentile mission; as in Isa 56 it could have reflected eschatological hope that the nations would come as proselytes to Zion.

Of the two motifs (corruption and Gentiles), only the former finds some direct echo in the Johannine account. There Jesus says: "Do not make my father's house a house of merchandise" (2:16). Even so, while this may include concern about corruption, it is primarily a reaction against the presence of commercial activity in the temple court, not to its being carried out in a corrupt manner. The tradition may reflect influence from Zech 14:21b MT, "There shall no longer be traders in the house of the Lord of hosts on that day."[218]

The fourth evangelist notes that the disciples later applied Ps 69:10 to Jesus' activity and its consequences: "Zeal for your house will consume me" (2:17). In doing so, the evangelist not only indicates that this action of Jesus will contribute to his arrest and trial, a factor passed over in his passion narrative, but also portrays Jesus as treating the temple with respect (indeed, "zeal"!) as God's house. The second motif, Gentiles, may be indirectly present in the johannine account in the light of the fact that using the Gentile court for such merchandising transactions at least affected the way the area could function, potentially affecting Gentiles, but John's account does not make the link explicit.

Let us assume that the Johannine description of the scene preserves an earlier interpretation than that represented in the mixed quotation in Mark 11:17. Then we have a tradition according to which Jesus objects to the presence of commercial activity as such in the temple, which he describes

---

[218] The context of Zechariah is one concerned with the holiness of Jerusalem, right down to its cooking pots! But we cannot assume an allusion to the removal of traders would imply espousal of what is in the context. Cf. also Mal 3:1, "The Lord shall suddenly come to his temple," associated with the messenger who will prepare his way. A christological reading of the allusion to "the Lord" here may have been in the minds of those who passed on the anecdote, but no evidence is present in the extant texts.

directly as his Father's house. The commercial activity includes not only money changers and dove sellers but also those selling sacrificial animals.[219] The use of Psalm 69 in the Johannine tradition presents Jesus' actions more as an attempt at reform ("Zeal for your house") than as an act of judgement. The possible allusion to Zech 14:21b also coheres with this understanding. In Mark the detail about Jesus' prohibiting carrying material in the temple might also suggest that Jesus was originally concerned at behaviour in the temple, ie. with reform.[220]

One would certainly expect the temple authorities to have objected to Jesus' action. It would have been seen as unnecessary interference in their domain; they had their own temple police! And more to the point, they had authorised these activities in the temple. He had no right to interfere. In reality, had Jesus embarked on a clean up of the outer court, the authorities would have soon put a stop to it. The outer court was expansive and well guarded, especially during festivals.[221] Jesus' action must have been confined enough in space and time, not to expose him to immediate arrest. This already suggests an action of a symbolic nature, rather than a general clean up.

What was being said by the symbolic act? Was it primarily a protest against the clutter? One can easily imagine such a protest. The temple is to be a place of worship, including these outer courts; look what it has become! This is my Father's house! The problem with this reforming image is that both Mark and John indicate that Jesus' action has a direct bearing on his execution. Execution just for over zealous protests in the temple? Both, however, bring another factor into play: Jesus' prediction about the temple's destruction and its replacement. John even has it accompanying Jesus' action in the temple. Whether John is correct or not, we must read Jesus' actions as those of one who also predicted the temple's destruction. That puts a different complexion on the event and on Jesus' attitude towards the temple.

---

[219] V. Eppstein, "The Historicity of the Cleansing of the Temple," *ZNW* 55 (1964), pp. 42–58, reports that Caiaphas introduced the selling into the outer court as competition for the four suppliers operating on the Mount of Olives. But see the discussion in Evans, "Cleansing or Portent," pp. 265–267, raising doubts about the reliability of the tradition in relation to dating and about Eppstein's assumption that prior to Caiaphas no selling took place in the outer court.

[220] Dunn, *Partings*, pp. 48–49, relates this to the hope for the Messiah expressed in Ps Sol 17:30, who was expected to purify Jerusalem and assemble Gentiles proselytes, though he also contemplates that "purification of the Temple involved also its destruction" (p. 49).

[221] On the fact that it must have been a minor act; otherwise there would have been intervention by the authorities who oversaw the area, see Borg, *Holiness*, p. 172.

Already the Johannine use of Psalm 69 suggests strongly that Jesus' zealous act in the temple led finally to his death. The johannine version also
preserves an account of an interchange which immediately followed Jesus'
deed. In it he responds to the Jews' request that he validate his authority for
such action by saying: "Destroy this temple and in three days I will raise it
up" (2:18). The saying is a variant of the logion found on the lips of false
witnesses in the Jewish trial scene of Mark's passion narrative, where it
misrepresented but substantially preserved what Mark and, later Matthew
believed, was a genuine prediction of Jesus. Jesus was announcing the destruction of the temple, not in the form, "I will destroy . ." (that was the false
testimony in 14:58),[222] nor probably in the form, "You (ie. the Jews) destroy . .", but as something God would do.

"In three days", if it belongs to the original logion and has not been introduced on the basis of resurrection tradition, would mean "in a short time."
The hope for a new temple to replace the old was not unique to Jesus.[223]
Behind Mark 13, now replete with apocalyptic imagery encouraging Mark's
readers to see the events of their own time, lies further evidence of Jesus'
prediction of the temple's destruction. The extent of early tradition is disputed and the form of Jesus' words may be irrecoverable. Possibly he employed the standard Danielic metaphors of abomination. Possibly we should
find original material only behind 13:2.

Announcing that God would destroy the temple is more than predicting
that it will be destroyed; it is saying God will do it and that implies judgement. The evidence that Jesus announced God's destruction of the temple
makes it unlikely that Jesus was pleading for reform. What would be the
point? There is no trace of Jesus' saying, "Unless you reform, God will
destroy." The tradition suggests Jesus was more pessimistic about the temple than that.

Was Jesus, then, attacking the temple by his actions? John's version would
not support that. It is not assumed in the question of the Jewish authorities,
who ask by what authority he is acting, a question echoed in the Markan
tradition. If Jesus' actions had been an attempt symbolically to put an end to
the cult by removing from worshippers the access to animals and birds for
sacrifice and to money changers for appropriate coinage and by stopping the
carrying of temple vessels, the authorities clearly missed the point. On the
other hand, the authority question only really makes sense on the basis that

---

[222] So Sariola, *Markus*, p. 228.
[223] On the hope for an eschatological temple see 1En 90; 91:13; Tobit 13:10; 14:5–7;
4QFlor f. 1–3:1–6; 11QT 29; Sib Or 3:280–294; Sib Or 5:414–433; 2 Bar 68; TBenj 9.

Jesus is wanting to change (ie. reform) things. The more likely alternative is that Jesus' action would have been ambiguous; what they contemplated as reform (according to the Johannine and Markan tradition) had gone beyond reform. It attacked activities which themselves represented or were a mani- festation of the reason why God would destroy the temple.

What was the problem? To some degree an answer cannot be given with- out considering the broader issue of the relationship between the historical Jesus and the temple system. Some preliminary observations are pertinent. Nothing suggests Jesus attacked the temple as such, nor its sacrificial cult as set out in Torah.[224] It is his Father's house. It belongs to the holy institu- tions of the Torah. He participates in its cult. The evidence points rather to what the temple system had become in Jesus' day.[225] God's judgement in destroying the temple will be because of what it has become, not because of what it was meant to be.

The traditions of Jesus' action in the temple suggest a strong reaction to the commercial clutter of the outer court. Use of the outer temple court area was frequently a matter of dispute.[226] Access to on site animals and birds for sacrifice and currency exchange was a service. For some, however, this user friendly service broke the personal nexus which existed when a person brought their own sacrifice.[227] Was this also Jesus' concern? Nothing indi- cates that it was. Potential pollution may have been a concern of some.[228] The earliest tradition appears only to highlight the merchandising in the tem- ple and the problem was primarily the location. Probably the concern of the historical Jesus was that introduction of such activity distracted from the purpose of the temple as a place of worship.

The fuller picture of likely historical traditions indicates that there were

---

[224] Yet it is in this sense that Sariola, *Markus*, p. 217, believes that the pre-Markan tradition should be understood; similarly Gnilka, *Markus II*, p. 129; F. Hahn, *Der urchristliche Gottesdienst*, SBS 41, (Stuttgart: KBW, 1970), pp. 29–30. Against the view that the tradition obscures what was once an attempt at political revolution, see Dunn, *Partings*, p. 47, citing S. G. F. Brandon, *Jesus and the Zealots*, (Manchester: Manchester Univ., 1967).

[225] The Qumran covenanters also predicted a replacement for the old temple in part on the grounds that the present temple was polluted (see 4QFlor; cf. also 11QTemple 29).

[226] So B. D. Chilton, *The Temple of Jesus. His Sacrificial Program within a Cultural History of Sacrifice*, (University Park, Penn: Penn State Univ Pr, 1993), pp. 101–111. See also Nineham, *Mark*, p. 304, and Branscomb, *Law*, p. 127. For the view that Jesus was objecting to the use of the Gentile court as a street: Sariola, *Markus*, p. 217; Pesch, *Markusevangelium II*, p. 198.

[227] See Chilton, *Temple*, p. 109.

[228] Pollution of the temple was a long standing concern which expressed itself in various ways. Cf. 1 En 10:17–21; TMos 5:4–6; 6; 9:6–7; PsSol 4:11–12; CD 4:17; 20:23; 4Q390 2:9; TLevi 15:1; Jos *JW* 4:201–202, 386–388.

other matters of concern which Jesus had with the temple authorities which need to be weighed in his despair and words of judgement.[229] This would have included corruption and exploitation, quite independently of whether this occurred in the individual dealings of the traders. There is strong evidence to suggest that Jesus judged the temple authorities as hopelessly corrupt and out of touch with true faith. His response was not reform, but judgement. Thus any allusion to Zech 14:21b, "There shall no longer be traders in the house of the Lord of hosts on that day", need not then necessary indicate only reform; it would indicate where the problem lay, because of which God's judgement was to come upon the temple.[230]

Yet there is a fine line between predicting God's judgement on what the temple has become and attacking the temple itself. Jesus' actions could easily be misconstrued, intentionally or otherwise, as an attack on the temple. The more public support, the more dangerous such a stance. Both Jesus' action and his prediction in relation to the temple were open to such interpretation. Any move against these activities was a move against the temple authorities which had permitted them and might easily be construed as tantamount to a move against the whole temple system itself.

It is possible then to see Jesus' actions as a symbolic prophetic action expressing God's judgement against the temple. It was not originally an attempt at reform, a 'cleansing', but a prediction of God's judgement on the present system by attacking some symptoms of abuse. It is, in one sense, the action of the frustrated reformer and clearly identifies one of the major issues which gave offence. Jeremiah's prediction of the temple's destruction is a close analogy. In other words, we are not dealing with an approach that is anti-temple and so, by implication, anti much that is contained in Torah. Rather the attitude towards Torah reflected in the tradition is of one grieved at abuses in the temple and therefore expressing God's judgement on the present temple authorities and on the temple.[231] An action such as this, which both highlights the abuse and symbolises God's anger and impending judgement, would be seen by temple authorities as an affront against God's temple and might be construed to the Romans as an assault on Roman authority, since they stood as guarantors of the temple and the central insti-

---

[229] Oakman, "Cursing fig trees," pp. 264–266, suggests that Jesus' objection is to the way the temple authorities used the temple "as a system of exploitative redistribution for the benefit of the few" (p. 266). Cf. also Bauckham, "Demonstration," pp. 81–83.

[230] See also Brown, *Death of the Messiah*, p. 455.

[231] So also Brown, *Death of the Messiah*. p. 458. See also Brown's extensive discussion of Jesus' prediction (pp. 438–454).

tution of the Jewish people.[232]   I think the strongest evidence points in this direction.[233]

So far our discussion of material seeming to come originally from Jesus has not shown Jesus at any point acting against the Law.   Rather what we have found is concern about application of Law in relation to the temple. Practices should not be allowed which impede access of people to worship. Jesus' primary concern was abuse of various kinds by temple authorities, only one of which receives attention in the anecdote.   Predicting God's judgement on the temple because of the corruption of its leaders is not the same as attacking the institution itself.   Probably Jesus reflected the prophetic contrast between a focus on attitude and human need as more significant than concern with externals, though this is not explicit and, as with the prophets, not an either or.   The tradition preserves Jesus' concern for the temple as God's house.

The prediction of a new temple replacing the old, or at least the destruction of the old, is a position consistent with someone upholding Torah, including its cultic provisions, as already Jeremiah illustrates.[234]   However this leaves open the extent to which Jesus' new hope of a temple (if it existed) envisaged a purified rebuilt temple.   Mark's tradition may well have captured something of the spirit of Jesus in having him speak of the hope for a temple which will be a house of prayer for all nations.   The question needs further consideration in the light of all material concerning Jesus and the Law which has a claim to authenticity.

In summary, behind both Mark's and John's tradition is an account of Jesus' action in the temple in relation to both sacrifices (including animals) and currency exchange dealers.   Probably John's tradition is closer to the original issue, when he depicts Jesus' concern for the temple as God's house and the effect which the location of such activities on site had for people.   In his action he challenged the authorisation given for such activities in the temple

---

[232] So K. Müller, "Möglichkeit und Vollzug jüdischer Kapitalgerichtsbarkeit im Prozess gegen Jesus von Nazaret," in *Der Prozess gegen Jesus. Historische Rückfrage und theologische, Deutung*, QD 112, edited by K. Kertelge, (Freiburg: Herder, 1988), pp. 84–110, here: 82.   In an important review of the legal evidence he concludes that the charge against Jesus would have been accurately reflected in the title on the cross and represented *perduellio* on the basis of Jesus' prophetic symbolic action and his temple word.   In agreement: Dautzenberg, "Eigenart," pp. 147–150, 154, 165–170.

[233] On the fact that as an act it must have been minor; otherwise there would have been intervention by the authorities who oversaw the area, see Borg, *Holiness*, p. 172.

[234] On this see also Evans, "Predictions".

by the temple authorities. The authority issue is still preserved, though variously, in both versions. The temple logion may have its original place in the tradition. Even if it does not, it supports an interpretation of Jesus' act as not only defying the ruling, but also using the occasion to symbolise God's judgement, though it needs to be seen that this element has to be supplied from the wider context.

Whether or not the act and the prediction of judgement belong together, neither portrays Jesus as acting contrary to Torah. What impresses is Jesus' concern about the temple as his Father's house. The nature of the concern relates to the place and may still be reflected in the interpretative hand which introduced the Isaiah quotation in the pre-Markan tradition. The presence of the commercial activities may have been seen as impeding Gentiles in particular. At some stage this will have been seen as an allusion to the Gentile mission. "House of prayer" may, but need not, imply a contrast, inclusive or exclusive, with sacrificial activities. It did for Mark and may have done already at some stage in pre-Markan tradition. At the point where the contrast became exclusive we have an abandonment of commitment to Torah, characteristic of Mark. At the earlier stages this will not have been the case. All the more striking, then, is Mark's dramatic symbolic use of the narrative within the composition 11:1 – 13:37 to present Jesus as the one who replaces the temple condemned by God to destruction for the abuses of its leaders and who replaces it with a new temple, the community of faith and prayer.

1.6.3 Conclusion

Within 11:1 – 13:37 we find evidence of strong Markan composition, comparable in extent with 6:6 – 8:26 and similarly concerned with an issue of Law, the temple. Jesus' journey takes him to the heart, to the temple. The temple is a major theme underlying the whole section. By intercalating the temple incident with the cursing of the fig tree Mark had Jesus declare God's judgement on the temple. Mark has linked the issue of Jesus' authority with the replacement of the old temple by the new community of faith. Clearly for Mark, Jesus' authority as Son of God makes this possible.

Associated with this replacement are notions of judgement against the temple because of the corrupt behaviour of its keepers and their rejection of God's beloved Son. Associated with this replacement is also a value system which disparages the external and cultic in favour of the internal and ethical. This value system, already applied in Mark 7:1–23, underlies the thesis of the new temple of the community. It is a radical application of what were

originally inclusive contrasts in the prophetic tradition. Within this perspective Mark still portrays Jesus as valuing the temple, but primarily as a
place of prayer, and that, for all peoples. Corruption and clutter had made
this impossible. The linkage between focus on externals with hypocrisy and
abuse is implicit in the section as a whole.

Mark's Jesus supersedes Torah and, with regard to the temple and its cult,
abrogates it. In Mark's time the destruction is at hand, if not already recent
history. This external event will have provided added confirmation for Mark
of his position. The new temple is one built on the cornerstone which the
builders rejected, living therefore by the authority of Jesus, the Messiah and
Lord at God's right hand, and his radical reworking of Torah according to
which at the centre of God's will is the call to love God and neighbour, not
as a summary of all laws, but as a criterion for all of life. The heritage of
Israel, its vineyard, is now in the hands of a new community.

1.7 Mark 14:1 – 16:8 in Review

1.7.1 Mark 14:1 – 16:8

The confrontation with the temple authorities is heightened in the passion
narrative. In 14:1–2 Mark shows the chief priests and scribes carrying out
the intentions already espoused by the Pharisees and the Herodians in 3:6.
There the plot arose in response to Jesus' claims to authority and his interpretation of the Law. The chief priests and scribes made the plot their own
also in response to the issue of Jesus' authority, especially because of his
action in the temple and his use of the vineyard parable against them (11:18;
12:12). In this way Mark achieves a linkage between the earlier controversies and the passion.

Mark contrasts their response to Jesus in 14:1–2 with that of an unknown
woman who anoints Jesus' head in the house of Simon the leper (14:3–9).[235]
The similar Lukan anecdote portrays Simon as a Pharisee who raises issues
of propriety (Luke 7:36–50). Here in Mark, there is no controversy over
Law; only the same kind of contrast between religious male leaders and a
truly pious woman which we found also in 12:38–44 (the widow's mite).
Luke was not wrong to extrapolate as he has. Socially the presence and the

---

[235] Westerholm, *Scribal Authority*, pp. 68–69, notes the potential breach of purity laws
in Jesus' eating in the house of a leper (Mark 14:3); however, the epithet, "leper," may, as
he suggests, refer to a previous state.

behaviour of the woman would evoke the suspicion that she was wanton and possibly a prostitute. But this is not Mark's concern. She is, on the contrary, a model of discipleship. In the irony of the narrative she does what the disciples should have done: she anoints the Messiah! Those present (the disciples) fail to reach her level of understanding. Mark swings the narrative in contrast again in 14:10–11, to recount Judas' collusion.

The pattern of contrasts continues in 14:12–16. Jesus has the disciples prepare for the passover and then celebrates it (14:17–25). Jesus' celebration of the Passover, which includes the actions of breaking bread and saying a blessing over the cup, belongs to Jesus' Jewishness in Mark. It was a normal a part of his piety as attendance at synagogue. Jesus' entry a week previously also coincides with normal Jewish practice, although Mark shows no interest in this aspect nor in the rites of immersion which accompanied such visits.

Mark passes on the tradition according to which Jesus identified himself with the bread and the wine and invested them with atoning significance. Mark might well have exploited the event to set it in contrast to the temple system or, at least, to aspects of it concerned with atonement, but neither here nor in the only other allusion to Jesus' vicarious death (10:45) is there any indication that this was Mark's intent. That allusion is, in any case, incidental to Mark's primary purpose, which is to present Jesus as the serving one. This coheres with the fact that Mark's emphasis generally is on Jesus' path of suffering, whereas the interpretation of that death as a atoning act did not play a central role in his theology. He was not the author to the Hebrews or Paul!

In what follows Mark contrasts Jesus' faithfulness with the disciples' failure, from Judas to Peter to all the disciples who will abandon him. Jesus is faithful in prayer, submits to arrest[236] and faces the high priest. In the trial of Jesus the temple theme returns. Mark reports the evidence of false witnesses who reported Jesus as having said: "I will destroy this temple made with hands and in three days build another not made with hands" (14:58). From the wider context and from the formulation itself it is clear that Mark has a carefully nuanced understanding of the falsity. The hearers already know that Jesus has predicted the temple's destruction (13:2) and the major section, 11:1 – 13:37, had highlighted it as an act of divine judgement. What is more, the contrast, "made with hands" and "not made with hands", absent

---

[236] On the suggestion that the cutting off of the "servant of the high priest" we should see an anti priestly act rendering a priest unfit to serve through mutilation see the critical discussion in Brown, *Death of the Messiah*, pp. 273–274.

from all parallel versions of the logion, reflects Markan dualism. Though the hearers would probably not have known it, we know that elsewhere other versions of the saying are deemed authentic (John 2:19; cf. also Matt 26:61). Apparently the falsity lies for Mark primarily in the claim that Jesus himself would do this.[237] Otherwise it appears to stand and, indeed, reflects the heart of Mark's understanding of the temple.

The temple "made with hands" is to be destroyed – by God – and another temple will replace it, one not made with hands. While, in Hebrews, "not made with hands" refers to a heavenly temple (9:11), in Mark it refers to the community as a temple, a concept fundamental to Mark's concern in 11:1 – 13:37. While "made with hands" may sometimes be associated with polemic against idolatry (its use in LXX; cf. Isa 21:9; 31:7; 46:6; cf. also Acts 7:48), it would be too severe to infer this meaning here and so see in these words a disparagement of the temple as idolatrous. Mark's Jesus does not behave as though the temple is in itself idolatrous; nor does the high priest's response assume Jesus implied such a thing.[238] Yet Mark doubtless understands Jesus to be expressing more than an inclusive contrast. Mark 7 shows that he is more likely to have considered the temple dispensable because it belonged to the irrelevant, external form of religion.

The accusation of which Jesus is found guilty, blasphemy, seems to rest on his acceptance of the designation, "Christ, the Son of God". The juxtaposition of messiahship and the temple motif, both here and in the crucifixion scene, may well be deliberate and reflect the belief that the new temple is to be the work of God's anointed Son of David, a juxtaposition noted in our discussion of 12:28–34,35–38.

The accusation of blasphemy most likely reflects accusations made by Jews against Christians' claims for Jesus.[239] Mark had foreshadowed it in the accusation of blasphemy in 2:7, where scribes assume Jesus is claiming to act independently of God and taking to himself divine prerogatives. Does Mark assume that the authorities might legitimately convict Jesus of blasphemy for making such claims, had Jesus not indeed been the Christ, the Son of the living God? In other words, was it simply a matter of a false claim? Or did the accusation of blasphemy depend on a misreading of what "Christ, the Son of God" meant? The latter was the case in the charge of blasphemy in 2:7, where Mark's Jesus exposes the charge as based on a false

---

237 So Brown, *Death of the Messiah*, pp. 447–448.

238 So also Brown, *Death of the Messiah*, p. 440.

239 Cf. Brown, *Death of the Messiah*, p. 526. See also his extensive discussion of blasphemy, pp. 532–547. See also the discussion of blasphemy in relation to my treatment of 2:6–7.

understanding of Jesus' relation to God. He is the authorised Son of Man. Here it is not so clear. The charge of blasphemy may be directed at Jesus' assent, but its primary focus appears to be Jesus' claim in 14:62 that he would come as Son of Man on the clouds of heaven and seated at God's right hand. It is probably related to the claim to sit at God's right hand. Mark does not enable us to understand their reasoning in detail. Mark assumes his hearers will be able to make some sense of the charge, but recognises it as false. Given Mark's understanding that Jesus' claim is legitimate, he would the claim in itself as contravening Torah.

In what follows the accusation of messiahship is twisted in a political direction. It stands over the cross, both literally and figuratively, as the charge against Jesus. Mark makes good use of the irony which this tradition offers, for Jesus is indeed the Jews' Messiah. Thus Barabbas is offered in exchange for Jesus; Jesus is mocked, dressed in purple, crowned with thorns and hailed in mockery; his accusation reads, "King of the Jews," he is crucified between two brigands; he is mocked both as would be destroyer and rebuilder of the temple and as messiah; and it is left to a Gentile to acclaim him, "Son of God." Throughout, Jesus is portrayed as remaining firm and taking solace, like a devout Jew, in prayer and finally in the words of Psalm 22:1.

In the crucifixion scene the temple motif reappears in the words of the mockers (15:29). The effect is to recall the accusation at the trial of Jesus, but also to prepare for the drama which follows. For Mark tells us that at Jesus' death the curtain of the temple was split from top to bottom (15:38). The temple will indeed be destroyed! Jesus' prediction is vindicated; the event is a divine portent foreshadowing God's judgement on temple and the temple authorities for their rejection of Jesus.[240] Mark gives no indication which curtain was meant, the outer curtain visible at the entry or the curtain separating the Holy Place from the Holy of Holies. It does not appear to matter, since the tearing means judgement. This seems the most natural

---

[240] So Brown, *Death of the Messiah*, pp. 1102. He suggests also that God's wrath here in rending the veil answers the wrath of the high priest at the trial in rending his garments (p. 1100). He also suggests that this understanding of the torn veil may have developed in the decades before the destruction, in response to concern that Jesus' prediction had not been fulfilled (pp. 450–451). Vögtle, A, "Das markinische Verständnis der Tempelworte," in *Die Mitte des Neuen Testaments. Einheit und Vielfalt neutestamentlicher Theologie. FS für E. Schweizer*, edited by U. Luz, and H. Weder, (Göttingen: Vandenhoeck und Ruprecht, 1983), pp. 362–383, here: 373–378, believes that Mark understood the event as signifying the end of the old cultus (therefore the tearing of the inner curtain) and its replacement by the new community based on the saving work of Christ. This assumes that for Mark Jesus' death is salvific in a singular sense, a view not strongly attested in Mark as we have seen. I am not sure that Mark would share the assumptions about space which

reading of the text and best reflects the motif as Mark has been developing it. It is a matter of speculation whether more is intended. Could it also convey the idea that God has abandoned the temple?[241] But that may misread Mark's assumptions, who probably considered that it had always been a temple made with hands and destined only to be a house of prayer. For the same reasons I consider it unlikely that he sees this as the event which removes the barrier between sacred and profane.[242] In the light of Jesus' quotation of Isaiah, "My house shall be called a house of prayer for all nations" (11:17), one could suggest that the event symbolises that the temple's purpose is now to be fulfilled; there is access "for all nations".[243] A Gentile centurion immediately acclaims him Son of God (15:39). This is possible, but entails complex symbolism. The primary focus is judgement.

The narrative colouring of darkness and of the patterns of three hour intervals serve to enhance the climactic quality of the event: the rejection of Jesus by the Jewish and Roman authorities and his acknowledgment by God, by the Gentile onlooker and by the faithful women (15:38–41). The Gentile and the women bring a certain defiance to expression in the text, for these, who are not insiders according to the Law, now bear witness to God's truth. In the same defiant spirit Mark had recounted the anointing of Jesus by the unknown woman.

In 15:42–47 Mark portrays Joseph of Arimathea acting in accord with respect for Torah and the sabbath. The women, too, are true to Torah in their preparations. Mark says they have been with Jesus from the beginning. These details are incidental to the narrative, but the presence of the women raises potential purity issues. For Mark they are in all probability not an issue and may well reflect the strength of women within his own Christian setting.[244] The Jewish context is presupposed and the observance uncontroversially part of the setting.[245] Mark's brief narrative of the resurrection celebrates God's response, yet leaves the hearer to complete the sequel, as even the women are overcome by fear.

---

this interpretation requires of him. For him the temple always was only "a temple made with hands".

[241] Cf. Brown, *Death of the Messiah*, p. 1135, who points out that Mark achieves this meaning by use of the word, "sanctuary," ναός, in 14:58; 15:29,38.

[242] Cf. Malbon *Narrative Space*, pp. 109, 120–126.

[243] Cf. Hooker, *Mark*, p. 378.

[244] On the prominent role of women in Mark see M. A. Beavis, "Women as Models of Faith in Mark," *BibTheolBull* 18 (1988), pp. 3–9; S. L. Graham, "Silent Voices. Women in the Gospel of Mark," *Semeia* 54 (1992) pp. 145–158; E. S. Malbon, "Fallible Followers: Women and Men in the Gospel of Mark," *Semeia* 28 (1983),. pp. 29–48; W. Munro, "Women Disciples in Mark?" *CBQ* 44 (1982), pp. 225–241; Fander, *Die Stellung der Frau*.

[245] So Weiss, "Sabbath," p. 16.

1.7.2 Conclusion

Mark's concern to emphasise that Jesus is Christ and Son of God continues
in the passion narrative. With regard to Jesus' attitude towards Torah, Mark
also continues the theme of the destruction of the old temple and the creation of the new, possibly linked to Jesus' messiahship, though the link is not
explicit. This juxtaposition is present on both occasions when the temple
theme occurs, in Jesus' Jewish trial and in his mockery and death. Jesus is
the authority who is beside and beyond Torah and effectively announces the
replacement of its temple. The splitting of the curtain is a portent of God's
judgement. Mark does not develop the motif of the new temple further in
this division, although there may be hints in Mark's characterisation of the
faithful. They include the lowly women, the Gentile centurion, the traditionally excluded, and will include the restored disciples. These will constitute the new temple.

For the rest, Jesus is portrayed as naturally Torah observant, particularly
with regard to the preparation and celebration of the passover in Jerusalem,
including the actions of breaking the bread and giving thanks, blessing the
wine, and singing the Hallel. In the trial Mark assumes Jesus' innocence of
the charge of blasphemy, as he had in 2:7–10. Similarly, the actions of Joseph
and the women in relation to the burial and sabbath law naturally reflect
Torah observance. For Mark these details are naturally part of the story.
Finally, it is to be noted that Mark does not employ the last supper narrative,
with its reference to the body and blood of Christ as atoning, to enhance the
theme. We can only guess at possible links he could have made, but gives
no indication that he had.

1.8 Jesus' Attitude towards the Law in Mark – Conclusions

1.8.1 Jesus' attitude towards the Law according to Mark

In Mark the final source of authority is God. Jesus is God's Son. Mark has
God affirm this at the baptism. Mark offers little which enables us to define
the nature of the relationship, nothing about pre-existence, nothing about
miraculous conception. Yet Mark leaves his hearers in no doubt: Jesus acts
with God's power and authority. It is evident in his miracles and exorcisms,
his summoning of disciples, his declarations of God's will, his role at the
end of history, and, not least, in his resurrection. As this divine power and
authority is the starting point of the gospel, both in the narrative prologue

and ideologically, it must be the starting point for consideration of Jesus' attitude towards Torah. Christology is the given.

Given this christology, what are the options? One is that this christological authority replaces all other authority. This could mean ignoring other authority or discrediting it. Another is that this authority realigns the other authority in a manner which gives it a subordinate role, perhaps also by replacing or discrediting only parts of it. A further alternative is that it coexists with the other authority without defining the relationship.

In Mark's narrative world Jesus, the Son of God, is not God's only manifestation of authority. God has acted before. This comes most clearly to the fore in the parable of the rebellious tenants, but is assumed throughout. More than that, Mark's Jesus belongs within a history of God's action: he is its climax. This continuity is established by reference to what God had said in that history through the prophets. More than that, Mark believes that God's will is preserved within the scriptures, which we know as the Law and the Prophets. Mark presents Jesus as fulfilling hopes expressed in these scriptures. They are not thereby replaced. Mark's Jesus continues to make reference to them in argument.

For Mark, then, Jesus is God's Son, who exercises divine power and authority, but this is complicated by the fact that manifestation of God's will already exists in the scriptures and is known and revered as God's Law. Mark's solution is not to discredit Torah, replacing it by Jesus. Nor it is to subordinate Jesus to Torah; that would contradict his claim of absolute authority for Jesus. But in his portrait of Jesus, Mark could not ignore the relationship of Jesus to existing religious tradition which also had divine sanction. The neatest solution would have been to talk in terms of total replacement or, at the other extreme, simply of an 'add-on' which in no way called previous tradition into question. For Mark, neither was possible.

Mark's Jesus is beyond being a teacher of the Law. He exercises an authority which enables him both to affirm it in parts and to supersede it. It is at this level that we need to see that much of Jesus' teaching and exercise of authority relates not to the Torah at all, but to his distinctive mission. Such teaching material includes: the manner of response to the preaching of the word (4:1–34); the instructions which the disciples should follow for their missions (6:7–11); the challenge to fearless confession in the face of danger (8:34–38); warnings concerning humility and the dangers of intolerance and offensive behaviour towards fellow believers (9:9:33–50); the welcoming of children (10:13–16); right attitudes towards possessions and towards positions of leadership (10:23–45); the need to be a community of faith and prayer (11:22–25); exhortation concerning coming persecution, false prophets and messiahs, and the signs of the end of time (13:1–37); the celebration of the Lord's Supper (14:22–25); and, not least, teaching about himself as suffering Son of Man who will die and rise again (8:31; 9:33; 10:33–34). Indeed, most of the teaching material in Mark relates directly to the disciples and the community which they will build on his foundation. He speaks as Lord of the Church. It is ultimately from this perspective that we must see also his pronouncements on what is now appropriate of the Law's demands.

His purpose in writing, therefore, is to present Jesus as Son of God, as good news (1:1), not to provide a treatise on Jesus' attitude towards Torah. Yet it was impossible to do the former without attention to the latter. The absence of the word, νόμος ("law"), in Mark, in no way means that Mark avoided the issues. They are central to the conflict motif which dominates the plot; they are also often incidental, even unintentional. Mark's complex response to the issues is best seen within the parameters of continuity and discontinuity. The usefulness of this framework is that it sets the discussion in the context of the relationship between Mark's Jesus and Mark's understanding of God's action in history.

1.8.2 Continuity

Much of this is incidental or assumed. For Mark Jesus was a Jew. As a Jew he attended the synagogue on the sabbath (1:21; 6:2). He prayed and gave thanks for food according to Jewish custom (6:41; 8:6; 14:22). He made preparations for and celebrated Passover (14:12–26). He wore tassels on his garment (6:52). He appealed to Jewish scriptures in argument (2:25–26; 10:3–8). He employed biblical imagery (4:3–9; 12:1–9). He prayed in the language of the psalms (14:34; 15:34). He cited decalogue commandments to counter abuses or to refer to what God required (7:10; 10:19; cf. 10:10–11) and probably concurred with John's criticism of Herod for breach of marriage kinship laws (6:17–18). He identified the two greatest commandments, citing two passages from Torah (12:29–31). In relating to Gentiles he assumed Jews were God's first priority (7:27). He heals the Gentile woman's child without entering the Gentile's house (7:24–30). He called twelve disciples (in some way reflecting the twelve tribes of Israel; 3:14). He was offended when a leper crossed forbidden barriers and firmly sent him off to the temple to do as Torah prescribed (1:40–45). He enters the temple and teaches there, citing scripture which describes it as God's house (11:11,15–17; 11:27 – 12:44). Those close to him are reported to have observed sabbath law in tending to his burial (15:42–47). Mark's Jesus refutes charges of violates the Law by blasphemy (2:7–10; cf. 14:61–64) and sorcery (3:22–30).

Mark enhances the sense of continuity. In the prologue he portrays Jesus as the one whom the scriptures foretold (12–3). In a double move Mark does this also for John the Baptist and then has John announce Jesus, also with prophetic authority (1:2–8). Thus for Mark, the God who acclaims him at baptism is clearly the God of salvation history (1:9–11). Mark interprets the transfiguration scene in a way which affirms this continuity and repeats the double move of the prologue by identifying John with Elijah (9:2–13). A number of the miracle stories echo Old Testament themes typologically (e.g., Exodus motifs: the feedings and the walking on the water; the Psalms and Jonah: the stilling of the storm; Elijah/Elisha tradition: the healings of the women, the feedings). It is likely that the Mark who included the transfiguration scene also sensed many of these connections. Mark appears to have deliberately used imagery of Israel in developing his argument in 6:6 – 8:26 to show that Jesus' community may include both Jew and Gentile. As already noted, the parable of the rebellious tenants (12:1–9) sets Jesus in line with the prophets; he is both the climax and unique; for he is the beloved son. Especially from the entry scene onwards Mark emphasises Jesus' messiahship as fulfilling the hopes of scripture. Mark would probably have been aware of the echoes in the passion narrative of Psalm 22.

A Jewish hearer of the story would also make other assumptions. These include that Jesus would have undergone appropriate purification procedures after contracting uncleanness in touching a leper, being touched by a menstruant woman, returning from Gentile territory, and on coming to Jerusalem for the Passover and such personal things as nocturnal emissions. Mark makes no mention of these. His silence could be interpreted as ignorance; more probably he knew of the issues and deemed them irrelevant or unnecessary.

Were we to focus only on these items of continuity, it would be possible to contemplate the 'add-on' model for Jesus' attitude to Torah as Mark's view. Jesus would be God's latest, even God's final, initiative, fulfilling scriptural hopes. He comes to add to what has gone before, but in no way to diminish or dissent from it. It is all from God. God's authority holds it all together. The effect would be then to endorse what has gone before and to supplement it. But there is another side to Mark's story.

1.8.3 Discontinuity

In its starkest expression, discontinuity surfaces in Mark's commentary on Jesus' statements about food laws: καθαρίζων πάντα τὰ βρώματα ("declaring all foods clean," 7:19c). As we have seen, it should not be read in isolation. It simply represents Mark's summary of the import of Jesus' words in 7:1–23. The effect of these is to set aside some major sections of written Torah. It is clear from the context that this abrogation derives from certain basic principles. One is reflected in 7:15 and its exposition in 7:17–23, which contrasts external things (entering a person) and internal moral attitudes linked to behaviour. The beginning of the episode shows that more is involved than food, though that is Mark's primary focus. There is also no need to be concerned with ritual purification of hands (and cups, pots, kettles and beds). At stake are purity laws and food laws. While the narrative begins with a dispute over particular Jewish applications of biblical law, effectively it ends up denying the principle of the biblical law itself. Treating external items as unclean is depicted as absurd. In the same spirit food laws are held up to ridicule: the food does nothing more than pass through the stomach and then into the toilet!

The stance represented by Mark's Jesus in 7:1–23 signifies a major break with Torah, especially if the attack on purity law is extended to such central matters as Israel's special identity and the temple. Mark's use of 7:1–23 within the composition of 6:6 – 8:26 shows that he was aware of the implications of this abrogation for determining the place of Gentiles in relation to Israel. In miniature the encounter with the Syrophoenician woman which immediately follows in 7:24–30 sets out Mark's stance. Israel's priority in salvation history is acknowledged ("first"), but all other barriers fall. The wider context illustrates this. The bread of Jesus is for Jew and Gentile alike. In 5:1–20 and 21–43 Mark had already used symbolism to juxtapose God's action in Jesus both in Gentile and Jewish land. But especially in constructing 6:7 – 8:26, with 7:1–23 at its centre, Mark demonstrates that he was aware that above all the clean - unclean barrier (especially in relation to food, but also hands, household items, and, not least, land) held Jew and Gentile apart. Jesus declared the barriers invalid. To say he abolishes or abrogates them is not enough, since his argument is based on showing that such things cannot have the value apportioned to them and, by implication, never did have. Yet Mark can have Jesus do this, without surrendering the sense of continuity implied in salvation history.

The stance of disregarding purity barriers probably also plays a role in 2:13–17, though the primary focus of the latter is Jesus' eating with immoral people. In the light of Mark's stance on purity, we may assume that Mark would have deemed any objections to Jesus' behaviour on purity grounds as irrelevant and invalid.

Mark's treatment of the temple theme also reflects the principles of 7:1–23. Primarily Mark has Jesus confront corruption and failure in the temple system. That still coheres with a stance of continuity, setting Jesus in line with prophets like Jeremiah, as we have seen. But there are three features which reflect the more fundamental critique of the cult itself. They are: the designation of the Jerusalem temple as one "made with hands"; the use of the scribe's contrast between the greatest commandments and sacrifices; and the ideal of the temple as a house of prayer (for all nations). In isolation each of these needs to be no more than a statement of relative priority, but taken in the broader Markan context they should be understood as denying the value of the cult system as a whole. This is confirmed by Mark's vision of the alternative: the community of faith and prayer. Mark might have used the last supper and the understanding of Jesus' death as vicarious polemically against the cult, but nothing indicates this.

Mark's portrait of Jesus' attitude towards the Law is coloured, therefore, not only by the absolute claims he makes for Jesus, but also by a distinctive value system. This set of values goes beyond the relative contrast between cultic or ceremonial law and ethical law which had been present in some of Mark's traditions and cohered with the biblical tradition of the prophets.[246]

---

[246] Cf. Hos 6:6 and related texts referred to above in discussing the two great commandments. See also on the inwardness of the Law: Jer 31:31–34; Ezek 18:31; 36:26; Sib Or 5:265–266; TBenj 5; Aristeas 168; Jub 1:22–25; Sir 2:16; 32:15; Wisd Sol 7:7; 9:17; 1QH 12:10; 13:11; 4Q504 2:13; 4Q434 fr. 2, 4:10–11; 4Q436 1:4–6; ApocAdEv 13:5–6; 4 Ez 3:20; Jos *Ap* I 178; on spiritualisation of the cultic: Sir 3:3, 30; 35:1–5; Arist 146–150; Judith 16:16; 1QS 5:6; 8:1–16; 9:3–6; Ps Phoc 228; 2 En 45; Sib Or 4:8–11; Jos *JW* 5:458; and on spiritualisation of circumcision: Deut 10:16; 30:6; Jub 1:22–25; 1QS 5:5; 1QH 10:7; 4Q434 1:4. Philo is careful to avoid exclusive antitheses in contrasting ritual and cultic laws and their symbolic value. He attacks insincerity and hypocrisy, demanding that outward acts be accompanied by inner repentance: *De Cher* 95–96; *Quod Det Pot* 20–21; *De Immut* 7–9; 102–103; *De Agric* 130; *De Plant* 107–108; *De Vit Mos* II 107–108. He also rails against 'superstition', which he frequently links with hypocrisy; e.g., *De Cher* 42; *Quod Det Pot* 24; *De Immut* 103, 164; *De Plant* 107. He can also speak disparagingly of meaningless rituals (e.g., *De Cher* 42) and of babbling (*De Cher* 48). He comes close to dispensing with the cult in arguing that "genuine worship is that of a soul bringing simple reality as its only sacrifice" (*Quod Det Pot* 21) and that God accepts the guiltless even if they offer no sacrifice (*De Plant* 108; similarly *De Vit Mos* II 108). Although he ridicules concern about clean animals and unblemished priests, it is always in the sense that such concerns, separate from inner purity, have no meaning. The same applies to his repeated assertions that no building of timber or stone suffices as a dwelling for God, eg., *De Cher* 99–100; *De Plant* 126. Here Philo shares the view that the universe is God's temple not only with Isa 64–66; Wisdom 13–14, but also with many philosophers of the period. H. W. Attridge, *First Century Cynicism in the Epistles of Heraclitus*, HarvTheolSt 29, (Scholars: Missoula, 1976), pp. 13–23, cites among others the fourth epistle of Heraclitus, Zeno, Seneca and Plutarch. Philo rejects those who emphasise the symbolic meaning and neglect the literal, perhaps even effectively

For Mark's Jesus it is not a matter of priorities, but a matter of absolute values. Purity laws and food laws are not just of lesser importance; they have no status, for such things cannot affect real purity, since they belong only to the external.[247] The same logic extends to the temple itself. It could be a place of prayer and worship, and as such, God's house, but nothing more than that. This rationalising stance, present already in Mark's tradition, defies not only many laws of Torah, but also major principles which underlie them and, beside his christology, forms the basis for Mark's understanding of Jesus' attitude towards the Law.

---

abrogate it (*De Migr Ab* 89–93). The only other direct evidence for a Judaism which dispenses with parts of Torah is found in Strabo XVI 2,35–39. See Klinghardt, *Gesetz*, pp. 288–293. It appears to derive from Hellenistic Jewish sources mid to late second century BCE. It contrasts Moses' foundation of the sacrificial cult, without elaborate processions, to the one God, at Jerusalem, with later developments through the priesthood which led to the introduction of practices based in "superstition": food laws, circumcision, excision and "such like". Mark is closer to those whom Philo attacks, but different since there is no sign that it is symbolism that drives Mark. He is closest to those influences which appear in Philo's use of "superstition" and are reflected in his still inclusive antitheses which nevertheless speak disparagingly of outward rituals (for Philo: on their own).

[247] For this kind of critique of religion as reflecting pagan thought of the time see the important overview of H. W. Attridge, "The Philosophical Critique of Religion under the Early Empire" in *Aufstieg und Niedergang der Römischen Welt II.16.1*, (Berlin: de Gruyter, 1978), pp. 45–78; see also his *First Century Cynicism*. He refers to the widespread reaction in many philosophers of the time against gory sacrifices and a preference for inwardness or seeing the world as a temple. Often this accompanied a stance in which the philosopher still participated in the cult, while holding radical views which spiritualised the significance of the rites. This can be seen in the contrast between the strong rejection of religion in Zeno, the Cynic Diogenes, Oenomaus of Gadara and Demonax with the more inclusive stance of Antisthenes, the letters of (pseudo-) Heraclitus, Dio Chrysostom, Epictetus and Seneca, and also Philo. Common criticisms included immorality at festivals, anthropomorphism and the immorality of the gods, the nature and effects attributed to sacrifices, the idea of providence, charlatanism, materiality of images and pointlessness of external rituals, and the neglect of ethics and individual piety, frequently associated with the idea of belonging in the world as God's temple. This is a generalising summary of a range of approaches; see Attridge for differentiated detail.

This kind of influence is evident in Philo. It is also found in Paul's letters (eg. Rom 2:12–16,25–29) and in Hebrews, where at times the inclusive antithesis between ritual and cultic law, on the one hand, and the spiritual is broken and the latter disparaged as dispensable. See also F. G. Downing, *Christ and the Cynics*, JSOT Manuals 4, (Sheffield: JSOT Pr., 1988), pp. 129–130; see also his "Law and custom: Luke-Acts and late Hellenism" in *Law and Religion. Essays on the Place of the Law in Israel and Early Christianity*, edited by B. Lindars, (Cambridge: Clarke, 1988), pp. 148–158, here: 154–155.

1.8.4 The Commandments

The stance of Mark's Jesus sets him at odds with much of Torah. Yet Mark stops a long way short of abandoning Torah altogether. Neither Mark's christology nor his rationalising dualism demanded a total abandonment of Torah. We have also noted the strong sense of continuity in Mark with God's actions in the past and with scripture. 7:1–23 illustrates well Mark's differentiated approach to Torah. For as well as having Jesus dismiss Torah requirements, it has Jesus use Torah against abuses associated with corban. Jesus cites the decalogue commandment about honouring parents. Then, as a contrast to the irrelevance of foods we eat, Mark highlights the relevance of evil attitudes flowing from within: "sexual immorality, theft, murder, adultery, greed, wickedness, deceit, licentiousness, the evil eye, slander, pride, stupidity" (7:21b–22). All are ethical; none, ritual or cultic. These are moral values, including a faint echo of the decalogue in the early items. It is clear, therefore, that Mark represents Jesus as at least espousing the moral commandments of the decalogue.[248]

This is confirmed in his account of Jesus' encounter with the rich man (10:17–21). Keeping the moral commandments of the decalogue, here loosely summarised, belongs to the essential requirements for those who seek eternal life. They are not optional or preparatory. For Mark, this means more than exact compliance with demands; it entails attitude and commitment. On the one hand, that means commitment to discipleship and the willingness to abandon wealth and give to the poor. On the other hand, it means letting one's life be determined by the two central principles of love for God and love for neighbour. 12:28–31 makes this clear. Mark has Jesus cite these as Torah commands. For Mark they are not a summary of the Law, as if they imply adherence to the whole Law in this spirit, since Mark's Jesus dismisses ceremonial and cultic law as irrelevant. Loving God has, for him, nothing to do with temple ritual of sacrifice and careful observance of purity provisions. Rather loving God and loving neighbour are made to function as a summary of what Mark's Jesus believes that God requires, including those demands of the Law which are still valid. They also provide the ethical foundation for the way he understands and interprets these demands. What they mean in practice is determined by the values already indicated:

---

248 So Dautzenberg, "Frühes Christentum," p. 245, who emphasises that Mark's Gentile Christianity, like that of the pre-, post-, and pauline communities, is concerned to uphold the ethical commands of Torah represented in the ten commandments and the two great commandments. Mark's Christianity is not ready to give up its Jewish heritage. See also his "Gesetzeskritik," pp. 56–58.

christology and rationalising dualism. Therefore to love God means also to follow Jesus. It does not mean to observe ritual and cultic law. To love others means to live morally in accord with the principles enunciated in the decalogue. But as 7:1–23 has shown, the focus is not compliance with commandments, but fulfilling them in accordance with the principle of caring for people.

Thus, within the framework provided by his dualism and by his upholding of the moral values of the decalogue, Mark sees the command to love as providing the fundamental ethical principle to be applied in concrete situations. This attitude informs Jesus' stance in his disputes in 2:1–12; 2:13–17; 2:22–28 and 3:1–6, his injunction to the rich man to sell all and give to the poor (10:17–22; cf. also 23–25) and, with a similar focus on use of wealth, his criticism of the scribes in 12:38–40.

The attitude of radical concern for people in need is striking and occurs mostly in the form of aphorisms. 2:9 ("Which is easier, to say to the paralytic, 'Your sins are forgiven,' or to say, 'Rise and take up your pallet and walk'?") cleverly poses an alternative which can be answered on two levels: ability and legality. The effect is to ridicule the assailants' preoccupation with legality and to focus on the right and the necessity to respond to a human being in need. 2:17a ("It is not the well who have need of a doctor, but rather the sick") is also a refusal to entertain an issue of Law (moral and, perhaps, ritual) by focusing instead on human need. 2:27 ("The sabbath is made for people, not people for the sabbath") also frustrates attempts to define appropriate legal behaviour on the sabbath. It appeals to an understanding which sees the sabbath as gift rather than demand. 3:4a ("Is it lawful on the sabbath to do good or to do harm?") is similar in its provocative assault on the interpreters. In effect it argues that human need must have highest priority in determining sabbath law.[249]

Such aphorisms appear in a number of Markan anecdotes and probably stem as such from tradition.[250] Mark's strong emphasis on Jesus as author-

---

[249] 10:9 probably also originates as a response to inner Jewish discussions of Law interpretation, rather than as a conclusion of an argument. Like the other aphorisms it probably functioned as a challenge to the process rather than as a ruling. Understood as a metaphor, "What God has yoked together let no human being separate", states the obvious: do not undo what God has done. It confronts concentration on undoing with the higher principle: what God has done and wills. It lent itself to becoming a ruling, and, with the added scriptural argument, became so in Mark's version.

[250] These include 2:1–12; 2:15–17; 2:23–28; 3:1–6; 7:1–23; 10:2–12 (cf. also 2:18–22; 12:13–17) and contain the following aphorisms:

"Which is easier, to say to the paralysed man, 'Your sins are forgiven,' or to say, 'Rise and take up your pallet and walk'?" (2:9).

ity causes a shift in the nature of Jesus' argument within many of these traditions.[251] Implicit appeals to human need (eg. 2:9; 2:17a; 2:27; 3:4a) become in Mark appeals to human need on Jesus' authority, which, in end
effect, become claims to Jesus as rival authority (2:10; 2;17b; 2:28). Mark
is ultimately not commending Jesus on grounds that his words and deeds are
good, though that is still present, but on grounds that he is the Son of God
and as such wields God's power and authority.

Within this framework individual commandments retain their divine authority. This is particularly evident in Jesus' teaching about divorce and
remarriage (10:2–12) and, indirectly, in the stance of John the Baptist to
Herod's marriage (6:18). In 10:2–12 Mark has Jesus appeal to God's will in
creation that the two be one flesh against the Mosaic provision of divorce.
10:11 (ἐπ᾽ αὐτήν, "against her") appears also to appeal to concern for the

---

"Those who are well have no need of doctor, but those who are sick" (2:17a).
"The sabbath was made for human beings, not human beings for the sabbath" (2:27).
"Is it lawful on the sabbath to do good or to do ill, to save life or to kill?" (3:4).
"There is nothing outside of a human being which going into them defiles them, but the
things coming out of a human being are what defile them" (7:15).
"What God has joined let no human being separate" (10:9).
"The things of Caesar give back to Caesar and things of God to God" (12:17).
"The wedding guests cannot fast while the bridegroom is with them" (2:19a).

All embody a contrast or alternative. All are clever aphorisms. In 2:27 and 10:9 this is
between human beings and God. Human beings also feature in 7:15. 2:9 and 3:4a pose
alternatives as a way of making a point. 2:17a is proverbial; perhaps also 2:19a. 2:27,
7:15 and 10:9 are categorical statements. 12:17 takes the form of a provocative exhortation. These aphorisms, with or without their anecdotal setting, reflect a consistent stance
of a very clever mind. They appeal, rather than declare. Their authority is self contained.
They have an 'off hand', almost casual, character in their dismissal of casuistry. They are
not rulings in Law and hardly go beyond provocative challenges to start again, but at least
they indicate a new starting point which is not inappropriately summed up in the modern
phrase, 'people matter most'. To claim too much for them as if they really deal with
matters of Law is absurd and unfair. People who make laws must take them into account,
but then their work has hardly begun.

251 Whoever added 2:10 has rendered 2:9 no longer a self contained argument. It is
overshadowed by a claim to authority. I am inclined to think that this is Mark's work here
and also in 2:17b, 2:28 and 3:4b. In 2:23–28 we find in addition to 2:28 the biblical
argument from precedent in 2:25–26, making the case that human need may justify setting
side sabbath law. It is not an abrogation of sabbath law, but an issue of its applicability.
Whoever added it understood the orientation of 2:27 (and 3:4a) well, but went beyond the
original meaning of 2:27 to stress need: David's men were hungry; by implication so were
the disciples. This changed the story, but also the nature of the argument. It is now an
argument by appeal to an external authority. We see the same process in 10:2–9 where the
provocative aphorism which contains its own argument has been supported by scriptural
argument, appeal to an external authority, which then, in effect, turns 10:9 into a ruling, to
which the floating logion about divorce and remarriage was subsequently attached, probably by Mark and certainly in a form edited by Mark.

wronged woman. The sharpness of the abrogation is blunted, however, by the assertion that the concession regarding divorce was aimed at hardening the Jews' hearts or alternatively was a concession because of their hardened hearts and, thus, by implication should be revoked. Here we see three sets of values combine: the prohibition of adultery, as in the decalogue; the appeal to God's intention; and concern for the wronged woman. These combine to counter the provision for divorce. The dualist criterion does not play a role. Mark argues within scripture, theologically. Scripture is not absolute; therefore he can have Jesus dismiss the divorce law as a concession or provocation. The nature of Jesus' argument does not suggest that it ever should have had validity, so that we should not read this as Jesus changing or abrogating law, so much as affirming part of the Law as valid and part as invalid, much as happens with the ceremonial and cultic law.

Mark's Jesus differentiates within Torah. Food laws, purity laws concerned with externals, the sacrificial cult – these are no longer accepted as Torah. More, they are denigrated as useless. On the positive side we have: the Torah command to love God, expressed, for instance, in prayer and in the new community of faith, but not, as in Torah, in adherence to cultic and ritual law; and we have the Torah command to love neighbour, understood universally as any human being, and expressed both in the ethical commands of the decalogue and in related ethical injunctions.

1.8.5 Loose ends

Loose ends remain. The sabbath commandment also belongs to the decalogue. In neither dispute concerning the sabbath (2:23–28 and 3:1–6) does Mark's Jesus indicate either dismissiveness or abrogation. Instead, he argues, broadly, that in the determination of sabbath law human need should be taken into account. It is not, however, left at that. Mark affirms: Jesus is Lord also of the sabbath (2:28). Yet neither this statement nor the preceding verse (the sabbath was made for people) implies that sabbath no longer matters for Mark. Rather, Jesus abrogates to himself the right to determine what is appropriate on the sabbath and enunciates the principle that the sabbath is primarily gift (2:27; 3:4).

Mark is silent about what constitutes sabbath observance for his community. He reports, without evaluative comment one way or other, the observance of sabbath by Joseph of Arimathea and the women in the preparation for Jesus' burial (15:42–47). Probably he would have reduced the command to what lies in the decalogue and not acknowledged the authority of further extrapolations in Torah, written or oral. He certainly shows no sign of sensing any problem in the activities on the sabbath in 1:21–34. The fact that he apparently operates with a Greco-Roman reckoning of days need not imply non observance. The problem with positing sabbath observance in Mark's community is that elsewhere temporal differentiations in terms of holiness are disparaged in the same category as spatial distinctions (cf. Gal 4:10). In the case of the sabbath and, at least, of the Passover, this does not appear to be Mark's stance.

It is uncertain to what extent Mark perceived in 2:1–12 a dispute about the Law. Its present focus is the charge of blasphemy, which for Mark is manifestly false, both here and in the Jewish trial. It is like the charge of exorcising demons by the power of Beelzebul (3:22–30), a major law issue, but for Mark without foundation and therefore irrelevant for discussing Mark's view of Jesus' attitude towards Torah. Associated with it, however, may also be the sense that Jesus acts outside established authority. Mark was aware that this was an issue also with John the Baptist. Mark, in any case, has Jesus dispute the attempt to imply some monopoly in relation to declaring God's forgiveness which would exclude himself (and John) and with his aphorism urges that healing the sick and declaring God's forgiveness should be on the same level. Ultimately the aphorism is arguing that human need should determine appropriate behaviour not institutional authorisation. In Mark's story, Jesus' claim to authorisation as Son of Man, makes the christological claim paramount. It still would imply disputing any temple monopoly in the matter, but it is not clear that Mark would have perceived this as a conflict with Torah (which, in reality, it was not).

Another loose end is Mark's attitude towards leprosy. Is a leper still 'unclean' for Mark, in accordance with Torah? This might appear to be so, especially since Mark's Jesus enjoins that the man obey Torah provisions by going to the priest and making an offering. There are two issues here, leprosy as unclean and use of the temple cult. As we saw, it is unlikely that Mark sees this as a mere ploy, just using the ritual to get at the priests. It is more likely that Mark still acknowledges that lepers were a problem in society (though not "unclean" in ritual terms) and treats the Mosaic provision as a rite for reintegration. Mark intends to set Jesus in a good light in relation to Torah before the controversies which follow.

A final loose end is Mark's intercalation of the healing of the bleeding woman within the story of Jairus' daughter. In doing this Mark seems to have been aware of the woman's uncleanness according to Jewish law, since his language reflects the relevant passages in Leviticus. Making the intercalation shows an awareness that her being healed was like a resurrection. Does this mean that Mark sees Jesus making her ritually clean whereas before she was ritually unclean? This would imply Markan adherence to this aspect of the purity code. Would not Mark have believed that such barriers were invalid? But if he did, does that not make nonsense of what his inter-calation achieves? In fact, it does not. For there is some evidence that non Jewish cultures might also marginalise her; but, more to the point, just her continuing history of suffering, which is all that Mark emphasises, makes sense of the intercalation: she is restored to life. Mark does not have to adhere to Jewish purity law to appreciate what the healing would mean for her and probably did not. His narrative, aside from the possible allusions to Leviticus, which may, in any case, be drawn from his tradition, shows no interest in the many purity issues which the intercalated stories raise. He describes her plight primarily in terms of physical distress, not ritual es-trangement. For Mark, we may assume purity barriers with regard to women were no longer applicable and this may well also be reflected, indirectly, in his rather belated note in the passion narrative that women had been in Je-sus' companions from the beginning (15:40–41).

In discussing this final loose end we encountered an area of eloquent silence, already noted in discussing assumptions of hearers about continu-ity. Was Mark aware of all the purity issues involved in the intercalated stories? If so, did he simply ignore them as irrelevant? Or was he ignorant? The issue also arises with the preceding episode: the healing of the demo-niac at Gerasa which is shot through with Jewish ethos in relation to purity (pigs, cemeteries, Gentile land, unclean spirit). Mark's sensitivity to the barrier issues in his major composition, 6:6 – 8:26, and his extensive famili-arity with the Old Testament stories, make it likely that he was not ignorant. Instead he chose to ignore them because they were not (for him, personally, in all likelihood, no longer) relevant. The silence is eloquent, because we may assume that Mark knew that Jesus would have been placing himself in danger of impurity, but deliberately chose to ignore it.

1.8.6 Conclusion

For Mark, then, Jesus is the absolute authority under God. He stands in continuity with God's action of old, recorded in the scriptures. His own deeds echo God's deeds in the past and he fulfils scripture prophecy. Yet with regard to the Law he differentiates. The authority for this differentia-tion is given in Mark's christology. The basis for the differentiation is a rationalising dualism which denies ritual and cultic law as having to do with externals such as food and outward purifications and belonging to a temple made with hands. Above all Mark's composition in 6:7 – 8:26 and his treatment of the temple motif after chapter 11 reflects this value system and show that Mark had a direct interest in addressing the issues.[252] This has come through strongly as a result of the sequential compositional analysis and deserves greater attention. Mark represents Jesus not as abrogating such law, but as dismissing its value altogether. He is not, therefore, concerned with distinguishing written and oral law. Jesus' authority and the dualistic criterion apply equally to both. What remains is love for God, expressed in the community of faith, the new temple, which fulfils the temple's original purpose of being a house of prayer for all nations (and only that), and love for neighbour. The latter is associated with the ethical values of the decalogue interpreted in a way which emphasises inner attitude as well as behaviour and the discernment of God original will and intention.

Beside this Mark appears to assume sabbath observance, but as God had originally intended as determined by Jesus. Mark apparently has no difficulty retaining traits of Jesus' Jewishness (attendance in the synagogue, travel to the temple, celebration of the passover, even initial hesitancy about the leper and rebuff of a Gentile, and using temple provisions for reintegration of lepers into society). Mark probably knew and assumed much more about Jesus' Jewishness; his silence probably reflects his view that much observance was irrelevant to true religion. There is no indication, on the other hand, that he bedevilled ritual and cultic observance and the temple. He does not have Jesus attack it as idolatrous or demonic, but only as without relevance for true holiness. Nor does he pursue a thoroughgoing disparagement of all ritual and ceremony as such: he assumes the worth of, at least, John's baptism, probably knows the celebration of the Lord's Supper as a rite and has no compunction in reporting Jesus' intention to celebrate the Passover.

Mark's approach raises theological issues, which he shows no signs of addressing. His Jesus dismisses much of the Law. Abrogation might have been easier to deal with. Then one could propose that God had given interim laws, now to be put aside by better laws; but that is not the character of his argument. Jesus dismisses their value altogether. How then did they come to be in Torah? It is unlikely that Mark saw them as demonic in origin or as bad laws given deliberately by God (cf. Ezek 20:5). As we have already noted, he never has Jesus attack them in this way. Only in relation to divorce law might Mark have such a thing in mind, where he has Jesus de-

---

[252] Dautzenberg, "Frühes Christentum," p. 245, argues that Mark's community would most likely include former God fearers for whom matters of Jewish Law which fascinated the pagan world such as sabbath and food laws could not be passed over.

clare the provision either a concession to human weakness or a provocation. But this is far from certain and nothing indicates that Mark saw other laws as provocations. The idea is not unlike one of Paul's lines of thought about the Law (Gal 3:19; Rom 5:20). But it is not so applicable to ritual and cultic law.

With regard to the temple and temple sacrifices Hebrews develops an explanation based on seeing the cultic law as given by God to provide a foretaste and a shadow of the true heavenly temple and truly effective sacrifice to be achieved by Christ. Mark shows no signs of doing this with regard to Jesus' death as a sacrifice or to any other aspect. For him the new temple is the community of faith, not the temple in heaven. The logic of Mark's position demands that he would see ritual and cultic law as given by God, but he offers no clue as to purpose. Clearly he must have differentiated what was valid within Torah from what never had validity. Mark is more in tune with those portions of Hebrews that portray cultic law as worthless (7:18; 9:13–14).

Mark, like Paul and Hebrews, has crossed the line from inclusive antitheses to exclusive antitheses. This move sanctions the jettisoning of much of Torah. The authority for the move is christological, but the ideology which informs it derives from rationalising critique of religion in the Hellenistic world of the time. Mark stands under this influence, and expresses it in his own distinctive way. The move doubtless also reflects the story of Mark's community. Inclusiveness has become a hermeneutical criterion, as it had for Paul. It stems from the love which Mark affirms. Combined with an ideological critique of religion, it offers a fascinating model for interpreting scripture in the cross-cultural context in any age, where established, even divinely sanctioned, categories of exclusion are called into question. One can extend a Markan perspective on scripture from inclusion of Gentiles to inclusion of many others, excluded on grounds of their social status (slaves), gender, race, age, sexual orientation or disability.

The move provokes theological issues which Mark leaves unaddressed and will find resolution for some in an even stronger dualism (Mark is the preferred gospel among gnostics) and for others (not least, Matthew and Luke) in a desperate attempt to reaffirm the Law's integrity.

Chapter 2

Jesus' Attitude towards the Law according to Matthew

2.1 Recent Research

The literature related to Jesus' attitude towards the Law in Matthew is extensive. Mostly the theme features as part of a wider study; this is symptomatic of the nature of the material. Thus one can expect in a treatment of Matthew's christology or ethics or relation to Judaism some treatment of the Law theme. Conversely to treat the Law without reference to these themes misses important connections. It is significant that Gerhard Barth's major treatment of the Law appears in one volume together with the redactional studies by Bornkamm on eschatology and ecclesiology, and by Held on miracles.[1]

Barth begins his study of Law in Matthew by drawing attention to the central significance of the theme of judgement in Matthew, by which Matthew has Jesus underline the importance of doing God's will (pp. 54–58).[2] He sees Matthew expounding Torah on two fronts. One front is against lax Christians who believe the Law has been abolished or modified (7:15–23; 24:10–11). With this in mind he has Jesus strike out against any suggestion that Torah has lost validity. The other front is against rabbinic casuistry. In response, Matthew emphasises that Jesus maintains the validity of the Law and has Jesus expound the centrality of love in interpreting Torah (Barth refers especially to 22:34–40; 12:9–14; 7:12; 23:23; 12:1–8; 18:12–35; pp. 58–88, 149–154). In developing this response, Matthew shows Jesus as not

---

[1] G. Barth, "Das Gesetzesverständnis des Evangelisten Matthäus," in G. Bornkamm, G. Barth, H. J. Held, *Überlieferung und Auslegung im Matthäusevangelium*, WMANT 1, (Neukirchen-Vluyn: Neukirchener, 1960, 2nd edn, 1970, expanded with Bornkamm's article on Mt 28:16–20), pp. 54–154; English: G. Barth, "Matthew's Understanding of the Law," in: G. Bornkamm, G. Barth, H. J. Held, *Tradition and Interpretation in Matthew*, (London: SCM, 1963, 2nd edn, 1982), pp. 58–164.

entirely rejecting rabbinic tradition, but rather differing concerning the basis for interpretation. Thus sabbath is practised, but not in the rabbinic mode of strictness; and purity laws apply, but are given less priority than inward purity (pp. 83–86). Yet in the context of confrontation of his rabbinic opponents, Matthew has Jesus go so far as even to abrogate certain Old Testament commandments (Barth cites here the fifth antithesis, 5:38–39, on retaliation; pp. 86–88).

Beside the demand of the Law is the call to discipleship which, Barth argues, effectively also interprets the Law and sets it within the call to perfection, not primarily in an ethical sense, but as following the way of the suffering Jesus (pp. 88–98). Discipleship and radical fulfilment of the Law become one and the same thing (p. 96). Accordingly, Matthew's christology includes the notion that Jesus came to effect God's will, God's righteousness; he expresses it in his love and lowliness; the Law belongs within that greater whole (pp. 96–98, 117–143). It is not replaced by a new or messianic law (pp. 143–149).[3]

Barth's treatment raised important issues. It began with judgement and ended with christology. I hope to show that these belong even more closely together conceptually than Barth has shown. His treatment also brought out the tension between the authority of Law and christology which would dominate research in the area. Does one totally integrate the other? Are there abrogations? Would this have mattered to Matthew?

Reinhard Hummel[4] argues that Matthew's gospel reflects a developing Christian *halakah* within his community, evident in his tendency to justify Jesus' approach by reference to scriptural argument. "Matthew's church has it own Christian *halakah*, alongside the Pharisaic; its own rules for community and devotion, alongside the Jewish ones; its own tradition of the Law beside that of the rabbis; its own church discipline, while it is still itself subject to Pharisaic jurisdiction; its own teaching authority, which it sets beside the seat of Moses, on which the 'scribes and Pharisees' sit."[5] Like Barth, he

---

[2] In doing so he draws attention to Bornkamm's contribution to the same volume, "Enderwartung und Kirche im Matthäusevangelium," pp. 13–47.

[3] In this he responds to the earlier work of B. W. Bacon, "Jesus and the Law. A Study of the First 'Book' of Matthew (Mt 3–7)," *JBL* 47 (1928), pp. 203–231; and, earlier still, J. Wellhausen and J. Weiss (Barth, "Gesetzesauslegung," p. 143 n. 1). See also G. D. Kilpatrick, *The Origins of the Gospel According to St. Matthew*, (Oxford: Clarendon, 1946).

[4] R. Hummel, *Die Auseinandersetzung zwischen Kirche und Judentum im Matthäusevangelium*, BETh 33, (Munich: Kaiser, 1966).

[5] Hummel, *Auseinandersetzung*, p. 64. "Die Kirche des Matthäus hat ihren eigenen, christlichen Halachoth neben den pharisäischen, ihre eigene Gemeinde- und Frömmigkeitsregeln neben den jüdischen, ihre eigene Gesetzestradition neben der der

sees 5:17–20 as, in part, directed against antinomists, and designed to underline the validity of Torah. Without νόμος there is only ἀνομία (p. 69). The antitheses are directed against Torah as understood by the rabbis. Thus Hummel gives full weight to 5:20, "Unless your righteousness exceeds that of the scribes and Pharisees you shall not enter the kingdom of heaven." Like Barth, he sees only the fifth antithesis (on retaliation) abrogating a provision of Torah, and that, under the influence of the love command (pp. 72–73). Matthew does not reduce Torah to the command of love, as Schweizer had suggested.[6] Matthew even allows some rabbinic *halakah* to stand (23:23).

According to Hummel, in taking over traditions in 23:16–22; 5:23–24; and 8:4, Matthew exhibits a conservative, positive stance towards the temple (pp. 78–82). Its destruction is an eschatological event because of the guilt of Judaism in crucifying Jesus and in rejecting the church (pp. 85–90). As Messiah, Jesus is Lord of the temple (12:6; pp. 90–94). But Matthew does not attack the cult as such. Nor does he spiritualise it. Hosea 6:6 is used not against the temple, but "against those who, even after the catastrophe, have not yet grasped that the temple has been eschatologically taken over and overcome through the Messiah, the sacrificial cult, through the love command".[7] Matthew understands neither 20:28 ("The Son of Man did not come to be served, but to serve and to give his life a ransom for many") nor 26:28 ("This is my blood of the covenant poured out for many for the forgiveness of sins") in sacrificial terms. For forgiveness is the fruit of the authority of Jesus, also given to the community (9:9), and based on the love command (pp. 101–103). Matthew sees unbelieving Israel as cut off from its traditions; its past has become the tradition of the church (p. 150). The radical interpretation of Torah, through linking it with discipleship, has the effect of destroying the narrow definition of Israel and opening it to Gentiles. Individual Jews must decide between Pharisaism and the church. Matthew assumes a periodising which distinguishes Jesus' earthly ministry to Israel from the post Easter mission of the disciples to the Gentiles (pp. 141–142).

Hummel has thus pushed the line of Barth in locating Matthew and his

---

Rabbinen, ihre eigene Kirchenzucht, während sie selbst noch unter pharisäischer Jurisdiktion steht, ihre eigene Lehrgewalt, die sie neben den Lehrstuhl des Moses stellt, auf dem die 'Schriftgelehrten und Pharisäer' sitzen."

[6] E. Schweizer, "Matthäus 5,17–20 – Anmerkungen zum Gesetzesverständnis des Matthäus," *TheolLitZ* 77 (1952), pp. 479–484.

[7] Hummel, *Auseinandersetzung*, p. 100, "gegen diejenigen, welche auch nach der Katastrophe noch nicht begriffen haben, dass der Tempel durch den Messias und der Opferkult durch das Liebesgebot eschatologisch überholt und überwunden sind."

community in close proximity to Judaism still further. Hummel saw that relationship as being of a kind that dialogue, or, at least, justification, can take place, in part, on their terms (*halakah*). At the same time others, like Strecker and Walker, were pushing in the opposite direction, arguing that separation from Judaism lay well in the past and that consequently the issue of authority was clearly resolved along the lines that Jesus alone was the authority; thus he could quite readily uphold or abrogate Torah.[8] Hummel's comments about the temple raise important issues, especially since cultic law is so important within Torah. How can one supersede cultic law and yet still argue by *halakah*? How does argument by *halakah* relate then to the strongly christological arguments which he assumes in expounding the replacement of the temple? Is the role of christology in Matthew's understanding of the law being given sufficient weight? One of the problems for Hummel is that the actual evidence in Matthew for halakic argument is limited to only a handful of passages. Nevertheless the presence of such argumentation at all on the lips of Matthew's Jesus raises important questions about the way Jesus saw the Law.

Hübner[9] argues that Matthew believes fulfilment includes modification. He sees this illustrated in the command to love enemies. In his view, this command, together with the positive formulation of the golden rule, implies criticism of the content of Torah. Hübner speaks directly of conscious abrogation (pp. 196–197). Accordingly, Matthew's Jesus is not for the Law for its own sake, but interprets Law on this basis. He uses the idea of reward to torpedo contemporary Pharisaic-legalistic notions of merit (p. 205). Matching a tendency among the prophets, Jesus stands over the Law (p. 202). According to Hübner, 28:18 and 11:27 show that Jesus' authority from God is to be identified primarily in his teaching (pp. 198–201). Miracles and scripture references function to confirm this.

Nevertheless, wherever possible, Matthew also waters down tradition which is critical of the Law (for instance, Mark 7 and Matt 11:13) and seeks to convey a positive attitude towards the Law on the part of Jesus (eg. 22:36,40 cf. Mark 12:28). Thus Hübner highlights tension which exists within Matthew: Matthew incorporates traditions critical of the law, and traditions,

---

[8] G. Strecker, *Der Weg der Gerechtigkeit. Untersuchung zur Theologie des Matthäus*, FRLANT 82, (Göttingen: Vandenhoeck und Ruprecht, 1962, 3rd edn, 1971); R. Walker, *Die Heilsgeschichte im ersten Evangelium*, FRLANT 91, (Göttingen: Vandenhoeck und Ruprecht, 1967) and see the discussion of this trend in G. N. Stanton, *A Gospel for a New People*, (Edinburgh: T&T Clark, 1992), pp. 131–142.

[9] Hübner, *Gesetz*.

like 5:18, "rejudaising" the Jesus tradition, as he puts it (p. 196), and does so without smoothing out all the differences. Overall, however, Hübner believes that Matthew's tendency is to reverse the rejudaising trend and to see the issue of Jewish Gentile and Jewish Christian relations as a thing of the past (p. 206). Thus Hübner concludes: "To interpret Matthew on the basis of 5:18 should really be a thing of the past! By contrast, however, it is going too far and contradicts the balancing tendency of the first gospel, to describe him as a 'radical antinomian' (Walker)."[10] Hübner's work raises acutely the issue of the significance of such traditions within Matthew's portrait of Jesus.

Frankemölle argues that Matthew's understanding of Torah is similar to that of Deuteronomy.[11] Torah is primarily the revelation of God's will and describes not the preconditions of the covenant, but the covenant relationship itself (p. 299). Matthew, therefore, has Jesus appeal to covenant principles. In these love is central and focuses on inwardness (cf. Deut 6:5; 7:9; 10:12; 26:16; p. 302). Jesus does not replace or suspend the Law; nor does he reject scribes and scribal tradition (so 23:2–3), as long as it conforms to right teaching (pp. 294–295). Rather he is its authorised end-time interpreter. His gospel of the kingdom is the proclamation of God's will and at the same time the hermeneutical criterion of all *halakoth* (p. 304). The evidence for the covenant link is, however, not strong. It does nevertheless point to one possible resolution: that in Jesus the eschatologically new justifies the reinterpretation of the old.

To this general tendency belongs the line of interpretation, according to which Matthew sees Jesus as the messianic interpreter of the Law.[12] The

---

10 "Mt von Mt 5,18 aus zu interpretieren sollte eigentlich der Vergangenheit angehören! Demgegenüber ist es aber völlig überspitzt und widerspricht der ausgleichenden Tendenz des ersten Evangelisten, diesen als 'radikalen Antinomisten' zu bezeichnen (*Walker*)." Hübner, *Gesetz*, p. 206.

11 H. Frankemölle, *Jahwebund und Kirche Christi. Studien zur Form- und Traditionsgeschichte des 'Evangelium' nach Matthäus*, NTAbh 10, (Münster: Aschendorff, 1974), p. 294.

12 On this see H.-W. Kuhn, "Das Liebesgebot Jesu als Tora und als Evangelium. Zur Feindesliebe und zur christlichen und jüdischen Auslegung der Bergpredigt," in *Vom Urchristentum zu Jesus. Für Joachim Gnilka*, edited by H. Frankemölle and K. Kertelge, (Freiburg: Herder, 1989), pp. 194–230, 218, who points to P. Schäfer's article, "Die Torah der messianischen Zeit," in *Studien zur Geschichte und Theologie des rabbinischen Judentums*, AGJU 15, (Leiden: Brill, 1978), pp. 198–213; see also R. Mohrlang, *Matthew and Paul. A Comparison of Ethical Perspectives*, SNTSMS 48, (Cambridge: CUP, 1984), pp. 23–25; D. C. Allison, *The New Moses. A Matthean Typology*, (Minneapolis: Fortress, 1993), pp. 185–190, 320–323; and earlier: W. D. Davies, *Torah in the Messianic Age and/ or Age to Come*, JBLMonSer 8, (Philadelphia: SBL, 1952).

question is then to what extent such an expectation entailed the notion that the Messiah would also abrogate Law. Another approach is to focus on the prophetic aspect of fulfilment. Thus Trilling[13] argued that for Matthew the normative function of the Law and the Prophets remained in force, only the predictive function (11:13) ceased. The "fulfilment" idea was a magic key that enabled Matthew to deal with continuity and discontinuity. Sand[14] argued that the linking of the Law with the prophets indicated that Matthew understood the Law only as interpreted in the prophets. However this disjunction does not easily fit 7:12; 22:40; 11:13. Banks sees Jesus effectively fulfilling and so replacing the Law in his ministry; his attacks are not on written, but oral law.[15] Can such a distinction be maintained? Meier[16] says the Law came to an end in Jesus' death and resurrection. But does this sit well with 5:18, 20 or 23:2–3, which appear to assume ongoing validity of the Law?

Suggs[17] argues that for Matthew Jesus is Torah. This resolves the tensions which arise between the claims of 5:18–19 and the antitheses (pp. 113–114). There is, therefore, no need to appeal to inconsistency on Matthew's part in not being aware of tensions among the traditions which he uses.[18] "Matthew knows no problem at all because he appeals *always* to the Torah even when he appears to contradict it. For him, Jesus is Wisdom-Torah" (p. 114). Jesus is the Torah present where two or three are gathered together in his name (18:20). Suggs appeals to *mAboth* 3:2, "When two sit (together) and there are words of Torah between them, there the Shekinah sojourns between them" (p. 115). The tension still remains, however, and, in one sense, becomes

---

[13] W. Trilling, *Das wahre Israel. Studien zur Theologie des Matthäus-Evangeliums*, SANT 10, (Munich: Kösel, 3rd edn, 1964), p. 160. He also believed that according to Matthew Israel's rejection of the Messiah resulted in the church becoming the true Israel (referring especially to 21:43; 27:25). K. Syreeni, *The Making of the Sermon on the Mount. A procedural analysis of Matthew's redactoral activity. Vol 1*, AASF.DHL 44, (Helsinki: Suomalainen Tiedeakatemia, 1987), pp. 188–189, 194–196, also argues that "fulfil" is the key and combined with Matthew's use of "law and the prophets" for the Law, and the formula quotations, effectively enabled Matthew to hold two things together, thus affirming no change yet a radicalised understanding of Law.

[14] A. Sand, *Das Gesetz und die Propheten. Untersuchung zur Theologie des Evangeliums nach Matthäus*, BU 11, (Regensburg: Pustet, 1974), pp. 188–189.

[15] Banks, *Law*, pp. 217–218; "Matthew's understanding of the Law," pp. 235–238.

[16] J. P. Meier, *Law and History in Matthew's Gospel. A Redactional Study of Mt 5:17–48*, AnBib 71, (Rome: PontBibInstPr., 1976), pp. 89, 168.

[17] M. J. Suggs, *Wisdom, Christology, and Law in Matthew's Gospel,* (Cambridge, MA: Harvard Univ, 1970).

[18] Here he attacks Bornkamm ("Enderwartung," pp. 22–23).

even more acute: how can Torah incarnate negate itself? And does Matthew really make such an identification?

Mohrlang[19] argues that for Matthew the whole Law remains valid (p. 9). His approach resembles that of Barth and Hummel in many respects. Thus he argues that Matthew is not for written law and against oral law, since this would contradict 23:23 (p. 14). Mohrlang also confronts the widespread tendency to explain away the conservative elements in Matthew as tradition which Matthew would not have taken seriously (especially in relation to 23:2–3 and 23:23).[20] He suggests that Matthew's focus was on the hypocrisy of the scribes and Pharisees, not so much their teaching. With regard to these references, he writes: "I judge that their presence in the text is very likely a hint of his basic respect for the scribal function of interpreting the Mosaic law, and an acknowledgment of the need for oral tradition in general" (p. 14). He draws attention to evidence of Christian scribes within the community (13:52; 23:34; p. 15). At the same time he acknowledges a tension which these statements produce with others in the gospel, which Matthew may or may not have reconciled (p. 14; see also p. 22).

According to Mohrlang, the antitheses are directed against prevailing interpretations of Torah, not Torah itself (pp. 19–20), especially against Pharisaic interpretations. On the whole, like Barth and Hummel, he sees Matthew "waging battle on two fronts: on the one side, against some unspecified antinomian threat or charge; and on the other, against the misplaced priorities of the Pharisees. With regard to the former, he defends the abiding validity of the entire law; with regard to the latter, he emphasises the right interpretation of the law – even though this leads him at times to contradict not only parts of the scribal tradition but also individual commandments of Torah itself" (p. 22).

He notes Suggs's claim that the inconsistency is to be resolved by seeing that Matthew understands Jesus himself as Torah incarnate and suggests that, at least, something like this provides an explanation, but more along the lines that Matthew saw Jesus as Messiah, Lord and Son of God (p. 23). With regard to christology, he deems that there is too little evidence to say that Matthew viewed Jesus as a new Moses (p. 23). "The crucial point is this: Matthew presents Jesus not as a new lawgiver, but as the giver of a new interpretation of the law" (p. 24). "And yet, Jesus is much more to Matthew

---

[19] R. Mohrlang, *Matthew and Paul. A Comparison of Ethical Perspectives*, SNTSMS 48, (Cambridge: CUP, 1984).

[20] Mohrlang, *Matthew*, 14; cf. Trilling, *Israel*, pp. 211, 215; Strecker, *Gerechtigkeit*, pp. 34–35.

than just the authoritative interpreter of Torah . . . he is *Lord*, the Messiah, the Son of God" (p. 25). Jesus' teaching is not referred to primarily under the category of νόμος. Against Hummel, he disputes that Matthew's approach is primarily *halakah*, because too little of Jesus' teaching in Matthew resembles *halakah*, though some is present. Jesus' compassion oriented yoke is light, even with its emphasis on radical obedience to the deepest intent of the Law (p. 26).

Vouga[21] notes that Matthew removes the Markan idea of Christ alone as authority and reinstates the validity of Torah (p. 179). Generally Matthew understands the Law as the normative expression of God's will. Matthew employs the following criteria for interpreting the Law: mercy, as attested in the practice of Jesus; the second table of the decalogue; the will of the creator and the double command of love. Sabbath and ritual purity laws are not abolished, but made subordinate to ethics (pp. 182–183, 255).

In the view of Amy-Jill Levine[22] Law is still in effect for Matthew, not abrogated (pp. 160, 180–181); that includes circumcision (pp. 182–184). Matthew uses a salvation historical schema according to which Jesus' mission is first confined to Israel, and after Easter expanded to Gentiles.[23] Matthew's primary concern is however not ethnicity but position; he is countering a centralised elite and advocating inclusiveness.[24] With regard to the Law, it remains in force even for the Gentiles. She finds evidence for Gentiles upholding the full Law in Antioch in Paul's letters (p. 185). Matthew's concern (e.g., in 12:1–14) is correct interpretation, not abrogation, of Law

---

[21] Vouga, *Loi*.

[22] A.-J. Levine, *The social and ethnic dimensions of Matthean Salvation History. "Go nowhere among the Gentiles . . ."* (Matt 10:5b, Studies in the Bible and Early Christianity 14, (Lewiston: Mellen, 1988)

[23] Thus references to Gentiles (Ruth, Rahab, the magi, the centurion, the Canaanite woman) are merely anticipatory in Matthew; they do not become disciples (Levine, *Salvation History*, p. 165). In the cleansing of the temple Matthew omits the words "for all Gentiles" (p. 170). Matthew is not interested in Gentile-Jewish ethnicity issues. He tones down Gentile references in the healing of the Gadarene demoniacs, has Jesus reaffirm the restriction of the mission in relation to the Canaanite woman, deletes Jesus' tour through Gentile territory, and deletes reference to Jairus' synagogue connections (pp. 112, 120, 133–151). Only with the great commission does the gospel extend to Gentiles. She argues that in 28:19 ἔθνη means Gentiles, but that this should be understood as an extension of the mission to Israel, not its replacement (pp. 14, 43, 180–196). The result is that Jews and Gentiles are set on an equal footing; a separate Israel "ceases to exist in the gospel's purview" (p. 242).

[24] Jesus turns to the marginalised: women, lepers, toll collectors, sinners. She notes a progression in 8:1–15 from Jewish man to Gentile man to Jewish woman (leper, centurion, Peter's mother-in-law), all excluded from the cult (Levine, *Salvation History*, p. 122). The sons of the kingdom in 8:11–12 are a socio-economic reference to those in power, not

(pp. 38, 248–249). He also portrays Jesus as faithful to the majority of Pharisaic traditions (p. 160). He acknowledges that the scribes sit on Moses' seat, but requires that all pronouncements be measured according to the principle of mercy rather than sacrifice (p. 248).

Matthew is concerned to reject claims for Jerusalem as the centre as the personification of elitism (p. 100). "The tearing of the veil indicates that the Jewish cultus will cede its authority to the non centralised, non hierarchical church; it portends the ultimate demolition of spatial boundaries" (p. 168). The sacred space is where the disciples gather (p. 100). A tension remains: how would Matthew reconcile upholding Torah with such an attitude towards the temple and space which is to a large degree enshrined in Torah?

Also setting Matthew within a strongly Jewish context, and therefore as Torah observant, is Overman.[25] He makes the point that within the Judaism of the period we are considering, "The law emerged as both the common ground and battleground between competing factions and communities. It was by means of the law that the sectarian communities were able to legitimate their own position and denounce that of their adversaries" (p. 24). According to Overman, "Matthew's community accurately lives out the law" (p. 89), despite the charges of their opponents to the contrary. It is "a sectarian community, as evidenced by its hostility toward the parent group in its setting, by its developing internal structure, and by its suspicious view of the civil realm and those outside the group" (p. 107; see also pp. 106–140). 23:2–3 shows that the scribes and the Pharisees have power in the broader Matthean community setting (p. 145). It is "mostly, if not thoroughly, Jewish but in the process of turning to the wider Gentile world" (p. 158), a community located most plausibly in Tiberias or Sepphoris (p. 159).

Affirming Overman's findings about Matthew's Jewishness and stance on the Law is Alan Segal.[26] He notes, however, that Matthew "does not completely ignore Jesus' criticism of the law" (p. 7). Matthew 15 is more than an attack on Pharisee values, because purity laws were special also for

---

to ethnic Israel (pp. 126–127). Israel does not reject Jesus; individual Jews (like individual Gentiles) and, above all, Jewish leaders, do, especially those defending the status quo from a position of power (pp. 217, 260–263). "Their" synagogues is an indication of rejection of townspeople, not of Israel (pp. 156–157). The focus is not ethnicity, but position (pp. 94–95). Even 27:25 ("the Jews") still allows lots of exceptions (p. 268).

[25] J. A. Overman, *Matthew's Gospel and Formative Judaism. The Social World of the Matthean Community*, (Minneapolis: Fortress, 1990).

[26] A. F. Segal, "Matthew's Jewish Voice," in *The Social History of the Matthean Community. Cross-Disciplinary Approaches*, edited by D. L. Balch, (Minneapolis: Fortress, 1991), pp. 3–37.

many others. He suggests that "it is not clear that the sentiments he articulates would have cast his community outside of Judaism. Rather it seems likely that the sentiments he articulates could have had a place within Hellenistic Judaism. Sociologically, then, we should think of Matthew's community as a rather left-wing one in terms of obedience to Torah. But it is not one that claims to be beyond Jewish law entirely, as is Paul's" (p. 7). Segal sees Matthew's position as heir to Peter's compromising position in Jewish communities over eating with Gentiles, which is in turn reflected in Peter's response in Gal 2 (pp. 14–23). Matthew wards off Paulinists on the one side and overly strict Jewish Christianity on the other: Christian Pharisaism (p. 22). He assumes circumcision is no longer demanded in the Matthean community in the light of Acts 15. Matthean Christians might have remained within Judaism and their stance on the Law fitted within the spectrum of Jewish law observance (p. 31).

Matthew's gospel reflects, however, a growing rift with the emerging rabbinic leadership (p. 32). "The hostility to Pharisees one sees in the First Gospel provides one piece of evidence that Christians were still concerned with what was happening in Jewish communities and synagogues, still found there, and greatly vexed by some of the positions they heard from Christian Pharisees inside and outside of synagogues" (p. 35). Segal also refers to rabbinic traditions of concern about the teaching of two powers in heaven as indicative of rabbinic polemics against Christians (pp. 32, 36). He sees 21:33–45 and 27:15–26 as suggesting a replacement theology, though not necessarily demanding a complete separation from Judaism (p. 37). Thus Segal shows greater sensitivity than does Overman to the tensions. His approach raises the issue whether Matthew is responding to Christian Pharisees.

Wong[27] argues that the different tendencies identified in Matthew are to be explained not by Matthew's preservation of older traditions, but by a strategy of including divergent stances to enable both Gentile and Jews in his community to feel at home. Accordingly Matthew begins the sermon on the mount with a particularist, Israel-oriented section (5:17–20), and concludes it with a universalising of Torah in the golden rule (7:12; pp. 33, 36–52). Matthew has used the word, πληρῶσαι, deliberately to enable Christian Jews to read it as upholding the validity of Torah and to enable Christian Gentiles to read it differently, as something Jesus has fulfilled (p.

---

[27] Kun-Chun Wong, *Interkulturelle Theologie und multikulturelle Gemeinde im Matthäusevangelium: zum Verhältnis von Juden- und Heidenchristen im Matthäusevangelium*, (Freiburg, Switzerland: Universitätsverlag; Göttingen: Vandenhoeck und Ruprecht, 1992).

42). He sees a similar deliberate ambiguity in ἕως ἂν πάντα γένηται ("until all things happen/are done" 5:18; p. 43). Correspondingly Wong seeks to show that while Matthew speaks about the inviolability of the Law, he treats the Law very freely, omitting circumcision and relativising sabbath and purity law. He finds an analogy in the summaries of the Law in Philo's *Hypothetica* 7:1–9 and Josephus's *Contra Apionem* 2:190–219, written with sensitivity to Gentile readers (pp. 58–62). The dual focus of Matthew is evident in terms depicting non believers or expelled believers: τελώνης for Jews and ἐθνικός for Gentiles. This is a more extreme variant of Barth's original position about two fronts. What others see as unresolved tensions resulting from Matthew's portrait, Wong sees as a deliberate cross-cultural strategy. This raises issues both of Matthew's integrity (a fair question), but also of whether it strains credibility to attribute to him such a subtlety. 5:17–19 expresses much more than a cultural preference.

In his collection of essays, with revisions and additions, Stanton[28] only indirectly addresses the issue of Torah in Matthew's community. Of related interest are his observations from sociology and conflict theory about Matthew's community as sectarian, where he draws an interesting parallel between Matthew's relation to the Pharisees and the Damascus Document's relation to the Essenes.[29] Both exhibit characteristics of a community having cut itself off from the parent body. Both have a strong sense of persecution. Both portray their break from the original community through the coming of a new teacher, yet at the same time still share many characteristics with their community of origin. Strong invective stands beside strong evidence of closeness. Differentiation becomes important, as in Matthew's choice of ἐκκλησία rather than συναγωγή. The closer the communities, the more intense the conflict. The community exhibits strong group cohesion and only secondary development of formal authority structures. They legitimate themselves by showing other leaders have forsaken original path, and by repeated assertions of being true fulfilment.

Thus Stanton rejects the notion that Matthew writes as a Jew for a community still within the fold of Judaism, but also the view he is a Gentile, or writing for a predominantly Gentile church, living at some distance from

---

[28] Stanton, *Gospel*.

[29] Stanton, *Gospel*, pp. 89–107, using L. M. White, "Shifting Sectarian Boundaries in Early Christianity," *BJRL* 70 (1988), pp. 7–24; J. Blenkinsopp, "Interpretation and the Tendency to Sectarianism: An Aspect of Second Temple History," in *Jewish and Christian Self-Definition*, Vol 2, edited by E. P. Sanders, (London: SCM, 1980), pp. 1–26; L. Coser, *The Functions of Social Conflict*, (London: Routledge and Kegan Paul, 1956).

Judaism.[30] Rather Matthew reflects intense rivalry, a recent break, continuing antagonism and the need for the community to defend itself (see also p. 156).[31] Thus Matthew consistently portrays Jewish leaders in a negative light, associates scribes and Pharisees with synagogues ("their" synagogues) in contrast to the *ekklesia* of his community. "Whereas the reading of torah and instruction in it were central in the synagogue, in the church the commands of Jesus took precedence" (p. 130). The kingdom has been transferred to a new people which includes Gentiles (8:11–12; 15:12; 21:41,43). 28:15 shows Matthew's community defining itself over against the Jews. With regard to crucial texts, he argues that ἔθνη ("nations" or "Gentiles") in 28:19 is inclusive of Israel (in the light of 10:10,18; 24:9–14; see also pp. 158–161). 10:5–6 belongs to the past of the community. 23:2–3 must not be read in isolation from what follows, as if it indicates blanket approval. 17:24–27 (paying temple tax) and 24:20 ("not on the sabbath") reflect strategies of avoiding offence (pp. 192–206).

On some points Stanton remains unclear. On p. 329 he asserts that in 12:1–8 "the Sabbath commandment is not abolished; it is subordinated to the kindness and mercy of God". Yet on p. 204, discussing the same passage, we read: "If, as I have argued in Chapter 5, Matthew's community has cut its ties completely with Judaism, Matt 12.1–14 could well have been taken to legitimate abandonment of the sabbath." The sociological perspectives make an important contribution to understanding the dynamics of the setting and provide a plausible explanation. They form an important background for the task of discerning what then emerges as the attitude of Matthew's Jesus to the Law; they do not answer it.

---

[30] Stanton, *Gospel*, pp. 113–145.

[31] Agreeing with Stanton, see also D. A. Hagner, *Matthew 1–13*, Word Bib Comm 33A, (Dallas: Word, 1993), pp. lxviii–lxxi. Cf. also U. Luz, *Das Evangelium nach Matthäus (Mt 1–7)*, EKK I/1, (Zurich: Benziger; Neukirchen-Vluyn: Neukirchener, 1985), pp. 68–72, who argues that Matthew's community finds itself at a turning point as it comes to terms with the failure of the Jewish mission and a new openness to Gentiles, which raised issues, still unresolved, about the relation of Torah to Gentiles. See also Stanton, *Gospel*, pp. 169–171, in which he claims that Matthew shows evidence of accusations being made in his time against the christology of the community, which correspond to those which feature in later Jewish tradition: that Jesus was a magician and a deceiver. Hence Matthew highlights the charge that Jesus was possessed by (or was! 10:25) Beelzebul (9:34; 12:24,27; pp. 173–178). He allows the charge that he was a deceiver (27:63–64) to answer itself (p. 179). He also highlights Jesus as Son of David and in such contexts Stanton notes that strong Jewish reaction occurs (2:3; 9:27–28; 12:23; 21:9,15), reflecting that this was an issue of his day (pp. 180–185). In addition he believes that Matthew reflects an early form of the two parousia scheme which appears in the second century, according to which messianic prophecies unfulfilled in Jesus' ministry will be fulfilled at the second coming (pp. 185–189).

Saldarini[32] is closer to Overman in making a strong case that Matthew and his group still see themselves as being part of Jewish community (pp. 7–8). Recently expelled from the synagogue assembly (pp. 52, 101–103), they still see themselves as faithful to Torah, as expounded by Jesus (pp. 124–164), and offering Israel the only true option for what it means to be a Jew in the late first century. In this they set themselves in contrast to early forms of the rabbinic movement which had been more successful with rival claims. Matthew's community finds itself therefore in transition. In its alienation (especially because of the actions of local Jewish leadership, pp. 44–67) it is engaging more in openness towards non Jews and welcoming Gentiles among its members (pp. 68–83). Saldarini, therefore, locates Matthew at a point where his community is on the way towards a situation where in the next generation it, together with his gospel, will be incorporated into the predominantly Gentile church.

Saldarini demonstrates that Matthew's handling of the Law issues show that he is familiar with what were issues in Judaism of his day and claims that Matthew's response falls within the range of discussion of the period (pp. 125–156). The ten commandments are the core of the Law for Matthew and "more fundamental than purity regulations" and "categorically binding over sectarian traditions". . . . "the foundation of Jesus' special emphases in his teaching". Other key qualities are: "justice, mercy, faith(fullness) and Godlike perfection" (p. 162). "Matthew's interpretation of biblical law is neither an abrogation nor a surpassing of that law, but a correct understanding and fulfilment of it" (p. 162). The key to Jesus' authority is "Jesus' relationship with God, high status, and divinely given knowledge and mandate (3:13–17; 11:25–27)" (p. 163).

Saldarini's suggestion about where Matthew's group finds itself must be brought more closely into relation with Matthew's christology. The issue comes clearly into focus in the controversies about the sabbath, for instance, at the point where Jesus asserts that he is greater than the temple. Saldarini

---

[32] A. J. Saldarini, *Matthew's Christian-Jewish Community*, (Chicago: Univ. of Chicago Pr., 1994). K. R. Snodgrass, "Matthew's Understanding of the Law," *Interpretation* 46 (1992), pp. 368–378, also emphasises that Matthew's view is that Jesus was positive towards the Law, but that it should be interpreted from the prophetic perspective of love and mercy. Cf. earlier Hummel, *Auseinandersetzung*, who argues that Matthew's community finds itself within Judaism, though not participating in the synagogue, and that Matthew's Jesus uses methods of *halakah* to justify his stance. The criticism by R. E. Menninger, *Israel and the Church in the Gospel of Matthew*, Amer. Univ. St. VII, 162, (New York: Peter Lang, 1994), pp. 15, 126 of Hummel is that Hummel underplays the significance of christology in Matthew's thought (referring to 10:32–33).

notes the claim but without discussing its implications.[33] The issue is implicit in his comment, "The author of Matthew wrote a narrative about Jesus the Son of God and Messiah, not an instructive discussion of the law like the Mishnah or a commentary on Scripture like the midrashim" (p. 125). What implications does the immensity of this claim have for the place of the Law in Matthew and for the place of Matthew's community?

Menninger[34] sets the parameters well for the discussion of the Law in Matthew by noting that three factors should be borne in mind: Matthew is writing in a Jewish-Christian milieu; he is still in debate with the synagogue about correct interpretation of the Law; and he needs to relate the coming of Jesus as the fulfilment of Israel's hopes to his interpretation of the Law. He argues that for Matthew, Jesus has replaced the Law as the authority of the true Israel. Thus much of Jesus' teaching is unrelated to the Law. The Law is not bad, but belongs to the previous era of *Heilsgeschichte*. This is part of Menninger's main thesis that for Matthew the church is the true Israel, who are the new tenants of the vineyard of the kingdom (21:43). He sees Matthew's community as now outside the fold of Judaism, but still living in proximity to Judaism and strongly Jewish in ethos. His main argument is christological: the coming of the Messiah brings new revelation, surpassing and supplanting the old. Accordingly he emphasises the passages like 12:7 (Jesus as "something greater than the temple"). He sees Matthew's version of the dispute over purity law as no less radical than Mark's; and on 5:18–19 argues that 5:18 implies that the old Law had been fulfilled and replaced by the coming of Jesus and that 5:19 refers not to the old law but Jesus' commandments. But this attempt to resolve the tension by explaining away 5:18–19 remains problematic.

This review of some of the more important contributions of recent research raises a number of questions. Should we assume that Matthew intends a coherence in his gospel? Coherence is called into question where, for instance, difficult conservative traditions like 5:18 and 23:2–3, are discounted as traditional and as no longer carrying weight. On the other hand, this becomes more complicated with the realisation that actual coherence and intended coherence are not the same. Did Matthew just not notice the tensions? Alternatively, he did, as Hübner suggests, and chose to live with

---

[33] Saldarini, *Community,* p. 130.

[34] Menninger, *Israel and the Church*, pp. 103–133. Menninger operates with two key concepts, true Israel and remnant, both of which, as he acknowledges are not directly present in the gospel.

them, or, as Wong proposes, deliberately exploited them to appease divisions in his community. Barth's suggestion of two fronts would make it plausible, sociologically, that in addressing one group Matthew might make statements which conflict with his intentions in relation to the other. Then there is the question whether Matthew intends his statements to be informative or to function in some other way: to provoke, or to provide stereotypes, as, perhaps, in the case of "the scribes and the Pharisees" or in the case of the theses against which the antitheses are directed.

At the simplest level we could pose alternatives like: Did Matthew's Jesus replace the Law entirely, written and oral? replace only parts? replace only oral tradition? Did he differentiate within Torah? On what basis? Ethical against cultic and ritual? Decalogue against the rest? Intention against behavioural prescription? The reality is more complex than these alternatives presuppose.[35] There have been significant advances in our understanding of the Jewish world of the late first century, which have brought to light the extent to which Matthew's gospel reflects familiarity with Jewish issues of the time. This is brought out clearly especially by Saldarini and Stanton.[36] It is reflected in the shift in scholarship away from the view that Matthew is Gentile or primarily occupied with a Gentile setting. Associated with this is the realisation that Judaism, pre-70 CE, was diverse, and that this diversity did not suddenly cease in the decades following the war. Matthew's apparent familiarity with disputes reflected in early rabbinic tradition and his focus predominantly on Pharisees seem to indicate that his community must still be in some relationship with such circles.

People have differed about whether Matthew saw his community as within or outside of Judaism.[37] The distinction is itself problematic. Is "Judaism"

---

[35] Another complicating reality is contemporary concerns in Jewish Christian relations. How far is judgement coloured by concern to show the superiority of one's own faith community, Jewish or Christian, or by ecumenical concern to minimise differences between Judaism and Christianity. These are not matters of idle preference, but have been energised by the horror of genocide this century and the shameful heritage of antisemitism in western Christendom. Faith in a relationship means believing it can deal openly with differences, and with the truths and fictions we believe are real.

[36] See also Luz, *Matthäus I*, pp. 71–72 who summarises the significant parallels which have been noted between Matthew and Johanan ben Zakkai, including: priority of mercy (also using Hos 6:6) over ritual and cultic law, openness towards Gentiles, a concern with the centrality of ethical norms, a pro-peace stance in relation to the Jewish war and a strong emphasis on future judgement. See also P. Sigal, *The Halakah of Jesus of Nazareth according to the Gospel of Matthew*, (Lanham: Univ of America Pr., 1986), pp. 154–159.

[37] Contrast the attitudes of Harrington and Luz. D. J. Harrington, *The Gospel of Matthew*, Sacra Pagina 1, (Collegeville: Liturgical, 1991), begins his commentary with the statement that he is writing his commentary "from a 'Jewish' perspective – one that I

the local "synagogue", ie. the local gathering? Is it a range of people and groups sharing a basic framework of thought? Are the Jews whom Philo disparages for not holding both literal and allegorical interpretation (*De Migr Ab* 89–94) still Jews? The "synagogue" is probably too narrow; what evidence is there that all Jews came together in such gatherings? Were there not "synagogues" and "synagogues"? Matthew's group has been expelled and now calls itself an ἐκκλησία (ecclesia). Would that imply separation from Judaism? Hardly, in itself. In the past people have applied the "curse" of the *minim (Birkah Ha-Minim)* to the discussion, but this has become problematic on grounds of dating.[38] On the basis of Matthew, evidence of conflict and alienation is compelling, with or without a formal edict. The sectarian characteristics of the community have been well documented. These suggest not an abandonment of the heritage of Israel, but rather a claim to have it right and that others have it wrong.

Part of the conflict with deviant groups relates not just to exclusion from power, but also to dispute over what is admissible or inadmissible in belief. Those expelling Matthew's group doubtless had this in mind. Matthew's group doubtless laid its counterclaim. It is not for us to arbitrate but to describe. The issue of Matthew's portrait of Jesus' attitude towards the Law is inseparable from Matthew's own attitude towards the Law and that of his community. At stake, then, were not just claims, but whether claims matched reality.

In claiming a positive attitude on Jesus' part Matthew may provide evidence consistent with that or evidence inconsistent with it. The assessment

---

believe is demanded from the text itself" (p. 1). He sees Matthew's community as one alongside other Jewish communities, apocalyptic and early rabbinic, with which it was in tension, grappling with what it meant to be Jewish after the destruction of the temple and finding that answer in Jesus as the authoritative interpreter of Torah (p. 17). By contrast Luz, *Matthew I*, p. 71, argues that Matthew is no longer within the framework of Judaism. It is a response not to the destruction of Jerusalem, but to the implications of the Jewish rejection of Jesus.

[38] W. D. Davies, *The Setting of the Sermon on the Mount*, (Cambridge: CUP, 1966), pp. 256–315, had defended the thesis that Matthew is a Christian response to Jamnia. W. D. Davies and D. C. Allison, *A Critical and Exegetical Commentary on the Gospel according to Saint Matthew Vol I. I–VII*, (Edinburgh: Clark, 1988), pp. 136–137, see Matthew being composed at the general time when the benediction was being formulated. See the discussion urging caution in Stanton, *Gospel*, pp. 142–145; Hagner, *Matthew*, pp. lxviii–lxix; Saldarini, *Community*, pp. 18–19, 220–221; Luz, *Matthäus I*, pp. 70–71; and generally on the benediction: R. Kimelman, "*Birkat Ha-Minim* and the Lack of Evidence for an Anti-Christian Jewish Prayer in Late Antiquity," in *Jewish and Christian Self-Definition*, Vol 2, edited by E. P. Sanders et al., (Philadelphia: Fortress, 1981), pp. 226–244, 391–403; W. Horbury, "The Benediction of the *Minim* and Early Jewish-Christian Controversy," *JTS* 33 (1982), pp. 19–61; Overman, *Matthew's Gospel*, pp. 35–71.

of consistency will depend not simply on the logic of coherence, but on the criteria. Measured by his own criteria Matthew's evidence may be consistent or not consistent. Measured by the criteria of his opponents, doubtless it was not. In exploring Jesus' attitude towards the Law according to Matthew, we shall need also to be sensitive to Matthew's criteria.

The issue of criteria has also become important in measuring coherence in attitudes towards the Law within (the rest of?) Judaism of the time. Earlier assumptions of a monolithic approach are being abandoned. Whether widely tolerated or not, diverse interpretations existed in Jewish groups of the time, without apparently implying that their Jewishness was called into question. It is no longer meaningful, for instance, to cite Jesus' attitude towards divorce or oaths in the antitheses as necessarily anti Torah. The boundaries were often blurred. Even the distinctions between written law of the Pentateuch and other laws, part of the Jewish ethos, are sometimes blurred.

On the other hand, there were common features which we might identify as Jewish and thus as criteria for Jewishness. They included monotheism, the sense of nationhood as Israel, the authority of the Law as the basis of covenant, and the holiness of land and temple.[39] These are interrelated. The Pentateuch, the written Law, is the primary source. Temple or cultic laws are an important part of Torah. In discussing Matthew's attitude towards the Law we need to take into account, therefore, the issue of criteria.

Does Matthew add to these (eg. christology)? Or does he seek to extrapolate from existing criteria? Is he operating with a scheme according to which Jesus is, by implication, already part of the existing criteria, ie. predicted by the Scriptures? If so, is the implication of such prediction an addition which upholds continuity or introduces continuity, and, if the latter, how is this continuity understood? Is it good to better or bad to good or a combination of both? If abrogation is entailed, are there theological implications and does Matthew deal with them and how? Where is Matthew located on the map in relation to Marcion on the one hand and strict Torah adherence, on the other?

In what follows I want to listen to the text, not only for references, direct and indirect, to the Law, but also for what are the underlying criteria which appear to surface in the text of Matthew. For understanding Matthew's (and Matthew's Jesus') approach to the Law is about finding it on the map of Matthean values. Just to focus on particular passages where Law issues are paramount or to conduct a thematic or word study would run the danger of not seeing the issue in perspective. This is all the more the case because

---

[39] So Dunn, *Partings of the Ways*, pp. 18–36.

Matthew is not primarily writing about the Law; he is writing about the one he hails as Christ, the Son of God. The absence of the Law theme from sections of Jesus' teaching in Matthew, for instance, is also significant.

In this chapter I employ the same method as I used in Mark. It is not my intention to provide a detailed treatment of all Law issues in the text. My focus lies elsewhere. It is the attitude implied or expressed. Where such issues arise I shall mostly refer the reader to current discussion and engage in detailed response only where the matter directly affects our theme.

2.2   Matthew 1 – 7 in Review

2.2.1   Matthew 1:1 – 4:22

"The beginning of the good news" (Mark 1:1) has become in Matthew 1:1 the story of Jesus' genesis, which already sets the parameters of the drama to follow. The genealogy (1:1–17) indicates that from the beginning Matthew is concerned to relate Jesus to the heritage of Israel. He is a son of Abraham; and, in particular, he is the Messiah of the Davidic line, even if, finally, only by adoption. Within this strong affirmation of Jesus' belonging to Israel are the five women, each associated in some way with sexual scandal and with the Gentile world.[40]   Perhaps Matthew intends to counter a Jewish explanation of Mary's pregnancy that might have circulated in the same way as the alternative explanation of the empty tomb mentioned in 28:11–15.[41] The effect is to assert God's involvement in the irregularity. It is also, perhaps, to alert the reader to a characteristic of the story of God's action which follows in the ministry of Jesus: attention to those not usually included or at least given second place, including Gentiles. A tension with the norm is, therefore, already built into the genealogy, but nothing indicates that this norm is Torah. It is the norm in the sense of the usual, the dominant pattern (of genealogies!), the standard way of doing things and, by implication, a tension with those who maintain the norm.

---

[40] See R. E. Brown, *The Birth of the Messiah. A Commentary on the Infancy Narratives in the Gospels of Matthew and Luke*, (New York: Doubleday, 2nd edn., 1993), pp. 71–74.

[41]   Brown, *Birth*, p. 72 n. 23, rejects this suggestion on grounds that the women's presence would not make Mary's adultery more acceptable. The point would not be that their presence justifies her adultery, but that they were used by God even though negative reports and rumours were made about them. For detail on the accusation as it appears in Jewish and pagan literature see Brown, *Birth*, pp. 534–537.

God subverts the norm in the story of Mary's miraculous conception (1:18–25) and, at the same time, the story gives us a clearer focus on the place of Law. For Matthew has Joseph act in accordance with Law (1:19).[42] He is righteous. This righteousness entails his choosing which part of Torah to apply and how. That is already an important indicator. Joseph's righteousness is reflected not only in Torah conformity, but more especially in Torah interpretation: he takes the compassionate option among the possibilities offered by Torah. For he does not drag her to court (Deut 22:20–21, 23–24), but chooses rather the less public way of divorce (Deut 24:1–4).[43] He is not rebuked for this initiative, but lifted beyond it when he hears what really happened (1:20).

Into Joseph's world of hopes and norms God has entered with a new initiative. This initiative is for his people: Jesus will save "his people" (Israel) from their sins (1:21).[44] We are still in the world of Israel. Then Matthew tells us through the prophecy from Isaiah 7:14 that he shall be called, "Emmanuel, which means 'God with us'" (1:23). The term is rich in associations. Within its Isaianic context the child is a sign that Judah will not be abandoned to the might of Israel and Syria (Isa 7–8). Within its Matthean macro context it finds an echo in the promise that Jesus, in turn, will be with his own when they gather (18:20) and until the end of time (28:20).

The promise that God will dwell with the people is a major eschatological hope (eg. Isa 43:5; Ezek 34:30; 37:27; Zech 2:10–12; 8:3; 11QTemple 29:7–10; Jub 1:17,26).[45] Often it is related to the belief that God dwells with his people in the temple (eg. Ezek 37:26–27). Associated with the promise that Jesus will save his people from their sins, the promise that he will be Emmanuel could be evoking the understanding that Jesus should be

---

[42] So M. N. A. Bockmuehl, "Matthew 5:32; 19:9 in the light of Pre-rabbinic Halakhah," *NTS* 35 (1989), pp. 291–295, here: 294–295, who notes that Matthew share the assumption that illicit sexual union renders continued marriage impossible.

[43] So Brown, *Birth*, pp. 125–128; Luz, *Matthäus I*, p. 104. Cf. A. Wouters, *"...wer den Willen meines Vaters tut." Eine Untersuchung zum Verständnis vom Handeln im Matthäusevangelium*, BU23, (Regensburg: Pustet, 1992), pp. 209–213, who argues that Joseph is "righteous" primarily because he seeks the will of God. He claims that the Law actually offered no direct solution: he neither wanted a trial nor would he have been conforming to Torah's concern for getting rid of corruption from Israel by divorcing her quietly. I doubt whether Matthew sensed such a problem.

[44] So Saldarini, *Community*, p. 29. Matthew's Israel will expand to include Gentiles, so that this should not be seen as ignoring them. Nevertheless it shows Matthew's orientation.

[45] So Davies and Allison, *Matthew I*, p. 218.

understood in terms of the temple. One of the things the temple cult achieves is forgiveness of sins. Is Matthew hinting that Jesus needs to be understood as taking his place beside the temple or as its replacement? In 12:6 in dispute with the Pharisees over action in the grain fields Jesus argues that "something greater than the temple" was there. Should Matthew mean that Jesus will take the place of the temple,[46] this would have major implications for understanding Jesus' attitude towards the Law. It would also raise the issue of manner and timing: when would Jesus replace the temple and how would such a change be understood? These are issues to which we shall return, where I shall argue that the evidence in the rest of Matthew does not support such a view.

Tension becomes acute in the account of Herod and the magi (2:1–18). The focus is messiahship, which had been announced in the genealogy (1:1,17) and given a first role definition in the angel's announcement in 1:21 ("he shall save his people from their sins"). Herod and all Jerusalem prefigure the violence which will lead to Jesus' death. The magi prefigure the response of the Gentiles.[47] The holy family reflect the image of the holy people, Israel. They flee to Egypt and return thence. And, earlier, they escape the plotting of a foreign king just as Israel escaped Balak's plans (Nu 22–24). Jesus, the star of Jacob, has arisen (Nu 24:27). The tapestry of allusions underlines Matthew's claim that Jesus is Israel's Messiah and that those who belong to him are truly Israel.

In these two chapters Matthew has made extraordinary claims for Jesus. He is Israel's Messiah. But, more than that, he is the Son of God, divinely created through Mary. Matthew passes over what the implications of this might have been for his childhood and development. Instead he takes us to the Jesus hailed at his baptism as God's Son. Matthew leaves us in no doubt that Jesus carries divine authority. It is important to note this foundational principle of Matthew's story, because it means that when we discuss Jesus' attitude towards the Law, we must always bear in mind that, whatever the status of the Law, Jesus, himself, has divine authority. It means, therefore, that one option is ruled out from the beginning: that Jesus' authority is less than that of Torah. Such an option might view the Torah as having divine

---

[46] Cf. T. L. Donaldson, *Jesus on the Mountain: a Study in Matthean Theology*, (Sheffield: JSOT Pr., 1985), pp. 184–186, who speaks in terms of Matthew's Jesus replacing Zion.

[47] Saldarini, *Community*, p. 70, rightly points out that we are dealing here with only a rudimentary and inchoate response. Similarly Levine, *Salvation History*, p. 165. See also Donaldson, *Mountain*, p. 185, who sees Matthew having Jesus replace Zion (cf. Isa 60:6). But Ps 72:10–11 speaks of the king.

authority directly from God, whereas Jesus' authority was by creation and delegation. But, even then, in substance there could be no conflict: for both express God's will. For Matthew, Jesus' divine authority is beyond question. This issue is how it stands beside the authority of the Law.

The account of John the Baptist (3:1–12) no longer belongs to the beginning of the story, as the final climax of scriptural prediction, as it did in Mark, but represents a further stage in its development, a continuing story of scripture fulfilment. As in Mark, John's appearance in Matthew is somewhat unmediated (3:1). Probably for both evangelists and for their hearers this was not so. The fulfilment of scripture puts John on side with God's initiatives in the story and so with Jesus. For Matthew, this solidarity is so strong that John effectively preaches the same message of the kingdom of God as do Jesus and, later, the disciples (3:2 "Repent; for the kingdom of heaven is at hand!" cf. 4:17 "Repent; for the kingdom of heaven is at hand"; 10:7 "The kingdom of heaven is at hand"). It extends also to the offer of forgiveness of sins, provided in John's case through baptism. As in Mark, Matthew's account reports that people confessed their sins at their baptism by John (3:6).[48] Jesus, too, would save his people from their sins and be Emmanuel, "God with us". John's baptism of forgiveness belongs then to God's new initiative. Matthew and his hearers doubtless appreciated that this was controversial in the light of institutional interests in cultic rituals for dealing with sin. The transition to the scene that follows may reflect this tension; the Pharisees and Sadducees appear. It has John grasp the initiative.

Matthew has John confront the integrity of the Pharisees and Sadducees, calling them a brood of vipers, and warning them of self complacency before the impending judgement (3:7–10). This contrasts sharply with the picture of emerging confrontation between Jesus and scribes and Pharisees in Mark. The attacks find their echo in Jesus' words against the scribes and Pharisees in ch. 23 and in his warnings to disciples about fruit in 7:19. The issue is not that they refuse John's baptism; they come for it (3:7). The issue is that they do not show the signs of genuine repentance. Wanting to undergo the rite without that is what John attacks. Matthew also has John attack their claim to be children of Abraham. The implication is: to be a child of Abraham is not a guarantee that one will escape the judgement.

John's quip that God can create sons of Abraham from stones is not a disparagement of Abrahamic descent.[49] Matthew has, after all, shown Jesus'

---

[48] So rightly Luz, *Matthäus I*, pp. 146–147; cf. Davies and Allison, *Matthew I*, pp. 300–301.

[49] Rightly Saldarini, *Community*, p. 42.

Abrahamic descent in the genealogy and introduced him as Son of Abraham. The point is rather that one cannot presume on God's favour on such a basis. The image of God making sons from stones (perhaps a Hebrew/Aramaic pun),[50] may also evoke for the hearers the later inclusion of Gentiles.[51] Allusion to Gentile inclusion has already featured in the genealogy and the magi story.

John confronts the Pharisees and Sadducees with judgement. Judgement is also the central theme in Matthew's account of John's predictions (3:11–12; cf. also 3:10), whereas the theme is hardly present, if at all, in Mark's account. The effect in Matthew is to give Jesus, the one introduced as Israel's Messiah and the world's Saviour, a strongly forensic function. It is a second major statement of Jesus' role after 1:18–25. Jesus will save his people from their sins and will be Emmanuel. Now we learn: he will be the judge to come. Jesus is John's coming judge. He will baptise with the Holy Spirit and fire. He is about to gather the wheat and burn up the chaff.

Taken with the confrontation of the Sadducees and Pharisees. This portrait of Jesus as judge also makes an important statement about Jesus' relation to Law; for judgement will be in accordance with Law. Already Matthew has indicated through John's preaching that obedience to the Law is more than ritual observance and goes beyond a sense of divine election. Jesus will be the one to exercise such judgement and will do so in accordance with the Law. This is an important motif and Matthew will make this role of Jesus more explicit as the gospel goes on.

It is this Jesus, Israel's Messiah, the Son of God, the world's coming saviour and judge, who receives the divine affirmation at his baptism (3:13–17). The link with John especially highlights his role as delineated by John, the world's judge. The focus on judgement, with its demand of righteousness as the criteria for judgement, began with John's assault on the Pharisees and Sadducees and with his predictions of the judge to come. It provides the context for understanding Matthew's account of Jesus' baptism. We see this when Matthew has John protest his unworthiness to fulfil the deed, but has Jesus assert in response: "We must fulfil all righteousness" (3:15).

That obviously included, for Matthew's Jesus, being baptised by John. Jesus is committed to total righteousness. It recalls the commitment of his adoptive father, Joseph, to act in accordance with righteousness. It is probably

---

[50] See Davies and Allison, *Matthew I*, p. 308.

[51] So Davies and Allison, *Matthew I*, pp. 308–309; Brown, *Birth*, p. 68, sees a possible allusion also to the promise to Abraham that in him blessing will come to all nations.

also appropriate to see in Jesus' words a programmatic statement. Jesus is concerned with fulfilment of righteousness, which in the context is very much focused on behaviour: doing what God wills, but also carries with it by implication fulfilment of God's plans set forth in the predictions of the Old Testament. It will find its echo in Jesus' programmatic statement in 5:17, 20 ("Do not think that I have come to abolish the Law and the Prophets. I have not come to abolish but to fulfil them . . . For I tell you, unless your righteousness exceeds that of the scribes and Pharisees you will not enter the kingdom of heaven"). It also finds an echo later in Matthew's description of John as having come "in the way of righteousness" (21:32). In the broadest sense righteousness means: keeping God's law, though law here includes more than Torah: it includes being baptised by John.[52]

It is then the impeccable one who is impeccably obedient who is to fulfil John's predictions and be judge of all the world. John baptises Jesus; the Spirit descends. By the Spirit he is equipped to baptise in Spirit, one of the judging images used of him by John. God acclaims him for all to hear as his beloved Son. The effect is to recap what has been said thus far in the gospel about Jesus. He is God's Son, Israel's Messiah, the world's judge, and his role is defined in particular in terms of judgement. He will act as judge. He stands for obedience to God's will.

The temptation scene in Matthew recalls the Israel typology of the infancy narratives (4:1–11). Like Israel, God's son (cf. 2:15), Jesus is led into the wilderness. Unlike Israel, Israel's Messiah does not fail in the wilderness. He remains faithful, warding off the wiles of the tempter with words of Torah. This reinforces the impression that Matthew is concerned, much more than Mark, to portray Jesus as the one who truly represents Israel and fulfils its Torah. At the same time, Matthew allows us to see Jesus in an exemplary role: he does not break fast for the sake of food; in "the holy city" he does not seek glory through wonder working; he does not accept authority except from God. Fasting is affirmed, as in 6:16–18. Wonders are noted as at least ambiguous, as in 7:21–23. The quest for power is eschewed, as in 20:24–28. Again Matthew is allowing us to see important criteria for discerning God's will.

---

52 Cf. H. Giesen, *Christliches Handeln: eine redaktionskritische Untersuchungen zum* δικαιοσύνη *Begriff im Matthäusevangelium*, Eur. Hochschulschriften 181, (Frankfurt: Peter Lang, 1981), pp. 27, 31, 41, 76, who argues that the plural in Jesus' reply to John, "It is fitting for us to fulfil all righteousness" (3:15), is a statement about Jesus and the disciples and so is programmatic for the gospel as a whole. It refers more naturally in the context to John and himself, who are here directly in view; the disciples are not.

The final scene of the temptation will find its echo in 28:16–20 where Jesus will declare his authorisation to power over all things in heaven and on earth, but by God's hand. There may be another faint echo of the mission to the Gentiles here, as perhaps also in Matthew's note that after Jesus' arrest Jesus moves to "Galilee of the Gentiles" (4:12–16). But the final temptation scene also highlights another important motif for Matthew's christology and attitude towards the Law: authorisation. It shows that Matthew does not envisage Jesus as somehow incarnating God because of his miraculous creation. Rather the model is typically within the frame of legal thought: Jesus is authorised. It is a christology of divine delegation applying to one divinely created.

Matthew's Jesus exercises this divinely given authority to call disciples (4:18–22) and generally to make demands. Israel's Messiah, the nation's Saviour, and the universal judge, calls the first disciples. Who they are and what they are to become is determined by who it is who calls them. When we read the first summaries of Jesus' preaching (4:17) and activity (4:23–25), we do so already clear about his mission. As with John the Baptist (3:2), Jesus' message of the kingdom is one of impending judgement and the opportunity to repent (4:17), a message given later also to the disciples in almost identical terms (10:7).

Within 1:1 – 4:22, then, Jesus' attitude towards the Law is closely related to christology. Jesus is Son of Abraham, Son of David, Israel's Messiah. He is the miraculously created Son of God, God's new initiative. He will save his people from their sins and bear the name Emmanuel. His story matches (and, in obedience surpasses) the story of Israel. He is the coming judge, equipped with the Spirit. He exemplifies total obedience and looks alone to God for authorisation for his demands.

The focus is strongly on judgement to come: hope for those who repent; wrath for those who do not. This christology necessarily sets Jesus in relation to God's Law or will. To this point in Matthew this includes being baptised by John and may be designated as righteousness. In the realm of discerning God's will Matthew allows us already to detect the values with which he operates. Joseph exemplifies the principle that interpretation of Law should favour the compassionate option. John makes clear that outward ritual (baptism) and claims to election on the basis of ethnicity without corresponding behaviour count for nothing. Jesus demonstrates that breaking commands (the command to fast) to meet material need, pursuing miracles at the expense of obedience, and seeking power, are failure before temptation.

The section exposes tensions between Jesus and his antagonists. The genealogy shows God siding with those who do not conform to the norms of society. The story of the magi prefigures the crucifixion by political and religious authorities and all Jerusalem. The names of Jesus, depicting him as saviour from sins and as God dwelling with his people, could be indicating rivalry with the temple, but, seen in the light of the gospel as a whole, probably do not. The sequence from John's baptism for the forgiveness of sins to the attack on Pharisees and Sadducees may reflect a sensitivity over institutional claims. Probably the tempter's options reflect stances which Matthew would have his hearers identify and reject.

The overall effect of this opening is to identify who Jesus is, his unique creation, equipment, authorisation, and role. The latter is described in a manner which raises the issue of his relation to the Law and puts heavy emphasis on attitude and behaviour. He is both judge and, with the promise of forgiveness, saviour from judgement. For Matthew's Jesus as judge to come the role of Law becomes central: what is God's will, by which all will be judged? It is also central in the sense that Matthew has Jesus identify his chief concern as fulfilling all righteousness. What is the relation between Jesus' understanding of God's will and written Torah? These are central issues because of the way Matthew has introduced his gospel. In this opening section, with its strong emphasis on Jesus' identity and his role as judge, Matthew has established the basis on which they will be addressed in what follows.

2.2.2 Matthew 4:23 – 5:16

Matthew 4:23 is rightly recognised as beginning a new major section. It forms an inclusion with 9:35. Both are summaries which report Jesus' teaching in the synagogues, preaching the gospel of the kingdom and healing every disease and sickness. 4:24–25 reports the response, also in summary form, and adding reference to exorcism. 4:17 had already reported Jesus' preaching in summary; it was the same as John's (3:2). When the common summary of John's and Jesus' message is read in the context of Matthew's narrative thus far, the message of the kingdom emerges as a proclamation of the coming judgement and of the hope of salvation from judgement through forgiveness of sins. The effect of 4:17 is to continue the focus on judgement and on Jesus' role as judge to come.

The new element in the summaries of 4:23 and 4:24–25, compared with 4:17, is Jesus' activity as teacher and as healer and exorcist. We have to wait until 8:1 – 9:34 for a first glimpse of Jesus as healer and exorcist. Why is the judge to come doing such things? In effect, Matthew has John raise this issue in 11:2–6, to which we shall return. If 8:1 – 9:34 portrays Jesus as healer and exorcist, 5:1 – 7:29 portrays him as teacher. It is within this framework that Matthew has constructed the first detailed instance of Jesus' teaching, the so-called Sermon on the Mount.[53] Here is the teaching of Jesus the judge. By taking Mark's detail of Jesus' ascent up a high mountain to appoint disciples (Mark 3:13) and making it the occasion of a lengthy exposition, Matthew evokes, probably intentionally, the image of Moses.[54]

---

[53] H. D. Betz, *The Sermon on the Mount* (Minneapolis: Fortress, 1995), exegetes the Sermon on the Mount on the basis that it is an independent entity, not as a part of the Gospel of Matthew. He argues that it represents an *epitome,* a summary of teaching, for which he points to parallels both in Jewish and non Jewish literature. But the similarities remain at a fairly general level, the form not sufficiently distinct, to warrant building too much on it. See the criticism of C. E. Carlston, "Betz on the Sermon on the Mount – A Critique," *CBQ* 50 (1988), pp. 47–57, here: 50–51, and D. C. Allison, "A New Approach to the Sermon on the Mount," *EphTheolLov* 64 (1988), pp. 405–414, which remain, to my mind, valid. Allison points also to Matthean compositional features of the sermon (use of triads and eschatological triad in the conclusion; pp. 406–409) and an extensive number of semantic and thematic links (pp. 410–411) in arguing convincingly that the case for extensive Matthean composition is strong. He also points to the weakness of some of Betz's arguments from Hellenistic parallels (eg. about visual perception, p. 412), and the questionable assumption that the sermon is a systematic summary of Jesus' teaching and therefore able to be categorised as an *epitome* (p. 412; see also pp. 413–414 on the lack of christological titles and references to Jesus' death and resurrection).

See also Stanton, *Gospel*, pp. 295, 310, 325, who addresses not only the formal category, but also the claim by Betz that the theology of the Sermon is so different from that of Matthew as a whole. One needs to take Betz into account in arguments from Matthean redaction, especially in any claim that Matthew edits and expands the sermon on the plain. It is not possible to deal with these complexities in this study. For the purposes of my analysis in this chapter I shall make reference to Betz, because it is the same text which he exegetes.

[54] For the notion of Jesus as a new Moses in Matthew's typology, see the full treatment in Allison, *New Moses.* On 5:1–2, see pp. 172–180 and also pp. 324–325, where he criticises Donaldson, *Mountain,* (see pp. 112–113) for playing down Sinai allusions in the text. Donaldson's argument rests heavily on the inclusio which he sees between 15:29–31 and 4:23 – 5:1, both reflecting Zion typology. He claims that in developing the inclusio Matthew presents Jesus not as a new Moses giving a new Law, but as Messiah and Zion as the place of Torah instruction (pp. 113–119). I would consider it not unrealistic that Matthew may have assumed allusions to both Sinai and Zion. Cf. also J. A. Grassi, "Matthew as a Second Testament Deuteronomy," *BibTheolBull* 19 (1989), pp. 23–29, who points to similarities between Matthew and Deuteronomy. In particular he draws attention to the Sinai and related motifs associated with the mountains (esp. the sermon on the mount, the transfiguration and the great commission): the promise, "I will be with you," the antitheses recalling the commandments of Sinai; the imagery of the transfiguration (light, Moses, the cloud, "listen to me!" Deut 18:15). He also points to the motifs of succession and the ekklesia. In all, the Sinai typology is undeniably present, but not, to my mind, in such a way as to justify the claim that Matthew sees "this gospel of the kingdom" as the new equivalent of "this book of the law", Deuteronomy, as Grassi claims.

The discourse addresses Jesus' disciples, but the crowds are also in view, quite literally (5:1), and as potential disciples in earshot of his teaching, according to 7:28. In it Jesus' declares God's will, in promise and reward. In the light of the gospel thus far one might have expected some teaching about repentance and forgiveness of sins, but that belongs rather to the preaching of the gospel. Here is instruction for those who have responded, who have repented. But the framework established thus far, of life now in the light of judgement to come, continues to dominate throughout, from the beatitudes (5:1–12) to the warning about false prophets and false foundations (7:15–28). The judge to come, Israel's Messiah, the divinely created Son of God, who proclaims judgement and salvation from judgement, is declaring God's will, Torah according to Jesus.

Within this instruction comes a major section about the Law and the Prophets, with particular focus on the written Torah (5:17–48). This section belongs within the instruction and properly so, since written Torah is concerned with instruction of the faithful. It would be wrong to describe the instruction of the discourse as a whole as Jesus expounding written Torah, for much of the instruction, unlike 5:17–48, is not directly related to Torah as in the Law and the Prophets. In the broader sense, however, Jesus' sermon is Torah, instruction of God's will. The fact that this is so raises the fundamental question: what is the relation of Jesus' teaching of God's will to what Matthew understands as God's Torah given in the Law? The formal reality of having a section dealing with written Torah within Jesus' discourse shows, in itself, a close relationship.

The so-called beatitudes in Matthew (5:3–12) represent promises for the faithful, but function also as exhortation, as promises frequently do. Some describe plight; others describe attitude.[55] The values implied in the genealogy reappear: people on the margin, the lowly of spirit, those who thirst for justice, those who mourn, the persecuted are to receive the promised kingdom. Yet Matthew is also promoting attitudes consistent with such solidarity: lowliness of spirit, gentleness, hungering and thirsting after righteousness, compassion, purity of heart, and peacemaking. With some,

---

[55] The matter of which express ethical attitude and which plight or whether all express one or the other is still very much open to debate. See the recent discussion in Luz, *Matthäus I*, pp. 198–216 and Betz, *Sermon*, pp. 110–153, favouring an ethical attitude for all but the last two; Davies and Allison, *Matthew I*, pp. 329–269, favouring plight for the first four and last two; similarly Hagner, *Matthew*, pp. 91–96: the first four reflect the spirit of Isa 61:1; Harrington, *Matthew*, pp. 77–85: "The Beatitudes sketch the attitudes that the Matthean Christians should manifest and allude to the suffering that they endured (5:4,10–11)" (p. 82).

both aspects may be simultaneously present (poor in spirit; lowly and gentle; hungering and thirsting for righteousness). Many of these traits echo the injunctions and promises of the psalms and prophets (Isa 61:1–2; Ps 37:11; 42:3; 24:4). The primary focus is probably attitude. The first eight are embraced by concern for righteousness, a strong Matthean concept, already noted as programmatic in 3:15, and soon to reappear in 5:20. Here as there it is about doing God's will. The values hailed in the beatitudes belong, for Matthew, to life under God's Law and effectively set the parameters for its interpretation. The judge and saviour quite properly announces what counts in the last.

Such life is salt and light to the world; it demonstrates God's presence by deeds of goodness (5:13–16). The salt image appropriately portrays goodness as proactive, not being good in itself, but bringing good to the world. The alternative, judgement, being cast out and trodden under foot, makes a striking metaphor. The imagery of being light to the world strongly reflects Israel's self understanding (Isa 49:6; cf. Rom 2:19) and, juxtaposed to "the city set on a hill", evokes the imagery of Zion and Israel. Matthew is laying claim to these images for his community. The transition to the theme of Law in 5:17–20 may well indicate that Matthew has in mind the eschatological hope that the peoples will be drawn to Zion and from Zion's hill God's Law would be proclaimed (Isa 2:2–5),[56] just as in 5:1–2 he is probably evoking the image of Moses and Sinai.

This first section of Matthew's Sermon on the Mount is already of great importance for understanding his attitude towards the Law. For his narrative thus far had portrayed Jesus as judge and saviour. In the sermon Matthew's Jesus, the coming judge, is declaring the will of God, laying down the principles of judgement, made explicit in 16:27: the Son of Man will render to everyone according to their works. This is the basis of their reward, seen both negatively and positively. The laying down of the principles of judgement is happening already in 5:3–12 and 13–16 and already here important parameters are set. They include the focus on the marginal, evident earlier in the genealogy. Consistent with this (and with Joseph's righteousness for which one should strive with purity of heart) is a strong emphasis on

---

[56] So J. Dumbrell, "The Logic of the Role of the Law in Matthew 5:1–20," *NovTest* 23 (1981), pp. 1–23, here: 14–16, who draws attention to the importance of Zion imagery and its connection to the Law as explaining the sequence of the sermon, here, from these statements to the theme of law; see also K. M. Campbell, "The New Jerusalem in Matt. 5:14," *SJT* 31 (1978), pp. 335–363 and earlier: G. von Rad, *The Problem of the Hexateuch and Other Essays*, (Edinburgh: Oliver & Boyd, 1966), pp. 232–242.

compassion and active peacemaking. It is probably in this active sense that we should understand the salt and light metaphors. At the same time Matthew makes it clear that Jesus' call is not away from Israel, but to be Israel (the light of the world, the city on the hill). Thus in Matthew, already to this point in the narrative, Jesus is being portrayed as standing in very close association with exposition of God's will. This is the immediate setting for 5:17–48.

2.2.3 Matthew 5:17–48

Matt 5:17–48 continues the focus on God's will. It forms an important section within this instruction and flows coherently from what precedes, especially if an allusion to Zion typology evokes the image of Torah instruction going forth from Zion. It is not the beginning of instruction in God's will; this has been happening already since 5:3. Nor will it be the end of it; it continues from 6:1 – 7:28. It can therefore be misleading to separate the section from its broader context or subsume the discourse as a whole under its theme. It is even more misleading to treat the passage without due regard to what has emerged in the gospel thus far, in particular, the strong christological claims to authority. The hearer listens to 5:17–48 as part of the instruction of Jesus, Israel's Messiah, the divinely created Son of God, who will judge the world.[57]

The passages falls into two main parts: statements of principle in 5:17–20 and exposition of six aspects of Torah in 5:21–48. The opening statement is of primary significance for the whole passage, indeed for Matthew's picture of Jesus as a whole. Nothing in the narrative thus far would suggest that Jesus intended to overturn Torah. The strong negative, "Do not think that I have come to abolish the Law or the Prophets", is either just a rhetorical device to prepare for the positive statement[58] or, as is more likely, it also

---

[57] S. Westerholm, "The Law in the Sermon on the Mount: Matt 5:17–48," *CriswellTheolRev* 6 (1992), pp. 43–56, here: 44–47, makes the valid observation that Matthew only comes to address the Law after first having established that Jesus proclaims the kingdom of God. This sets all else, including, the Law in perspective, so that Jesus both fulfils sacred history and transcends the demands of Moses, with "a more perfect embodiment of the divine will" (p. 47). On the importance of the kingdom see also G. Strecker, "The Law in the Sermon on the Mount," in *The Promise and Practice of Biblical Theology*, edited by J. Reumann, (Minneapolis: Fortress, 1991), pp. 35–49, here: 37, who points to 5:20 and its concern with the kingdom.

[58] So Banks, "Law," 226, who points to the similar non polemical use of "Do not think" in 10:34; similarly Strecker, *Bergpredigt*, p. 57; Giesen, *Christliches Handeln*, p. 221.

reflects an alternative view known to Matthew. That is implied by 5:18–19. That alternative view might be held by Christians who believe Jesus absolves them of need to observe the Law or by Jewish critics who believe that Jesus' teaching leads to neglect and even deliberate transgression. 5:19 may envisage the former and perhaps refer to neglect of only parts of the Law. At the same time Matthew may also be warding off criticism, perhaps evoked by such views, perhaps by Christian malpractice, perhaps by a (mis)reading of his own position as wanting to portray Jesus as effectively abolishing Torah.[59]

For Matthew, Jesus stated categorically that he came to do the opposite of abolishing the Law and the Prophets. In the light of the preceding context, where Jesus demands good works, this most naturally means something like: they are to be taken with the utmost seriousness. Keep the whole Law! The verses which follow 5:17, namely 5:18–19,20, and 21–48, confirm this. The orientation of the statement is clear: it is in the opposite direction of abrogation; it is confirming and upholding the validity of the Law and the Prophets.[60] This must, then, be the sense of "fulfil" in the positive statement: "I have not come to abolish, but to fulfil." πληρῶσαι "fulfil" is particularly appropriate because elsewhere Matthew uses it of scripture fulfilment in Jesus' ministry. The mention of the prophets may have led to its use here,

---

[59] Barth, "Gesetzesverständnis," p. 62, suggests that the view being rejected is that of antinomists who believe Jesus came to abolish the Law; similarly Hummel, *Auseinandersetzung*, p. 68; I. Broer, *Freiheit vom Gesetz und Radikalisierung des Gesetzes*, SBS 98, (Stuttgart: KBW, 1980), pp. 24–25. Betz, *Sermon*, p. 173, sees 5:17–20 responding to the accusation that Jesus' interpretation was not controlled by clear principles, had the effect of undermining Scripture and Torah, and thus produced a heresy (p. 173). He sees this danger evident in the teaching and behaviour attacked in 5:19; 7:15–20,21–23. He sees in 5:17–20 a statement of principles of interpretation and draws attention to similar awareness in Greco-Roman literature of the importance of not simply applying laws but also taking into account motivation and volition (pp. 167–172). He also suggests, pp. 175–176, that 5:17 may well be caricaturing reported sayings of Jesus such as we see reflected in Gosp Ebionites frg. 5: "I have come to abolish sacrifices and if you do not cease sacrificing, the (divine) wrath will not cease from you"; Gosp Egyptians frg 3: "I have come to abolish the works of femaleness"; and the words attributed to the Marcionite Marcus in Adamantius *De recta in deum fide* XV: "This is what the Judaists wrote, the (version): 'I have not come to abolish the law but to fulfill (it).' But Christ did not speak in this way; he said rather: 'I have not come to fulfill the law but to abolish (it).'" He assumes such attitudes also find their echo in reports in later rabbinic literature. See also I. Broer, "Die Antithesen der Bergpredigt. Ihre Bedeutung und Funktion für die Gemeinde des Matthäus," *BibKirch* 48 (1993), pp. 128–133, here: 131, who sees Matthew putting the case against criticism from the Jewish community.

[60] Cf. D. L. Balch, "The Greek Political Topos Περὶ νόμων and Matthew 5:17,19 and 16:19," in *Social History of the Matthean Community*, edited by D. L. Balch, (Minneapolis: Fortress, 1991), pp. 68–84, here: 76–79, who argues that Matthew maintains a "polarity,

but the focus in the context is more in line with 3:15, "to fulfil all righteousness". There it means doing what God demands. Here the focus is not so much on Jesus' doing God's will,[61] but on Jesus' causing God's will to be done.

In this sense Matthew is portraying Jesus' mission as one of seeking to cause God's will to be done, fulfilling God's will as manifest in the Law and the Prophets.[62] The emphasis here is on Law in particular and upholding it[63] and giving instruction so that it is rightly fulfilled.[64] The focus in the context is not on Jesus replacing the Law.[65] That would be no answer on

claiming not to 'abolish' the laws, but granting the power to 'loose' them" (p. 78), pointing to a similar polarity in treatments of the Law in Josephus and Dionysius of Halicarnassus (pp. 72–75). He understands the antitheses as loosing parts of Torah. He also makes a connection with 16:19 in the claim that this power to "loose" Torah provisions is given to Peter and the disciples (pp. 78–79) and explains how Matthew can justify giving up the command to circumcise and the restriction of 10:5–6 by having Jesus authorise a Gentile mission in 28:18–20 (pp. 79–84). But is "loosing" about deleting Torah requirements or about judgement? Also it is by no means certain that Matthew's community does not presuppose circumcision.

[61] Cf. J. Schniewind, *Das Evangelium nach Matthäus*, (Göttingen: Vandenhoeck und Ruprecht, 1964), p. 54.

[62] See Barth, "Gesetzesverständnis," p. 65; Giesen, *Christliches Handeln,*, p. 145, who speaks of Jesus fulfilling God's law and of Christians also being called to fulfil God's law; Dumbrell, "Law," pp. 19–20 who favours the idea that law continues its validity, pointing to the Zion eschatology background of the context. According to Saldarini, *Community*, pp. 161–162, fulfilling the Law takes place in Jesus' deeds and his "teachings, which lay bare the true meaning and requirements of the law" (p. 161); similarly Luz, *Matthäus I*, p. 239.

[63] Cf. G. Dalman, *Jesus-Joshua. Studies in the Gospels*, (London: SPCK, 1929), pp. 57–59, who suggests that behind πληρῶσαι "fulfil", lies קים meaning "uphold", "confirm"; similarly D. Daube, *The New Testament and Rabbinic Judaism*, (London: Athlone, 1956), pp. 153–154. Cf. also Betz, *Sermon*, pp. 178–179, exegeting the sermon in isolation from its Matthean context, who argues that the meaning is primarily legal and corresponds to the Hebrew, קים, and should be understood in the sense that "Particular laws are intended not simply to be complied with but to be 'fulfilled' by serving as instruments for meeting the demands of justice." The Matthean use of πληρῶσαι "fulfil" demands something more than "uphold".

[64] A. H. McNeile, *The Gospel according to St. Matthew*, (London: Macmillan, 1915), p. 58; speaks in terms of Jesus bringing out the true meaning of the Law; similarly F. V. Filson, *The Gospel according to Saint Matthew*, Black's NT Comm., (London: A&C Black, 1960), p. 83, Strecker, *Gerechtigkeit*, p. 147; *Die Bergpredigt. Ein exegetischer Kommentar*, (Göttingen: Vandenhoeck und Ruprecht, 1984), p. 57; Hagner, *Matthew*, p. 106; but while this may apply to 5:21–48, it is doubtful whether this sense to is be inferred into πληρῶσαι, "fulfil", in 5:17. Nor is there any direct indication in 5:17 itself that the focus in the expression, "Law and the Prophets," is ethical law, as Strecker, *Gerechtigkeit*, p. 144, maintains, although that is the primary focus in 5:3–15 and 21–48 (but not in 6:1–18).

[65] Against Banks, *Law*, pp. 207–210; "Matthew's understanding of the Law," pp. 229–231, where he draws attention to 11:13 which he would interpret similarly. Cf. also Meier,

either front and would come too close to meaning the opposite of 5:17. On the other hand, the statement must be read in the light of Matthew's christology.[66] In the opening section of his gospel Matthew has established Jesus' authority and it is in this authority that he has Jesus give the discourse. The opening section inevitably raised the question: how does God's authority in Jesus relate to God's authority in the Law and the Prophets. Matthew seems bent on saying: no conflict. In all it is God's authority; yet, given salvation history, Jesus brings something new. The new is not abrogation of the old. Matthew presents it rather as a matter of Jesus upholding the integrity of the Law and Prophets by giving them authoritative interpretation. This we might expect of the one who is to come as judge. The christological motif of Jesus as judge continues to inform the discourse. Whether, beyond that, Matthew is influenced by an understanding of the Messiah as Law giver or interpreter of the Law remains uncertain. Nothing in the context suggests this is so.[67] We may recognise an allusion to Mt Zion in 5:16, but that need not imply an allusion to the motif of Messiah.

The strong sense of continuity with the Law and the Prophets, expressed in the idea that Jesus sees them as expressing God's will and has come to see that it is done, receives its confirmation in 5:18–19. According to 5:18, not

---

Law, pp. 75–85, 165; Menninger, *Israel*, pp. 106–108, who argues that the addition of "or the prophets" to an original word of Jesus about the Law shifted the focus from the Law to the scriptures as a whole and enabled Matthew to use πληρῶσαι in a way that suggests that what Jesus said and did fulfils the hopes of the Law and the Prophets and so replaces Law. According to Betz, *Sermon*, p. 178, the "or" in the sermon acknowledges the different nature of each authority, one given directly by God, the other indirectly through the Spirit, but both are seen here under the perspective of Law.

[66] R. Hoppe, "Vollkommenheit bei Matthäus als theologische Aussage," in *Salz der Erde – Licht der Welt: Exegetische Studien zum Matthäusevangelium. FS für Anton Vögtle zum 80. Geburtstag*, edited by I. Oberlinner and P. Fiedler, (Stuttgart: KBW, 1991), pp. 141–164, here: 148–149, argues that "fulfil" adds a christological aspect, present in ἦλθον, "I have come", in 3:15 and in the fulfilment quotations. Accordingly Jesus does not set aside Law, but fulfils the Law and the Prophets in a way that both leaves them still valid, but no longer as the ultimate measure of authority; he is.

[67] Cf. Kuhn, "Liebesgebot," pp. 217–219; Broer, "Antithesen," p. 131; K. Pantle-Schieber, "Anmerkungen zur Auseinandersetzung von ἐκκλησία und Judentum im Matthäusevangelium," *ZNW* 80 (1989), pp. 145–162, here: 156; Hagner, *Matthew*, p.106. On the Messiah as interpreter of Torah, see Schäfer, *Studien*, pp. 198–213; see also Allison, *New Moses*, pp. 185–190, 320–323. Allison's concern is to support his thesis, that "Matthew 1–5 presents Jesus as the new lawgiver, the eschatological revealer and interpreter of Torah, the Messiah who brought the definitive, end-time revelation, a revelation for the heart, as foretold by Jeremiah's ancient oracle" (p. 190). Allison argues that Jesus brings new Law in the sense that he both upholds Mosaic law and on divorce and loving one's enemy his teachings "go Moses one better" (p. 323). Allison also draws attention to 11QTemple as an analogy, which was both new yet not seen as an abandonment of Pentateuchal law.

the tiniest detail[68] of the Law is to be changed, "until all[69] comes about" or "is done" (ἕως ἂν πάντα γένηται). Like πληρῶσαι "fulfil", γένηται includes both the sense of doing what is commanded and fulfilling what is predicted, in other words, having God's will done.[70] The emphasis on obedience to commandments in 5:16 and 17 and in 5:19–20, not to speak of 5:21–48, precludes reading ἕως ἂν πάντα γένηται as implying the temporary validity of Torah until it is changed by Jesus or until it is fulfilled in Jesus' ministry[71] or his death and resurrection.[72] The point of the instruction for Matthew is that he wants his community to know that it is still in force and will be until eternity.[73]

Hence 5:19 threatens severe demotion in the kingdom of God for any who teach modification of the least command. In harmony with its context, the reference is to commands of written Torah which Jesus has come to champion.[74] If this has more than hypothetical relevance in Matthew's time,

---

[68] The specific reference is to features of the Hebrew text. Betz, *Sermon*, p. 182, suggests the saying intends a deliberate allusion to the Hebrew text and implies a rejection of the notion which appears later in *Ps Clem Hom* 3.51.2–3 that the original Torah was oral and that the written version included invalid additional material (eg. re. sacrifices). This assume the presence of such tradition in the first century, which cannot be shown.

[69] Barth, "Gesetzesverständnis," p. 66, notes that Matthew's "all" is directed against those wanting to modify Torah's demands (also in 3:15; 23:3; and 28:20).

[70] This means that ἕως ἂν πάντα γένηται may include reference to future eschatological fulfilment at the end time, but also includes reference to God's will being effected in the interim, so that it is not simply repeating the first ἕως clause about heaven and earth passing away. Cf. Davies and Allison, *Matthew I*, p. 495; Hagner, *Matthew*, p. 107. Sand, *Gesetz*, p. 38, notes the similar expression in the Lord's Prayer: "Your will be done" (6:10).

[71] Cf. Banks, *Law*, pp. 217–218; "Matthew's understanding of the Law," pp. 235–237; E. Schweizer, *Das Evangelium nach Matthäus*, NTD 2, (Göttingen: Vandenhoeck und Ruprecht, 1973), p. 64, who also suggests Jesus brings a new law, the law of love; Menninger, *Israel*, pp. 109–110. He goes on to argue, following R. A. Guelich, *The Sermon on the Mount*, (Waco: Word, 1982), p. 148, that 5:18 incorporates two opposite approaches in the "until" clauses: one, that of the synagogue arguing permanent validity; one, that of the Church, arguing fulfilment in Jesus' ministry (pp. 110–111). This is forced.

[72] Meier, *Law*, pp. 59–65; 30.

[73] For the suggestion that this is an indirect criticism of the Law since it implies that the Law is not eternal, see Dumbrell, "Law," pp. 19–20; Mohrlang, *Matthew*, p. 9; Davies and Allison, *Matthew I*, p. 490; against this Strecker, *Gerechtigkeit*, p. 143, *Bergpredigt*, p. 58, who argues that 18b reflects a popular expression for "never". Similarly Broer, *Freiheit*, pp. 43–44. The focus of the context is not putting limitations on the Law's applicability, but underlining its validity. So also Saldarini, *Community*, p. 8. Betz, *Sermon*, p. 184, argues that it also reflects apocalyptic thought and offers the additional thought: "the Torah will not simply pass out of existence, but will be replaced by salvation itself, which, after all, is its content."

[74] So D. A. Carson, "Matthew," in *The Expositor's Bible Commentary*, Vol 8, edited

which is likely, it means that some have, indeed, been modifying Torah in ways that Matthew would see Jesus here proscribing and also that Matthew, nevertheless, does not see fit to exclude them altogether.[75] But it is not as though Matthew's main point is to offer a concession here, as if he were to say: "Despite all I have said, I want you to know that we are not excluding those who do." The emphasis is entirely negative and discouraging. This means we should treat 5:19 with great caution as evidence of a concessional attitude. To this I shall return when considering the way these statements function.

5:20 reinforces the impression of the continuing validity of the Law when it demands that the disciples' righteousness must exceed that of the scribes and Pharisees.[76] The verse presumes a high degree of concern about fulfilment on their part, rather than their hypocrisy and corruption so lambasted elsewhere in Matthew; otherwise it would be something of an anticlimax.[77] More significantly, the vocabulary used here, "righteousness",

---

by F. E. Gaebelin, (Grand Rapids: Zondervan, 1984), pp. 1–599, here: 146; R. T. France, *Matthew. Evangelist and Theologian*, (Exeter: Paternoster, 1989), p. 195; cf. Menninger, *Israel*, p. 112, who argues that the "commandments" are Jesus' commandments; similarly Banks, "Matthew's understanding of the Law," pp. 238–240. Betz, *Sermon*, pp. 186–188, however, argues that "these least commandments" refers ironically to Jesus' commandments and does so in deliberate contrast to Pharisaic traditions which prioritise commandments in accordance with the difficulty they pose in compliance, viewed primarily from the perspective of detailed observance. He notes 11:28–30 as expressing a parallel idea. This makes sense, he argues, of the judgement: to become least in the kingdom is surely the punishment not for teaching and transgressing the least command, but the greatest. Betz bases his interpretation also on making a distinction between ἐντολαί and νόμος, the former, referring to Jesus' exposition of the written Law, the latter, to the written Law itself. Nothing in the immediate context suggests such a distinction. Betz can arrive at such an exegesis because he see 5:17–20 as enunciating four principles. But, surely they cannot be taken in isolation from one another even in Betz's hypothetical source (and certainly not in the Matthean context). The close relationship between 5:17–18 and 5:19 most naturally implies that the commandments of Torah are the intended reference in 5:19; better, these commandments as interpreted by Jesus. On contrasts between greater and lesser commandments cf. 4 Macc 5:19–21, which rejects suggestions that less weighty sins are less serious. Similarly *mKidd* 1:10; *mMakk* 3:15; *mHull* 12:5, but for the general distinction between lesser and weightier matters of the Law see Matt 23:23; *mAboth* 2:1; 4:2.

[75] Cf. Betz, *Sermon*, pp. 185, 188–189, who speaks of "an apostate teaching apostasy" (p. 185). He agrees with J. Weiss, *The History of Primitive Christianity*, 2 vols, (New York: Wilson and Ericksson, 1957), II p. 753, in seeing in ἐλάχιστος an allusion to Paul (cf. 1 Cor 15:9).

[76] Menninger, *Israel*, pp. 113–114, does not convince when he proposes that not two levels of righteousness are contrasted, but two different systems: obedience to Jesus' Law and obedience to Old Testament Law.

[77] Cf. Betz, *Sermon*, p. 193, suggests that the implied criticism includes both hypocrisy

links what is being said in the preceding paragraph both to the conditions set
out in the beatitudes which enjoin a thirst after such righteousness and to the
exposition which follows in 5:21–48, which conclude with the demand that
believers be "perfect as their heavenly father is perfect".[78]

One could hardly have a clearer statement about Jesus' attitude towards
the Law than what we find here in 5:17–20. They appear to be stating that
the entire Torah, inclusive of ritual, ceremonial, food, circumcision laws, is
to be continued until the end of time. There are, however, some tensions, in
particular, between 5:19 and 5:18.[79] The latter demands obedience down to
the letter; the former apparently concedes exceptions. We have already noted
that 5:19 should not be misread as intending to announce an exception. Its
function is primarily negative, in support of 5:18. Its internal logic also
makes one suspicious. One would expect, formally, that those teaching
abandonment of the greatest commandments would be made least in the
kingdom. The point is obviously not eschatological reversal. The rhetorical
juxtaposition is, "least command" – "least person". The rhetorical play may,
in effect, be a colourful way of saying; there will be no room in the kingdom
of heaven for such people.[80] It is only if we take the saying literally that we
must acknowledge that for all its negativity the saying implies inclusion. It
is very tenuous to build reconstructions of Matthew's place in early

---

and the attitude of mere compliance with the written law and its interpretation through
tradition.

[78] Betz, *Sermon*, pp. 190–193, rightly points out that the focus of 5:20 is the
righteousness which will count before God's throne and refers here to performance. But
then he distinguishes this from the way Matthew would have interpreted righteousness:
imitation of the righteousness of Christ. Such a distinction is open to question, especially
if we understand such righteousness to include following the exposition of Torah by Jesus
who also lived it out. On the possibility that the Sermon on the Mount reflects current
discussions about higher and lower forms of justice, see his treatment on pp. 194–197.
Betz notes that the criticism here of an inadequate level of righteousness on the part of the
scribes and Pharisees has no precise parallels elsewhere in the New Testament. Even 23:2
does not constitute a parallel, because the chapter addresses abuses. Hoppe,
"Vollkommenheit," pp. 159–164, makes the point that this perfection must be more than
keeping commandments, as 19:16–22 shows. He argues that it is not primarily ethics, but
discipleship and thus marks the significance difference between Matthew's community
and Judaism. But that is not the focus of either 5:20 or 5:48.

[79] So Betz, *Sermon*, p. 185; Strecker, *Gerechtigkeit*, p. 145; Hübner, *Gesetz*, p. 27.
Cf. Wong, *Interkulturelle Theologie*, p. 42, who argues that Matthew deliberately intends
that 5:17–20 to be open to be taken in two ways, to enable both Jews and Gentiles in
Matthew's community to identify with it. This strains the integrity of the text.

[80] So Hoppe, "Vollkommenheit," pp. 149–150, who argues for an alternative considered
by Luz, *Matthäus I*, p. 238, that 5:19 should not be seen as casuistry, but as a rhetorical
statement supporting, not providing an exception to 5:18.

Christianity (eg. relation to Pauline Christianity) on what is at most a minor secondary implication.

5:18 is also susceptible of a literal or a metaphorical interpretation. It can be read literally and would be reflected in resistance to changes to written texts of the Law and the Prophets. It can, however, be seen just as a striking metaphor for stating that no commandment is to be waived. In a broader sense, it could also imply less than a literal fulfilment and even include some abrogation.[81] How much of a metaphor is it? Is Matthew thinking quantitatively or qualitatively? Does he envisage adherence in the sense of the fulfilment of every single commandment or is the statistical totality of both 5:18 and 19 itself metaphorical for a total attitudinal commitment? Or is it both? Only the context can decide.

The echo in 5:20 of the "righteousness" set out in the various beatitudes suggests that the focus is not ritual and ceremonial law. But 5:17–20 does not, in itself, imply anything with regard to such emphases within the Law. Perhaps that kind of weighting is implied in 5:19, but this is far from certain. We cannot find a resolution without careful examination of 5:21–48. Even then we will need to leave open the extent to which the strictures of 5:17–19 still apply to the Law in its entirety. To some degree nothing in the immediate context makes an answer possible; we will need to consider the question in the light of the material in the gospel as a whole.

In 5:21–48 Matthew has set the material within a pattern of two groups of three, the first section of each being introduced by a fuller formulation of the contrast which is implied in each. In it, "You have heard that it was said to the ancients", alludes to God's word through Moses to the people of Israel. Coherence within the broader context thus makes it unlikely that Matthew sees Jesus attacking Torah commandments. Yet in each case Old Testament commandments are cited with or without additions. The starkness of the antithetical form goes beyond a contrast of opinions in interpretation. The most plausible explanation is that Matthew sees Jesus citing commandments as they were being heard, ie. interpreted.[82] The status of his antithetical

---

[81] So Barth, "Gesetzesverständnis," pp. 65–66 n. 4

[82] Daube, *Rabbinic Judaism*, p. 56, shows that "one who hears" frequently refers to one who interprets, often negatively. Thus Betz, *Sermon*, p. 208, makes the point that the thesis being attacked is not the commandment itself, given by God, but its literal interpretation, either left unexpressed or present also by addition. "The SM introduces here a critical difference between what God has in fact said and what the tradition claims God has said." It also does not assume that age of a tradition guarantees its worth. See also pp. 216–217; similarly Hagner, *Matthew*, p. 112; Kuhn, "Liebesgebot," pp. 213–214, who on p. 216 summarises the force of the first five theses as follows: 1. (Only) the person who (really) commits murder must be brought to trial; 2. (Only actual) adultery is to be

statement is, however, not a second opinion,[83] but an authoritative declaration made on his own God given authority. Thus Jesus' words in the antithesis, "but I tell you," do not set Jesus in competition with God (or Moses), but express the authority which belongs to the divinely created Son of God, Israel's Messiah, the one who will come as the world's judge. He comes not to abolish, but to uphold and expound Torah on the basis of the authority which is his.

In all cases Jesus adds authoritative comment designed to uphold the commandment. This is the essence of the contrast, but this is not to deny that in applying commandments more strictly, Jesus at times significantly adds to or modifies the original. At times this includes modifications which would entail a change of more than a "jot or tittle", so that it is apparent that the stricture of 5:18 is employing hyperbole. On the other hand, 5:17–19 make it likely that Matthew saw 5:21–48 as fundamentally upholding, rather than abolishing Torah.

5:21–22 show Jesus going beyond the commandment about murder to outlaw the attitude of hatred which lies behind murder and expressions of anger which flow from this attitude.[84] The point does not lie with the particular words cited, nor with the legal instances envisaged. These serve rhetorical purposes and ultimately encompass all such activity together as standing under divine judgement.[85]

5:23–24 apply the same attention to attitudes of anger and hatred in enjoining temple worshippers not to offer sacrifices without first dealing with conflict in their relationships with others.[86] Matthew, writing after the

---

avoided; 3. The institution of a bill of divorce is evidence of (divine) sanction of divorce; 4. With regard to swearing falsely, it is (only) required that you keep your oaths (vows) made to God; 5. The *ius talionis* allows the right to demand compensation (whatever form it may take).

[83] Cf. Daube, *Rabbinic Judaism*, pp. 55–62, who cites forms of refutation of opinion in rabbinic tradition, using the phrase, "But you must say". This falls short of the authority expressed here, but the differences should not be exaggerated. See the discussion in Betz, *Sermon*, pp. 208–209.

[84] Betz, *Sermon*, pp. 218–219, shows that Jesus leaves the decalogue prohibition in tact, but takes up its interpretation in 21c, using its formulation, but challenging it as interpretation. For similar teaching on anger see Sir 1:22; TDan 2–5; TGad 3–5; cf. also Arist 168; 4 Macc 2:1–23; Ps Phoc 57–58, 63–64.

[85] The instances are not to be taken as extensions of criminal law, but function satirically and at the same time as a means of changing the focus from criminal to moral law. So Betz, *Sermon*, pp. 219–220.

[86] Betz, *Sermon*, pp. 222–223, brings out the drama of the saying, by noting how the point of remembering comes at the final step in the procedure of sacrificing: placing the gift on the altar. He also points to the related text in Did 14:2 and discusses similar concerns about ethics and sacrifice in Hellenistic literature (pp. 224–226).

temple's destruction, must be preserving this logion for the attitude it enjoins rather than with any particular concern for temple worship. That does not suggest either a negative or positive approach to temple law, itself. He has already portrayed Jesus' concern for personal reconciliation in the beatitude given the peacemakers (5:9) and will do so later in the gospel (6:14–15; 18:12–35).

Matthew may well intend that the injunction in 5:25–26, with which this segment closes, to reach agreement with an adversary in law, be taken quite literally as a further application of right attitude between people; its primary concern is dealing with anger.[87] It falls thus within the Torah exposition of Jesus who applies Torah to everyday situations of life.

Throughout the segment Matthew shows us Jesus' putting the focus on attitudes assumed to underlie murder and encouraging behaviours which give expression to the reverse of such attitudes, reconciliation instead of hatred, making peace instead of war, and, at least, in imagery, declaring such attitudinal behaviour as the appropriate basis for acceptance before God, thus applying the demand of 5:20 to this area of concern.

Similarly, the second segment, 5:27–30, represents an exposition of Torah which makes it stricter.[88] The traditional prohibition of adultery becomes a proscription of adulterous attitudes towards a woman (5:27–28).[89] The logion which follows demands radical discipline under the image of plucking out the offending eye or cutting off the offending hand (5:29–30).[90]

Associated with such strictness is also the shorter third segment, 3:31–32, which gives us Matthew's version of the prohibition of divorce, found also in 19:9 in Matthew's revised version of Mark 10:11–12. The thesis, "Whoever divorces his wife, let him give her a bill of divorce", is not a

---

[87] See the discussion of alternatives in Betz, *Sermon*, pp. 226–228. 5:26 reflects the hopeless situation of being in jail at the time (pp. 229–230). Cf. Strecker, *Bergpredigt*, p. 72, who sees Matthew allegorising the trial scene and therefore alluding to the final judgement.

[88] Betz, *Sermon*, p. 231, suggests that the hearer might rightly supplement the citation of the commandment with: "and whoever commits adultery shall be answerable to the court", in parallel to the previous antithesis. The focus of the law interpretation being attacked is its literal character.

[89] On the erotic psychology of the time and role of the eye in it, see Betz, *Sermon*, p. 232. Adultery infringed the rights of another male. He outlines the possible meanings of the phrase πρὸς ἐπιθυμῆσαι αὐτήν: "for the purpose of desiring her", "with the result that he desires her", "for the purpose of arousing her desire", opting for the first (pp. 233–234. He also draws attention to many Jewish texts with a similar theme from the period (pp. 234–235). See, for example, TBenj 8; PsSol 4:4–5.

[90] On the common use of cutting off limbs as a metaphor for seriousness in both Hellenistic and rabbinic literature, see Betz, *Sermon*, pp. 238–239.

direct quotation of the Law, but a summary of one aspect of Deut 24:1–4. Matthew's Jesus is attacking the application of this Law which treats divorce as a matter of course.[91] Matthew's version of the logion has been shaped in a community where Jewish Torah prevails. This is evident in the inclusion of the exception clause, on grounds of πορνεία, probably "sexual immorality",[92] and in its reflection of Jewish law according to which only the husband can divorce. Jesus' declaration does not call the divorce provision into question, as in Mark's version, but applies it with greater strictness.[93]

By contrast, the prohibition of oaths, 5:33–37, has the effect of ruling out

---

[91] So Betz, *Sermon*, p. 244. On divorce practice of the time and its background, see pp. 244–248. He notes two opposing tendencies in interpretation in the period: greater stringency, even outlawing divorce, and greater liberalisation.

[92] So Betz, *Sermon*, p. 250; G. J. Wenham, "Matthew and Divorce," *JSNT* 22 (1984), pp. 95–107, here: 104; C. L. Blomberg, "Marriage, Divorce, Remarriage, and Celibacy: An Exegesis of Matthew 19:3–12," *TrinJourn* 11 (1990), pp. 161–196, here: 173–182; Bockmuehl, "Matthew 5.32; 19.9," pp. 294–295, who refers to 1QapGen 20.15; Philo *Abr* 98; and Matt 1:19, which illustrate the assumption that illicit sex destroys the marriage relationship. Matthew uses the broader term, πορνεία, rather than the specific word for adultery, moiceía. For the view that porneía refers to incestuous marriage see Meier, *Law*, pp. 147–150; B. Witherington, "Matthew 5.32 and 19.9 – Exception or Exceptional Situation," *NTS* 31 (1985), pp. 571–576. The saying would then be particularly appropriate for dealing with dissolution of marriages of Gentiles contracted contrary to biblical law. Cf. also Fitzmyer, "Matthean Divorce Texts"; Nolland, "Prohibition of Divorce," pp. 21–25.

[93] Commonly Matthew is seen as allowing only adultery as an exception and in this way falling in line with the stricter interpretation Deut 24, perhaps under the influence of the position later attributed to Shammai. So, for instance, Strecker, *Bergpredigt*, p. 76–80; Saldarini, *Community*, pp. 147–151, esp. 150; Vouga, *Loi*, p. 106; see also Sigal, *Halakah*, pp. 83–118. In treating the statement forbidding divorce with its exception clause as part of the prematthean sermon of Q, Betz, *Sermon*, pp. 248–259, points out that one reading of Deut 24 is that the granting of a bill of divorce cancelling a marriage only applies where a woman has been rendered unclean. This is the case with the woman wanting to remarry her first husband, since it is presumed she will have had other relationships. This is the situation which Deut 24 addresses, not divorce in general. It is in line with this interpretation that Jesus' prohibition, according to the 'SM', applies only where such impurity, here sexual immorality, has taken place. The guiding principle is that no act of law should render anyone unclean. It is not wrong to divorce someone rendered unclean, indeed, to receive her back would render the man unclean. It is wrong to divorce a woman who is not unclean, because it forces her into uncleanness. This coheres also with Paul's allowing divorce of an unbelieving partner, since the partner is already unclean and so his or her status would not by changed by the divorce. The implied argument of 5:31–32 would, then, be different from Matt 19:3–12, which interprets Deut 24 differently as a concession (p. 257). In both, however, remarriage is forbidden. Within the context of Matthew's gospel as a whole, however, it is doubtful whether Matthew understood 5:32 differently from 19:9. On other suggestions of the background of the divorce saying see also the discussion and notes on Mark 10:1–12.

Torah provision for oaths.[94]   This may be seen as a pitting of Jesus' authority against that of Torah, but, more likely, Matthew sees it as an upholding of Torah by making it even stricter.   It was a stance which did not place Matthew's Jesus outside the framework of Jewish discussion of the time.[95] Josephus tells us of some Essenes, who having made oaths at initiation, then abstain from all oath taking as part of their religious commitment (*JW* 2.135). The reasons which Matthew presents for applying such a prohibition are various.   Swearing by heaven or earth or Jerusalem is assumed to entail an abuse because these are in special ways treated as belonging to God (5:34–35).   The text reflects traditional Jewish reverence for the city, Jerusalem. But 5:36 argues differently: swearing by one's head is forbidden, because one has no power to change hair colour.   Presumably, in a different way, what belongs to God, here God's power, is being forbidden as a basis for human oaths.   The assumption seems to be that an oath made on the basis of a surety that, in fact, God provides, and not the swearer, is invalid.   5:37 limits this still further by making people swear only on the basis of something they, themselves, produce, and, even more specifically, the words: "Yes, yes; no, no."[96]

Taken as a whole, this segment is the first to offer justification for Jesus' demands and appears to do so on the basis of undermining oaths altogether, by arguing that one can offer as a surety only what one can be responsible for oneself.   But the prohibition goes, in fact, further than the justification requires, which at most sets up a new pattern for oath giving related only to one's own strong affirmation or denial.   Considered in association with the

---

[94]   On the place of oaths in the ancient world see Betz, *Sermon*, pp. 259–263. The formulation of the prohibition in 5:33 reflects Hellenistic Jewish *halakah* (pp. 263–264). Betz argues that the proposal which underlies 5:33 is that to deal with perjury, it is better to upgrade oaths to promises, vows, to God (p. 266).   See also Saldarini, *Community*, p. 152–153. According to Betz, the Sermon rejects oaths altogether in a combination of arguments, relating to options of the time, because of their presumptuousness and miscalculation in the power they seek to exercise in relation to God and oneself, but finally because of the moral priority of directness in language. Additions amount to perjury and stem from evil. So Betz, *Sermon*, pp. 266–274. He suggests the reference to Jerusalem reflects the location of the community which produced the sermon in Jerusalem (p. 269). But Jerusalem was of central significance for most Jews, including diaspora Jews.

[95]   So I. Broer, "Anmerkungen zum Gesetzesverständnis des Matthäus," in *Das Gesetz im Neuen Testament*, QD108, edited by K. Kertelge, (Freiburg: Herder, 1986), pp. 128–145, here: 131; Sanders, *Jewish Law*, pp. 50–56; Vermes, *Religion of Jesus the Jew*, pp. 34–35.

[96]   Some consider that the effect of 5:37 is that Matthew's Jesus has not removed oaths altogether. So Strecker, *Bergpredigt*, p. 84, pointing to the similar formulation in 2 En 49:10; similarly Vouga, *Loi*, p. 243. See also Davies and Allison, *Matthew I*, pp. 535–536 (but cf. conflicting comments on p. 538).

earlier segments, this prohibition stands consistently on a line which is directed against destructive (here, manipulative) attitudes and behaviour in human relations.

5:38–42 contrast between the principle of equivalent retaliation which formed part of the Jewish legal system, "an eye for an eye and a tooth for a tooth," (and forms part of most legal systems!) and a teaching of Jesus which directly contradicts it. Matthew does not seem to be dealing with these statements in their original sense as a principle for determining restitution and penalty in a forensic context. Instead he appears to assume that these were principles being applied more generally to interpersonal behaviour. It is this use that Jesus challenges.[97]

Jesus lays down a stricter law which rules out retaliation altogether. He enjoins that one should not offer resistance to the evil person. The text lists three instances: striking on the cheek, being sued for one's undergarment, and being pressed by the military to carry a load for a mile. Only the first directly relates to retaliation. But the other two belong generally to resisting what are seen as evil people. Matthew's Jesus counsels both submission and generosity, offering double what is asked for. The segment ends with an application of the principle even to those who are not seen as "evil", namely anyone who asks for anything and, as an instance, those asking for a loan.

The specific applications do not come into conflict with Torah; they go beyond it. They do not place Matthew's Jesus outside the range of Jewish discussion of the time.[98] They run in the direction of asking more of people, rather than less. Far from abrogating or watering down Torah, they are making Torah stricter at this point. This is consistent with the previous five antitheses. Matthew's Jesus is concerned with heightening Torah's demand, even when such strict interpretation effectively rules out certain Torah provisions.

The final segment also has Jesus offering a teaching in contrast to what people have been hearing (5:43–48). The expansion, "and hate your enemy", is a provocative expansion representing the implications of a particularist

---

[97] See the excellent discussion in Betz, *Sermon*, pp. 277–285, who shows that the concern is not to revoke Torah, but to outlaw its literal interpretation as justifying retaliation. Non retaliation belongs within the perspective of the Golden Rule as a means of seeking the change in evildoers. Jesus' own behaviour illustrates the point. The Sermon is dealing primarily with human relations in conflict, not with cases of law and compensation. Betz shows the way the principle of retaliation was being widely questioned in the Hellenistic world of the time, including the instance of striking a person (pp. 285–289). The Sermon interprets the *ius talionis* not as a principle of law, but in the context of ethical relationships and does so by interpreting it in the light of the Golden rule, which is its preventive, positive, counterpart (pp. 292–293).

[98] So Broer, "Gesetzesverständnis," p. 132; Betz, *Sermon*, pp. 277–285.

understanding of "you shall love your neighbour".[99] Matthew sees Jesus as offering teaching which goes beyond such an understanding. Matthew's Jesus enjoins love for enemies and prayer for persecutors. It is interesting that, as in the segment on oaths, so here, Matthew's Jesus supports his teaching by argument. The first is an argument by analogy: we should do as God does, in indiscriminately having sunshine and rain come to the just and unjust.[100] The second is an argument from self interest: reward will come to those who go beyond the norm of what any person, even toll collectors and pagans/Gentiles, would do.

Reward (5:46) plays a significant role also in the following sections (6:1–18).[101] It is striking that in 5:46–47 toll collectors and Gentiles[102] are singled out as ordinary and unworthy citizens. The same negative attitude comes elsewhere in Matthew: toll collectors in 18:17; Gentiles in 6:7,32; 18:17; 20:19, 25. Matthew does not appear to sense any tension between this and the first argument, indeed, the theme of the whole segment, of doing as God does in avoiding discriminatory behaviour and attitudes, indeed, loving even one's enemies. Matthew probably saw the use of toll collectors and Gentiles in the argument from reward as nothing other than instancing typical behaviour and not as discriminatory in itself.[103] The contrast is even more striking because anecdotes about Jesus' open and accepting behaviour towards toll collectors have been paradigmatic within the tradition. One cannot escape the conclusion that at these points Matthew is closer to Jesus' critics than to Jesus and this coheres with his conservatism generally.

---

[99] So Betz, *Sermon*, p. 304; who cites Luz, *Matthäus I*, p. 310; Guelich, *Sermon*, pp. 225–227. Hating enemies is not part of Old Testament or rabbinic teaching, but was a popular notion of the world of the time and a matter of discussion in philosophical school, where, for instance, Plato opposed it. See Betz, pp. 305–308.

[100] The sermon cites only part of Lev 19:18, omitting "as yourself". Betz, *Sermon*, pp. 302–303, suggests this is because it wants to focus on God as model in the interpretation and that therefore such an addition would be inappropriate. On God's love in nature as the model for human love, see PsSol 5:6–8.

[101] Cf. Hübner, *Gesetz*, pp. 203–205, who seeks to contrast Matthew's approach with that of Pharisaic Judaism; the latter appealed to reward as a goal; the former portrays reward as a result (p. 204). While this may be the case in 25:31–46, it will not hold elsewhere, especially in 6:1–18 and reflects a stereotyping of Pharisaic Judaism as seeking salvation by merit which owes more to the conflicts of church history than to first century Judaism.

[102] A negative attitudes towards Gentiles, is reflected also in 22:7; 24:6–7. See Saldarini, *Community*, p. 77. Cf. Levine, *Salvation History*, p. 11, who argues that ἐθνικὸς in Matthew now means pagan rather than Gentile; similarly p. 32 re. 6:32.

[103] Betz, *Sermon*, p. 320, notes the issue for Matthew, but assumes Matthew tolerated the tradition as reflecting an attitude of the past not his own. This is not satisfactory.

Matthew concludes the segment with a reformulation of its first argument, but now generalised: the disciples should be perfect as God is perfect (5:48). This also echoes 5:20, the demand for righteousness, and so both brings to a conclusion the six antitheses and embraces them within the demand for righteousness. There is both a quantitative and a qualitative aspect to such perfection and righteousness. The qualitative difference is that it is based on Torah now interpreted by Jesus. In that sense it includes following Jesus, but not as an extra. For to follow Jesus is to keep the commandments. At the same time, the quantitative difference lies in the fact that a different quality of understanding Torah leads to greater righteousness.[104]

Taking 5:17–48 together as a whole, we see that in it Matthew emphasises Jesus' continuity in matters of the Law and the Prophets. This coheres with his focus on Jesus' fulfilment of Old Testament prophecy elsewhere in the so called formula quotations. In this passage the focus is especially the Law. The rigorous demands of 5:18–19 and the way Torah is treated in 5:21–48 belong together. The demand for total obedience expressed in 5:20 and 5:48 frames the antitheses. But the rigour of 5:18–19 is expressed not in literal fulfilment, quantitatively, but, qualitatively, in a radical restatement of Torah demands.

In this process of radical restatement, Matthew has Jesus expand the focus of the prohibition of murder and adultery to include all attitudes and actions which potentially lead to such acts. The tendency of such expansion is clearly in the direction of greater demand. The same tendency is apparent also in the contrasts which follow. Divorce is permitted on much more strictly defined grounds than apparently had become common practice. Oaths, allowed only under certain provisions, are virtually forbidden altogether; their intention to uphold truth is maintained by a commitment to non manipulative use of language. Rules which were being applied to allow retaliation and hate of enemies are replaced by a command to submit generously and to love and pray for enemies. The new teaching, therefore, places greater demands on adherents of the Law, and is, in that sense, stricter.

The focus throughout is on having a more generous, positive attitude towards people. This is obvious in the first and the last two antitheses (murder, retaliation, loving neighbour). It is probably also determining those

---

[104] E. Lohse, "'Vollkommen sein'. Zur Ethik des Matthäusevangeliums," in *Salz der Erde - Licht der Welt: Exegetische Studien zum Matthäusevangelium. FS für Anton Vögtle zum 80. Geburtstag,* edited by I. Oberlinner, and P. Fiedler, (Stuttgart: KBW, 1991), pp. 131-140, here: 137-140, argues that this is not a quantitative difference, but only qualitative: receiving God's goodness as gift (as in the beatitudes) and following Jesus.

on adultery and divorce, if the concern is with wronging people. It is also present in the forbidding oaths as a means of manipulation. The attitude coheres with the focus in the beatitudes on positive behaviours and attitudes towards people[105] and with the Matthean version of the Golden Rule in 7:12.

In his God given authority Jesus declares God's will in relation to each. But in doing so he is not shown making free floating or arbitrary claims.[106] There are values which inform his stance. We have already noted the coherence given to Jesus' interpretation by the strong emphasis on attitude and on a positive approach to people. The clear implication throughout is also that Jesus' words interpret and apply the true intention of the commandments. In other words the Law has authority and Jesus uses his authority and wisdom to uphold the Law's authority and expound what that authority demands. In the first three antitheses and the fifth Jesus does this by implication only, offering declarations only. But their force is derived from this dual authority: that of the Law, itself, and that of Jesus uniquely qualified to interpret it. Yet beside the dual appeal to authority, the first two antitheses also make an implicit appeal to common human experience: the link between attitude and behaviour. A similar appeal to common experience (of abuse) probably underlies the statement on divorce. On oaths Matthew's Jesus offers explicit arguments. They, too, appeal to common human experience (pointless oaths and the evil of manipulation in communication), but also to theology in the strictest sense (against attempts to manipulate God). In the final antitheses the appeal is primarily theological again: God's generosity, though again linked with human experience.

---

[105] Betz, *Sermon*, pp. 204–205, proposes that the antithesis have been constructed on the basis of Lev 19:18, the command to love one's neighbour which features in the final antithesis and is focused on broken relationships. The "Torah commandments are 'fulfilled' in the sense that with the love-commandment, the whole Torah is fulfilled" (p. 205).

[106] Betz, *Sermon*. pp. 209–210, makes the point that these claims appeal to the meaning of the scripture being interpreted, do so in the light of the love command, sometimes illustrated by examples, proverbs, rhetorical questions, and in a way which assumes they can be understood and further applied to concrete situations. They, therefore, differ, from the parallels which Daube adduces from academic rabbinic discussion (Daube, *Rabbinic Judaism*, pp. 55–62), on the one hand, and from direct claims based on christology on the other. In Matthew, however, Betz's latter observation needs qualification. His main point, however, still stands even for Matthew. Cf. also H. Weder, "'But I say to you...' Concerning the Foundations of Jesus' interpretation of the Law in the 'Sermon on the Mount'," in *Text and Logos. The Humanistic Interpretation of the New Testament*, SPHomSer, edited by T. W. Jennings, (Atlanta: Scholars, 1990), pp. 211–228, here: 221–225, who notes that the statements of Jesus appeal to no external authority, or, at most, appeal to what nature teaches. Betz's observations are more satisfactory. Cf. also his "Die 'Rede der Rede'. Beobachtungen zum Verständnis der Bergpredigt Jesu," *EvTh* 45 (1985), pp. 45–60, here: 47–51.

These values help govern Matthew's understanding of Jesus' approach to the Law. They form an important part of the 'mix' of authority. We might identify them in summary as: having positive regard and love for people (though Matthew is not always consistent here, as his stereotyped references to toll collectors and Gentiles show); valuing attitude as well as behaviour; honouring and loving God; and imitating God's love and righteousness.

Matthew was setting Jesus' declarations against the ways that Torah was being heard in his day, hence the antithetical form. The positions taken by the Matthean Jesus fall within the range of debate about Torah interpretation in his time and should not be seen as abrogating Old Testament Law.[107] Matthew certainly sees it that way.[108] Jewish contemporaries of Matthew may well have agreed, although we might expect also mixed reactions. It is another question whether in actual substance Matthew's Jesus departs from Torah. A material comparison of the texts of Matthew and written Torah had led many in the past to that conclusion. But the greater tendency to set these texts within their socio-religious context and the growing knowledge and understanding of that context have led to a much greater reluctance to draw such a conclusion in recent years and rightly so.[109]

It is also important to identify the social function of 5:17–48. The primary focus in Jesus' authoritative declarations about God's will in Torah is to

---

[107] See the important discussion in Broer, "Gesetzesverständnis," pp. 131–133, who concludes with regard to the antitheses (in particular, on oaths and retaliation): "Das von den Antithesen geforderte Verhalten wird auch in jüdischen Belegen gefordert und übersteigt so den Rahmen des dem Judentum Möglichen nicht" (p. 131). ("The behaviour demanded in the antitheses is also demanded in Jewish texts and so does not exceed the range of what was possible in Judaism.") As evidence for this he draws attention, in particular, to Müller, "Gesetz". Cf. Strecker, *Bergpredigt*, p. 65, who sees the antitheses expressing Jesus' distance in relation to Torah: "Der Kyrios steht über der Tora; seine Autorität ermöglicht es, Torakritik zu üben" ("The Lord stands above the Torah; his authority makes it possible for him to engage in criticism of the Torah"). See also pp. 74, 98–99.

[108] So Davies and Allison, *Matthew I*, p. 492, who write: "We cannot think that he believed the teachings of 5.21–48 to contradict the Torah. In other words, in Matthew's eyes the tension between Jesus' teaching and the Mosaic commandments was much less that in the eyes of many modern scholars." Similarly Luz, *Matthäus I*, p. 241.

[109] Cf. K. Syreeni, "Matthew, Luke, and the Law. A Study in Hermeneutical Exegesis," in *The Law in the Bible and its Environment*, Publications of the Finnish Exegetical Society 51, edited by T. Veijola, (Helsinki: Finn. Exeg. Society; Göttingen: Vandenhoeck und Ruprecht, 1990), pp. 126–157, here: 133–141, who argues that unlike Luke, Matthew operates within a text world which is remote from his own and therefore tolerates the contradiction of having Jesus affirm the Law and then progressively contradict it, especially from the third antithesis onward. See also D. Zeller, "Jesus als vollmächtiger Lehrer (Mt 5–7) und der hellenistische Gesetzgeber," in *Studien zum Matthäusevangelium. FS W. Pesch*, SBS, edited by L. Schenke, (Stuttgart: KBW, 1988), pp. 299–317, here: 301–305, who

reinforce the identity of the Matthean community as having claim to right interpretation of Torah.[110] It is directed primarily to the community, not to outsiders. It is also giving concrete instruction to the community in what it means to do the will of God.[111] The community clearly holds both the authority of Torah and the authority of Jesus together. It does not want to see contradiction between the two and so Matthew emphasises consistency. Strong assertions in the interests of identity reflect what the community wants. In making such assertions in antithetical mode, Matthew imputes a counter stance to those from whom he has Jesus distance the community. It is open for discussion the extent to which in doing so, he has accurately described opposing positions or caricatured them.

2.2.4 Matthew 6–7

While 5:21–48 forms a unit in which the major statements of 5:17–20 find exposition, the remainder of the Sermon on the Mount presents teaching of Jesus only indirectly related to issues of the Law. Yet upholding God's Law as an aspect of doing God's will is never far from the surface. This is evident in 6:1–18, which deals with three major aspects of Jewish piety: almsgiving, prayer, and fasting. 6:1 sets them under the heading of the key term, "righteousness". Greater righteousness (5:20), for which believers are to hunger and thirst (5:6) and for which they will be persecuted (5:10), includes

---

claims that the antitheses are in fact set against the commandments of Torah and not just their interpretation. Jesus is neither a new Moses, nor a prophet, nor a messianic teacher (p. 306). Instead Zeller suggests the model of the Hellenistic King as Lawgiver. This model explains Jesus' divine authority, his issuing of new laws, with a similar divine authority, a gentleness, even the form of the laws and that Jesus as king is exemplary (pp. 305–315). He points to use of such an image of Moses by Philo (*Vit Mos* I 334; II 4; *de Praem* 55). This fails to take the obviously Jewish context of Matthew sufficiently into account.

[110] I. Broer, "Das *Ius Talionis* im Neuen Testament," *NTS* 40 (1994), pp. 1–21, here: 11–21, argues that the fact that Matthew portrays the *ius talionis* as the Old Testament and Jewish norm says more about the relation between his community and the Jewish community from which his has separated than it does about the practice of the former (p. 20). Whether consciously or not, Matthew's antitheses function to establish the identity of the community. This explains, he suggests, how there can be such a discrepancy between what Matthew describes as Old Testament and Jewish Law and current evidence of Judaism of the time (on this see pp. 5–6).

[111] Cf. Strecker, *Bergpredigt*, p. 69, who interprets the strictness as Matthew's attempt to have the law function as judge, in effect, as a basis for calling for repentance. The idea that Matthew was engaging in an evangelistic ploy, by seeking to induce guilt through the antitheses, in preparation for the relief offered by the gospel, is a misreading of Matthew's purpose, indeed undermines it.

these practices. But they are treated not primarily as a matter of Torah interpretation nor in relation to particular Jewish ordinances. The same applies to the Lord's Prayer which also strongly reflects Jewish origins.

The teachings of 6:1–18 are directed to a Christian community which identifies itself over against the "hypocrites". These are clearly Jewish outsiders and are following normal Jewish practices, even if for the wrong reasons and in the wrong way. Jesus' instructions do not conflict with Torah. Yet they indicate distance not only from abuses, but also from current Jewish practices. This is reflected, in particular, in Matthew's emphasis on privacy.[112]

The basic teaching consists of three matching formulations which condemn hypocrisy and enjoin behaviour which will earn God's reward (6:2–4,5–6 and 16–18). Making a show in front of others is contrasted with discreet, undemonstrative actions. In the segment on prayer (6:5–15) we also find an exhortation not to babble like Gentile worshippers (6:7–8), but to pray in a manner set out in what we know as the Lord's Prayer (6:9–13). It is followed by a saying which reinforces the sentiments of part of that prayer, warning that those who do not forgive others will not receive forgiveness from God (6:14–15). Jesus, the teacher, is instructing the community about appropriate piety and at the same time warning them of the consequences of false piety.

There follow a series of teachings in three loosely knit clusters of three themes each. The first consists of 6:19–24. 6:19–21 warns about the hoarding of riches, directing the disciples again to seek their reward in heavenly riches. 6:22–23 is a warning against the evil eye of greed, by way of a parable of the eye setting the whole body in light or in darkness. 6:24 contrasts the claims of Mammon and God.

6:25–34 address the related theme of anxiety about basic material needs, such as food and clothing. In enjoining lack of anxiety, Jesus argues from the state of nature, birds and plants, in particular, to persuade the disciples that they can trust that God will also take care of them. Within the wider context , the closing words, which call the disciples to seek first God's kingdom and righteousness (6:33), form a link both with the beginning of the section we are considering, by recalling the injunction to seek heavenly

---

[112] See K. Syreeni, "Separation and Identity: Aspects of the Symbolic World of Matt 6.1-18," *NTS* 40 (1994), pp. 522-541, who argues that Matthew is setting over against Jewish piety a Christian piety removed from the eyes of Jewish opponents and from view of other believers. It is no longer Jewish piety (pp. 527–531). Hypocrites are not just scribes and Pharisees as in Mt 23, but, more generally, Jews (p. 527). Matthew's use of this material reflects not only separation from Judaism but also a sensitivity to the pagan world, so that the community probably understands itself as "a third race" (p. 538).

riches, and with the major theme of righteousness which spans ch. 5 and reappears also in 6:1. They recall the promises of the beatitudes to the poor in spirit and those who hunger for righteousness.

7:1–11 begins with teaching about judging others (7:1–5), warns against exposing what is treasured to those who will not appreciate them and even abuse them (7:6), and promises God's answers to the prayers of those who ask, as a parent would respond to a child (7:7–11). 7:6, coming after the warnings about judgement, may well be citing an instance where judgement should be exercised: namely, over against the Gentile world which fails to appreciate the holy.[113]

Only in 7:12 do we return to a deliberate link with the Law and the Prophets. It comes as a comment on the Golden Rule: "Whatever you want people to do to you, do also to them; for this is the Law and the Prophets." Matthew appears to be using this as a summary that is inclusive rather than exclusive. He is not attempting to reduce the Law and the Prophets to this rule, in a way that excludes anything, but to identify this as underlying all their provisions. Yet there is much in Torah for which it is quite irrelevant, especially ceremonial and cultic law; they are obviously not in Matthew's mind at this point; nor have they been, except incidentally (5:23–24).

The words, "the Law and the Prophets", recall 5:17. The effect is to embrace all of the intervening material within the framework of "the Law and the Prophets" and to portray Jesus' teaching as an authoritative exposition of what the Law stands for. This means that we should not see 5:17–48 as dealing with Torah related issues, followed by other kinds of teaching in 6:1 – 7:11 unrelated to Torah. Instead Matthew sees the whole within the context of Jesus' authoritative exposition of God's will given in the Law and the Prophets and interpreted by love.

This receives confirmation in what follows. For, if 7:12 brings the teaching to a conclusion with reference to the Law and the Prophets, the first of the exhortations which follow employs a common image for describing the call

---

[113] On this problematic text see Betz, *Sermon*, pp. 493–500. He notes the parallel with the words of Jesus to the Syrophoenician woman (Mark 7:24–30; Matt 15:21–28), but argues that within the Sermon the focus is more likely to be heretics, "perhaps the Samaritans (cf. Matt 10:5) or Gentile Christianity under Paul's leadership" (p. 500). From a Matthean perspective I believe that it probably retains its Gentile associations, but understood in the sense of pagans. It is tied up with how Matthew uses the word ἐθνικοί elsewhere. H. von Lips, "Schweine füttert man, Hunde nicht – ein Versuch, das Rätsel von Matthäus 7:6 zu lösen," *ZNW* 79 (1988), pp. 165–186, shows that the behaviour here described would have run contrary to norms of the day and therefore be a symbolic way of saying; acting wrongly will reap dangers. In the context he believes that it must mean judgement (p. 184).

of God's Torah in the Old Testament in Jewish literature, the image of the
two ways (7:13–14).[114] The narrow path leads to life, the broad path, to
destruction. Matthew is probably aware that by using these metaphors he is
strongly identifying Jesus with the Law.

The warning against false prophets who do not bear fruit (7:15–20) and
against those who masquerade as followers of Jesus (7:21–23) sets obedience
to Jesus' teaching of God's Law as the primary criterion of divine
judgement.[115] Jesus' words in 7:19 that trees which do not bear fruit will be
cut down for fire echo John the Baptist's threat to the Sadducees and Pharisees
word for word (3:10). Disciples or Sadducees and Pharisees, in Matthew all
are to be judged by one Law, by one judge. Charismatic activity will no
more win the judge's favour than Abrahamic descent or the rite of baptism,
if people have not pursued righteousness (7:21–23). Matthew has Jesus, the
judge, dismiss them in the words of Ps 6:9 as "those who perpetrate
wickedness" or "lawlessness".

Barth saw in the final word, ἀνομία, translated, "wickedness", a direct

---

[114] Deut 11:26; Jer 21:8; TAsher 1:3–5; 2 En 30:15. For further references and
discussion see Davies and Allison, *Matthew I*, pp. 695–696.

[115] Barth, "Gesetzesverständnis," pp. 68–69, understands these as the Christian
antinomists whom Matthew had been attacking in 5:17–20. He identifies the same group
in 24:11–12 (p. 70). Saldarini, *Community*, pp. 104–106, who argues that in 7:15–20
Matthew may be attacking rival Jewish teachers; but only in 7:21–23 does it become fellow
Christian leaders. He cites the discussion in D. Hill, "False Prophets and Charismatics:
Structure and Interpretation in Matthew 7, 15–23," *Biblica* 57 (1976), pp. 341–348, here:
336–339. Against this D. Trunk, *Der messianische Helfer. Eine redaktions- und
religionsgeschichtliche Studie zu den Exorzismen im Mattthäusevangelium*, Herd. Bib. St.
3, (Herder: Freiburg, 1994), pp. 225–226, argues that they are particular itinerants with an
antinomian slant. "False prophets" come from within and therefore 7:15–20 cannot refer
to rival Jewish teachers. Those of 7:21–23 and 24:11–12 are people influenced by them.
Betz, *Sermon*, pp. 326–327, assumes that 7:15–20 attacks leaders of Gentile Christianity
of the Pauline type and that 7:21–23 describes their victims who have neglected obedience
to Torah while engaging in charismatic activities (see also pp. 528–529, 540–541). Betz
speculates that the position of the Sermon is that of the pillars at the Jerusalem council,
not their conservative Jewish Christian opponents, so that the issue of neglecting Torah is
not about circumcision and the like, but about love, as explicated in the Sermon. He also
notes the absence of the title, "Lord," from the Sermon and assumes it to have been
recognised as characteristic of the Gentile community (pp. 547–548). The evidence for
this is however very slim; acclamation or address of Jesus is not present elsewhere in the
sermon. He notes that it is extraordinary that the author admits that Gentiles can do these
things in the name of Jesus, but says the Sermon shows "obvious disinterest in any form of
ecstatic experience" (p. 550). I doubt that the evidence warrant this claim. See also the
earlier criticism of Betz in Carlston, "Betz," pp. 51–52. Strecker, *Bergpredigt*, pp. 167–
168, rejects the view that Matthew has the group in mind already in 5:17–20; nor does he
recognise reference to a particular group here.

reference to the Law, νόμος, and so to antinomians (cf. also its use in 24:12 in connection with false prophets). This may be so, but the word on its own was common for describing wickedness and did not necessarily always have the connotation which its etymology suggests.[116]

Building on sand or on rock sets out the stark alternatives again in 7:24–27. Jesus the judge has spoken. Matthew equates keeping Jesus' words (7:24), doing the will of the Father (7:21), bearing good fruit (7:17), and entering the narrow gate (7:13) as right responses to Jesus' message set out in the Sermon on the Mount. While much of the material has no direct relationship to the written Torah (especially 6:19 – 7:11, and to some degree 6:1–18), the whole belongs together as Jesus' exposition of Law, both literally, in 5:21–48, and by extension as the proclamation of God's will in 6:1 – 7:11. Matthew associates them closely. For Matthew there are not two authorities, Jesus and Torah, but one.[117]

It is significant that Matthew describes the crowds' response to Jesus' teaching using the words which Mark had used to describe Jesus' teaching in the synagogue when he healed the demoniac: "The crowds were amazed at his teaching; for he was teaching them as one having authority and not as their scribes" (7:28–29; cf. Mark 1:22). Mark makes this comment without directly indicating the substance of the teaching. Matthew has more than compensated for this. But while in Mark the contrast is starkly between Jesus and the scribes, in Matthew it is Jesus' interpretation of the Law contrasted with theirs. The subtle change from "the scribes" to "their scribes" in Matthew reflects this; for in Matthew Jesus is the scribe par excellence![118]

Reviewing Matthew 6–7, we note its strong emphasis in the final sections, the conclusion of the sermon as a whole, on judgement. Jesus is speaking as judge to come. The challenge, here, is directed to the community and constitutes a call to total obedience. It also identifies alternative Christian teachings which Matthew would see as undermining such obedience. 7:15–27 speaks in terms of Jesus' teaching and looks back on the sermon as a whole. But this teaching is not something independent of Torah. By returning directly to the Law and the Prophets in 7:12 Matthew shows that he sees not only 5:17–48, but also the intervening teaching in 6:1 – 7:11 as belonging

---

[116] So Mohrlang, *Matthew*, pp. 16–17; Carlston, "Things that Defile," p. 85; Hill, "False Prophets," pp. 338, 340; Davies and Allison, *Matthew I*, pp. 718–719.

[117] Betz, *Sermon*, pp. 564–565, links the image of the rock with the image of Peter as the rock, suggesting that Matthew preserves awareness that Peter was once held such a foundational role, but that it belonged to the past.

[118] See also Saldarini, *Community*, p. 103.

within the context of Jesus' exposition of Torah. Direct interpretation of
written law and general extrapolation of God's will are seen as one. Thus
Matthew has Jesus employ the image of the two ways, commonly used of
God's law, to refer to responses to his own teaching.

Details of practical devotion in 6:1–18 reflect a strongly Jewish
background, including the Lord's Prayer, but differ from common Jewish
practice, thus reflecting a distinctive community. None imply disrespect of,
or non compliance with, Torah. Much of the rest of the teaching has parallels
in Jewish expositions of God's will in the period. As in 5:47, there are still
indications of viewing the Gentile world through conservative Jewish eyes
as alien in its religious practices (6:7), greed (6:31), and, perhaps, its hostility
and insensitivity to the holy (7:6).

2.3 Matthew 8 – 20 in Review

2.3.1 Matthew 8:1 – 9:35

In 8:1 – 9:34 Matthew presents reports of Jesus' activities. There are three
groups of three miracles (8:1–15; 8:23 – 9:8; 9:18–34) and, between them,
material of a different kind. As a whole the passage includes evidence of the
activities which are mentioned in summary in 4:23 and 9:35, which provide
its framework, and in more detail in 4:24–25 and 8:16–17. They also provide instances of the activities which Jesus will enumerate in his response to
John the Baptist's query in 11:2–6. But, beyond that, these stories present
important insights about who Jesus is and about the contrasting responses of
faith and unfaith to his work.

Matthew begins in 8:1–4 with the story of the healing of the leper which
Mark had used at the end of his first division (1:40–45) and immediately
before the controversy stories of 2:1 – 3:6. Matthew has already used the
summary from Mark 1:39 as the basis for the framing statements of 4:23 and
9:35. Immediately prior to 8:1, in 7:28–29 he has used material from the
opening exorcism of Mark's gospel, 1:21–28, to describe the crowds' reactions to Jesus' teaching in the Sermon on the Mount. It is an episode which
he otherwise does not recount. Bornkamm may well have been right when
he suggested that Matthew's reason for deleting the story itself was because
of sensitivity that it (and therefore the following episodes, Mark 1:29–31,32–
34) took place on the sabbath.[119] When Matthew does use the following

---

[119] Bornkamm, "Enderwartung," p. 29 n. 1.

Markan episodes (the healing of Peter's mother-in-law and the evening healings, 8:14–15,16–17), they are no longer linked with the sabbath.

In reproducing Mark's story of the leper's healing (Mark 1:40–45) in 8:1–4, Matthew makes significant changes. He transfers Jesus' anger or sternness and the man's disregard for Jesus' command to silence to the healing of the two blind men in 9:30–31. The overall effect is to reserve the focus for Jesus' healing power and for his exhortation that the man fulfil the Law's commands.[120] Unlike Mark, Matthew can assume his readers are familiar with the purpose of this law and so omits that it is "for purification". This first episode confirms the picture of Matthew's Jesus as upholder of the Law. On the other hand, Matthew mentions Jesus' act of touching the leper without any indication of implications for Jesus' purity.

The healing of the centurion's servant (8:5–13) entails an encounter with a Gentile. The latter puts his request and, after Jesus' response, addresses Jesus a second time in which he declares himself unworthy to receive Jesus under his roof. Jesus then agrees to healing at a distance, just as he will with the Canaanite woman's daughter (15:21–28). Many, reading the story in isolation from its Jewish context, see in the centurion's statements primarily an expression of humility. But Matthew's Jewish hearers would have a much clearer grasp of the issues. Here was a Gentile seeking help from Jesus, a Jew, which would entail his entering a Gentile dwelling. The centurion is sensitive to the purity issues involved. Luke's Peter deals with a similar issue in Acts, also with regard to a centurion, and spells out the problem: "You know that it is not lawful for a Jewish man to associate with or visit a Gentile" (Acts 10:28).[121] The centurion's statement is not a gesture of humility, but an acknowledgment of the purity issue. He spells it out, "I am not worthy for you to come under my roof."

The fact that he does so after Jesus has already made a response raises questions about the nature of that response. The words, ἐγὼ ἐλθὼν θεραπεύσω αὐτὸν (8:7), may be translated as either a statement: "I will come and heal him"[122] or a question: "Am I to come and heal him?"[123] If

---

[120] εἰς μαρτύριον αὐτοῖς ("as a testimony to them") refers to reporting information as required, not to giving testifying to count against them. So rightly Luz, *Matthäus II*, p. 10. He suggests it also secondarily includes reference to testimony to the people that the Messiah is Torah observant. Perhaps. See also Davies and Allison, *Matthew II*, p. 16; Hagner, *Matthew*, pp. 199–200.

[121] Cf. *mOhol* 18:7, 9, which declares the dwelling places of Gentiles unclean.

[122] So Gundry, *Matthew*, pp. 142–143; Hagner, *Matthew*, p. 204.

[123] So U. Wegner, *Der Hauptmann von Kafarnaum (Mt 7,28a; 8,5–10.13 par Lk 7,1–10). Ein Beitrag zur Q-Forschung*, WUNT 2.14, (Tübingen: J. C. B. Mohr [Paul Siebeck],

they are a statement, then the centurion is raising the purity issue and proposing an alternative strategy to a Jesus, who had already declared he was coming. If they are a question, then they should be understood as an initial rebuff, like the rebuff given the Syrophoenician woman. The centurion's response acknowledges the issue at stake for Jesus as a Jew and then argues an alternative strategy. I am inclined to think the latter will have been the understanding in Q and possibly also in Matthew (see also the relevant discussions on Luke and Q in the chapters below).

Interestingly, Jesus does not go to the Gentile home, but heals at a distance, just as he will in the case of the Canaanite woman in 15:21–28. Matthew is showing Jesus conforming to Jewish Law, or, at least, an interpretation of it which in the anecdote the centurion and probably Jesus himself share. The prefiguring of the Gentile mission, both in the encounter and in Jesus' words in 8:11–12, which will find fulfilment only after Easter (28:18–20), alerts us to the fact that on their terms such a Gentile mission raises major Law issues. To these we shall return.

The centurion's words are also important for understanding faith and christology in Matthew. The centurion likens his own exercise of authority to that of Jesus' authority. In doing so he acknowledges Jesus' authority. While Matthew does not portray him as following Jesus, he is a model of true faith. Faith means acknowledging the authority of Jesus. The narrative strongly contrasts the Gentile's faith with the unfaith of Israel. Matthew generalises this contrast by including Jesus' prediction of the entry of Gentiles into the kingdom and the exclusion of "the sons of the kingdom" (8:11–12). The contrast in its Matthean context reads most naturally as one between Gentiles and Jews, not between elite Jews and other Jews,[124] or Palestinian and Diaspora Jews.[125] The point is: unbelieving Jews, like unbelieving Gentiles, will be excluded. It is not a rejection of (and abandonment of mission to) Israel as a whole.[126]

The third healing, that of Peter's mother-in-law, follows in 8:14–15, before a first summary in 8:16–17. Here, as in the healing of the centurion's servant, Jesus performs his healings by his word, a distinctive Matthean emphasis. Both the healing of Peter's mother-in-law and the summary of healings follow

---

1985), pp. 375–380; Gnilka, *Matthäusevangelium II*, p. 301; Luz, *Matthäus II*, p. 14; Davies and Allison, *Matthew II*, pp. 21–22.

[124] Cf. Levine, *Matthean Salvation History*, pp. 126–127. So Luz, *Matthäus II*, p. 15; Hagner, *Matthew*, p. 205.

[125] Cf. Davies and Allison, *Matthew II*, pp. 28–29.

[126] See Saldarini, *Community*, p. 42, against generalising this as total exclusion of Israel: after all, the patriarchs will be there and other Jews as well. See also pp. 70–71. He shows that contrasts between Israel's faith and outsiders was not uncommon in the biblical

Mark 1:29–34, but, as noted above, any link between these events and the sabbath has been removed. Attached to the summary of healings is a characteristically Matthean formula quotation demonstrating Jesus' fulfilment of Isa 53:4, "He took our infirmities and bore our diseases." Matthew sees in it a literal reference to Jesus' healing ministry.

The first cluster of three reports Jesus' compassion towards three people disqualified from full participation in the cult: a leper, a Gentile, a Jewish woman. Perhaps Matthew assembles the stories deliberately to make this point.[127] However, nothing else directly suggests this. The first two portray an image of Jesus as concerned with fulfilment of the Law, but, unlike the focus of the great sermon, with purity law in particular.

At the beginning of his narrative of the stilling of the storm and before he narrates the next cluster of three miracles, Matthew includes two encounters on the theme of discipleship. In one, a would be disciple who is a scribe asserts his intention to follow Jesus anywhere (8:19–20).[128] It is further indirect evidence that Matthew's community included scribes (cf. 7:29). In the other, "another of his disciples" wants to delay the voyage so that he can attend to the burial of his father (8:21–22). Jesus' response to him sets immediate following as a higher priority than obligations to the dead. In doing so, Jesus effectively sets such personal allegiance above an obligation, not specifically enshrined in Torah, but widely seen as an implication of honouring one's parents.[129] Matthew gives no indication that he sees in Jesus' demand a call to disregard a Torah obligation. By placing the encounter within the context of actual and not would-be disciples, and one of them a scribe, Matthew represents Jesus as expressing his demands of members of the Christian community. The storm stilling itself supplements the demand for total obedience with the demand for total trust in the face of danger.

---

tradition. The centurion should not be seen only as a rounded symbol of the Gentile church: he does not follow Jesus (p. 72).

[127] So Levine, *Matthean Salvation History*, p. 122.

[128] See J. Kiilunen, "Der nachfolgewillige Schriftgelehrte. Matthäus 8.19–20 im Verständnis des Evangelisten," *NTS* 37 (1991), pp. 268–279, who makes a strong case against the view that the scribe should be seen in a negative light, against J. D. Kingsbury, "On Following Jesus. The 'Eager' Scribe and the 'Reluctant' Disciple (Matthew 8. 18–22)," *NTS* 34 (1988), pp. 45–59. It is more likely that, given the context, Matthew should mean us to see in the man a potential disciple. This fits the ecclesial theme of the context better.

[129] On the importance of such burial obligation see M. Hengel, *The Charismatic Leader and his Followers*, (Edinburgh: T&T Clark; New York: Crossroad, 1981), pp. 3–15; "Jesus und Tora," pp. 158–159; Sanders, *Jesus and Judaism*, pp. 252–255. See also Davies and Allison, *Matthew II*, pp. 53, 56–58; Hagner, *Matthew*, p. 217; Vermes, *Religion of Jesus*, pp. 28–29 and the discussion in the chapters on Luke and Q.

In his retelling of Mark's account of the stilling of the storm (8:18–27; cf. Mark 4:35–41) and of the healing of the Gerasene demoniac (8:28–34; cf. Mark 5:1–20), Matthew has them foreshadow the eschaton, with its attendant threat of danger and chaos and the victory of the Son of God over evil powers. Matthew removes traits which might suggest Jesus is just a practising exorcist. In effect the passages reinforce the predictions already made by John the Baptist and reinforced at Jesus' baptism: here is the Son of God who makes his demands as the master of the deep and is victor over all evil. Aside from that, Matthew offers no reflection on the location of the exorcism in Gentile territory (Gadara). His Jewish readers would surely have been sensitive to the purity issues (Gentile territory, pigs, tombs), but Matthew makes nothing of it. He omits Mark's reference to a mission beginning in the Decapolis (cf. Mark 5:20). Matthew is being consistent; the extension of the mission to include Gentiles must wait until 28:18–20. Matthew's doubling of Mark's single demoniac reflects Matthew's strategy to convict Israel for its unbelief by the evidence of twofold witness. Matthew is playing (hard!) with Jewish forensic Law (cf. Deut 17:6), and will repeat the strategy both in a similar transformation of Bartimaeus (Mark 10:46–52) into two blind men and in the doubling of that story itself in 20:29–34 and 9:27–31.[130]

Matthew's version of the healing of the paralytic (9:2–8; cf. Mark 2:1–12) is without the dramatic entry through the roof. It also omits the scribes' ground for alleging blasphemy, namely, "Who can forgive sins but God alone?" Possibly this was because Matthew knew the passive, "Your sins are forgiven," could not be other than an announcement of God's forgiveness. Yet the charge of blasphemy may still imply that the scribes saw it differently. For Matthew the charge is wrong not because Jesus is God, but because he is authorised to act with divine authority as the Son of Man saying makes clear.[131] When Matthew has Jesus highlight the evil thinking in their hearts, he is probably strengthening the link, already present in Mark, with the Jewish trial where the accusation of blasphemy next comes to expression. He adds a new conclusion which broadens the scope of such authorisation beyond Jesus, undoubtedly, to the Church: the crowds "glorified God that he had given such authority to human beings (ἀνθρώποις)" (9:8). Matthew not

---

130 See also my discussion of the episode, W. R. G. Loader, "Son of David, Blindness, Possession, and Duality in Matthew," *CBQ* 44 (1982), pp. 570–585, here: 580–582.

131 So Luz, *Matthäus II*, p. 37; cf. Davies and Allison, *Matthew II*, p. 91, who, despite drawing attention to the Son of Man saying, still appear to share the scribes' comprehension of the event, when they write: "He has acted not as a channel of forgiveness but as its source."

only dismisses any breach of the Law, but extends the claimed authority to the community.[132]

Forgiveness of sins featured very early in the gospel: in the etymological exposition of the name, Jesus (1:21); and also, by implication, in John's ministry of baptism. It is also implied in the call to repentance which comes on the lips of John (3:2), Jesus (4:17) and, later, the disciples (10:7). In our discussion of the Markan passage we noted that it should not be presumed that according to Law forgiveness was the monopoly of the cult. On the other hand, it is entirely credible that claims to mediate divine forgiveness would raise controversy. The claim of Jesus (and the Christian community) to do so belongs in a grey area, so far as issues of Torah observance are concerned, and so does not imply conflict or abrogation of Torah. It would, if the claim presumed to replace instances of such authority established by Torah, but that is not clear at this point.

In introducing Mark's sequel episode about the call of Levi and Jesus' eating with toll collectors and sinners (9:9–13; cf. Mark 2:13–17), Matthew uses the same word, ἄνθρωπον, ("human being"), to describe the disciple whom Jesus calls, as he had used in 9:8 to allude to the authorisation of the disciples to forgive sins ("to human beings"). Matthew is underlining the authority which discipleship will entail. Apart from the change of name, from Levi to Matthew, giving rise to speculation about the gospel's authorship, the passage is notable for Matthew's addition of Hosea 6:6: "Go and learn what this means: 'I desire mercy and not sacrifice'." Matthew will do the same in the controversy over plucking grain on the sabbath in 12:7. By inserting the appeal to Hosea into the middle of Jesus' reply and thereby separating "Those who are well have no need of a doctor, but those who are sick" from "I have come not to call righteous but sinners", Matthew reinforces the argument of compassion for the needy and justifies Jesus' mission through scripture.[133] The wider context must determine whether Matthew understood the contrast (mercy and not sacrifice) exclusively or as a matter of relative priority. So far his strong statements about upholding the Law would favour the latter and this will be confirmed. As with the contrast, "righteous – sinners", Matthew understands it inclusively.

Matthew's version of the controversy over fasting is also similar to Mark's

---

[132] Hummel, *Auseinandersetzung*, pp. 37–38, rejects the suggestion of Bultmann, *Synoptic Tradition*, pp. 15–16, that this should be understood narrowly as another version of the "keys" of authority of 16:19; rather it is linked with the emphasis on compassion reflected in 9:2 and 9:13. It is surely both.

[133] Hummel, *Auseinandersetzung*, pp. 38–40, noting this, speaks of Matthew turning the issue in the direction of a halakic discussion.

(9:14–17; cf. Mark 2:18–22). In Mark the episode stands at the structural centre of 2:1 – 3:6. In Matthew it is less prominent. Matthew's account simplifies the contrast between the time of Jesus' earthly ministry and the time of fasting. The images of the patch and the wine remain. Their application in Matthew is not immediately apparent. Nothing indicates a contrast between Jesus and the Law.

At the beginning of the final cluster of three miracles, Matthew includes a very trimmed account of Mark's long narrative, which combined the healing of a woman suffering from bleeding for 12 years and the raising up of a sick 12 year old girl who died while Jesus was on the way to heal her (9:18–26; Mark 5:21–43). Gone is the name, "Jairus", and his designation as "a leader of the synagogue". Gone is also Mark's juxtaposition between Jesus in Gentile territory (Gerasa) and Jewish territory; Matthew narrated that exorcism two episodes back (8:28–34). The girl is already dead. Jesus heals the woman and raises the girl to life. Two Matthean additions reflect Jewish colour: there are flute players at the mourning (9:23); the woman touches Jesus' tassel (9:20). This enhances the sense of Jesus' Jewishness. The focus of the narrative falls on Jesus as the healer and as the one who raises the dead. Again purity issues (Jesus being touched by an unclean woman, and then entering the leader's house) are passed over without comment.[134] As in Mark, Jesus' claim that the girl is not dead, but sleeps, might be seen as ruling out the danger of corpse impurity.

With Matthew 9:27–31 we come to another instance of Matthew's doubling (see the discussion on 8:28–34, above). It is in fact double doubling and reflects, as we saw, Matthew's use of the requirement of the Law that there be at two or three witnesses at a capital trial (Deut 17:6). Mark's Bartimaeus (Mark 10:46–52) has become two blind men and the anecdote has been told twice, once here and once, corresponding to its original position in Mark, just before the entry into Jerusalem (20:29–34). The blind men give traditionally valid testimony to who Jesus. He is Son of God and Son of David.[135] The final miracle in the cluster, the exorcism of the dumb demoniac (9:32–34), is another doublet (cf. 12:22–24). Both evoke the charge that Jesus is in league with the prince of demons and prepare for the counter charge that not Jesus but his accusers are demon possessed. We shall return to the charge below.

---

134 Saldarini, *Community*, p. 139, notes this here and in 8:28 (entry into Gentile territory) and 9:10–11 (eating with sinners), but sees them as indicating that Matthew gives priority to healing and teaching, without implying that the purity issues were invalid.
135 See Loader, "Son of David".

9:35 returns us to the summary of 4:23. Within this framework we have received from Matthew a mini portrait of Jesus' ministry. Jesus appears as authoritative upholder and interpreter of the Law in Matthew 5–7, modifying existing commandments to make them stricter, but determined by the criterion of compassion, and adding wider material which now counts as God's Torah for the community. In 8 – 9 there is further evidence that Matthew sees Jesus in this light. He has removed and reordered Markan material to avoid laying Jesus open to the charge of breaching sabbath law. Following Mark, he has Jesus command the leper to fulfil Torah purity provisions. He respects the centurion's acknowledgment of unworthiness to have Jesus enter his house. Matthew may well intend that we see in Jesus' first response the same kind of reluctance he will show in later encountering the Canaanite woman. He refers to Jesus' wearing tassels.

Matthew's own Jewish ethos is reflected in the way he employs the legal requirement concerning witnesses to duplicate stories of healing (9:27–31; 20:29–34; cf. Mark 10:46–52) and exorcism (9:32–34; 12:22–24), and to double Mark's characters to produce two demoniacs and two blind men (twice!). He also adds the Jewish colour of flute players accompanying the mourning for the dead girl. On the other hand, we miss any reflection on purity issues in Jesus' touching a leper, being in Gentile territory, and being touched by an unclean woman. Matthew has also dismantled Mark's hints of the Gentile mission in the Decapolis and his juxtaposition of Jesus' deeds in Gentile territory and in Israel (Mark 5:1–20 and 21–43). On the other hand, as with the women in the genealogy and the magi, he prefigures the post Easter expansion of mission to the Gentiles in the centurion's faith and the associated prediction of 8:11–12.

Jesus' distinctive authority comes through in his demand that a disciple set aside obligations toward a dead parent. This is striking, but nothing indicates that Matthew saw it as a breach of Torah. Like Mark, he has Jesus dismiss charges against him that he breaches the Law by blasphemy, in declaring forgiveness of sins, by appealing to Jesus' authorisation. Matthew adds that this authority extends also to his disciples (9:8). In another case he justifies Jesus' behaviour and his mission by reference to the words of Hosea 6:6, that God demands mercy and not sacrifice. Neither the claim to be authorised to declare God's forgiveness nor the practice of eating with toll collectors and sinner represents a breach of Torah. The latter reflects a clash of priorities in interpreting Torah. The former, the claim to authorisation to forgive sins, while not controverting Torah, is a much greater cause for concern for Jesus' opponents, because it raises the relation of Jesus' authority to other authorities, and, in particular, to the authority of Torah.

Thus, as in his teaching in 5–7, so in his activities portrayed in 8:1 – 9:34, compassion for people, especially those in need, features prominently, especially in the healings. 8:17 notes that it fulfils Isa 53:4. In the dispute over mixing with outcasts he has Jesus call on Hosea 6:6. In 9:27 he responds to the appeal: "Son of David, have mercy on me!" Compassion also stands at the head of the section which immediately follows.

2.3.2 Matthew 9:36 – 13:52

9:36 – 10:42 consists of instructions to disciples. It is set within the context of Jesus' compassion for the crowds: "And Jesus seeing the crowds had compassion on them, for they were harassed and helpless like sheep without a shepherd." Matthew found this statement, with its biblical allusion to Israel as sheep without a shepherd (cf. Nu 27:17) in Mark's account of the feeding of the five thousand (Mark 6:34). He has relocated it and heightened it by adding, "harassed and helpless". Matthew is about to describe Jesus' response to Israel's plight. He begins with the naming of the twelve (10:1–4) and initial instructions for their mission (10:5–15). Within these instructions we find the striking prohibition, without parallel in Matthew's Markan source or in Q, that the disciples are to avoid Gentile and Samaritan territory, and conduct their mission only in Israel (10:5–6). Within the overall context of Matthew's gospel this reflects the divine mission strategy which applies equally to Jesus (15:24 "I have not been sent except to the lost sheep of the house of Israel"). The expansion of the mission to include Gentiles must wait until after Easter (28:16–20).

In the interim the mission begins with Israel. In the warnings about persecution in the following verses (10:16–23) we find an echo of this beginning. The Son of Man will come before the disciples have used up all the cities of Israel as places to which to flee (10:23). In Matthew's day disciples were obviously still able to find refuge in Jewish territory and were still engaged in mission there, even though the mission had long since been opened to the Gentiles.[136] It is striking that no explicit connection is made in the instructions between the prohibition to go to the Gentiles and Samaritans and purity issues.

In 10:11–14 Matthew has Jesus exhort the disciples to seek worthy lodgings. This could pertain to being Torah observant, because entering

---

[136] See Menninger, *Israel*, p. 32 against the view of D. R. A. Hare, *The Theme of Jewish Persecution of Christians according the Gospel of St. Matthew*, SNTMS 6, (Cambridge: CUP, 1967), pp. 80–129, that the persecution texts in 10:17,23; 23:34 refer to the past not to Matthew's current community. See also Saldarini, *Community*, p. 60.

homes would have raised issues of purity.[137] Yet in 10:14 the issue of worthiness seems related to response to the greeting of peace, welcome or rejection.[138] The behaviour enjoined in 10:14, shaking dust off the feet, may be analogous to shaking Gentile dust off one's feet,[139] but the focus here seems again not to be Jewish purity issues, but responsiveness to the gospel.

The instructions in 10:1–14 and in the rest of the chapter are like those in 6:1 – 7:28. They represent God's Law for the disciples. There are also direct similarities in content, such as the use of nature as an example of God's care for his own (sparrows and the hairs of one's head: 10:29–30; cf. 6:26–30); and the declaration that open confession or rejection of Jesus will be the criterion for divine judgement (10:32–33; cf. 7:15–23). In the struggle for right allegiance new priorities will be set in relationships, including, by implication, the overriding of priorities set by Torah itself (10:34–39; cf. 8:22).

By placing the material on the mission of the disciples immediately after the summary of Jesus' own activity and before John the Baptist's query about Jesus' identity in 11:2–3, Matthew effectively associates Jesus' mission with theirs in the discussion which follows. Already by formulating their message in terms identical with both Jesus' and John's message (3:2; 4:17; 10:7), Matthew has brought them close together. 10:1 establishes the basis of this link: Jesus gave them authority. The delegation of authority has already been implied in 9:8. They are now to go out to heal and exorcise like Jesus, to preach and teach, and to be his representatives as he is God's representative. They, too, will face the charge of being Beelzebul (10:25). But to welcome them is to welcome Jesus and to welcome the one who sent him (10:40–42). Matthew is developing his christology of authorisation using the envoy model and has now extended it to his doctrine of ministry. The resultant system of authority is also closely related to the authority of the Law; the close relationship between the two is presupposed and the nature of that relationship continues to be an issue.

John's question in 11:3 might well be shared by a first hearer of the gospel. Had not John announced the fiery judge of the end time? Instead we have had reports of teaching and healing. Jesus' answer in 11:4–6, replete with allusions to Old Testament prophecy of the wonders of the end times (Isa

---

[137] Cf. *mDemai* 4:6 which speaks of a man entering a city where he knew no one and asking, "Who is there here that is trustworthy? Who is there here that pays Tithes?"

[138] So Hagner, *Matthew*, p. 272.

[139] So Hagner, *Matthew*, p. 273; but cf. Luz, *Matthäus II*, p. 101.

29:18; 35:5–6; 61:1), reassures; but it also redirects the focus. Jesus' activities, illustrated in the previous chapters, are already signs of fulfilment of prophetic hope. For Matthew these are "the deeds of the Messiah" (11:2); Matthew has added this to his source (cf. QLk 7:18). The effect is to add greater definition to Matthew's christology: on earth he is the Messiah;[140] in the end he will come as judge in fulfilment of John's predictions.

The return in Matthew 11 to John the Baptist also represents a new beginning for the hearer. We are back with John the Baptist. Matthew underlines John's eschatological role, using special Q sources. John marks the turning point in history, the last of the prophets predicting the kingdom; he introduced Jesus in whom it now already begins to come to expression and faces rejection (11:11–12). In 11:13–14 he has Jesus explain: "For all the prophets and the law prophesied until John. And if you want to receive it, he is Elijah the one who is to come." The effect is to make Jesus' ministry the climax of history and the fulfilment of scripture, including the Law. Here the Law seems to be treated, along with the prophets, primarily in its function of predicting what will be in the end times, rather than in a regulatory sense. Nothing here implies that the Law (or the Prophets) cease their application or jurisdiction.[141]

The juxtaposition of John and Jesus continues with the imagery of children in the market place (11:16–19). The accusation against John was demon possession because of his asceticism. The accusation is striking, because John, therefore, shares this accusation with Jesus (9:34; 12:22–24) and the disciples (10:25). Against Jesus the accusation is gluttony and drunkenness, on the one hand, and keeping bad company, on the other. This had already been the issue in 9:9–13. Behind the charge is the assumption that a Torah observant Jew would not behave like this. The words recall Deut 21:20 about the rebellious son: "This son of ours is rebellious and contentious, he does not obey our voice, he is a reveller and a drunkard." From the perspective of the accusers both John and Jesus are acting contrary to Torah.

---

140 Cf. 4Q521 fr. 2 col. 2, which contains a similar collection of wondrous deeds as part of future hope, with allusion to Isa 61:1 and Ps 146. A reference to a Messiah appears at the beginning of the fragment; the deeds, however, are portrayed as deeds of God, the Lord.

141 Barth, "Gesetzesverständnis," pp. 59–60, notes that Matthew has changed the Q form of the saying, preserved better in Lk 16:16, which could, he thinks, be understood to imply that "the law and the prophets" were valid only up until John. Matthew rejects the Hellenistic Christian view of the Law. See also Davies and Allison, *Matthew II*, pp. 256–257. On the Q saying see my discussion of Q, below. Cf. Menninger, *Israel*, pp. 107–108, who argues that 11:13 implies that Jesus completes and brings to an end the Law.

By implication, Matthew asserts that both are Torah observant. Jesus' response to criticism both of John and himself is to speak of wisdom: "Wisdom is justified on the basis of her deeds." How are these words to be understood?

Does Matthew read this just as a loose personification, as much as to say: consequences of decisions (ie. of a person's wisdom) will tell you what was wise and what was not.? In this case Matthew would be arguing that the results of John's and Jesus' ministry will show whether they were right or not. This would be similar to the emphasis in both John and Jesus on fruit as the evidence of goodness (3:8,10; 7:16–20; cf. also 12:33). It is a typically Matthean emphasis. Here the deeds, fruit, are to be taken as evidence that John and Jesus are wise. Or does Matthew understand wisdom here as an allusion to wisdom as God's heavenly assistant (as in Prov 8:22, 31; Sir 1:1–9)? If so, does Matthew perhaps know the identification of wisdom and Law in Sirach 4:23 (also Bar 4:1)? Then the deeds will show that John and Jesus act in accordance with God's wisdom, God's will, in the broadest sense, Torah, and perhaps also that they are in some sense wisdom's envoys. This was probably the emphasis in Q in which Jesus' reply reads: "Wisdom shall be vindicated by her children" (cf. Luke 7:31–35). Matthew's version of the statement must be read in the light of the focus on deeds and that means in the light of the immediate context.

The following verses upbraid cities for failing to respond to Jesus' miracles (11:20–24). The immediate focus on Jesus' miracles makes it likely that these are part of what is being referred to as wisdom's deeds in 11:19, rather than just deeds of ethics, although both are to be seen as putting God's will into effect. Thus, as in 11:2–5, the emphasis in 11:20–24 is on miraculous deeds as proof. They show that Jesus is who he claims to be. In 11:25–26 Jesus gives thanks that "these things" have been hidden from the wise and revealed to babes. Assuming a correlation among (i) "deeds" in 11:19, (ii) "miracles" in 11:20–24 and in 11:2–5, and (iii) "these things" in 11:25, Matthew means us to see in all a reference to Jesus' ministry. The cities failed to grasp what the miracles indicated, namely who Jesus is. 11:27b confirms that this is the focus ("No one knows the Son except the Father and no one knows the Father except the Son and the one to whom he wishes to reveal him"). In 11:27a another variant of the same argument occurs: "all things" had been given Jesus by the Father. The reference here is to Jesus' authorisation. The circle is complete: the Father has authorised the divinely created Son; the Son knows the Father and reveals him. This occurs in Jesus' deeds, which, as miraculous manifestations of the divine, ought to convince people that he is who he is.

What, then, are we to make of the allusion to wisdom and its/her deeds in 11:19? Restricting "deeds" to miracles would fit 11:20–24 and 11:2–5, but not 11:25–27, nor the image of John in Matthew; for he performs no miracles. It is better then to allow "deeds" in 11:19 to include more than miracles. It is, after all, "deeds"! The "deeds" are revelatory to the truly wise (11:25–26). It helps to recognise that Matthew is not speaking of miracles per se, but of Jesus' miracles as manifesting a particular quality. They are the deeds of compassion, narrated in 8:1 – 9:34 and summarised in 11:2–5. They are, then, not different from the idea of appropriate fruit. To make sense of Jesus' statement in 11:19 as a defence both of Jesus' and John's behaviour, the "deeds" of 11:19 must include both miracles and other actions, indicative of God's involvement. Whether miraculous or not, the deeds of Jesus and John are sufficient defence against the accusations hurled against them. They show both to be acting in accordance with God's will. They are not acting contrary to Torah.

Would Matthew have also seen in Jesus' words an allusion to the figure of wisdom, like Q, or especially to wisdom associated with Torah? 11:28–30 suggests this is likely: "Come to me, all who labour and are heavy laden, and I will give you rest. Take on my yoke and learn from me, because I am gentle and lowly in heart, and you will find rest for your souls; for my yoke is easy and my burden is light." Matthew's imagery appears to be related to the imagery used in Sir 51:23–27, in which Sirach exhorts people to come near and take upon themselves the yoke of wisdom, associated in Sirach with the Law, to find serenity:

> Draw near to me, you who are uneducated, and dwell in the house of learning. Why do you miss out on these things and why are your souls so very thirsty? I have opened my mouth and declared, "Buy for yourselves without money. Place your necks under my yoke and let your soul receive education; it is nearby for you to find. See with your eyes that my toil has been little and I have found great rest for myself.

The passage alludes to the call of the prophet in Isa 55:1–3 and of wisdom in Prov 1:20–23; 8:1–36; Sir 24:19–22. Jesus' appeal is not on behalf of the written law nor one that competes with (or has nothing to do with) the yoke of the written law. Rather, understood in the light of 5:17–20, it is Jesus' appeal to submit to his teaching, which Matthew sees as upholding and rightly expounding God's will expressed in Torah. Matthew appears to have Jesus use the traditional image of wisdom summoning people to come and learn. It also lies behind the preceding context. Knowing God, being known by God and making God known (11:27) are something attested widely of wisdom

(Job 28:12–27; Sir 1:6–9; Bar 3:32; Wisd 8:4; 9:1–18; 10:10.[142] 11:25–26 also uses common wisdom motifs. Matthew will have understood the allusion to wisdom in similar terms to the way it is used in Sirach, where wisdom is identified with Torah. It remains, however, at the level of occasional imagery, rather than of fundamental theology; otherwise its absence elsewhere is too difficult to explain. Nothing, therefore, suggests that Matthew espouses a theology which sees Jesus as either Torah- or Wisdom-incarnate.[143]

---

[142] So Davies and Allison, *Matthew II*, p. 272.

[143] Cf. F. Christ, *Jesus Sophia: Die Sophia–Christology bei den Synoptikern*, ATANT 57, (Zurich: Zwingli, 1970); Suggs, *Wisdom*, pp. 99–106, who argues that Matthew portrays Jesus as speaking as Sophia and Torah. Against this C. Deutsch, *Hidden Wisdom and the Easy Yoke. Wisdom, Torah and Discipleship in Matthew 11:25–30*, JSNTS 18, (Sheffield: JSOTPr, 1987), pp. 134–135, argues that Matthew presents Jesus in 11:28–30 as Wisdom incarnate, but not as Torah incarnate. "Whereas the image may be related to the figure of the teacher and his interpretation, in the Jewish sources, the focus is on the learning of Torah or wisdom. The image of the yoke in Mt 11.28–30, however, occurring in parallel with the clauses 'Come to me' and 'Learn of me', focuses on the person of Jesus, who is both Wisdom itself and the Sage who interprets wisdom. So taking up the yoke of Jesus becomes a correlative of discipleship, with that discipleship including 'obedience to the Law as interpreted by Jesus' and an understanding of the mysteries of the Kingdom as disclosed by him" (p. 135). 11:28–30, as its parallel, Sir 51:23, indicates, is the call of the Sage, not of wisdom itself (p. 138). "In so far as Jesus' teaching includes interpretation both of the religious tradition and of the eschatological moment at hand (and still to come), the description of his role in 11:25–30 and 11:2 – 13:58 resembles most that of the Qumran teacher" (p. 138). See also her "Wisdom in Matthew: Transformation of a Symbol," *NovT* 32 (1990), pp. 13–47, here: 36–39.

These are significant observations in which Deutsch points to the broader context: to narrow Jesus to a teacher of Torah or even its embodiment misses too much of the rest of Jesus' teaching in Matthew, not least 11:25–27! She also counters Stanton's view (*Gospel*, p. 375) that the yoke has no reference to Torah, but refers primarily to the yoke of discipleship, pointing out that this denies the links with Law interpretation in what follows (p. 178 n. 78). F. Christ, according to Deutsch, overdoes the identification with Torah, finding it in the revelation of 11:27 and in the call 11:28, with Jesus himself as the mystery, wisdom and law (*Jesus Sophia*, p. 118). Deutsch also distances herself from H. D. Betz, "The Logion of the Easy Yoke and of Rest (Mt. 11.28–30)," *JBL* 86 (1967), pp. 10–24, here 24, who says that "rest" corresponds to the presence of the risen Lord. Stanton makes a valid point that 11:27, the mention of Jesus as "Son", would not lead the reader to think of "wisdom" in the immediately following verse (*Gospel*, p. 370). The issue, however, is to what degree we may assume hearers would detect an echo of the call of the sage in Sir 51 and an echo of Torah associations with yoke. The following context speaks for the allusions to Torah. The preceding context speaks for the association with wisdom. But from neither are we justified in speaking of an incarnation of wisdom or Torah in Matthew. Had this been the case we should have expected further signs of it in Matthew. See also Davies and Allison, *Matthew II*, p. 295. For a denial of the presence of wisdom christology altogether in Matthew see M. D. Johnson, "Reflections on a Wisdom approach to Matthew's Christology," *CBQ* 36 (1974), pp. 44–64.

The employment of wisdom imagery to portray Jesus as purveyor of God's Torah and its promise of life matches the portrait we have of Jesus from the Sermon on the Mount where Jesus upholds Torah, expands and expounds it, and promises its benefits, as in 11:28–30. The yoke of Torah, as expounded by Jesus, is, in contrast to the burdensome interpretation of the scribes and Pharisees, not burdensome;[144] it is the way to life and rest. By using Jewish Torah imagery, Matthew keeps Jesus closely within a Jewish understanding of Torah and stresses continuity between old and new.[145] The focus on Jesus in these terms coheres with the theme of the following episodes which depict Jesus as expounding Torah.[146]

Thus in 12:1 Matthew returns to his Markan source and offers his version of the controversy over the disciples' plucking grain on the sabbath (cf. Mark 2:23–28).[147] From the outset he makes explicit the allusion to hunger, which in Mark is only implied. Jesus' first response to the Pharisees charge is, as in Mark, the reference to David feeding his hungry men, but trimmed of the inaccuracies of the Markan version. He then adds a further argument: the Torah has priests work on the sabbath in the temple.[148] Matthew, writing

---

[144] So Deutsch, *Hidden Wisdom*, pp. 41–43. Jesus' "rest" is not freedom from the Law's demands, but the presence of Jesus helping the disciples to bear the yoke. The interpretation of the scribes and Pharisees is contrasted with Jesus' interpretation of Torah in the passages which follow (p. 43). Similarly Suggs, *Wisdom*, pp. 107–108. On the image of yoke see Sir 6:23–31; 51:23–26; 2 Bar 41:3; 2 En 34.

[145] Cf. Allison, *Moses*, pp. 218–233; D. C. Allison, "Two notes on a Key Text: Matthew 11:25–30," *JTS* 39 (1988), pp. 477–485, here: 479–483, who suggests that allusions to Jesus as the new Moses may lie behind the passage. He points to the parallel with Exod 33:12–13, which speaks of reciprocal knowledge between God and Moses (in that order, as here) and associates it with the promise of "rest" (33:14). He also sees a hint of Moses typology in the use of πραΰς, a favourite appellation of Moses (Nu 12:3 LXX). Such influence is possible, but not as prominent as the wisdom/Torah connection, which supplies not only motifs, but also form: the invitation, which not present in the Moses material. B. Charette, "'To proclaim liberty to the captives.' Matthew 11.28–30 in the Light of OT Prophetic Expectation," *NTS* 38 (1992), pp. 290–297, argues that neither Wisdom nor Law is Matthew's concern in 11:28–30, but Jesus' messiahship as the lowly one ("learn from me that I am meek and lowly") and his fulfilment of prophetic hope of rest for the captives. This would then echo the hopes of 11:2–5. This may be so, but beside the Wisdom and Torah allusions. Allusions she adduces to prophetic material concerning "rest" are too scattered to establish significant parallels.

[146] So Deutsch, *Hidden Wisdom*. p. 43

[147] Mohrlang, *Matthew*, p. 10, suggests that Matthew deliberately moved the sabbath episodes so that they took place after the sermon on the mount which sets the Law teaching in perspective and deliberately after 11:25–30 for the same reason.

[148] Cf. E. Levine, "The Sabbath Controversy according to Matthew," *NTS* 22 (1976), pp. 480–483, who suggests that Matthew is referring here not to priests working in the

for his community, and not for the synagogue, nevertheless engages in halakic argument which must have meant something for his hearers. He assumes they share his view about the authority of the Law and the scriptures. The issue is not primarily defending what happened in Jesus' day, though that matters to Matthew, but justifying the stance now taken by the Matthean community. That stance emerges in the episode to follow, which is closely linked.

While at one level Matthew's arguments are halakic, at another they transcend such argumentation. Already in the allusion to David, there is probably an implicit allusion to Jesus as David's Son, the Messiah. But especially in the argument about the priests working on the sabbath, Matthew goes beyond analogy. Here he has Jesus claim: "I tell you, something greater than the temple is here" (12:6). It comes immediately before Matthew's second allusion to Hosea 6:6: "If you knew what it means, 'I desire mercy and not sacrifice,' you would not have condemned the guiltless" (12:7) It is likely that Matthew is responsible for these additions and that they should be taken closely together. They are an important statement about Jesus' authority.[149]

Something greater is happening here than the temple, ie. what happens in the temple. It expresses itself in the person of Jesus and in his compassionate interpretation of the Law. This Jesus is claiming authority to interpret sabbath Law. It is not a claim against the Law. It is however one which unmistakably highlights Jesus' authority. This is also the implication of the way Matthew has rewritten Mark 2:27-28, to preserve only the christological claim, which he then presents as the ground rather than the conclusion for what precedes:[150]

---

temple, but to a practice debated between Sadducees and Pharisees about whether one could reap the 'omer offering on the day of the Passover (*mMen* 3) In this the Pharisees took the more lenient view. Here Jesus would be alluding to their own rulings. On the legitimacy of temple service on the sabbath, see Jub 50:10–11; CD 6:18; 10:14–23.

[149] Cf. Barth, "Gesetzesverständnis," pp. 75–78, who, while rightly noting the legal character of Matthew's argument which wards off the dangerous implications of Mark, avoids addressing the issue which the christological claim of 12:5–6 raises (Jesus is "something greater than the temple"), simply noting these verses would have been independent tradition; similarly Sigal, *Halakah*, p. 132 ("something greater" means the need); Luz, *Matthäus II*, p. 231 ("something greater" is "mercy"); Mohrlang, *Matthew*, p. 10; Saldarini, *Community*, pp. 130–131. Cf. Banks, *Law*, p. 117, who writes: "It is a question of authority rather than legality as such which is at stake"; similarly, pp. 127, 110–111. For R. H. Gundry, *Matthew. A Commentary on his Literary and Theological Art* (Grand Rapids: Eerdmans, 2nd edn., 1994), p. 223, the neuter, μεῖζόν, "something greater", focuses on the quality of what Jesus is rather than just his identity.

[150] Against Hummel, *Auseinandersetzung*, pp. 40–44, who argues that here, as in 9:13, the Hosea passage is inserted immediately before the christological claim in a way that the former legitimises the latter.

"For the Son of Man is Lord of the sabbath" (cf. Mark 2:27–28 "And he said to them, 'The sabbath was made for man, not man for the sabbath, so that the Son of Man is Lord also of the sabbath'.").[151]

It is the particular relation to the temple which makes priests' work on the sabbath appropriate. It is the particular relation to Jesus which, according to Matthew, makes what the disciples are doing on the sabbath appropriate. The weakness of the argument is that the priests prepare for worship, an activity particularly enjoined for the sabbath, whereas the disciples are simply meeting their own needs. But Matthew overlooks this weakness because meeting human need is a priority which overrules the sabbath and because the one to whom the disciples relate is superior to the temple.[152] Meeting human need in mercy is more important than sacrificing, even sacrifice on the sabbath.[153] Thus Matthew is combining both Jesus' superiority to the temple and the principle that mercy matters more than sacrifice. The claim of Jesus' superiority over the temple may not be exclusive,[154] any more than the contrast between sacrifice and mercy should be understood in this way, but it is striking. Yet for the hearer, there can be nothing surprising in the claim of ultimate authority for Jesus. Matthew has never left us in any doubt about that from the beginning and has just reiterated it in 11:27.

What are the implications of these arguments for Matthew's understanding of Jesus' attitude towards the Torah? As we have just noted, they bring to expression a christology which has been assumed throughout. Thus far the authority of Jesus and the authority of Torah have not clashed. On the contrary, Matthew has been at pains to emphasise that Jesus is bent on making

---

[151] Menninger, *Israel*, pp. 122–123, highlights the significant christological claim of this verse which goes beyond sabbath interpretation (not "also of the sabbath" as Mark 2:28). Cf. Hübner, *Gesetz*, pp. 118–123, who suggests that Matthew and Luke may be using an additional source, Q.

[152] There is no hint here that Jesus claiming the rights of priests for himself and his men. Cf. D. Daube, "Temple Tax," in *Jesus, the Gospels, and the Church. In Honor of W. R. Farmer*, edited by E. P. Sanders, (Macon: Mercer UP, 1989), pp. 121–134, here: 127.

[153] Cf. Hummel, *Auseinandersetzung*, pp. 40–44, who argues that the point of the Hosea quotation is not to justify the disciples' behaviour; the example of David addresses that as something to embarrass the Pharisees; rather it is to justify the doing of good deeds, the issue of the following pericope, and relates to the contrast between temple service and the work of Jesus. Similarly D. Hill, "On the Use and Meaning of Hosea VI.6 in Matthew's Gospel," *NTS* 24 (1978), pp. 107–119, here: 114–119. While both sabbath passages belong together and find their resolution in 12:12b, there is no need to deny the relation of the Hosea text to its narrative context in 12:1–8.

[154] Cf. Donaldson, *Mountain*, pp. 184–186, who understands Matthew as portraying Jesus as the replacement of the temple. In him God is with us and will remain with us always.

sure that Torah is observed and adds much more. It is, of course, Torah as expounded by Jesus, but nevertheless Torah. Yet with the massive authority which Matthew's christology presupposes there had to be tensions. One has already surfaced in 8:21–22 where Jesus puts following the call to discipleship ahead of duty to the dead, although, as we saw, there is no specific burial law which it contravened and Matthew probably did not sense it as an issue. Here Matthew has Jesus assert his own superiority over the temple. It is one thing to assert the superiority of deeds of loving kindness over temple rituals; it is another to assert the superiority of Jesus over the temple. Yet even this is not abrogation.[155] Within Matthew's Jewish community where Jesus' authority is recognised, it is still a matter of one part of God's Law overriding another: obligation to Jesus overrides all other obligations.

Viewed from a Jewish perspective outside the community, Matthew's Judaism might be seen as odd, but unproblematic, as long as its teacher was interpreting Torah, however authoritatively. It became problematic when that authority was being used to waive Torah requirements. This might have

---

[155] So Barth, "Gesetzesverständnis," pp. 75–78; Hummel, *Auseinandersetzung*, pp. 44–46; Daube, *Rabbinic Judaism*, pp. 67–71; Davies, *Setting*, pp. 103–104; Mohrlang, *Matthew*, p. 10; Vouga, *Loi*, pp. 46–48; Wong, *Interkulturelle Theologie*, p. 80; "The Matthean Understanding of the Sabbath: A Response to G. N. Stanton," *JSNT* 44 (1991), pp. 3–18, here: 6–8; Sigal, *Halakah*, pp. 119–136; Broer, "Gesetzesverständnis," pp. 138–141, who makes the additional point that one should not necessarily conclude from this nor from 24:20 that the sabbath was an issue for Matthew's community; Segal, "Matthew's Jewish Voice," pp. 6–7, arguing that Matthew rejects only the Pharisaic interpretation of the sabbath law; Overman, *Matthew's Gospel*, pp. 80–82, arguing that in Matthew's view the disciples were not breaking sabbath law, but that Matthew takes the charge seriously; similarly D. J. Harrington, "Sabbath Tensions: Matthew 12:1–14 and Other New Testament Texts," in *The Sabbath in Jewish and Christian Traditions*, edited by T. Eskenazi, D. Harrington, W. S. Shea, (New York: Crossroads, 1991), pp. 45–56, here: 46–54, who writes of Matthew's concern to maintain the liberal interpretation of sabbath law by Jesus while remaining sensitive to his community as sabbath observant (p. 52); the "something greater" he sees as primarily a reference to the community (but inclusive also of Jesus and the kingdom; p. 48). See also M. Limbeck, "Die nichts bewegen wollen! Zum Gesetzesverständnis des Evangelisten Matthäus," *TheolQuart* 168 (1988), pp. 299–320, here: 314–319, who argues that Matthew assumes common ground with the his Jewish opponents that there are clashes at times in law in which one part of law may override another, but argues that what overrides is not God's honour, but God's mercy. Torah is indeed upheld, but the mercy principle is used in its interpretation. He also points to the significance of the sequel where Matthew has Jesus cite Isa 42 to show that Jesus' way is to seek the victory of God's way of justice which consists in gentleness and sensitivity in application of Torah. Cf. Strecker, *Gerechtigkeit*, p. 32–33 who interprets the passage as implying Jesus has annulled sabbath law; Menninger, *Israel*, pp. 119–120, who argues that the point of comparison with David is primarily christological for Matthew: David could set aside Law; Jesus has set aside Law.

been tolerated to some degree; but beyond a certain point it no longer represented interpretation of Torah; it meant a rival Torah. Matthew's christological argument, here, exposes a tendency toward the latter. The Son of Man is Lord of the sabbath, but this is still being used to declare what is appropriate on the sabbath, not to abrogate it.

The concern to stay within the framework of Torah is still evident in the other sabbath episode (12:9–14). Matthew's account of the healing of man with the withered hand on the sabbath has Jesus engage in legal argument,[156] much as one might have expected in an intramural Jewish discussion. He even omits from his source the provocative questions of Jesus about doing good or harm, saving or killing on the sabbath (cf. Mark 3:4b). Perhaps Matthew sensed that this response of Jesus failed to take seriously enough the issue of Law involved. Instead, Matthew has the opponents ask directly about legality (12:10) and has Jesus respond on their terms with halakic argument (12:11–12, "Who among you, if he had only one sheep and if it fell into a pit on the sabbath, would not take hold of it and lift it out? How much more valuable is a human being than a sheep?").[157] The conclusion: "So it is lawful to do good on the sabbath" (12:12b) brings us back to Matthew's focus in the previous episode on mercy and must be read within that wider context. It goes far beyond what the halakic argument will allow and is so loose as to come near to abolishing sabbath law, but stops short.

In 12:15–21 Matthew has drawn on Mark 3:7–12. He reduces it to a very brief summary. On the one hand, he had already used part of it in 4:24–25 and 5:1 (cf. Mark 3:7,8,13). On the other, he has deleted from it the reference to exorcisms and to the acclamations of demoniacs that Jesus is "Son of God". Instead, as in his use of Mark 1:32–34 in 8:16–17, he uses the summary to portray Jesus as acting in humility and in accordance with the scriptures: Isa 42:1–4.

> Behold my servant/child in whom I am well pleased,
> my beloved in whom my soul delights;
> I shall put my Spirit on him
> and he will announce judgement/justice to the nations.
> He will not be contentious or shout out,
> nor will anyone hear his voice in the streets.

---

[156] So Barth, "Gesetzesverständnis," pp. 73–74, who points out that Matthew's redaction both implies continuing sabbath observance and places it in within the perspective of love for others. See also Hummel, *Auseinandersetzung*, pp. 44–45; Levine, *Matthean Salvation History*, pp. 38, 248; Sigal, *Halakah*, pp. 136–142; Sand, *Gesetz*, pp. 43–45; Davies and Allison, *Matthew II*, p. 328.

[157] Cf. the much stricter position which forbids such action in CD 11:13–14; 4Q265 fr. 7,1:5–7, which disallows rescue of an animal, but allows rescue of a human being.

He will not break a bruised reed,
nor snuff out a smouldering wick,
until he has brought judgement/justice to victory.
And in his name the nations will put their hope.

It is a fitting replacement of the acclamation from the lips of demons; it begins with words which recalls the event of Jesus' baptism: "Behold my servant/child (παῖς) in whom I am well pleased, my beloved in whom my soul delights; I have put my Spirit on him." The rest of the quotation is also important for the portrait of Jesus in Matthew and recalls the way Jesus' role had been defined by John before Jesus' baptism as judge to come: "He will announce judgement/justice (κρίσις) to the nations." It goes on to predict his humility and gentleness and ends: "until he brings judgement/justice (κρίσις) to victory. And in his name the nations will put their hope."

This divine witness has the effect of bringing together major elements of Matthew's portrait: servanthood/sonship; baptism; justice/judgement; humility and gentleness; and the Gentile mission. For our purposes the statements about Jesus and judgement or justice are important. They belong together well with the baptism imagery, because John announced Jesus as judge.[158] κρίσις can encompass both judgement and justice as the criterion for judgement. Matthew is thus reinforcing Jesus' role as the judge to come who makes known God's justice in the present. It is in this perspective that Matthew considers Jesus in relation to the Law. Making known God's justice means making known God's Torah, which includes the application of written Torah as well as expansions of it and additions to it given by Jesus.

The reference to gentleness in the Isaiah quotation, "He shall not strive or cry aloud, nor shall anyone hear his voice in the streets. A bruised reed he shall not break or quench a smouldering wick" (12:19–20a) also recalls his gentle spirit proclaimed in 11:28–30. The effect is to surround Jesus' exposition of the Law in 12:1–8 and 12:9–13, on either side, by statements related to Jesus as interpreter of the Law. The gentleness finds its exposition in Jesus' application of "justice", God's Law in the face of human need.

The impression that Matthew means us to pause and recollect at this point in the narrative is reinforced by the presence in 12:22–24 of a doublet of the

---

[158] Barth, "Gesetzesverständnis," pp. 117–120, notes the importance of the passage for Matthew's christology of the lowly servant, but misses the emphasis on judgement. Instead, where he addresses κρίσις, he speaks of God's "Recht", "justice" (pp. 132–133). The is a common deficiency and denies the important correlation with Matt 3. It is repeated in Hagner, *Matthew*, p. 338; cf. Luz, *Matthäus II*, pp. 247–248.

miracle with which the section 8:1 – 9:34 ended (9:32–34).[159] There, at the healing of a dumb demoniac, the Pharisees accuse Jesus of being in league with Beelzebul. Here, the same occurs, except that the man is, in addition, blind, and the crowds raise the issue whether Jesus is Son of David. Matthew seems to have introduced these features from the immediately preceding story in 9:27–31, where the blind men hail Jesus as Son of David. The effect is to take us back to where Matthew left off in describing Jesus' activity and back to the issue of conflict with the Pharisees.

The conflict, announced in 9:34, identified in 10:25 and 11:18 as also directed at the disciples and at John, erupts now in full scale in 12:25–45. The prophetic word cited in 12:18–21, reaffirming Jesus as judge, yet also underlining his gentleness and vulnerability, is finding immediate fulfilment. Jesus argues against their accusation that he is in league with Beelzebul, threatening his opponents with judgement if they fail to see his exorcisms as the work of the Spirit (12:31–32). Jesus the judge reasserts, as had John, that future judgement will be on the basis of fruit (12:33), and, like John, addresses his opponents as a "brood of vipers" (12:34; cf. 3:7). People's words will betray them on the day of judgement. By their fruit they will be known. The emphasis is on both the healthy tree, the right heart, on the one hand, and the fruit, the words which result. This is a standard emphasis of the Matthean Jesus (12:33–37). Matthew's Jesus' has applied the same principle to John and himself in 11:19. Their deeds will vindicate their wisdom.

Next, Matthew has Jesus respond to the request for a sign by using the image of Jonah's three day stay in the belly of the whale as a sign of his own resurrection (12:38–40). But beside this he has Jesus predict that the Ninevites and the queen of the south would take the stand for the prosecution against his accusers. Each reference ends with a claim about Jesus' superiority: he is greater than Jonah and greater than Solomon (12:41,42). This is not a claim in relation to prophetic writings or wisdom literature, but serves simply as an *a minore ad maius* argument, as it did in 12:6, to emphasise the deserved condemnation. Matthew ends the conflict by having Jesus turn the tables on his accusers. Not he, but they are possessed (12:43–45).

Matthew's version of Jesus' family coming to speak with him (12:46–50) no longer has the strong negative overtones we find in Mark (3:21–22,31–35). Matthew has omitted all traces that they disapprove of Jesus or fear for

---

[159] On the Matthean exploitation of the motif of two witnesses, which lies behind the duplication, see Loader, "Son of David."

his sanity. The infancy narratives portray quite another picture. Rather the narrative serves in Matthew to enable Jesus to include as his family all who do the will of his Father in heaven. This is not only a common Matthean formulation, but also reflects a constant Matthean theme. For Matthew, Jesus' major concern is to have people "do the will of God." This means doing God's will as expounded by Jesus who has come to extrapolate the meaning of the Law and the Prophets for that end and will judge all according to their performance, based on that criterion.

As in Mark, this provides a transition to the collection of parables (13:1–53; cf. Mark 4:1–34). Matthew has considerably expanded the Markan selection. The focus is strongly on appropriate response to Jesus' message, rather than on the miraculous harvest; Matthew even omits the parable of the seed which matures to harvest in secret (cf. Mark 4:26–29). The disciples are those who do understand and, in contrast to Mark (4:10–13), Matthew emphasises that they are now seeing and hearing what many prophets and righteous longed to see and hear (13:16–17). This belongs to Matthew's understanding of Jesus as the one who brings the activity and teaching which belongs to the climax of history.

The parables of the wheat and weeds, the mustard seed, the leaven and the dragnet all reflect Matthew's focus on righteous deeds as the basis for judgement. The parables of the hidden treasure and the pearl emphasise the degree of commitment expected. Matthew emphasises that the disciples do comprehend Jesus" meaning (13:51) and likens "every scribe trained for the kingdom of heaven" to a householder who produces from his treasure new and old (13:51–52).[160] It reflects Matthew's concern to portray Jesus and, here, also his disciples, as teachers who uphold and expound Torah in ways that bring out continuity between old and new. It is also noteworthy that here, as already in 8:19 (cf. also 7:29), we meet the term "scribe" used of a Christian teacher, indicating a strong sense of social continuity with the Jewish community.

Within 9:36 – 13:52, 9:36– 11:1 deals , in particular, with Jesus' authorisation of his disciples. It is a further application of the delegation model and implies not only that the disciples share Jesus' task of healing preaching and

---

[160] A. J. Hultgren, "Things New and Old in Matthew 13:52," in *All Things New. Essays in Honor of Roy A. Harrisville*, edited by A. J. Hultgren et al., (St Paul: Luther Northwestern Theological Seminary, 1992), pp. 109–118, here: 113–116, considers the options: (a) the Law and the Prophets over against Jesus; (b) pre-Easter over against post-Easter Jesus and opts for a combination: the Law and the Prophets and the Jesus tradition over against needing to find a new word for current situations.

teaching; they also have authority. This had already been hinted at in 9:8 and will return for fuller treatment later in the gospel. Matthew does not relate the restriction of the disciples' mission (corresponding to Jesus' own limited mission to Israel) to issues of Torah. Nor do these appear to feature in his instructions about hospitality, as they might have. Much of the material in this chapter is instruction. Some of this argues by appeal to nature (sparrows and the hairs of one's head); most is direct instruction and command. But all should be seen as part of a whole: Jesus teaches as the one authorised to declare God's Torah. He is the judge to come.

The effect of 9:36–11:1, after the depiction of Jesus' deeds in 8:1 – 9:35, is to bind the ministry of Jesus and the future ministry of the disciples together. In ch. 11 Matthew brings the hearer back to the issue of Jesus' identity. Any listener to John would have expected Jesus to have come as judge. Instead he has been doing other things and commissioning the disciples to do the same. Matthew, therefore, has John ask the question. The result is an important series of statements about Jesus' identity, including his relation to John, which also have importance for Matthew's view of Jesus' attitude towards Torah. Matthew's introduction already gave a first clue: these are the deeds of the Messiah (11:2). Both John and Jesus are portrayed as standing in a line of fulfilment with the Law and the Prophets (11:13). But both are under attack. Focussing on Jesus, Matthew argues, on the basis of his deeds, including his miracles, that he is to be seen as the one authorised by God, who has the unique relation of sonship with God and makes God known.

These claims also come to expression in 11:28–30 which presents Jesus as offering the true exposition of Torah to his contemporaries. It associates Jesus with Torah, and perhaps also with the traditional figure of wisdom, as associated with Torah in Sirach. It is not a claim that Jesus is Torah or wisdom incarnate, but should be seen as part of a wider conceptual framework in which Jesus, by his unique authority, expounds God's will as judge to come.

The association with Torah in 11:28–30 prepares for Matthew's reedited versions of the sabbath disputes, which directly follow. There Matthew has Jesus offer two kinds of argument. Jesus claims to be greater than the temple and the Lord of the sabbath. Yet beside this is halakic argument, in which Jesus appeals to the priority of compassion for human need. They are combined in such a way that Torah remains in tact. Compassion (9:36), mercy (12:7), doing good (12:12), continue to determine Torah interpretation and to characterise Jesus' approach. Matthew portrays Jesus' deeds as Messiah (11:2–5) and his healings in this light (12:15–21). But the combination produces results which put relation to Torah under strain, for instance, in simplifying the criterion for what is allowed on the sabbath to "doing good." Similar tensions lie behind the demand that a disciple neglect responsibilities for the burial of his father (8:22) and the teachings about family loyalties in 10:34–39 (cf. also 12:46–50).

Following the sabbath episodes, in 12:15–21, Matthew employs Isa 42:1–4 in a manner which recalls Jesus' baptism and his role as judge to come, as announced by John. It also forms an inclusion with 11:28–30, emphasising Jesus' gentleness as interpreter of Torah. Jesus then speaks as judge to come in the debate with the scribes over the charge that he is demon possessed. The same motif and orientation underlies the parable chapter which focuses on responses to Jesus and their consequences at the judgement.

Matthew's text continues to claim that Jesus fulfils and champions the Law and the Prophets. Matthew is consistent in portraying Jesus very much within a continuity, so that his coming represents not replacement of Torah, but its exposition and expansion. Accordingly the Christian community teachers, probably like Matthew himself, can see themselves as standing in the scribal tradition of interpreting God's Law and so bearing witness to the treasures of both old and new.

2.3.3 Matthew 13:53 – 16:20

In this section Matthew follows his Markan source closely, but with significant modifications. In 13:54–58 he offers an abbreviated version of Jesus' appearance in his home town synagogue (Mark 6:1–6). In Matthew, the question, "Where does this wisdom come from and these miracles?", might evoke the close association already implied between Jesus and wisdom in 11:28–30. It serves to confirm the criterion announced in 11:19 ("Wisdom is justified by her deeds"). In Matthew, there is also a much more direct connection with Jesus' parable teaching (which immediately precedes) than in Mark, where a series of miracles (4:35 – 5:43) intervenes between the parables (4:1–34) and the visit (6:1–6). Matthew has already used these miracles in the great collection of Jesus' deeds in 8:1 – 9:34. Matthew still retains Jesus' words about rejection, including a reference to his own household, but omits reference to his kin (13:56; cf. Mark 6:4).

Matthew then follows the Markan sequence, which links Jesus' words about rejection as a prophet with the account of John the Baptist's execution (14:1–12). Matthew abbreviates the account of Herod's pondering about Jesus' identity (14:1–2). The result is that it no longer matches Jesus' conversation with his disciples at Caesarea Philippi (cf. 16:12–14), as it did in Mark (6:14–16; 8:27–28). Similarly Matthew has heavily abbreviated

Mark's version of John's death (14:3–12; cf. Mark 6:17–29). Unlike Mark, Matthew has John's own disciples report the affair to Jesus (14:12), continuing the consistency with which Matthew brings John and Jesus more closely together than in Mark.

Matthew continues with the Markan sequence of the feeding of the five thousand (14:13–21), the walking on the water (14:22–33), healings at Gennesaret (14:34–36), teaching on purity (15:1–20), the encounter with the Canaanite woman (15:21–28), healing by the lake (15:29–31), the feeding of the four thousand (15:32–39), the request for a sign (16:1–4), the warning about the leaven of the Pharisees and Sadducees (16:5–12), and the discussion at Caesarea Philippi (16:13–20). The only major omission is the healing of the blind man at Bethsaida (cf. Mark 8:22–26). He has more than made up for this by double use of Mark's account of the healing of blind Bartimaeus (9:27–31; 20:29–34; cf. Mark 10:46–52).

Before commenting in more detail on the episodes within this section, I want to make some observations about the section as a whole, especially since it played a key role in Mark. Within Matthew's use of this large section of Mark there are significant variations. Within Mark we noted the important role which Mark 8:14–21 plays in shedding light on the section as a whole. When we look to 16:5–12, the equivalent segment in Matthew, we find that Matthew has made significant changes. The warning in Mark 8:14 about the leaven of the Pharisees and Herodians has become a warning about the leaven of the Pharisees and Sadducees. This is been a standard description of the opponents of John and Jesus in Matthew. In what follows he then moves the focus from the number of baskets as such (12 and 7) to the extent of the miracle in each case (16:9–10; cf. Mark 8:19–20). For Matthew uses the feedings not for their numerical symbolism, as had Mark to celebrate the participation of both Jews and Gentiles in the blessings of the kingdom, but for the weight they bear as miracles. This is also reflected in the feeding narratives, themselves. To each he adds after the numerical figure: "not including women and children" (14:21; 15:38). The focus on the massiveness of the miracles recalls the vindicatory function of miracles in 11:19. Accordingly Matthew has removed from the feeding of the five thousand much of the imagery of Israel (the image of the sheep without a shepherd, used earlier in 9:36; the sitting in 100s and 50s). The feedings no longer represent Israel and the Gentiles. Rather both are events echoing Israel's past (manna in the wilderness) and its future hope (especially the feeding of the four thousand linked with Zion typology, as we shall see).

Matthew has also changed the focus of the teaching section from being concerned with issues central to the Gentile mission, rejection of food laws

(Mark 7:1–23), to being concerned with deprecating Pharisaic interpretation of purity laws. Accordingly the encounter with the Canaanite woman no longer relates to it in the way as it does in Mark, namely, to underline the falling of the barriers and the inclusion of Gentiles.[161] Rather it functions, as did the encounter with the centurion, as an example of Gentile faith to shame Israel and, at most, only prefigure later Gentile involvement.

He has also removed reference to Gentile territory in 15:29–31(cf. Mark 7:31–37), omitting the specific healing of the deaf mute and replacing it with a summary of a broadened range of healings. He has also integrated it with the account of the feeding of the four thousand which follows, so that it echoes his account of the feeding of the five thousand, into which he had also introduced a reference to healing. The result is a narrative (15:29–39) which reflects Zion typology and no longer represents a feeding of Gentiles as in Mark. Matthew has also destroyed the neat coupling in Mark between the healing of a deaf and dumb Gentile by spittle in 7:31–37 and the blind Gentile of Bethsaida by spittle in 8:22–26, signs of positive Gentile response in contrast to the deafness and blindness of the disciples.

Therefore, while using Markan material, Matthew has fairly thoroughly dismantled the Markan composition, so that it no longer celebrates the inclusion of Jew and Gentile in the kingdom based on rejection of "offending parts" of Torah. The material now serves another purpose, still focused on teachings, but centred on interpretation and authority.

We turn now to the individual episodes. In Matthew the feeding of the five thousand, to which we have already given considerable attention, is primarily a miracle testifying to Jesus' power and, with the feeding of the four thousand, acclaims the blessings of the gospel for Israel. The strongly christological emphasis of Matthew's feeding of the five thousand continues in his account of Jesus' walking on the water (14:22–33). If the former reflects Matthean undoing of a major Markan theme in the section, the latter reflects in Matthew a new emphasis which Matthew brings, which have a direct bearing on the authority of the Church and its leaders as Jesus' successors in interpreting Torah.

Matthew makes substantial additions to the account of the walking on the water (14:22–33). Not only does he add that the disciples acclaim Jesus as Son of God, an element absent from Mark's account, but he also has Jesus invite Peter to walk on the water. There is an implicit cross reference back to this event in the authorisation of Peter in 16:16–18. There, too, Matthew adds the acclamation of Jesus as Son of God and then has Jesus declare

---

[161] So rightly Davies and Allison, *Matthew II*, pp. 543–544.

Peter to be the church's foundation and give him authority to bind and loose, assuring him that the Church will be victorious against hell's gates. In 14:22–33 Peter's authority to walk over the deep symbolically represents the authority over the powers which Jesus gives him explicitly in 16:16–19. In 18:18, Matthew will attribute this same authority of Peter's to the Christian community. It has been given authority to declare God's will, ie. to interpret Torah.

The acclamation of Jesus as Son of God in this scene (14:33) also has the effect of removing the drama of Peter's confession in 16:16; it is no longer the first statement of recognition of Jesus as Messiah, as it had been in Mark 8:29. Correspondingly Matthew has altered the form of the question to the disciples at Caesarea Philippi to "Who do people say that I, the Son of Man, am?" There is no question of the disciples' not knowing that he is the Son of Man, already established as a term of authority (8:20; 9:6; 12:8; 13:41). The effect is thus to put the major emphasis of the passage on the authorisation which Jesus gives to the church through Peter, the emphasis matched here in 14:22–33 by the addition of Peter's walk on the water. This change in orientation also explains Matthew's treatment of Herod's questioning, noted above; it no longer functions as an inclusio with the Caesarea Philippi episode as it had in Mark.

The brief summary of Jesus' healing activity which follows in 14:34–36 (using Mark 6:53–56) corresponds in Matthew's macrostructure to the summary he has created in 15:29–31. This appears to enhance the sense of symmetry, with the two feedings and the two summaries corresponding, though it is not a neat pattern, since the walking on the water breaks it and the second summary has been integrated with the second feeding. We note that Matthew preserves Mark's reference to Jesus' κράσπεδον ("tassel" 14:36; cf. Mark 6:56), which reinforces the impression of Jesus' Jewish piety, especially before the following discussion on purity laws. Matthew had already introduced reference to Jesus' κράσπεδον in the account of the healing of the woman with the flow of blood (9:20).

Without doubt, however, as in Mark, the teaching of Jesus about purity, 15:1–20, forms the centre of the section as a whole and provides the reference point for Jesus' warning about the teaching of the Pharisees and Sadducees in 16:5–12. Matthew sees no need to explain the rite of hand washing for his readers (cf. Mark 7:3–4). We must assume, that his hearers were sufficiently familiar with such rites. In omitting the explanation Matthew also removes what in Mark was not only an explanation, but also an implicit disparagement of such outward rites. Matthew also generalises the accusation: "Why do your disciples transgress the tradition of the elders?

For they do not wash their hands when they eat bread" (15:2; cf. Mark 7:5 "Why do your disciples not live according to the tradition of the elders, but eat with unwashed hands?"). The reference is, therefore, no longer to a particular occasion, as in Mark, where it possibly even refers to eating the loaves which had been miraculously multiplied (cf. Mark 7:2).

Matthew has also rearranged the original Markan sequence of Jesus' assault on his questioners. Mark's Jesus had used Isa 29:13 to attack their hypocrisy (7:6–8), followed by an attack on their abuse of the *corban* law (7:9–13).[162] Now in Matthew the Isaiah quotation concludes the attack on abuse of *corban* law (15:7–9). In the rearrangement Matthew has ensured that the words of Jesus, "Abandoning the command of God you hold to human traditions" (Mark 7:8) no longer stand on their own as a generalisation, but apply to the particular instance of abuse of *corban* law (15:3). Similarly he has once again omitted Markan disparagement ("And you do many such things like this," Mark 7:13). These changes indicate that Matthew still respects aspects of the tradition of the elders.[163]

In 15:11 Matthew reformulates the controversial logion of Mark 7:15. He replaces "There is nothing outside of a person which entering him defiles him" with "Not what enters the mouth defiles a person". Matthew's version makes a clearer reference to food. His version of the second half is closer to Mark, but also adds reference to "the mouth", thus removing the potential allusion to defecation: "but what comes out of the mouth, this defiles a person"; cf. Mark: "but the things coming out of person are what defile the person." He also introduces the reference to mouth in 15:17 and 18 (cf. Mark 7:18,20).[164]

Matthew then inserts 15:12–14 in which Jesus acknowledges the offence this caused the Pharisees and attacks them as blind guides. Only then does he move to have Jesus explain the controversial saying. His abbreviated version is more in the form of an elaboration of the saying: what enters the mouth, goes to the stomach and from there to the toilet (15:17). Matthew omits Mark's reference to its significance, including Mark's own conclusion that Jesus thus declared all foods clean (Mark 7:19c). Then, following Mark, he states the significance of what comes from within (15:18,19,20a). Matthew

---

[162] On the background to discussion of releasing people from oaths, see Saldarini, *Community*, p. 156.

[163] So Vouga, *Loi*, p. 86.

[164] On the relationship of the forms of the logion among Mark 7:15; Matt 15:11 and Thom 14, see the discussion in Dunn, "Purity," pp. 42–44, who also believes a form of the saying lies behind Mark 7:18b,20. On Thom 14 see also our discussion in the chapter on Thomas below.

has trimmed the list of what comes from within and defiles by bringing it more into line with the decalogue categories. Finally he has Jesus add a conclusion to the whole, not present in Mark: "To eat with unclean hands does not defile a person" (15:20b).

In appending this conclusion Matthew shows that he shares with Mark the assumption that the accusers connect impure hands with food defilement and assume this can defile the eater.[165] What does this conclusion imply with regard to purity laws in relation to food? We have seen that Matthew has dismantled Mark's focus on Gentile mission, so that it is likely that categories of clean and unclean foods are not primarily in view. Nevertheless Jesus' contrast in 15:11 could offend, as the report of the disciples in 15:12 indicates.

The question is: does Matthew imply that Jesus is abrogating all purity laws with regard to food and thereby ruling out the particular instance raised? That would imply that Jesus abrogates all relevant parts of Torah.[166] Omission of Mark's famous aside (7:19c "declaring all foods clean") would be more a reflection of style than of content. Or is his argument, that it is more important to focus on ethical attitude and behaviour than on such concerns with ritual purity?[167] This interpretation is more complicated, because it means taking the contrast in 15:11 as one of degree,[168] yet still having Matthew conclude that eating with unwashed hands does not (through allegedly contaminating the food) make a person unclean. The logic would have to be: purity issues are less important; and this particular teaching about purity is, in any case, unnecessary.[169] Matthew's argument does not say

---

[165] See the discussion of Mark 7:1–23 in the previous chapter. Hübner, *Gesetz*, pp. 180–183, drawing attention to the fact that normally unclean hands and foods rendered thereby unclean do not make people unclean. He argues that only such foods are in view in 15:11.

[166] So Banks, *Law*, pp. 139–140, 143–145, who argues that Matthew may even preserve the more original form of the saying in 15:11; similarly Broer, *Freiheit*, pp. 114–122 and "Gesetzesverständnis," pp. 141–142; Menninger, *Israel*, pp. 122–126.

[167] So Saldarini, *Community*, pp. 134–139, who argues that Matthew counters only tradition which is not, or not well grounded in scriptural law, but in no way accepts Mark's abrogation. Similarly Hummel, *Auseinandersetzung*, pp. 46–49; Mohrlang, *Matthew*, pp. 11–12; Davies and Allison, *Matthew II*, pp. 517, 537; Levine, *Matthean Salvation History*, p. 160; Luz, *Matthäus II*, p. 425; Overman, *Matthew's Gospel*, pp. 82–84; Vouga, *Loi*, p. 88, who sees Matthew drawing a line of demarcation between his community and Hellenistic Jewish synagogue.

[168] Barth, "Gesetzesverständnis," pp. 83–84, believes Matthew would have understood 15:11 inclusively, as a relative contrast as 23:23; similarly Davies and Allison, *Matthew II*, p. 531; Luz, *Matthäus II*, p. 425.

[169] So Booth, *Purity*, pp. 221–223.

that explicitly, but it seems to be implied. This makes better sense of Matthew's omission of Mark's conclusion in 7:19c. It also coheres with 15:12–14 where Matthew has Jesus attack the Pharisees not for adherence to Torah, but as guides. It is their interpretation which he is attacking. The alternative would make of 15:20b a rather odd conclusion. For it would have Matthew end on a minor issue, having launched an argument and conclusion of much greater significance, abolishing purity and food laws as a whole. As it is, 15:20 represents a position with which all but extremists would agree. The cause of offence is the generalisation in 15:11, which does not seek to abolish, but does call into question the kind of emphasis which these Pharisees espoused.

While Matthew retains Mark's basic contrast between what comes from without and what comes from within, he has removed the implied ridicule present in Mark. His mention of the toilet (15:17) no longer functions disparagingly. Matthew has reworked Mark's contrast so that it is now much more clearly about the setting of Torah priorities. Matthew's version of the list of evils coheres with his focus elsewhere on making love and compassion the priority in Torah interpretation.

It is hard not to see here, too, a sensitivity being shown by Matthew, particularly in the matter of food laws. If his community is as strongly Jewish as many features of his gospel seem to indicate, we may assume his community observed food laws. On the other hand, viewed from the macrostructure, what is it, then, that makes the "leaven of the Pharisees and Sadducees" something to avoid, as 16:5–13 teaches? It is surely not just their insistence on handwashing. It is probably more than just their hypocritical interpretations such as the use of the *corban* law. The concern is not with the problem which food and purity laws pose for the Gentile mission. The butt of Matthew's critique appears rather to be the quality of their interpretation of the Law, exemplified by the handwashing dispute and the abuse of the *corban* law. This corresponds, in turn, to Matthew's vilification of them in chapter 23. It is that they are "blind guides" (15:12–14).

This conclusion coheres with the fact that Matthew links the encounter with the Canaanite woman (which follows in 15:21–28) less clearly with what precedes than does Mark. In Mark it instances Jesus' breaking through the traditional barriers of purity by responding to a Gentile in Gentile territory[170] and so illustrating what Mark has derived from Jesus' teaching.

---

[170] Some even doubt Matthew intends to indicate that the event took place in Gentile territory. So Levine, *Matthean Salvation History*, p. 137; Davies and Allison, *Matthew II*,

In Matthew the barriers are held in tact.[171] She must batter them three times before she achieves a positive response. In response to her first request Matthew interposes the disciples between her and Jesus (15:22–23). To some degree this ameliorates Jesus' sharp refusal as it is recorded in Mark.[172] The disciples want to send her away. Instead of responding positively to their demand, Jesus replies that he is sent only to the lost sheep of the house of Israel (15:24). This Matthean addition matches Jesus' own command to his disciples to exercise their mission at first only in Israel (10:5–6). Later the mission opens to the nations, as surely all hearers would have known (28:18–20). This has the effect of setting Jesus' response not so much in the context of traditional Jewish-Gentile relations, but of Jesus' own mission. Even the saying about taking the children's food and giving it to dogs now falls within that perspective (15:26). This is the time of bread for Israel; it is not yet the time of bread for Gentiles.

Jesus finally rewards the woman's persistence with the declaration: "O woman, your faith is great. Let it what you want happen" (15:28). Jesus' response is now not, as in Mark, to the substance of her argument, but to her faith.[173] The woman stands, like the centurion whose servant was healed despite initial rejection (8:5–13), as an example of true faith in contrast to Israel's unfaith. This does not rule out the possibility that Matthew sees in her, as in the centurion, a foreshadowing of later Gentile response, but the focus is primarily that her faith shows up Israel's unfaith.[174] Thus she

---

pp. 546–548; Harrington, *Matthew*, p. 235; Saldarini, *Community*, pp. 72–73. The issue is whether εἰς τὰ μέρη (15:21) means "towards" or "into". Cf. cf. Luz, *Matthäus II*, p. 433. Saldarini also notes Matthew's omission of Mark's mention of Jesus entering a house, possibly because it was a Gentile house.

[171] So Levine, *Matthean Salvation History*, pp. 133–151, esp. 133; Saldarini, *Community*, pp. 72–73.

[172] Cf. Levine, *Matthean Salvation History*, p. 132, who shows some ambivalence about the reference to dogs, preferring "puppies" in her heading, but acknowledging that it was an ethnic insult (p. 151).

[173] So E. A. Russell, "The Image of the Jew in Matthew's Gospel," *ProcIrBibAssoc* 12 (1989), pp. 37–57, here: 44.

[174] Cf. Levine, *Matthean Salvation History*, p. 139, who denies that her addressing him as the Jewish Messiah with the words, "Son of David," is a confession of faith. I agree in the sense that full Gentile confession of faith must come only after the great commission for Matthew. The woman's response, like that of the centurion who appreciates Jesus' authority, is faith in the sense of recognition of who Jesus was and what he could do. See also Donaldson, *Mountain*, p. 132. Cf. also E. Wainwright, *Towards a Feminist Critical Reading of the Gospel according to Matthew*, BZNW 60, (Berlin: de Gruyter, 1991), pp. 238–247, who suggests that the issue in the story, including the reference of "dog", is not only that she is a Gentile, but also that she is a woman and reflects debate over the inclusion of women in the liturgical life of the Matthean community. This is

acclaims Jesus as "Son of David"; which the Pharisees had failed to do! She is even described as Canaanite, Israel's traditional enemy in the land. A further echo of the story of the centurion is the healing of a dependant at a distance. The distance may reflect issues of unwillingness to enter a Gentile house, although, as in Mark, this receives no attention. Matthew's use of the anecdote is, therefore, different from Mark's. It does not illustrate Jesus' abandonment of the barriers set by Torah.

The summary of healings and the feeding of the four thousand (15:29–39) now serve further to illustrate Jesus' supernatural powers. They effectively duplicate the healing and the feeding of the five thousand (14:13–21). It is no longer a feeding of Gentiles in Gentile territory as in Mark; therewith the potential purity issues, passed over in Mark, disappear. Matthew sets the scene on a mountain (15:30). On the mountain "the crowd saw the mute speak, the maimed made whole, the lame walk, and the blind see and glorified the God of Israel" (15:31).[175] On the mountain the four thousand hungry are fed. The scene is effectively a return of focus to eschatological fulfilment in Jesus' ministry, as set forth in Jesus' reply to John (11:2–5). There are strong allusions here, as there, to Isa 35:5–6. The feast on the mountain recalls the great prophetic promises about Zion (eg. Isa 25:6; Jer 31:7–14; cf. also Mic 4:1–7).[176] What in Mark symbolised inclusion of Gentiles is in Matthew a celebration of fulfilment for Israel.

The request of the Pharisees and Sadducees for a sign (16:1–4) meets with a double response. Jesus tells them they should read the signs of the times as they do the seasons, and he refuses a sign, except for that of Jonah, already mentioned in 12:39. Here, and in Jesus' discussion with the disciples about bread in 16:5–12, Matthew associates Pharisees and Sadducees, as he had in John's invective at 3:7. In doing so Matthew effectively lumps the pre-70 Sadducees and the dominant Pharisees of his own time together as one, without discrimination. The conflict in teaching is a conflict alive in his day. 16:5–12 serves to encourage greater faith in Jesus as the one who performed such marvellous miracles with the bread and therefore as the teacher whose authority surpasses that of his opponents. Seen in the light of

---

reflected in use of one of the liturgical formulae of the community on her lips., "Have mercy on me, Lord" (15:22). This may well be so, although it is not the primary focus of the passage.

[175] Praising "the God of Israel" is here not an indication of Gentiles. According to Luz, *Matthäus II*, p. 440, it reflects the liturgical language of the Psalms used in Matthew's community (cf. Ps 41:14; 72:18); similarly Levine, *Matthean Salvation History*, p. 162; cf. Gundry, *Matthew*, p. 319.

[176] On its Zion symbolism, see Donaldson, *Mountain*, pp. 124–129.

15:1–20, it is an appeal to accept Jesus as the true interpreter of God's will, God's Law.

The omission of Mark's narrative of the healing of the blind man at Bethsaida breaks not only the correspondence which existed in Mark between the two Gentile healings by spittle and the symbolism which these acts conveyed (Mark 7:31–37; 8:22–26), but also breaks the connection between the end of this section and the end of Jesus' public ministry outside of Jerusalem, which Mark had achieved through the equally symbolic linking of the blind man at Bethsaida and the blind Bartimaeus (Mark 8:22–26; 10:46–52). Matthew, too, is sensitive to the symbolic potential of such healings, but has chosen not to use the healing at Bethsaida. He uses only Mark's story of the healing of Bartimaeus, twice (once, at the conclusion of Jesus' ministry outside of Jerusalem, in its original position, 20:29–34; cf. Mark 10:46–52; and once, at the conclusion of the collection of Jesus' deeds in 8:1 – 9:34, in 9:27–31). Both times Matthew makes of Bartimaeus two blind men sets up a contrast between their acknowledgment of Jesus as "Son of David" and the lack of faith not of the disciples, as in Mark, but of Israel's leaders. To the same end he introduced the Canaanite woman's acclamation of Jesus as "Son of David" (15:22).

The omission of the Bethsaida narrative also has the effect of creating a more direct transition from the discussion about teaching to the authorisation of Peter in 16:16–19. Thereby Matthew lays the foundation for the theme of teaching about the Church in the chapters which follow. As already noted, Matthew breaks Mark's suspense of presenting here the disciples' first confession (16:13; cf. Mark 8:27). Instead Peter affirms what they have all affirmed before (16:16; cf. 14:33); thus the focus falls on his authorisation. The language of keys and of binding and loosing (16:19) is at home in the context of discussion about Torah and its application (so already QLuke 11:52; also Rev 1:18; 2 En 40:9–11; *bSanh* 113a).[177] Here it most likely focuses on teaching, but 18:15–19 will show that already here Matthew probably has in mind the application of God's Law to behaviour and to situations calling for judgement in the believing community. Even Matthew's use of such metaphors shows that he understands teaching within the framework of teaching about attitude and behaviour. Teaching and application of God's Law in the community will be informed by Jesus' teaching. Jesus' teaching is about God's will. For Matthew, that means Torah as expounded by Jesus and all other instructions given under his authority.

---

[177] See the discussion in Davies and Allison, *Matthew II*, pp. 635–641.

The section 13:53 – 16:20 is remarkable for the way it reveals Matthew's compositional orientation. We noted it early in the way Matthew destroys the inclusion between Herod's pondering of options about Jesus' identity and the disciples' reporting similar options at Caesarea Philippi. The explanation belongs to the way Matthew changed the focus of the latter scene from christology to ecclesiology. The emphasis is on Peter (and the church) as bearer of authority to interpret and declare God's Law, in subjection to Jesus. It accounts for the expansion of the episode about walking on the water. It belongs in turn to the contrast found already in Mark between Jesus' teaching and that of the Pharisees; but here Matthew's concerns differed from Mark.

Mark had structured the material to emphasise the legitimacy of the Gentile mission. Matthew has dismantled Mark's structure; he makes the same material read quite differently. At the heart of it is still the discourse evoked by the handwashing dispute, but it now amounts to conflict over rival interpretations of Torah, not to its partial abrogation. Jesus does not declare all foods clean. The issue is not inclusion of Gentiles. The teaching of the Pharisees and Sadducees either encouraged disobedience or added unnecessary requirements. Matthew's omission of disparaging and generalising material about Jewish practices indicates sensitivity to a stronger Jewish constituency and respect for the tradition of Torah interpretation in which he is also engaged. Thus the encounter with the Syrophoenician woman now becomes an encounter with a Canaanite whose faith serves as a contrast with Israel. The barriers are not breached as in Mark, for Jesus' (and the disciples') mission is only to the Jews. The inclusion of Gentiles, whom the woman prefigures, is a matter for the future.

Matthew's Jesus emerges then as the true interpreter of Torah. His teachings should be followed, not those of the Pharisees. His deeds (the feedings, walking on the water, healings) both recall the deeds of the God of Israel and fulfil Israel's visions of hope. His deeds continue to legitimate his claim. He is the Son of God with absolute authority. Yet, as in the sabbath controversies, he does more than declare teaching. He argues it and uses the criterion of the priority of ethical attitude and behaviour in determining appropriate interpretation of Law. He passes onto Peter and the Church the authority to transmit and apply his teachings. They are the true scribes and interpreters.

2.3.4 Matthew 16:21 – 20:34

In 16:21–27 Matthew follows Mark's account of Jesus' first prediction of his passion, Peter's response and Jesus' instruction about discipleship closely up until 16:27 where he significantly changes the warning in Mark about those who are ashamed of the Son of Man. Now, instead of reading as a threat that the Son of Man will be ashamed of them before his Father when he comes (Mark 8:38–39), the version in Matthew simply takes up the announcement of the Son of Man's coming and adds: "and he shall repay all according to their behaviour," a formulation taken from Ps 62:13. Some of the changes may be because Matthew already has a version of the saying in 10:32–33, drawn from Q. The changes, however, also reflect a major emphasis of Matthew. In this major statement Matthew is reasserting that Jesus is the judge to come. He is not just the witness at the last judgement, as the Markan source implies. Jesus will judge all according to the measure of Torah as expounded by him. Matthew is returning us again to the theme with which Jesus' ministry began and which underlies his understanding of Jesus' preaching and teaching. Jesus, the Christ, the Son of God, who calls disciples, will be the world's judge before whom all must give account. So he was announced by John. So it remains. This is the message of the kingdom.

We see this emphasis reflected also in the way Matthew has reworked the following verse. Where Mark 9:1 read, "And he said to them, 'Truly I tell you there are some standing here who will not taste death before they see the kingdom of God come in power'," Matthew 16:28 reads: "Truly I tell you, 'There are some standing here who shall not taste death until they see the Son of Man coming in his kingdom'." Matthew has introduced the Son of Man motif, thus bringing it into closer association with the preceding verse.

Matthew's version of the transfiguration follows Mark closely, but Matthew now portrays Jesus' metamorphosis in terms much more reminiscent of Moses on his return from Sinai and drops the laundry imagery (17:1–8). To this focus on Moses imagery belongs also Matthew's change of Mark's "Elijah with Moses" (9:4) to "Moses and Elijah" (17:3). Matthew still retains Mark's eschatological frame of reference, in which these are seen as figures of the end time. Thus he retains the discussion about the coming of Elijah in the person of John the Baptist in 17:10–13. But the change in order may suggest that Matthew is, perhaps, also focusing now on Moses and Elijah as representatives of the Law and the Prophets. This would mean he is using the scene to underline that Jesus fulfils both and exercises, above all, the role of Moses as upholder and giver of Torah. It is interesting that Matthew has changed the order further so that the disciples' response of fear, which occurs in Mark as a result of the appearance of the three (9:6), has become one of worshipful reverence. It is now in response to the heavenly words that this is God's beloved son and they should "listen to him" (17:6). The latter words, taken from Mark 9:7, quote Moses' exhortation concerning the coming of a prophet like himself in Deut 18 15.

These features of the narrative present Jesus as one who stands above all in succession to Moses in his role as giver of the Law. As in Mark, Matthew's transfiguration story should be seen as an apocalyptic vision, a foretaste of what is to come. The transfiguration scene in Matthew belongs also closely with what precedes, as it does in Mark. But in Matthew the prediction speaks of Jesus coming in his kingdom as the son Man, the judge. Seen in this light, the transfiguration depicts Jesus the judge as the beloved Son. Thus the heavenly voice which had identified him at his baptism as the judge predicted by John does so again and adds appropriately, "Listen to him!" Again we are encountering the twofold focus of Matthew's christology: Jesus will come as judge; yet he has already come. In his present coming he is Israel's Messiah, the divinely created Son of God, whose deeds are signs of eschatological hope being fulfilled and whose words declare and interpret God's Law.

Remaining with Mark's sequence, in 17:14–21 Matthew heavily abbreviates the healing narrative which follows the transfiguration (Mark 9:14–29). In doing so he has Jesus rebuke the disciples rather than the crowd for lack of faith (17:17; cf. Mark 9:19) and adds the promise that faith as small as a grain of mustard seed can move mountains (17:20). This echoes the Markan saying which follows the temple expulsion in Mark 11:22–23, which Matthew will also use again at the same point (Matt 21:21). The saying replaces Mark's emphasis on the need for prayer (cf. Mark 9:29). It effectively removes the set of links which Mark had established in 9:28–29; 10:27; and 10:52 to prepare for the image of the new community of prayer, the new temple in 11:15–25. As he dismantled Mark's compositional structure and focus in Mark 6:7 – 8:26, so he will remove the Markan focus on the community of faith as the new temple which Mark develops in 11:1 – 13:37.

Continuing the Markan pattern, Matthew goes on to Jesus' second prediction of his passion (17:22–23), but follows it with a passage unique to Matthew, about the collection of the temple tax (17:24–27). Peter affirms that Jesus does pay the temple tax. Jesus intervenes, arguing that the families of kings are usually exempt from the royal taxes. He then presses the analogy to the effect that he (and his followers) have a relation to the temple (or, better, to God) analogous to that of the royal family to the king and should, therefore, be exempt. Compliance is then a concession not to give offence, a stance which is given divine approval: a coin in a fish's mouth.

Payment of temple tax is based on the provision in Ex 30:11–16 for all males to make a one off half shekel offering at the time of the census. Subsequently it became the basis for the half shekel temple tax, a practice which seems to be reflected in its early stages in Neh 10:33. Its legitimacy was open to debate.[178] Who paid was also subject of debate, especially in relation to priests. Nothing indicates a priestly claim here on the part of Jesus.[179] Nor does Matthew treat it as an issue of Law observance.[180] One might consider that Matthew was having Jesus claim a unique relationship with the God of the temple. He is the unique Son of God, created by God through miraculous conception, who alone knows the Father and has been uniquely authorised by him. He therefore not only belongs to what the temple represents, but is, himself, greater than the temple (cf. 12:6). But Jesus' argument is about "the sons of the kingdom". He obviously has not only himself, but also Peter in mind. Then, at most, it is a defence which asserts that Jesus and his own should be free, but one almost any Jew could have argued.[181]

The events of the narrative reflect a time when the temple was still standing. The freedom which Jesus claims for himself and Peter need not imply that he sees the temple as irrelevant or obsolete or that he replaces it.[182] Coming as it does within the context of instruction to the community, it may well be intended by Matthew to portray Jesus' advice to his own Christian Jewish community. In Matthew's time the tax was, in any case, no longer directed to the temple, but as the *fiscus judaicus* to the temple of Jupiter in Rome (so Jos *JW* 7: 218). Matthew's was probably sound advice.[183]

---

[178] See the discussion in Luz, *Matthäus II*, pp. 529–531.

[179] Cf. Daube, "Temple Tax," pp. 127, 131.

[180] So rightly Hummel, *Auseinandersetzung*, p. 104.

[181] So Luz, *Matthäus II*, p. 534.

[182] Cf. Hummel, *Auseinandersetzung*, p. 104, who considers that Matthew's tradition may reflect a Hellenistic Jewish influenced community which had distanced itself from the temple and cult, but notes that Matthew still sees the tax as being raised for God (17:25–26). See also Luz, *Matthäus II*, pp. 533–534.

[183] Saldarini, *Community*, pp. 144–146, makes the point that in Matthew's gospel Jesus is made into an example for Christian Jews facing the *fiscus judaicus*. Cf. J. Gnilka, *Das Matthäusevangelium,* 2 vols, HTKNT, (Freiburg: Herder, 1986), *II*, pp. 115–116, who argues that Matthew would not have this in mind, but would remain focused on the temple as though it were still standing, as did rabbinic discussion of temple law. But against this, Matthew's is not an halakic discussion of that kind.

To read into the story another agenda, such as an attempt on Matthew's part to prepare his community for giving up cultic law, is unwarranted.[184]

In chapter 18 Matthew portrays Jesus as giving further instruction to the disciples, relevant to their community life. In 18:1–5 Matthew rewrites Mark's account of Jesus' response to the disciples' dispute about who was the greatest (Mark 9:33–37). In doing so he sets the discussion within the context of what counts in the kingdom of heaven, enjoining both childlike humility as well as acceptance and support of such childlike believers. 18:6–9 continues with warnings against causing these to stumble.

18:10–14 narrates the parable of the lost sheep to illustrate the attitude to be taken towards those who go astray from the community. The context continues to be one of concern about community members (cf. Luke 15:1–7). Immediately following is a rule for dealing with such ones who go astray and about reaching a verdict in the local congregation about possible expulsion (18:15–20). Here we find the local congregation exercising the function of law given to Peter in 16:16–18. But, in addition, we find the promise that when they do so Jesus will be in their midst. This is so close to similar Jewish traditions that Shekinah will be present with the two or three who gather to study Torah, that it is likely Matthew draws on such tradition here. Not only during his lifetime, but also in post resurrection days, Jesus champions Torah and, like God's Shekinah, will dwell with God's people who seek to understand this Torah (cf. *mAboth* 3.2, 3). This promise will also form the climax of the gospel, where it follows authorisation of the disciples to teach what they have been taught (28:20). The focus both here and there is on teaching and its application. The promise also echoes the angelic announcement to Joseph that Jesus will be "Emmanuel, God with us" (1:23).

Matthew has already expressed concern for compassion and reconciliation in exercising such community Torah by having the parable of the lost sheep introduce the ruling (18:10–14). He reinforces it in what follows: Jesus teaches about forgiving seventy seven times (18:21–22) and reinforces the message in the parable of the unmerciful servant (18:23–35). The orientation

---

[184] Cf. G. Dautzenberg, "Jesus und der Tempel. Beobachtungen zur Exegese der Perikope von der Tempelsteuer (Mt 17,24–27)," in *Salz der Erde – Licht der Welt: Exegetische Studien zum Matthäusevangelium. FS für Anton Vögtle zum 80. Geburtstag,* edited by I. Oberlinner and P. Fiedler, (Stuttgart: KBW, 1991), pp. 223–238, here: 236–238, who sees Matthew's use of a story which reflects criticism of the cult, as an attempt to portray Jesus' relationship with the cult as one of accommodation and so to prepare his community for giving up cultic law. He finds a similar relativising of cultic law in 9:13; 12:7 and 23:23.

in ch. 18 is thoroughly consistent with the approach taken in the Sermon on the Mount. Matthew's Jesus interprets Torah strictly against offences, but enjoins compassion in seeking the straying sheep of the community and in forgiving those who have wronged them (cf. 5:23–24; 6:14–15).

In Matthew 19, as in Mark 10, the scene changes. Jesus enters Judea. Nevertheless what follows continues in the general area of instruction for the believing community. In his version of Jesus' discussion about marriage and divorce in 19:3–12, Matthew reverses Mark's order. He has Jesus begin his response to the Pharisees' question about divorce with the creation material instead of with the words, "What did Moses allow/command you?"(Mark 10:3; cf. Mark 10:2–12). This removes the offence which Mark's account might potentially evoke by having Jesus cite Moses only to contradict him. Instead Matthew has the Pharisees introduce the question about Moses, thus removing any implied disparagement. Jesus can then explain Moses' provision as a concession, but without the potentially negative overtones of Mark. Matthew is once again exercising greater sensitivity in the light of his Jewish Christian context.

In addition, Matthew has Jesus continue the discussion by declaring what is now effectively a strict interpretation of the existing Mosaic provision. He thus replaces Mark's private conversation between Jesus and the disciples in which divorce and remarriage is forbidden altogether, by either party, and in which Moses is thus overruled (19:9; cf. Mark 10:11–12). Matthew also reverts to a form of declaration which fits Jewish Law in having only the man able to divorce. The overall effect is that Matthew's Jesus upholds Moses' provision and defines the only acceptable ground for its application as πορνεία.[185] Here we have Jesus as interpreter of the Law and not, as in Mark, overturning it. To it Matthew appends teaching about voluntary singleness, probably an option taken by some itinerants of the time (19:10–12).[186]

In 19:13–15 Matthew's account of the children coming to Jesus is simple (cf. Mark 10:13–16). It does not have the injunction that we should be like children, because Matthew has used that already in 18:3. The only significant addition may be that he suggests that people brought children to Jesus not

---

[185] Betz, *Sermon*, pp. 256–257, draws attention to the difference in interpretation of Deut 24:1–4 between 5:31–32 and here. There Deuteronomy is interpreted as only dealing with the situation where a defiled woman seeks remarriage to a former husband, forbidding it. It is not a concession, allowing divorce, as 19:3–12 and its Markan source presupposes. But doubtless Matthew interpreted both in the same way, of divorce as in 19:3–12. See also the discussion of 5:31–32 above.

[186] So Vouga, *Loi*, p. 103. Cf. Wisd 3:14.

only that he should touch them, but also that he should pray for them. This gives to Jesus' action a stronger religious and Jewish flavour and removes the potential danger present in Mark of perceiving Jesus as a kind of magical figure. Perhaps Jesus' activity is even modelled on what a Jewish scribe might be expected to do (cf. Gen 48:14–15).

Matthew has exercised considerable freedom in rewriting the account of the rich man's encounter with Jesus (19:16–22). To begin with, he reedits the initial exchange to remove any suggestion that Jesus might be denying he is good. He then conforms the list of commandments and their formulation, now on the lips of the inquirer, to the decalogue. To the decalogue he adds the summary command: "And you shall love your neighbour as yourself." The latter addition reflects a consistent Matthean concern (cf. 7:12; and the double use of Hosea 6:6 in 9:13 and 12:7) and will form a link with 22:39. Matthew is bringing Jesus and the Torah, represented here by the decalogue, into close association.

The other remarkable change is Matthew's transformation of the man into a young man and his introduction of the words, "If you want to be perfect" (19:21). The two are playfully related since "perfect", τέλειος, also means "mature, grown up". It is about the young man growing up! But the passage makes an important distinction between keeping Torah within a normal Jewish framework of expectations and keeping Torah as defined by Jesus, which brings with it the demand of total discipleship. Matthew does not see two levels of requirement, let alone two levels of discipleship,[187] but recognises that some people have not yet made the transition to acknowledging Torah as it now stands. In this sense the words about becoming "perfect" reflect 5:48: "Be perfect as your heavenly Father is perfect." Torah according to Jesus must be fulfilled, a righteousness which exceeds that of the scribes and Pharisees (5:20).[188] This is the requirement for all. Matthew does not see discipleship as an extra, over and above Torah observance. Rather to follow Torah truly can be nothing other than following Jesus who is its true interpreter. The potential is there for one call to obedience to clash with the other, but Matthew consistently seeks to avoid such an idea.

---

[187] Against the view that Matthew contemplates two levels of Christian discipleship, see Barth, "Gesetzesverständnis," pp. 89–96; E. Lohse, "'Vollkommen sein,'" pp. 137–140.

[188] Mohrlang, *Matthew*, p. 18, does not allow the words, "If you would enter life, keep the commandments", as evidence that Matthew believes keeping the Law is necessary for entering the kingdom (though he believes this is Matthew's stance), because, he argues, it derives from Mark. But this is the very methodological fault he was finding with those prepared to dismiss the significance of 23:2–3 and 23:23 a few pages earlier! (p. 10).

The discussion about the implications of Jesus' demands about poverty (19:23–30) follows Mark's narrative closely and preserves the same solution: ultimately only God makes salvation possible. But Matthew adds his version of the Q tradition that, beyond this, the disciples will exercise judgement over Israel at the eschaton (19:28; cf. Luke 22:28–30). They are now the community of the judge who interprets Torah and will finally use Torah at the judgement. The theme of judgement, and with it the application of Torah, is never far from Matthew's thinking. The disciples, already commissioned to bind and loose on earth (16:16; 18:18), will share this role in the future. Jesus and the Law belong in Matthew with an understanding which gives the Church a major role in interpreting and executing Torah. This, in turn, must determine Matthew's own self understanding of what he is doing in his gospel.

Mark's narrative concludes at this point with Jesus declaring: "Many who are first will be last and last, first" (Mark 10:31). Matthew preserves this (19:30) and has it serve as the transition to a set on instructions to the community about leadership. Initially he uses it neatly as a framework for the parable of the labourers in the vineyard (20:1–15), in 20:16 reversing its sequence. This has the effect of using the parable of the hired labourers as a warning to long time Christian leaders against arrogance. Jesus' third passion prediction, 20:17–19, now serves to continue the theme of leadership. Like Mark, Matthew contrasts it with the ambition of James and John (and, in Matthew, also their mother; 20:20–28). As in Mark, the discussion concludes as it began, with the example of Jesus who came to serve and to give his life a ransom for many (20:28). As in Mark, we find no particular reflection here on the possible consequences of Jesus' death for understanding Law and cult.

Matthew brings the narrative of Jesus' public ministry outside of Jerusalem to conclusion with the account of the healing of two blind men (20:29–34), just as he brought the sample of Jesus activity in 8–9 to an end using substantially the same story (9:27–31 linked with the duplicate of the exorcism, 9:32–34; cf. 12:22–24). One may suspect he got the idea from Mark who also used such healings symbolically at the end of major sections (8:22–26; 10:46–52). The story serves a symbolic purpose. By changing Mark's single Bartimaeus into two blind men, Matthew reflects Jewish legal tradition about the validity of two witnesses, as he does also in the doubling of the story itself and in changing the one Gerasene demoniac (Mark 5:1–20) into two Gadarene demoniacs (8:28–34). He uses the two blind men who acclaim Jesus, Son of David, as a contrast with the spiritual blindness of Israel's leaders who refuse to acknowledge him.[189]

Within the passage 16:21 – 20:34, which deals primarily with instruction of the disciples for their life as a Christian community, we have a continued emphasis on Jesus as bearer of Torah, both during his ministry and beyond it, including at the end of time. At the end of time, as Son of Man, he will judge all according to their behaviour, measured doubtless according to Torah. The association of Jesus and Torah lies behind the more strongly Mosaic imagery in which Matthew portrays Jesus in the narrative of the transfiguration. This sets the tone for what follows in which Jesus as judge to come and bearer of Torah instructs the community.

In what follows Matthew's Jesus instructs the community across a range of issues, but always in continuity with Torah. The strategic advice to pay the temple tax indicates that Matthew's community is identified as Jewish. It implies no criticism of the cult as such or of Torah. Jesus operates as the true interpreter and bearer of Torah in Matthew's significantly modified version of the discussion about divorce law. Jesus' teaching now amounts to a stricter definition, rather than as what could be interpreted as an abolition of Moses' divorce law. Matthew has also significantly reworked the encounter with the rich man not only to have it more accurately reflect decalogue prescriptions, but also to typify the move demanded of Jews: that they should conceive total commitment to Torah as necessarily including following Jesus. In this, Jesus is not an authority competing with Torah, nor a duplication (or incarnation) of Torah, nor an additional authority beside Torah, but the divinely created Son of God and judge to come who, in continuity with Torah, upholds it, interprets it and declares God's will for the present.

It is not surprising that in a section concerned with the community's role, Matthew has Jesus' role as interpreter and bearer of Torah given to the community. We had seen this already with Peter in 16:16–18. Here we find the same authority given the community in the context of making judgement about its own membership in the post Easter period (18:15–20). Jesus also promised the disciples similar authority for the judgement day (19:28). Between the time of his ministry and his return he also promises to be present when the community whom he has authorised to teach exercises Torah and applies his teachings (18:19–20). Matthew speaks of Jesus as later Jewish tradition spoke of God's Shekinah, being present where even a few study Torah.

---

[189] On the symbolic use of duality in relation to these and other anecdotes in Matthew, see Loader, "Son of David".

2.4 Matthew 21 – 28 in Review

2.4.1 Matthew 21:1 – 22:46

Apart from his introduction of another formula quotation and having Jesus fulfil it all too literally (sitting on two animals!), Matthew's account of the entry into Jerusalem links it more closely than Mark with the preceding episode. He has the crowd, like the two blind men, hail Jesus as Son of David (21:1–9; cf. Mark 11:1–10). The words, "Hosanna to the Son of David; blessed is he who comes in the name of the Lord; hosanna in the highest" (21:9) will find their echo in 23:39 where Jesus looks forward to his final, triumphant coming to Jerusalem: "You shall not see me from now on until you say, 'Blessed is he who comes in the name of the Lord'." For Matthew this is and remains the holy city. Here in 21:1–9 Israel's Messiah enters the holy city. The crowds also acclaim him as "the prophet, Jesus of Nazareth in Galilee" (21:11). Matthew has Jesus immediately enter the temple and expel those who bought and sold, and overturn the tables of the money changers and pigeon sellers (21:10–13). This is a departure from Mark's order, who has Jesus first enter the temple and look around and then only on the following day enter the temple and perform this act (Mark 11:11; 11:15–17). Matthew therefore loses the inclusio effect of looking around at the temple, which Mark had achieved between 11:11 and 13:1–2.

In making them a single sequence of events, Matthew may well be directing us to see a closer link between what happens at the entry and what happens in the temple event.[190] Is there a link between the understanding of Jesus as Messiah and his action here?[191] Perhaps more significant is that the one performing this act is identified just prior to this as a prophet (21:11). Does Matthew see this as a prophetic act? The notion of Jesus as a prophet and as suffering the fate of a prophet recalls the response of Jesus in his home synagogue (13:53–58). It will find further echoes in the following passages, where the Jewish authorities show themselves sensitive to the crowd's view that Jesus is a prophet (21:46) and similarly in 23:34–39, where Jesus' rejection and death is interpreted in line with Israel's rejection of the

---

[190] On the rhetorical structure of Mt 21–23 see R. Grams, "The Temple Conflict Scene: a Rhetorical Analysis of Matthew 21–23," in *Persuasive Artistry, FS G. A. Kennedy*, JSNTS 50, edited by D. F. Watson, (Sheffield: JSOTPr, 1991), pp. 41–65. He notes that the whole is flanked by Jesus' entry and the prediction of his future reentry (21:1–11 and 23:39) and by Davidic messianic claims (21:9–11 and 22:41–46; pp. 47–48) and follows a typically Matthean pattern of threes.

[191] See the discussion of the same issue in the chapter on Mark, above.

prophets. Quite possibly Matthew intends that we should see Jesus' deed in the temple as a prophetic statement. If so, what does it mean?

Matthew's reordering of Mark's narrative means that the hearer does not have the cursed fig tree as a clue. It comes later in 21:18–19. In addition, Matthew omits Mark's detail that Jesus forbad people to carry implements in the temple courtyard (cf. Mark 11:16). Would he have sensed this as unrealistic or, perhaps, as too radical, implying an attack on the cult system as such, as it might have been understood in Mark? The effect of this omission is to juxtapose Jesus' action against the sellers, buyers and moneychangers and his words more strongly than in Mark.

Matthew also omits from Jesus' words "for all nations", thus removing the possible allusion to the significance of the event as taking place in the Gentile court or as having relevance for Gentiles. The Gentile theme is not in view.[192] Instead, Jesus' words stop at declaring the temple should be a place of prayer. Possibly Matthew is viewing Jesus' attack as a reproach for the commercial activity in the temple and understands by the word, λῃστῶν, "brigands, robbers", also corrupt practices. Alternatively, Matthew may be viewing Jesus' action as symbolic of judgement against the temple leaders, rather than against these particular people. He may also have recent history in mind, when λῃσταί did take possession of the temple.

Matthew adds that Jesus continued in the temple with acts of healing (21:14–16). Children acclaim him, "Son of David". By contrast, the Jewish authorities find their responses offensive. We have already noted the way Matthew used this confession in contrasts between faith and unfaith in 9:28–31; 12:22–24; 15:21–28; 20:29–34. It is at this point that Matthew narrates that early the following day Jesus curses the fig tree and reports the immediate effect (21:18–19). As in Mark, it is followed by a discussion with the disciples in which Jesus assures them of the power of faith to move mountains in answer to prayer (21:20–22). But the cursing of the fig tree and subsequent discussion seem no longer to function as a commentary on the significance of the temple expulsion, as they do in Mark. Matthew has removed the structural interlocking of the cursing of the fig tree with the temple expulsion. He has departed from the Markan scheme which prepares the hearer to see the community as the new temple.

---

[192] Grams, "Conflict Scene," pp. 49–50, suggests the omission is because Matthew's focus is broader than Gentiles; it envisages a change of worshippers and worship leaders, symbolised in Jesus' healing the lame and blind and in the acclamation of the children. The disciples, entrusted with the keys and the power to bind and loose (16:19; 18:18) and instructed in the ways of humble leadership (Mt 18–20), are to be the new leaders of Israel.

We should probably see both the temple expulsion and the cursing of the fig tree in Matthew as demonstrations of God's judgement on the Jewish authorities for their failure to believe in Jesus.[193] Neither functions any longer as implicit criticism of the temple, nor supports the notion that the community of faith is a new temple, as in Mark. Similarly, later in his account of Jesus' trial before the high priest Matthew does not take up Mark's description of the temple as made with hands (cf. Mark 14:58). Rather the theme of Israel's rejection of their Son of David has been the main feature of the narrative, already since the healing of the two blind men in 20:28–34. What Matthew has done avoids any implied critique of the cult as such. He will portray the temple's destruction as judgement upon its leaders, removing any implied disparagement of the system itself.

21:23 – 22:14 contains Matthew's version of the question about Jesus' authority and of Jesus' response. After the initial interchange, 21:23–27, Matthew has inserted a new response, the parable of the two sons (21:28–32). He then continues with Mark's extended response which uses the parable of the vineyard (21:33–46; cf. Mark 12:1–2). He then adds a third element, the parable of the wedding feast (22:1–14), to make a characteristic Matthean cluster of three. The three parables speak of responses to John, Jesus, and the disciples, respectively.

The initial question and answer in 21:23–27 is almost identical with Mark. While in Mark it picks up the particular theme of Jesus' authority as a centre of controversy from the beginning of his ministry, in Matthew the comparison with John may well also recall for the hearer John's witness to Jesus as the judge to come (3:11–12). In addition, for Matthew not only are John and Jesus linked in authority. They also proclaim the same message of repentance and the kingdom, as do also the disciples (3:2; 4:17; 10:7; all three also face the charge of sorcery: 9:34; 10:25; 11:18).

It coheres with this that Matthew begins Jesus' response to the chief priests and elders of the people with the parable of the two sons and with the focus on John. Again Matthew portrays John in terms strikingly similar to those used of Jesus (21:28–32). Thus Matthew has the parable highlight different responses not to Jesus, but to John: contrasting the response of toll collectors and prostitutes to John with the response of the chief priests and elders of the people (21:31–32 "Truly I tell you, the toll collectors and prostitutes will enter the kingdom of God before you. For John came in the way of righteousness and you did not believe him, but toll collectors and prostitutes believed him. But, seeing this, you did not in the end repent and believe

---

[193] Similarly Saldarini, *Community*, pp. 54–55.

him"). Significantly Matthew describes John as coming "in the way of righteousness" and even makes response to John's message the basis for entry into the kingdom of God. John, like Jesus, is seen as bearer of Torah's demand and promise, just as 11:16–19 had linked them as the doers of wisdom's works. Here their commonality is stressed. Matthew would also have said of Jesus that he came in the way of righteousness as providing the basis for entry into the kingdom.

In 21:33–46 the theme of judgement against Israel's leaders for their rejection of the prophets, of John and of Jesus himself, continues as Matthew offers his version of the parable of the wicked tenants.[194] Matthew speaks of a series of groups of servants being sent, rather than single emissaries. His version has the son killed outside the city, establishing a closer correspondence with Jesus' death. Matthew's addition that the chief priests and the Pharisee feared to arrest Jesus because the people thought he was a prophet (21:46) is a reference back to Jesus' first entry into the city and continues the theme of the leaders' rejection of the prophets. It also reinforces the link with John, for 21:26 had reported that the crowd also held John to be a prophet.

The parable concludes in Matthew, as in Mark, with the observation that the vineyard's owner will do away with the wicked tenants and entrust the vineyard "to other vineyard keepers" (21:41: Mark 12:9). But Matthew elaborates in two ways. He adds after "vineyard keepers": "who will produce the fruit at its due time" (21:41). Then after the allusion to Ps 118:22, the image of the rejected stone made the cornerstone, he returns to the motif of the "other vineyard keepers" in 21:43 and applies it to the chief priests and the elders of the people: "Therefore I tell you, the kingdom of God will be taken away from you and given to a people (ἔθνει) which will produce its fruit."[195] The "therefore" suggests that in some way the change in vineyard keepers is related to the image of the stone. It is an image for Jesus' rejection and resurrection, but probably also alludes to the rejection which the community itself has experienced.[196] Associated with it for Matthew is the change to a new set of vineyard keepers. The logic appears to be that the

---

[194] The focus is not Israel, but the leaders, so Saldarini, *Community*, pp. 58–59.

[195] So Saldarini, *Community*, pp. 60–63; cf. Menninger, *Israel*, p. 152; Gnilka, *Matthäus II*, p. 230, who speaks of the idea of a "third race". It is important, however, to see that the focus of conflict in all three parables is not with Israel, but its leaders (teachers), and that therefore the focus is neither an ethnic nor a third race alternative to Israel, but a replacement of Israel's leaders by the community. It is the vineyard keepers who slay the messengers, not the vineyard!

[196] Similarly Stanton, *Gospel*, p. 152.

rejected one and his people will now take over as keepers of the vineyard. In other Matthean imagery, they will be entrusted with the keys of the vineyard (cf. 16:16–19). It is not a contrast between Israel and Gentiles, but between the chief priests and elders of the people, on the one hand, and Jesus and his people whom he will authorise, on the other. Matthew is not setting ἔθνος ("people, nation") in contrast to λαός ("people", often in relation to Israel), but using it neutrally to refer to another set of people. For in Matthew's case it is not a matter of replacing the ruling authorities with another set of ruling authorities; the authority is not again to be entrusted to a few but to the community as a whole (the community of Jesus' followers). In this Matthew remains close to the Markan understanding of the parable, which as we have seen, is also best understood in the context of authority and leadership.

Two further aspects require comment. For Mark, Ps 118:22 belongs to a network of allusions to the community as a new temple, replacing the old. This is not Matthew's view, as already indicated by the way he effectively dismantles it in dealing with Mark's material about Jesus' action in the temple. Yet Matthew does use the image ecclesiologically, to signal the change in vineyard keepers. A new group, a people, the people of the rejected one, replace not the temple, but the old vineyard keepers, the temple authorities. In this way Matthew both avoids the implied criticism in Mark of the cult and so of Torah and resets the perspectives so that the issue is who has authority to interpret Torah. For, in Matthew's thinking, interpreting Torah belongs within the message of the kingdom, the way of righteousness.

The second aspect reinforces this trend. For Matthew emphasises in 21:43 that the kingdom of God is to be "given to a people who bring forth fruit" (21:43). Matthew has consistently had John and Jesus use the fruit imagery as a metaphor for doing what God requires (3:8–10; 7:15–20; 12:33). Matthew is applying the phrase, "bring forth fruit", to the Church. Christian community is life under Torah as interpreted by Jesus. This is an important theme which continues in these final chapters. The Christian community will also be accountable. Matthew is not just reporting the failure of Jesus' contemporaries.[197]

Matthew concludes this second parable with the note that the chief priests and the Pharisees knew that Jesus was speaking about them (21:45–46). The mention of Pharisees, not named among the questioners in 21:23, but

---

[197] If we take 21:44 as part of the original text of Matthew, we find here a further threat of judgement on Jesus' contemporaries. The verse appears to allude to the crushing of evil realms in Nebuchadnezzar's dream in Dan 2:34–35,44–45, by a new stone, symbol of a new kingdom.

doubtless assumed to be present, connects Matthew's story with concerns of his own day, where it was above all the Pharisees who had laid claim to be the true keepers of the vineyard.

Judgement against the vineyard keepers is also the theme of the third parable which forms part of Jesus' response to the question about authority (22:1–14). Perhaps the imagery of kingdoms already present in the allusion to Nebuchadnezzar's dream in the imagery of the rock in 21:44 helped forge the link to the image of the king in 22:1–14. The reference to the marriage of the king's son recalls the sending of the beloved son in the vineyard parable. Matthew does not, here, have the son announce the invitations and summon the guests. Others do this. Within the Matthean context, therefore, we should probably see in these messengers of the kingdom, Christian missionaries. The destruction of Jerusalem in the recent history of Matthew's community was God's judgement on the Jewish leaders, in particular, for rejecting these messengers.[198] The same point is made in 23:34–36, where Matthew has Jesus merge Israel's past history of rejecting prophets with its coming history of rejecting his sages and scribes. The invitation to others on the streets would be understood by Matthew as identifying his own community. They are the street people. Matthew may also now include Gentiles among these, but that is not the primary focus.[199] In the expansion of the parable to warn about appropriate dress at the feast, Matthew is addressing his own Christian community. Like the warnings in 7:21–23, it demands that they live according to the Torah, the Torah according to Jesus.

Matthew has considerably developed Mark's account of the authority question and Jesus' response. Matthew has transformed Mark's questioning scene with a single parable response (Mark 11:27 – 12:12) into a questioning scene with a threefold parable response which focuses in turn on John the Baptist, Jesus, and the disciples. In it he reasserts the claim of all to be true bearers and interpreters of Torah and depicts the destruction of Jerusalem as God's judgement on Israel's leaders and teachers for rejecting their missions. This emphasis will find a strong echo in 23:34–39.

Matthew recounts the exchange over paying taxes to Caesar (22:15–22),

---

[198] So Saldarini, *Community*, pp. 63–64; similarly Levine, *Matthean Salvation History*, p. 213.

[199] Cf. Saldarini, *Community*, p. 64, who argues that only Israelites are intended by Matthew, the fruits of the mission to Israel. This seems to me too rigid, although the point is taken. Would Matthew have limited the secondary application of the warning in the parable about right garments in this way? I agree, however, against most commentators, that it is not understood by Matthew primarily as a reference to the Gentile mission. Cf. Gnilka, *Matthäus II*, p. 239; Schweizer, *Matthäus*, p. 275; Gundry, *Matthew*, p. 438.

in much the same way as in Mark, as an attempt by the Pharisees and Herodians to find grounds against Jesus. Jesus remains Torah faithful, avoiding extremism on the one hand and compromise of God's dignity on the other. The encounter with the Sadducees (22:23–33) is also similar. Matthew's community would have been familiar with the levirite provisions which underlie the question.

Matthew's treatment of the following episode concerning the greatest commandment (22:34–40) differs significantly from Mark's (12:28–34). No longer do we have one of the scribes asking an open question. Instead Matthew introduces the Pharisees as wanting to do one better than the Sadducees, who had just failed in their attempt to expose Jesus. The question on the lips of their spokesperson is putting Jesus on trial. Unlike Mark, Matthew does not have Jesus first acclaim that God is one. Instead he proceeds directly to a citation of Deut 6:5, and adds the statement: "This is the greatest and first commandment" (22:38). Then, following Mark, he cites Lev 19:18, "You shall love your neighbour as yourself." He then omits the Markan comment: "There is no other commandment greater than these" (Mark 12:31b) as well as the rest of Mark's account. Mark had the scribe respond approvingly, repeat the commandments cited and add that these are more important than burnt offerings and sacrifices, to which Jesus responded by declaring him not far from the kingdom of God (12:32–34). Matthew has none of this. This accords with Matthew's purpose. He has shaped the encounter as a hostile one, like the two which precede it. Those scribes are far from the kingdom in Matthew's view and nothing has changed.

In the process Matthew has avoided allusion to the cult. The contrast with sacrifices would have cohered well with Matthew's sentiments elsewhere; he has twice cited Hosea 6:6, which may lie behind Mark's story (9:13; 12:7). But he would not have identified with the way Mark had made it serve as a disparaging contrast between the new temple and the old temple as one made with hands and concerned with external irrelevancies. Instead Matthew has Jesus return to his major concern. Jesus adds: "For on these two commandments hang all the Law and the Prophets" (22:40). It confirms Matthew's focus on "the Law and the Prophets", echoing his declaration in 5:17 that Jesus came not to abolish them, but to make sure they are fulfilled. It also echoes his comment on the golden rule in 7:12, "for this is the Law and the Prophets". The passage is important also for confirming Matthew's particular approach to "the Law and the Prophets". They are to be interpreted in the light of the first and second great commandments.[200] The effect in

---

[200] On the centrality of the law of love for Matthew see Barth, "Gesetzesverständnis," pp. 70–73.

the narrative is to pit his Torah interpretation against that of the former vineyard keepers.

In 22:41–46 Matthew again adds reference to the Pharisees to underline the contemporary relevance of the passage. As in Mark the passage concerns the true understanding of messiahship (12:35–37). It is an issue which would probably have featured in the tensions leading to the isolation of Matthew's community. The Messiah must be seen more than "the Son of David". This is much more significant in Matthew than in Mark because it is this appellation which has appeared so frequently on the lips of the crowd. The effect, as in Mark, is to challenge an approach to messiahship which fails to see the Messiah as also David's Lord. Matthew's hearers know that he is the divinely created Son of God and judge to come. The passage serves to reaffirm who Jesus is and, by implication, to reassert the guilt of the leaders for rejecting him. Matthew ends the episode with the note that the Pharisees had no answer and dared no further questions. With this Matthew rounds off the interchange with the Jewish leaders. In ch. 23 he has Jesus deliver judgement against them. To this we turn in the following segment.

In 21:1–22:46 Matthew sharpens the focus on the rejection of Jesus by Jewish authorities and sets it in contrast to the crowd's acclamation of Jesus as Son of David.[201] Within the section Matthew has consistently deleted or changed items which in Mark served to criticise the cult and to suggest that it was to be replaced by the community of faith. The inclusio created by the motif of looking around at the temple (Mark 11:11; 13:1–2) has gone. He has dismantled the intercalation of the temple episode within the cursing of the fig tree and separated the two events. Jesus' action in the temple represents God's judgement against the Jewish authorities, who will reject Jesus as they have rejected the prophets. The image of the rejected stone no longer suggests a new temple; it symbolises the change of vineyard keepers. The dismantling will continue with Matthew's rewriting of the temple logion in the Jewish trial to exclude the contrast: "made with hands,   not made with hands", and to turn it into a true statement about Jesus' power, not his intention (26:61; cf. Mark 14:58).

In this section Matthew focuses strongly on the Jewish leaders. The issue of authority is paramount. At dispute is not the Law or the Prophets, but who is to hold the keys to their interpretation and the declaration of God's will. It is important to see this, since it tells us about Matthew's theological

---

[201] Saldarini, *Community*, pp. 52–64, rightly argues that the final public teaching of Matthew's Jesus is wholly devoted to attacking the religious leaders.

mind-set and confirms the centrality for him of Torah. Not that it is only about Torah; but it includes Torah. For in Matthew's view Jesus is not in competition with Torah; he upholds and expounds it as part of his total task to proclaim the kingdom, call for repentance and teach God's will. In the conflict Matthew does not isolate Jesus, but sets him in solidarity with the prophets, but especially with John, on the one hand, and the disciples, on the other. Thus we find again the extraordinary overlap between John and Jesus: John comes in the way of righteousness; in response to John's message one enters the kingdom or fails to do so. The crowd, says Matthew, sees both as prophets. Both are rejected.

Matthew emphasises that the Christian community will also face rejection, like John and Jesus. The vineyard parable now serves to spell out the consequences of the rejection of Jesus: the Jewish authorities are to be replaced by the community of faith. Under their teaching and administration of Torah the fruits of righteousness will not fail. They are the ones commissioned to teach what Jesus commanded and are the true successors of Jesus, John and the prophets. The parable of the wedding feast speaks in Matthew of their mission and interprets Jerusalem's destruction as God's judgement on the leaders for their failure to acknowledge that the way of Jesus and John, the way of righteousness, is the way to the kingdom. In establishing this solidarity Matthew is not complacent about the fallibility in his community and so warns them, too, of the demands of righteousness.

Matthew gives the interchanges between the Jewish leaders and Jesus a contemporary relevance for his community by introducing the Pharisees. The passages about the greatest commandment and the Son of David highlight the central issues at stake: Torah interpretation and christology. Torah must be interpreted in the light of the great commandments; there is no question about its validity. Matthew sees to it that any such hints present in Mark are obliterated. Christology must include Matthew's understanding of Jesus as the divinely created Son of God, authorised by God as judge to come and interpreter of God's will. Such a christology undergirds the claim to interpret Torah and declare God's will.

2.4.2 Matthew 23:1–39

Where Mark has three verses of text which portray Jesus' attack on the hypocrisy of the scribes (12:38–40), Matthew has a whole chapter of 39 verses. Matthew 23 contains important statements bearing on Matthew's understanding of Jesus' attitude towards Torah. He begins by having Jesus affirm that the scribes and Pharisees sit on Moses seat[202] and to enjoin the disciples to do what they say, not what they do (23:2–3). While Matthew has Jesus go on to attack hypocrisy, this opening statement is potentially of wide ranging significance. Is it just a rhetorical ploy to set up the contrast which follows[203] or use of a relic which Matthew no longer takes seriously?[204] Matthew is usually too careful for that.[205] Or does it really mean that Matthew is having Jesus acknowledge the teaching authority of the scribes and Pharisees in matters of Law? [206] This is the most natural reading of the text.

How can this be when he has just been showing that they, the former vineyard keepers, are to be replaced? Is 23:2 understood by Matthew as a reference to what applied only in Jesus' day[207] or to what also applies in Matthew's own day?[208] Nothing in the immediate context excludes the latter possibility. On the other hand, in the wider context, Jesus has given the

---

[202] See the discussion of the motif of the "seat of Moses" in rabbinic tradition in H. J. Becker, *Auf der Kathedra Mose. Rabbinisch–theologisches Denken und antirabbinische Polemik in Matthäus 23,1–12*, ANTZ, (Berlin, 1990), pp. 17–51, who notes that rabbinic evidence is late, but that Matthew provides evidence for its use in Greek speaking Judaism in the late first century and probably reflects rabbinic claims of the period.

[203] So Banks, *Law*, p. 176; D. Garland, *The Intention of Matthew 23*, SuppNovT 52, (Leiden: Brill, 1979), pp. 20–21, 54. Cf. Grams, "Conflict Scene," p. 60, who sees irony in 23:2–3 which is resolved in Jesus' statement that people should not do as they do.

[204] So Strecker, *Gerechtigkeit*, pp. 16, 138, who dismisses its relevance for Matthew by assigning it to tradition and seeing it as contradicting 16:11–12; similarly France, *Matthew*, p.194 n. 58, who suggests that the passage be read along the lines: "You may follow their teaching if you like, *but* don't imitate their behaviour." This is not what the text says!

[205] Becker, *Kathedra*, pp. 86, who makes the point that Matthew gives it prominence and draws attention to the emphasis here and elsewhere on "all" (so: here 23:2–3 and 28:20; 5:18; pp. 90–91). It coheres with 23:2–3 that Matthew does not attack tradition itself or play tradition off against written law (pp. 91–94).

[206] So Barth, "Gesetzesverständnis," p. 80; cf. Gundry, *Matthew*, p. 455, who argues a distinction between their administration of the Law in general which they do not obey and their special traditions which they do and suggests that Matthew intends the former.

[207] Cf. S. H. Brooks, *Matthew's Community. The evidence of his special sayings material*, JSNTS 16, (Sheffield: JSOTPr, 1987), pp. 116–117, who explains these opening statements within the context of his theory that the chapter represents the stages in the history of the Matthean community and suggests a similar chronicling through Matthew 10 (pp. 117–118). This is another form of denying their validity in Matthew's text and assuming Matthew includes material which he consciously disavows for the sake of an historical account, but for which he offers no temporal or other clues!

[208] Cf. B. T. Viviano, "Social World and Community Leadership: The Case of Matthew 23:1–12,34," *JSNT* 39 (1990), pp. 3–21, here: 11–13, who argues that the word ἐκάθισαν means "have taken their seat" and now sit, a reference to the authoritative claims of Jamnia. But the words must also make sense in the narrative context of Jesus' ministry.

disciples such authority (28:18–20; 18:18; 16:16–19). This might suggest
that Matthew is reporting what Jesus said to the disciples as something which
applied at the time of the ministry of Jesus. Matthew is quite capable of
such historical sensitivity. He employs it in portraying the pre-Easter mission
as limited only to Israel (10:5–6; 15:24; cf. 28:18–20). It would cohere with
such an interpretation of 23:2, that when speaking of the disciples' exercise
of authority, Matthew is careful to have Jesus use the future tense (16:16–
19; 18:18). Matthew would be reflecting here, again, his strong sense that
Jesus, and later, the disciples, stand in a Mosaic succession of Law
interpretation. But there are problems. It is unlikely that Matthew means
only to report the past. His inclusion of the Pharisees with the scribes suggests
contemporary relevance. How is this to be understood?

It is not clear that he sees their sitting on Moses' seat as legitimate. Yet
nothing suggests illegitimacy. The criticism is levelled at their practice, not
their teaching. That is also extraordinary, because the issue between Jesus
and the scribes and Pharisees has been not only practice, but also
interpretation of Torah. A more probable alternative is that Matthew is
alluding to politico-religious realities, particularly of his own time and
setting.[209] There, the scribes and Pharisees administer community law and
the Matthean community is forced to comply.[210] This can be so, even when
the Matthean community is estranged from the synagogue. For then it is an
even more significant issue. Matthew's Jesus enjoins compliance with what
the Pharisees and scribes prescribe. If seen in this light, the contrast seems
to be between their role in public life and their behaviour in private life. By
and large Matthew's Jesus can live with their role in public life, just as he
has Jesus agree to payment of the temple tax. Matthew's concern is with the
abuses in their behaviour, but also with their priorities in teaching and
interpretation. Acknowledging that they sit on Moses' seat is primarily an
acceptance of their public administrative role, but it is not an endorsement
of their ethics or Torah interpretation overall. I believe that seeing it in this

---

[209] So E. Lohmeyer, *Das Evangelium des Matthäus. Nachgelassene Ausarbeitungen
und Entwürfe zur Übersetzung und Erklärung, für den Druck erarbeitet und herausgegeben
von W. Schmauch*, KEK Sonderband, (Göttingen: Vandenhoeck und Ruprecht, 4. Aufllage,
1967), pp. 334–335; Gnilka, *Matthäus II*, p. 274. Saldarini, *Community*, pp. 7, 46–52,
argues that Matthew is intent on delegitimating the Jewish leaders. It is resistance from
within typical of a marginalised group (eg. egalitarianism). He acknowledges the likelihood
that in Matthew's community the scribes and Pharisees had attained significant power.
They had expelled Matthew's group from their assembly (p. 52).

[210] Garland, *Matthew 23*, pp. 42–43, notes that not all Pharisees had the authority
attributed to them in 23:2, so that one may ask whether the combination scribes and Pharisees
had special significance for Matthew.

way makes sense both of the statement as it stands and of Matthew's approach to Torah elsewhere and to their interpretation and practice of it.[211]

Having exhorted the disciples to obey their words, but not follow their practice, Jesus goes on to attack the scribes and Pharisees for imposing heavy burdens upon people by their laws, while not lifting a finger to help them (23:4).[212] The assumption here is not that the burdensome laws are wrong, but that they are demanded without adequate support for those who are to fulfil them. Matthew may well be evoking among his hearers some recollection of Jesus' own invitation to take up the yoke of God's Law as one that is light and not heavy (11:28–30). With the support Jesus offers the commandments are no longer burdensome.

23:5–7 attacks the parading of their piety, their broad phylacteries, the size of their fringes, their choice of leading seats in feasts and in synagogues, and their fondness of being greeted publicly, especially as "rabbi". The latter may reflect the titular use which was probably becoming current around the time Matthew was writing. This would lend support to the view that Matthew sees what we have here as applying to his own day.

The appellation, "rabbi," serves as the link to 23:8–12, in which Matthew has Jesus forbid that the disciples have themselves called "rabbi," or "father". Rather they are to serve in humility and find from that their reward. It belongs to the Matthean understanding of leadership that it is the community who have been entrusted with the authority of being keepers of the vineyard, not an elite among them.

There follows a series of pronouncements of judgement, directed against the scribes and Pharisees, introduced with the formulation: "Woe to you, scribes and Pharisees, hypocrites" (23:13,14,15,23,25,27,29). The first attacks their blocking entry to the kingdom of heaven and refusal, themselves, to enter (23:13). It is important to note the implication: they should instead

---

[211] See now also the discussion in M. A. Powell, "Do and Keep what Moses Says (Matthew 23:2–7)," *JBL* 114 (1995), pp. 419–435, who suggests that the reference is not "to their role as teachers at all, but to their social position as people who control accessibility to Torah" (p. 431).

[212] Cf. Becker, *Kathedra*, p. 144, who believes 23:4 means that they teach difficult *halakah* without taking it on themselves. Jesus also teaches heavy commandments. But they are light because they bring life and freedom from other burdens (pp. 147–148). Matthew has Jesus criticise the scribes for ignoring love, which is, in turn, Jesus' teaching about the kingdom of heaven (pp. 166–168). Limbeck, "'Nichts bewegen'," argues that the expression reflects legal discussion and means: being not willing to make changes. He sees the attack as directed primarily against dangers within Matthew's own community of inflexible use of the powers to "loose" (pp. 302–311). The former may well be so, but not the latter. The issue belongs to the delegitimation of scribes and Pharisees outside Matthew's Christian community. See Saldarini, *Community*, pp. 7, 46–52.

be like John and Jesus (and the community), proclaiming the kingdom, repentance and the way of righteousness. The issue is the way they handle Torah. If they handled it rightly they would open the way for people into the kingdom.

The second woe takes up Mark's attack on their exploitation of widows and on their demonstrative prayers (23:14). The third mocks their efforts to make proselytes whom they make into people worse than themselves (23:15). This probably reflects the experience of Matthew's community of persecution or rejection coming with the intensity which often characterises converts. It doubtless relates to their manner of interpreting Torah. Like the first woe, it indicates that the Matthean church is facing considerable opposition in its mission from within the Jewish community.

23:16 introduces another woe, but without the set formula. It clearly has the same addressees in mind, labelling them "blind guides" and attacking their unreal distinctions in laws about oath taking. He attacked the scribes and Pharisees as "blind guides" in 15:14 for their way of interpreting Torah. Matthew has already indicated Jesus' more radical teaching on oaths in 5:34–37.

The woe in 23:23 assails the scribes and Pharisees because they put the emphasis too much on the lesser commandments of tithing and too little on "justice and mercy and faith". Matthew obviously understands the tithing commands to have validity – they are not to be left undone; but priority belongs to the others. This confirms the impression that Matthew assumes the validity of Torah and its application, even in areas such as tithing.[213] Matthew's categories appear to reflect the categories of pre-mishnaic discussion.[214] Here in 23:24, as in 23:16, Jesus again addresses the scribes and Pharisees as "blind guides". Straining out a gnat while swallowing a camel is another way of making the same point as 23:23: they observe laws about minutiae, but fail in what matters. It is also an allusion to a particular application of corpse impurity law, but does not imply its abolition in any way.

The woe in 23:25–26 uses issues about purifying vessels to attack preoccupation with externals and neglect of 'internal' issues of morality.[215]

---

[213] So Saldarini, *Community* pp. 50–51. Cf. Garland, *Matthew 23*, pp. 140, who dismisses 23:23: "from an earlier tradition which cannot be pressed too far theologically" (p. 140); France, *Matthew*, p. 194 n. 58, who suggests Matthew implied an "if you wish"!

[214] On this see the discussion in the chapter on Q of Q11:42 below.

[215] On the purity issues reflected here see in relation to the underlying Q saying, see J. Neusner, "'First Cleanse the Inside'," *NTS* 22 (1976), pp. 486–495; also Saldarini, *Community*, pp. 139–140, who emphasises Matthew's familiarity debates about purity within the Jewish community. And see further in the chapter on Q, below.

The contrast recalls Jesus' statements about food (15:11,17–20). It does not necessarily imply rejection of matters concerned with external purification, but ranks them as of secondary importance compared with moral purity. Preoccupation with the external manifests blindness of the Pharisees. The woe of 23:27–28 uses the practice of whitewashing tombs to develop the contrast between the scribes' and Pharisees' concern about outward rightness, while neglecting inner, moral impurity. Again the point is not to attack either the white washing of tombs or attention to externals, but doing so at the expense of neglecting what in Matthew's view of Torah has higher priority. Similarly in 23:29–32 their practice of erecting and adorning the tombs of prophets and the righteous and bewailing their murder is not being attacked. It is being exposed as inconsistent with their own murderous rejection of the prophets and righteous of their own day.

These verses form a transition to a longer exposition of the murderous behaviour of the scribes and Pharisees (23:33–36). Jesus addresses them in words which echo John's confrontation of the Pharisees and Sadducees: "Snakes, brood of vipers, how shall you escape the judgement of Gehenna?" cf. 3:7, "Brood of vipers, who warned you to escape the wrath to come?" Perhaps Matthew is again deliberately evoking Jesus' connection with John as he did in 21:23 – 22:14, where the rejections of John, Jesus and his missionaries are linked together. Jesus declares: "There I am sending you prophets and sages and scribes, some of whom you will kill and crucify, and some of whom you will beat in your synagogues and pursue from city to city" (23:34). The reference is clearly to members of the Christian community, as it had been in 22:1–14. The identification of "sages and scribes" beside "prophets" reflects the strongly Jewish nature of Matthew's community which saw itself as authorised to exercise the role of sage and scribe, including interpretation of Torah.

Jesus' statement concludes: "So that all the righteous blood poured out on the earth may come upon you, from the blood of Abel the righteous to the blood of Zechariah son of Berachiah,[216] whom you murdered between the sanctuary and the altar. Truly I tell you all this will come upon this generation" (23:35–36). The "so that" expresses purpose and reflects the theological view that God allows this rejection to happen in order that not only their guilt but also the guilt of their forbears (23:31–32) may be avenged on their generation in one full sum. This is both a vehement attack on the

---

[216] For the identification of Zechariah, including possible allusions to the Zechariah killed during the siege of Jerusalem by two Zealots, see Saldarini, *Community*, p 240 n. 31. Cf. Jos *JW* 4:335–344.

leaders and an explanation of what happened in the destruction of Jerusalem. This, and the suffering which accompanied it, was God's act of vengeance, according to Matthew.

Matthew's source has this statement of Jesus (23:34–36) as the words of "the Wisdom of God" (Q/Luke 11:49–51). Matthew's change is doubtless deliberate. Why? Probably because of his consistent emphasis on the chain of authorisation from Jesus to his own. In making the change is he deliberately suppressing reference to the wisdom imagery? This is possible, but unlikely. He has retained the image of wisdom in 11:19. There, too, it is associated with the theme of rejection. As we have seen, Matthew is probably aware of its association in tradition with Torah and with the wise when he writes 11:25–30. It may also be reflected in the lament of Jesus which immediately follows in 23:37–39, "Jerusalem, Jerusalem, killing the prophets and stoning those sent to her, how often I wanted to gather your children, as a hen gather her chickens under her wings, and you refused." Matthew's community might hear it as a cry of the risen Jesus, but narrative integrity demands that we see it as a statement about the past. How can Jesus be claiming this about himself in the past? The most probable explanation is that he identifies himself with the role attributed in tradition to wisdom, the sender of the prophets (cf. Prov 1:21–33; Bar 3:14–15; 1 En 42:1–2). The fact that this idea is already present in the tradition behind 11:16–19 makes this more likely. Matthew probably envisages Jesus speaking as a prophet under inspiration the words of God's wisdom. This is more likely than that we have suddenly appearing here (perhaps for the second time only; cf. 11:19–30) a full blown christology of pre-existence in the form of Jesus being the incarnation of Wisdom; for if such were the case, its absence elsewhere would be inexplicable.

In line with the prophets (also with John, the prophet, and with the prophets whom he will send), Jesus speaks as a prophet. The judgement follows the lament: "Behold your house is left to you, desolate. I tell you, you shall not see me from now on until you say, 'Blessed is the one who comes in the name of the Lord'." (23:38b–39). Jerusalem's "house" is the temple.[217] Jesus is predicting its destruction. He is also announcing his departure from the people of Jerusalem. Perhaps associated with this is an allusion to the

---

[217] So Gundry, *Matthew*, p. 473. Gnilka, *Matthäus II*, p. 304, believes it could mean both city and temple, pointing to Jer 7:12 and 1 En 89:51,54 where the author refers to both as God's house. But in Matthew 23:37–39 this is difficult if the city is being addressed. On the similar imagery used of Jerusalem's fall in 5 Ezra 1:28–33, see Stanton, *Gospel*, pp. 266–267.

absence of Yahweh, for Jesus is Emmanuel. They will not see Jesus until he once again enters Jerusalem (cf. 26:64). Then they shall acclaim him blessed. "Blessed is he who comes in the name of Lord" (Ps 118:26) was the greeting at Jesus' first entry (21:9). With this inclusio Matthew completes Jesus' words to Jerusalem. It also reflects a strongly Jewish eschatology centred on Jerusalem.[218]

Matthew 23 belongs closely together with the previous chapters as the final section dealing with Jesus' ministry in Jerusalem. Its ending forms an inclusio which links Jesus' past and future entry into Jerusalem. The theme of rejection, especially in 23:32–39 strongly echoes the theme of rejection in those chapters and in a similar way links together the prophets, John, Jesus, and the disciples, all under the image of rejected prophets. The allusion to the sending of disciples not only as prophets, but as sages and scribes, coheres not only with the strongly Jewish ethos of Matthew, but also with the self-understanding of Matthew's community as portrayed by Matthew. Jesus has authorised them to do as he did: to proclaim the kingdom, announce repentance and expound God's will in a manner which stands in the succession of true interpreters of the Law.

In Matthew 23:2–3 Matthew has Jesus acknowledge the politico-religious reality that the scribes and Pharisees are in power and enjoin compliance. The attacks which follow primarily target abuses (hence the frequency of "hypocrites"), but also false priorities. Matthew's Jesus maintains his consistent emphasis on ethical attitude and behaviour. But the chapter is remarkable also for its inclusiveness. It is not attacking practice of written law or even its detailed elaboration and application, for instance, in what should be tithed, washed, sworn, strained (gnats), or done to honour the dead; it is attacking failure to put the priorities where Matthew's Jesus argues they should belong: justice, mercy and faith. The implication is also that, were they to do this, they, too, would open the kingdom of heaven to people. Matthew does not dispute this.

What emerges is a Jesus who belongs within the scribal tradition and attacks the failure of its practitioners. Yet at the same time this is no internal argument on common ground. Jesus speaks not as a scribe, but as the divinely

---

[218] This creates difficulty for Levine's view, *Matthean Salvation History*, that "the tearing of the veil indicates that the Jewish cultus will cede its authority to the non centralised, non hierarchical church; it portends the ultimate demolition of spatial boundaries" (p. 168). The sacred space is where the disciples gather (p. 100). 23:39 indicates that Matthew has not demolished the spatial boundaries entirely.

created Son of God, authorised to be judge. As such he knows Torah and how it should be applied. When he speaks in the words of God's wisdom of events of the past, this should be understood not as a rare surfacing of a high Matthean christology which sees Jesus as pre-existent wisdom or Torah. He speaks under prophetic inspiration. His prediction of God's judgement on Jerusalem through the taking away of the temple is a lament. There is no hint of cult critique. On the contrary the chapter ends with a note of hope centred again on Jerusalem, when Jesus shall enter her once more and his enemies declare him blessed. This is a rare glimpse of an aspect of Matthean eschatology which, again, is strongly Jewish in its orientation on Jerusalem.

2.4.3 Matthew 24:1 – 25:46

The omission of Mark's account of the widow's mite, Mark 12:41–44, makes the transition from Matthew 23 to Matthew 24 much more direct. Mark has a brief account of woes against the scribes (12:38–40), the account of the widow and her mite (12:41–44), then Mark 13 in which Jesus foretells the destruction of the temple and the end of the world. Matthew goes directly from the woes to the prediction of destruction, thus underlining the one as the consequence of the other.

Matthew 24 follows Mark 13 closely, but with significant variations. In Mark the disciples' viewing of the temple (13:1) recalled Jesus' similar looking around in 11:11, and formed part of the network of temple imagery through which Mark disparaged the old temple and portrayed the community of faith as its replacement. Matthew does not share this view, as we have seen. In 24:2 Matthew's Jesus formally predicts the temple's destruction: "Truly I tell you, not one stone shall be left on another, which shall not be thrown down."

A new section begins when the disciples ask Jesus when this would happen and what would be the sign of his coming (added by Matthew in the light of 23:39) and of the end of the age (24:3). Matthew's Jesus warns about deceivers who will claim, "I am the Christ" (24:5; cf. Mark 13:5, "I am," meaning "I am the one"). Matthew may be alluding to messianic claimants who appeared in Judaism during the turbulent years before the temple's destruction. Much of the material which Matthew found in Mark 13:9–12 about both Jewish and Gentile persecution he has moved to 10:17–22, where it became part of Jesus' instruction to the disciples about their mission. He retains Mark 13:13, "You shall be hated by all people because of my name," in the form, "You shall be hated by all nations because of my name" (24:9b). By "nations" (ἐθνῶν) Matthew doubtless means all nations including Israel.

This coheres with what follows, where he refers to offence and betrayal within the community (24:10).

At this point Matthew adds that false prophets will be successful in leading many astray (24:11–12). In this context he speaks of ἀνομία, which, he says, will increase with the result that the love of many will flag. ἀνομία may simply mean, "wickedness" and often does. It could possibly mean "lawlessness", ie. non observance of the Law, reflecting the word's etymology. The same issue arose in our discussion of 7:21–23. The statement would then reflect Matthew's insistence that believers uphold Torah as interpreted now by Jesus with the central focus on love. Some have, therefore, seen here an allusion to the kind of problem alluded to in 7:15–20 and 21–23 and perhaps being countered on one front in 5:17 (see the earlier discussion of these passages). This may be so, even without the rather uncertain argument from etymology. Certainly love is the central feature of the Law according to Matthew, so that failure of love reflects neglect of Torah as expounded by Jesus.

24:14 includes an allusion to the expansion of the mission to include Gentiles, which Matthew reports in 28:18–20. Matthew's version of the Danielic prediction of Jerusalem's woes follows Mark's with minor variants (24:15–22; cf. Mark 13:14–20). The abomination is now portrayed as a thing, not a person. More interesting is Matthew's addition in 24:20. To Mark's version of the exhortation that the disciples should pray that their flight not take place in winter, Matthew adds, "nor on the sabbath" (cf. Mark 13:18). It may reflect Matthew's concern for Law observance;[219] but it could also be envisaging practical difficulties which would arise on a sabbath.[220] Either way, such a change may indicate memory of what happened at the time of flight; or it may now be seen as relevant for any future flight.

In 24:23–24 Matthew follows Mark in predicting false christs and false prophets who will perform miracles (Mark 13:21–23). Both appear to be distinct from the false prophets of 24:11–12. Matthew may be alluding again

---

[219] So Gnilka, *Matthäus II*, pp. 323–324. Wong, *Interkulturelle Theologie*, pp. 79–80, believes it reflects sabbath observance in Matthew's community; and "Sabbath", pp. 14–17, where he suggests Matthew's community faces persecution from Romans and that some members are sabbath observers. Schweizer, *Matthäus*, p. 295, believes Matthew's community kept sabbath, but with a freedom for which flight would not present a problem; the allusion to sabbath here is a relic of tradition.

[220] So Gundry, *Matthew*, p. 483, who refers to problems of getting supplies because of Jewish observance, not because of their own. Barth, "Gesetzesverständnis," p. 86, thinks the concern is about giving offence to others; similarly Banks, *Law*, p. 102; Stanton, *Gospel*, pp. 203–205.

to those mentioned in 24:5. Their behaviour, described only by Matthew as luring people into the wilderness, fits what we know of movements in the period of the Jewish war. Matthew's following description of the coming of the Son of Man uses the imagery of lightning and the gathering of vultures (24:27–28), then remains close to Mark, but with some additional apocalyptic colouring (24:29–31). Matthew is portraying the coming of Jesus, the Son of Man, as judge.

Matthew's use of the fig tree metaphor would not carry an allusion to the temple as it probably does in Mark (24:32–33; cf. Mark 13:28–29). Jesus' words, "Heaven and earth shall pass away, but my words shall not pass away" (24:35), remain embedded among predictions of the end, as in Mark (13:31). In Matthew they would, perhaps, evoke for the hearer the wider range of Jesus' teaching as interpreter of Torah and perhaps even the memory of the similarly formulated word of Jesus in 5:18: "Until heaven and earth pass away not one jot or tittle shall pass from the Law until all is fulfilled."

After the Markan material, Matthew now adds a series of parables based on Q material to exhort the disciples to be ready before Jesus the judge (24:37–44,45–51; 25:1–13,14–30; cf. already 24:27–28). They reflect typical Matthean emphasis on ethical attitudes and behaviour. Nothing is said about such matters as keeping sabbath, tithes, and observing purity laws. The allusion to Noah's generation stresses "eating and drinking, marrying and giving in marriage" aims not to attack those activities as such, but to emphasise that people carried on their lives without sensing the danger of judgement which Noah proclaimed (24:37–39). 24:40–44 similarly emphasises suddenness. 24:45–51 focuses more directly on inappropriate behaviours. Speaking of slaves entrusted to run the household creates an analogy with the way Matthew understands the disciples; Jesus has authorised them to run his church. Perhaps the image of abuse of such power and debauchery alludes to dangers which Matthew sees in his community. Matthew has Jesus make a direct shift to contemporary terms when he has him condemn them to share the lot of "the hypocrites" (24:51; cf. Luke 12:46 has "with the unbelievers"). Unfaithful disciples will be no better off than the Jewish hypocrites whom Jesus has condemned (similarly 24:11–14).

The same focus on continued readiness is central in 25:1–13, which also underlines faithful obedience to Jesus' teaching as essential for salvation. The cry of the foolish girls, "Lord, Lord," and his response: "I do not know you," echo the warning of 7:21–23. There Jesus says that he will declare, "I never knew you," to those who cry to him, "Lord, Lord," and appeal to public

Christian achievements, but have not lived according to the Father's will. The parable of the talents in Matthew reinforces the demand that Christ's servants exercise their gifts (25:14–30).

The climax of Jesus' public ministry is another demand that disciples live out their faith in good works (25:31–46). It is a symbolic depiction of the last judgement. Again the focus is on Jesus as the judge to come. 16:27 had already indicated, that the Son of Man would judge all according to their behaviour. Characteristic behaviours which are approved in 25:31–46 include feeding the hungry, giving drink to the thirsty, taking in the stranger, clothing the naked, visiting the sick and the imprisoned. Since 24:3 Matthew has been describing Jesus' words to his disciples. Here, as his final major teaching, he depicts universal judgement. It is not to satisfy the curiosity of the disciples about what will happen to others. It still forms part of Jesus' exhortation to them. It reveals the criteria of judgement which will apply to them as it will apply to all and confirms Jesus' understanding of God's will, including his attitude towards Torah. Acts of kindness and compassion count more than anything else.

Reviewing 24:1 – 25:46, we note that Matthew's prediction of the temple's destruction shows no trace of anti-cultic attitudes. Matthew's version of Jesus' predictions appears to reflect knowledge after the event, including knowledge of the activities of messianic and prophetic claimants of the time. It reflects experience of persecution and the expansion of the mission to include Gentiles. It may allude to rival Christian teachers (false prophets) who, to Matthew's mind, encourage disregard of the Law, but that is uncertain. The added warning about the sabbath may, but need not, reflect concern about sabbath observance.

From 24:26 onwards the focus is on the coming of Jesus as judge in a number of parables. Through these Matthew's Jesus addresses the disciples. Effectively they depict the judge warning of the kinds of behaviours which will bring judgement. For failure he sees the same punishment as he will mete out to "the hypocrites", an allusion to the scribes and Pharisees. The focus is strongly ethical. There is no mention of cultic or ritual law. The behaviours enjoined pertain, in part, to leadership: not abusing responsibility; using one's abilities for the kingdom. Possibly the parable of the girls is directed in particular at the kind of abuses outlined in 7:21–23. The theme of Jesus as judge to come reaches a climax in the final depiction of judgement and reveals that as judge Jesus is concerned with acts of compassion. By this law all are to be judged. This is consistent with Matthew's presentation of Jesus' attitude towards Torah and how it should be interpreted throughout the gospel.

2.4.4 Matthew 26:1 – 28:20

Matthew's passion narrative follows the Markan order closely. It sets a fourth Son of Man passion prediction at the outset (26:2), heightens the disciples' failure and darkens the figure of Judas. Like Mark, Matthew passes over any purity issues in relation to the anecdote that a woman anointed his head in the house of Simon the leper (26:6–13). As in Mark, Jesus and his disciples meet together for the Passover Meal and at the conclusion sing the Hallel (26:17–30). In the last supper Matthew's version of the word about the wine adds: "for the forgiveness of sins." (26:28). Blood being poured out for forgiveness of sins is probably sacrificial imagery, or, at least, understood as vicarious. In 1:21 Matthew had interpreted Jesus' name as indicating that he will save his people from their sins (1:21). In the light of subsequent and parallel Christian tradition one might expect some indication elsewhere in the gospel that for Matthew forgiveness is based on Jesus' sacrificial or vicarious death, as it is here. But, as in Mark, nothing indicates it is central to Matthew's understanding of the gospel of forgiveness and, as in Mark, the only other possible reference (20:28; cf. Mark 10:45) is incidental to the point being made about humility. John, Jesus and the disciples proclaim repentance with the implied promise of forgiveness. The Lord's Prayer assumes God will forgive sins (6:7–13). Matthew notes that the authority to forgive sins is delegated to the disciples (9:8). Matthew regularly makes God's forgiveness a model for disciples. Forgiveness seems primarily rooted in the attitude of God, not in an act of vicarious or sacrificial atonement, although Matthew knows the tradition and, by his addition, ensures the link. Equally, there is no suggestion, as in Hebrews, that this in any way calls into question cultic law, which also included provision for forgiveness.

In the Gethsemane account and the arrest scene (26:36–58) there is little of direct relevance to the theme; at most, perhaps, Jesus' protest that he "sat" as he taught in the temple (26:55). This was the common teaching stance of rabbis, but also of others. Within the arrest scene Matthew's distinctive additions have Jesus remind the hearer of who Jesus really is and that as such he could call on angelic intervention, but refuses to do so in order that scripture may be fulfilled (26:52–54).

More significant is Jesus' appearance before the Sanhedrin (26:59–66), for, although Matthew follows the Markan material, he makes some significant changes. He removes the ambiguity of Mark's comment that false witnesses reported that Jesus had predicted he would destroy the temple (cf. Mark 14:57). Instead, and in contrast to false witnesses who came forward earlier, there are now two (ie reliable) witnesses (26:61). They report Jesus as saying that he could destroy the temple (not necessarily that he would!). And, more significant, Matthew has removed from the saying the Markan contrast between the temple "made with hands" and one "not made with hands" (cf. Mark 14:58). Matthew had already dismantled Mark's disparagement of the temple and his hints that the believing community would be the new temple. Here he does the same. The effect is to have Jesus make a claim about what he might have been able to do, but, like calling on angelic support in 26:52–54, refused to do.

For the rest of the Jewish trial account, Matthew follows Mark in having the high priest charge Jesus with blasphemy and adds no stronger evidence to enlighten its background as a legitimate charge. He does, however, have the high priest swear an oath (26:63). Alert hearers might remember Jesus' declaration, forbidding such oaths (5:33–37), thus setting the high priest in a bad light. Even more striking, therefore, is Matthew's addition to the account of Peter's denial, that he took an oath in denying that he knew Jesus (26:72).

The account of Judas' remorse and return of money to the treasury (27:3–10) reflects issues of Jewish Law as the chief priests rule that blood money cannot enter the temple treasury, but this is a secondary feature in the narrative. The account of the trial before Pilate in Matthew (27:11–26) is noteworthy for the added details that Pilate's wife intervenes (27:19), that Pilate washes his hands (27:24) and that the Jews issue the fateful cry that Jesus' blood would be on them and on their children (27:24). The sequence reflects the practice of the Law in Deut 21:6–8 LXX which provides for washing hands of innocent blood associated with declaration of freedom from blood guilt. The description of Pilate washing his hands also echoes Ps 26:5–6. The cry recalls Jesus' judgement on the scribes and Pharisees for rejection of the prophets in 23:35–36: "All these things will be required of this generation." Here the Jerusalem crowd reinforces the prediction and relates it directly to the killing of Jesus.[221] As in Mark, the inscription over the cross reads that Jesus is "King of the Jews" and subtle ironies indicating Jesus is truly the royal Messiah abound. In Matthew they strongly recall the themes of the infancy narratives.

In his version of the mockery under the cross and the splitting of the

---

[221] See Saldarini, *Community*, p. 33, who argues that it should be seen as referring only to the Jerusalem people, not all Jews.

temple's curtain (27:38–54) Matthew is no longer interested, as was Mark, in making a point about the old and new temple, although he retains Mark's reference to the temple in the mockery of Jesus (27:40). Instead he uses the episode to highlight Jesus as the Son of God. Thus, in a way that echoes the temptation narrative, he has the mocker add: "If you are the Son of God" (27:40), and adds to another: "He believed in God; let him rescue him now if he wants him. For he said, 'I am the Son of God'" (27:43). Here we also find echoes of the portrait of the suffering wise, mocked for claiming to be a child of God (Wisd 2:12–20). This sets the scene for the response to the great astounding events which follow at Jesus' death.

Whereas in Mark the rending of the curtain immediately precedes the centurion's acclamation and symbolises judgement and the replacement of the old temple made with hands, in Matthew the rending is just the beginning; there follows the great eschatological earthquake and the resurrections in the holy city (27:51–53). Seeing these (the earthquake and what happened subsequently), the centurion and those around him make their response: "Truly this is the Son of God" (27:54). The rending of the curtain, while still probably understood as an act indicating God's future judgement,[222] is now subordinated to a more significant theme: the presentation in apocalyptic colouring of Jesus as the Son of God. It is no longer associated, as in Mark, with disparagement of the cult.

In the addition here about the earthquake, we find traces of Jewish sensitivity typical of Matthew. He speaks of "the holy city" and "the holy ones" (27:52–53; cf. 4:5). A strongly Jewish background also explains Matthew's addition that the chief priests and Pharisees sought guards for the body and later concocted the rumour that the disciples had stolen the body (27:62–66; 28:11–15). Matthew is reporting anti Christian propaganda alive in the Jewish community ("This rumour has been spread among the Jews to this day").[223]

The women show the same respect for the sabbath as they do in the Markan narrative in coming to the tomb only after the sabbath (28:1; cf. Mark 16:1–2). The meeting with Peter and the disciples, promised in Mark's brief narrative (16:7) and in Matthew's to the disciples as a group (28:7), actually takes place in Matthew. He reports it in 28:16–20. Again on a holy mountain, like Moses (cf. 5:1–2; 15:29; 17:1; esp. 4:8), Jesus commissions his disciples.

---

[222] Cf. Gnilka, *Matthäus*, p. 476, who mentions two possible interpretations: the end of the old cultus and access for all to the presence of God. Neither is indicated in Matthew.

[223] Saldarini, *Community*, pp. 35–36, argues that the reference to "Jews" here does not necessarily imply separation from the Jewish community. Nevertheless it implies a strong sense of alienation.

11:27 had already affirmed that he is the authorised one: "All things have been given me by my Father". In 28:18 it appears in the form, "All authority in heaven and on earth has been given to me." This could allude to heavenly authority now being added to his earthly authority.[224] It probably also relates directly to the expansion of the mission to all the world. As in 11:27, the focus of this authority is less rule than teaching authority, though in both 11:27 and 28:18–20, and throughout Matthew, God's rule comes to expression primarily in Jesus' teaching. Thus he sends the disciples to teach what he has taught them and promises to be with them forever (28:19–20). As we noted in relation to 18:20, his promise to be with them to the end of the age recalls the promise that God's Shekinah will be present where two or three study Torah. Teaching and study is also the context in 28:20. The promise also echoes the designation of Jesus as Emmanuel, God with us, in 1:23.[225]

In 28:19 Jesus expands the mission. The limits of mission to Israel have fallen away. Whether τὰ ἔθνη means "Gentiles" or "nations", the implications is that the mission to Gentiles is an expansion rather than a replacement of the mission to Israel, for 10:23 assumes it is still in progress.[226] By his words in 28:19 Matthew has Jesus extend what originated as John's baptism to become baptism "in the name of the Father, the Son and the Holy Spirit." Matthew has brought what Acts portrays as significant early developments of the early church to a single point in time.

Matthew makes no mention of circumcision of Gentiles. It is not easy to

---

[224] Levine, *Matthean Salvation History*, p. 175.

[225] Donaldson, *Mountain*, pp. 183–186, links this reference to Jesus' presence (who is God's presence) with Zion and temple typology. Jesus is therefore replacing the temple and the place where God is found. Other evidence in Matthew does not support this view.

[226] G. Tisera, *Universalism according to the Gospel of Matthew*, Eur. Univ. Studies XXIII 482, (Frankfurt: Peter Lang, 1993), pp. 305–306, summarises the arguments for an inclusive understanding of τὰ ἔθνη: its meaning corresponds to its use in 24:9,14; 25:32; it reflects the emphasis of the context on "all"; it echoes 26:13; and 10:23 presumes a continuing mission to Jews. Matthew believes in a continuing mission to Israel and does not give up the special term λαός. See also J. P. Meier, "Nations or Gentiles in Matthew 28:19?" *CBQ* 39 (1977), pp. 94–102; Wouter, *"...Wer den Willen meines Vaters tut"*, pp. 372–376; Stanton, *Gospel*, pp. 158–161; Saldarini, *Community*, pp. 78–81; Menninger, *Israel*, pp. 43–44, though his implied argument that Israel is included because the true Israel is now the church is forced. Cf. also Levine, *Matthean Salvation History*, pp. 14, 43, 180–196, who argues that τὰ ἔθνη does mean Gentiles, but in the sense of an extension of mission, not an exclusion of mission to the Jews. For the view that τὰ ἔθνη refers to Gentiles and does not include Israel, see D. J. Harrington, *Light of All Nations. Essays on the church in New Testament Research*, Good News St 3, (Wilmington: Glazier, 1982), pp. 110–123; Walker, *Heilsgeschichte*, pp. 111–113. It does not differentiate adequately between judgement on Israel's leaders, on Jerusalem and on Israel, and so interprets 28:19 too readily as a replacement of Israel.

interpret the silence.[227]   At no point thus far does he indicate the dropping of
a single commandment of Torah, even though he makes it clear that some
are very secondary. Given his expressed priority for ethical attitude and
behaviour, circumcision would almost certainly take a low priority. The
question is whether the liberal approach, evident in handling sabbath law
might, when applied to circumcision, still insist on it in all cases or in any.
Factors outside Matthew must be weighed, including the attitude of other
Jews to the requirement and the relation of Matthew's community to other
Christian groups who had apparently ceased to demand it. Could Matthew
have had Jesus declare what he does in 5:18, knowing that circumcision had
been waived? I believe the balance of evidence favours not reading the
silence in 28:18–20 as implying abrogation.

Matthew 26–28 does not add greatly to our findings on Jesus and the Law.
Perhaps of most significance is Matthew's change of the temple imagery. At
most there is a hint of its destruction. The rending of the curtain probably
symbolises its doom; but gone is the Markan disparagement of the old and
the theme of its replacement by a new temple not made with hands, the
community of faith. Instead Matthew's concern is to highlight Jesus as the
Son of God with apocalyptic signs and power.

Within the narrative are occasional additions reflecting a strongly Jewish
milieu (particularly those concerned with Judas, Pilate's wife's dream, Pilate
washing his hands, the earthquake and resurrections, and the rumour of the
stolen body). In addition Jesus and his disciples are portrayed as faithful
Jews observing Passover and the women as observing sabbath. Matthew
makes capital out of Jesus' teaching on oaths to expose the high priest and
shame Peter. There is no reflection on the possible implications of Jesus'
death or the eucharist for understanding the validity of sacrifice and the cult.

The closing scene reflects major emphases of the gospel. It confirms that
Matthew understands christology within a legal framework of authorisation.
The same framework of thought applies to his understanding of the disciples'
commission. This understanding persists in Matthew's description of mission
as a call to make disciples and to teach. Even the promise of Jesus' presence
reflects this pattern of thought: it echoes promises made to those who teach
and study Torah. Within the same ethos is the way the extension of the
mission to the Gentiles also requires special authorisation. Finally the failure

---

227 For discussion see Saldarini, *Community*, pp. 156–160. That they did not
circumcise, but kept a minimum of laws: Davies and Allison, *Matthew II*, pp. 537–538;
Segal, "Matthew's Jewish Voice," p. 31; that they did: Mohrlang, *Matthew*, pp. 44–45;
Levine, *Salvation History* , pp. 182–184.

to mention circumcision in the mission instructions probably reflects that it is taken for granted.

2.5 Jesus' Attitude towards the Law in Matthew – Conclusions

2.5.1 Jesus, judgement, and the Law

In the Matthean birth narratives we learn primarily who Jesus is. There is little about what he is to do. At most there is a hint in the interpretation of his names, Jesus, "he will save his people from their sins" and Emmanuel, "God with us". It is not until we reach the narrative of John the Baptist's preaching that we receive a clearer indication. Here we find Matthew has formulated the summary of John's message in words identical to those used for the summary of Jesus' message, "Repent, for the kingdom of heaven is at hand" (3:2; cf. 4:17). We also find John foretelling Jesus and his role: Jesus is the judge to come. Both aspects, the common message and role definition play a significant role throughout the gospel. Both are relevant for understanding Matthew's view of Jesus' attitude towards the Law.

The similarity of Jesus' and John's message is evident elsewhere in the gospel. Thus John confronts the Pharisees and Sadducees with the words: "Brood of vipers, who warned you to flee from the wrath to come?" (3:7); Jesus confronts the scribes and Pharisees similarly: "Snakes, brood of vipers, how will you escape the judgement of Gehenna?" (23:33). He uses "brood of vipers" of the Pharisees also in 12:34. In 3:10 John declares: "Every tree which does not bear good fruit shall be cut down and thrown into the fire"; Jesus makes an identical declaration in 7:19. But more than these instances of common formulations, Jesus' emphasis throughout the gospel reflects the same warnings that judgement will be according to works.

Accordingly in 21:23–27 Matthew not only takes up Mark 11:27–33, where the chief priests and scribes and elders question Jesus about his authority and where Jesus answers by linking his authority with John's. He also expands it with the parable of the two sons and has Jesus declare John as having come "in the way of righteousness" and his preaching as opening the way into the kingdom (21:28–32). Here, John, too, is associated with toll collectors and sinners, an accusation made against Jesus (11:19). Both John and Jesus, but also the disciples, face the accusation of being in league with demons (9:32; 10:25; 11:18). Similarly, not only does Matthew share with Mark the sense that John's death foreshadows Jesus' rejection and death; he rewrites the story so that John's disciples themselves come to Jesus to report the event, underlining the closeness and continuity between the two (14:12).

A similar identification occurs in the explanation of the parable of the children playing in the market place. There Matthew uses the tradition in which Jesus pairs his own sending with that of John and has Jesus declare in defence of them both: "Wisdom is vindicated by her deeds" (11:16–19). Immediately before this he had been emphasising the significance of John's role as marking the turning point from which the message of the kingdom is brought to the world (11:7–15). Both John and Jesus belong to the period towards which the Law and the Prophets have been prophesying (11:13).

The effect of this close identification is twofold. In part it ensures that John stands in continuity with Jesus. He also preached the kingdom. But, in terms of actual content, it is more significant that it has the effect of making Jesus more like John with regard to the focus of his message: Jesus proclaims judgement. This, in turn, puts a strong emphasis on Law and by implication on Jesus' relation to Torah. This is reinforced by the fact that John, in fact, announces Jesus as the coming judge, the second aspect noted above.

John the Baptist identifies Jesus as the judge to come. The narrative effect of the encounter with John and then the giving of the Spirit and the voice from heaven at Jesus' baptism is to confirm this. Jesus is the one who, John announced, would come to bring judgement and baptise with Spirit and fire. At his baptism God anoints him with the Spirit and declares him his beloved Son. As we shall see there are far wider ramifications, but the effect of reinforcement of Jesus' identity as the one announced by John must be given full weight. It means that Jesus not only proclaims God's judgement, but does so as judge to come. This makes him distinct from John. He is God's divinely created Son, before whom John is unworthy. John equates to the traditional expectation of Elijah (11:14; 17:10–13). Jesus is the judge to come. But both are part of God's eschatological initiative. Both must fulfil all righteousness, as Jesus reminds John. Both announce God's judgement.

Within the Matthean narrative, John's original prediction about Jesus helps make sense of his later doubt, reported in 11:2. Jesus was not fulfilling the judging role. The response in 11:3–6 is not a denial of his coming role as judge; it points rather to a distinction between Jesus' role on earth and his role at the end of time. Jesus is the judge to come, but now he is exercising roles which also belong to end time expectation and indicates that these validly precede the exercise of judgement itself. These are wider ramifications of Jesus' baptism which John did not comprehend. In ch 11 Matthew differentiates between John and Jesus while also still holding them closely together. John is, indeed an eschatological figure, but least in the kingdom of God, whose inauguration takes place with Jesus, himself (11:11). A similar difference exists between the picture of John's life as an ascetic in the explanation of the parable of the children playing in the market place and the depiction of Jesus' ministry as one of present celebration (11:16–19).

But, for Matthew, it is still the judge to come who preaches, teaches and heals on earth. We find this confirmed in 12:15–21, where Matthew makes remarkable use of Isa 42:1–4. It has the effect of bringing together: an allusion to Jesus' baptism and anointing by the Spirit, a reassertion of his ministry as preacher of judgement, a statement about his gentleness, echoing his style of Torah interpretation (11:28–30), and a hint of the mission to the Gentiles. Jesus, the judge to come, proclaims judgement. But the juxtaposition shows that this activity must be seen within the broader context of Jesus' ministry. This means, in turn, that the way the judge relates to Torah must also be seen in that light.

I have deliberately begun with the link between John and Jesus, because it is how the gospel begins. It also establishes grounds for the expectation that judgement and Jesus' role as judge significantly colour Matthew's understanding of Jesus and his attitude towards Torah and are present throughout the gospel.

Warnings that judgement will be by works are a consistent feature of Matthew's gospel. It is the essence of Jesus' final teaching to his disciples in Matthew 24:37 – 25:46 and is symbolically portrayed in the climax of this teaching in 25:31–46. It also forms the climax of Sermon on the Mount (7:24–27; and see also 7:15–23) and is the frequent theme of parables. Judgement by works applies equally to Jews and Christians. The harvest will sort the wheat from the weeds (13:33–43), the good from the bad fish (13:47–50), the new keepers of the vineyard must also produce fruit (21:41), and those belatedly invited to the feast must wear the appropriate garments (22:11–14). Crying, "Lord, Lord," or sporting Christian achievements is no compensation when the oil has run out (7:21–23; 25:12–13). Those who fail will have their lot with the hypocrites (24:51). Righteousness must even exceed that of the scribes and Pharisees (5:20). All will be judged according to their behaviour (16:27).

Jesus not only announces judgement throughout the gospel; he is, as John had announced, frequently portrayed as the one who will judge. This he will do as Son of Man on his throne of glory (25:31–46); and as Son of Man he will judge the behaviour of all (16:27). It is he who will confront those who make claims on his lordship and who will reward the righteous (7:21–23; 25:1–46). Significantly, however, Matthew also announces a role for the disciples in future judgement (19:28), as he also authorises them to continue his teaching and the exercise of judgement within the community of faith (28:18–20; 18:15–20; 16:16; 14:22–33; 9:8).

The announcement of judgement belongs, as it did with John, with the announcement of the kingdom. In this task, too, the disciples share (10:7). For judgement in Matthew is at the same time the occasion for reward and blessing, a constant feature in Jesus' teaching. The good news, according to Matthew, is primarily that the judge has come to announce the basis of judgement and to hold out the promise of blessing to those who hear his word. This is done most directly in the beatitudes (5:1–11). The kingdom's rule is manifest above all in the teaching of God's Law.

Jesus' role as judge is an aspect of Matthew's broader christology. It belongs within and reflects Matthew's understanding of Jesus' authority. Matthew operates with an authorisation christology. Jesus is the divinely created Son of God, but Matthew does not call him God or assume immediate divine knowledge. Rather in Matthew's understanding the Son has been authorised by the Father. This shows in his defence of the act of forgiveness: "The Son of Man has authority on earth to forgive sins" (12:5). It is reflected also in 11:27a, "All things have been given to me by my Father" and in 28:18, "All authority in heaven and on earth has been given to me." The notion of authorisation is central. Thus Matthew's christology reflects a legal framework of thought. Jesus, too, is obedient. He refuses at accept authority from any other source. Authorisation is authorisation to expound God's will and that includes Torah. Jesus has received his authorisation as Son of Man and judge to come. He has received authorisation to declare forgiveness of sins.

He has also been authorised to authorise others. Thus this strongly legal framework of thought determines the way Matthew understands the church. Jesus has Peter walk on the water (14:28–31). By this event Matthew foreshadows Jesus' authorisation of Peter as the foundation of the church which prevails against the gates of Hades. Jesus gives Peter the keys and the authority to bind and loose (16:16–19). The same authority is assumed for the local church community (18:18). The authorisation is understood in strongly legal terms and includes the right to interpret and administer God's will, in effect, Torah on earth. Matthew understands this authorisation in terms similar to what is claimed by the scribes. They, too, bind and loose and have the keys to the kingdom (23:13; cf. 23:2–4). Accordingly it is no surprise that Matthew's church also includes scribes (8:19; 12:51–52; 23:34). In 7:28–29 Matthew even portrays Jesus as being a scribe, contrasting his with the authority of "their (Jews') scribes". Matthew's scribes are to be seeing scribes, unlike the those outside his community who are blind guides (23:16, 24; cf. also 15:14). One day it is the disciples who will sit on twelve thrones judging the tribes of Israel (19:28). They have also been authorised for mission, first to Israel and then to the world. The mission is described in terms of making disciples and teaching. It all falls within a consistent framework.

We have shown that both John and Jesus shared a similar focus on judgement. John's definition of Jesus' role as judge to come matches Jesus' emphasis on judgement and his role as judge throughout the gospel. Also Matthew's understanding of both the authority of Jesus and of the church belongs within same legal framework of thought and is analogous to the way he described the role of the scribes who interpreted Torah. It is in this setting, therefore, that Matthew's approach to Torah is to be seen. Even before we discuss his particular application of Torah, this framework strongly suggests that Torah will have a central role in Matthew's thought.

The christology of Jesus' authority and, within it, his role as judge, provides the primary background for understanding how Matthew perceives Jesus' approach to the Law. It is important, however, that other christological motifs not be ignored. Here I am reluctant to speak of titles because motifs and titles do not always coincide. For instance, Matthew frequently uses Son of Man in describing Jesus' future role as judge, but not exclusively so. It is here that I want to comment on the relative significance of three further motifs.

The first may be identified as wisdom, sometimes as wisdom and Torah christology. We have noted that Matthew portrays both John and Jesus in relation to this wisdom. Referring to their activities, Jesus declares that wisdom will be vindicated by its behaviour (11:19). Matthew appears to understand this as saying that the deeds of John and Jesus will be shown in the long run to be the deeds of wisdom. The implication is that both can be seen as wisdom's envoys, like the prophets. Matthew is not assuming a spiritual hierarchy which would interpose wisdom as a being between God and Jesus. The claim to exclusive mutual knowledge between Jesus as Son and God as Father in 11:27b and therefore the ability to make God known echoes similar claims made of wisdom. The image of the wise man as God's Son appears also to be reflected in the passion narrative (Wisd 2:12–20). Jesus invitation to people in 11:28–30 to take on his yoke echoes the invitation spoken by prophets and sages in the name of wisdom. Its closest parallel is in Sirach where it is linked with Torah (Sir 51:23–27; cf. also "Where did he get this wisdom and these powers from?" Matt 13:54). Matthew also appears to use similar imagery in 23:34–39 and may envisage Jesus speaking with prophetic inspiration, as wisdom, of Jerusalem's rejection of the prophets.

Matthew is clearly aware of such imagery. Some have proposed that Matthew's use of wisdom typology implies he is laying the claim that Jesus is wisdom or Torah incarnate and see in this both the basis for continuity and for the freedom of Matthew's Jesus to change or add to the Law. Apart from not finding evidence of the latter, I find the claim that Matthew sees Jesus as wisdom or Torah incarnate not well founded. The use of such imagery is too isolated to indicate that Matthew understood it in this way. On the other hand, its presence in 11:16–30 and probably behind 23:34–39 does suggest Matthew is aware of it. Its use in 11:28–30 suggests he knew it already as wisdom imagery associated with Torah as in Sirach. It also stands in close relation to the notion of wisdom as the sender of prophets, as both 11:16–19 and 23:34–36 testify. However it does not have the prominence of the judge motif. It remains at the level of imagery.

Frequently, people appeal to Jesus' messiahship when discussing Matthew's account of Jesus and the Law, usually in order to explain Jesus' teachings either as a new Law or a new interpretation of the Law.[228] There is, at most, some evidence for the latter in relevant Jewish literature. It is more difficult, however, to find a specific link in Matthew between Jesus' messiahship and his interpretation of the Law. Messiahship is of major significance in Matthew from the beginning. Jesus' deeds are the deeds of the Messiah, but there are no particularly messianic traits associated with Jesus' exposition of the Law in the Sermon on the Mount. Leading up to the Sermon on the Mount the motif of Jesus, the Son of God, as judge has been far more prominent and on occasions of dispute over the Law Jesus refers to himself as Son of Man. At most, one might point to the juxtaposition which Matthew inherits from Mark of the question about the greatest commandments and Jesus' question about the Son of David (22:34–40,41–46; cf. Mark 12:28–34,35–37), but this is late in the narrative as a whole and shows no sign that Matthew is giving it special emphasis. Therefore, while not denying the importance of messiahship in Matthew, I do not find it having a prominent role in relation to Jesus' dealing with the Law. This indicates, I think, that we should be rather hesitant to appeal to traditions about messianic interpretation of Torah when discussing Matthew.

Finally mention should be made of a motif which makes its appearance but twice and then only by implication. In 18:20 and 28:20, both concerned with either decisions about Law or teaching of God's Law, Jesus promises

---

[228] See Schäfer, *Studien*, pp. 198–213; Allison, *New Moses*, pp. 185–190, 320–323.

his presence, in 18:20 even among two or three. The similarity between this promise and the claim that God's Shekinah accompanies even a few who study Torah makes it likely that Matthew's christology is influenced from this background. It reinforces again the Jewish context of Matthew's christology.

A motif which features directly in association with Jesus' teaching about the Law is that of Moses. Moses typology doubtless underlies Matthew's description of Jesus ascending the mountain to deliver the so-called Sermon on the Mount. Possibly imagery of Zion as the place of Torah instruction also plays a role. Moses typology may also play a role in 11:27 and 28–30, although wisdom Torah imagery is stronger. Moses typology also features in a number of other contexts in Matthew. There can be no doubt that it plays a role in Matthew's portrait of Jesus and the Law. It takes its place, however, within the wider context of Matthew's christology which is much more than a Moses prophet christology. The actions of Jesus, the divinely created Son of God, authorised as judge to come, do echo those of Moses. This is especially so, when he deals with the Law, because the Law was given through Moses. But the emphasis is on Jesus' authority, which far surpasses that of Moses, so that the typology must be seen as subordinate to the more dominant christology of the Son of God destined to be judge.

2.5.2 *Jesus' positive attitude towards the Law*

Jesus as judge and as the one who proclaims such judgement is, of necessity, also the one who declares law. This is the context for understanding the way Matthew relates Jesus to the Law. Hypothetically, Jesus might have proclaimed a new Law, replacing the old, or one quite independent of it. In reality, our text portrays Jesus in strong continuity with the written Torah and the prophets. He announces that he has come to uphold the Law and the Prophets and to ensure they are fulfilled (5:17), even to the finest detail (5:18) and threatens to demote any who teach otherwise (5:19). He claims to be teaching the Law and the Prophets in a nutshell (7:12; 22:40). He stands, with John, as the fulfilment towards which the Law and the Prophets looked forward (11:13).

Our review of the gospel material has shown that Matthew has Jesus offer a radical interpretation of the demands of Torah. From condemning actions of murder and adultery, he goes to the root of the problem, to condemn the attitudes which lie behind them (5:21–26,27–30). Only sexual immorality may justify divorce (5:31–32; 19:3–9). Honest communication removes all need for oaths (5:33–37). Fairness in relationships is transposed into generosity (5:38–42); selective loving becomes love for all, even enemies (5:43–48). While some of this may entail forbidding what written Torah allows (eg. oaths), Matthew, it seems, understands none of this as abolishing Torah or changing it. Jesus remains consistently within the strict parameters set by 5:17–19, understood qualitatively as a metaphor demanding total commitment to Torah.

This demand is characteristic of Matthew's portrait of Jesus throughout the gospel. Matthew deliberately removes signs that might indicate otherwise. Thus he has refashioned Mark's account of the discussion about divorce (10:2–12) to remove any sense of contrast between Jesus and Moses and has realigned Jesus' divorce logion so that it is now understood as a strict interpretation of Deut 24, not, in any way, its abrogation. Where Mark has Jesus explicitly reject Torah (7:1–23), Matthew has made significant changes in the direction of showing that Jesus differs with the Pharisees (and strongly) on matters of Torah interpretation, not over Torah provisions themselves. He also omits Mark's disparaging explanations and generalisations about the tradition of Jewish Law interpretation (eg. Mark 7:2–3,13b) or directs them so that they apply now only to certain abuses not to the traditions themselves (eg. the use of *corban*; cf. Mark 7:8). He deletes Mark's conclusion about Jesus "declaring all foods clean" (Mark 7:19c). He understands Jesus' contrast between what enters and what comes out of a person (15:11) as a statement about priorities: ethical attitudes and behaviours are much more important in determining purity than laws pertaining to food. In his hands the passage becomes an attack by Jesus on unnecessary demands (like hand washing) and on the abuse of *corban* (15:1–20), not on written Torah nor its tradition of interpretation in general.

Within the broader surrounding context of this passage, which includes the feedings, Mark had expanded the contrast between Jesus' teaching and that of the Pharisees. With considerable subtlety, exploiting the image of teaching as bread, Mark had used the two feeding stories to celebrate the inclusion of Gentiles with Israel in the feast of the kingdom. Jesus' rejection of food laws had made it possible. His crossing the barriers in response to the Syrophoenician woman and his presence in Gentile territory symbolised the inclusion. This skilful composition is a feature of Mark's gospel and central to understanding his view of Jesus' attitude towards the Law. It is all the more striking that Matthew has dismantled this achievement of Mark. Its centrepoint, the teaching on impurity, no longer rejects food laws. The encounter with the Canaanite woman now functions as an exception, a foil to Israel's unfaith. The barriers are affirmed, with only a hint that she, like the centurion, prefigures a future inclusion of Gentiles. The feedings celebrate fulfilment of Israel's hopes for Israel, not for Israel and the Gentiles, and function as miraculous vindication of Jesus and his teaching. Earlier Matthew had also dismantled the Markan symbolic contrast between the 12 year old Jewish girl and woman bleeding for 12 years (5:21–43), on the one hand, and the encounter with the Gentile demoniac in Gerasa (5:1–20), on the other. These kinds of changes reflect that Matthew was aware of what Mark had done and deliberately sabotaged it.

Matthew also dismantles Mark's development of the temple motif, which lies especially behind Mark 11–13 (but also features in the passion narrative, not least, in 14:58). Mark had portrayed the community of faith and prayer as the new temple, replacing the old, and had composed 11–13 to bring this message across. Here, too, Matthew disagrees with Mark. He dismantles the intercalation of the temple scene within the cursing of the fig tree (21:10–19; cf. Mark 11:11–21). He removes the juxtaposition of the temple and the community of prayer (21:12–13 and 21–22; cf. Mark 11:15–25). He changes the focus of the image of the building stone (Ps 118:22; 21:42–44; cf. Mark 12:10–11). He deletes the scribe's contrast between the great commandments and sacrifices (cf. Mark 12:28–34). Similarly, in the Jewish trial scene, Matthew has removed what in Mark is a disparaging contrast between the temple made with hands and the one not made with hands (26:61–62; cf. Mark 14:58). He has also reshaped the narrative of Jesus' crucifixion and death so that the focus now falls on Jesus the Son of God, borne witness to by apocalyptic signs, not on the rending of the temple curtain, which becomes just one in a series of signs (27:38–54; cf. Mark 15:29–39).

Matthew still has Jesus predict God's judgement on the temple, but removes any hint of cult critique which would then also be critique of Torah. Even in 12:6, where Matthew has Jesus claim that he represents "something greater than the temple", this is not disparagement of the temple. The discussion of temple tax (17:24–27) similarly reflects no cult criticism; in Matthew's day the issue had become one of not giving offence. It coheres with this that Matthew gives no indication that he sees Jesus as replacement of the temple. Where he might have done so, for instance, in his use of the name, Emmanuel, for Jesus (1:23), and in the last supper tradition (26:26–30; cf. 20:28), he is silent. Even the Sadducees and Pharisees in Matthew come to John not to dispute the validity of his rite compared with those established in the temple, but to submit themselves to it (3:7).

It is hard to find in Matthew any indication that he saw Jesus abrogating, let alone rejecting, parts of the Torah. In the controversies over the sabbath, Jesus calls on his own authority as Lord of the Sabbath, but does so in such a way as to support his own halakic argument and establish a principle for interpretation of sabbath law (12:1–8,9–13). He does not abrogate the sabbath as such. Like the charges of sorcery (9:32; 12:24–27), the allegations of blasphemy in the dispute over his declaration of forgiveness (9:3–8) and at his trial (26:65) are for Matthew manifestly false, not because he thinks Jesus is God, but because he knows he is the divinely created Son of God who is authorised to act on God's behalf. Similarly the dispute about Jesus' mixing with toll collectors and sinners (9:10–13) is for Matthew a matter of conflicting Torah interpretation. Even in reporting Jesus' words to a disciple to leave family burial duties to follow him (8:22), there is no indication that Matthew saw this as an abrogation.

The impression Matthew gives is rather that Jesus was Torah observant and expected that of his followers. This is the most natural reading of what he says in 5:17–20 and Matthew appears to understand it so. It is what we might expect of a son of Abraham, of the Jewish Messiah and of the judge to come. Already Joseph's righteousness (1:19) reflects commitment to Torah. Matthew's use of fulfilment quotations and of typology to link Jesus with Israel and Moses would lead to the same conclusion. Such obedience is demonstrated in the temptation account (4:1–13). It is reflected both in the Moses typology underlying the Sermon on the Mount and in the way Matthew has Jesus set his own teachings within the framework of statements about the Law and the Prophets (5:17; 7:12). Whether expounding the right understanding of commandments, including appropriate attitudes in sacrificing (5:23–24), almsgiving, prayer and fasting (6:1–18), or teaching about trust (6:25–34), for Matthew these represent extrapolation of Torah. It coheres with this that Jesus sends the leper to the temple (8:1–4), hesitates to enter a Gentile house (8:5–13), wears tassels (9:20; 14:36), restricts his disciples' mission, like his own (15:24) to Israel (10:5–6) and is suspiciously distant towards Samaritans and Gentiles (8:7; 15:21–28; cf. also 5:47; 6:7,32; 7:6; 18:17). He enjoins submission to scribes and Pharisees in power in his community (23:2–3) and his Torah observance appears to have had room for much that was practised in his day as extrapolation from Torah, including particulars concerning tithing (23:23), purifications (cf. 23:25–26), corpse impurity (cf. 23:24) and honour of the dead (cf. 23:27,29), even though he insists they must never take higher priority than the demand for justice, mercy and faith (23:23). He is sensitive to danger in speaking of flight on the sabbath (24:20), he celebrates Passover (26:17–19) and his close acquaintances observe the sabbath in preparing to come to his tomb (27:62–66).

Matthew's is a strongly Jewish ethos. The city is the holy city (4:5; 27:53); two witnesses make a valid case (the doubling of figures and of pericopes;

8:28–34; 9:29–31 with 20:29–34; 9:32–34 with 10:22–24); Joseph is constrained by marriage laws (1:19); the chief priests refuse blood money (27:3–10); "your sins are forgiven" must mean "God forgives them" (9:2–8); entering a Gentile centurion's house would be inappropriate (8:5–13); washings are a standard form of Jewish purification (cf. 27:24); levirite marriage laws make the Sadducees' question possible (22:25–33). The disciples are like a city on a hill, possibly an allusion to Zion (5:14); they will sit on twelve thrones, judging the tribes of Israel (19:28); they are the new keepers of the vineyard (21:33–44).

At this point we should also mention Matthew's silences. At a number of points Law issues would have arisen through Jesus' behaviour or the behaviour of the disciples. Jesus' contacts with the leper (8:1–4), with the women with a flow of blood (9:20–22), potentially with a corpse (9:23–26), and his presence in Gentile territory (8:28–34) are passed over without comment about the purity issues involved. Jewish values are assumed without comment. Similarly in the instructions to the disciples for their mission to Israel hospitality is mentioned and "worthy" hosts, but relevant issues of purity, such as untithed food, are passed over without mention (10:5–15).

Even more significant, because of its importance in early Christianity's disputes with(in) Judaism, is circumcision. Does Matthew's silence about circumcision when depicting the expansion of the mission to include Gentiles imply its abrogation? It seems not to be so. In any case, even if it were, Matthew, it seems, would probably not consider it a breach of Torah.

There is, therefore, no indication in Matthew's gospel of abrogation of circumcision, food, purity, or other ceremonial laws. Matthew consistently seeks to hold to the strong commitment to Torah obedience set out in 5:17–19. The issue with the Pharisees is not whether to uphold Torah, but how to do so and how to relate the authority of Jesus to the authority of Torah.

2.5.3 How Jesus interprets the Law

Within the context of Torah observance Matthew portrays Jesus as having a distinctive approach. We found important hints of this approach already in first sections of the gospel. The genealogy betrays a stance which challenges the norm: beside the men are maligned women (1:1–18). Matthew is siding with women and outsiders. Siding with outsiders is present also where Gentiles exemplify a positive response to Jesus (the magi, 2:1–12; the centurion, 8:5–13; the Canaanite woman, 15:21–28), but also in the positive responses of the leper (8:1–4), the woman with the flow of blood (9:20–22), the blind (9:29–31; 20:29–34; 21:14), and the many others who sought healing from Jesus or acclaimed him, not least the children in the temple (21:15–17). When Matthew has Jesus hail the "poor in spirit" blessed(5:3), he probably includes these. This stance is not primarily reactive – against the authorities; it is pro-active: a commitment to the needy. The same active understanding is reflected in the images of salt and light (5:13–16). This commitment determines Jesus' interpretation of Torah.

Joseph's response also throws light on the approach Matthew espouses (1:19). He chooses the most compassionate option in Torah, not trial, but quiet divorce. The same values are enshrined in the beatitudes. They includes promises to needy and suffering, but their primary focus is to hold out promises which will facilitate attitudes of lowliness, peacemaking and compassion (5:3–12). The righteousness and purity they espouse are to be understood in this way. The quantitative demand for total obedience to Torah must stand beside the qualitative demand for this kind of righteousness. In both senses it surpasses the righteousness of the scribes and Pharisees (5:20).

Much of Jesus' distinctive Torah interpretation in Matthew reflects the value of compassion for the needy. It is present in all of the antitheses and encompasses them by linking the demand for righteousness and for perfection with being like God who is portrayed as compassionate (5:20,45,48). At a number of other points we see this criterion operating. It is there when Matthew identifies the golden rule with the Law and Prophets (7:12). It appears to be present in the declaration of forgiveness in 9:2, although the focus is rather more on authority. It is certainly present in the use of Hosea 6:6, both in the context of Jesus' eating with toll collectors and sinners (9:13) and in the healing on the sabbath (12:7). In the latter such "doing good" is declared the principle for sabbath law interpretation (12:12). Compassion motivates Jesus' commission of the disciples (9:35), is reflected in the deeds of the Messiah (11:5) and in Jesus' invitation to people to bear his yoke (11:28–30). Its ease reflects the quality of his demands, not their lack of quantity. Gentleness is one of the themes in Isa 42 which Matthew uses to reaffirm Jesus' mission (12:19–20). As in Mark, Jesus' feeding of the multitudes is motivated by compassion (15:32). Matthew adds love for neighbour to the list of commandments detailed to the young man (19:19). In confrontation with the scribe he marks it out as central beside the command to love God (22:34–40). In the attack on the scribes and Pharisees he contrasts their preoccupation with minor tithing with the prior demand of mercy, justice and peace which they neglect (23:23). In bemoaning the effects of false prophets and their teaching in the days to come he bemoans above all the demise of love (24:12). Finally, in the depiction of the judgement scene, where he appears as judge, the criterion by which all will be judged is compassion (in action) or lack of it (25:31–46).

Determining that compassion is the criterion for Matthew's interpretation of the Law is not the same as saying that he replaced Torah by this command or used it to abrogate certain parts of the Law. The evidence cited above shows that Matthew had a place for a wide range of practices which were not directly ethical or related to compassion (eg. the sabbath, Passover, food laws). These included practices which went beyond the written law, whether as part of Jewish extrapolation of the Law or as distinctive practices linked with his own community. The latter include baptism (28:20) and doubtless the eucharist (26:26–29) and the distinctive Christian forms of almsgiving, prayer and fasting (6:1–18). Jesus also fasted (4:2). Matthew does not disparage the external. The issue is the coherence of the inward and outward, as he has John make clear to the Sadducees and Pharisees, who, in Matthew, come to be baptised (3:7–9).

This orientation towards love appears, in particular, in relation to three special concerns of Matthew: hypocrisy by those who make demands, slackening of demands, and abuse of power. The first, hypocrisy, is, above all, directed at the scribes and Pharisees (esp. ch. 23; but cf. 6:1–18, without this identification, but clearly directed at outsiders in the Jewish community). The second, slackening of demands, is with Christians who acclaim Christ and perform miracles, but fail to keep the commandments (7:21–23). They are like the girls without oil (25:8–12). They cry, "Lord, Lord," but fail to live lives of righteousness. They are probably also represented in the guest without the right garments (22:12–14) and among the goats in 25:31–46. Their leaders may well be the false prophets of 7:15–20 and 24:11–12 as a result of whose activity love wanes. 5:19 may also allude to them. The third concern, abuse of power, may be alluded to in Jesus' third temptation: power seeking. It appears strongly in the warnings of 24:45–51 and in Jesus' instructions to the disciples about humility (20:1–28; cf. also 18:12–35).

2.5.4 *The Authority of Jesus and the Authority of Torah*

Matthew leaves us then in little doubt about the basis of Jesus' interpretation of Torah. This must, however, be seen in a broader theological perspective. Matthew has not made love an absolute that overrides all else. God is the absolute authority for Matthew. Jesus is authorised to speak for God, not for himself. Similarly Torah is authority because it is given by God. Matthew appeals to reverence for what belongs to God and recognition of human limitation (5:34–37). Matthew sees behaviour in terms of doing God's will.

The two great commandments make this clear: both loving God and loving neighbour (22:34–40). Such righteousness includes not only almsgiving (6:1,2–4), but also fasting, prayer (6:5–18) and baptism (22:20). Things are to be said or done primarily because God commands them. This is evident even in the antitheses where the authority of Jesus' exposition assumes the underlying authority of Torah itself; they spell out how the command should be understood and upheld. But Matthew's Jesus also goes beyond juxtaposing love for God and love for neighbour. Integrating both is the command to be perfect as God is perfect (5:48). Matthew appeals to God's own loving to motivate human loving (5:45). God not only commands love; God loves. Thus Matthew can appeal to God's attitude and action towards people as exemplary and towards birds and plants as assuring (5:9,45; 6:25–34). Occasionally Matthew employs the common Jewish form of arguments, as in the sabbath controversies, but always closely associated with the criterion of need.

Matthew does not, therefore, separate the appeal to authority from the appeal to love. The appeal to love is subordinated to the former because it is God's will and reflects God's own attitude and action. Matthew's strictly theological perspective explains how threats and promises commonly reinforce commands. Matthew's perceptions also determine the way he sees Jesus applying love to various situations. At some points even what appear to be common prejudices support instruction, such as in the disparaging treatment of toll collectors and Gentiles (5:46–47).

To this point we have considered Jesus' attitude towards Torah in Matthew, by considering the criteria which governs his interpretation of it. But mostly Matthew has Jesus present both his interpretation of Torah and his own teaching with unargued authority. Jesus is the one who declares, "but I say to you." Matthew never gives the impression that Jesus is merely another interpreter of Torah, albeit, a better one. While he never portrays Jesus as contravening or abrogating Torah, he never suggests, either, that Jesus is subordinated to Torah. Matthew has made it clear that Jesus is the divinely created Son of God. He is the judge to come. This dominates the opening chapters and is fundamental for the whole, as we have seen. Reading Matthew, one does not have the impression that Jesus is primarily a Law interpreter. His role is much larger. Accordingly, only occasionally do disputes centre on issues of Torah interpretation.

Jesus is Israel's Messiah. He is the divinely created Son of God, come to call Israel to repentance in the light of the kingdom and its message of hope and judgement. These claims for Jesus mean that Matthew is holding two things together: the authority of Jesus and the authority of Torah. He clearly understands that they cohere. They cohere theologically: the one God who gave the Law and the Prophets, has sent the one of whom they spoke. Torah's authority and Jesus' authority are one. This is the import of his statement in 5:17–20. It shows that Matthew sees the whole in a salvation historical perspective. Jesus fulfils in both senses. He fulfils hopes and he acts in accordance with Torah to ensure it is done.

Such a juxtaposition of old and new raises many issues and possibilities. It is clear that Matthew portrays Jesus as not only interpreting Torah; he also gives much teaching which goes beyond or is not directly related to Torah and does so on his own authority. How does Matthew understand the relationship of this new person and these new teachings to Torah? The answer is almost certainly in terms of continuity. Even many of Jesus' new teachings he sets within the framework of Torah, as is evident in the Sermon on the Mount, where Matthew is probably responsible for the antithetical form. Falling outside of this category are primarily the mission instructions. All else is really application of Torah to new situations such as community life.

There is nevertheless potential tension in appealing to two kinds of authority. We see it in the sabbath controversies, where argument by analogy, appeal to compassion and appeal to authority combine. Is not the upshot, it is allowed to do good on the sabbath, almost a waiving of sabbath law? It falls short of that. The same tension is apparent in Jesus' demand that a would-be disciple abandon his obligation to bury his father (8:22). It is not uncommon for interpreters of the Law to acknowledge that in certain circumstances one part of the Law overrides another. But here the one part of the law is Jesus' demand. We have mentioned that one possible interpretation of Matthew's silence about circumcision is that he interpreted Jesus' mission command as overriding the demand for circumcision. Matthew obviously would not sense a contradiction between such demands and 5:18; but, on the other hand, we believe it more likely that Matthew still assumes circumcision.

Another area of major tension is declaration of forgiveness of sins, an authority exercised by John, Jesus and the community. It does not contravene Torah, but raises major problems about authorisation, which do not surface in Matthew's account of John's ministry, but then become a charge of blasphemy with Jesus (9:2–8). The extent of Jesus' authority, beyond any instance foreseen in the Law, evoked the charge. The appeal to authorisation does not completely meet the charge. Anyone can claim authorisation. The more Jesus' authority is emphasised, the easier it would become to move from having his demand override Law on some occasions to having it override Law on all occasions. In the apparently recent openness towards Gentiles,

Matthew would face the issue of circumcision and food and purity laws as had others. There is no sign that he has already resolved such issues, or, at least, done so by modifying Torah demands.

Unquestionably Matthew portrays Jesus as God's new initiative in fulfilment of Israel's hope set forth in the scriptures. Yet Matthew does not appear to play the new against the old. He omits Mark's programmatic account of the exorcism in the synagogue in which the crowds acclaim Jesus' "new teaching with authority" (Mark 1:21–28, esp. 27), preserving only the contrast between Jesus' authority and that of the scribes (Mark 1:22) and then as a contrast between Jesus and "their" scribes (7:29). Matthew does not appear to be using the sayings about old and new patches, old and new wine, to contrast Jesus' teachings with the teachings of Torah (9:17). The contrast seems to be rather contrasting interpretation. In the same vein the saying about the scribe of the kingdom who brings out both old and new (13:51–52) reflects Matthew's inclusiveness of both. Matthew emphasises continuity.

In Matthew's presentation of Jesus and the Law we find a consistent emphasis on continuity between the old and the new. The new consists in the fact that written Torah now receives a new expansive interpretation, incorporating a radical interpretation of the old in the direction of outlawing attitude as well as actions and setting all under the perspective of love for God and love for neighbour. Incidental changes or alterations which this exposition may entail do not amount, in Matthew's understanding, to abrogation of any part of Torah; attempts at abrogation are to be resisted, even though Matthew knows that some Christian teachers teach them. (5:19).

The relation between the old and the new authority becomes concrete in Matthew's rewriting of Mark's account of the rich man who approaches Jesus (19:16–22: cf. Mark 10:17–22). Matthew has enhanced the statement about the commandments. They are now more clearly identified as decalogue commandments; Matthew supplements them with the command to love one's neighbour. Where Mark has Jesus declare the man's observance of the commandments lacking in one thing, Matthew has the man ask Jesus what he still lacks. Matthew then has Jesus restate his earlier assertion of the man's goal in different terms: "If you want to be perfect" (19:21; cf. "If you want to enter eternal life" 19:17). Matthew is restating what he implied in the Sermon on the Mount: "Be perfect as your heavenly Father is perfect" (5:48). The command which follows, "Sell all you have and give to the poor and you will have treasure in heaven and come follow me," is not an extra, but an exposition of the original demand. Thus for this man selling all and giving to the poor echoes the command to love one's neighbour. Following

Jesus is, indeed additional, but only in the sense that following Jesus entails keeping the commandments and, conversely, there can be no true keeping of the commandments if they are not kept in accordance with their exposition by Jesus.

The passage is paradigmatic for Matthew's understanding of Jesus' attitude towards Torah. Matthew has Jesus shift the focus from his own authority to God as the ultimate authority. He sees God's authority undergirding the Law's authority as setting out the basis for entering eternal life. He characteristically puts the emphasis on ethical commandments of the decalogue supplemented by the love command which is his basis for interpreting them. In doing so he makes sure they are recognised as parts of the written Law. On the other hand, while he passes over other parts of the Law in silence, we know from elsewhere that he does not disregard them. While he juxtaposes Jesus' authority and Torah authority in such a way as to emphasise continuity, true Torah obedience must now include following Jesus, who demands complete fulfilment of its requirements in accordance with his exposition. The demand to follow Jesus is not derived from Torah, but from Jesus' own God given authority.

2.5.5 *Matthew's Jesus and the Law in new Perspective*

In research on Jesus' attitude towards the Law according to Matthew there have been some fundamental changes over recent years. One important aspect is a change in assumptions about what might or might not be deemed to fall outside of Judaism of the time. Clearly what even Barth and Hummel, for instance, still considered as abrogations of Torah (see the research review above), are now rightly seen as falling within the possibilities of Torah interpretation of the time. These radical interpretations accordingly play a lesser role in determining the nature of Matthew's relationship with wider Judaism. This strengthens the coherence of the case made by Barth, Hummel and Mohrlang, that Matthew's Jesus has a positive stance towards the whole of Torah, including its tradition of interpretation, and primarily attacks abuses of the latter and false priorities. This position is confirmed most recently also by Saldarini. As our analysis has shown, there is, therefore, no need nor justification for seeking coherence in Matthew by assigning some sayings to the baggage of tradition (Strecker, Trilling), by rationalising tensions as a deliberate ploy (Wong), by resolving them by making Jesus Torah incarnate (Suggs), or by imposing a christological interpretation on texts about the Law which either have them declare the Law no longer valid (Meier) or have them apply to Jesus' commands independent of the Law (Banks,

Menninger). Some tensions, such as the extent of the mission, resolve themselves within Matthew's salvation historical perspective (Levine).

Part of our changed understanding of Judaism of the time has also been the recognition of the centrality of the temple to Judaism, even after the destruction of the temple. It is therefore no longer possible to talk about the temple as though it is separate from Torah. This makes problematic the claim of Levine, that Matthew envisages abrogation of the temple.

The Judaism of Matthew's time is no longer seen as monolithic, as historians have reassessed the nature of the traditions about post 70 CE Judaism. As Saldarini acknowledges, in Matthew's setting the emerging strength of Pharisaic Judaism is apparent and Matthew reflects alienation from this form of Judaism which has assumed power in the community. Sociological studies confirm this analysis, according to which Matthew and his community are exhibiting the traits of a marginalised group (Stanton, Overman, Saldarini).

My review of Jesus' attitude towards the Law in Matthew fits well into this picture. Matthew has taken hold of Mark's account of Jesus which portrays him both as rejecting and as disparaging parts of Torah, purified the tradition of all such implications and, using the more strongly Torah favourable traditions found in Q and in independent material, has fashioned a gospel which primarily sets forth the authority of Jesus, but does so in a way which still holds place for Torah. He has done so for the Christian community. The attacks on the scribes and Pharisees are not directed at Christian Pharisees within the Christian movement (cf. Segal); they are identified too clearly with the Jewish leadership and with those who crucified Jesus for that. Nor are the attacks externally directed apologetic or polemic. They are for internal consumption, to strengthen identity and self understanding as the community comes to terms with its identity. Matthew's Jesus upholds Torah and sees his ministry in terms of both fulfilling the hopes of the Law and the Prophets and making sure that Torah is rightly understood and fully obeyed.

Matthew and his community lean heavily in the direction of interpreting Torah in accordance with the command to love and of subordinating ritual and cultic law to this priority, while not abandoning it. At the same time, obedience to authority is the foundation of Matthean thought in such a way that threat of judgement on those who dispute this authority becomes a central feature in Jesus' proclamation. This stands in a certain tension with the focus on love and mercy. But this is inevitable in a system which motivates primarily by appeal to authority. Something of this is present in all the gospels, but most strongly in Matthew. It reflects a certain way of understanding Torah. If Matthew seeks to uphold the authority of the whole Law, interpreted by central commands of love, Mark's Jesus calls for compassion which can dispense with parts of Torah. John will, as we shall see, dispense with Torah altogether; obedience is an aspect of personal allegiance. Luke is much closer to Matthew but from a less authoritarian perspective. For Matthew, Jesus is the judge to come, offering the grace of forgiveness and instruction, and warning of the consequences of rejection.

Chapter 3

Jesus' Attitude towards the Law according to Luke

3.1 Recent Research

Literature on the theme in Luke-Acts is extensive, even more than with Matthew. An appropriate starting point in modern times is the work of Hans Conzelmann,[1] who pioneered redaction-critical study of Luke. For Conzelmann, Luke's portrayal of the attitude towards the Law on the part of Jesus and of the early church must be seen in the context of Luke's salvation historical schema (p. 147). "Adherence to the Law is associated with a definite phase in the Church's development, during which it is strictly observed" (p. 147; similarly pp. 159–160). The Law belongs to a past epoch, even though it maintains its position as a principle (Luke 16:16–17; pp. 160–161). It can be used apologetically to expose Israel's failure, but it functions primarily with the Prophets as prophecy (p. 161). "The period of the Church's beginning is characterised by universal adherence to the Law" (p. 147). Hence the links with the temple, both early in Acts and in the ministry of Jesus. The Cornelius episode and the Apostolic Council show how it came about that Gentile Christianity no longer keeps the Law. Scripture justifies the move (Acts 15:16–17). The Law is not timeless, but belongs to redemptive history, preparing the way for the gospel, as Israel prepares the way for the Church. "The idea of the Law is not developed into a theological concept" (p. 160). The contrast made by Luke's Paul in Acts 13:38–39 rests on Luke's understanding of the Law as burdensome (p. 160).

Haenchen[2] speaks of Luke struggling throughout Acts with the problem

---

[1] H. Conzelmann, *The Theology of Saint Luke*, (London: Faber and Faber, 1960), first published as *Die Mitte der Zeit* (Tübingen: J. C. B. Mohr [Paul Siebeck], 1953, 2nd edn., 1957).

[2] E. Haenchen, *Die Apostelgeschichte*, KEKNT III, (Göttingen: Vandenhoeck und Ruprecht, 1968, 1st edn, 1956).

of the Law free Gentile mission (pp. 89–90). He sees the solution similarly to Conzelmann. According to Luke, the first Christians were faithful to Torah; then God intervened to institute the Gentile mission. But Luke is still concerned to show that the Law is not neglected. Paul continues to keep it and Gentiles keep what the Old Testament asks of them (p. 91). Otherwise they are freed from the Law which is burdensome (p. 100).

Both Conzelmann's and Haenchen's approach give the Law a function primarily within the framework of redemptive history. Its observance is a function of continuity, not a contemporary concern. Hübner[3] basically adopts the starting point of Conzelmann, but goes beyond his general observations to address a selection of key gospel passages about the Law (those dealing with the sabbath and with purity). Thus he believes that Luke portrays Jesus as Torah faithful and as not calling the Law into question, because Luke wants to show that this abrogation takes place at the time of the church (p. 208). He sees Luke wanting to avoid indications that Jesus abrogated Mosaic Law. Thus Luke omits Mark 10:2–9 and reinterprets 16:16 so that it no longer implies the Law ceases to have validity (p. 207). This allows Luke to portray the beginnings of Jesus' life in strongly Torah observant colours.

Hübner sees the vision in Acts 10 as abolishing ritual impurity as such, in relation both to foods and to people. This abolition was not in place, however, during the time of Jesus' earthly ministry. It applied only from the time of the risen Jesus, the period of the church (pp. 190–191). When Luke wrote the gospel, he already had this change in mind for Acts. Hübner argues that Luke's omission of Mark 7:1–23 as part of the great omission, 6:45 – 8:26, is partly because of doublets which it created with 11:37–41 and Acts 10 and partly because he wanted to locate the teaching about foods closer to where he deals with the Gentile mission (pp. 182–185). In the section on woes, where Luke deliberately distributes the woes between Pharisees and scribes according to their roles (p. 186), Luke's Jesus attacks the Pharisaic, not the OT understanding of purity in 11:38–41 (p. 188).

Thus, according to Hübner, Luke integrates the Law issue within his salvation historical scheme of promise and fulfilment (p. 208). Beside resur-

---

[3] Hübner, *Gesetz*. Luz, *Gesetz*, pp. 131–134, reflects the Conzelmann–Hübner line of approach. He sees the Law issue as less prominent in the Gospel than in Acts, where Luke is concerned to show God's purpose was to establish a Law free Gentile church and does so through Peter's report of his vision and encounter with Cornelius and through James' scriptural warrant for the move. The Law functions primarily in the context of promise and fulfilment for Luke and belongs to the past stages of salvation history. Luke is concerned also to show Paul and early Christian leaders as Torah observant to ward off criticisms against Paul.

rection, scripture fulfilment also legitimates Jesus' authority after Easter. Jesus fulfils the Law in the sense of fulfilling what it predicts (pp. 209–211). "Jesus is supported by the authority of the Law; he does not stand in authority over the Law" ("Jesus ist von der Autorität des Gesetzes getragen, nicht aber steht er autoritär über dem Gesetz" p. 211). Generally Hübner concludes that Luke used traditions which were in conflict (p. 207). On the one hand, they included the rejection of the *ius talionis* (6:27–30) and of divorce (16:18), although Luke does not directly refer to the Old Testament provisions they annul. On the other hand, Luke includes the conservative statement in 16:17, although Hübner believes that we must conclude from 16:18 that Luke cannot have given 16:17 its full weight (p. 207).

Hübner's study represents an advance, both in nuancing Conzelmann's approach, but also in addressing important selected texts. He assumes that Luke's texts, or at least the traditions which he uses, imply abrogation of some laws, even though Luke plays this down. As we shall see, these common assumptions are open to question. An adequate treatment must examine all the relevant material. Hübner also depends heavily on conclusions about the significance of Peter's vision and the council of Jerusalem.

A radically alternative approach which questions these assumptions came in the brief yet incisive challenge of Jervell.[4] He challenges the assumption that Luke had no interest in the Law except as a matter of history (p. 134). He raises the issue of the relevance of the Law issue for Jewish Christianity of Luke's time; in particular, for the issue of identity with Israel. He disputes that Luke assumes the church is the new Israel, replacing the old (p. 135). Luke, he claims, was dealing with more than history.

In doing so, Jervell notes that Luke's distinctive terminology in dealing with the Law is conservative and Jewish: "law of the Lord" and "law of the fathers" (Luke 2:23,24,39; Acts 22:3); "customs which Moses delivered to us" (Acts 6:14; 15:1; 21:21; 28:17); "Moses being preached" (Acts 15:21); "the living words" (Acts 7:38); "to speak against Moses, the law" (Acts 6:11,13,14; 21:21,28; 25:8; 28:17); and the comparative frequency of "the law of Moses" and "Moses" as a reference to the Law (pp. 136–137). Jervell argues that for Luke the Law is Israel's Law; his interest in Moses is primarily as Law giver. Luke "is most concerned about the ritual and ceremonial aspects of the law. The law is to him not essentially the moral law, but the mark of distinction between Jews and non-Jews" (p. 137). "The heart of the law is circumcision (Acts 15:1,5; 16:3)" (p. 137).

---

[4] J. Jervell, "The Law in Luke–Acts," in *Luke and the People of God. A New Look at Luke–Acts*, (Minneapolis: Augsburg, 1972), pp. 133–152, originally published in *HTR* 64 (1971), pp. 21–36.

Jervell notes the early Christians' allegiance to the temple and their focus on purity, expressed in strict separation from Gentiles, and that even Cornelius keeps all of the Law except circumcision. Similar strictness is reflected in the infancy narratives and in the absence of criticism of the Law in the gospel. Allegations of abrogation levelled at Stephen's Jesus are rejected by Luke as false (p. 138). The focus in rewriting the discussion about the greatest commandment (10:25–37; cf. Mark 12:28–34) and in Jesus' confrontation about tithing (11:37–41; cf. Matt 23:23) is no longer a hierarchy of values in the Law. "Love is not conceived as far more than sacrifices (Mark 12:33)" (p. 139). Luke avoids disparaging Moses on divorce; instead, Jesus' divorce teaching illustrates "the perpetual validity of the Mosaic law" (p. 139). Luke possibly knew Mark 7, but his own approach does not disparage the "customs of the fathers". Neither Luke's account of Jesus' words about cleansing cups and plates, where he highlights almsgiving, nor his treatment of the sabbath reflects anti-Law stances (p. 140). In the latter, Luke shows that the Law demands that people be set free. Torah observance runs through Luke and Acts. The claim that myriads of Jewish Christians are Law observant (Acts 21:21) would not make sense if Jesus had been shown as indicating otherwise (pp. 140–141).

For Jervell, then, Luke does not see the attitudes toward the Law reflected in the gospel as relics of the past. They are attitudes which Luke still espouses. Luke's represents the most conservative stand on the Law in the New Testament. His concern to defend Christians against allegations of neglect of the Law shows that the issue is not peripheral for him. Luke sees speaking against the Law as belonging together with speaking against Israel as the people of God and against the temple. He portrays James as concerned that people charged Saul with committing such a sin. In this context "this sin refers primarily to the ritual aspect (21:21ff.,28ff.)" (p. 141).

According to Jervell, "Luke's view of the law is bound up with his ecclesiology" (p. 143). Jewish Christians remain Israel; they are the true Israel who "believe *all things* in the law and the prophets, which includes the acceptance of the circumcised Messiah promised to the people and now come" (p. 142). The Gentiles are associated with Israel; the apostolic decree is merely an application of relevant sections of the Law which apply to them: "Perhaps Luke consciously refers to what Lev 17–18 demands from the 'strangers' that sojourn among Israelites" (p. 144). Gentiles are not free from the Law, only from the requirement of circumcision. He rejects Conzelmann's claim that, according to Luke, the church kept the Law only until the decree (p. 145), arguing that this would then justify the charges against Paul. "For Luke it is impossible that the law should be abrogated, replaced, or conceived as an epoch" (p. 145).

This is a thoroughgoing attempt to claim contemporary relevance of the Law in Luke's view both for Jewish and Gentile Christians. It belongs to Jervell's thesis that the inclusion of the Gentiles is an extension, not a replacement of Israel. Such claims about the Law find strong support in the gospel. They also seek to do justice to Luke's emphasis on Torah observance by Paul and by other Jewish Christians throughout Acts. But such an approach entails arguing a particular interpretation of Stephen's speech, Peter's vision, and the apostolic council. It also raises the question whether surrender of the command to circumcise Gentiles does not undermine the argument.

For Banks[5] the issue is related to Luke's primary focus. Jervell's position would make the Law central. In contrast, Banks writes: "Luke's foremost interest appears to be in the character of Jesus' ministry and its general relationship to Judaism rather than with the specific issue of the Law" (p. 107). This should not be lost sight of, as can easily happen in the study of particular themes. On the debates and controversies, he concludes: "In Luke, the issue of the Law and Pharisaic reaction is even further in the background and he appears to incorporate material dealing with it only when it serves to point up the saving preaching and healing ministry of Christ, and the corresponding stress on love and compassion in his teaching" (p. 172). Banks's interpretation, here, coheres with the way he handles 16:16–18 as at first sight "an anomaly in the gospel, for nowhere else have we found Lucan interest in the Law itself" (p. 219). The "retention of vv. 17–18 probably results from his faithfulness in preserving the tradition (cf. 14:2ff.) even when it does not yield to his particular concerns" (p. 220). This negation of 16:17–18 as traditional is unsatisfactory and reflects that Banks sees it countering his thesis, as, indeed, it does.

Overall he concludes that of the synoptic evangelists Luke is least concerned with the question of Jesus' attitude towards the Law (p. 246). He rejects the belief that Luke's omissions and reorientations together with 16:16–18 imply a fundamentally conservative attitude towards the Law on Luke's part (p. 247). Rather the demands of Christ's mission take priority over Law; in Jesus' ministry the Law is fulfilled, even though this is not to explicitly stated (p. 248). What Banks affirms about christology, however, is more convincing than what he says about the Law. The issue is how to take the christology seriously and yet relate it to what Luke actually says about the Law.

---

[5] Banks, *Law.*

Turner[6] addresses Luke's attitude towards the Law in the context of his
study of the sabbath and Sunday in Luke Acts. He finds that Luke's stance
in the sabbath controversies is to show that messianic work continues irrespective of the sabbath (pp. 100–108). This does not imply abrogation, but
is also not interpretation of sabbath law. Generally he argues that "Jesus'
attitude to the law seems to involve elements of affirmation and yet, simultaneously, degrees of abrogation" (p. 108). He cites seven main texts which
have been used to argue a conservative approach on Luke's part. The instruction to the leper (5:14) should be seen as necessary for his rehabilita-
tion and primarily as an occasion for witness (p. 109). The response to the
lawyer's question about eternal life (10:25), read in its context, transcends
the demands of the Law (pp. 109–110). The injunction not to neglect tithing
(11:42) may be simply rhetorical (p. 110). The reference to unclean graves
merely addresses the Pharisees on their own terms (p. 110). Of 16:16–18
and 16:29 he writes, "The law's eternal validity is certainly maintained, despite the dawning of the new age, but it has been transcended and changed
by being sucked up into the powerful vortex of Jesus' messianic teaching
and demands" (p. 110). As evidence for this he cites 16:18, which exceeds
the Law. Similarly he reads 18:18–21 as indicating that for Luke Jesus "transcends and surpasses" the Law (p. 111).

In addition, Turner makes the point that Luke's Jesus never enjoins study
of the Law; subordinates the Law to his own activities and in 11:41 applies
parallel insights to those of Mark 7:18–23 (p. 111). He reinforces his argument, that "Jesus fulfils and surpasses the law" (p. 111), with reference to
the predictive function of the Law and suggests that the best explanation of
the Law material in Luke is to see it in the context of the promise of the new
covenant. He acknowledges the difficulty in use of this concept, which appears only once, but argues, I think without success, that it should be assumed as the framework of Luke's thought (pp. 112–113).

He also takes Acts into his purview, criticising Jervell's thesis that Luke
sees both Jew and Gentile as belonging in the one people of God, Israel, and
having one Law. He argues that Luke intends Peter's thrice repeated vision
to state a change not only with respect to Gentiles but also, and partly as its
ground, a change in food laws (p. 116). He rightly calls into question the
adequacy of claiming that the apostolic decree represents Old Testament
Law applicable to Gentiles, since it is too selective (p. 117), but goes further, claiming that Acts 15 implies the council "made a break in principle

---

[6] M. M. B. Turner, "The Sabbath, Sunday, and the Law in Luke/Acts," in *From Sabbath to Lord's Day. A Biblical, Historical and Theological Investigation*, edited by D.
Carson, (Grand Rapids: Zondervan, 1982), pp. 99–157.

with the law" (p. 118). He sees Peter's statement in Acts 15:10–11 as implying critique of the Law in relation not only to Gentiles but also to Jews (pp.
118–119). "The mainspring of Luke's theology is not the restoration of Israel and the church's nomism, but the lordship of Christ by the Spirit and its
corollary, a new covenant people" (p. 119). Luke's portrait of a Law observant Paul is apologetically motivated by the rise of Jewish nationalism
and the resurgence of nomism in Jewish Christianity (pp. 122–123). On
sabbath observance he concludes that factors such as habit and religious
conservatism, social and religious community pressure, and the theological
conservatism in the Jerusalem leadership explain its continuance in Jewish
Christianity. An effect of this by association is that Gentiles would expect
that it was also incumbent on them (pp. 124–128).

Turner identifies many of the key texts and the effect they have on the
question as a whole. At a number of points our analysis will differ. Important in his presentation is that, like Banks, he acknowledges the full weight
of the new, the coming of the Messiah. But in doing so, does his thesis that
Jesus surpasses and fulfils the Law sufficiently take into account the way
Jesus engages the Law?

In his monograph on the Law in Luke Acts, Wilson[7] notes diversity both
within the Gospel and between the Gospel and Acts. The Gospel portrays
the figures of the infancy narratives and Jesus himself as Torah observant
(pp. 20–24). He notes that passages such as Luke 16:17; 10:25–28, and
16:29,31 imply that the Law is valid and that keeping the Law is the way to
salvation (pp. 13–18). The focus on Law obedience is, above all, love of
God and love of neighbour, but he shows that Luke does not condemn Pharisaic scruples, but only the neglect of essentials (11:42; p. 18). Jesus condemns failure to keep the Law (pp. 25–26). Yet, on the basis of the account
of Jesus' encounter with the rich ruler, Wilson argues that for Luke the Law
must be supplemented (pp. 27–29). "Care for the poor could have been seen
as fulfilment of the law, but the call for radical poverty and personal discipleship could not" (p. 28). Jesus' teaching in the sermon on the plain is not
portrayed as teaching of the Law, as in Matthew, but as Jesus' teaching beyond the Law (p. 29). Thus he argues that Luke 16:16–18 brings together
both the statement that the Law remains valid and that this validity is not
absolute, since 16:18 would have been understood as abrogation of the Law
(pp. 29–30, 43–51). He sees similar abrogation of the Law in the sabbath
controversies, in which, he claims, Jesus justifies transgression of the Law
on the basis of his authority (pp. 31–39).

---

[7] S. G. Wilson, *Luke and the Law*, SNTSMS 50, (Cambridge: CUP, 1983).

The Law is accordingly subordinate to Jesus (p. 35). Wilson writes: "It is not stated, of course, whether Jesus kept the laws on cleanliness and tithing, though it is implied that he did not" (p. 42). He notes the absence of major Markan passages on the Law (esp. Mark 7:1–23 and 10:2–12), but explains the former by its absence from Luke's version of Mark and the latter by Luke's lack of interest in issues of Law (pp. 52–55). 11:37–41, which has similarity with Mark 7, does not imply rejection of purity laws (p. 42). He concludes: "The variety of Lucan material on the law and the absence of any clear signs of reflection on it, in marked contrast to Matthew and Mark, suggest that the question of Jesus' attitude towards the law was not a problem for Luke or his readers, at least at the time he composed the Gospel" (p. 57). Thus Luke's lack of interest allows him to bring together in the gospel some inconsistency: Jesus upholds the Law as God's way to salvation, demands more than the Law, and also abrogates parts of it. In a careful study of Luke's terminology Wilson closes off the option of explaining these differences by playing off customs against laws (pp. 1–11). Rather Wilson lets the inconsistencies stand. The discrepancies are sharpened through interpreting the divorce logion, 16:18, and the sabbath controversies as representing abrogations, and in turn, by modifying the sense of 16:17 in that light.

Wilson sees a more consistent position in Acts. Here Luke is concerned with the Law, particularly in defending Paul against charges of being against the Law (pp. 63–67, 108–110). For Jewish Christians the Law is still in force. Even Peter's vision he sees not as abrogating Law; rather Luke understood it primarily as justification for Peter's contact with the Gentile centurion (pp. 68–70). "The effect of the vision is thus that Peter abandons his conservative (Palestinian?) position for a more liberal (diaspora-Jewish and Christian?) stance" (p. 71). Peter's speech hails Law observance but the assumption throughout (unlike in some passages of the gospel) is that keeping the Law is not enough (13:38–39; pp. 59–61).

According to Wilson, Luke is nowhere critical of Jewish Law observance in Acts (p. 61). The reference to its weight in 15:10–11 is not such that would imply it should not be shouldered (p. 60). In contrast to Jervell, Wilson argues strongly that the apostolic decree is not the application of Law to Gentiles on the basis of Lev 17–18, but reflects rather what Luke understands as an apostolic solution inspired by the Spirit and one which probably bore similarity to demands made of Gentiles by synagogues (pp. 74–101). He detects a tension between the rebuttal of the charge against Stephen, that he taught that Jesus would change laws (6:14), and Jesus' own attitude in the gospel, for instance, towards the sabbath (pp. 62–63, 111). He notes also a tension between Peter's vision and the decree, which would be removed if we read the decree in ethical terms with the Western text, but he sees this as a secondary development (pp. 98–101). He sees the effect of the decree being: "Gentiles are free from the law or 'customs of Moses' because they are not their customs but the customs of the Jews, Gentiles have their own religious and cultural roots which, like those of the Jews, can be taken up and fulfilled by the gospel of Christ" (p. 106).

Thus Wilson claims that "Luke's view of the law is that it is the *ethos* of a particular *ethnos*" (p. 103). He notes a tendency in Josephus, and to a lesser degree in Philo, to present Jewish Law to the world using the neutral language of "custom" (pp. 4–11, 103, 113). Wilson sees this as belonging together with a magnanimity towards pagan piety, as expressed in Acts 14:15–17, but also with the tendency among writers of the period to give brief summaries of the Law which focus on ethics (p. 103). The reduction of Jewish Law to the level of ethnic customs raises issues of how Luke might understand scriptural authority. He has shown that "customs" still mean the Law; are we to believe that the Luke of the positive statements about the Law in the gospel, which are probably stronger than Wilson allows, can now in Acts reduce such laws to the same level as the customs of any other people? Wilson notes the problem, especially in the fact that it does not cohere with Luke's use of the Law and the Prophets as scriptural authority in prediction; but he believes the tension is Luke's. Luke's primary focus in allusions to the Law and to Moses is in their predictive rather than their legal function (pp. 2–3, 56, 112). Are such inconsistencies to be explained by Luke's general lack of interest in the issue of Law and by the belief that even in Acts it is secondary to the defence of Paul? But inconsistency is Wilson's thesis. He writes: "That Luke has a consistent view throughout his two volumes must be proven rather than assumed, and there is always the danger that the more consistent view of Acts will be imposed on the Gospel" (p. 55).

Juel[8] is close to the view of Jervell. He notes that "Luke's Jesus is even more scrupulous about aspects of the law than Matthew's" (p. 103). Luke has Jesus avoid meetings with Gentiles (omitting the Syrophoenician encounter, having the centurion negotiate by delegation) and keeps Jesus away from Gentile territory. He assumes the Law forbids contacts with Gentiles (so Peter in Acts 10:28; p. 104)). Peter's vision is not about abrogating food laws, but accepting what God cleanses: Gentiles (p. 105). Even Cornelius is all but a Jew. The apostolic decree applies appropriate Torah to Gentiles

---

[8] D. Juel, *Luke–Acts. The Promise of History*, (Atlanta: Jn Knox, 1983).

(pp. 106–107). "Like the thousands of Jewish believers in Jerusalem who are zealous for the law, the whole church lives in observance of the commandments" (p. 107).

The opposite stance is reflected in Blomberg.[9] He begins by acknowledging the pious Jewish observance in the infancy narratives and among the earliest Christians, especially Paul, and Luke's omission or abbreviation of passages which in Mark or Matthew are critical of the Law (pp. 54–55). Among these he cites the omission of Mark 2:27; 7:1–23; 10:2–12. He also notes key summaries of proclamation, pre- and post-Easter, which are formulated in terms of Old Testament Law: Luke 10:25–28; 18:18–20; 16:17 with 16:29. With these he notes Luke's strong emphasis on fulfilment of predictions of the Law and the prophets in 24:27,44; Acts 3:22; 7:37 (pp. 55–56). But he goes on to contrast the views of Jervell and, "more nuanced", Wilson, on the one hand, and others like Banks, who, with most commentators "until recent years", concluded that the Law was not a significant issue for Luke or who see Luke's attitude towards the Law largely in terms of typological or midrashic concerns (p. 56). He strongly supports the latter view.

In terms of method Blomberg argues the value of considering the material sequentially (p. 56). He begins by emphasising that the infancy narratives, as well as demonstrating Law observant piety, also demonstrate expectation of change in the relationship between God's people and the Law; they, therefore, prepare the reader for such change (p. 57). Thus typological correspondence reinforces expectation of the new. Luke 3–4 declares the new has arrived. In 4:31 – 5:16 the announced miracles are in evidence. Reference to the Law (in sending the leper to the temple) is an incidental detail not stressed (p. 58). In 5:17 – 6:11 "Jesus repeatedly displays his authority over and above the oral and the written law" (p. 58). Sabbath law is broken with Jesus' authority (pp. 58–59). The focus on Jesus' authority continues in the sermon on the plain and beyond into ch. 7. "Through his first seven chapters Luke has set the pace for his entire work which, far from disclosing a nomistic theology, reveals Jesus breaking down legal barriers and shattering Jewish stereotypes rather indiscriminately" (p. 59). These are already major claims and reflect Banks' insistence that christology be taken seriously. The emphasis on looking at the material in sequence is one I also strongly espouse. However Blomberg's reading of the controversies, that in them Jesus abrogates Law, is open to question.

---

[9] C. L. Blomberg, "The Law in Luke–Acts," *JSNT* 22 (1984), pp. 53–80. His approach is followed most recently by D. Bock, *Luke 1:1 – 9:50*, (Grand Rapids: Baker, 1994), pp. 39–40.

Yet, argues Blomberg, Jesus is not antinomian; he affirms the double love commandment (10:25–28) and rebukes the Pharisees' neglect of justice and love of God (11:42; pp. 59–60). Potentially Jesus' statement about purity in 11:41 comes close to Mark's radical conclusion about abrogation in 7:19 and indicates that Luke's omission of Mark 7:1–23 within a larger omission should not be read as dissent (p. 60). Luke 16:16–17 implies that "the Law is valid in the age of this world. But with the end of this 'Weltzeit' and the arrival of the kingdom of God and the Son of Man, the Mosaic Law loses its validity and becomes superfluous" (p. 61). "The Law has not passed away without failing to accomplish everything for which it was intended" (p. 61). In this sense not one stroke of a letter has failed; all is being fulfilled. The divorce logion is thus an example of change, not continuity. Blomberg concurs with Banks that Luke understands the commandments in the account of the encounter between Jesus and the rich ruler, as a mere springboard for the demand to follow (p. 61). He suggests that the emphasis on the new (new covenant in the Lukan last supper) and on scripture fulfilment implies that "the requirements of the new age might in some way be different" (pp. 61–62). He urges that the demands of the Law should be seen as fulfilled in part by Jesus' ministry and sacrifice, while others are fulfilled in Christ's ethical demands (p. 62). Blomberg points to the prophetic hope that God's instruction would be proclaimed to the nations from Jerusalem (cf. Mic 4:1–2) and claims that through the development of the travel narrative and through his focus on Jerusalem Luke is claiming that Jesus' teaching has taken the place of the Law as God's instruction (p. 62).

In relation to the gospel, Blomberg assumes a number of things, all of which require further examination. They include: that Jesus abrogates the Law in 16:18; that 16:17 relates primarily to fulfilment of prediction; that 16:16 implies the Law belongs to a past epoch already from the point of view of Luke's Jesus; and that this fulfilment takes place in Jesus' death as a sacrifice and in his teaching focused on ethical commandments.

Blomberg interprets references to the disciples' links with the temple in Acts as incidental and without significance (p. 62). When Peter speaks of Jesus in terms of Deut 18:15–20, it has nothing to do with claiming continuity with the Law (pp. 62–63). Blomberg questions whether Luke intended that we should believe that all the allegations made against Stephen were false, suggesting 6:11, slander against Moses, not designated as false witness, may reflect genuine critique of the Law on Stephen's part (p. 63). Peter's vision confirms abolition of the food laws and of purity restrictions on table fellowship with Gentiles (p. 64). Luke envisages integrated Christian communities (as in Acts 19:8–10); this implies that God had "made no distinction between us and them" (Acts 15:9) and therefore that neither Jews nor Gentiles are obliged to be totally Torah observant (p. 64).

For Blomberg, Mark 7:19 reflects Peter's own reflections; he suggests the vision would not have been a surprise for him (p. 65). Luke, he believes, shows awareness of the issue in 11:41. Blomberg reads Paul's statement in 13:38–39 in the light of his letters as a declaration that forgiveness is solely on the basis of faith, by grace, through Christ alone (p. 65). The apostolic decree is not an application of Old Testament Law (pp. 65–66), but an appeal to Gentiles to show sensitivity to Jewish Christians. It is to be read as a caring strategy not a Torah commitment ("If you keep these, you will do well" 15:29); as such it is similar to Paul's strategy of being a Jew to Jews and a Gentile to Gentiles (1 Cor 9:19–20). Paul's circumcision of Timothy and his making a vow at Cenchreae do not reflect commitment to Law observance (pp. 66–67). The charges against Paul in Acts 21:21 and in the hearings which follow are, indeed, false, but only because they imply deliberate acts on Paul's part, not because he was Torah observant (pp. 67–68).

Blomberg concludes by noting that Luke does not distinguish oral and written Law. Jesus challenges both, as he challenges both ethical and ritual law (p. 69). Where people keep the Law in the Gospel and Acts, it is largely incidental (p. 70). Luke's focus is separation from Judaism and from Jewish Law. "Those who keep the Law throughout Luke's gospel do so rightly, from a salvation-historical perspective; the new covenant is not inaugurated until the complex of events stretching from the crucifixion to Pentecost" (p. 70). Blomberg's exegesis of 16:16–18 stands in some conflict with this. Luke sees all of the scriptures fulfilled in Christ. "For Luke, the law is preeminently prophecy" (pp. 70–71). On this basis Blomberg qualifies Wilson's observation that Luke has not integrated the predictive and prescriptive understanding of the Law (p. 71).

Thus Blomberg eradicates the Law issue by putting all the focus on prophecy; but will the texts stand this strain? Blomberg has reasserted the problems which Acts poses for interpreting Luke's view of the Law, especially, Stephen's stance, Peter's vision, the apostolic decree and the nature of Paul's Torah observance as strategy, not conviction. While he may be accused of reading Paul into Acts' picture of Paul, the questions Blomberg raises in this respect must remain central.

Within his work on the Jews in Luke-Acts, J. T. Sanders[10] argues that Luke's treatment of the Jews reflects his concern about ongoing tension between Gentile Christianity and Jewish Christianity in his own time. Phari-

---

[10] J. T. Sanders, *The Jews in Luke–Acts*, (London: SCM, 1987).

sees represent Jewish Christians. They are both associated with Jesus and criticised because of their insistence on Jewish *halakah*. They are not directly linked with those who killed Jesus, but ultimately put into the same category, for Luke champions the cause of Gentile Christianity against their attempts to impose Law observance on Gentiles. "In order to triumph over such an onslaught, Luke fires, as we Americans would say, shotgun blasts at his opponents and hits a rather wide target" (p. 315).

Within this context Sanders treats Luke's attitude towards the Law. He disputes Wilson's view that attitudes towards the Law and towards Pharisees vary from the Gospel to Acts (pp. 124–128). In particular, he disputes Wilson's exegesis of the sabbath passages and the statements about the Law in 16:16–18, arguing that Luke's consistent position is that Jesus attacks only *halakah*, never the Law itself (pp. 169, 172–173; 190–191, 194–195, 199–202). The apostolic decree represents for Luke the application of appropriate Law to the Gentiles, based directly or indirectly on Lev 17–18, and possibly also reflecting early stages of the Noachic laws (pp. 115–116, 121–122).

Emphasis at the beginning of the gospel and the beginning of Acts on observance of the Law reflects Luke's interest not in Law observance as such, but in linkage between eras (p. 117). The resolution of the apostolic council is not a compromise between Jewish and Gentile Christianity, but a choice in favour of Gentile Christianity. It is the result of recognising that dietary laws disagree with God's will, that God wills the Gentile mission and that the Law is burdensome (pp. 118–119). Luke is concerned "to invalidate the Jewish Christian position" (p. 119), not to provide a way for both communities to live together or have table fellowship (pp. 119–121). "The proper basis for association of Jews and Gentiles together in the church is, for Luke, God's abrogation of the Torah (except for those laws intended specifically for Gentiles)" (p. 121). "Luke is at pains to show how the early church, like the early Jesus, sought a home of piety and devotion in Judaism, but it would not. And so Jesus and the church turned from Judaism and the Jews to the Gentiles, and Christianity became a Gentile religion, and all the Jewish laws in the Torah were rendered null and void, and Torah-observant Jewish Christians became hypocrites" (p. 128; similarly pp. 129–131). Luke does not reckon with a mission to Jews after the conclusion of Acts and if any did convert their continued observance would be "a matter of personal preference" (p. 129).

The chief difficulty with Sanders's comments concerning the Law is his insistence on the Apostolic Council as a turning point not only for Gentiles but also, by implication, for Jews. This scheme has Jewish Christians Torah observant until that point; after that Torah observance seems not required or at least only optional. But this does not make sense of Paul or Luke's defence of Paul in the remainder of Acts. Would Sanders's Luke still have room for a Law observant Paul? Apparently not, and this is the problem. Sanders does not adequately explain how Luke can disown all of Jewish Christianity, yet still be concerned to portray Paul as genuinely Law observant.

Esler[11] argues "that, as far as Luke and his readers were concerned, the crucial factor in the establishment of the sectarian status of the Christian community *vis-à-vis* Judaism was the institution of table fellowship between Jews and Gentiles, and that this was still a live issue in his own community" (p. 111; and for the argument, itself, pp. 71–109). This necessitated Luke's serious treatment of the Law. He notes the importance of Law obedience in the infancy narratives, but also argues, as did Blomberg, that these portray a waiting for something more which implies that the Law "is incapable, *per se*, of bringing salvation to Israel" (p. 113). He points to Acts 13:38–39 as explicating this theme. But "the mission of Jesus represents the culmination of the law, not its abrogation" (p. 113). Those who are truly Torah observant accept Jesus; those who reject Jesus act contrary to the Law's hopes (pp. 113–114). Esler speaks of Luke nevertheless showing signs of sensing the incompatibility between a Christianity inclusive of Jews and Gentiles and Judaism. He sees Luke seeking to disguise it. This is a significant perspective which Esler uses to account for the inconsistencies which Wilson brought out.

He follows Wilson closely in showing how Luke portrays Jesus as both Torah observant (eg. with the lepers) and as upholding obedience to Torah as the way to life (Luke's conservative redaction in 10:25–28 of Mark 12:28–34). On the latter he notes that Luke may well mean this to be understood in the light of what he says elsewhere, namely, that more is required to achieve fulfilment of the commands of love than by relying only on the Law (p. 115). He sees Luke's transfiguration account as elevating the Law and the Prophets more highly than in Mark. Esler agrees with Banks and Wilson in emphasising the centrality of christology in the sabbath controversies, but rejects Wilson's view that sabbath was not an issue for Luke. He points out that only Luke notes the Torah conformity of the women who rested on the sabbath after Jesus' death (23:56). He counters Wilson also by referring to Acts 1:12 and 20:7–12, which reflect the sabbath's relevance for Luke's

---

[11] P. Esler, *Community and Gospel in Luke–Acts. The Social and Political Motivations of Lucan Theology*, SNTSMS 57, (Cambridge: CUP, 1987).

community (p. 116). He observes that in Luke's community Jews would observe the sabbath, while Gentiles would not, but all would gather on the sabbath evening, claiming both Jews and Gentiles would have been thus reassured, "the Jews because the Mosaic rule had not been revoked and the Gentiles because their failure to observe the sabbath was compatible with Jesus having transcended the Law, as well as being validated by Luke's account of the Apostolic dispensation in Acts 15" (p. 117). This assumes a rather sophisticated collusion between both groups in holding together such variant stances, perhaps too much so. He also sees Jesus respecting yet transcending Law in the encounter with the ruler (Luke 18:18–30).

Esler, like Wilson, speaks of Luke's Jesus challenging the Law. Thus he cites Jesus' refusal to let a disciple bury his father (9:60; p. 117), but, unlike Wilson, sees Luke being aware that this and statements about abandoning family would have constituted a breach of Law for Jews and were only to be relieved by claiming the Christian community as the true family (p. 118). He notes Jesus' attacks on Israel's leadership for not keeping the Law (10:29–37; 11:42–43; 16:19–31; pp. 118–120). He finds in Luke 16:17 a strong affirmation of the Law's validity. He sees in the juxtaposition of 16:17 and Jesus' divorce logion in 16:18 a ploy by Luke to argue that Jesus' words intensify rather than abrogate Torah. Luke is establishing a contrast between these demands and the failure of the Pharisees to keep the Law (16:15; pp. 120–121). Noting Luke's omission of Mark 7:1–30, he agrees with Hübner that Luke still addresses the issues it contains (in 11:37–41,44 and Acts 10), so that they remain important for Luke (pp. 121–122). Omission of Mark 10:3–9 was to avoid offending Jewish Christians with its disregard of Deut 24 and to spare Gentiles an unnecessary report of a Jewish controversy (p. 122).

Dealing with Acts, he notes early Torah observance which is echoed later in the portrait of Paul's observance of the Law in 21:20. In Acts 6–7 he claims that "some of the tensions as to the place of the law which can be detected in Luke's Gospel suddenly burst to the surface." (p. 123). The defence offered by Stephen to the charges made against him consists in part in a rejection of the right of the Sanhedrin to judge on two grounds; its forbears had rejected Moses and it fails to interpret Moses correctly. Abrogating the right to interpret Mosaic tradition to himself and the Christian community, Stephen also justifies his right to dispense with some of its provisions, a stance, which, Esler believes, matches Jesus' approach in the Gospel (pp. 123–125). He believes Luke wants us to see Stephen as attacking the temple and as representing an emerging group of Greek speaking Christian Jews whose acceptance of godfearers had evoked the accusations against

Stephen (pp. 145–161). The point of the Cornelius episode is the legitimising not of the Gentile mission, but of table fellowship (p. 96). Not the vision
but the direction of the Spirit persuades Peter to respond (10:20–21; pp. 93–
94). The pressure for circumcision was also because of the problem of table
fellowship between Jews and non-Jews. That is the focus of the apostolic
decree based on Lev 17–18. Such table fellowship which called into question the separateness of Israel remained an issue in Luke's community, which
included a significant component of Jews (pp. 93–109).

While Luke defends Paul as Torah faithful, this is, Esler claims, "the en-
ergetic advocacy of an impossible belief", even when based on Luke's portrait, because Paul regularly lived and ate with Gentiles (pp. 127–128). Esler
also concludes, in general terms, that "Luke's keen desire to depict Christian fidelity to the law runs up against the hard facts of the case" (p. 129).
Rejecting Wilson's claim that Luke is ambiguous or ambivalent, he argues
that Luke knows what he is doing and goes to "such great lengths to argue
what is ultimately an impossible case" because he wants "to satisfy some
need of the community for whom he wrote." He sees this need as that of "a
significant number of Jews in his community whose grip on the gospel was
under threat on account of criticism from Jews, or from conservative Jewish
Christians, that they were endangering the Jewish *ethnos* and the Mosaic
law" (p. 129).

Esler assumes inconsistencies: Jesus upholds and abrogates Law; the same
tension is reflected in Acts. While differing at points from Wilson on matters of interpretation, for instance, the sabbath, he upholds the fact of inconsistencies; they are not a sign of ambivalence, but reflect Luke's attempt to
defend the indefensible. Luke comes out as perhaps naive, perhaps deliberately deceptive, more the latter in Esler's account. This is an important
sociological attempt to account for perceived tensions. It is not without its
problems; its assumed reading is at many points open to question.

By contrast Vouga[12] believes that the issue of the Law is no longer alive
for Luke; hence Luke's omission of Mark 2:27 and his focus on Jesus as Son
of David (p. 52–61). Luke is not concerned with debate with Jews in his
contemporary world; they are ciphers for unbelief and belong to the past (p.
67). In the account of Jesus' encounter with the ruler (18:18–30) Luke sees
obedience to the ethical commandments of the decalogue and obedience to
Jesus' call to discipleship as one and the same; Jesus' demands thus take up
and complete the Law, which Luke sees as preliminary to the gospel (pp.
132–133). Luke's understanding of the Law as ethical demand reflects

---

[12] Vouga, *Loi*.

tendencies in Hellenistic Judaism and Hellenistic Jewish Christianity. In this sense he interprets the Law as the way to salvation in the discussion with the lawyer (10:25–28; pp. 152, 183, 187).

Issues of dispute with Judaism and within Christianity over Law have become a thing of the past (pp. 152, 186–187). The scriptures, including the Law, have become a source in which Christians may seek understanding of God's demands (pp. 151–152). Luke presupposes the Law as he presupposes Israel in relation to the church and its mission. Luke avoids giving the impression of a rupture between the periods of salvation history. The apostolic decree heralds a new phase in which the community is freed from the ritual prescriptions of the Law which had impeded it, but not from the Law itself (pp. 184–185). Vouga explains Luke's omission of Mark 7:1–23 is by pointing to the treatment of the issue in Acts 10 within the perspective of salvation history and by the presence of similar material in 11:39–52.

Luke's distance from the past controversies enables him to use the Law positively, but now understood within a solely ethical framework. Vouga's position closely reflects that of Hübner and Conzelmann. He limited his treatment, however, to controversies and the antitheses in the gospel tradition. This makes an assessment of the whole of Luke-Acts difficult. The result is that Vouga does not sufficiently take into account passages which are indicative of more contemporary interest in the Law and in its lasting authority than Vouga allows.

Klinghardt[13] dismisses Wilson's reason for Luke's interest in the Law in Acts, namely, defence of Paul against criticism, as without evidence (p. 7). He prefers Stegemann's explanation that conflict with Jews was taking place before pagan courts.[14] In discussing 16:16–18 in its broader context, he argues that Luke is challenging the notion of election based on an ethnic understanding of Abraham as father which had led to separation based on purity concerns (pp. 29, 31–36). This, together with abuses of wealth among Pharisees, is the target of Luke 16 (p. 39). In this, Luke belongs, argues Klinghardt, to a Jewish tradition of attacking such abuses.

While Luke upholds purity laws, he sees almsgiving as affording protection against contamination (pp. 29, 37, 50–51). Contamination comes especially through sexual immorality (p. 29). Klinghardt's claim for this function of almsgiving rests on texts which attribute some atoning function to

---

13 M. Klinghardt, *Gesetz und Volk Gottes. Das lukanische Verständnis des Gesetzes*, WUNT 32, (Tübingen: J. C. B. Mohr [Paul Siebeck], 1988).

14 W. Stegemann, *Zwischen Synagoge und Obrigkeit. Zur historischen Situation der lukanischen Christen*, FRLANT 152, (Göttingen: Vandenhoeck und Ruprecht, 1991).

almsgiving; but none of the texts cited support the notion that almsgiving makes one impregnable to uncleanness (p. 50 n. 20: Prov 10:2; 12:22; Dan 4:27 Theod.; Tob 4:10–11; Sir 3:14). The assumption that almsgiving renders one impregnable is not well supported. If it were so, would it not have much wider implications than just relations to Gentiles? It would effectively make one immune from all impurity, but Luke does not appear to assume such immunity and Klinghardt argues that Jewish Christians still observe the whole Law.

Klinghardt sees the Gentiles in Luke's community as mainly poor and the Jewish Christians as mainly rich. This gives particular weight to the challenge directed to the Pharisees (p. 67). These, within Luke's community, resist the influx of Gentiles and the financial burden they bring (p. 68). Klinghardt sees the Lukan community as still closely linked with Judaism, though in conflict with it, hence the strong association between attacks on the riches of Pharisees and application of the same concerns to Christian Pharisees.

Klinghardt sees Luke's Jesus consistently affirming the Law (so in 16:16–18). Forgiveness is not new, but newly institutionalised in baptism (Acts 13:38–39; pp. 99–107). He sees the apostolic decree as the application of those Torah provisions to Gentiles which relate to the eradication from the people of Israel of what pollutes (pp. 186–200, 205–206, 217). Luke assumes Gentile observance of much of the Law beside these commandments, as is testified of Cornelius, without however the demand of circumcision (pp. 205–206). For Klinghardt's position the possibility that uncircumcised Gentiles could be accepted within the Judaism of the time becomes very important.

For Luke the encounter with the ruler has become teaching not about becoming a disciple, but about being one. It reflects application of the Law, both in relation to outsiders and to insiders (almsgiving; p. 132). In the encounter with the lawyer he sees Luke influenced in two ways: by Jewish law and by contemporary values of the pagan world. In relation to the latter he emphasises friendship values, well illustrated in the parable of the Good Samaritan (pp. 152–155).

On the temple, Klinghardt notes the positive attitudes reflected in the narratives of Jesus' infancy and of the beginnings of the church (pp. 267–269, 273). The temple functions as a place of teaching and prayer (p. 273–274); it is linked with Gentile mission (Luke 2:25–32; Acts 22:17–21); pp. 276–279). But in general Klinghardt sees Luke accepting ethical and ritual, but not cultic law (p. 306). Thus he sees Luke rejecting the temple, but, otherwise, upholding the Law. The rejection of the temple, he argues, is rejection not of the Law, but of an interpretation of the Law. He sees this reflected in Stephen's speech, which, in turn, reflects a stream of Hellenistic Judaism, influenced by pagan cult criticism (pp. 284–303). Berger, with whom Klinghardt completed his dissertation, had earlier proposed the existence of such a tradition reaching into the first century.[15] It represented a universalist understanding of Law and was reflected in Hellenistic Judaism and influenced Luke at this point. This is a crucial hypothetical assumption for Klinghardt's construction, but its primary evidence is late (*PsClem Rec* I 33–39).[16] Furthermore it is not possible to separate cultic from ritual law as easily as Klinghardt assumes. Purity law is closely related to the temple. The problem is that Luke shows believers (including Paul) as also Torah observant in relation to the temple. Is Luke really disparaging the temple? Can it be that such an attitude underlies Luke-Acts, but surfaces only in the Stephen episode? Why then does Jesus send the lepers to the temple and have Mary make the offering for purification?

Klinghardt's work contains other speculation in relation to the Law, for instance, that Luke sees John the Baptist as the priestly Messiah coming before the royal messiah who will bring changes, in particular, in relation to purity laws (pp. 70–77, 80–82). His exegesis of the sabbath controversies is also speculative, arguing that Luke's concern is to vindicate Christian sabbath worship and the rights of itinerants to gather food (pp. 228–230, 234–240).

Klinghardt's attempt seeks to make sense of Luke's approach in the light of Luke's supposed situation. Its strength is that it argues for a coherent stance on Luke's part. It takes Luke's concern to stress Law observance seriously and does not treat it as a ploy to argue an unarguable case. Klinghardt tries to come to terms with a reading of Stephen as temple critical yet Torah faithful on the basis of the theory of an alternative interpretation in Jewish tradition which could dispense with the temple. The issue is important; the solution, too speculative. Klinghardt's image of Luke's community being like other sectarian communities of Judaism (he points to similarities with Qumran: the two Messiahs, use of Deut 18:15–18; distance from the cult; the shared possessions; concern with purity; p. 309) is helpful, but has he heard Banks's caution about the centrality of christology? A strength of his analysis is that, beside Jewish sensitivity, he draws attention to Luke's sensitivity to pagan thought of the time, especially pagan Hellenistic virtues (eg. shared possessions; sexual ethics; friendship).

---

[15] Berger, *Gesetzesauslegung*, pp. 16–31, 538.

[16] See the critique in H. Hübner, "Mark vii 1–23 und das 'Jüdisch–Hellenistische' Gesetzesverständnis," *NTS* 22 (1976), pp. 319–345, esp. 325–345. See also the discussion in my notes on Mark 10, above.

Fitzmyer[17] argues that for Luke the Law remains normative in all periods of salvation history. He points to the many instances of conscious Law observance in the infancy narratives (pp. 176–177). Jesus declares that keeping the commands to love God and neighbour is the way to eternal life (10:25–28; p. 177). Fitzmyer finds the Law's validity affirmed in Luke 16:17. He does not see 16:18, the saying on divorce, which follows in the "loose unit which does not hang well together", as intended by Luke to modify this (p. 180). The prohibition is "not directly contrary" to the Old Testament (pp. 197–198 n. 11). The parable of the rich man and Lazarus assumes the Law's validity (16:29,31), as do Jesus' instructions to the lepers (5:12–16; 17:11–19; p. 180). Fitzmyer also notes Luke's use of the Law (and the Prophets) in a predictive sense (p. 181). 16:16 implies both the Law's continuing validity and that it is now supplemented (pp. 180–181); similarly, the encounter with the rich ruler (18:18–25; pp. 181–182). Fitzmyer rejects Wilson's view that the sabbath controversies show Jesus challenging the Law (pp. 183–185); the issues are rather appropriate interpretation of sabbath law.

The period of the church is also marked by the continuing validity of the Law according to Fitzmyer. This is evident in early Christian practices, in Stephen's refutation of allegations to the contrary, and in the deliberate portrait of Paul as Law observant (pp. 185–186). The Law remains God's Law throughout. On Paul's claim at Pisidian Antioch (13:38–39), Fitzmyer argues that it amounts to a claim that "forgiveness is offered for *everything* – which the Law never offered" (p. 187), that is, it is a claim that the gospel supplements the Law. Will the text allow this? The Law and the Prophets provided for inclusion of Gentiles in the reconstituted Israel (pp. 194–195). For Fitzmyer, the apostolic decree is to be understood on the basis of Lev 17–18 (p. 202 n. 45). Here is a position, like Jervell's, emphasising coherence and consistency. It depends on particular interpretations of Acts passages which are central for any understanding of the Law. The same questions must be asked of Fitzmyer as those asked of Jervell. Are Stephen's speech, Peter's vision, the withdrawal of the Old Testament command to circumcise, adequately accounted for?

Syreeni[18] argues that Luke's attitude towards the Law "has its driving force 'from below', ie. from the concrete reality, which it takes for granted and seeks to interpret" (p. 136). That concrete reality is one "where the difference between Jews, Christians, and Gentiles is an observable fact" (p.

---

[17] J. A. Fitzmyer, "The Jewish People and the Mosaic Law in Luke–Acts," in *Luke the Theologian. Aspects of his Teaching*, (London: Chapman, 1989).

[18] Syreeni, "Matthew, Luke, and the Law."

139). Gentile Christians observe the apostolic decree which Luke sees as authorised by the apostles and also legitimated by its link with the Old Testament. They "do well" to keep it (15:29; pp. 139–140). Apart from that, the Law no longer played a role for Luke's Gentile community; Luke had no need to christianise it or demonise it. He treats it from the perspective of an outsider (p. 145). Therefore including conservative ideas about Torah "cost him nothing" (p. 146). Luke is concerned about salvation historical continuity between his own community and Israel. In that process he transforms Paul into a pious Jew and portrays Jesus as Torah observant. He deliberately omits or modifies Law critical tradition, so that Jesus preaches the validity of the Law as a way to salvation (Luke 16:29–31; 16:16–18; 10:25–28).

Syreeni sees, however, a change in Acts where Luke has Paul declare the Law to be deficient for salvation (13:38–39) and Peter declare it impossible to keep (15:10; pp. 146–147). Syreeni explains Luke's different positions partly by emphasising his concrete, person focused, attitude; for instance, he makes nothing of the implications of Peter's vision for food laws; it is about Gentiles (pp. 147–148). Partly Luke's salvation historical concern explains the inconsistencies: the Law functioned as promise and as basis for realising the need to repent; but, either way, faith in Christ is now necessary (pp. 149–150). "In all cases, however, a sensitive reader will realize that the Law of Moses and the traditions of Israel are treated with an outsider's unconcerned piety. The law was a respectable symbol from the past just as the Jerusalem temple was" (p. 150). This is another attempt to come to terms with inconsistencies. Here, it is achieved primarily on the basis of the Conzelmann model, which assumes that Luke is looking back as an outsider. The matters are so far past that he can afford inconsistencies. But does this give sufficient weight to the claims made for the Law, for instance, in 16:17?

Neyrey[19], whose contribution to understanding the symbolic world of Mark we have already noted, has done the same for Luke-Acts, with the same insightful sensitivity to purity and boundaries. In dealing with maps of places he espouses Dahl's interpretation of Acts 7:7, which identifies "this place" with Jesus (p. 286).[20] I find this unconvincing (see the discussion of

---

[19] J. H. Neyrey, "The Symbolic universe of Luke–Acts: 'They Turn the World Upside Down'," in *The Social World of Luke–Acts. Models for Interpretation*, edited by J. H. Neyrey, (Peabody: Hendrickson, 1991), pp. 271–304.

[20] N. A. Dahl, "The Story of Abraham in Luke–Acts," in *Jesus in the Memory of the Early Church*, (Minneapolis: Augsburg, 1976), pp. 66–86, here: 74–75.

the passage below). Thus Neyrey believes that the allegations against Stephen are, in fact, true: he spoke against the temple (p. 286); Neyrey then fails to deal adequately with the positive representations of the temple. He illustrates from Lukan material the disregard of maps of person, times and the body. In depicting Luke's defence of Jesus' purity, he draws attention to Jesus' pedigree and his occasional observances to show that he "was no stranger to the rules which denote covenant membership" (p. 289).

The analysis needs to go further and ask: what did his compliance imply? Neyrey shows that, as in Mark, Jesus is unaffected by crossing boundaries in relation to the unclean; Luke considered him a person authorised to cross them, a "limit breaker". Neyrey does approach the issues of scriptural authority for Luke, proffering the suggestions that Luke sees the Law and the Prophets primarily in their prophetic role and espouses distinctive lines of interpretation. Thus Luke favours a more open Abrahamic and Davidic understanding of covenant than a Mosaic Sinai one and generally upholds the notion of reversal as characteristic of God's action.

The avowedly abstract model is useful in the questions it raises, but Neyrey's application of it presents difficulties precisely because he does not discuss relevant passages exegetically, omits others (like Luke 16:16–18) or opts for particular exegetical interpretations (eg. on Stephen) which are very much in dispute.

Salo[21] employs Conzelmann's salvation historical scheme to provide a framework for his understanding of the Law (pp. 31–32). Accordingly, both in the time before Jesus, reflected in the infancy narratives, and in the time of Jesus' ministry, the Law remains the way to salvation. During Jesus' ministry it sometimes stands beside Jesus' own demands that people follow him and renounce possessions, although the latter is seen as an implication of the true practice of Torah (pp. 104–111, 152–157). At no point does Jesus contradict the Law; Luke even shows him respecting the observances of the Pharisees and having positive social contact with them. The issues of conflict are over abuses, especially failure to give to the poor and the imposition of unnecessary restrictions in interpreting the Law. Luke omits elements in his sources which suggest there are distinctions within the Law; all stipulations are to be obeyed (pp. 122–127). He also omits traditions which could create the impression that Jesus was critical of Torah, such as Mark 10:2–9 on divorce. Luke is forced not to omit the logion, 16:18, but seeks to

---

[21] K. Salo, *Luke's Treatment of the Law. A Redaction–Critical Investigation*, Annales Academiae Scientiarum Fennicae Dissertationes Humanarum Litterarum 57, (Helsinki: Suomalainen Tiedeakatemia, 1991).

convey the impression that it is not inconsistent with Torah (pp. 148–149). Salo assumes it was in tension with Torah. Apart from this, Salo assumes a consistent picture in the gospel.

According to Salo, Luke displays a certain ambivalence in handling the charges against Stephen (pp. 172–189). They are false, yet true. Jesus will destroy the temple and the laws will be changed. But, since that is yet to come in Luke's scheme, he has Stephen's speech not answer the charges. What it does do, according to Salo, is show Stephen as upholding the validity of the Law, while at the same time criticising the move from the tent of witness to the temple building. The criticism is not the building itself, but the corruption it came to house. Thus Luke is not anti cultic. Paul continues to use the temple. Luke does, however, see the financial institutions which it houses as the cause of abuse and has Stephen argue that worship of God cannot to be centralised in the temple in that way. The temple, including in its cultic role, still has a central role for Luke's players, but its destruction does not mean irrecoverable loss (pp 183–188). Luke also deliberately hides other Law issues which he knew had arisen with the Hellenists, such as circumcision and the acceptance of a eunuch, because he preserves the moment of change for the events surrounding Peter and the conference at Jerusalem (p. 189).

The vision of Peter functions in Acts primarily to declare Gentiles clean (pp. 205–207). Luke makes this jump possible by portraying Peter as thoroughly Law abiding and Cornelius, similarly, except for circumcision. Circumcision features indirectly in the narratives through mention of the circumcision party (p. 207). Salo credits Luke with considerable subtlety in handling the change. Thus, beside Cornelius' piety, Luke employs miraculous phenomena (angels, visions), to confirm the validity of the development (p. 207). But while the focus is that Gentiles have become clean, Luke deliberately composes Peter's vision, so that it is open to wider interpretation, including interpretation by some as abolishing food laws (pp. 208–210). He even makes this easier by inaccurately including some clean animals in those which appear. "The author skilfully and intentionally wishes to leave the vision open to different interpretations" (p. 210). Is this too subtle? It recalls Esler's claim about Luke deliberately allowing diverse interpretations of the sabbath. Salo sees Luke using Peter as a symbol of the right behaviour for Jewish Christians; it is to accept Gentile Christians and to enter their homes; for they have been cleansed and the coming of the Spirit on them proves that (pp. 211–214).

Salo argues that Acts 13:38–39 means "that Judaism, including its legal system, cannot provide an adequate basis for salvation" (p. 218). "Judaism does not (or at least not any more) possess salvation, but rather justification can be obtained only by becoming a believer" (p. 220). Luke avoids Paul's polemical references to the Law, because he believes Jewish Christians may observe the Law as long as they also follow Christ (p. 221). Salo relates this to the notion of Conzelmann that Acts 15 will bring a new epoch (p. 221). Here Salo understands Peter's statement about the burden of the Law as primarily negative. It is inconsistent with Luke's views elsewhere, since it questions the validity of the Law not only for Gentiles but also for Jews. Luke's own view is to be found in the speech of James (pp. 237–243). The change relates only to Gentiles. They are not obliged to keep the whole Torah but only what is set out in the apostolic decree (pp. 244–245). The decree is an important symbol in Luke's community and makes table fellowship possible. Luke understands it to be Mosaic, apostolic and legitimised by the Spirit (pp. 251–252). Salo's claim about Peter is remarkable in the light of the role he sees Peter playing for Luke. Is it credible?

Salo sees Luke addressing issues of his own community which included both Gentile and Jewish Christians, perhaps even in separate communities (p. 296). Luke is a Gentile with the knowledge of Jewish issues which one might expect of one living in a mixed community where most Jewish Christians were not first generation converts. Luke's inaccuracies are mainly related to the temple which had long been destroyed (so: Jesus' presentation in the temple; the timing of the Passover; and Paul's Nazirite vow. p. 297). Overall his concern is legitimation: of the Gentile church with only limited legal requirements and of table fellowship for Jewish-Christians (pp. 298–299). Luke's emphasis on such unity still leaves loose ends, such as how a Jewish Christian observing food laws could have fellowship with a Gentile, but here Peter's example serves as a model (pp. 300–301). But would a Peter who, according to Salo, issued such radical statements at the council, work as a model for such Jewish Christians? Salo sees much of Luke's understanding as being based on pragmatism, such as Paul's circumcision of Timothy, but also the apostolic decree (pp. 301–302).

This brief review can scarcely do justice to the authors involved, all of whom contribute significantly to the discussion. I have sought to outline only what I consider salient points for our discussion. At a number of points through this chapter I address the contributions in greater detail or deal with matters not noted in the review.

There are a number of issues which emerge from this survey. The first is the importance of considering all the material. Conzelmann's comments belong to a larger whole and remain at the level of generalisations. Works like those of Hübner, Banks, and Vouga limit themselves to certain passages and so do not do justice to much of the rest of the material. To some extent Klinghardt's work faces the same danger. His focus is on key texts: Luke 16:16–18; 18:18–31; 10:25–37; Acts 15; the sabbath controversies and the temple. Inevitably shorter works like those of Jervell, Blomberg, and Fitzmyer limit their scope, although the latter also provides the backing of a substantial commentary. Wilson's is the first monograph length treatment. He offers a systematic treatment of the gospel and then Acts, grouping the material in categories of being pro-Law, supplementing Law and Law critical. In this he is followed closely by Esler. But Wilson also acknowledges that this is problematic, noting that a treatment of the issue in the sequence in which they appear in Luke's writings has much for it (p. 12).

One of the strengths of Blomberg's article is that he argues on the basis of sequence, pointing out that the infancy narratives establish expectations as to how the rest of the gospel should be understood (p. 56). Salo, who disputes Blomberg's interpretation at this point (p. 62), also chooses a sequential treatment, but only in the sense that he deals with selected passages in the sequence in which they come in Luke. A proper sequential treatment can deal more adequately with issues such as salvation historical perspective in the material, upon which many have based their interpretations. As in treating the other gospels I have opted for the sequential approach and in doing so to review all of the material. This makes it easier to assess the relative significance of passages within the fabric as a whole by detecting their role within their broader narrative context. It is not the only way to proceed, as I have noted in my general introduction, but it does, I believe, offer distinct advantages, not least, because it differs from most treatments thus far.

Some basic questions relevant also for other chapters have a major impact on research findings here. How do we draw the line between what is interpretation of Law and what is abrogation of Law? This is particularly important in dealing, for instance, with the divorce logion, 16:18, and the sabbath controversies. Most specialist Judaists assure us that what we have before us need not be seen as abrogation, but belongs within the range of interpretation of the Law in the period.

Much more difficult are the areas of temple criticism and the abandonment of the requirement that Gentiles be circumcised. It is incontrovertible that Luke envisages a change, at least, in Law interpretation regarding circumcision. Is it to be seen as abandoning part of Torah or as just interpreting it differently and so remaining within the range of possible interpretation of the time? Klinghardt raises the latter issue directly (pp. 183–185); it continues to be a matter of some dispute.[22] With regard to temple criticism much hangs on the interpretation of Stephen's speech. Does it attack the temple in such a way as to attack the Law? Does it assume Law and temple can be separated and attack the temple from a Torah observant stance? Is such a separation thinkable, documented? Or is the attack not on the temple, but on abuses?

Also of great importance is the reading of Peter's vision. Is it to be read only in the light of its direct use in the narrative, to declare Cornelius (and Gentiles) clean? Does that constitute a breach of written Torah? Or would it be seen as coming within the bounds of dispute about interpretation of Torah? Or does Luke also assume abrogation of food laws as set out in the vision? Does it replace Mark 7 in Luke's scheme of things?

Acts bristles with controversial exegetical issues: others include the meaning of Paul's contrast in 13:38–39; of Peter's remarks about the weight of the Law in 15:10 (a confession of sin or an implicit attack on Torah?), of the apostolic decree (application of Torah to Gentiles? pragmatic laws? or advice of the apostles freeing Gentiles from Torah?).

There is a range of possible understandings concerning Luke's view.

1. Both Jewish and Gentile Christians still remain Law observant with regard to what applies to them (the change in demands with regard to circumcision being interpreted as compatible). Klinghardt's is closest to this position, especially if we were to understand what he says about the cultic as not contrary to Law.

2. Both Jewish and Gentile Christians still remain Law observant with regard to what applies to them, except for the imposition of circumcision, overridden by the Jerusalem decision (so Jervell, Juel, Fitzmyer).

3. Jewish Christians remain Torah observant and Gentile Christians are to keep only the selection of the Old Testament laws which apply to Gentiles, ie. those set out in the apostolic decree, and the ethical commandments (Salo).

4. Jewish Christians remain Torah observant and, as a result of the Jerusalem council, Gentile Christians are free from the requirement

---

[22] See J. L. Nolland, "Uncircumcised Proselytes?" *JSJ* 12 (1981), pp. 173–194; J. J. Collins, "A Symbol of Otherness: Circumcision and Salvation in the First Century," in *To See Ourselves as Others See Us*, edited by J. Neusner and E. S. Frerichs, (Chico: Scholars, 1985), pp. 163–186; B. Wander, *Trennungsprozesse zwischen Frühem Christentum und Judentum im 1. Jh. n. Chr.*, Texte u. Arbeiten z. Neutestamentlichen Zeitalter 16, (Tübingen: Francke Verlag, 1994), pp. 168–171

to obey Torah, but are enjoined to live according to the apostolic decree in sensitivity to Jewish Christians and to keep ethical commandments (Wilson, Esler).

5. Jewish Christians and Gentile Christians are no longer bound to keep the Law since the Jerusalem Council, but only Jesus' teaching, which takes up and fulfils all relevant Law requirements; the decree is an injunction to sensitivity (Blomberg, and, differently, J. T. Sanders).

As far as the attitude of Luke's Jesus is concerned, the range also varies. The main options are that Jesus was consistently Torah observant and enjoined Torah observance, that he was above Torah and that his Jesus' teaching and behaviour was sometimes Torah observant and sometimes not. The salvation historical approach sometimes sees Jesus' and Jewish Christian Law observance as persisting only up until the apostolic council. Others argue that Jewish Christian Law observance persisted. It is possible to dismiss the later developments in Acts as belonging to a new stage in history. Alternatively one could argue that they reflect what Luke must have thought was also the mind of Jesus during his ministry and interpret passages like 16:16–18 accordingly. The effect this has will depend on how one assesses the developments in Acts; are they consistent with Torah observance or not?

A fundamental issue is whether one assumes coherence within the double work. Wilson warns that it must be demonstrated. That can be approached from the other side; assume consistency in an author, until shown otherwise! I believe this approach to be better. Great caution is appropriate when people suggest that the author is only passing on a tradition (Banks), pleading an unwinnable case which blinds him to contradictions (Esler), lacking interest and therefore allowing inconsistencies to stand (Wilson), or deliberately creating ambiguities for community political reasons (Esler, Salo). We must also raise questions about the extent to which it is possible to explain inconsistencies through Conzelmann's scheme of salvation history. Is the Torah observance of the first Christians and of Jesus' forebears and Jesus himself adequately explained as a relic of a past epoch? It would be easier to do so if we did not have indications that appear to give permanent validity to the Law. While the assumption of coherence must, to my mind, be the starting point, it should never be used to force coherence on the text where it is not present. Do we have such occasions in Luke's doublework?

Finally, consideration of the Law in Luke must take into account that, as with the other gospel writers, Luke is writing primarily about Jesus, not about the Law. He is writing about Jesus as God's divinely created Son who

bears his ultimate authority. To discuss Law issues without relating the issue of the Law's authority to that of Jesus is to remain in a vacuum. This is
the strength of the argument of Banks and Turner. There are other major
issues which impinge on our understanding of Luke's approach to the Law.
For instance, if Luke's eschatology has a place for the restoration of Jerusalem, or if he envisages Israel as expanded rather than expended by the Gentile mission, this, in turn, has implications for how we will assess the role of
the Law given by God to Israel. One way to ensure respect for this broader
context is to examine the double work as it stands in sequence and seek to
sense the issue of Law within the whole story as it unfolds.

3.2 Luke 1:1 – 9:50 in Review

3.2.1 Luke 1:1 – 4:13

The Lukan infancy narratives of John and Jesus are strong in Jewish colouring. The expressions of hope with regard to the two are formulated in strongly
Jewish terms (1:68–79,51–55,30–33). Zechariah praises God that he is re-
deeming his people (1:68), saving them from their enemies (1:71,74). In
relation to John, Zechariah acclaims that he will "give knowledge of salvation to his people in the forgiveness of sins" (1:77). This is a prophecy of
John's baptism (to which we shall return below).[23] Mary proclaims that God
will depose the mighty, lift up the lowly and come to Israel's aid (1:52,54).
Simeon declares that Jesus is to be a light for the Gentiles (2:29–32). Luke
portrays Simeon as "looking for the consolation of Israel" (2:25). Anna
reports her joy to people who were similarly "looking for the redemption of
Israel" (2:38). Luke has portrayed these hopes as primarily about to find
fulfilment in Jesus, but also in events of Acts. For Luke, as we shall see, the
hopes for Israel's liberation expressed in the infancy narratives are not fully
exhausted by the first coming of Jesus, but remain part of his eschatology
(cf. Acts 1:6).[24] Such hopes, in any case, no more imply change or abroga-

---

[23] As we shall see, Luke does not see John's baptism as in conflict with the Law. W.
Wink, *John the Baptist in the Gospel Tradition*, SNTSMS 7, (Cambridge: CUP, 1968), pp.
72–79, argues that Luke sees John the Baptist as Messiah of Aaron. Against this: Brown,
Birth, pp. 268–269, who rejects the suggestion, because it assumes there existed at the
time such an association with the Elijah expectation, does not match expectations evident
in Qumran and because Luke makes nothing of John's priesthood.

[24] See the overview of evidence in the conclusion of this chapter. See also, for instance, M. Bachmann, *Jerusalem und der Tempel. Die geographisch–theologischen
Elemente in der lukanischen Sicht des jüdischen Kultzentrums*, BWANT 109, (Stuttgart:

tion of the Law, as Blomberg suggests,[25] than they do when they are expressed elsewhere in Jewish literature.

Not only the hopes, but also the setting reflects strong Jewish piety and faithful Law observance. Sometimes this is incidental, in keeping with the strongly Jewish context. Thus Luke portrays Zechariah in his priestly duty in the sanctuary of the temple (1:5–23).[26] Mary and Joseph are in the first stage of Jewish marriage when she falls pregnant as a result of divine intervention (1:26–27). John and Jesus are circumcised on the eighth day (1:59; 2:21a). Luke relates both occasions as the setting for the naming (1:59–64; 2:21a).[27] Simeon and Anna, people led by the Spirit, are both associated with the temple (2:25–27,36–38).

But sometimes Luke puts the fact of Law observance directly in the foreground. Thus he highlights that Joseph and Mary observe the purity laws after childbirth and make the offering of the first fruits (2:22–24), citing appropriate portions of the Law (Ex 13:2,12,15; Lev 5:11; 12:8).[28] Luke repeats reference to these actions as Law observant in 2:27 and again in 2:39.[29] At the same time his eagerness to emphasise fulfilment does not prevent some inaccuracy: only Mary needs purification, but Luke speaks of *their* purification; only the offering of the first fruits requires that people go to the temple, not purification; Luke also omits any mention of payment of the five shekels to redeem the child (cf. Nu 18:15–16).[30]

Kohlhammer, 1980), pp. 365–369, who emphasises that the temple and Jerusalem are the focus of Luke's eschatological hope, especially as expressed in the infancy narratives (cf. 2:25,37–38,49).

[25] Cf. Blomberg, "Law," p. 57.

[26] Salo, *Law*, p. 48, notes Luke's stress on Zechariah and Elizabeth as examples of Jewish piety who eagerly and joyfully obeyed the Law, noting that this coheres with an appreciation on Luke's part of covenantal nomism. Brown, *Birth*, p. 280, suggests that Zechariah's failure to bless the people is matched by Jesus' blessing of the disciples in 24:50–52.

[27] On the uncertainty about the link between circumcision and name giving see Brown, *Birth*, p. 369.

[28] Salo, *Law*, pp. 49–52, argues that Luke himself has created 2:21–24 which reports Jesus' circumcision and naming, and the presentation and purification.

[29] J. A. Fitzmyer, *The Gospel according to Luke*, AB 2, (New York: Doubleday, 1981), p. 421, comments that Luke's repeated emphasis on the Law here (2:22a,23a,24a,27,39) is "to stress fidelity to the Mosaic Law. The new form of God's salvation comes with obedience to this Law."

[30] Brown, *Birth*, pp. 447–450, notes these tensions within 2:21–24. He suggests Luke's account is influenced both by his use of Samuel typology and by his own lack of adequate knowledge. Salo, *Law*, pp. 52–53, suggests Luke's report of "their" purification is either an inaccuracy or is intending to show even greater piety than the Law demanded. Luke's inaccuracy here and in the omission of the payment of 5 shekels to redeem the first born

Luke has Mary and Joseph also make pilgrimage to the Passover (2:41–51).[31] Jesus, the boy, is a child prodigy in the temple, listening to the teachers and asking them questions (2:46). Later there will be conflict. Here there is no hint of disapproval or disdain for the temple. The picture Luke succeeds in creating is that of truly pious Jews, Torah observant, being caught up into the divine plan, in fulfilment of Israel's hopes.[32]

In introducing John's ministry in 3:1–6, Luke has rewritten and expanded his Markan source in such a way that the narrative has strong echoes of what was said in the infancy accounts. This includes the sense of commitment to true piety understood to include living in accordance with Torah. John is identified again as the son of Zechariah (3:2). He comes preaching baptism for the forgiveness of sins (3:3; cf. 1:77). Luke, who has already used Malachi 3:1 (1:76), which formed part of Mark's opening prophetic text (Mark 1:2–3), instead expands the Isa 40 part of that text by two additional verses. Mark read: "The voice of one crying in the wilderness, 'Prepare the way of

---

(Nu 18:15–16) reflect not ignorance of the Law on Luke's part, he suggests, but has to do with his concern to convey the general impression of Law observance rather than concern with detail (pp. 53–55). J. Nolland, *Luke*, Word Biblical Commentary 35A, (Dallas: Word, 1989), pp. 110, 113, 117, similarly emphasises that Luke wants to show Jesus fulfilling the law. "Their" purification may reflect that Luke sees it as a family matter or that he stands under the influence of Hellenistic thought according to which both were unclean (p. 117). F. Bovon, *Das Evangelium nach Lukas (Lk 1,1 – 9,50)*, EKK III/1, (Zurich: Benziger; Neukirchen–Vluyn: Neukirchener, 1989), p. 140, links the presentation of Jesus with the notion of holiness (1:35) and interprets the scene in terms of Jesus' offering to the Father and the transfer of the holiness of the temple to Jesus. This reads far too much into the passage. Accordingly he sees the emphasis on the Law as just to make the transition smooth from the old to the new. F. W. Horn, *Glaube und Handeln in der Theologie des Lukas*, (Göttingen: Vandenhoeck und Ruprecht, 1983), p. 273, believes Luke's inaccuracies about the Law's practices are indications of his distance from the Law; similarly F. G. Downing, "Law and custom: Luke–Acts and late Hellenism," in *Law and Religion. Essays on the Place of the Law in Israel and Early Christianity*, edited by B. Lindars, (Cambridge: Clarke, 1988), pp. 148–158, here: 149.

[31] So Salo, *Law*, pp. 55–59, as Luke's redactional work.

[32] Salo, *Law*, p. 62, writes: "Nowhere in Luke–Acts do we meet so much legal terminology packed so closely together. We do not have any criticism of the law or hints of it being abolished. We find no hint that the coming new age would mean any change with respect to the law. Obeying the ordinances was a proper way of serving God. If changes in the legal practices should come, readers are quite unprepared for them" (p. 62; contrast Blomberg, "Law," p. 57). The coming change is not in the role of Law but in salvation (p. 63). Cf. Brown, *Birth*, pp. 236, who sees Luke's purpose in the infancy narratives as primarily to assure his Gentile readers of salvation historical continuity. Luke is not appealing to Jewish Christians. His view of the temple and its ritual is nostalgic, rather than motivated by conflicts with Jews or Jewish Christians of his day. His nostalgia may also be reflected in his use of songs of the poor from the Jerusalem Jewish Christian community (pp. 353–354). But does nostalgia and salvation history suffice?

the Lord! Make his paths straight'" (Isa 40:3). Luke adds Isa 40:4–5, "Every valley shall be filled and every mountain and hill made low; the winding paths will be straight and the rough made smooth. And all flesh shall see the salvation of God." The result is that they come to a climax with the hope for "the salvation of God", a major motif of the infancy narratives.

In the infancy narratives Luke had already defined John's role as turning the people of Israel back to God in the spirit of Elijah (1:16–17); here, therefore, his words of warning to the crowd (3:7–9) and his exhortation to ethical behaviour (3:10–14) are understood as part of that eschatological task. In Luke, John's preaching aims at a threefold response: repentance, baptism, and changed living. They belong together as a whole; hence John's warnings and exhortations which undercut a sense of security based on being children of Abraham (cf. John 8:33–39). Not ethnicity but ethical practice counts.

People prepared to change their ways and receive the cleansing baptism receive God's forgiveness. There are two issues here in relation to the Law: forgiveness and election. Luke shows no sense that the promise of God's forgiveness for those who repent contradicted provisions of Law, although Luke knows from Mark that the chief priests, scribes, and elders of the people were uncomfortable with John's claims (Luke 20:1–8). Rather, in the light of the narrative thus far, hearers would understand such sins to be sins against the Law and the accompanying exhortations to be expositions of God's Law. With regard to election, what John taught belonged within the biblical tradition of judgement, reflected strongly in Deuteronomy. The allusion to making children of Abraham from stones may in Luke be more than a strong assertion of God's freedom; it may already hint at inclusion of others in the family of Abraham apart from those who are his descendants.

The exhortations in 3:10–14 envisage three groups: the crowds, the toll collectors and soldiers. Possibly they are all already sons of Abraham. Possibly Luke would mean his hearers to see soldiers as Gentile, though originally they would probably have been Jews in the service of Antipas. In any case we find the same issue here as in the account of Jesus' preaching at Nazareth (4:16–30): a hint of inclusion not only of outcasts and marginalised, but also of Gentiles. We shall return to the Law issue there.

The infancy narratives had also said much about Jesus' role as the divine saviour, so that when John predicts his coming as judge (3:16–17), his words are to be heard within the context of this broader understanding. They do not have the same definitive role which they have in Matthew's account, though they include judgement as one of his tasks. Luke even introduces them with the report that some had wondered whether John was the Messiah

(3:15). The effect is to recall that messianic christology of the infancy narratives and to cause the hearer to understand the statements which follow in 3:16–17 in the light of it.

In addition, Luke will have the promise of baptism with the Spirit fulfilled on the Day of Pentecost (Acts 1:5), not in an act of future judgement. Luke's portrait of the role of the Spirit at the beginning of Jesus' ministry doubtless has this correspondence with the beginnings of the church in mind. Accordingly, Luke subordinates the act of baptism to the reception of the Spirit and to the heavenly acclamation which reaffirms the identity of Jesus. According to Luke, this means affirming that he is the Son of God by divine creation through the virginal conception (3:21–22). It is significant, and characteristic of Luke, that he adds that Jesus was praying at his baptism. This reinforces the continuity with the praying pious of the infancy narratives. After the baptism, Luke is also concerned to reaffirm Jesus' solidarity both with Israel's and with humanity's past and does so through his version of the genealogy (3:23–38). There is thus a strong sense of continuity with faithful Israel as portrayed in the infancy narratives.

Luke's focus on Jesus as bearer of the Spirit ("filled with the Holy Spirit" 4:1) and as Son of God continues in 4:1–13 where both Jesus' exposure to temptation and his victory in temptation demonstrates his possession of the Spirit. "If you are the Son of God" introduces the first and third temptation in Luke and so sets the whole in this perspective. Jesus, the Son of God, the Spirit bearer, answers the devil's wiles with words of the Law. In the Lukan gospel this continues the strong impression of true Torah piety which surrounded both John and Jesus from the beginning. There, too, Luke associated such piety with the activity of the Spirit.

Luke's order of the three temptations reflects his interests: the final temptation is in Jerusalem at the temple.[33] This probably reflects the fact that Luke will make Jerusalem the goal of Jesus' ministry, the place of his Easter appearances and of the beginnings of the Church. It may also reflect the continuing importance of Jerusalem in Luke's thought, including his eschatology.

The emphasis on Jesus' Jewishness, on his belonging to those who are truly Torah observant, is very strong in these opening chapters. At the same time Jesus' identity as Son of God and bearer of the Spirit both represents something new and belongs in continuity with divine action in the past. Luke

---

[33] For the view that Luke is responsible for this order as matching the pattern of Jesus' life, see Fitzmyer, *Luke*, p. 507; Bovon, *Lukas I*, p. 193; I. H. Marshall, *The Gospel of Luke. A Commentary on the Greek Text*, NIGNT, (Exeter: Paternoster, 1978), p. 167.

gives no indication of conflict between this Jesus and the authority of Torah in these chapters.

3.2.2 Luke 4:14 – 6:49

Luke's first detailed account of an action of Jesus' ministry again stresses Jesus' traditional Jewish piety: he enters his home synagogue on the sabbath, as was his usual practice.[34]   Luke has Isa 61:1–2 (with expansion from Isa 58:6) function as a statement of Jesus' calling which refers back to his baptism: the Spirit of the Lord is upon him and has anointed him.[35]   This reinforces, again, the role of the Spirit.   In the words of the prophecy he has been sent to proclaim good news to the poor, release to the captives, recovery of sight to the blind, to free the oppressed and to proclaim the year of the Lord's favour.   This is an important clarification of Jesus' role as the anointed Messiah.[36]   How Luke understands these words becomes clear from the narrative of Jesus' activities in the rest of the gospel.   Luke's Jesus declares that these scripture hopes are fulfilled (4:21), one of many occasions where Luke portrays Jesus as fulfilling scripture promises.   The prophetic words portray Jesus primarily in the role of deliverer and saviour, in accord with the predictions of the infancy narrative.   They do not focus on Jesus in relationship to Law.   However in the course of fulfilling this calling, Jesus' activities will raise issues related to the Law.   This is already apparent from what follows in this scene.

---

[34] So Marshall, *Luke*, p. 181; Fitzmyer, *Luke*, p. 530; W. Wiefel, *Das Evangelium nach Lukas*, THNT 3, (Berlin: Ev. Verlagsanstalt, 1988), p. 106; Salo, *Law*, pp. 67–68; cf. Banks, *Law*, p. 91, who suggests it was rather only for mission purposes. Similarly Turner, "Sabbath," pp. 101–102. But nothing in the text suggests this was the case. Regular attendance was the proper pious practice according to Josephus, *Ap* 2:175; *Ant* 16:43; Philo *Hyp* 7:12.

[35] Possibly in using this text Luke is alluding to the jubilee year (cf. Lev 25:10). Marshall, *Luke*, p. 184; Wiefel, *Lukas*, p. 106; Bock, *Luke*, p. 406. See also Turner, "Sabbath," pp. 101–102, who rightly argues the lack of evidence for the view that Luke is having Jesus link "his mission with the sabbath in order to make the day a fitting memorial of his redemptive activity", citing S. Bacchiocchi, *From Sabbath to Sunday. A Historical Investigation of the Rise of Sunday Observance in Early Christianity*, (Rome: Pont. Greg. Univ., 1977), p. 21. 11QMelch also links the jubilee year with Isa 61:1–2. In 4:25–27 Bovon, *Lukas*, p. 215, sees Luke extending the image of the jubilee beyond the land of Israel to the whole earth and so here envisaging inclusion of both Jews and Gentiles. This is uncertain. In any case there is no hint elsewhere that the jubilee motif plays a role in Luke's thought.

[36] For the link between Isa 61:1–2 and royal messianic expectation, see the new Qumran text, 4Q521, fr. 2 col. 2, which begins with a reference to the Messiah, than reports God's action in terms of Isa 61:1.

The synagogue scene in 4:16–29 appears to operate on two levels, one, to narrate a particular event, but at a second level, to foreshadow the story of Jesus and the early church in miniature. Initial positive response turns to rejection. At first all speak well of him (4:22a). The slide begins with the interpretation which tried to put Jesus in his place: "Is this not Joseph's son?" (4:22b), perhaps already intended by Luke to evoke a wry smile: we, the hearers, know just how much Joseph had to do with it! This, then, slips enigmatically into confrontation, where Jesus apparently senses a twofold accusation (4:23). It is not clear why they would confront Jesus with the proverb, "Doctor, heal yourself!" The second accusation is less enigmatic: he should do miracles in Nazareth as he had in Capernaum (activity assumed in 4:14–15). It sounds like a re-run of the temptation scene (cf. 4:9–12). The upshot is Luke's shortened version of the logion about a prophet's rejection in his own country (4:24), shorn of reference to family and kin (cf. Mark 6:4) because the infancy narratives have shown them as pious Jews. Jesus then contrasts the response of Elijah and Elisha to the needs of a Gentile widow and of a Gentile leper with their response to the widows and lepers in Israel (4:25–26). The immediate context is the claim that Jesus should do miracles in Nazareth and not just Capernaum. It is, on the face of it, a conflict between Nazareth and Capernaum, not one between the self righteous and the needy or marginalised; nor between Jews and Gentiles.

Nevertheless, at a second level, Luke may well have had the larger scene in mind: the gospel will turn to the Gentiles. The home town rejection of Jesus because he favours Capernaum would also symbolise rejection by the Jews both of Jesus because he went to outsiders and of the church because it turned to Gentiles.[37] Later, in Acts 13:46 Paul will declare to the Jews of Pisidian Antioch: "It was necessary that the word of God be preached first to you. Since you refuse it and reckon yourselves unworthy of eternal life, behold, we are turning to the Gentiles." Paul repeats the same sentiment in 28:28. It also underlies Luke's version of the parable of the great feast (Luke 14:16–24). There there are two steps: a turning to the marginalised; then a turning to Gentiles.

The issue in 4:16–29 is not presented as a matter of Law, but almost as one of envy and rivalry. The issue with the Gentile mission is much more than that, but its implications are left unexpressed, except in the sense that scripture upheld the validity of the actions of both Elijah and Elisha in responding to Gentiles.

---

[37] So Nolland, *Luke*, pp. 200–201.

After this programmatic scene Luke takes up the story with which Mark opens his account of Jesus' ministry, the exorcism in a synagogue at Capernaum (4:31–37; cf. Mark 1:21–28). 4:23 had already indicated that Capernaum had been a place of positive response, probably a successful healing; thus this scene helps reinforces the contrast with Nazareth. Like Mark, Luke mentions Jesus' teaching authority at the beginning: "his word (λόγος) was with authority" (4:32; cf. Mark 1:22 "He was teaching them as one who has authority and not as the scribes"), but omits Mark's contrast with the scribes. At the conclusion he replaces Mark's formulation ("What is this? A new teaching with authority. He commands even the unclean spirits and they obey him" 1:27) with the words: "What is this word (λόγος)? For with authority and power he commands unclean spirits and they depart?" (4:36). In putting it this way, Luke has omitted Mark's reference to this as new authority.[38]

Thus Luke's account removes Mark's focus on conflict. Law issues do not appear to concern Luke here, though they are potentially present at a few points. These include that the exorcism and the healing which follows happen on a sabbath; that the demons are described as "unclean" and that Jesus is addressed as "the holy one". Luke shows no sign of sensing a sabbath issue here[39] nor of intending a reflection on purity issues, except in the general sense that Jesus is victorious over evil powers. Nor does the presence of the demoniac in the synagogue carry any negative connotations for the synagogue itself. The focus is solely on demonstrating Jesus' power to fulfil the ministry for which he has been anointed.

In 4:38–39 Luke rewrites Mark's account of the healing of Peter's mother-in-law (1:29–31), turning it into an exorcism . The quotation from Isaiah 61:1–2 in 4:16–20 is finding its fulfilment: captives are being set free. Luke continues by using Mark's summary account of healings which follow on the same evening (4:40–41; cf. Mark 1:32–34). They offer further evidence of fulfilment. Luke adds that the confronted demons acknowledge Jesus as "Son of God" and that they knew he was "the Christ" (4:41). The effect is to reinforce for the hearer that it is the one introduced as Son of God and Christ who is active here.

Luke continues to follow Mark in 4:42–43 (cf. Mark 1:35–38) and for the first time speaks of Jesus' preaching the good news of the kingdom of God,

---

[38] So H. Merkel, "Israel im lukanischen Werk," *NTS* 40 (1994), pp. 371–398, here: 386. Bovon, *Lukas*, p. 219, links the omission to Luke's addition in 5:39, which he sees as favouring the old.

[39] Salo, *Law*, p. 92.

an element not present at this point in Mark's account. In part Luke is returning to the earlier Markan summary of Jesus' preaching (Mark 1:14–15). This is indicated by his inclusion at this point of the call of the disciples, which in Mark follows this summary (Mark 1:16–20; Luke 5:1–11). He is also recalling Jesus' commission in the words of Isaiah 61:1, "to proclaim good news to the poor" (4:18). In using Mark's account of the call of the disciples Luke has expanded it with the report of the miraculous catch of fish (5:1–11). The effect is to heighten the symbolism of mission and bring the focus of the narrative back to 4:16–30. For there he had hinted at the mission of the early church beyond the religious people of Israel. Thus, when Luke finally returns to the order of Markan material he had been following, the healing of the leper (5:12–16; cf. Mark 1:40–45) echoes Jesus' reference to Naaman, the Syrian. Luke is composing with 4:16–30 in mind.

Luke retains Jesus' command that the leper fulfil the Law's provisions by showing himself to the priests and making the appropriate offering. This reads very naturally as typical of the Torah observance already noted in the infancy narratives. Nothing suggests fulfilling Torah obligation is just a stunt to confront the priests with Jesus' miraculous ability. Rather it is like Mary's fulfilment of her obligations and reflects the obligation to present the evidence to the priests that one has been made clean, public authentication.[40] It may include the sense of witnessing to them about what Jesus had done, but only at a secondary level. Apart from the explicit exhortation to obey the Law, Luke offers no comment about other Law related aspects of the passage. Thus he offers no reflection on the propriety of the leper's approach, omits Jesus' initial response and any hint of anger. He also gives no indication of sensing problems with Jesus' touching the leper.[41] Luke would have understood Jesus' words, "Be made clean", not as a priestly declaration of purity status. The latter will occur after the leper obeys Jesus' injunction to follow the Law's provisions and go to the priest.

It is likely that, as in Mark, the story of the leper's healing, is intended to prepare the hearer for the controversies which follow. But unlike Mark, Luke has given no hint of controversy with teachers of the Law; on the contrary, Jesus' commitment to the Law merely confirms the strong impression

---

[40] So Nolland, *Luke*. p. 228. Cf. Turner, "Sabbath," p. 109; Salo, *Law*, pp. 71–72, who argues that Luke means that Jesus' opponents should be confronted with the evidence that he is observant of the Law. Similarly, Bock, *Luke*, pp. 476–477. But what preparation has there been for such antagonism in the text thus far?

[41] Banks, *Law*, p. 105, suggests that Jesus, like Elijah, Elisha and the priests, would have been considered by Luke to be immune from contamination in touching the leper . Similarly Salo, *Law*, pp. 69–72. Luke shows no interest in the issue (pp. 69–70).

from the beginning that Jesus and his forebears represent true piety and are careful observers of the Law. The rejection at Nazareth had more to do with provincialism than with Law at the primary level; the broader conflict is hinted at only at the secondary level.

When Luke does finally come to recount controversy, he does so on a large scale. To begin with, in recounting Mark's first controversy story (Mark 2:1–12), Luke gives greater prominence to the fact that Jesus was teaching (5:17–26). He then has Pharisees and teachers of the law gather from every village of Galilee, from Judea and from Jerusalem, obviously to hear Jesus. Thus Mark's reference to "some scribes" (2:6) has become a major assembly of Pharisees and teachers of the Law! This sets the stage for potential conflict.[42] Luke adds further that "the power of the Lord was on Jesus to heal" (5:17), recalling Jesus' anointing and his powerful ministry of healing. We are no longer dealing with a small scale interchange as in Mark; we have a major encounter.

Luke substantially follows Mark's account of the dialogue, so that the reader is left with the picture of Jesus as Son of Man claiming authority to forgive sins. The large body of representatives of Jewish tradition held it to be blasphemous, for it claimed to do what God alone can do (Nu 15:30–31; Lev 24:10–24). The concern about Jesus' forgiveness of sins reappears in 7:47–49. "The power of the Lord" in Jesus (5:17) and the tangible evidence of its effect in the healing is already a strong defence. Luke underlines it by adding that the crowds exclaimed they had seen *paradoxa* (5:26) and that the man went home glorifying God (5:25). Luke knew that John the Baptist's baptism for forgiveness of sins was similarly controversial (20:1–8), although nothing is said about it evoking a charge of blasphemy. For Luke there is no question: Jesus has the authority. He is, therefore, not claiming to be God. He is not transgressing Torah. He is acting with divine authorisation.[43]

Luke's account of the conflict about eating with toll collectors and sinners (5:27–32) also follows Mark closely, with minor variations (cf. Mark 2:13–17). Luke removes any ambiguity about the connection between Levi's

---

[42] So Salo, *Law*, p. 73, who notes that introduction of the description, "teachers of the law", heightens the issue of conflict. Similarly Nolland, *Luke*, p. 234.

[43] Salo, *Law*, p. 76, rightly notes that Luke is defending Jesus' authorisation to forgive sins, not his declaration of God's forgiveness. The authorisation claim renders the blasphemy accusation invalid. It is however important to give this distinction its full weight; Jesus does, in fact, declare God's forgiveness, but has been authorised to do so. Bovon, *Lukas*, pp. 247–248, rightly notes that this indicates that forgiveness of sins in Luke is a relationship not dependent on the cross.

call and the meal; here Levi hosts the meal. The extent to which the objections are on grounds of purity or of morality are no more clear in Luke than they are in Mark. On the other hand, Luke has the complaint as one made not about Jesus, but about the disciples.[44] This may be a clue about the issues of Luke's day, which are probably reflected in the issues in Acts, where ritual purity issues, not morality purity issues, were at stake. This makes it unlikely that the controversy here in Luke's story is only about moral issues. The issue, however, is not Gentile impurity; for we are hearing about Jews. It is about both their impurity and their immorality, the former, doubtless because of disregard of laws concerning proper tithing and preparation of food.[45]

Luke adds to Jesus' statement of purpose that he come to call sinners the words: "to repentance" (5:32; cf. Mark 2:17). Elsewhere when Luke has similar charges brought against Jesus, he has Jesus answer them similarly: Jesus is reaching out to sinners to bring about change in them (Luke 15:1–7,8–10; 19:1–10). The addition, "to repentance", reinforces the validity of Jesus' behaviour: it bears worthwhile fruit. The addition of "to repentance" also changes the character of the statement as a whole; it has Jesus reject an absurdity; people do not call the righteous to repentance. Luke does not understand "the righteous" as a reference to the scribes and Pharisees as self righteous.[46] They are not complaining that Jesus has not called them. Rather the saying in Luke reflects that fact that Luke knows that there are people who are well and righteous; his infancy narrative is full of them! Luke's Jesus justifies his actions on the grounds that they are a strategy for bringing toll collectors and sinners to repentance. Overall, Luke presents Jesus in this passage as in conflict with the opinions of the scribes and the Pharisees, not with the Law, itself.

Luke has merged what follows in Mark into the same scene, so that the conversation continues with the Pharisees' question about fasting and praying (5:33–39; cf. Mark 2:18–22). The focus is not only on fasting in itself, as in Mark, but on frequent fasting and praying in contrast to the fact that the disciples eat and drink (5:33). The effect is to remove the implication that the disciples never fast. Luke adds praying. It is one of his positive themes. The issue is not, therefore, about fasting and praying as such, but about their frequency. More particularly, it is about characteristic ways of being: as-

---

[44] So Salo, *Law*, p. 78.

[45] Cf. Salo, *Law*, p. 71, who argues that the issue was primarily purity laws. Similarly J. D. Kingsbury, *Conflict in Luke. Jesus, Authorities, Disciples*, (Minneapolis: Fortress, 1991), p. 87.

[46] Cf. Kingsbury, *Conflict*, p. 88.

ceticism or open joy. Fasting will have its place in the days of the Church when it awaits Christ's return. The issue here is not Law, but, at most, the practice of piety.

Luke's version of the parables of the patch and the wine (5:36–39) varies from Mark's (2:21–22). Where Mark speaks of sewing unshrunk cloth on an old garment, Luke speaks of tearing a piece from a new garment to sew it onto an old one. This is a rather violent image. Luke's Jesus points out the implications of such a procedure: it will destroy the new garment and not match the old. Destruction, not shrinkage, is what Luke has in mind. On the other hand, Luke stays closer to Mark in speaking of the danger of new wine bursting old wine skins, noting the loss of both. Both images, the patch and the wine, imply that it is destructive to both the old and the new to try to implant the new in the old in some way. From the previous context of conflicts it is most natural to read the old as referring to the way of the scribes and Pharisees and the new as representing the way of Jesus and his followers. The primary concern with the first image is with the destruction of the new. In the second the old skins are burst, but the real value is the new wine. The message seems to be: resist accommodating the new to the old. The issue is not about the gospel and the Law, but about the way of Jesus and the way of the scribes and Pharisees. Luke adds to the wine image the comment that no one drinking the old wine will want the new, because the old wine is better. This is good wine wisdom, but appears to be used ironically to explain the resistance of the Pharisees.[47]

In his version of the conflict over plucking grain on the sabbath (6:1–5) Luke again follows Mark closely (cf. Mark 2:23–28). For Luke "some of the Pharisees", rather than just "the Pharisees" (Mark 2:24), ask the question. For some Pharisees in Luke are very positively disposed towards Jesus. These Pharisees ask their question of the disciples, whereas in Mark they ask it of Jesus about the disciples. These variations may not be greatly significant.[48] Luke adds that the disciples rubbed the grain and ate it. The

---

[47] Similarly Fitzmyer, *Luke*, p. 597; Kingsbury, *Conflict*, pp. 88–89; G. Nebe, *Prophetische Züge im Bilde Jesu bei Lukas*, BWANT 127, (Stuttgart: Kohlhammer, 1989), p. 164; Nolland, *Luke*, p. 250; Bock, *Luke*, p. 522.; Salo, *Law*, pp. 78–86, who argues that irony is the best explanation of the final statement. He adds that Luke may be applying it to Jewish Christians of his own day (p. 85). He sees the point of contrast in both parables being to counter attempts to make Judaism Christian or Christianity Jewish as being destructive for either. They are to be kept separated. Cf. Merkel, "Israel", pp. 385–386, who argues that Luke defends the old against Pharisaic innovation.

[48] So Salo, *Law*, p. 87; D. B. Gowler, *Host, Guest, Enemy, and Friend. Portraits of the Pharisees in Luke and Acts*, Emory Studies in Early Christianity 2, (Frankfurt: Peter Lang, 1991), p. 207, who points to the use of "some of" the Sadducees in 20:27 as not having special significance. Cf. Klinghardt, *Gesetz*, p. 228, who argues that the change to

effect is to underline the nature of what the Pharisees saw as the offence, work on the sabbath, and to point to the reason: the need to eat food. This was already implied in Mark, but becomes more explicit through the link with the David story which is concerned with food and hunger. The point of the David story is that there was precedent for overriding (sabbath) law in the case of human need.[49]   There may be a subsidiary hint of the link between Jesus, the Messiah and Son of David, and David. But the main argument does not appear to be: because of who he was, David could override the Law; so, because of who he is, the Son of Man may override the Law.[50] Rather Jesus has authority to determine appropriate sabbath practice, as he has authority to declare God's forgiveness.[51]   The issue is interpretation of sabbath law.[52]

Luke's Jesus offers four kinds of argument. In citing David, three kinds of argument are combined: appeal to scripture or scriptural precedent, appeal to the moral claim of human need and appeal to the example of an authority figure. The fourth argument is appeal to Jesus' own authority as Son of Man, possibly also indirectly reinforced by the Davidic messianic link. Formally it is possible to read Luke as laying all the weight on the latter and none, in particular, on the first two kinds of arguments.[53]   This could lead to the view that, being Lord of the sabbath, Jesus can dispense with it on occasions or altogether. The remaining sabbath episodes and the reference to sabbath observance elsewhere in the two volume work (Luke 4:16,31; 13:10; Acts 13:14–15,42,44)[54] suggest that Luke does not understand Jesus as either abrogating or sanctioning abandonment of sabbath law.[55]

"some of the Pharisees" is because there are Pharisees in his community (p. 228). But elsewhere Luke is not so careful (cf. already 6:7).

[49] Cf. Klinghardt, *Gesetz*, p. 229, who believes that Luke uses the David reference to justify the right of missionaries to the holy.

[50] Cf. Turner, "Sabbath," pp. 103–104.

[51] Cf. Luke 6:5D "On the same day he saw someone working on the sabbath and said to him, 'Man, if you know what you are doing, you are blessed; if however you do not know, you are accursed and a transgressor of the Law'." This does not reflect the Lukan attitude, but rather Pauline thought, but see also the discussion below in ch. 6.

[52] So Sanders, *Jews in Luke–Acts*, pp. 172–173; Kingsbury, *Conflict*, p. 89; Nolland, *Luke*, p. 257; Bock, *Luke*, p. 525; Bovon, *Lukas I*, p. 271; Salo, *Law*, pp. 87–88, 90.

[53] So Banks, *Law*, pp. 121–122; Wilson, *Law*, pp. 33–34. He writes: "The claim to lordship over the sabbath ultimately subordinates the sabbath to Jesus and does not merely establish him as arbiter of sabbath disputes. If the sabbath is subordinate to Jesus so is the law" (p. 35); Blomberg, "Law," pp. 58–59; Vouga, *Loi*, pp. 50–52. Cf. Esler, *Community*, p. 117.

[54] So Salo, *Law*, p. 90; Esler, *Community*, p. 116.

[55] Cf. H. Schürmann, *Das Lukasevangelium. 1. Teil*, HTKNT III/1, (Freiburg: Herder, 4. Auflage, 1990), p. 305; Gowler, *Host*, p. 208: Jesus is above the law.

Like Matthew, Luke omits the statement: "The sabbath was made for people not people for the sabbath" (Mark 2:27). If Luke intends an allusion to Jesus' authority as Davidic Messiah, one could understand that Luke would see 2:27 as an interruption to the flow of thought.[56] Alternatively, or perhaps additionally, he sensed the dangers of generalising such a principle or found the example of David sufficiently made the point.[57] Probably he is also not interested in the style of argument which Mark 2:27 represented, but sees the claim of Jesus' lordship as sufficient.[58]

Similarly, Luke stays close to Mark in the account of the healing of the man with the withered hand on the sabbath and has Jesus offer the same arguments (6:6–11; cf. Mark 3:1–6). Luke omits Jesus' anger at the hardness of his opponents' hearts and the severity of their response. Instead of plotting to kill, they are portrayed as asking the question: "What are we going to do with Jesus?" As in Mark, Jesus' response argues that human need justifies Jesus' action on the sabbath.[59] I find the suggestions that Luke is making a claim here about either the church's healing practices on the sabbath[60] or about its worship practices on the sabbath without sufficient foundation.[61]

---

[56] In a different way christological argument also motivates Matthew's omission of Mark 2:27. This makes the suggestion of Hübner, *Gesetz*, pp. 117–122, that Matthew and Luke know a Q form of the story unnecessary.

[57] Vouga, *Loi*, pp. 50–52, suggests that Luke omits 2:27 because Law issues are no longer alive in his time; his focus is christology, including Jesus as Son of David, which best explains the smooth transition for Luke from 6:4 to 6:5. Salo, *Law*, pp. 89–90, links it the development of Sunday worship (celebration of communion; Acts 20:7), for which 2:27 would be confusing. It is not, he believes, because Luke would read it as critical of the Law (p. 89). Cf. Klinghardt, *Gesetz*, p. 229.

[58] Banks, *Law*, pp. 121–122, sees Luke perceiving the relationship between the scripture reference to David and the christological statement as one of premise to conclusion.

[59] Cf. Bank, *Law*, 130–131, who argues that Luke's concern is not the ordinance of the sabbath or Jesus' authority in treating it, but "a desire to highlight those works of Jesus which bring salvation and healing to men, which as v.16 makes clear, especially occur on that day" (p. 131). But that would imply a special status for the sabbath in Luke which Banks wants to deny! Vouga, *Loi*, pp. 66–67, argues that for Luke there is no longer any need to justify Jesus' activity in relation to the Law; the focus is edification of believers and exposure of unbelief expressed through figures of the past. Wilson, *Law*, p. 36, argues that Luke's aim is "to illustrate the character of Jesus' mission and the nature of the opponents rather than to reflect upon the legal implications of Jesus' words." But then why four sabbath stories and so much sabbath observance in Luke?

[60] Cf. Schürmann, *Lukasevangelium*, pp. 306–310; Bacchiocchi, *Sabbath*, pp. 32–38; and in relation also to the other sabbath healings: W. Grundmann, *Das Evangelium nach Lukas*, THNT 3, (Berlin: Ev. Verlagsanstalt, 1971), p. 280; Banks, *Law*, pp. 121, 130.

[61] Cf. Klinghardt, *Gesetz*, p. 230, who suggests the issue is not healing, but Christian preaching on the sabbath. He also sees 13:10–17 and 14:1–6 as halakic defence of the sabbath observance of Luke's community, not sabbath critique (pp. 231–234), and be-

Luke will repeat the argument from human need in the two similar sabbath controversies in 13:10–16 and 14:1–6, where Jesus also faces the need to defend healings on the sabbath. We shall consider the significance of all three after we have treated each individually. There is no sense either here or in the other controversy stories that Luke sees Jesus as contravening Torah.[62] The principle of Torah observance, reflected in the infancy narratives, still applies here. Nothing in the narrative thus far has suggested that Luke or Luke's Jesus intended a departure from this principle. The conflicts pertain not to the Law itself but to its interpretation.[63]

For Luke the primary interest is not Torah, nor Jesus' relationship to Torah, but Jesus, himself, as the one sent to announce something new which brings good news, healing to those who are in need and the opportunity for sinners to repent. The question is whether this means that Luke sees Jesus in his mission as fundamentally above Law[64] or as claiming that he upholds and rightly interprets it. The evidence thus far point towards the latter option.

Luke has changed the original Markan order of the next two episodes in preparation for the so called sermon on the plain. He first presents Jesus' selection of twelve apostles (6:12–16; cf. Mark 3:13–19), then has the crowds gather for healing and teaching (6:17–19; cf. Mark 3:7–12). Then in this context, with the crowds within earshot, he has Jesus present his teaching (6:20–49). We are at a point of transition in the gospel. Since 5:17 Luke has had Jesus deal with those who challenge his understanding of God's will. The focus is now returning to the fundamentals of Jesus' mission itself.

Luke adds his introduction to the Markan material: not only does Jesus go up onto a mountain, as in Mark 3:13; he does so to pray and remains in prayer all night. We are back with the kind of piety reflected in the infancy narratives. This confirms that it is no transitional relic of salvation history. By portraying Jesus in this way Luke is legitimising Jesus' approach against other claimants to leadership in piety with whom he has been in conflict and is underscoring the authority for what he is about to do: choose twelve apostles. The symbolic significance of choosing twelve would not be lost on Luke's hearers. It links Jesus and his apostles to Israel. Effectively it is a

---

lieves they are more than that: they are seeking to justify Christian missionary activity in synagogues (pp. 234–240). The issue is more than work; it is worship. Similarly Salo, *Law*, pp. 91–93. This appears to me to exceed the evidence. Klinghardt speculates that Luke may also be addressing pagan critique of the sabbath (pp. 241–154).

[62] Cf. Rordorf, *Sunday*, p. 66.
[63] So Salo, *Law*, pp. 91–93.
[64] So Turner, "Sabbath," pp. 105–108.

rival claim to leadership over against those who have challenged him. Perhaps also the mountain symbolism, evoking Sinai, reinforced the claim.

This symbolism continues perhaps in 6:17–19 where Luke rewrites Mark 3:7–12, a summary account of healings at the seaside, so that they become healings on the plain amid crowds of disciples and people from wide and far. Luke removes the acclamation of Jesus as Son of God, which has had used earlier (4:41; cf. Mark 3:11). There are also echoes of Jesus' exorcism and authoritative word in the synagogue (4:31–37). We have returned full circle. The effect is to re-present Jesus as doing the work of his calling according to Isa 61:1–2.

The opening announcement of Jesus' discourse of blessing to the poor (6:20) also recalls Jesus' use of Isaiah 61:1. He was anointed to proclaim good news to the poor. The reward of the kingdom of God connects also to the reiteration of Jesus' purpose in 4:43, where Luke uses Mark 1:15. The effect is to give particular focus to the teaching which follows. It is, after all, also the first piece of extended teaching in Luke and an important clue therefore about what he understands Jesus' message to be.

Significantly, Luke has these words addressed to the disciples. They are the poor, the hungry, those who weep and who face persecution (6:20–23). The promises of reversal of their present fortune are matched by woes to disciples who prosper now (6:24–26). The direct address to the disciples continues in the exhortation that they love their persecutors (6:27–28). This continues from the theme of the fourth promise and fourth woe. Turning the other cheek, releasing one's inner as well as one's outer garment and giving what people demand of one and not demanding it back, also belong in the context of disciples' facing dangers, but may have in mind more than direct persecution (6:29–30). By 6:31, a formulation of the golden rule, the focus seems to have moved away from the specific situation of persecution to, more generally, how disciples should behave in human relationships.

Loving, doing good, and making loans should extend beyond the circle of those liable to reciprocate. Otherwise disciples will do no better than what sinners do (6:32–35a). Extending these behaviours in this way is to emulate God's mercy towards both the just and the evil and so be true children of God (6:35b–36). The argument which underlies the whole exhortation to this point is theological: the disciples should react as God reacts. Such behaviour contrasts with what sinners might also do.

The promise of reward already features in these exhortations, but only in the following verses is it at all specified. Those who do not judge or condemn, who forgive and give shall not be judged, condemned; they shall be forgiven and receive in abundance (6:37–38). These set the rules for the community of disciples.

6:39–40 addresses the need for the disciples to prepare themselves for leadership, to be teachers like Jesus. 6:41–42 returns to the theme of judging others, using the image of the mote and the beam, but perhaps, because of the context, now thought of as applying to disputes among leaders. 6:43–45 uses the images of fruit, figs and grapes, to emphasise the need to address oneself to right inner life as a basis for right external behaviour. The teaching concludes with the image of right and wrong building to illustrate the consequences of responding to or rejecting Jesus' teaching (6:46–49). Luke will have in mind the disciples, here, too, when he has Jesus speak of some who will address him as "Lord, Lord," but not do as he says.

What is striking in this block of teaching, compared with the expanded version of Matthew, is that Luke has Jesus at no point relate it to the theme of Torah. This need not mean Luke sees Torah as irrelevant or sees Jesus' teaching as replacing Torah. To this point in the narrative we might indeed assume that Luke would see Jesus as thoroughly consistent with Torah, but Luke does not make an issue of it. It is not a central theme for him here. Jesus is certainly not, in Luke, primarily an interpreter of the Law. Yet most of what occurs is a declaration of God's will, Torah in the broadest sense. Whatever its source, Luke uses this material without any need to relate it to the Law such that would leave traces in the text. This is Jesus' teaching of God's will. It is set neither above or below the Law. Its relation to the Law is not worth mentioning. This is probably because Luke saw it as wholly consistent with a positive attitude towards the Law. In the broader frame of Luke's narrative Luke has dealt with challenges to Jesus' attitude towards the Law and shown them to be without foundation. They are now sufficiently resolved as to be left out of view.

3.2.3 Luke 7:1 – 9:50

Luke follows the block of teaching with the account of the healing of the centurion's servant (7:1–10), which contrasts the centurion's faith with Israel's lack of faith. To some degree, the centurion, as a Gentile, points forward to the centurion, Cornelius, in Acts 10–11. The Jews address the man's worthiness: he loves the people of Israel and built the people a synagogue (7:5). This is an extraordinary level of commitment and recalls what Luke will report about Cornelius' depth of Jewish piety (10:2,22,35). Nothing indicates that Luke is mentioning such detail dismissively. It is as respected here as it is in the infancy narratives. In response to the request, Jesus sets out to heal the servant. Unlike the account in Matthew (and Q), Luke's Jesus does not rebuff the request (cf. Matt 8:7). Nevertheless Luke does not have Jesus encounter the centurion. Instead there is a delegation. This may already reflect Luke's sensitivity to purity issues. In the message he sends, the centurion addresses them directly: he is unworthy to have Jesus come under his roof, precisely the problem addressed in Acts 10:28. The centurion's faith is evident in the way he speaks of his own authority as an analogy for that of Jesus and in his trust that Jesus can deliver. It is good Lukan christology. The healing takes place at a distance; Jesus did not enter the centurion's house. It is a fascinating piece which highlights major issues, not least, the positive role of pious Law observance and the problem for Law observance of including Gentiles. The passage signals the latter; but it waits for Acts for a resolution.

Like much that has gone before in previous chapters, the passage recalls the programmatic scene with which Luke's account of Jesus' ministry opened (4:16–30). The centurion is like Naaman, the Syrian general (4:27). This probably accounts also for Luke's inclusion of the episode which follows, namely the raising of the widow of Nain's son (7:12–17). It is a clear echo of the healing of the son of the widow of Zarephath by Elisha, to which Luke's Jesus had also alluded in his sermon in the synagogue at Nazareth (4:25–26). The people acclaim Jesus as a great prophet (7:16). Luke shows no sense of impropriety or danger in Jesus' touching the corpse of the dead child.

In 7:18–23 Luke returns the focus to John the Baptist, by narrating how he seeks confirmation that Jesus is the one to come. This may reflect a sense of discrepancy between John's announcement of Jesus as coming judge and his activity, though, as we have seen, Luke has not given this the emphasis which we found in Matthew's account. The effect of the narrative, here, is to reaffirm for the reader Jesus' own statement of purpose, given in the reading of Isaiah 61:1–2 in his home synagogue (4:16–20). In this sense the passage belongs closely with what has immediately preceded. Jesus' answer alludes directly to the Isaiah quotation, as well as blending with it other Old Testament expectations of miracle and of healing in the last days (cf. Isa 29:18; 35:5–6; 42:18; 26:19).

In the passage which follows, Luke's narrative has Jesus hail John's eschatological significance in terms which cohere closely with the infancy narratives, while preserving the distinction made there between the two (7:24–27). John was not yet part of the new kingdom of God (7:28). Luke then notes the response of the people and the toll collectors who had been baptised by John (7:29). They see in Jesus' words a vindication of God, probably understood as a vindication that John was right in what he announced. By contrast Luke declares that the Pharisees and lawyers, who had refused his baptism (once confronted with John's terms; 3:7–9), had set aside what was God's will for them (7:30).

In 7:31–35 Luke continues the close connection between Jesus and John which this assumes. Luke's Jesus portrays both John and himself as children of wisdom rejected by their contemporaries, but in whom wisdom would be vindicated. The image changes from God being vindicated (7:29) to wisdom's being vindicated (7:35). Luke has Jesus allude to wisdom elsewhere in relationship to his mission (11:49–51), so that we should assume that he is using the image here of wisdom acting as God's agent. However, differently from in Matthew, there is no apparent connection, here, between wisdom and Torah. The theme of the Law is, however, indirectly in view, in as much as the material here recalls the series of conflicts which precede, particularly the accusations levelled against Jesus and his disciples for mixing with toll collectors and sinners and "eating and drinking" (5:27–39). It comes into direct view again in what immediately follows. The charge of drunkenness and gluttony may also the reflect the instruction in Deut 21:20 about treatment of a rebellious son. For Luke such charges are manifestly false.

In 7:36–50 Luke brings a further controversy narrative. Jesus dines with a Pharisee. Already that detail implies sufficient acceptance of Pharisee norms on the part of Jesus as to make such fellowship possible.[65] Thus Luke's Pharisees bear indirect testimony to a certain level of recognition of Jesus' approach to the Law on matters that concern them, even if at many points they are in conflict.[66] This host is shocked that Jesus, as a prophet, lets a sinner touch him.[67] It calls into question Jesus' prophetic credentials, on the assumption that, had he known, he would have forbidden it. It turns out that Jesus does know about her. The Pharisee probably assumes she is both immoral and unclean, but the issue for Luke seems to be not Jesus' exposure to ritual impurity, but his willingness to have contact with a known sinner. This is shown in the fact that Jesus focuses on her sin and its forgiveness, not on issues of her possible impurity.

---

[65] So Salo, *Law*, pp 94–95.

[66] This makes Wilson's claims, *Law*, p. 42, that "It is not stated, of course, whether Jesus kept the laws on cleanliness and tithing, though it is implied that he did not" rather doubtful.

[67] Banks, *Law*, p. 105, referring also to Jesus' touch of the leper, rejects the suggestion that there were any ritual considerations raised by her action or that Jesus overrode them with the principle of love. He argues that they would not have applied to situations like this, especially since here and in 8:44, it is the women who take the initiative, not Jesus. But where purity laws apply, who takes the initiative is irrelevant.

The narrative also contrasts the Pharisee's response with that of the woman, who presents herself as repentant and as showing love to Jesus. Jesus reinforces his stance with a parable arguing that people forgiven much will love much. Jesus declares her sins forgiven, much to the consternation of Jesus' table companions, who ask: "Who is this, who also forgives sins?" The passage reflects a typical Lukan concern with repentance and a characteristic contrast between the approach of a Pharisee and one of a sinner. It may well be Luke's own creative rewriting of the Bethany anointing (Mark 14:3–9), using conflict dialogue from the healing of the paralytic (5:17–26). Unlike in the latter, Luke says nothing about a charge of blasphemy. Luke may imply that the Pharisee thinks it, but nothing is said; only a very evocative question which the hearer can readily answer, "Who is this, who also forgives sins?" Thus no Law issues are addressed directly. Luke's account leaves issues of ritual impurity out of the picture. The focus is on the different attitude towards people between Jesus and his host; that is an issue of how Law is applied. For Luke, Jesus is doing nothing contrary to what the Law demands.

Luke follows this account by a general summary statement about Jesus' activity of preaching the kingdom of God, but noting the presence of other women in his company who had also become disciples (8:1–3). Luke passes over in silence the purity issues involved of having an accompanying group which involved women. Instead his focus is on their following and on the fact that they provide funding and minister to the needs of Jesus and the disciples, an echo of the role of other prominent women of the time in the lives of teachers and philosophers.

At this point Luke returns to the Markan source, significantly abbreviating the parable of the sower and its interpretation, but using it to highlight the need for a response to the word of God which is from the heart and which endures (8:4–15; cf. Mark 4:1–20). Luke includes Mark's sayings about appropriate response (8:16–18; cf. Mark 4:21–25), but then skips over the remaining parable material (cf. Mark 4:26–34), taking up instead the account of Jesus' family coming to him, from earlier in Mark and in abbreviated form (8:19–21; cf. Mark 3:20–21,31–35). Luke reformulates its message to correspond to the language of the parable; his family are those "who hear the word of God and do it". In the process he omits all indication of family disapproval; his family is not trying to rescue him because he is beside himself (cf. Mark 3:20–21,31); that would not sit well with the infancy narratives. Rather they are simply not able to get near to him because of the crowd (8:19).

Returning to the Markan order, Luke also abbreviates the accounts of the stilling of the storm (8:22–25; cf. Mark 4:35–41) and the exorcism of the Gerasene demoniac (8:26–39; cf. Mark 5:1–20). In the latter there is no hint of purity issues with regard to the Gentile location, the tombs or the pigs, though Luke doubtless knew of their significance for Jews. Luke even allows the man to proclaim his healing in that region, though this is not portrayed as the beginning of a Gentile mission. There follows the account of the raising of Jairus' daughter and the healing of the woman with the flow of blood (8:40–56; cf. Mark 5:21–43). While retaining Mark's figure of twelve in association with both women, Luke does not appear to use it symbolically as does Mark. Nor does Luke show any cognisance of purity issues in this passage (the woman touching Jesus; Jesus entering, unclean, into the house of the synagogue leader; Jesus touching the corpse of the child). These stories function largely to illustrate the time of fulfilment of the prophets (especially Isaiah 61:1) as announced by Jesus (4:16–20) and confirmed to John (7:22).

The commissioning of the twelve follows directly after this episode (9:1–6; cf. Mark 6:7–13), because Luke had already used Mark 6:1–6, the sermon at Nazareth. It was the setting for Jesus' opening proclamation (4:16–30). Luke may intend a symbolic link between the commissioning and the previous episode through use of the recurrent numeral, twelve. He may intend a similar symbolic use of the numerals in presenting two commissionings, one, here, of twelve and the other, in 10:1–12, of seventy. These may symbolise the two missions, one to Israel, the other to the nations. If so, this would have to be at a secondary level (as in 4:16–30), since in their narrative context both missions are clearly focused on Israel. While in 9:1–6 Luke uses the Markan account as his base, he does so also with an eye to consistency with the commissioning of the seventy, based on Q material. Among other things this leads to his introduction into the former of the command that the disciples are to proclaim the kingdom of God, a set Lukan expression for Christian preaching (9:2).

Luke uses Mark's note that Herod ponders the options about who Jesus might be, Elijah, a prophet or John risen from the dead (9:7–9; cf. Mark 6:14–16). He then omits the detail about John's death (Mark 6:17–29; cf. Luke 3:19–20). At this point Luke embarks on major adjustments. With Mark, he has the disciples return from their mission and has Jesus feed the five thousand (9:10–17; cf. Mark 6:30–44), but this now occurs in Bethsaida. Mark's narrative at this point goes on to record the disciples' setting out for Bethsaida, Jesus' walk on the water, healings, teaching about purity, encounter with the Syrophoenician in Gentile territory, a further healing there, the feeding of four thousand, the Pharisees' request for a sign, Jesus' warning about their teaching, and, finally, arrival at Bethsaida where Jesus healed a blind man (Mark 6:45 – 8:26). Instead, Luke has omitted all of this and relocated the feeding of the five thousand to Bethsaida, thus enabling him to pick up Mark's narrative thread.

In doing this Luke has not only removed Mark's careful symbolic composition which emphasises the legitimacy of the Gentile mission; he has also removed the central passage where Mark has Jesus offer radical teaching on purity (Mark 7:1–23). He may have compensated for the former at a secondary level by including the two different commissionings. They even make a similar use of the numbers twelve and seven (here, seventy; cf. Mark 8:16–21). But the discussion on purity has gone. So has the associated encounter with the Syrophoenician woman (cf. Mark 7:24–30). Luke preserves the theme of the Gentile mission for Acts. There Luke will have his own composition which links purity issues (Peter's vision) and the mission, but in a much modified form. For there, all the emphasis falls on the purity of people and, apparently, none on food laws generally or their disparagement.[68] The apostolic decree, if it is more than an obligation to sensitivity, shows Luke as more conservative than Mark concerning food.

Luke retains the reference to Bethsaida, but probably envisages it as Jewish rather than Gentile. He will omit Mark's reference to Caesarea Philippi (cf. Mark 8:27; Luke 9:18). There are echoes of Mark 7:1–23 in 11:37–41 (specifically the motif of purification before eating and the words "declaring all foods clean" Mark 7:19c in 11:42, "all things will be clean for you") as we shall see, but the focus has been narrowed to issues of bathing before meals and the washing of vessels. Luke also uses the warning about the leaven of the Pharisees (Mark 8:14) in 12:1. These echoes and especially the omission of the radically disparaging material of Mark 7:1–23 raise the question whether the omission was intentional. Absence of the material was, at least, convenient, but I consider deliberate omission more likely.[69] By making this omission Luke has deleted Mark's account of Jesus abrogating

---

[68] Cf. Hübner, *Gesetz*, pp. 182–185, 190–191, who argues that Luke has merely postponed the issue to Acts 10, where Peter's vision effects the same. Similarly Esler, *Community*, pp. 121–122. Even if this were so and Luke had presumed divine sanction for abrogating the food laws, he has done so without the associated disparagement.

[69] So, for instance, Merkel, "Israel," pp. 386–387, who believes Luke considered it too radical; Fitzmyer, *Luke*, pp. 770–771, because it avoided having Jesus enter the areas of Tyre and Sidon. Cf. Wilson, *Law*, pp. 52–55, who believes that Luke's copy of Mark did not have this section. Similarly Blomberg, "Law," p. 60, argues that Luke's omission should not be read as dissent. See also now M. Pettem, "Luke's Great Omission and his View of the Law," *NTS* 42 (1996) pp. 35–54, who also concludes that "Luke omits Mark 6.45–8.26 from his gospel because it contradicts his understanding of God's law" (p. 53).

and disparaging laws of Torah. Within the sequence of the Lukan narrative such considerations cannot bear great weight, since the hearer is probably unaware of the omission. It is, however, important for the attempt to reconstruct Luke's intention.

Another effect of Luke's great omission is that it brings Herod's quandary about Jesus' identity (9:7–9) closer together with Jesus' question to the disciples about his identity (9:18–21). Luke adds, characteristically, that Jesus was praying. He omits Peter's wrong understanding of messiahship (cf. Mark 8:32–33) and thus juxtaposes Jesus' prediction of his own suffering directly with that of the suffering of those who will follow him fearlessly (9:22–27; cf. Mark 8:34–38). The focus is faithfulness in suffering. Even Jesus' transfiguration has been made into a vehicle for predicting his passion as Moses and Elijah are shown speaking with him about his "exodos" (9:28–36; cf. Mark 9:2–10). The scene may recall for the hearer Moses' ascent to Sinai. Luke adds that Jesus' face shone (9:29; cf. Exod 34:29–35). The disciples saw his glory (9:32; cf. Exod 33:18). Again Luke adds that Jesus was praying. At a secondary level Moses and Elijah may represent the Law and the Prophets,[70] but, if so, the focus would be primarily on their prediction of his suffering and death. The heavenly declaration recalls for the hearer the statement at Jesus' baptism, as it does in Mark, but Luke omits the subsequent discussion about John (cf. Mark 9:11–13). The passage does not address issues of Law, except in as much as Moses represents its predictive function and Moses typology sets Jesus in continuity with God's actions in history.

Luke follows Mark in bringing the narrative of the healing of the possessed boy, albeit in abbreviated form (9:37–43a; cf. Mark 9:14–29). He leaves aside, however, the reflections about faith and prayer which begin the Markan theme of the community of faith as the new temple. Instead he proceeds directly to Mark's second passion prediction, from which he omits the reference to resurrection (9:43b–45; cf. Mark 9:31). The effect is to place greater emphasis again on Jesus' prediction of his death . He follows Mark's account of Jesus' teaching on humility (9:46–48; cf. Mark 9:33–37) and of Jesus' rebuttal of John's intolerance towards another acting in Jesus' name (9:49–50; cf. Mark 9:49–50). In Mark there follow warnings against offences (Mark 9:42–50). Luke will introduce these at a later point (14:34–35). Instead in 9:51 he moves on to rewrite Mark 10:1, making it not only

---

[70] Cf. Nolland, *Luke*, p. 499; C. F. Evans, *Saint Luke*, (London: SCM, Philadelphia: Trinity, 1990), pp. 416–417, who deny such an allusion. On the issue of whether Luke intends a reference here to Moses as prophet or as the law, see also Salo, *Law*, pp. 97–99, who concludes that both aspects are probably present.

the turning point where Jesus sets off on his fateful journey to Jerusalem, but also the beginning of a large block of passages with no parallel in Mark.

3.2.4 Conclusion

Luke's gospel begins with scenes of Jewish piety. Conformity to the Law is part and parcel of such piety, but in 2:22–24 and associated verses Luke makes a special point of emphasising it. In the opening chapters there is a close association between expressions of conformity to the Law and expressions of strongly Jewish hope. Luke sees the latter coming to fulfilment not only in John and Jesus and in subsequent history but also in the eschaton. This suggests that Luke sees conformity to Torah as much more than a relic of a past age or a temporary transitional phenomenon. It is, in fact, what we find in the chapters which follow. For Jesus, himself, exhibits a similar piety. This is evident in his prayerfulness and obedience when tested, on the one hand, and in his expressed attitude towards the Law when challenged, on the other.

Similarly John's confrontation of the crowd about reliance on their descent from Abraham and his call to repentance reflect Israel's prophetic tradition. They do not call the Law into question; they assume its demands, especially its ethical demands. More controversial is his baptism, but the tensions which Luke later reports that it evoked are fundamentally about tension with institutionalised authority. Luke similarly sees Jesus' authorisation to declare God's forgiveness as in no way contravening Torah.

Luke alerts us to conflict at a number of points. They mainly result from an emphasis on the universal. The sermon at Nazareth is at one level dealing with local provincialism; at a secondary level it raises the issue of Gentiles, an issue which involves Law. But generally the Law is a secondary issue; the primary issue is that Jesus comes as Spirit anointed deliverer. After the rejection at Nazareth Luke's account uses Markan material which shows Jesus in conflict with teachers of the Law. He does so in a way that initially deletes the contrast between the old and the new and between Jesus' authority and that of the scribes. The infancy narrative had placed Jesus firmly on the side of those who rightly uphold Torah. Jesus' response to the leper is to be heard in this light. Jesus' stance is much less ambiguous than in Mark. Only with the healing of the paralytic does Luke return to the matters of conflict. He reshapes Mark's first controversy story so that it becomes a major encounter with Israel's authorities. Here and in the controversies which follow, including those concerning the sabbath, Luke both asserts Jesus' authority and the validity of his interpretation of the Law.

The sermon on the plain is a declaration of God's will but at no point makes connection, positively or negatively, with the Law. We are probably correct to assume that Luke saw no tension between the two. Luke's version of the healing of the centurion's servant does not even have Jesus meet the Gentile, let alone enter his house, though the centurion is a devout supporter of Judaism. Luke's focus is his faith. The purity issues are present, but must wait until his account of Peter's meeting with the centurion, Cornelius, before they are addressed. Here as there, the centurion's piety in relation to Israel is applauded.

Throughout the section we have found that Luke passes over purity issues (contacts with the leper, with the unclean women, with corpses of dead children; entry into Gentile territory; having women in his company). Luke uses material which portrays both John and Jesus as rejected agents of wisdom, but, unlike in Matthew, there seems only an indirect connection between wisdom and Law: John and Jesus are both wrongly accused of acting contrary to Law. Conflict over Law is about interpretation. Jesus' opponents represent the old; he, the new. Jesus both asserts his own authority and asserts the priority of human need in determining the application of Law.

Luke's assumption is that such conflict will lead not only to the suffering and death of the Christ, but also to the suffering of the disciples. In this context the Law, apart from being an issue whose interpretation is in dispute, functions as part of scripture to prophesy such suffering. In the one clear case where Mark has Jesus declare a major aspect of Torah invalid, food laws, Luke has omitted the material, I suspect deliberately, because it would clash with his understanding of history and his own view as reflected elsewhere in his writings.

Luke's account in these chapters assumes that Jesus stands in continuity with the pious observers of the Law who attended his infancy. He keeps God's Law. He expounds God's will, often without specific reference to the written Law, but never in conflict with it. When he does face conflict, it is not over Torah but over its interpretation.

3.3 *Luke 9:51 – 19:27 in Review*

3.3.1 *Luke 9:51 – 11:13*

In 9:51 Luke signals Jesus' determination to go to Jerusalem. The hearer knows what Jerusalem has in store for him. Thus begins the so-called Lukan travel narrative, which links together mainly non Markan material related to the themes of discipleship. Apart from identifying its loose structure as a journey, it is difficult to find other overarching motifs, such as, for instance, that the journey in some way corresponds to the exodus of Israel (cf. 9:31) and portrays Jesus as a new Moses.[71]

In 9:52–53 Jesus is exposed to what Luke knows was a common response of Samaritans to Jewish pilgrims. The disciples want to emulate Elijah by calling down fire on them (cf. 2 Kings 1:10,12), but Jesus refuses (9:54–56). This typological trait hints that Jesus is both like Elijah, yet different from him. The final incident (9:61–62) in the following passage (9:57–62) includes a similar allusion to the Elijah stories, this time echoing the call of Elisha who was ploughing the field (1 Kings 19:20). The imagery is reflected in Jesus' response. But, again, what Elijah allowed, namely Elisha's farewell, Jesus does not allow. Luke is using the Elijah material to underline the demands of discipleship contained in the passage. In the first encounter Jesus emphasises his homelessness, and, by implication, the homelessness of those who follow him (9:57–58). This contrasts with the biblical promises of land and shelter, but Luke is not focusing here on the issue of biblical interpretation.

The second encounter has Jesus call a would be disciple to abandon family burial responsibilities (9:59–60). In any culture this would be an enormous challenge to existing values and Luke doubtless senses this, but shows no sign of seeing it as setting Jesus in conflict with Torah; nor does Torah regulate in such a way that he would be.[72] The same applies to the incident patterned on Elijah's call of Elisha. The demand is shocking and contrasts with usual cultural values, but Luke began with Jesus' determination to confront his fate in Jerusalem and shows Jesus calling for a similar all-out commitment from his followers. This had been Luke's concern already from 9:22, when he first has Jesus predict his suffering. Luke is not setting these incidents in relation to the issue of Jesus and the Law.

Jesus' sending out of the seventy (10:1–12) continues the emphasis on radical commitment among the disciples. The figure may well symbolise the wider Gentile mission to come, but at the literal level of the narrative Luke has Jesus send them as an advance party to cities and localities which

---

71 Cf. C. F. Evans, "The Central Section of Luke's Gospel," in *Studies in the Gospels. Essays in Memory of R. H. Lightfoot*, edited by D. E. Nineham, (Oxford: Blackwell, 1955), pp. 37–53.

72 So Salo, *Law*, pp. 101–102. Nolland, *Luke*, pp. 542, 544–545. Cf. Esler, *Community*, pp. 117–118, who considers this is a breach or challenge of Torah and that Luke knows it. See also the discussion in the chapter on Q and Matthew (8:22).

he was approaching. Luke offers no reflection on any purity issues entailed in their entering houses, as he does in Acts, so that we should best understand the envoys going to Jewish people, not Samaritans as Luke's geography at this point might suggest.

Luke's account twice instructs the disciples to eat the food provided for them: "Stay in the house eating and drinking what they provide" (10:7); "And into whatever city you enter and they welcome you, eat what is set before you" (10:8). Whether in a household or in a community, they are to eat what is provided. 10:7 justifies the instruction by arguing that a labourer deserves to be paid. That is the focus, not food purity issues. In 10:8 food purity issues may be in mind.[73] Here the instruction would not be permission to eat non kosher foods, since the setting is within Israel.[74] Luke will deal with such food issues in Acts. The injunction here in a Jewish setting does, however, reflect a setting of priorities which could come into conflict with any requirement not to eat untithed or wrongly prepared food. As such it probably reflects a contrast with Pharisaic interpretation, rather than with the Law itself.[75]

In 10:13–16 Luke's Jesus pronounces woes against unbelieving towns of Galilee. By having the woes immediately follow the commissioning Luke is showing that Jesus holds similar prospects of rejection before the disciples. In 10:17–20 Luke has the disciples report their successful exercise of authority over demons. Jesus acknowledges their success as the defeat of Satan, but redirects their joy to the assurance that they are chosen by God. Jesus' prayer of thanksgiving follows (10:21). It has the effect of affirming for the hearer that these simple disciples have become the bearers of divine revelation. 10:22 identifies again the source of that authority: Jesus, himself authorised and standing in a unique relationship with the Father. 10:23–24 reinforces, in turn, the unique position of the disciples of Jesus as those who have heard and seen what prophets and kings longed for. Thus Luke sets their unique position in the perspective of promise and fulfilment of scripture. As with the call and ministry of Jesus, so the disciples' commission and ministry relates only indirectly to the Law. The assumption is that they are Law observant, but in line with Jesus' priorities. Law issues come into view only when their interpretation and behaviour is challenged.

---

[73] Cf. Thom 14 juxtaposes the saying about eating and its equivalent of Mark 7:15; Matt 15:11, about the purity of what enters from outside.

[74] So Nolland, *Luke*, p. 553.

[75] Cf. Salo, *Law*, p. 104, who is content to suggest that it should not be read in the light of the apostolic decree, but nevertheless suggests that Luke leaves its interpretation open.

Having located the disciples clearly in the line of fulfilment of God's will in history, Luke turns to recount incidents which offer teaching for these disciples and their successors. The first is significant for showing Jesus and a Jewish lawyer agreeing that the way to life is to keep the twofold law of love for God and love for neighbour, as formulated in the Torah (10:25–29). At this point Luke appears to have used what occurs in Mark at the climax of Jesus' teaching ministry in the temple (cf. Mark 12:28–34).[76] In Luke the lawyer is asking the same question which the rich ruler puts to Jesus 18:18 ("Teacher, what must I do to inherit eternal life?" 10:25; cf. "Good teacher, what must I do to inherit eternal life?" 18:18). His Markan source had the lawyer ask at a more theoretical level about which commandment was greatest (Mark 12:28). Luke has no interest in such distinctions.[77] His focus is not to affirm a hierarchy among the commandments, either in an inclusive sense, as Matthew, or an exclusive one, which sets aside some parts of the Law, like Mark. All God's commandments are to be obeyed! Luke's focus is doing. He will have Jesus conclude: "You go and do the same!" (10:37; cf also 10:28, "Do this and you will live"). In addition, the emphasis is not: what single act must I do to qualify or enter, but what must I do and keep doing? In both, Luke puts the emphasis on doing.[78]

Jesus' response is therefore relevant not only for would-be disciples, but also for those who are already disciples. This would also have been the perspective of the lawyer, whose focus was not conversion, but right response to God. At one level, within Luke's narrative world, John the Baptist had already answered the question (3:10–14), an answer that, for Luke, remains valid. At another level, the obvious answer is: responding positively

---

76 Berger, *Gesetzesauslegung*, pp. 238–241, draws attention to the fact that both here and in 18:18–30 Luke has the same question asked: the way to eternal life. But whereas in 18:18–30 Jesus adds his own demand of almsgiving to the commandments, here almsgiving is portrayed as fulfilment of the command to love one's neighbour. The command to love one's neighbour goes beyond what the decalogue commandments require. The other difference is that here is that there is no call for discipleship; the call is to follow God. I doubt Luke would have acknowledged such differences.

77 So Jervell, "Law," pp. 138–139; Salo, *Law*, p. 109, who writes, "For Luke, all stipulations of the law are equally important, and therefore the claim of one single commandment being above another is omitted (Mk 12:28,31 par Mt)." See also Jervell, "Law," p. 139, who writes, "Love is not conceived as far more than sacrifices (Mark 12:33)."

78 So Salo, *Law*, pp. 107–111. M. Ebersohn, *Das Nächstenliebegebot in der Synoptischen Tradition*, MarbTheolStud 37, (Marburg: Elwert, 1993), pp. 227–234, who writes that the issue is about *doing* the Law, not about doing the *Law* (p. 232). Banks, *Law*, p. 170, argues that Luke has no theoretical interest in the status of the Law; instead the framework for the encounter and the parable expresses "the typical Lukan themes of salvation and compassion." This denies too much.

to Jesus.[79] But responding positively to Jesus means heeding his exposition of God's Law, such as we have in this passage. 10:25–37 is, therefore, not an erratic block which conflicts with Luke's christological claim.[80] Rather it interprets that claim. Luke's Jesus, like John, proclaims repentance for the forgiveness of sins; he declares God's will. Faith means responding to what Jesus teaches and acknowledging his authority. The passage must be read in this light. It brings to expression the assumptions which underlie Luke's gospel from the beginning: obedience to God's Law is foundational; it is the way to life.

In the parable Luke has Jesus contrast two kinds of response to the man's need and expose thereby the inadequacy of the response made by the Jewish religious functionaries (10:30–37). The story assumes that the priest and Levite act to avoid corpse impurity, even though the hearer knows that the man only looks dead.[81] Contracting corpse impurity would have been more serious had the priest and Levite been going up to the temple to serve, rather than on their way down from Jerusalem, but it is still there. A polemical jibe is hardly to be denied, given Luke's portrait of religious leaders to this point. They are judged by the criterion of love, just as the criterion of love had been set against the interpretations of teachers of the Law and the Pharisees in 5:17–26. Making the Samaritan the hero is also loading the story with polemical intent: it effects a reversal. The lowly and marginalised are Luke's heroes. It also reflects Luke's universalism: neighbour is broader than Israelite.[82] Luke uses the twofold love commandment to sharpen a contrast

---

[79] Klinghardt, *Gesetz*, pp. 152–155, argues that the encounter with the lawyer is to be understood in the light of the account of the disciples' mission which precedes it. It is, therefore, about how believing their message relates to keeping the Law in the quest for eternal life. This goes too far; Luke does not indicate that linkage. However, Klinghardt is right to suggest we must read the passage in its broader Lukan context. See also Esler, *Community*, p. 115, who notes that Luke may well mean the passage to be understood in the light of what he says elsewhere, namely, that more is required to achieve fulfilment of the commands of love than relying only on the Law (p. 115). This does not sufficiently weigh the extent to which for Luke Jesus' demands and those of the Law (of God) are much more closely integrated and that this reflects Luke's understanding of salvation and the Christian life.

[80] Cf. Wilson, *Law*. pp. 14–18.

[81] Cf. Banks, *Law*, pp. 105–106, who says there were no purity issues of oral or written law with either the Levite or the priest; similarly, *Salo*, p.110. But there were if the man might have seemed to have been dead – so Fitzmyer, *Luke*, pp. 884, 887.

[82] So Berger, *Gesetzesauslegung*, pp. 238–241; Klinghardt, *Gesetz*,, pp. 152–155, who points out that Luke's answer combines a universal understanding of the command to love neighbour with the strongly Greek emphasis on friendship. Accordingly, salvation is to become a member of the new community based on friendship and the giving up wealth; these are basis for understanding Law observance.

between commitment to observe purity law and concern for human beings in the interpretation of Torah. We may assume that Luke envisages that the lawyer, whose question arises from his aggression (he tests Jesus), is being rebuked along with his colleagues. Luke's focus is therefore both positive and polemical. He is critical neither of the cultus nor of the Law, but rather of its range of functionaries and the way they apply it.

The story of Mary and Martha does not directly relate to Law issues, though the position of women in the community which it assumes is noteworthy.[83] Luke introduces the next episode with another image of the praying Jesus (11:1–13). It introduces instruction about prayer, including the Lord's Prayer and the assurance that God responds to prayer. Jesus argues that even a reluctant friend bedded down in the middle of the night might respond if there is sufficient persuasion (11:5–8); therefore, surely God's response to us should be seen as the kind of thing any good parent would do (11:11–13). This is arguing theology by analogy with common human relationships.

This section is dominated by concern with the demands of discipleship. At the heart of these demands is obedience to Jesus' teaching and, in turn, at the heart of that teaching Luke has placed practical obedience to the Law's demands of love for God and for one's neighbour. Luke again claims the higher ground for Jesus in Torah interpretation.

3.3.2 Luke 11:14 – 16:31

11:14–23 depict Jesus responding to the allegation that he practices exorcism by being in league with Beelzebul, a gross transgression of Torah. In defence, Luke's Jesus asserts that Jesus casts out demons by the "finger of God" (11:20), like Moses before Egypt's magicians (Ex 8:15). This is followed by Jesus' teaching about demons who return in greater numbers (11:24–26). In 11:27–28 Jesus responds to a patronising woman's admiration with the challenge: blessed are those who hear God's word and keep it. Again the focus is on doing. 11:29–32 has Jesus condemn his generation for its unbelief and warn that the people of Nineveh and the queen of the south will sit in judgement on them. 11:33–36 continues the warning of judgement, using the imagery of light and darkness, sight and blindness. Luke appears to be using the whole complex, 11:14–36, primarily as a statement of judgement.

---

[83] Cf. Sanders, *Jews in Luke–Acts*, pp. 184–185, who sees Luke rejecting Martha as Law observant. The evidence does not support this. Luke does not make a connection between her kind of activity and Law observance.

Within it there may be a hint that Jesus' generation is, itself, bedevilled, an application of the returning demons which Matthew made explicit (Matt 12:43–45).

The focus on judgement also provides the setting for Luke's account of Jesus' confrontation with Pharisees in 11:37–44. First, Luke narrates conflict between Jesus and a Pharisee, because Jesus sits down to a meal without first immersing (11:37–41).[84] Jesus' response does not answer the issue directly, but, instead, contrasts the Pharisees' concerns with washing the outside of cups with their lack of attention to the inside of the cup, understood here metaphorically to refer to their own inner moral decadence (11:39).[85] He then points to God as the creator of both internal and external (11:40). The point is again that the internal should be given attention. But it still includes the external as worthy of attention.[86] The issue seems to be what kind of attention.

In 11:41 we have an enigmatic statement: "But give alms to the internal things, and behold all things will be clean for you."[87] Already the setting which describes Jesus eating without purification echoes Mark 7:1–23. Luke had earlier omitted this as part of his so-called great omission. This verse indicates that he knows the material and that the omission was deliberate. It represents Luke's version of Mark's "declaring all foods clean" (7:19).[88] It is therefore potentially of major significance for understanding Luke's approach to Jesus and Torah. The strange expression, "give alms to the things within", seems to be a metaphorical way of reinforcing the point of the previous argument. They should give attention to the heart, the inner moral life, in particular, to developing an attitude of generosity in giving to the poor. If they do so, "all things will be clean."[89] This applies, in the con-

---

[84] On this practice see Booth, *Purity*, pp. 200–201.

[85] So Nolland, *Luke*, p. 664.

[86] So Nolland, *Luke*, pp. 664–665.

[87] Nolland, *Luke*, p. 664, gives the sense as "give alms as an expression of what is inside".

[88] So Nolland, *Luke*, p. 665. He suggests that Luke is writing with reference to Gentiles, while having Jesus respond to Jews. He cites the example of righteous Cornelius who is clean. This seems to me to be foreign to the context.

[89] Klinghardt, *Gesetz*, p. 28, writes: "Pharisäische Almosen (zugunsten auch der Heiden bzw. Sündern in der Gemeinde) vollendet die eigene Reinheit in einer Weise, die die Kontaminierung durch Unreinheit überwindet: 'dann ist alles rein' (11,41)" "Pharisaic almsgiving (to the benefit also of Gentiles, that is to say, sinners in the community) completes their own purity in a manner which overcomes their contamination through impurity: 'then all is clean' (11:41)." For this view he acknowledges K. Berger. This appears to make too much of a systematic principle out of the contrast. The contrast is rather claiming that true piety is to be found in love for others; occupation with details of exter-

text, to washing oneself and to washing cups and, we may assume, to other vessels as well. It need not be read as contravening biblical purity laws and, probably, should not be taken in the Markan sense of declaring all foods clean.[90] Otherwise the narrative of Peter's vision in Acts 10:9–16 would indicate that Peter had missed the point of 11:41. Even then, as we shall see, the significance of the vision for Luke may be only metaphorical.

Three woes follow. In the first Jesus attacks the Pharisees' attention to matters of tithing while neglecting issues of justice and the love of God (11:42). The contrast is not exclusive; tithing is still enjoined. Unlike Matthew, Luke does not express the contrast in terms of greater and lesser commands (Matt 23:23). As we noted in discussing 10:25–29, the encounter with the lawyer, for Luke all commands are equally to be obeyed.[91] The tithing here goes beyond what the Law requires (Lev 27:30–33; Nu 18:12; Deut 14:22–29; 26:12–15, and see the discussion of the Q version in the following chapter). It reflects Pharisaic extension of these laws. Luke does not attack these extensions as such.[92] He enjoins that the tithing requirement be obeyed.

Next he attacks the Pharisees' striving for public privilege (11:43) and alleges they are like unmarked tombs which people walk over unawares (11:44). The metaphor uses the belief that walking over tombs unawares makes one unclean (Nu 19:16).[93] The woes continue in 11:45–46, directed now to lawyers[94] for imposing heavy legal demands, but not helping people fulfil them. The burdens imposed are their interpretations of the Law. Luke's Jesus is not attacking the Law itself.[95]

They also build the tombs of prophets while not realising that they thereby

---

nal washings matter much less. Cf. also Salo, *Law*, pp. 120–122, who argues that the point is not to dismiss Old Testament Law (which is not at stake) nor even Pharisaic practices as such, but to assert the priority of almsgiving.

[90] Cf. Blomberg, "Law," p. 60, who argues that potentially Jesus' statement about purity in 11:41 comes close to Mark's radical conclusion about abrogation in 7:19 and indicates that Luke's omission of Mark 7:1–23 within a larger omission should not be read as dissent (p. 60). Similarly, Turner, "Sabbath," p. 111.

[91] So Jervell, "Law," pp. 138–139; Salo, *Law*, pp. 122–123.

[92] Wilson, *Law*, p. 18; Salo, *Law*, p. 123, draws attention also to 18:9–14, where the fact that the Pharisee tithes is not the problem; his attitude is. Nolland, *Luke*, p. 666, makes the point that Luke has exaggerated the contrast by speaking of comprehensive tithing, but still retains the notion that tithing is required. Cf. Turner, "Sabbath," p. 110, who suggests the injunction to obey may be only rhetorical.

[93] So Salo, *Law*, p, 124.

[94] The change of title both draws attention to the interpreters of the law and associates the Pharisees with them. So Salo, *Law*, p. 124.

[95] So Jervell, "Law," p. 140; Salo, *Law*, pp. 124–125.

show their solidarity with those who killed them (11:47–48).[96] To this latter accusation Luke has Jesus add a prediction by wisdom, pictured here as God's agent who will send them prophets and apostles (11:49–51). Wisdom then links the rejection of these future envoys with the murder of prophets throughout history from Abel to Zechariah and declares that the current generation will pay for all of this. Like the use of wisdom in 7:35, wisdom, here, is not brought into relation with Torah, but stands in the context without further elaboration.

The final woe accuses the lawyers of taking away the key of knowledge and refusing to gain access to knowledge for themselves and hindering others from gaining access (11:52). By knowledge Luke doubtless means the knowledge of God preserved in scripture and especially in the Torah. As teachers of the Law they had been entrusted with its key. Luke's Jesus does not dispute this underlying assumption, but upbraids them for failing to fulfil their task rightly.[97] In 11:53–54 Luke reports that the conflict with the scribes and Pharisee continued outside.

In 12:1 Luke again draws on material he had omitted from Mark. He warns about the leaven of the Pharisees, designating it as hypocrisy (cf. Mark 8:15). In Mark it had been the teaching of the Pharisees attacked in 7:1–23 which effectively excluded Gentiles. By placing the warning here in 12:1, immediately after the confrontations of 11:37–54, Luke directs it against the Pharisees' abuse of the Law attacked especially in 11:37–45, which he designates here as hypocrisy. 12:2–3 warns that all such hidden evil will be exposed. Disciples need not fear persecution, presumably coming from Jesus' opponents, but fear only God (12:4–5). Analogies from nature, God's care about a single sparrow and about the hairs of our head, ground a call for trust in God in the face of such danger (12:6–7). Luke clearly assumes that conflict with Pharisees will bring the disciples in danger of their life. This implies that they will be drawn into conflict between Jesus' interpretation of Torah and that of the Pharisees, as outlined in the woes.

The challenge to hold faith in face of persecution also underlies the promise and warning in 12:8–9. The Son of Man's response before God at the last

---

[96] Salo, *Law*, p. 125, points out that no evidence supports the assumption here that at this time Jews were building such tombs, but, in any case, the practice, itself is not being attacked.

[97] Salo, *Law*, pp 126–127, points out that for Luke the Pharisees are treated less severely than the scribes in the woes. Luke still holds hope that Pharisees will convert and become Christian Pharisees. He suggests that their applications of Law are not in dispute here. With the scribes Luke sees only hopeless opposition which blocks people, including Pharisees, from becoming believers. Luke does not envisage Christian scribes.

judgement will correspond to the disciples' confession or denial of Jesus before people in the present. The theme continues with the warning not to blaspheme the Spirit and with the assurance that the Spirit will teach believers what they are to say when they face trial (12:10–12). The two are clearly linked; blaspheming the Spirit means denying the Spirit's witness to Jesus.

The focus shifts in 12:13–15 to warnings about greed, which continue with the parable about the rich fool in 12:16–21. The connection between fearing the Pharisees and avoiding greed is readily explicable from 11:39 and 16:14–15, where Jesus accuses the Pharisees of greed (16:14–15). The disciples are not to emulate the Pharisees. In urging simple trust in God's providence, Jesus again argues from nature (ravens, lilies and grass; 12:22–32; cf. 12:6–7). Disciples should give away their possessions to the needy and seek lasting treasure in heaven (12:33–34). They should await the coming Son of Man in readiness, as servants waiting for the master's return from a wedding feast and alert to the dangers of burglary (12:35–40). Luke then has Peter ask about the parable's application (12:41). Jesus' reply focuses on the right exercise of leadership in the community of disciples, a role Peter will go on to fulfil (12:41–48). Warnings that Christian discipleship will lead to family divisions follow in 12:49–53, juxtaposed to Jesus' own sense of the suffering he must face. None of this is directly related to Torah; yet it coheres strongly with Jesus' exposition of Torah in the parable of the Good Samaritan.

Jesus' exhortation that disciples should read the signs of the times (12:54–56) and settle their differences among each another not through the public courts (12:57–58), stands in the context of judgement. Jesus sounds like John when he uses the ruthless Roman slaughter of Galileans in the temple and the collapse of a tower to warn about coming judgement and to call people to repent (13:1–5). These are minor but important indications about Luke's view of Jesus' preaching. Its effect is to emphasise the kind of repentance which John enjoined: consistent behavioural change. The parable in 13:6–9 reflects the same focus: there is still chance to repent.

13:10–17 changes scene. Jesus again shows his Jewish piety by attendance at the synagogue.[98] That detail is incidental. The main focus is on Jesus healing a woman on the sabbath in a synagogue. The synagogue leader argues that such healings should be left to the other six days of the week. Jesus responds by arguing from analogy. As it is acceptable practice to untie and water animals on the sabbath, so it is acceptable to release the woman from the bind of Satan on the sabbath. The dispute is in the realm of sabbath

---

[98] So Salo, *Law*, p. 131.

law interpretation. Luke reports that Jesus' answer put his opponents to shame. In itself the argument is not strong and hardly meets the leader's criticism, because daily watering of animals is a necessity, whereas acts of healing an individual are not.[99] This shows that the difference between Jesus and his opponents lies at a deeper level; Jesus refuses to take seriously the kinds of concerns which they bring to sabbath law. Concern to respond to human need overrides concern to protect sabbath observance. Jesus is not challenging the sabbath law; he is defending his practice as appropriate to the sabbath.[100] The episode echoes 6:6–11 and 14:1–6, which follows shortly.

13:18–21 present the parables of the mustard seed and the leaven. It seems they are linked with what precedes very loosely, perhaps by the promise that such deeds of Jesus will lead to greater success. 13:22 reminds us of Jesus' journey to Jerusalem, expressing, perhaps, the same theme. Jesus' own journey of danger may provide a loose link to the exhortation that people strive hard to enter the narrow gate, because few will achieve it (13:23–24). The warning takes up the imagery of a householder who will keep the door shut despite the cries of those outside who claim his acquaintance (13:25–27). By contrast, Jesus offers a vision of Abraham, Isaac, Jacob and prophets in the kingdom of God, joined by many others from all directions of the compass, but with his own contemporaries excluded (13:28–30). This is obviously not a statistically exclusive statement, since many do respond.

In 13:31–33 Luke has the Pharisees report Herod's intention to kill Jesus, a hint already, perhaps, of his role in Jesus' trial. Jesus responds with direct reference to Jerusalem as his place of death, like one of the prophets. In 13:34–35 Jesus bewails Jerusalem's murderous response to the prophets and her refusal to respond to his attempts to bring her caring. Jesus is identifying himself with the sending of people before his own time. Quite possibly Luke envisages Jesus as identifying himself with God's wisdom as in 11:49–51. The declaration that Jerusalem's house is taken away is the first announcement of the temple's impending destruction. It is not critique of the cult as such, but of Jerusalem and its leaders. Jesus also announces he will return to the city and be welcomed with the words of Ps 118:26. People will welcome him with the same words at his entry into Jerusalem in 19:38, but 13:35 is referring not to this event, but to the parousia, which will take place

---

[99] The leader argues similarly to the "general rule" attributed to Akiba *mShabb* 19:1, "Any act of work that can be done on the eve of Sabbath does not override the Sabbath, but what cannot be done on the even of the Sabbath overrides the Sabbath." (also *mPes* 6:2; *mMen* 11:3).

[100] So Salo, *Law*, p. 132.

after "the house is taken away".[101] It assumes a role for Jerusalem in the eschaton. It echoes the kind of eschatological hope expressed in the infancy narratives and elsewhere (eg. Acts 1:6).

14:1–6 offers a third instance of controversy over Jesus' healing on the sabbath, this time in the house of a Pharisee who had invited him to attend a meal. As in 7:36 the fact of Jesus' dining with a Pharisee is important indirect evidence of how Luke perceived Jesus' piety.[102] It is of a kind that such an invitation on the part of a strict Pharisee is thinkable. As in 13:10–17 and 6:6–11, the issue is interpretation of sabbath law,[103] not its disregard or abrogation. As in 13:10–17 Jesus argues from analogy; as it acceptable to rescue a child or an ox which had fallen into a well on the sabbath, so it is acceptable to heal on the sabbath. The analogy is again weak, because it compares an emergency situation with one where the healing could be performed on any other day.[104] It seems written not from the perspective of serious ongoing dialogue about Law interpretation with Jewish authorities, but from a distance, where the Jewish objections are not taken seriously, but trivialised. Luke's Jesus, by implication, has no time for that kind of sabbath interpretation. Seen in the context of the other two episodes we must conclude that Luke sees Jesus as observing sabbath law and acting in consistency with it when he heals and therefore as rejecting what he characterises as the trivialising interpretations of the Pharisees. They are illegitimate, because, in the view of Luke's Jesus, they fail to take seriously the compassion which the Law enjoins.

Within the same meal setting Luke has Jesus offer a practical strategy to avoid being embarrassed in the current seating etiquette at meals (14:7–10). It is a parody on current practices. It also functions as a parable, for Luke has Jesus conclude on a different plane with words about divine judgement and reward: "Those who exalt themselves will be humbled and those who humble themselves will be exalted" (14:11). Further advice follows in 14:12–14 where Jesus suggests people not make banquets for their friends and rela-

---

[101] So Nolland, *Luke*, pp. 742–744; J. B. Chance, *Jesus, the Temple and the New Age in Luke–Acts*, (MercerUP, 1988), pp. 130–132. See also Allison, "Matt 23:39 = Luke 13:35b," pp. 75–84. cf. Fitzmyer, *Luke*, pp. 1035–1036, who sees an allusion to both.

[102] So Salo, *Law*, p. 132.

[103] So Merkel, "Israel," p, 288. Cf. P.–G. Klumbies, "Die Sabbatheilungen Jesu nach Markus und Lukas," in *Jesu Rede von Gott und ihre Nachgeschichte im frühen Christentum. Beiträge zur Verkündigung Jesu und zum Kerygma der Kirche. FS für Willi Marxsen*, edited by Koch, D.–A. et al., (Gütersloh: Mohn, 1989), pp. 165–178, here: 173–178, argues that the focus of Luke in all three sabbath healings is christology; the sabbath aspect belongs merely to the setting.

[104] So Salo, *Law*, p. 133.

tives and the rich who are able to repay the favour, but for the poor and needy, who cannot. Such behaviour reaps reward from God. It is obviously a provocative saying, a touch unrealistic at a practical level, but designed to urge a change in lifestyle toward concern for the needy.

The same concern is reflected in the parable of the great feast which immediately follows (14:16–24). It has become to some extent an allegory. The poor and needy symbolise ordinary Jews, like the first disciples who are also called "the poor", but should also be seen as including those who are literally poor and marginalised. The people of the highways symbolise the Gentiles. Expansion to the Gentiles will raise issues of Law. Luke passes over them here. 14:25–27 urges total discipleship even when it means family division and 14:28–35 urges the same disciplined response, illustrating it by preparations for war and by the need to keep salt pure.

Conflict with Pharisees and scribes about Jesus' eating with toll collectors and sinners sets the scene for the three parables of chapter 15. In the similar controversy which Luke took over from Mark in 5:27–32 (cf. Mark 2:13–17), Luke had added to Jesus' words, "I have not come to call the righteous, but sinners", the phrase: "to repentance". Luke has Jesus conclude the parables of the lost sheep and the lost coin with the same theme: "I tell you, there will be joy like this in heaven over one sinner who repents rather than over ninety-nine righteous who have no need of repentance" (15:7; similarly 15:10). Luke justifies Jesus' mixing with toll collectors and sinners on the grounds that he seeks to lead them to repent. In putting it this way Luke's focus is on their moral sin (of which they are to repent), not their impurity.

Within Luke's version of Jesus' answer to these accusations about his company, the parable of the prodigal son serves to illustrate repentance and to counter complaints against acceptance of such penitents. It is not clear whether Luke is also seeing the parable as justifying Jesus' mixing with, and therefore acceptance, of toll collectors by eating with them, whether or not they have repented. Probably not. The issue, relevant for Luke's community, would have been one of warding off criticism that the acceptance of sinners, especially Gentiles, into Christian faith communities represented disregard for traditional teaching to avoid such company with Gentiles, probably on both moral and purity grounds. Maybe Christian Pharisees within his community were espousing such teaching. The parable itself turns in part on Jewish sensitivities; the low point is reached where the man is sent out to tend pigs, unclean animals! Luke would be aware of this; but his focus is elsewhere: acceptance of sinners and warding off criticism which the parable exposes as mean and unnatural, in contrast to the spontaneous love shown by the Father.

Luke's version of the parable of the unjust steward focuses on appropriate use of riches (16:1–13), including practical advice about the advantages of having contacts with the rich.[105] This may relate, in turn, to the presence of toll collectors in Jesus' company. 16:14–15 has Jesus respond to the Pharisees' ridicule of his approach to riches with another attack on their hypocrisy and greed.

There follows the statement: "The Law and the Prophets are until John; from then the kingdom of God is being preached and all are forcing their way into it" (16:16).[106] It belongs closely together with what follows: "But it is easier for heaven and earth to pass away than for one stroke of the Law to fall. Whoever divorces his wife and marries another commits adultery and whoever marries a woman divorced from her husband commits adultery" (16:17–18). In the Lukan context the point is to say that, despite the new age of the kingdom, the Torah still applies and that this is evident in the instance of Jesus' exposition of marriage law which Jesus applies in the strictest possible terms.[107] Conzelmann writes, "Until now there was 'only' the law and the Prophets, but from now on there is 'also' the preaching of the Kingdom".[108] 16:16–17 continues Jesus' confrontation of the Pharisees. Their application of divorce is an instance of their greed.[109] The following

---

[105] For the view that originally the parable at the core of the section was a bold attempt by Jesus to portray himself under the guise of a rogue, who forgave debts without proper authority, see W. R. G. Loader, "Jesus and the Rogue in Luke 16,1–8A. The Parable of the Unjust Steward," *Revue Biblique* 86 (1989), pp. 518–532.

[106]. Cf. Klinghardt, *Gesetz*, pp. 70–77, who speculates that Luke sees John and Jesus as priestly and royal Messiah, respectively, a notion he uses to strengthen the image of John as primarily preacher of the Law. He interprets 16:16 in the sense that in proclaiming the Law John, as priestly Messiah, prepares the people for Jesus, the royal Messiah, who confirms John's teaching about the Law, but, as the one gifted with the Spirit, goes beyond Israel (p. 80).

[107] So Jervell, "Law," p. 139. Klinghardt, *Gesetz*, pp. 81–82 n. 7, draws attention to studies of the expectation that at the eschaton there would be changes to Torah. In this he notes clarifications which Elijah is believed to bring: concerning purity of families and unresolved rabbinic disputes. He also notes that actual changes pertain to central purity laws: unclean animals or animals not ritually slaughtered and relations with unclean women. With Schäfer, he believes that such discussions derive from within Hellenistic Judaism. Much of this is speculative and dependent on late sources.

[108] So Conzelmann, *Theology*, p. 23; similarly Klinghardt, *Gesetz*, pp. 19, 82; Salo, *Law*, pp. 143, 145, 160–161; Fitzmyer, "Law," p. 180; Nolland, *Luke*, pp. 820–821, Luke means the Law is still in force and permanently valid (not just for a fixed time); J. B. Tyson, *Images of Judaism in Luke-Acts*, (Columbia: Univ. of Sth Carolina, 1992), p. 71.

[109] So Nolland, *Luke*, pp. 821–822, who takes 16:18 as meaning: divorce in order to remarry (pp. 821–822); H. Moxnes, *The Economy of the Kingdom: Social Conflict and*

parable reinforces this concern, when it berates the greed of the rich man (16:19–31).

Luke appears to sense no tension between 16:18 and the Law's provision for divorce.[110] He may have been aware that Jesus was not the only one to interpret Torah in this way (cf. CD 4:21).[111] He later omits the Markan discussion which includes a version of the logion (cf. Mark 10:2–12), probably because its setting could be read as casting Moses in a poor light.[112]

Given the context, the focus of 16:17 is primarily ethical.[113] That is clearly Luke's concern in applying the Law, but it would be wrong to read it as exclusively ethical.[114] Attempts to harmonise 16:17 with 16:18 by suggest-

---

Economic Relations in Luke's Gospel, (Philadelphia: Fortress, 1988), pp. 149–150, who emphasises that Luke means the Law is in force and the Pharisees by their greed transgress it. He strongly emphasises the economic power of the Pharisees and the importance of almsgiving in Luke (pp. 151–153).

[110] So Tyson, *Images*. p. 71; Fitzmyer, "Law," pp. 197–198 n. 11. Cf. Salo, *Law*, pp. 146–147, who suggests that Luke did sense contradiction between Jesus' divorce teaching and the Law, but sought to hide the conflict, omitting Mark 10:2–9 (see also pp. 149–150). On p. 148, however, he notes that is questionable whether such stricter application would really have been seen necessarily as contradicting Torah. Cf. Hübner, *Gesetz*, p. 207; Horn, *Glaube*, pp. 276–278; Wilson, *Law*, pp. 29–30, 43–51, who uses his belief that 16:18 would be read as abrogation of the Law to argue that Luke 16:17 cannot be absolute.

[111] Klinghardt, *Gesetz*, p. 28, argues that in 16:18 Luke is consciously applying laws originally applicable only to priests to the community and so making a special claim of purity for his community. I doubt such a Pharisaic interest on Luke's part; it is not evident elsewhere. With Berger, he sees 16:18 as typical of Pharisaic extension of priestly law to lay people (pp. 88–89). See also the discussion of Matt 5:32 above. Such law (Lev 21:7,14) forbids priests to marry women who have already has sexual relations with another man on grounds of her impurity and evidence shows that such extension was being applied (Jub 33:9; TRub 3:15; 6:4–5; TLev 9:10; *mSota* 5:1; Jos *Ant* 4:245; PsPhoc 205; p. 88 n. 9). Pagan Hellenistic parallels also indicate emphasis on marital faithfulness as a virtue, both in philosophical contexts (especially Pythagorean) and in cultic settings (pp. 89–94). Thus Klinghardt sees Luke appealing in 16:18 to two fronts (p. 95).

[112] So Salo, *Law*, pp. 148–149.

[113] So Nolland, *Luke*, pp. 820–821.

[114] Horn, *Glaube*, pp. 71–72, believes that Luke looks back on a past epoch and uses the Law here only to describe ethical behaviour, especially giving to the poor. He argues that Luke treats ceremonial laws only as customs, so that 16:17 should be read in only a limited sense. Luke is concerned to show continuity and does so on the basis of this understanding of the Law (pp. 87–88). Giving to the poor is the heart of Torah for Luke (pp. 89–120). Thus Horn argues that for Luke Law observance is primarily a way of indicating continuity in salvation history (pp. 273, 275–276). On the other hand, he rejects the idea that Luke espouses the ethical as Law and jettisons the ceremonial as custom, because Luke does not hold fast to such distinctions (cf. Acts 21:21; 28:17; 25:8; p. 274), though he believes that Luke's language opened that possibility. According to Horn, Luke assumes that Jewish Christians fulfil the Law and that Gentiles maintain continuity through the apostolic decree (p. 275). Luke is concerned to stress both continuity and

ing that in 16:17 Luke means only the Law as fulfilled by Christ[115] or as taught by him run contrary to the role of the Law in the gospel thus far.[116] Similarly it is unsatisfactory and unnecessary to dismiss these verses as relics of tradition.[117] 16:18 would not necessarily have been understood as abrogating Torah. 16:17 suggests that Luke did not take it in this way. He is not, therefore, forced into a compromise by including it.[118] Rather the whole is a consistent unit emphasising strictness. It confronts the Pharisees, and those who would identify with them, with the Law's demands. In these demands the emphasis is to fall, above all, on love and generosity towards the needy. The result is that Luke has Jesus state what our review has already found: Jesus, according to Luke, remains Torah observant, like his family before him. With the coming of the kingdom nothing has changed concerning the Law's validity.

The theme of riches and their abuse continues in the parable of the rich man and Lazarus (16:19–31). Its final verse takes into view both the teaching of Moses and the prophets, on the one hand, and that of the post Easter community of Jesus, on the other: "He said to them, 'If they do not listen to Moses and the prophets, nor will they be persuaded is someone should rise from the dead'." Luke clearly assumes that to follow the Law and the prophets, which must include generous giving to the poor, is the way of salvation.[119] This again raises issues about Lukan christology. Luke has no dif-

---

coincidence between the Law and Jesus' teaching. In doing so, Luke understands the Law primarily as the demand to love one's neighbour. He is not interested in setting this command in relation to others in terms of priority. This orientation is reflected in 10:26 and is the context for understanding 16:17, which is not a statement of principle, but something to be taken closely with its context, which stresses moral attitudes. 16:18 shows that it is not to be taken literally (pp. 276–278). I would have thought 16:18 shows that it is to be taken strictly.

[115] Cf. Blomberg, "Law," p. 61, who appeals to the use of the word pese˜in "fall" to argue that "the Law has not passed away without failing to accomplish everything for which it was intended" (p. 61). In this sense not one stroke of a letter has failed; all is being fulfilled. The divorce logion is also thus an example of change, not continuity. This ignores the strong focus on ethical demand in the context.

[116] Cf. Marshall, *Luke*, pp. 626–630; Sanders, *Jews in Luke–Acts*, pp. 199–202, who suggests Luke means 16:16 as scripture prophecy and by 16:17 that only some of the Law is still upheld, including 16:18 on divorce.

[117] Cf. Banks, *Law*, p. 219, who writes of 16:16–18 as, at first sight, "an anomaly in the gospel", arguing that the retention of 16:17–18 "probably results from his faithfulness in preserving the tradition (cf. 14:2ff.) even when it does not yield to his particular concerns" (p. 220).

[118] Cf. Esler, *Community*, pp. 120–121; Salo, *Law*, pp. 148–149.

[119] So Wilson, *Law*, pp. 17–18; Fitzmyer, "Law," p. 180; Klinghardt, *Gesetz*, p. 29, sees here an attack by Luke on ethnic understandings of having Abraham as father, already

ficulty in claiming continuity between the messages of Jesus, John, and the
Law and the Prophets. It is not only because he perceives them in a continuity of redemptive history. He also sees them demanding the same response
and the same continuing behaviour. The Jesus of Luke is not supplanting
the Law nor adding a requirement over and above the Law. The kingdom is
evident in the new manifestation of the Spirit in Jesus' ministry. Jesus' coming as the anointed Christ, the divinely created Son of God, represents new
power, a new initiative, new acts of liberation; but all this reinforces the
message of repentance; it does not replace it. Luke does not envisage a new
God or new source of redemption, just a greatly expanded access to the one
who is its source.

This section contains some of the most important material in the gospel
concerning Jesus' attitude towards the Law. It shows Jesus vigorously asserting the Law's claims while strongly rejecting the approach of his critics
which are shown to be trivial or hypocritical and based on greed. For all
Luke's claims, some issues remain unresolved, not least, those concerned
with relating to Gentiles. There is also the sense that Luke makes his claims
about Jesus to persuade the faithful; he is not entering serious dialogue with
Jews outside of his community. It is quite another question whether what he
claims about Jesus' Torah faithfulness would win their assent.

3.3.3 Luke 17:1 – 19:27

Luke 17 turns again to instruction for the disciples and their future community. It warns against causing other disciples to fall, enjoins mutual confrontation and forgiveness, encourages faith, and warns against pride and
self satisfaction (17:1–10). In the healing of the ten lepers (17:11–19), Luke
has Jesus instruct them that they should show themselves to the priest, just
as he had with the leper in 5:12–16. Jesus remains observant of Law. Here,
however, the detail is more sparse and Jesus does not make physical contact.
All this is incidental, however, to the main theme which is that only one of
them, a Samaritan, returned to give thanks. He sets an example of gratitude.
There is polemical edge in the fact that it is again a Samaritan, one of the
despised, who is the hero (cf. 10:30–37).

In 17:20–21 Jesus turns away concern about the timing of the kingdom's

---

signalled by John in 3:8, which are made the basis of purity claims and separateness.
Similarly Salo, *Law*, pp. 150–152, who emphasises the link between the parable and the
address to the Pharisees in 16:14–15 and notes that the parable also implies that ethnic
membership alone is inadequate.

arrival, put on the lips of a Pharisee; Jesus declares that the kingdom is in their midst; but they refuse to recognise it. Jesus also urges the disciples not to take notice of predictions about when the Son of Man would come (17:22–23). Instead they should recognise that it will be preceded by suffering and rejection by this generation. People will be going about the normal business of living, when the end will suddenly come and the righteous will be taken off to salvation (17:24–37).

In 18:1–8 Jesus encourages the disciples to pray and not lose heart when, before the Son of Man's coming, they face suffering. 18:9–14 is linked to what precedes only loosely, by the theme of prayer. It offers another typically Lukan contrast between the response of a Pharisee and a penitent sinner. At stake is not the Pharisee's practices, but his attitude. At this point Luke returns to his Markan source. He picks up the thread at Mark 10:13–16, Jesus' welcoming the children. He had left off in 9:51 at Mark 10:1. He does not include Mark 10:2–12, having already included his own version of the divorce logion at 16:18, and perhaps wanting to avoid Mark's contrast between what Moses said and what Jesus said.[120]

Luke's version of the rich man coming to Jesus (18:18–23; cf. Mark 10:17–22) remains close to Mark's. Like Matthew, he trims the list of commandments to conform with that of the decalogue and reorders the list according to a common pattern which puts the prohibition of adultery first.[121] He also sets greater distance between Jesus and the inquirer: he is a ruler; Luke omits that Jesus loves him. It is consistent with Luke's emphasis that he has Jesus convey the message that it is necessary to keep the commandments if one is to inherit eternal life. As we have seen, Luke has the lawyer in 10:25 ask the same question. Jesus' response should not be read as formulating only the first step,[122] which would imply it was an inadequate response. We should not see obedience to the commandments, in itself, as deficient. The issue is the adequacy of the man's obedience. It lacks something. We must bear in mind that many would have answered like the ruler. A good many of those would have been among the Pharisees. The issue was not whether he had kept the commandments, but how well. Therefore Jesus' response in 18:22,

---

[120] So Merkel, "Israel," p. 387.

[121] On the order in Luke see Klinghardt, *Gesetz*, p. 127, who notes that putting the prohibition of adultery first reflects an emphasis present in Hellenistic Judaism and present in the apostolic decree.

[122] Cf. Banks, *Law*, p. 164, who claims that Jesus' reference to the Law in Luke's account "is primarily intended as an endorsement of its value as a testimony to, or its forming a springboard for, the more ethically–demanding and uniquely personal claim which follows." Similarly Blomberg, "Law," p. 61.

that the man sell all and give to the poor, is not to be seen as an additional demand, let alone a rival one to the Law's demand. Rather it is a confrontation with the Law's true meaning, just as the parable of the Good Samaritan had been in response to the same issue. Both here and there the focus is on compassion and care towards others. This is the constant feature of Jesus' attitude towards the Law in Luke.[123]

The command to follow should not be read as a second step required for salvation.[124] Jesus did not ask all to follow him in this way. But Jesus was claiming that in this case selling up and following was what was required; this demand exposed the qualitative inadequacy of the man's quantitative claim to have kept the Law. The challenge would show whether he really kept the commandments in the spirit in which they were intended. Luke could not think of obedience to the Law and obedience to Jesus as separable.[125] Jesus had come to declare God's will. Of course, obeying God's will also includes acknowledging those whom God has sent; that now means believing in God's Son.

The man fails to come to terms with this kind of obedience. In Luke's

---

[123] Klinghardt, *Gesetz*, p. 127, argues that Luke juxtaposes the decalogue command with the demand to give up property, the former focused on relationships with outside the community, the latter with behaviour within the community. According to Klinghardt, Luke changes the encounter from one about becoming a disciple to one about being one (p. 132).

[124] Vouga, *Loi*, pp. 132–133, emphasises that Luke is not setting Law against gospel, but sees them in continuity: 18:22 takes up and continues the point of 18:20. Cf. Wilson, *Law*, pp. 27–29, who writes, "Care for the poor could have been seen as fulfilment of the law, but the call for radical poverty and personal discipleship could not" (p. 28). Could it not be seen as putting the focus where it needed to be for the rich in their obedience to the Law? Esler, *Community*, p. 117, suggests that the Law is both upheld and transcended. Fitzmyer, *Luke*, pp. 1197, 1200, speaks of more than fidelity to the Law and of Jesus' response as drawing the man on. This seems to suggest to me that he is not adding something to the commandments, but expounding them in a fuller sense. Nolland, *Luke*, pp. 886–888, argues that there is clearly more required: relinquishing wealth and following Jesus, so that Luke's Jesus starts with what he already knows and Luke accepts him as pious like Zechariah, and Elizabeth, Joseph and Mary in the infancy stories. This assumes that Jesus did not understand the decalogue commandments as entailing what is enshrined in the love command. I doubt Luke would have made such a distinction.

[125] So also Salo, *Law*, pp. 152–153, who notes that the command to give to the poor is not an additional command. He writes: "Probably it is beyond the horizon of the author to make here a clear distinction between the commandments of the Torah and the orders of Jesus. Rather, there is a shift from the Torah (cited five commandments) to the ordinance of Jesus" (pp. 155–156). Between these mediates the demand to give to the poor. Thus, he claims, the text offers a different understanding from 10:25–28; 16:29,31: renouncing wealth for the sake of the poor and following Jesus. Even this distinction may be reading too much into the text. I shall return to this in the conclusions.

account, Jesus directs his teaching about the difficulty of rich people entering the kingdom to a wider audience than the disciples, unlike Mark (18:24–
25; cf. Mark 10:23). The same applies to the reassuring words that finally
only God can achieve the impossible and bring salvation (18:26–27). Finally Jesus reassures Peter that those who have left all will receive more
than ample compensation in this life and eternal life in the next (18:28–30).

Luke continues with Mark's third passion prediction in 18:31–34 (cf. Mark
10:32–34) and then skips over to Mark 10:46–52 to recount the healing of
the blind man (18:35–42; Bartimaeus in Mark). Luke omits the interim
Markan material about the ambitions of James and John (Mark 10:35–41)
and about lowliness in leadership (Mark 10:42–45). He preserves the latter
for Jesus' final discourse to the disciples at the last supper (22:24–27). Luke
accommodates the healing story from Mark within the narrative at the point
where Jesus enters Jericho, rather than as he departs, as in Mark, because he
now inserts in its place the account of Jesus' meeting with Zacchaeus (19:1–
10).

This latter includes complaints by people that Jesus went to eat at the
house of a sinner, recalling 15:1 and 5:27–32. Luke makes no comment on
any issues of Law which this may have entailed; he has already justified
mixing with sinners on the grounds of seeking to win their repentance and
this story exemplifies a model response (15:1–32). The focus, as Zacchaeus'
response shows, is primarily moral not ritual. His response, while delivered
in the present tense, should not be read as self defence, but as a declaration
of intent.[126] Zacchaeus' repentance includes restitution which satisfies (more
than satisfies) Torah requirements.[127] He also gives away half of his possessions. It is interesting that this stands in contrast with Jesus' challenge to
the ruler that he give up all (18:22). It confirms that Luke would not have
seen 18:22 as applicable to all. Yet the orientation is the same. Furthermore
what the rich ruler did not do (18:23) and the disciples found impossible

---

[126] Cf. A. C. Mitchell, "Zacchaeus Revisited: Luke 19,8 as a Defence," *Biblica* 71
(1990), pp. 153–176, who argues that Luke means not to portray Zacchaeus as a sinner,
but as a true child of Abraham, who rightly handles his money and makes restitution.
Similarly Fitzmyer, *Luke*, pp. 1220–1221. See, however, the criticism in D. Hamm,
"Zacchaeus Revisited Once More: A Story of Vindication or Conversion?" *Biblica* 72
(1991), pp. 249–252, who argues that Zacchaeus' so–called defence includes a confession
guilt: he has restitution to make. Similarly Nolland, *Luke*, p. 906. What would be the
point of the narrative, otherwise? To identify an exemplary toll collector?

[127] Nolland, *Luke*, p. 906, makes the point that while fourfold restitution appears in
some aspects of Jewish and Roman law and was being applied more widely, Zacchaeus'
response is to be seen as more than just the fulfilment of laws. Cf. also Klinghardt, *Gesetz*,
p. 57, who claims that Zacchaeus' act fulfils the requirements which Haberim imposed on
sinners for membership.

(18:25–26), Zacchaeus does. Accordingly Jesus declares: "Today salvation has come to this house" (17:9). His additional words, "For he also is a son of Abraham," reflect the inclusive focus of Jesus' mission to Israel; no son of Abraham is excluded. Jesus' closing words, "The Son of Man came to seek and save the lost" (17:10), recall the parables in 15:1–32. They had already refuted the charge laid here against Jesus. The fruits of Jesus' salvific activity quash all charges that Jesus acts contrary to Torah.

Luke next has Jesus address a parable to those concerned that his approach to Jerusalem may herald the coming of the kingdom (19:11–27). The parable reflects the image of kingdom by telling of a man who has gone off to be made a king. It then focuses on the behaviour of the servants who remain behind. In effect it answers concern about nearness of the kingdom with exhortation. As they await the parousia of Jesus the king, they should get on with the work of the kingdom as faithful servants.

3.3.4 Conclusion

Within Luke's travel section we continue to find Jesus focused primarily on his mission. This includes the prospect of suffering and the involvement of the disciples in both the mission and the suffering. Luke identifies Jesus with wisdom, particularly acting as the one who sends messengers to God's people; but there is no hint that for him wisdom and Torah are associated. Mainly Luke offers Jesus' teaching without bringing it into specific relation to Torah. Often it takes the form of direct instruction, sometimes with arguments from human relationships or from nature, mostly directed to life in the community of faith.

Within these chapters there are, however, a number of points where the Law comes into view. Some are incidental. That Jesus dines with Pharisees implies perceptions of Jesus as sufficiently Law observant to make this possible; Luke was aware of the issues as Acts shows. Jesus continues to appear as naturally pious, regularly praying. He enjoins the lepers to obey Torah's requirements. There is no indication that Luke senses a breach of Torah when Jesus calls a would-be disciple away from burial of his father, nor in the challenges to family loyalties, nor in the prominent presence of women. Purity issues are present in the imagery of the parables (the corpse in the parable of the Good Samaritan, the pigs in the parable of the Prodigal Son) and in the imagery of walking over graves unawares, but receive no direct attention. In the parable of the great feast Luke touches on the Gentile mission, but leaves potential Law issues unaddressed. Zacchaeus' response of restitution reflects and exceeds the demands of Jewish Law; his status as a son of Abraham warrants his salvation in Jesus' mission to Israel. Luke again hints at Jerusalem's role in eschatological hope, but offers no further detail.

Not all matters pertaining to the Law are incidental. In two accounts Luke's Jesus responds to the fundamental question: what must I do to inherit eternal life? On both occasions Jesus points to the Law. In 10:25–28 he points to the commandment to love God and one's neighbour and proceeds to expound the latter in the parable of the Good Samaritan. In 18:18–23 he points to the ethical commandments of the decalogue. Both passages make such adherence to Torah crucial. The same is assumed in the parable of Lazarus and the rich man (16:19–31). All three accounts imply a close connection between obeying the Law's demands and responding to the demands of Jesus.

Beside Luke's positive statements are attacks on others for failure to uphold the Law. Thus the parable of the Good Samaritan exposes lack of love in the representative religious leaders of the story. Both there and in the account of the grateful Samaritan leper there is a jibe at the prominent models of piety. The parable of the rich man and Lazarus reflects a similar view; it stands in the context of confrontation of the greed of the Pharisees. The same orientation is present in Luke's version of the encounter with the rich man, in Luke, the rich ruler. Jesus' challenge exposes the inadequacy of the man's approach. It may also be intended in the portrait of the mean elder brother in the parable of the prodigal son. In all the focus is on love and on giving to the poor.

This focus controls Jesus' response to criticism about healing on the sabbath. We saw in the previous section that, taken on its own, 6:1–5 might suggest that Jesus asserts his authority as Lord of the sabbath in a way that claims the right to dispense with it. The other arguments presented in 6:1–5 and the way Jesus defends himself in the other three sabbath controversies show that this is not so. Rather Jesus is claiming authority to interpret sabbath law aright. Jesus argues the legitimacy of his approach as valid interpretation. That approach puts human need foremost and exposes Jesus' opponents as concerned more with protecting rules than with people. Sabbath law remains; it is a matter of right interpretation. At the same time the claim made for Jesus' Torah faithfulness is directed at the faithful; it is not serious dialogue with Jewish partners outside Luke's community.

Another area of conflict is about Jesus' dining with toll collectors and sinners. Jesus' responses always imply the criticism is not primarily on ritual, but on moral grounds. Luke consistently represents Jesus' action as a strategy to secure their repentance. His behaviour is thus not only in conformity with the Law; it conforms to the Law's goals. The most blatant accusation of transgression of the Law is that Jesus is a sorcerer acting by the power of Beelzebub. This is flatly denied; rather "the finger of God", by which Moses wrought his miracles, is again at work.

The same orientation is evident in the way Luke's Jesus confronts the Pharisees in relation to their practices, rules about washing before meals and about washing cups and other vessels (11:37–41). Here Luke uses parts of the radical Markan passage of 7:1–23, which he has otherwise omitted. He restricts their application to such practices as the washings and leaves out Mark's disparagement of these practices. Luke argues that making almsgiving, generosity towards the poor, the focus in keeping the commandments, meets their true demand; attention to the finer detail of ritual purity, such as is exemplified in the concern about immersing and washing cups, becomes irrelevant. This is far from declaring scriptural Law on such things as irrelevant, as Peter's subsequent behaviour in Acts 10 confirms. A similar orientation is probably reflected in the injunction that the disciples not make a fuss about what is supplied to them as meals (10:8). What Luke's Jesus says about tithing confirms that his target is not the practices themselves, but neglect of the law of love. He upholds the application of tithing laws, even to minor foodstuffs. He acknowledges that the lawyers have, in the Torah, the key of knowledge. The problem is often designated as hypocrisy. It is also over preoccupation with fulfilling details of ritual law at the expense of justice and love of God. Luke dramatises the issue in his contrast between the Pharisee and the sinner: the attitude is under attack, not the scruples themselves.

It is in the context of such a confrontation that Luke's makes his most direct statement about the Law (16:16–17). It identifies the role of the Law and the prophets up till the time of John and the coming of the kingdom in Jesus, probably envisaging that role both as prophetic and as providing the source of discerning God's will. It then points out that the coming of the kingdom has in no way changed the validity of the Law, not a stroke of it. Luke reinforces the point by including Jesus' saying forbidding divorcing and remarrying (16:18). By appending Jesus' divorce logion Luke points the hearer towards an even stricter adherence than usual. Accordingly, Luke omits Mark's narrative about marriage where Jesus contrasts his teaching with that of Moses. In 16:16–18 Luke's Jesus makes it abundantly clear that in the time of the kingdom the Law is fully in force; greed and exploitation have no place. While the focus of the context is on use and abuse of wealth, Luke's attitude elsewhere towards practices of the Law would lead one to expect that he understood 16:17 as affirming the Law in its totality, as interpreted by Jesus.

At no point in this section does Luke portray Jesus' teaching as abrogating Torah or calling it into question. Where Luke needs to, he emphasises Torah's abiding validity and has Jesus counter unnecessarily restrictive interpretations. Mostly he offers Jesus' teaching without showing any concern to relate it to Torah. He neither sees conflict; nor is he concerned to portray Jesus as expounder of Torah. With Jesus the kingdom of God has come near, so that what he offers is new, in addition to the abiding demands of Torah, but in a way that leaves them in tact and in force. On the other hand the isolated allusions to future mission to the Gentiles keep alive the awareness that there are issues still to be addressed.

3.4 Luke 19:28 – 24:53 in Review

3.4.1 Luke 19:28 – 21:38

Luke's account of Jesus' entry into Jerusalem (19:28–40) stays close by his Markan source (Mark 11:1–10), but for a few minor details. One is the addition to the words of the crowd, "Peace in heaven and glory in the highest" (19:40). It is an echo of the angelic announcement at Jesus' birth (2:14). "Peace" is the link word for Jesus' lamentation which immediately follows: "If you, even you, had only known on this day the things that matter forpeace!" (19:41). A prediction of the city's siege and fall follows in 19:41–44. The effect of this announcement is striking since it establishes Jerusalem's destruction as a major theme in what follows and relates Jesus' rejection in Jerusalem to that event. It also gives the impression that Jerusalem matters to Luke. The ethos of Jewish hope, so marked in the infancy narratives, is making a return.

Like Matthew, Luke alters Mark's compositional structure at this point. He has Jesus go directly to the temple and make his confrontation (19:45–46). In it Luke mentions only a single act: expelling those who sold and, again like Matthew, he omits "for all nations" after Jesus' words: "It is written, 'my house shall be a house of prayer'." Luke does not relate the event to issues of Gentile involvement. That may be because he will deal with the issue of the Gentile mission only later, in Acts. But it may (also) be that Luke sees Jesus primarily attacking the presence of sellers in the temple.

Luke does not appear to treat the occasion as a symbolic prediction of judgement and destruction as one might expect after 19:41–44. For he has neither included the cursing of the fig tree nor picked up Mark's contrast between the old temple and the new temple of the community of prayer and faith (cf. Mark 11:12–25). There is not even an immediate sequel; for Luke goes on to speak of Jesus' teaching daily in the temple and of a continuing search by the authorities of a way to kill him (19:47–48). The action of beginning to clear the temple of sellers appears then in Luke as primarily an attempt to make it a better place for worship.[128] One might also suspect, given Luke's attacks on the abuse of wealth by religious authorities, that he sees such improvement as ridding the temple of its commercial enterprises and its potential exploitative practices, of which the sellers were just one instance.

This coheres with the early scenes in Acts where the first Christians continue to value the temple as central for their faith and make it their place of prayer. It also coheres with Jesus' use of the temple for teaching, a fact which Luke emphasises by framing the sections which follow, 20:1 – 21:36, with the words: "And he was teaching daily in the temple" (19:47; 21:37). In fact, Luke is so keen to emphasise Jesus' presence in the temple that he passes over any mention of Jesus' departure from the temple until 21:37. Within the broader Lukan scheme Jesus' presence in the temple echoes the infancy narratives where the temple had great prominence.[129] It also echoes the account of Jesus' presence there as a twelve year old, learning and asking questions. There is no indication here that Jesus is in a foreign place, a building created as part of Israel's fall from faith, as some interpret Stephen's speech. Jesus is at home. He belongs. The tragedy Luke portrays is that the temple's leaders do not welcome him.

19:47–48 describes Jesus' teaching in the temple and the hostile plans of the temple authorities, frustrated by Jesus' popularity. It functions primarily as the introduction for the confrontations which follow. Luke preserves Mark's first narrative where Jesus is questioned about his authority and answers by linking his own authority with John's (20:1–8; cf. Mark 11:27–33). Luke has linked John and Jesus already from conception and birth. As in Mark, the issue of authority is linked with what Jesus had just done in the temple, but Luke understands what Jesus had just done quite differently from Mark. Jesus acted primarily to reform temple worship not replace it.

---

[128] Similarly Nolland, *Luke*, pp. 936–937; Tyson, *Images*, p. 84; C. H. Giblin, *The destruction of Jerusalem according to Luke's Gospel: A Historical-Typological Moral*, AnBib 107, (Rome: BIP, 1985), p. 59.

[129] So Chance, *Jerusalem*, pp. 56–62. See also Bachmann, *Jerusalem*, pp. 138–170, who brings out the importance of the temple and Jerusalem for Luke, which is reflected in structural mirroring among the four main Jerusalem sections of the double work.

His version of Mark's parable of the wicked tenants (20:9–19) varies only in minor ways from Mark within the parable itself (cf. Mark 12:1–8). Like Matthew he conforms the fate of the beloved son to that of Jesus; he is first cast out of the city and then killed (20:15). He also has only one murder: that of the son. Like Matthew, Luke has additional words attached to Ps 118:22: "All who fall on that stone will be broken to pieces; and it will crush any on whom it falls" (20:18). This reaffirms the warning of judgement with which Luke began Jesus' days in Jerusalem (19:41–44). Jesus announces to the people that God will bring judgement on its leaders and will entrust the vineyard to "others" (20:16). By these "others" Luke doubtless means the disciples and the community of faith. The implication is that they will exercise the authority which Jesus has shown in caring for Israel and its heritage and will ensure that it bears fruit.[130] The vineyard is not to be destroyed or replaced; it is to receive new keepers. Part of that heritage is the interpretation of the Law; it is be interpreted in accordance with Jesus' teaching and its temple administered accordingly. The latter hope will fail.

Luke continues with the Markan source material in 20:20–26, telling of the attempt to expose Jesus over the issue of paying taxes to the emperor, and making explicit the hope of the questioners that this would provide evidence to present to Pilate (cf. Mark 12:13–17). This they will, indeed, do, according to Luke's account of the trial before Pilate (23:2), even though Luke shows here that the charge is false. Otherwise Luke stays close to Mark, as he does also in the discussion of the Sadducees' question in 20:27–40 (cf. Mark 12:18–27), which assumes knowledge of levirite marriage law. He omits as potentially too offensive Mark's generalising comment that they "err, not knowing the scriptures nor the power of God" (cf. Mark 12:24) and keeps the difference primarily to the matter of belief in resurrection. Even so, in Acts Luke will range the Christians with the Pharisees against the Sadducees on the matter of resurrection (cf. Acts 23:6–10).

Luke then omits Mark's next episode about the lawyer who asked which was the greatest commandment (Mark 12:28–34), because he has already made use of the first part of it in modified form in the encounter with the lawyer in 10:25–28 in connection with the parable of the Good Samaritan. This means he has omitted the second half of the episode, in which the lawyer contrasts keeping the love commandments with sacrifices and burnt of-

---

[130] Tyson, *Images*, p. 82. Sanders, *Jews in Luke-Acts*, pp. 211–213, argues that the focus is rejection of both the leaders and people in the words of the parable, but only the leaders in the narrative, because only later do the crowds turn against Jesus. But the people's response, "Oh no!" in 20:16, need not imply that they see themselves judged.

ferings, altogether. Instead he goes straight on to Jesus' teaching that the Messiah must be more than David's son (20:41–44). Here, too, he stays close to Mark (cf. Mark 12:35–37). The cumulative effect of these episodes in the Lukan narrative is to have shown that Jesus has rebutted attempts to discredit him and has countered by laying the foundations for an understanding of himself which will go beyond normal Jewish categories.

Luke continues to follow Mark closely, having Jesus attack the efforts of the Pharisees to make themselves prominent and their exploitation of widows (20:45–47; cf. Mark 12:38–40). As in Mark, the example of the poor widow's generosity, set in comparison with the rich (21:1–4; cf. Mark 12:41–44), also contrasts with the Pharisees' attitude. If in Mark the widow's response functioned more at the symbolic level as a foil to the Pharisees' greed, in Luke it recalls the real temple piety expressed in the infancy narratives and assumed throughout the gospel.[131] Luke continues the Markan order, following this by Jesus' announcement of the temple's destruction (21:5–6; cf. Mark 13:1–2). Luke doubtless also links the issue of the widow's poverty and the injustice it represents with this destruction, but without the Markan assumption that the community of faith, as a new temple to replace the old, will offer her hope.

Luke's version of the material in Mark 13 also shows largely minor variations. The whole discussion takes place still within the temple and not outside it, as in Mark, where it takes place on the Mount of Olives. In Luke it belongs to Jesus' public teaching, not to private instruction for the disciples. As we shall see, Luke's version of Jesus' predictions contains much more hope for Jerusalem and would, in that sense, be much less offensive to the Jewish hearer.

In 21:7–11 he makes it clearer than does Mark that the initial discussion is about the destruction of the temple (cf. Mark 13:3–8). He adds a characteristic warning against those who predict the imminent climax of history (21:8b). The predictions of persecution follow (21:12–19; cf. Mark 13:9–13), but Luke has Jesus make clear that these come before the events he is describing (21:12) and reassure the disciples, by reminding them that the one who counts the hairs of the head will continue to care for them (21:18: cf. 12:7).

Luke then rewrites Mark's account of the prediction, that the abominable one would appear in the temple (21:20–24; cf. Mark 13:14–20). Instead he speaks of abomination and sets it more clearly in the context of the siege of Jerusalem. The fall of Jerusalem is divine judgement. The passage closely

---

131 Similarly Bachmann, *Jerusalem*, pp. 331–332.

echoes Jesus' opening predictions about Jerusalem in 19:41–44. In 21:24
Luke has Jesus then predict that Jerusalem will remain trampled by the Gentiles, "until the time of the Gentiles is fulfilled." Luke appears to be rewriting Mark 13:10 ("The gospel must be preached to all nations"). The effect
in the Lukan narrative is to see Jerusalem's domination and desecration by
Gentiles as lasting until the climax of history to be described in 21:25–28.[132]
Without the intervening warnings about false prophets, which Luke omits at
this point (cf. Mark 13:21–23), the fall of Jerusalem and the climax of history are more immediately juxtaposed in Luke's sequence of events than in
Mark.

In the face of the climactic disasters and the coming of the Son of Man
the disciples and Luke's readers should, he adds, lift up their heads, because
their "liberation is at hand" (21:28). This recalls the use of similar language
about Israel's hopes in the infancy narratives (2:25,38; cf. also 23:51). It is
clear that Luke sees this "liberation" fulfilling those hopes. Bearing in mind
that Luke's Jesus is addressing the people of Jerusalem in the temple, not
the disciples on the Mount of Olives, as in Mark, this becomes a promise to
the people of Jerusalem.[133] Liberation includes for Luke removal of Jerusalem from Gentile control (cf. 1:71), though it includes more than that. Thus
here, too, we find a strong commitment on Luke's part to upholding the
traditions of Israel and this is consonant with his approach to Israel's Torah.

The parable of the fig tree, which Luke, following the Markan sequence,
takes over at this point (21:29–33; cf. Mark 13:28–32), may well function
not simply as a warning to read the signs of the time, but to see Jerusalem's

---

[132] Sanders, *Jews in Luke-Acts*, pp. 218–219, rejects the suggestion that Luke sees a
possible role for Jerusalem at the eschaton, arguing that the allusion is to Daniel (8:13–14;
9:26–27; 12:7), where what follows is the resurrection (12:1–3), and that there is no trace
of such a hope for Jerusalem elsewhere in Luke. He also rejects links with Rom 11:25.
But surely the reference to resurrection does not exclude such a focus on Jerusalem, but
rather strengthens it (cf. the tradition associating resurrection and Jerusalem in Matt 27:51–
53).

[133] For the view that Luke reflects here a role for Jerusalem at the eschaton see A. J.
Mattill, *Luke and the Last Things. A Perspective for the Understanding of Lukan thought*,
(Dillsboro: Western North Carolina Pr., 1979), pp. 134–145, who argues that Luke espouses belief in an eschatological hope which envisages the restoration of Jerusalem. He
points also to E. Franklin, *Christ the Lord. A Study in thew Purpose and Theology of
Luke-Acts*, (London: SPCK, 1975), pp. 13, 81, 102, 130, 204. See also D. L. Tiede, *Prophecy and History in Luke-Acts*, (Philadelphia: Fortress, 1980), pp. 89–96; Chance, *Jerusalem*, pp. 134–135, who appeals also to Acts 3:19–21; Luke 19:11; Acts 1:6 (pp. 132–134).
Cf. Giblin, *Jerusalem*, p. 91. Nolland, *Luke*, p. 1003, considers the idea of restoration a
possibility, but prefers to interpret "the time of the Gentiles" as the time when it is their
turn to face judgement.

fall and its possession by Gentiles as an indicator that the climax of history is near. This finds support in the fact that Luke has associated the description of Jerusalem's fall and of the events of the endtime more closely together. Luke appears to view eschatological fulfilment as including the restoration of the kingdom to Israel and the liberation of Jerusalem. This is a view he holds in common with other Christian writers of slightly later times, like Justin (*Dial* 80), who saw the land of Israel and Jerusalem as the location of the messianic reign of a thousand years and indicated the view was widespread. This makes sense of what Jesus predicts in 13:35: in Jerusalem at Jesus' parousia they will acclaim: "Blessed is he who comes in the name of the Lord" (13:35; cf. 19:38).

Luke has Jesus state explicitly that the kingdom of God will come in the lifetime of the current generation (21:32). He even omits Jesus' words of caution that not even he knows the day or hour, choosing rather to stop with Jesus' affirmation that his words are reliable for all time (21:33). The whole is set in the context of a warning to watch and be ready (21:34–36).

As already noted, the whole discourse takes place in public within the temple and in the light of its content in Luke this must be deemed appropriate. For while predicting the disasters which are to come, it shares the sentiments and aspirations of the pious Jews who first meet us in the opening chapters of his gospel who were "looking for the liberation of Israel" (2:38; cf. 2:25). The incorporation of Jewish national hope within Christian eschatology by Luke (or its retention) matches Luke's understanding of Jesus and the Law. Correspondingly, Luke concludes this section with the summary comment that Jesus exercised a daily teaching ministry in the temple and was received well by the people (21:37–38).

3.4.2 Luke 22:1 – 24:53

Luke begins the narrative of the passion, as does Mark, with reference to the Passover and to the aim of the Jewish authorities to destroy Jesus (22:1–2; cf. Mark 15:1–2). He omits the narrative of Jesus' anointing in Bethany (cf. Mark 14:3–9), because he has already used a similar story or, more probably, rewritten it, as one of his contrast stories at 7:36–50. Luke immediately reports the plot with Judas (22:3–6; cf. Mark 14:10–11). He continues to follow the Markan sequence, portraying Jesus as a normal pious Jew approaching Passover celebration, but with the same demonstration of miraculous foreknowledge as in Mark (22:7–13; cf. Mark 14:12–17).[134]

---

[134] Salo, *Law*, p. 159, notes that Luke, along with the other synoptic evangelists,

Luke proceeds directly to the narrative of the last supper (22:15–20; cf. Mark 14:22–25). He rewrites Mark's account, supplementing it with another version, reflected also in Paul's tradition (1 Cor 11:23–25), and reshaping it so that it reflects more closely the procedures of a Passover meal. Thus he takes the saying of Jesus which looks forward to drinking wine again in the kingdom (Mark 14:25) and creates from it two sayings, one relating to eating (the Passover meal) and the other to drinking the wine (22:16, 18). He then follows these by two further actions which come to constitute the eucharist (22:19–20). Like Mark and Matthew, Luke does not use the sacrificial imagery of poured out blood to reflect on the validity of temple sacrifices.

Luke's composition of the passage makes the transition to the announcement of Judas' betrayal quite dramatic. Jesus declares that the hand of the betrayer is with him on the table (22:21–23). Jesus' prediction evokes strife among the disciples. As a result of this sequence Luke can portray Jesus as giving final instructions to the disciples in the context of the supper, a farewell discourse much like a last testament (22:24–38). It gives Luke the opportunity to include material from Mark 10:41–45, which he had earlier omitted. Appropriate to the occasion, it deals with humility in leadership (22:24–27). In doing so, Luke has heavily abbreviated it to the essentials and rephrased Mark's only other possible reference to Jesus' vicarious death (Mark 10:45) in a way that removes the references to vicarious death altogether. For Luke the notion of Jesus' death as effecting salvation is not prominent and certainly not taken as implying replacement of cultic law.[135]

In the next segment of the speech, Luke's Jesus promises to give the disciples the kingdom; they will eat and drink with him there and will exercise functions of judgement over the twelve tribes of Israel (22:28–30).[136] This suits the narrative setting well (the meal image) and recalls the double prediction with which Luke had Jesus introduce the meal in the first place, that they would eat and drink with him in the kingdom (22:16,18). The hope expressed in 22:28–30 reflects strongly Jewish categories. The disciples'

---

misunderstands the date of the Passover, confusing the day of unleavened bread, 15th Nisan, with the Passover day, 14th Nisan, on which the lambs were slain. Since the temple no longer stood, the matter was not of great importance to Luke, to lead him to correct Mark at this point.

[135] Cf. Blomberg, "Law," p. 62.

[136] See also Chance, *Jerusalem*, pp. 66–85, on Luke's vision of the disciples' role at the eschaton. On the connection with the hope for the restoration of Israel see also J. Jervell, "The Twelve on Israel's Thrones. Luke's Understanding of the Apostolate," in *Luke and the People of God. A New Look at Luke-Acts*, (Minneapolis: Augsburg, 1972), pp. 75–112, here: 76–77.

role (judging includes ruling) will belong to their task as the new keepers of the vineyard.

The next segment (22:31-34) continues the focus on leadership. It alludes to Peter's future role, but connects this also to the prediction of his denial. Here Luke uses his Markan source (22:31-34; cf. Mark 14:26-31). Next, Luke has Jesus refer back to the previous commissioning of the twelve and reverse some of its limitations (22:35-38). Purses and bags are allowed, but, more surprising, so are swords. Quoting Isa 53:12, Jesus declares he is to be counted among the lawless. The natural sense of this passage is that the Law's authorities will seek to kill Jesus because they will consider him a transgressor of the Law, and that this will also endanger the lives of the disciples. They should therefore be ready to defend themselves when the occasion arises. The immediate application will be at Jesus' arrest. But in the light of this farewell discourse as a whole, it will apply also to the time when they exercise their mission in Christ's name in the world. For Luke, of course, Jesus is not "lawless"; he is Torah faithful; nor does he espouse breaking Roman law, although that is not the primary focus here.

It is interesting that this passage indicates that Luke was quite able to contemplate the need for change in Jesus' instruction as the disciples moved into a new situation. It raises the possibility that he might also envisage changes in the Law's instruction in changed situations. Whether this is so or the extent to which it is so will become apparent when we consider Acts.

In Luke's account, Jesus returns to his usual resting place (so 22:39; cf. 21:37) outside the city, on the mount of Olives. He reduces Mark's threefold account to a single instance of Jesus' prayer (22:39-46; cf. Mark 14:32-42), but adds, according to some manuscripts, dramatic detail highlighting the degree of Jesus' pain and emphasising that angels support him (22:39-46). The scene echoes the image of Jesus at prayer which Luke has inserted regularly throughout the gospel. The account begins and ends with Jesus' warning that his own also pray that they not enter temptation or trial. In the warning Luke may see a direct reference to the events which follow.

Luke' narrative of the arrest briefly recounts Judas' act of identification and Jesus' response (22:47-53; cf. Mark 14:47-53). It expands, however, the description of the attack on the high priest's servant. One of Jesus' company, presumably a disciple, asks Jesus if this is the time to strike and does so with effect. Jesus tells him, that that "was enough", the same expression he used when the disciples told him earlier they had only two swords (22:38). Jesus then heals the ear and confronts his assailants about the manner of the arrest. Luke's narrative reinforces the impression that swords are allowed for defence in such situations. Jesus does not rebuke the disciple. But it also shows Jesus limiting their use and responding to his enemies with compassion.

Luke reorders Mark at this point to tell of Peter's denial (22:54–63), of abuse from his captors (22:63–65) and to relocate the Sanhedrin hearing from night to morning (22:66–71; cf. Mark 14:43–72). Perhaps Luke is sensitive to Jewish Law at this point, which probably forbad night trial of capital cases.[137] The trial concentrates on two questions: whether Jesus is the Messiah and whether he is Son of God. Luke leaves aside the report of false witnesses about Jesus' prediction of the destruction of the old temple and its replacement by one made without hands (cf. Mark 14:58). This had formed part of Mark's thesis that the community of faith replaces the temple. Luke has not espoused that thesis. His Jesus is presented as seeking to reform the temple. An abbreviated form of the charge appears as a false accusation on the lips of Stephen's accusers in Acts 6:13–14.

The double question in Luke's trial narrative may be no more than Luke having the high priest ask two variations of the same question. To both Jesus refuses to give a direct answer, although Luke and his hearers know the answer is yes. Luke has Jesus ground this behaviour in their unwillingness to believe and respond. But possibly Luke deliberately distinguishes the two questions to show where the sticking point lay for the authorities. It was not with the claim of messiahship, a common enough claim at the time and one more relevant for Roman than Jewish legal concern, but with the claim to be Son of God. By Luke's day this was doubtless seen as offensive. Simply Jesus' concession that this is his claim was enough for the Sanhedrin. However Luke does not have them declare this blasphemous. In this sense we can say that Luke does not show Jesus as charged with breaking any Jewish law, although it is probably implied.

Luke, apparently better informed about the Jewish legal system, does not have them pass sentence, but rather proceed to involve Pilate, before whom they could now use the messianic claim and associated alleged criminal activity to ensure his execution (23:1–5 cf. Mark 15:2–5). Both Pilate and Herod find Jesus innocent of the charges which the Jewish leaders bring (23:6–12,13–16). Perhaps Luke is deliberately using the rule of the validity of two witnesses against the Jewish authorities by adding the hearing before Herod and also by reporting Pilate's multiple declarations of Jesus' innocence (23:4, 15, 22; cf. Deut 17:6). Luke has a much reduced version of the crowd's call for Barabbas, which he introduces without mention of the practice of a Passover amnesty (23:18–25; cf. Mark 15:6–14). Perhaps Luke knew better at this point, too.

---

[137] See the discussion in Brown, *Death of the Messiah*, pp. 357–363.

The narrative of the crucifixion follows Mark's sequence with some additions (23:26–48; cf. Mark 15:20–39).[138] The first of these is that he has Jesus turn aside and address weeping women of Jerusalem. He turns their thoughts to the disaster which would befall Jerusalem (23:26–32). This is consistent with Luke's emphasis on Jerusalem's fate already noted and, through the image of the green and dry wood, portrays what is about to happen to him as a foreshadowing of that disaster. It is a very Jerusalemite perspective.[139]

Luke's version of the mockery of Jesus omits reference to Jesus' alleged threat to destroy the temple, since Luke had already removed it from his narrative of the Jewish trial (23:33–38; cf. Mark 15:27–32). Instead he has him mocked twice as the Messiah and king of Israel. It is also at this point that Luke reports the superscription (23:38). At the beginning of the narrative many manuscripts portray Jesus as praying for forgiveness for his crucifiers, a pattern Stephen, too, will follow (23:34; cf. Acts 7:60), and an example of Jesus' radical teaching on love. Characteristically Lukan is the treatment of the two thieves, who have been made to represent positive and negative responses to Jesus (23:39–43). Jesus promises paradise after death to the repentant thief.

The account of Jesus' death (23:44–48) appears to explain Mark's three hours of darkness as an eclipse, but understood as an act of God (cf. Mark 15:33). It reports the splitting of the sanctuary curtain, but it is difficult to know how Luke would have understood this. In Luke it is not a response to his actual dying, but comes before it. This makes the rather speculative theories about Jesus' death effecting a way for Gentiles through the curtain to God or of God's reaching out to them[140] or of God's departure from the temple or of heaven being split open wide for universal access to the divine,[141] unlikely, though not impossible. It reads more naturally as an ex-

---

[138] Sanders, *Jews in Luke-Acts*, pp. 226–227, argues that Luke has the Jews crucify Jesus. Against this Nolland, *Luke*, p. 1136. Fitzmyer, *Luke*, p. 1496, says it is the Jewish leaders who lead him away to be crucified.

[139] Giblin, *Jerusalem*, pp. 105–106, notes this and also that it gives no indication, negatively or positively, about possible future conversion.

[140] J. B. Green, "The Death of Jesus and the Rending of the Temple Veil (Luke 23:44–49). A Window into Luke's Understanding of Jesus and the Temple," in *Society of Biblical Literature Seminar Papers 1991*, edited by E. H. Lovering, (SBL: Scholars, 1991), pp. 543–575, here: 550–557, argues that for Luke the rending of the veil symbolises the removal of barriers which the temple has come to represent, thus opening the way for the inclusion of the Gentiles. It does not symbolise the temple's destruction. Thus the temple remains a place of prayer, of teaching and revelation, but for all. Tyson, *Images*, p. 87, speaks of it as the reconquest of the temple as a place of prayer.

[141] Nolland, *Luke*, p. 1157, favours the view of D. Sylva, "The Temple Curtain and

pression of God's grief and anger at what is happening, including probably his anger in judgement.[142]   As a portent of judgement it is part of God's response to Jesus being crucified, like the eclipse.

Luke omits Jesus' cry of forsakenness, the confusion about his calling for Elijah and the attempt to keep him alive should Elijah come by giving him sour wine (cf. Mark 15:34–36). In Luke's account people had made such an offer in the setting of mockery (23:36). Instead, like a noble martyr, Jesus surrenders his spirit in obedience, speaking the words of Ps 31:6 before he dies: "Into your hands I commend my spirit" (23:46). The Gentile centurion, impressed by what he saw, acclaims Jesus "a righteous man", the crowds go home in deep distress, while Jesus' acquaintances, including many women watch at a distance (23:46–49).   Probably Luke reduces the level of the centurion's response, because he does not yet see the kingdom as open to Gentiles; that will come in Acts. But Luke may also have read Mark's account as meaning effectively the same thing: "a son of God".

Luke then continues with Mark's account of Joseph of Arimathea's initiative (23:50–56; cf. Mark 15:42–47). Significantly Luke adds that he is "good and righteous" and preserves Mark's description that he was one who "looked for the kingdom of God". In Luke's narrative he is thus like the pious of the infancy narratives, awaiting God's liberation of Israel. Both he and the women preparing the spices for burial observe the restrictions of the sabbath. Luke alone, among the evangelists, makes a point of emphasising their Torah observance (23:56). It is as relevant to emphasise this at end of Jesus' life as it was at it beginning, because obedience to Torah and sharing Israel's hopes are fundamental values which Luke's Jesus and Luke assume.

Luke then records the momentous discovery of Easter morning. In contrast to Mark 16:8, Luke has the women report the angelic announcement (given by two, not one man, as in Mark). The disciples respond with disbelief (24:1–11). Unlike Mark (and Matthew), Luke has them in Jerusalem at

---

Jesus' Death in the Gospel of Luke," *JBL* 105 (1986), pp. 239–250, that it means access between the divine and human sphere like at the death of Stephen (7:55–56) and in Luke 3:21. Brown, *Death of the Messiah*, pp. 1104–1106, rejects this view, because Luke uses the word σχίζω ("tear, rend") here, not "open", as he does in Acts 7:44–46 and Luke 3:21, where he replaced Mark's σχιζομένος ("torn open"). Cf. also R. L. Brawley, *Luke-Acts and the Jews. Conflict, Apology, and Conciliation*, SBLMS 33, (Atlanta: Scholars, 1987), pp. 127–132, who interprets the splitting of the curtain within the framework of belief in Jerusalem as the sacred city, the navel of the earth, the meeting point of heaven and earth.

[142] Brown, *Death of the Messiah*, pp. 1103–1104, favours the view that it is an expression of warning of judgement which will ensure (and does) if Jerusalem continues to reject the new message. Similarly Chance, *Jerusalem*, pp. 118–120. He also interprets "shutting the gates" in Acts 21:26 as an echo of tearing the curtain in Luke 23:45 (pp. 121–122).

this stage. The following scenes also take place in Judea (24:13–35). More important, the two disciples on the road to Emmaus continue Luke's focus on Jerusalem; with other Jerusalemites they had been hoping he would redeem Israel (24:18,21). They share the hopes of the faithful, from the infancy narratives to Joseph, from Jesus to the disciples of Acts 1:6. The incognito Jesus explains on the basis of Moses and the prophets that as the Christ he had to suffer (24:27). This is not the end of the story, nor of their hope.

After he has disclosed himself to them and they have rejoined the band of the disciples, Jesus appears again. Again he explains that all that was written concerning him in the Law of Moses and the Prophets had to be fulfilled (24:44–53). This now includes not only his suffering, death and resurrection, but also the preaching of repentance to all peoples, beginning from Jerusalem. Indirectly it continues the theme of Jerusalem's significance, raising the question that we are dealing here with more than a point of transition to world mission. Gentile mission is thus again announced, but without any reflection on Law issues. The Law, with the Prophets, is being fulfilled, but without any sense that it is thereby finished. Jesus' word of blessing at the ascension appears to echo Simon's blessing of the people in Sir 50:20–21. In a sense it also fulfils Zechariah's intent to bless the people in 1:21–22.[143]

3.4.3 Conclusion

There is little directly related to the theme of Jesus and the Law in these chapters but much that is indirectly relevant. Luke emphasises that Joseph and the women followers of Jesus are Torah observant. These together with the widow echo the pious of the infancy narratives. Luke has Jesus note that he will be falsely numbered with transgressors of the Law, but omits any such reference from the trial. Luke continues the image of Jesus as the man of deep prayer, notably on the Mount of Olives, and has Jesus celebrate Passover like a faithful Jew. His criticism of the Sadducees is not generalised as in Mark. As the risen one, on two occasions he also explains his suffering and resurrection in terms of fulfilment of the Law of Moses and the Prophets, without any indication that the Law thereby loses its relevance. Jesus is at home teaching in the temple. Luke has even transformed the

---

[143] Brown, *Birth*, p. 280. Nothing indicates that Luke intends it as a sign of the temple's destruction or Jesus' usurpation of high priesthood. So Chance, *Jerusalem*, pp. 62–64.

Markan apocalyptic discourse so that it can be portrayed as given publicly in the temple.

This reflects an emphasis within these chapters on Israel's hopes and, in particular, on Jerusalem's future. The disciples' eschatological role includes acting as judges and rulers over the twelve tribes of Israel. As in the infancy narrative, the righteous, like Joseph of Arimathea and the disciples on the road to Emmaus, long for the liberation of Israel, understood as identical with the coming of the kingdom. The parable of the fig tree now focuses on what has befallen Jerusalem and looks to the coming of the kingdom as its hope. Thus Luke writes from a perspective which looks back on the horrors of the Jerusalem siege, sees Gentile desecration of Jerusalem and incorporates the liberation of Jerusalem within Christian eschatology. Hence the focus on lamentation for Jerusalem's fate, introduced into the narrative at significant points: immediately after Jesus' entry and on the road to the cross. Jesus' own suffering foreshadows Jerusalem's suffering. Luke displays a decided sympathy for Jerusalem and its inhabitants. The Church's empowering and its mission will begin there. There, too, it will find its ultimate end, according to Luke. The disciples are the new keepers of the vineyard; they will sit on the twelve thrones. Gentile mission belongs within this perspective, but the Law issues it raises are not yet in view; even the Gentile centurion at the cross does not yet make a Christian confession. At one point Luke has Jesus reverse or modify previous instructions relating to mission. This at least opens the possibility that Luke could entertain such changes also in Torah provisions in a new situation, but that it still to be seen.

Luke has not taken up Mark's radical critique of the temple. His rewriting of Mark at this point has thoroughly removed any such hint. It is probable that Jesus' temple action should be seen as an attempt at reform, to make the temple a better place for worship and prayer. Luke omits all reference to Jesus' prediction that he is in any way bringing about the temple's destruction, let alone replacing it with himself and his community. He omits the contrast between sacrifices and love, even though he uses the related material about the great commandments earlier in the gospel. The torn sanctuary curtain in response to Jesus' suffering and before his death is possibly more an expression of divine grief and perhaps judgement which will come to the temple because of its leaders, than a reflection on the temple itself. Luke's account of the last supper also shows no hint of implying that Jesus' shed blood renders the temple cult obsolete.

Luke may also have a firmer grasp of Jewish legal practices. This may explain his placing the Sanhedrin hearing in the morning, rendering it at least legal, and his making the claim to be Son of God rather than the claim to messiahship the chief offence to the Jews. Correspondingly, it explains that Luke has the Jewish authorities bring the charge of messiahship to Pilate and that he drops reference to an alleged Passover amnesty. Luke also makes use of the force of two or more witnesses in a case of law in having both Pilate and Herod testify to Jesus' innocence and having Pilate himself do so three times.

3.5 *Perspectives from Acts*

Luke emphasises continuity between the message of Jesus and that of the early church. According to Luke 24:47 it will preach repentance for the forgiveness of sins in the name of Jesus. This is a fundamental clue to the link, borne out in Luke's portrait of the church's preaching. It is of great importance for understanding attitudes towards the Law. What has changed is the momentous event of Jesus' execution, his resurrection and the giving of the Spirit. The eschatological focus remains firmly linked to the hopes of Israel. Jesus is the appointed Messiah who will come to fulfil these hopes (Acts 3:20–21). The kingdom will be restored to Israel (1:6). Jesus is her saviour (13:24) and sole hope of salvation (4:12). Fundamental to this hope is belief in resurrection, Jesus' resurrection and that of all the faithful. Luke has Paul argue this as fulfilment of the promises of the Law and the Prophets (24:14; 26:22; 28:23; cf. also 3:22–24). This covenant blessing is also to be shared with the nations (3:25; 1:8); thus Luke recounts how the Gentile mission is born. The way to blessing is repentance and baptism, which has now gone beyond John's baptism to become baptism in the name of Jesus who is the saviour and to include the baptism with the Spirit which John predicted (1:5; 11:16).

The first disciples remain Torah observant Jews. They worship in the temple at the appointed times of prayer and preach there (2:46; 3:1; 5:12–13,20–21,42). Symbolically, Luke underlines the continuity with Israel by typology: Jesus appears on earth for 40 days; there are 120 pious awaiting God's promise in the upper room at Pentecost; the Pentecost outpouring of the Spirit is drawn with traditional motifs belonging to the legend of the giving of the Law at Sinai. The implication is not that there is a new Law replacing the old, but that what happens at Pentecost coheres with God's action in the past. What came to Jesus through the Spirit comes now to all who believe, though the focus is still on Jews. It has no more negative consequences for the Law's validity than did Jesus' ministry of the Spirit. The message is the same, but reinforced by what happened to Jesus and his vindication: it is a call to repentance. The call to repentance presupposes the validity of the Law, especially when taken in its true meaning, as interpreted by Luke's Jesus. Positively, the echo of Sinai reinforces the validity of the Law in Luke's account.

These typological echoes are, therefore, more than a claim that the church inherits Israel's traditions. For, according to Luke, Jewish Christians continue to be practising Jews. This is true, even of those who engage in mission to the Gentiles, like Paul. For, according to Luke, he defends his Torah faithfulness vigorously when it is impugned (24:17; 25:8). James (21:21–24), and even the Pharisees, fail to fault him in this (23:9), just as, earlier, the Pharisee, Gamaliel, saw no obvious offence among Christians in this respect (5:34). Similarly the Christians of Judea remain zealous observers of Torah (21:20).

In 4:12 Peter declares: "For there is salvation in no other; for there is no other name under heaven given among human begins by which we must be saved." This exclusiveness, however, is related to God's strategy for Israel's and the world's salvation. It assumes Jewish faith and Jewish hope and points to the way this hope will be fulfilled. It is not positing Jesus as an alternative to Torah as the way to approach God. For Luke Jews approach God by being Torah observant and recognising that Jesus has been sent as Messiah.

Beyond these general features, there are significant passages in Acts where the matter of Torah observance receives particular attention and which may add to our understanding of Luke and in turn, therefore, have some bearing on his understanding of Jesus' attitude towards the Law.

The first is the account of Stephen (6:1 – 7:60). According to 6:11 Stephen's opponents fabricate accusations against him, claiming that "he says slanderous things against Moses and against God".[144] This is sufficient for Stephen's arrest and presentation before the council. Luke then repeats more directly that the charges laid are false: "They put up false witnesses who said, 'This man never stops making statements against this holy place and against the Law. For we heard him say that this Jesus the Nazarene will destroy this place and change the customs which Moses gave us'" (6:13–14). Luke knows from Mark's account of the Jewish trial that the claims about Jesus in relation to the temple also came from false witnesses (cf.

---

[144] Tyson, *Images*, p. 112, believes the underlying problem in the conflict of Stephen with his fellow Hellenistic Jews was over dietary issues, but, as he acknowledges, this is not made explicit in Luke's composition of Acts which is our immediate concern. See also his "Acts 1:6–7 and dietary regulations in early Christianity," *Perspectives in Religious Studies* 10 (1983), pp. 145–161.

Mark 14:57). The most natural reading, here, is that Luke wants his hearers to consider these accusations as trumped up charges.[145] The two accounts of the charges, repeating three sets of two charges, come down to two main allegations. Stephen spoke disparagingly of the temple and of the Law. They assume that the claim of Jesus to destroy the temple implies disparagement of the temple and that his change of the Law disparages at least parts of it.

Nothing within the passage suggests that we should be especially sensitive to fine distinctions, as if Luke means that the false testimony is only partly untrue (cf. Mark 14:57–58). Nothing to this point has indicated this, either in relation to the temple or in relation to the Law.[146] Nor does Luke's usage justify the suggestion that Stephen attacked only cultic law.[147] The extent to which this may be so will depend on how we perceive Luke's understanding of subsequent history, both with regard to the temple and with regard to the Law.[148] The emphasis we have noted on Torah faithfulness of

---

[145] Cf. Blomberg, "Law," p. 63, who argues that 6:11, which is not directly designated as false testimony, may reflect Stephen's actual criticism. But both what follows and the use of ὑπέβαλον ("put up", often associated with false charges) suggest the opposite.

[146] C. K. Barrett, *A Critical and Exegetical Commentary on the Acts of the Apostles, Vol 1*, ICC, (Edinburgh: T&T Clark, 1994), pp. 319–320, 328–329, suggests that the falsity may not relate to substantial content and follows Wilson's view that Jesus changes the Law in relation to the sabbath. See Wilson, *Law*, pp. 62–63, 111. Pesch, R. *Die Apostelgeschichte*, EKK VI, (Zurich: Benziger; Neukirchen-Vluyn: Neukirchener, 1986), p. 238, says Luke believes the allegations are false about the Law and false about the temple in the sense that Jesus did not say that he, himself, would destroy it. G. Schneider, *Die Apostelgeschichte*, HTKNT V/1, (Freiburg: Herder, 1980), p. 439, believes that the quotation in 6:14 is not considered false by Luke in contrast to 6:11,13. Salo, *Law*, pp. 172–189, believes Luke shows ambivalence in handling the charges. They are false, yet true in the sense that Jesus will destroy the temple and the laws will, later in Acts, be changed. But, since that is yet to come in Luke's scheme, he has Stephen's speech not answer the charges. What the speech does do, according to Salo, is show Stephen as upholding the validity of the Law, while at the same time criticising the move from the tent of witness to the temple building. The criticism is not the building itself, but the corruption it came to house.

[147] Cf. Pesch, *Apostelgeschichte I*, p. 238; Schneider, *Apostelgeschichte I*, p. 439. Against this Barrett, *Acts*, pp. 328–329. See also Sanders, *Jews in Luke-Acts*, pp. 246–248, who argues that the accusations against Stephen are 'false' only in a *pro forma* sense (since they accuse Stephen, they must be false witnesses); Luke has no objection to their accusations. Stephen and, indeed, all Christianity à la Luke oppose the Temple and Mosaic custom" (p. 248). He argues that Luke distinguishes between God's Law and "the customs" from Moses. The true divine law is something different.

[148] Salo, *Law*, pp. 177–182, argues that the future tense in the allegations against Stephen that he declared Jesus would destroy the temple reflect Luke's understanding that this is indeed what came to pass in the 70 CE (pp. 179–180). Salo also believes that the idea that Jesus would change the laws will have its fulfilment in Acts 10–11 and 15. Yet, Salo still believes that, for Luke, they nevertheless remain false (p. 180).

the community, from the beginning to the end of Acts, not least, of Paul, should caution us against trying to detect too much subtlety. This issue is, however, complex.

The complexities begin with Stephen's speech in Acts 7. Luke presents it as Stephen's defence. The image Luke portrays of Stephen is one of true Jewish piety from the beginning. This is so already in 6:8 and is emphasised again in the closing scene (7:54–60). It is also reflected in the speech in which Stephen lays claim to his religious heritage. He acknowledges "this place" (7:7), which he is said to have slandered (6:13,14), as the place where God planned that his people should worship him.[149] He identifies positively the covenant of circumcision given to Abraham (7:8). Luke has Stephen again refer to the promise to Abraham (of "the place") in identifying the turning point which led to Israel's escape from Egypt (7:17). As the patriarchs abused Joseph, so the Israelites rejected Moses, whom Stephen portrays in almost superhuman colours (7:20–22). Luke portrays Stephen as being on Moses' side, because Moses had foretold the rising of a new prophet, whom he identifies with Jesus (7:37). Moses received the "living oracles" on Sinai (7:38). Similarly in 7:53 Stephen hails the Law as ordained through angels. To this point, though indirectly, Luke has already had Stephen successfully ward off the charges that he disparages "the place" and the Law or Moses.[150]

The charge against the Israelites was idolatry (7:39–41), which Luke has Stephen reinforce with the citation of Amos 5:25–27LXX. It hints at punishment through the Babylonian exile, although within the speech it addresses Israel's failings in the wilderness. In 7:44–47 the speech reaches a new phase. It affirms the tent of witness as constructed by Moses according to a heavenly prototype and its continuing role till the time of David. 7:47 reports David's desire to build a house for the God of Jacob. 7:48 reports Solomon's fulfilment of that wish.[151] Then Luke has Stephen add: "But the Most High does not dwell in what is made by human hands" and go on to cite Isaiah 66:1: "Heaven is my throne and earth my footstool. What kind of house will you build me, says the Lord, or what is my resting place? Has not

---

[149] Cf. Neyrey, "Luke-Acts," p. 286, who following Dahl, "Abraham," pp. 74–75, identifies "the place" with Jesus.

[150] Salo, *Law*, pp. 180–182, notes that, while Stephen's speech does not answer the charges directly, hints within it (such as "the living oracles") and its focus as a whole indicate that Stephen upholds the validity of the Law.

[151] Brawley, *Luke-Acts*, pp. 121–122, argues for θεῷ rather than οἴκῳ as the preferable reading in 7:46, indicating that David's seeking permission to build a temple was a sign of God's favour, as the temple itself became. But either way the sense of the passage is not substantially altered.

my hand made all of these?" (7:49–50).[152] The movement of thought from
"tent of witness" to the declaration that God does not dwell in what is made
by human hands is sudden and difficult.

The word, χειροποίητος "made with human hands", is used in the LXX
in attacking idolatry (cf. Isa 2:18; 10:11; 31:7; 46:6 LXX), but elsewhere of
the contrast between the earthly and heavenly temple (Heb 9:11). Does the
passage imply that the building of the temple was a sin, in contrast to constructing the tent of witness?[153] Were both constructions sinful acts, since
both were human made and not related to God's dwelling? Was neither of
the acts sinful, but only the way people came to treat what had been constructed?[154] Luke's Stephen certainly has no problem affirming that it is
right to have a place to worship God; he highlights that as part of the promise to Abraham (7:7).[155] The tent's construction appears sanctioned in 7:44,
when Stephen mentions that it was made according to the divine prototype

---

[152] Brawley, *Luke-Acts*, pp. 118–120, argues that Luke shares the view that the temple
will be replaced in Jerusalem at the eschaton by the presence of God, yet sees it now as
above all a place of prayer, teaching and proclamation. Stephen's attack is not on the
temple itself in contrast to the tabernacle, since he also attacks the failure of the wilderness generation (Acts 7:38–43; p. 121). He also draws attention to the fact that Luke
designates allegations of attacks on the temple as false (6:13; p. 122).

[153] So Pesch, *Apostelgeschichte I*, p., 257, who argues that it reflects pre Christian
attacks (see also pp. 246–247); Esler, *Community*, pp. 145–161, who also draws attention
to the legal argument applied in the speech, by which Stephen disputes the courts right to
interpret law and claims it for himself and the Christians. Barrett, *Acts*, pp. 337–339,
argues that while Luke has Stephen uphold the Law, he does portray him as attacking the
temple, using critique characteristic of Hellenism. He considers the possibility that 7:47–
48 may not be a stark antithesis, opposing the temple, and that Luke may not be associating χειροποίητος "made with human hands", with idolatry, but concludes that it is negative. Tyson, *Images*, p. 115, sees the building of Solomon's temple as an act of disobedience. Jesus has tried and failed to transform it from being a den of robbers; this is a hint
that the same will be the case for the church (p. 115). Closing of the gates (21:30) represents symbolically the end of Christian use of the temple (p. 184).

[154] Cf. Salo, *Law*, pp. 172–189, who sees Stephen criticising the move from the tent
of witness to the temple building. But the criticism is not the building itself, but the
corruption it came to house.

[155] Cf. Stegemann, *Synagoge*, 165–168, who argues that Stephen's speech counters
all human constructions for God's dwelling, not only Solomon's temple, and focuses in
7:7 only on the land as holy and sees the same focus in Paul's statement in 17:26. The land
is where the people are to serve God. God is bound neither to land nor temple (pp. 169–
171). Speaking against this holy place is more than speaking against the temple or cult; it
denies a special place; it also fits the period when the temple has been destroyed (pp. 172–
173). In Stephen's speech Luke is taking up accusations made against Christianity of his
time and clarifying them. Luke's attack is not thinkable as a variant of Jewish critique of
temple practice; it takes place at a time when Judaism is coming to terms with the destruction of the temple and represents a fundamental attack on the whole notion of holy places

(alluding to Ex 25:40; see also Heb 8:5). The temple's construction also seems sanctioned, because it is linked positively with God's favour to David. How far is 7:47, Σολομῶν δὲ οἰκοδόμησιν αὐτῷ οἶκον ("And/but Solomon built him a house") negative:? Is the δὲ a "but" referring only to the contrast between David and Solomon in the sense that David was not allowed to build it, but Solomon was? Or does it somehow imply contrast with God's will in the sense: God did not want it, but Solomon went ahead after all? The latter would be in clear defiance of the Old Testament accounts and create difficulties if it implied that already David's idea was sinful, since there is no hint of this in 7:46. The former interpretation suits better. But this means that somewhere there is a transition in thought between a legitimate tabernacle and temple to the stark comments in 7:48, which Luke has not supplied, but presumed. What did Luke have in mind here?

Possibly Solomon was a negative figure for him, as one who abused wealth, a major concern of Luke's. Then the sequence could be: Solomon built it. That was God's will, but the kind of person Solomon was led to treating the temple in ways which God did not intend; the "but" would contrast Solomon and David as persons not their actions or intentions in building the temple. Oddly enough, the Old Testament account has Solomon make the very point that Stephen makes with his allusion to Isa 66:1–2. At the dedication of the temple Solomon said: "Will God indeed dwell on the earth? Even heaven and the highest heavens cannot contain you, much less this house which I have built!" (1 Kgs 8:27). That need not have kept Luke from thinking primarily of Solomon's subsequent behaviour. Whether the Solomon factor was there for Luke or not, we are probably on the right track in sensing that the negative shift for Luke was not between the tabernacle and the temple, but between the temple and what it became. People came to have the wrong attitude towards it, as if it held God. This would cohere with Luke's portrait

---

(pp. 173–174). Similarly the accusation against Stephen and Paul that they teach non observance of the Law reflects accusations launched against Christianity of Luke's day (pp. 176–177). Luke's answer is to make a clear distinction between Gentile Christians and Jewish Christians who continue to observe Torah as, he is keen to argue, did Paul (pp. 177–179). Stegemann notes the parallels between the accusations against Stephen and Paul and the description of Antiochus IV's changes in 1 Macc 1:49 (including changing the laws, forbidding circumcision, causing apostasy; cf. also 2:15). The links also extend to setting Paul in analogy to Onias whose appeal to Seleucus was not a betrayal of his people (2 Macc 4:5), similarly Luke defends Paul against the accusation that he betrays Israel by including Gentiles (21:28; pp. 183–184). Judaism saw the Christians' attitude towards temple law and to Israel as assimilation to the pagan world comparable to the crisis of Antiochus Epiphanes.

of Jesus' criticism of the religious leaders and interpreters of the Law. Their attitude towards the Law distorted its function.[156] Their use of the temple made the whole system a place of abuse and exploitation.[157]

The prophetic text was not anti temple and should not be understood like that here. It is directed against a certain understanding of the temple. It is allied to the critique which Israel made of pagan cults and which also occurs in non Jewish writers of the period.[158] Undoubtedly Luke stands under the influence of both. But he stands on the side of those who respect cult,[159] but do not elevate it, rather than on the side of those who are ideologically anti-cultic and disparaging of the external.[160] I believe that such an interpreta-

---

[156] Schneider, *Apostelgeschichte I*, pp. 467–468, argues that in 7:47–48 Luke has Stephen not attack the temple as such but a false understanding of it. Similarly Chance, *Jerusalem*, p. 40; Brawley, *Luke-Acts*, pp. 118–120. C. C. Hill, *Hellenists and Hebrews. Reappraising Division within the Earliest Church*, (Minneapolis: Fortress, 1992), pp. 69–81, argues strongly that the speech of Stephen is neither law critical nor temple critical, but focuses on Israel's failure. In support of this view he points to the conclusions which Stephen draws, which are about failure to uphold Law, and to the weakness of the contrast which people have sought between the account of David's blessed intention and its realisation by Solomon of building a house for God, pointing out that the language reflects Ps 132:5 and 2 Sam 7:2,13 (pp. 71–72). The contrast is not between temple and tent, but between the truth that God does not dwell in things made with hands (p. 74). This attacks a tendency to locate God exclusively in the temple and has particular relevance in the period after its destruction; but is not anti-temple. "Accordingly it is not the institutions of Judaism, which are by definition good, but the unbelieving Jews themselves that are assailed" (p. 75). Similarly the severity of 7:39–43 is not directed against the tabernacle, but against unbelief (p. 79).

[157] So Salo, *Law*, pp. 183–186. The criticism is not the building itself, but the corruption it came to house.

[158] See Attridge, "Philosophical Critique of Religion".

[159] So S. Arai, "Zum 'Tempelwort' Jesu in Apostelgeschichte 6.14," *NTS* 34 (1988), pp. 397–410, here: 403–410, who argues that Luke expresses ambivalence towards the temple because Luke is dealing with issues of his own time in the face of criticism from Diaspora Judaism. Accordingly Luke emphasises through both Stephen and Paul that God cannot be bound to a place, while at the same time acknowledging that special significance which God gave to the place where the temple was built in salvation history.

[160] Cf. Klinghardt, *Law*, pp. 284–303, who argues that Stephen's speech belongs to a tradition of cult criticism which he finds attested generally in Hellenistic literature and in reference to the Jewish temple in Pseudo-Clementine literature. Luke has Stephen attack the cult on the basis of the Law as a particularising of what was meant to be universal. Unlike Mark, in Mark 10:4 (Moses' provocation for hardening Israel), Luke does not envisage change to the Law, but failure to fulfill it as leading to the construction of the temple. It therefore lacks, argues Klinghardt, the antijewish components which are characteristic of *ApostConst*. VI 20ff; *syrDidasc* 26 and probably also *PsClem Rec* 1:33ff and *Hom* 3:45ff (pp. 302–303). "So ist Kultkritik nicht zwangsläufig Gesetzeskritik, sondern eher Gesetzeshermeneutik. Dabei ist deutlich, dass diese Gesetzeshermeneutik eine Universalisierung intendiert: Der antihasmonäische Text *Strabo* XVI 2,35ff einerseits und

tion does best justice both to the passage itself in its context and to what we have discerned of Luke's attitude towards the cult elsewhere in his work. The pious of the infancy narratives, the Jesus who sends off the lepers and who seeks temple reform and makes it a place for his teaching, the earliest believers of Acts, and Paul, in its later chapters, were not masquerading about the temple, but rightly using it according to its original purpose as the holy place for prayer, worship and teaching.[161]

Within the framework of Luke's thought, therefore, the passage is more likely to be countering a particular understanding of the temple which fails to acknowledge that God is greater than the temple and cannot be so bound to it as its functionaries appear to assume. Thus for Luke's Stephen it remains "the place" and the place where believers continue to pray and even sacrifice. This coheres with the response of the Sanhedrin to Stephen's words. They are not pictured as taking offence at his comments here about the temple. What outrages them is Stephen's attack on their murderous response to Jesus and the prophets, and, above all, his claim to see the vindicated Jesus affirming him; for this amounts to a reaffirmation of what Jesus claimed at his trial. Here and elsewhere their fury is at the claim that they acted wrongly (7:51–57; cf. 4:1–2; 5:28).

The passage is important for the way Luke has associated the trial of Jesus and that of Stephen. Stephen also prays for his killers and dies as a martyr just as Jesus had done. His vision of the Son of Man at God's right hand echoes Jesus' warning to the Sanhedrin. Luke seems to have taken the temple theme from Jesus' trial, as he had it before him in Mark, and used it

---

Act 7 und *PsClem Rec* 1:36ff andererseits sind unter diesem Gesichtspunkt direkt vergleichbar" (p. 303). "Thus criticism of the cultus does not have to mean criticism of the Law, but rather interpretation of the Law. Accordingly it is clear that this interpretation of the Law has universalising as its purpose; the anti-Hasmonean text of *Strabo* XVI 2,35ff, on the one hand, and Acts 7 and *PsClem Rec* 1:36ff, on the other, are comparable when viewed from this perspective." In this way Klinghardt revives Berger's thesis of a universalist understanding of Law preserved in hellenistic Judaism and influencing Luke at this point. Despite the similarities among the texts he cites, ie. a change for the worse from an original set of laws, in each case the change is different. In the Strabo text it is the addition of food laws, circumcision and such like, to the sacrificial cult in Jerusalem; in the Pseudo-Clementine text it is the sacrificial cult itself which is the secondary development.

[161] Brawley, *Luke-Acts*, p. 123, argues similarly that the use of the temple both in the early life of Jesus and by Paul for purification (Acts 21:24–26) shows that it is not considered to be profaned by Luke. Cf. J. Bihler, *Die Stephanusgeschichte im Zusammenhang der Apostelgeschichte*, (Münster: Huber, 1963), pp. 161–178, who argues a change here in the evaluation of the temple. Against this is the consistency of use and respect for the temple throughout the double work.

in his presentation of Stephen. This includes not only the false accusation
of Jesus' intent to destroy the temple, but also the contrast between what is
and is not "made with hands". But it is significant that in doing so, Luke has
not followed Mark's line of having the community of faith become the new
temple, raised with Jesus after three days. Rather he has reworked the material so that its issue is now right attitude towards the temple and against the
restrictive theology of God to which having such a permanent construction
can so easily lend itself. This coheres with what seems to be Luke's understanding of Jesus' action in the temple: the removal of an abuse, not opposition to the temple in principle.

The next passage of major importance for our theme and for Luke (con-
sider the space he gives it!) is the story of Peter's response to Cornelius, the
Gentile centurion (10:1 – 11:18). Luke makes the issue clear as he sees it.
Continuing to be a practising Jew, Peter should have scruples about associating with non Jews, entering their homes and eating with them (10:28; 11:3;
cf. also 10:20 and Luke 7:1–11). To do so is "unlawful" (ἀθέμιτον), for
Gentiles are "unclean" (κοινὸν, ἀκάθαρτον; 10:28). Luke understands
Peter to be concerned about a breach of purity laws. It is not clear that he
would see it as a transgression of written Torah.[162] Probably not, because
nothing there forbids it. The issue is all the more striking because Cornelius
is not just your average Gentile. He is described by Luke as "fearing God
with all his household, giving alms and praying constantly to God" (10:2).
What did he lack? He was unclean and he was uncircumcised. Luke's focus
is the former, but his portrait of Cornelius already effectively calls any discrimination against him into question. This is reinforced when Peter declares: "In truth I perceive that there is no partiality with God, but in every
nation people who fear him and do what is right are acceptable to him"
(10:34–35). This is almost a different argument; it is not that Cornelius is
now deemed to be clean; he is deserving and that is only fair; God does not
discriminate. Yet it is clear that Luke's Peter has first to learn that God
declares Gentiles unclean, before all this can apply.

What turns Peter around is the vision of animals many of whom were
unclean (10:10–16), which Luke has him later recount to the Jerusalem church
(11:5–10). As a conscientious Jew, Peter refuses to eat unclean animals,
since he would thereby transgress Torah (unambiguously the written Torah;
Lev 11). The heavenly voice responds: "What God has purified

---

[162] Cf. R. J. Maddox, *The Purpose of Luke-Acts*, SNTW, (Edinburgh: T&T Clark,
1982), pp. 36–37, who argues that calling Gentiles clean changes the people of God. Peter
has transgressed the Law. God has abolished the Law.

(ἐκαθάρισεν), don't you make or treat as unclean!" (σὺ μὴ κοίνου; 10:15). The threefold repetition reinforces the vision's legitimacy. Divine intervention is sanctioning a departure from written Torah, or so it seems. But how does Luke understand it? He tells us that Peter cannot at first make sense of the dream (10:17). It then makes sense when he faces the prospect of going with Gentiles into a Gentile house. It is the Gentiles whom God has made clean. Peter tells Cornelius and his friends: "God has shown me not to call any person unclean or impure" (10:28). On the face of it the narrative reports a new divine initiative which changes the category of Gentiles. This seems to be reflected in the formulation: "What God has purified (ἐκαθάρισεν – aorist!) do not treat as unclean" (10:15).

There are obvious connections between the vision of unclean food and the issue of Gentile contact which Luke leaves unexpressed. One of the major concerns in contact with Gentiles was that they ate unclean animals, which, in turn rendered them unclean. Doing away with the distinction between clean and unclean animals therefore removes a major cause of Gentile contamination. The change in food laws implies the change in the status of Gentiles. Luke must have been aware of this connection. Otherwise it is striking that the vision is about food laws and its application ignores food laws and speaks instead of Gentiles being made clean.

There are two possibilities. Perhaps Luke has used a tradition about Peter's vision but has woven it into his composition in such a way that it now refers only to the new status of Gentiles and not to food laws at all. This would imply that for Jewish Christians biblical food laws still apply and claims by Jewish Christians in Acts to be fully Torah observant are not compromised.[163] There is much to be said for this understanding. It removes

---

[163] Jervell, "Law," p. 149, argues that Peter's vision meant that Cornelius was no longer deemed unclean and that therefore Peter's keeping company and eating with him did not contravene the Law; the issue was not Gentile mission as such. Similarly Wilson, *Law*, pp. 68–71; Juel, *Luke-Acts*, p. 105; Klinghardt, *Gesetz*, p. 212, who notes that the point taken from Peter's vision in the narrative is that it means Gentiles are not unclean; the reference to food is treated only as symbolic (p. 212). Neither it nor Klinghardt's key notion of almsgiving, as Klinghardt acknowledges, features in Peter's explanation of the event; Cornelius's piety and righteousness are the basis for his answered prayer (p. 213). Barrett, *Acts*, pp. 493–494, 516, notes that Luke's use of the vision suggests that he may not have seen in it abolition of the food laws, since both the way Peter uses it and the apostolic decree show no indication of such an abolition (cf. 10:28 and 10:14). He notes, "It is striking that whereas the dispute in ch. 11 begins with the legitimacy or otherwise of contacts between Jews and Gentiles and ends with the general question of salvation for the uncircumcised, that in ch. 15 moves in the opposite direction, beginning with the conditions of salvation and ending with what may appear to be rules designed to regulate table fellowship between (Christian) Jews and Gentiles" (p. 534).

the tension which results when the apostolic decree reaffirms food laws, although a different set of them. It also accords with the way Luke has Peter subsequently respond to and interpret the vision.

Alternatively, Luke intends the reader to understand the implicit connection between the declared change in the status of animals and the change in status of Gentiles.[164] We should then need to see Luke affirming Mark's view that all foods are clean, but disagreeing with him about both the source of this insight and the occasion.[165] It was not a teaching of Jesus, but arose only in the post Easter period as the Church was confronted with the issues of Gentile contact and came by direct revelation in a dream. If Luke is treating it in this way, it does raise the problems, noted above, when Jewish Christians are supposed to have remained faithful to Mosaic law and not taught otherwise. After all, its import is not just for Gentiles but also for Jews: food laws are no longer valid!

Luke describes the criticism which Peter's action evokes, predictably, as directed at his entering the house of Gentiles and eating with them (11:3). But neither here, nor after Peter recounts the whole episode in detail, is there discussion of the vision's wider implications about clean and unclean animals. It is passed over completely. The focus is joy at the response of the Gentiles. Already in describing Peter's critics as "those of the circumcision party" (11:3) Luke foreshadows where the new development will lead. Logically, declaring the status of Gentiles changed and thus opening the way to their hearing and response to the gospel, need have no bearing on circumcision. Now that they share the clean status of Gentiles they could surely also undergo circumcision, as do Jews and as would proselytes. Luke seems to assume that because Gentiles received the blessing of the Spirit, circumcision was rendered unnecessary, as if it normally functions as prerequisite for God's acceptance, even though those so blessed nevertheless undergo baptism. The success of the Gentile mission on this basis, without circumcision, helps provoke the need for the so-called Jerusalem conference which Luke records in 15:1–29.

It is very hard to believe that Luke could not have seen the implications which the vision of Peter has for Torah. Yet to maintain consistency with what we perceive to be Luke's stance elsewhere we feel compelled to conclude nevertheless that Luke did not draw from it the implication that God was abrogating laws of Torah. But are we then giving consistency higher

---

[164] Hübner, *Gesetz*, pp. 190–191; Pesch, *Apostelgeschichte I*, p. 339; Blomberg, "Law," p. 64; Turner, "Sabbath," p. 116; Tyson, *Images*, pp. 120–123.

[165] So Hübner, *Gesetz*, pp. 182–185.

priority than what appears to be the natural reading of the passage?[166] We shall need to return to this in the conclusion, where it should be weighed within a consideration of the whole.

Peter's experience, according to Luke, justifies inclusion of Gentiles in the community. They are no longer to be considered unclean. Therefore laws relating to their uncleanness no longer apply. This is still a long way from dispensing with food laws of various kinds and with circumcision. Luke assumes that the expansion of the gospel to Gentiles happened without the demand that they be circumcised. The issue is not addressed until it came to a showdown as a result of the insistence of Christian Pharisees. The "circumcision party" had at first not raised the issue of circumcision, but only of Peter's going to Gentiles and eating with them (11:1-2).[167] The mission of Paul and Barnabas had also neglected circumcision.

Before turning to the apostolic council where Luke has the matter dealt with, I want to comment briefly on Acts 13:38-39. Luke has Paul cite the advantage of the gospel for Jews: "Let it be known to you, gentlemen, brothers, that through this man forgiveness of sins is being declared to you (also) from all from which you were unable to be justified in the Law of Moses." This rather clumsy echo of Pauline tradition, in a rather unpauline, but characteristically Lukan way, identifies "forgiveness of sins" as the substance of the gospel and understands justification primarily as forgiveness.[168] It does

---

[166] Salo, *Law*, pp. 208–210, seeks to come to terms with the problem by claiming that Luke deliberately composes Peter's vision, so that it is open to wider interpretation, including interpretation by some as abolishing food laws. Luke, he says, even makes this easier by inaccurately including some clean animals among those which appear. "The author skilfully and intentionally wishes to leave the vision open to different interpretations" (p. 210). Is this credible?

[167] Esler, *Community*, p. 96, argues that the point of the Cornelius episode is not legitimising the Gentile mission, but table fellowship (p. 96). This is true to the extent that the case is not addressed as the legitimacy of the Gentile mission as such, but what their inclusion implies and that certainly raises the fellowship issue. Luke's use of the episode shows that he holds the two closely together. Fundamental is God's declaration about the cleanness and the confirmation given through the coming of the Spirit. But the first hurdle was certainly directly related to the issue of cleanness and what that implied for the contact which made the expansion possible; only as a result of that did the issue of circumcision arise (so rightly, Esler, pp. 93–94).

[168] Cf. Blomberg, "Law," p. 65, who sees it accurately reflecting Pauline tradition and arguing justification by faith alone without the law. See also Salo, *Law,* p. 218, who argues that Acts 13:38–39 means: "that Judaism, including its legal system, cannot provide an adequate basis for salvation" (p. 218). "Judaism does not (or at least not any more) possess salvation, but rather justification can be obtained only by becoming a believer" (p. 220). He credits Luke with avoiding direct criticism of the Law here only to avoid offending Jewish Christians who may still observe the Law as long as they believe in Christ (p. 221).

not say that prior to the gospel there was no forgiveness, as popular Christianity has often taught. Rather it speaks of more forgiveness than was possible before.[169]   Such a claim was implicit in John the Baptist's preaching; otherwise what was the point? Is Luke playing with statistics, here, in the sense: through Jesus we can forgive more?[170]   What were those sins which could not be forgiven previously? Or is the activity of John and Jesus a better clue? For there the difference does not seem to have been quantitative, but rather a matter of access. Luke would be understanding the Law of Moses as limited in what it could provide in offering people access to forgiveness. In John and then in Jesus, and in the preaching of the church, the usual access to forgiveness has been freed up, so to speak.[171]   It is a statement about the Law's inadequacy only in the sense that Israel also hoped for more. It need not be seen as attacking or disparaging the Law in itself and was probably not meant by Luke in such a negative light.[172]

According to Luke, by the time of the Jerusalem Council there are Christian Pharisees who are demanding circumcision as part of total observance of Mosaic Law (15:5). Luke has Peter recall his experience, noting God's equal favour to Jew and Gentile, again pointing out that the blessing came upon Gentiles only after faith and therefore arguing that additional requirements would be superfluous (15:6–9). But Luke has Peter support this plea, on the one hand, by arguing that to do otherwise would put God to the test, and on the other, by pointing to the difficulty they as Jews and their forbears have had in keeping the Law's demands (15:10). Apparently to want a re-

---

[169] Cf. Conzelmann, *Theology*, p. 160, who believes that the contrast rests on the notion that the Law was burdensome. This is not supported in the context and depends on a particular reading of Acts 15:10 which may, in itself, be in error.

[170] Cf. Fitzmyer, "Law," p. 187), who suggests that 13:38–39 amounts to a claim that "forgiveness is offered for *everything* – which the Law never offered".

[171] Klinghardt, *Gesetz*, pp. 99–107, argues that the new is not forgiveness of sins; that was already present in John's baptism and assumed in Judaism (pp. 99–107). "Gegenüber der Möglichkeit der Sündenvergebung durch das Erbarmen Gottes, die schon immer bestand, ist jetzt neu, dass Sündenvergebung als einmaliger Akt durch die Bindung an (Taufe und) Bekehrung quasi institutionalisiert ist: Sie gilt *jedem* der zum Glauben kommt, dh. sich bekehrt" (p. 109; similarly p. 113). "In contrast to the possibility of forgiveness through God's mercy, which had always been the case, the new element is that forgiveness of sins has been institutionalised through linking it with (baptism and) repentance: it is available for all who come to faith, ie. who repent" (my translation). I agree on the issue of access, but find the notion of its reinstitutionalisation without sufficient evidence. Klinghardt argues this in part on the basis of seeing a necessary relationship between 13:38–39 as *peroratio* and the *narratio* of the speech which focuses on the basis for this change: the enthronement of the Messiah as universal Lord (p. 108).

[172] So Wilson, *Law*, pp. 59–61; Cf. Tyson, *Images*, pp. 137–138.

versal of current practice would amount to putting God to the test, perhaps by disbelieving his involvement and doubting what he has revealed through that involvement: namely that Gentiles are clean and may receive the Holy Spirit. The hidden assumption is still that being declared clean and receiving the Spirit renders circumcision unnecessary. It is not a necessary conclusion. But one may assume that the logic is that the blessing renders any additional demand unnecessary – but then why baptise? Perhaps the thinking was: God's declaration and blessing affected the status of not just Gentiles as such, but Gentiles in their uncircumcision. To circumcise would amount to disbelief. This appears to be the understanding presupposed here.

Peter's second point seems even more extraordinary. The Law is too heavy a burden to put on Gentiles, because it has been too heavy a burden for us to carry.[173] A possible conclusion from such a reading would be that no one should be asked to bear it! But that is not Luke's conclusion, nor probably his understanding.[174] Luke is having Peter make the point that both Jews and Gentiles have been saved in the same way, by faith. Since they have been saved, without having any additional requirements imposed on them, and since there is obviously nothing deficient in their salvation, it would be inappropriate to impose such demands on them. Luke does not appear to be implying that such demands should not still apply to Christian Jews. It is doubtful that Luke understands "hard to bear" negatively, ie. as "burdensome". The Law's demands are to be borne; Luke has Peter acknowledge of the Jews: we have not kept them well.[175] In effect Luke is having Peter remind his Jewish colleagues that they are just as much sinners as Gentiles are. This cuts two ways: they should not spurn Gentiles and they should not impose on them what they fail to keep adequately themselves. Luke is at no point suggesting that this would be cause for Christian Jews to abandon the Law and is certainly not calling it into question. Luke assumes

---

[173] So Syreeni, "Matthew, Luke and the Law," pp. 146–147; Tyson, *Images*, pp. 146–147.

[174] Cf. Blomberg, "Law," p. 64, who believes it shows neither Jewish nor Gentile Christians are any longer to keep the Law. See also Turner, "Sabbath," pp. 118–119; Salo, *Law*, pp. 237–243, who considers that Luke knows Peter's statement is inconsistent with Luke's views elsewhere, since it questions the validity of the Law not only for Gentiles but also for Jews, but lets it stand. Luke's view, he believes, is to be found in the speech of James. Is it credible that Luke would allow such an inconsistency, particularly, in the character of Peter, who is otherwise a key exemplar for Luke?

[175] So J. L. Nolland, "A Fresh Look at Acts 15:10," *NTS* 27 (1980), pp. 105–115, here: 105; Pesch, *Apostelgeschichte I*, p. 78, sees Luke having Peter express Israel's sin and therefore its need of Christ, just like the Gentiles. Similarly Wilson, *Law*, p. 60; Klinghardt, *Gesetz*, pp. 111–112. The objection is not to imposing the Law on Gentiles but to imposing on them what applies only to Jews (p. 112).

continuing commitment on their part and this is confirmed in the assertions to this effect about Christian Jews, including Paul, in the rest of Acts.

Luke then has James affirm the inclusion of Gentiles, offering scriptural warrant from Amos 9:11–12 LXX: "'After these things I shall turn again and restore the fallen tent of David and I shall rebuild its ruins and set it upright, so that the rest of humankind may seek the Lord including all the Gentiles over whom my name is called,' says the Lord, making these things known long ago." By implication, James sees the expansion to include Gentiles as part of the restoration of the David's people. The focus here is the people, not the tent as temple.[176] He, too, appears to operate with Peter's assumption that God had acted to include people who were uncircumcised, which effectively meant that to circumcise them would be not to accept what God had done. James's proposal to impose limited restraints on the Gentiles is adopted by the council.

The upshot is that Luke allows for two groups in the church: Jews who remain Torah observant, but are freed to mix with Gentiles because God has declared them clean and are not obliged to insist on their circumcision; and Gentiles who must abstain from meat offered to idols, meat of carcases which have been strangled or have not been drained of blood, and *porneia* (probably illicit marriage relations).[177] These requirements appear to be based on Lev 17–18 where they are characterised as issues which justify exclusion of sojourners from the community.[178] When Luke has James refer to the

---

[176] So Chance, *Jerusalem*, pp. 37–41. Cf. A. G. van Aarde, "'The most high God does live in houses, but not houses built by men...': The relativity of the metaphor 'temple' in Luke-Acts," *Neotestamentica* 25 (1991), pp. 51–64, here: 54, 61.

[177] So Tyson, *Images*, p. 148. The decree is about four ritual issues, three concerning foods and one concerning either ritual prostitution or consanguineous marriages.

[178] Cf. Wilson, *Law*, pp. 74–101, who argues that there is no reference to Lev 17–18, but that Luke understands the apostolic decree primarily as an apostolic ruling inspired by the Spirit, not an application of Torah. But see the detailed treatment in Klinghardt, *Gesetz*, pp. 158–224, who reviews possible backgrounds of the apostolic decree. Its similarity with traditional combinations, idolatry-immorality and idolatry-food laws, is noted; but the reference to strangled food goes beyond these (pp. 160–169). Klinghardt notes that the so-called Noachic commandments and pentateuchal laws regarding "strangers in the land" include much that is not in the decree (pp. 177–180, 181–186). He finds the key to the content of the decree in the eradication formulae (what must be destroyed; Acts 3:21–22 shows Luke is aware of it; pp. 186–200). He argues that the decree identifies those particular laws for "strangers in the land" in Lev 17–18 which are associated with this formula of destruction. They are designed to keep the nation pure (blood: Lev 17:10; wrongly slaughtered meat: 17:13–14; sexual impurity/immorality: 18:6–29; idolatry: 17:7 and 20:3–5; p. 186). The upshot of his findings is that Luke is applying to Gentiles those parts of the Law which were focused, in particular, on Israel's ritual purity (pp. 205–206, 217).

reading of the Law in the synagogues, he is probably implying that such rules were not unfamiliar.[179] They may reflect a common Jewish stance. Probably Luke understood the decree as representing not only all that the apostles under the guidance of the Spirit required of Gentiles in terms of ritual law, but also all that the Law required of them in that respect.[180]

It would probably make meal fellowship possible in mixed communities, which, from James's comments about the extent of the diaspora, was liable to be almost everywhere.[181] But it would be a mistake to see the decree as focused solely on making table fellowship possible and to ignore it as application of Law.[182] If the concern were primarily table fellowship, it would be surprising that no mention is made of clean or unclean animals which would surely also be relevant. Does Luke assume that this distinction has been abolished for both Jew and Gentile anyway? It seems more likely that Luke has not understood Peter's vision in that way and so sees it as having no relevance to the conference concerns in that respect.[183] On the same

---

[179] So W. Radl, "Das Gesetz in Apg 15," in: *Das Gesetz im Neuen Testament*, QD108, edited by K. Kertelge, (Freiburg: Herder, 1986), pp. 169–174, here: 172–173, who argues that James' solution is not new; it is the standard one of the time; similarly Tyson, *Images*, p. 149.

[180] So Jervell, "Law," pp. 144–145; Juel, *Luke-Acts*, pp. 106–107; Sanders, *Jews in Luke-Acts*, pp. 115–116, 121–122; Tyson, *Images*, p. 149; Salo, *Law*, pp. 251–252. Cf. Conzelmann, *Theology*, p. 147, whose scheme assumes that Acts 15 marks a watershed after which adherence to the Law no longer applies. Similarly Turner, "Sabbath," pp. 117–118, who nevertheless rightly makes the point that the list in the decree is far from all the requirements which the Law has for Gentiles. According to Klinghardt, *Gesetz*, pp. 205–206, Luke assumes Gentile observance of much of the Law beside these commandments, as is testified of Cornelius, without however the demand of circumcision. For Klinghardt's position the possibility that uncircumcised Gentiles could be accepted within Judaism of the time becomes very important. He notes it as "gut denkbar" (p. 205; "quite thinkable"). He notes that women would be exceptions and suggests on the basis of Ex 12:49 LXX that the LXX author assumes there were uncircumcised proselytes and on the basis of Acts 13:43 (read with 13:16, 26) that Luke assumes the same (p. 184).

[181] Cf. Sanders, *Jews in Luke-Acts*, p. 119, who argues that Luke is concerned "to invalidate the Jewish Christian position" (p. 119), not to provide a way for both communities to live together or have table fellowship (pp. 119–121). "The proper basis for association of Jews and Gentiles together in the church is, for Luke, God's abrogation of the Torah (except for those laws intended specifically for Gentiles" (p. 121). "Luke is at pains to show how the early church, like the early Jesus, sought a home of piety and devotion in Judaism, but it would not. And so Jesus and the church turned from Judaism and the Jews to the Gentiles, and Christianity became a Gentile religion, and all the Jewish laws in the Torah were rendered null and void, and Torah-observant Jewish Christians became hypocrites" (p. 128; similarly pp. 129–131). The problem here is that later Luke in no way disparages Torah observance among Christian Jews.

[182] Cf. Esler, *Community*, pp. 93–109.

[183] Wilson, *Law*, pp. 98–101, notes the tension between Peter's vision and the apos-

grounds, the decree is hardly just strategic advice to avoid offence, on the Pauline model (1 Cor 9:19–23). The comment at the end of the letter, "From which if you abstain you will do well" (15:29), should not be taken as indicating optional good advice.[184] Rather they will do well, because this is God's will and applies God's Law.[185] There are no further demands which they would have to achieve before it could be said, that they had done well. Of course, there are, in addition, ethical commands, but Luke's focus here is ritual law. But even then, circumcision of Gentiles is still acceptable where occasion warrants it, such as when Luke explains how Paul had Timothy circumcised.[186] Luke appears then to have understood the decree as the application to Gentiles of what Luke believed the Law demanded of them. The exception proves the rule: circumcision. This exception required spectacular heavenly intervention for its legitimacy.

Another major sequence of events relevant for our theme is Paul's final visit to Jerusalem (21:17–26) and its sequel. Luke has James report to Paul about the huge numbers of Torah observant Jewish Christians in Judea (21:20). For Luke they are not an oddity or a particularly conservative group; they are normal Christian Jews.[187] As Jervell points out, the focus here is ritual not ethical law, thus indicating that Luke takes its observance seriously.[188] According to Luke, the accusers have been misinformed about Paul. People had been falsely alleging that Paul had been spreading apostasy from the Law of Moses among diaspora Jews by saying they need not circumcise their children nor observe Jewish ways (21:21; cf. also 21:28).[189] On the contrary, according to Luke, Paul has been Torah observant. Luke

---

tolic decree and that it would disappear if the decree were understood ethically, as came later to be the case.

[184] Cf. Blomberg, "Law," pp. 65–66.

[185] Cf. Wilson, *Law*, p. 106, who writes: "Gentiles are free from the law or 'customs of Moses' because they are not their customs but the customs of the Jews, Gentiles have their own religious and cultural roots which, like those of the Jews, can be taken up and fulfilled by the gospel of Christ" (similarly p. 103).

[186] Tyson, *Images*, pp. 149–150, argues that Acts 16:1–5 assumes the matriarchal principle applies and that Timothy would have been regarded as a Jew and should have been circumcised in the first place. Paul circumcised him It shows that Jews coming into Christianity still observe circumcision. Luke is demonstrating that the charge against Paul in 21:22 is false.

[187] So Jervell, "Law," pp. 140–141; Juel, *Luke-Acts*, pp. 107.

[188] Jervell, "Law," pp. 140–141.

[189] Blomberg, "Law," pp. 67–68, hardly does justice to the text when he argues that the charges against Paul in Acts 21:21 and in the hearings which follow were false only in the sense that they implied deliberate acts on Paul's part, not because he was Torah observant.

then reports a strategy, suggested by James, which Paul allegedly undertook to prove that this was so. It involved Paul's undertaking to pay on behalf of four of James's people what was normally required for the completion of a vow and the accompanying sacrifice (21:24–27).[190]

Luke sees this strategy as anything but an attempt to deceive; for Paul is, in fact, Torah observant. Later he has Paul speak of the purpose of his return to Jerusalem as being, among other things, to make sacrifices at the temple (24:17). Paul had, in any case, intended to undergo the requirements of purification (24:18). Paul's arrest, according to Luke, was all a misunderstanding: he had not brought a Gentile into the temple, nor had he transgressed the Torah in any way or taught others to do so (21:28–29; 24:6).

Luke's second volume contains much that pertains to the Law. Our focus is particularly on its significance for our understanding Jesus' attitude towards the Law as Luke would have seen it. In this we may assume that Luke would not portray attitudes towards the Law as legitimate in Acts which would have contradicted Jesus' attitude towards the Law portrayed in the gospel, unless he had indicated grounds for such a change. The question is also bound up with the issue of consistency in the overall picture of Luke's understanding of the Law. We shall return to that in the conclusion. I want here to summarise the relevant findings for our discussion from the review of the Acts material.

The Jewish disciples of Jesus are portrayed as consistently faithful to the Law throughout Acts, and that, with particular focus on both ritual and cultic issues. Luke makes a point at times of warding off all claims to the contrary, especially against Paul. The new element in the equation is the Gentile issue, which Luke had removed from his account of Jesus' ministry or at least sidelined. Luke's solution is to see circumcision waived by special divine initiative, but, apart from that, to see Gentiles as keeping the Law that applies to them (which Luke sees outlined in the decree) and to see Jews as not compromising their obedience when dealing with them.

With regard to his account of Peter, there are two main points of contention. Do his comments in Acts 15:10 imply disparagement of the Law as a burden for both Jew and Gentile or are they rather in the style of admission and assertion that Jews are equally sinners? The former would constitute a major tension with the positive assessment of the Law in the gospel and elsewhere in Acts. The latter is the more likely reading. The second is: does

---

[190] On the inaccuracies in Luke's understanding of the Nazirite vow, see Salo, *Law*, pp. 260–266.

Peter's vision imply that God has changed the food laws or is it just a meta-phor for the declaration that Gentiles are no longer unclean? The former option would not necessarily create tension with the gospel, since it would amount to a new decision in God's dealing with humanity. It would, how-ever, create tension within Acts, where on the most natural reading, Luke implies that the charges against Stephen as espousing changes in the Law are false and where such a liberal attitude toward food issues seems left out of account in the apostolic decree and the discussion which precedes it. More seriously still, it would give the lie to the claim that Jewish Christians who shared such a view were Torah observant and create massive inconsistency for Luke. The latter option makes better sense in the narrative as a whole: the vision is addressing the status of Gentiles, not food law.

That leads to two further areas of contention, Stephen and the apostolic council. Our review suggests that Luke would defend Stephen against the charges that he slandered the Law and the temple. His speech respects the Law's authority. Its comments about the temple are not an attack on the building itself or its predecessor, but on the abuses it has come to house as an institution (perhaps, in Luke's mind, already since Solomon).

The Jerusalem Council sanctions the practice of not requiring that Gen-tiles be circumcised. The issue here is whether not to impose such a demand is to disregard an important Torah provision. On the face of it this can hardly be denied (cf. Gen 17:12–14). This issue is whether Luke would have seen it this way. If he did, it could be seen as a change occasioned by a new situation, much as Jesus reversed his instructions about mission in Luke 22:35–38 (cf. Luke 10:4). He appears to assume that God's declaration that Gentiles are no longer unclean makes keeping that Law unnecessary. This rationalisation amounts to understanding that God had removed the need for them to be circumcised, though the requirement of circumcision still remained for Jews. Here we must distinguish between Luke's perception, on the one hand, and that of contemporary Jews and other Christians, on the other, many of whom would have seen an abrogation with extensive consequences for the status of the Law as a whole (eg. Paul).

The same must be said for the apostolic decree which appears to be un-derstood as guaranteeing that Gentiles are as Law observant as the Law de-mands them to be. James, the Spirit, and the Council make this inspired decision. The Law remains in force; the Gentiles keep only the ritual law requirements set out in the decree. They are not free from the Law. While Luke can use the apologetic language of customs to cover such things, he appears thereby not to disparage the Law or forget its divine origin. He wants to show that the Law is being upheld and doubtless believes in what he is saying. The same is probably the case when he reshuffles Paul's concepts in Acts 13:38–39. He does not intend to convey the impression that Paul disparages the Law or calls it into question. Rather he sees the gospel offering something more, much as was already the case in the ministry of both John and Jesus.

3.6 Jesus' Attitude towards the Law in Luke – Conclusions

3.6.1 Torah faithfulness

The most striking feature of Luke's presentation, both in the gospel and in Acts, is that there is an underlying assumption that both Jesus and those who surround him or later follow him are faithful to Torah. It is reflected in the gospel from the pious figures of the infancy narrative to Joseph and the women caring for Jesus at his burial, and in Acts from the early community centring its worship in the temple to Paul who comes to the temple to sacrifice. The details are uncontroversial and set out in the preceding pages.[191] As incidental detail it is significant enough. But Luke goes further. He makes a special point of underlining that actions are in obedience to the Law (so Luke 2:22–24; 23:55–56) and defends Paul against the charges that he transgressed the Law and taught others to do so. In all such cases we are dealing not primarily with ethical, but with both ritual and cultic law. As Jervell pointed out (see the review of research at the beginning of the chapter), even Luke's language about the Law reflects strong Jewish piety. This atmosphere of piety, understood in relationship to the Law, does not belong only to the gospel or only to the first phase of the Church, as Conzelmann and others assumed. It is consistently assumed throughout, as the controversies concerning Paul in the final chapters of Acts confirm. Such piety is both the seed bed and the setting for all that follows.

When we trace the development of the story, we note how this respect for the Law informs, and is reflected in, Luke's portrayal of the significant events.

---

[191] Zechariah and Elizabeth, Anna and Simeon; the circumcision of John and Jesus; Mary's purification and offering for her firstborn; Jesus' coming to the temple as a child prodigy; his regular attendance at synagogues, the regular mention of his prayerfulness, his observation of the Passover, his concern for the temple, his teaching in the temple; the presence of the disciples in the temple, their prayerfulness, the piety of Stephen, Peter observing the hour of prayer, Paul in visiting the temple, making Jewish vows, defended against all allegations that he is other than observant, the tens of thousand of Torah observant Judean Christians.

It informs the proclamation of the gospel. John proclaimed repentance for the forgiveness of sins. The call to repentance and the promise of forgiveness of sins remain central also for the message of Jesus and of the Christians in Acts. The repentance entails not only remorse for sins past, leading to forgiveness; it also means commitment to a changed life. Here the Law functions centrally as the expression of God's will. This would be only to be expected given the emphasis on true piety as faithfulness to Torah. It is implied in John's preaching, but, at times, made quite explicit by Jesus. This is not to say that Luke saw the will of God as expressed only in the Law. Clearly that is not the case, as the Sermon on the Plain, in contrast to the Matthean Sermon on the Mount, well illustrates. Luke presents much of Jesus' teaching without linking it explicitly to the Law. But the Law never loses its place. This is why Luke can have Jesus cite the Law when asked about what qualifies a person to inherit eternal life and, through the parable of Lazarus and the rich man, bewail the failure of people to heed the Law. In that context Luke has Jesus make his clearest commitment to the Law's abiding validity (16:16–17). It is to be upheld without exception. To see the divorce logion, which follows in 16:18, as an immediate exception is to attribute 'doublethink' to Luke and to fail to appreciate that he, like many of his contemporaries, would have perceived Jesus' strictness as strengthening, rather than weakening or abrogating the Law.

The preaching of the apostles follows a similar structure to that of John and Jesus. The difference is primarily that they now preach also about Jesus. But their message is not that he has replaced Torah or achieved salvation on the cross, rendering the Law obsolete. Luke knows the tradition about Jesus' vicarious death as part of his last supper tradition, but refers to it nowhere else. It is not central and he does not use it, as does the author of Hebrews, to negate the Law. Rather, in Luke, Jesus' death and resurrection vindicate his message. That message remains substantially the same. It calls for repentance, promises forgiveness and the Spirit and points forward to judgement and hope.

What John brought that was new over against what had gone before was the baptism for forgiveness of sins. What Jesus brought that was new over against John was the activity of the Spirit in his ministry. What the church leaders brought which was new over against Jesus was the message about Jesus and the pouring out of the Spirit on all, including Gentiles. But the common factor through all is that response to this new divine initiative should show itself in changed lives: repentance and life in accord with God's will in the community of God's people. That will is set forth in the Law and in Jesus teaching. This is why Luke can both affirm the Law as the way to salvation and affirm discipleship side by side. They are not in tension, nor do they represent two stages; for Jesus' message is the keeping of the Law and those who keep the Law will acknowledge Jesus and share the common hope for God's action in the future.

Paul's contrast in Acts 13:38–39 between limited forgiveness and unlimited forgiveness, as characterising what is possible through the Law of Moses and what is possible through the gospel, is best seen in the context of the contrast already implicit in John's baptism. It has less to do with quantity of forgivable sins and more to do with access to that forgiveness. It was not implying that the Law be abandoned or abrogated.

It is here that we can also consider the way Luke sees the Law and the Prophets functioning predictively. Luke merges the two functions in 16:16–17. The Law is one. Wilson must see the predictive role and the instructive role of the Law in tension, because he sees Jesus abrogating parts of Torah. Of this we found no convincing evidence. The Law's predictive function is also implied in the cries of those who observe it most closely. Thus the hopes of the faithful in the infancy narratives were not implied critique of the Law, as Blomberg suggested. The Law (and the prophets) taught them also to hope. This belief in hope furnishes the explanation for how Luke can present John and Jesus (and the Church) as faithful to the Law and yet as bringing something new. The hope is not for a change in the Law, but for fulfilment of what it predicts for those who remain faithful to the Law.

With regard to that hope we noted its centrality in the opening chapters of the gospel where it strongly reflects the language of Jewish national hope. Clearly these hopes are shown as finding their fulfilment in the birth of the child, Jesus, as Israel's Messiah, but they extend beyond that to the expansion of the gospel to the Gentiles and some of them will not find their fulfilment until the eschaton. These include hopes for Israel's liberation from her enemies. To such hope belong also a number of texts which speak of Jerusalem in terms of eschatology (13:35; 21:24,28; cf. also Luke 2:25, 38; 24:21; Acts 1:6). Luke has Jesus predict judgement upon the city and the temple's destruction (13:34–35; 19:41–44; 21:5–6,20–24; 23:27–31). But beyond that, Luke seems to affirm the Jewish hope for a future redemption of Jerusalem and of Israel. Jerusalem will be trampled by its enemies only for a time. The ultimate hope remains. He even appears to see it occurring in his own generation (21:32).

Luke frequently portrays events from a Jerusalem perspective, even portraying Jesus' own suffering as a foretaste of Jerusalem's suffering (23:27–31). His changes in the timing and content of the Sanhedrin trial over against Mark may show greater familiarity with the city and the laws of its institutions. For Luke Jerusalem remains the holy city and the place of hope. There is more going on here than can be explained by the valid observations about the role of Jerusalem in salvation historical terms as the goal of Jesus' ministry and the beginning point of the church. Already Paul keeps coming back to Jerusalem. For Luke, Jesus will come to Jerusalem as its Messiah. It will be liberated from the Gentiles who in Luke's time now desecrate it after the disaster of 70CE.[192]   Then its inhabitants will cry out to Jesus, "Blessed is he who comes in the name of the Lord" (13:35). The hopes of the pious (Anna, Simeon, Joseph of Arimathea, the disciples) will be fulfilled: the kingdom will be restored to Israel. While this does not relate directly to the issue of the Law, it has indirect bearing on it in that it confirms the strongly Jewish ethos of Luke's stance and so heightens the probability that he would see Jesus' attitude towards the Law as overall positive.

The same concern with Israel is also reflected in Luke's vision of the future of the church. It envisages rule over Israel, with the disciples on the twelve thrones. The vineyard parable also reflects Luke's belief that Israel and its heritage now has new vineyard keepers. The vineyard is not destroyed or abandoned. Changing the image, the great feast will include both the poor of Israel and, by expansion, the Gentiles. Both the extension of the invitation and the inclusion of Gentiles form part of the hope of the pious of Israel. It coheres with this strong sense of identification with Israel that Luke should accord the Law such great significance.

3.6.2 The old and the new

The hopes of the faithful, are, as we noted, primarily fulfilled in the birth of Jesus, the long awaited Messiah. In him something new has arrived. Sorting out the nature of the relation between the old and new is problematic.

---

[192] Brawley, *Luke-Acts*, pp. 125–126, who argues that the judgement on the city and temple is not final; 21:24 suggests it is only for a period as in Ezek 39:23; Zech 12:3. He relates this also to Luke's exoneration of the perpetrators of Jesus' death, who acted in ignorance (Lk 23:31,[34]; cf. Acts 3:17; 13:27). Luke's understanding of judgement on Jerusalem reflects an established pattern which combines judgement and restoration (cf. Deut 32; Zech 12:3; Amos 9:13–14; Joel 3–4 LXX; 1 Macc 4:11; 2 Bar 67–68). It coheres with this that the temple continues to be used even after the crucifixion (p. 126). Luke, he suggests, links Jerusalem and the temple, in part by false etymology (p. 123) and points to the way Luke can interchange the two (24:52–53; Acts 5:25,28; Luke 21:6–7 with 20–24; pp. 123–124). He suggests that the centrality of Jerusalem is not just to be explained in salvation historical terms, as a point from which to move on. It belongs rather within the widespread view of Jerusalem as the sacred city, the navel of the earth, the meeting point of heaven and earth, which he sees reflected in the temple as a place of visions in Acts (pp. 127–132).

The presence of the new, partly already in John, but especially in Jesus, and then in a broader way in the Church, had to entail dealing with the relation of old and new. Luke does contrast new and old garments, new and old wine, but to stress incompatibility between the way of Jesus and the way of the Pharisees, not between Jesus and the Law. Luke shows that already John's baptism for forgiveness of sins created difficulty. Apparently the temple personnel saw it as an issue of authority and must have inclined to declare John to be in breach of the Law. Luke only hints at this, but it is consistent with the image he gives of the stance they also took towards Jesus. It was also consistent with their particular style of interpreting the Law, which was concerned to protect propriety. Luke shows them challenging Jesus' authority as either demonic or blasphemous. Jesus flatly rejects both arguments, claiming God's authority and empowerment. Luke claims both John and Jesus as agents of God's wisdom and sets the authorities on the side of those who kill wisdom's messengers. Luke does not relate this directly to the Law, nor does he associate the figure wisdom with Torah. But ultimately such a claim put Jesus at odds with those who saw themselves as authorities and claimed that authority on the basis of the Law.

Luke shows Jesus as having two main issues with the Jewish authorities: hypocrisy and putting the emphasis in the wrong place. The two are closely interrelated. He relates hypocrisy particularly to being concerned with some aspects of Law while neglecting care for people. For Luke this is quite concrete and shows itself in misuse of wealth, greed and exploitation. In this context he confronts them with the Law and the need to take it seriously (16:16–17). In conflict with the teachers of the Law and the Pharisees Jesus is first and foremost a champion of the Law. The exchange with the lawyer in which Jesus tells the parable of the Good Samaritan makes the point clearly, both in the generosity it affirms and in the distraction it denounces. The same emphasis on an inadequate approach to the Law is exposed in the ruler, who claims he keeps the whole Law, but stumbles at the suggestion that he sell all and give to the poor. It is also present in the parable of the rich man and Lazarus.

Luke's version of the woes carries the same theme. Luke is not attacking the washing of cups or even tithing of minor foodstuffs, which he still has Jesus enjoin; he is attacking preoccupation with these, while neglecting love of God and justice. He can acknowledge that those who expound Torah have the key to knowledge. Attitude and orientation are all important, as the contrast between the sinner and the Pharisee illustrates. The same orientation toward human need explains Jesus' response to criticism about sabbath behaviour. Luke's Jesus does not abrogate the sabbath or dismiss its relevance. This is hardly thinkable given Luke's respect for it elsewhere. Rather Jesus dismisses his critics occupation with keeping laws rather than making people its focus.

In doing so, Luke's Jesus is hardly engaging in halakic argument; he disregards their arguments. In doing so he virtually appeals to common sense, at least a 'common sense' he presupposes many would share; and beside this he asserts his own authority to declare accordingly.[193] This appeal to common sense is also implicit in Luke's emphasis on use and abuse of wealth and the value of friendship, common in popular hellenistic ethics. In the encounters over the sabbath, but also in the woes, some of these fundamental Lukan values come to the surface. Luke identifies them as values of Jesus and as intended in the Law.

Central among them is the notion that God is not to be seen as primarily demanding obedience just because he is God and should therefore be obeyed. For on that logic one could not discriminate among commandments; every one would have to be obeyed down to the last detail. Such total and detailed observance would be an expression of love for God. How could it be otherwise? But Luke does not portray God in these terms. This is true even though he generally avoids indicating that some commands have greater weight than others, in contrast to Matthew, and, to a lesser extent, Mark. For that approach can still be an accommodation to the formal understanding of authority which we have described. Luke seems, in contrast, to have an understanding of God which assumes that God is most concerned with salvation, and making people whole, which Luke understands primarily in terms of healing, morality, and deliverance from oppression and poverty. It has not led him to abandon a ritual or purity value system, but for him this clearly plays only a subordinate role and, I suspect, is fast becoming irrelevant. It is this perspective that is missing in Jervell's analysis, who, otherwise, accurately describes what Luke wants us to hear. This underlying sense of values explains to my mind a number of peculiarities in Luke.

---

[193] Downing, "Law and custom," pp. 152–158, notes that 16:16–18 and generally Luke's understanding on the Law should be read in the light of pagan reaction to superstition and religious practices which harm or make no sense: sabbath, circumcision, God being bound in a temple. Luke's values very much reflect those of the learned world of the time. "It is in the light of the widespread critique, then of superstition, and especially Jewish superstition, that Luke presents Christians as properly pious, but without any 'superstitious' scruples that would preclude sabbath healing, suppose God bound to a temple site, demand burdensome or bizarre rituals of those of non-Jewish ancestry, or use traditions as an excuse for avoiding social contacts" (pp. 156–157). He draws attention among others to Seneca, *Moral Epistles* 95.48; Plutarch *Moralia* 169c, f; 170A; Philo *Spec. Leg.* 4.147; *De Mut.* 138; *De Praem.* 40. On pagan critique of the sabbath see also Klinghardt, *Gesetz*, pp. 244–252.

To begin with, Luke passes over so many incidents where purity issues would have been relevant. He does not appear to see the objections to Jesus' eating with toll collectors and sinners in that light, but concentrates instead on their moral sin and on justifying Jesus' presence with them as leading them to repentance. He indicates no sense of conflict with the Law in reporting Jesus' demand that a would be disciple turn from the burial of his father nor in the demands that people separate from their families and possessions. He makes no mention of the purity issues linked with Jesus' touching a leper, being touched by an unclean woman, touching corpses, entering Gentile territory, and has Jesus willing to override such concern to heal the centurion's servant. Yet he has Mary observe her time for purification, has Jesus send lepers to the priest, and makes Paul keep a Nazirite vow. But even then there are inaccuracies, consistent with someone affirming something as valuable, but not being directly involved. Observing such requirements is the norm, but is hardly central for Luke. This would make good sense also if we assume Luke himself is a Gentile, not a Jew. None of his main characters makes it central to their instruction. It comes into focus only where special circumstances make it necessary. This explains the way Luke treats these issues in Acts. There they become important because of special circumstances.

For Luke the coming of the Spirit on Cornelius and his friends is what makes all the difference. Circumcision can be left aside. And to get to that point Luke has Peter abandon scruples about encountering Cornelius on the grounds of a vision which effectively appeals again to Luke's understanding of common sense: how can animals be clean and unclean! Its real point, however, is: how can people be clean and unclean on ethnic grounds! Luke is on very shaky grounds, because this rationalising presentation, bolstered by appeal to miraculous coincidences, could imply not only abrogation of food laws, but of the purity system altogether. The exegete faces greatest difficulty here. Does Luke know what he is saying? Yet Luke shows no sign of taking more from the vision than an argument about the acceptability of Gentiles, so that we are left not knowing if he is being deliberately subversive[194] or naively reflecting his own ambiguity. My point is that Luke is

---

[194] This was the thesis of F. Overbeck, "Über das Verhältnis Justins des Märtyrers zur Apostelgeschichte," *ZWT* 15 (1872), pp. 321–330, which Jervell, "Law," p. 133, summarised as "stating that the author of Acts was unprincipled when he dealt with the law. On the one hand, Luke advocates justification by faith apart from the law (13:38f); on the other, Jewish Christians are obliged to keep the law unabridged, while Gentile Christians have only modified freedom from the law." Overbeck sees Luke's attitude to Jewish Christian adherence to the Law as without conviction, even though he sees Luke pretending it is important.

still operating within an understanding according to which it is necessary to obey the Law, but his orientation is such that he can affirm this, while effectively giving purity issues a low priority. This reflects fundamental ideological values, which are evident with the account of the vision itself. At one level it appears to appeal to God's declaration, almost as though God is issuing a decree. But effectively it is appealing against what Luke assumes people would agree was an absurd distinction. God sanctions this attitude. The same kind of appeal is implicit already in the account of Jesus' sermon in Nazareth. I find this more satisfactory than to assume Luke is being deliberately ambiguous as Salo suggests in relation to the vision.

It is interesting in this respect that Luke has not taken over the more radical stance of Mark on matters of Torah. He omits the section where Mark makes Jesus' teaching of purity a centrepiece for arguing the legitimacy of the Gentile mission and so also omits Jesus' radical teaching in which, Mark claims, Jesus renders all food clean. When Luke employs elements of this passage later, its focus has narrowed to dismissing the need for washing before meals. Even when he uses the story of Peter's vision in Acts, he appears to disregard its radical significance for food laws, choosing rather to apply it symbolically to the purity status of Gentiles. Luke was obviously not prepared to go as far as Mark.

The same difficulty reappears in the sequel in Acts 15. Luke can let circumcision go, just as he portrays Peter doing so earlier. Yet he appears to presume that to do so should be seen as coherent with faithfulness to Torah, because God has effectively made the Gentiles children of the covenant by pouring out the Spirit on them. It is a matter of dispute whether such a stand could be seen as still belonging within the realm of the possible in Torah interpretation. Luke's rationalisation is assumed again at the Council, but in a dangerously pauline sounding argument that salvation has put all on the same footing where they are saved by faith. Part of the argument may even disparage the additional requirements of the Law, but this is unlikely. It still, however, exposes a problem. How can Luke have Peter say this and yet also portray him as observant of the Law? The fact is that he does, so that for Luke the Law still stands, though he has effectively loosened its footing.

The decree, itself, is effectively a compromise, not between Jews and Gentiles, but between Luke's desire to affirm commitment to the Law and his ambivalence about its ritual demands. It is this kind of tension that has rightly led some to wonder whether Luke is motivated politically by the desire to placate, perhaps unconsciously, sensitive Jewish Christians, while still putting all of the emphasis otherwise on a strongly moral and ethical understanding of the Law.

Many would see a similar tension in Luke's handling of Stephen. I do not believe that the speech is anti temple, but it is critical of an attitude towards the temple. The use of "made with hands", with its associations of idolatry and its echoes of popular pagan critique of temple systems, confronts the temple leadership and implies they are disobedient like the wilderness generation. Luke's treatment of the Law elsewhere coheres well with what is said. The temple is still the holy place. It is the place of the pious. It is the place of vision for Paul's call to the Gentile mission.[195] Its rites are upheld. But Luke's Jesus confronts its abuses. We must not separate Luke's approach to the temple from his approach to the temple authorities and their retainers. Luke's attack is not on the temple, but on the abusive system and the approach to Law interpretation which it represents. There is a safety for Luke in this, since the temple no longer stands. Yet I believe his position in this is consistent. Had the temple still stood, and had the authorities not prevented it, Luke and his believers would have behaved towards it much as did Jesus and Paul and the pious of his story.[196]

---

[195] See Chance, *Jerusalem*, pp. 90–113, on the importance of the temple in association with the Gentile mission in both the gospel and Acts.

[196] J. H. Elliott, "Temple versus Household in Luke-Acts: A Contrast in Social Institutions," in *The Social World of Luke-Acts*, edited by J. H. Neyrey, (Peabody: Hendricksen, 1991), pp. 211–240, offers a typology for understanding Luke's view of the temple. He claims that we should see Luke favouring the household model against the temple system. The temple system represents exclusive space, run by a hierarchy, a centralised bureaucratic authority, economically controlling and exploitative. The household represents communal space, based on families (with fictive kin), with no public power, reciprocity, sharing of resources and inclusive. The temple forms an inclusio in the gospel, the household, in Acts. Luke shows the shift from the temple to the household. Elliott notes that the situation in Luke-Acts is complex, since Luke portrays respect for the temple as a place of prayer, purification and pilgrimage; however "the ministry of Jesus and his movement also is marked by what is perceived to be a flagrant disregard of the purity norms concerning persons, behavior, times and places" (p. 222). He rightly stresses the importance of seeing both the temple and the household within the systems which they represent.

It is not possible to respond in detail to the analysis, which sets out typical characteristics of both systems systematically. There are, however, some remarkable omissions. In a discussion sensitive to power issues, I would have expected to have found some discussion of the authority of Torah. This is especially important as part of "the full range of data" which Elliott rightly demands should be considered (p. 224), since it has enormous implications for how Luke perceives the issues raised by Elliott's typology on both sides. For, to some extent, the system which he sees Luke attacking, is enshrined in Torah and it is clear that for Luke the power has not been resolved on the basis of choice between two social systems, or simply between Torah and Christ. Elliott's typology raises the questions well, but offers few answers and is in danger of proffering ideological generalisa-

It is interesting that here, too, Luke is not prepared to go as far as Mark. He dismantles Mark's compositional focus on the destruction of the temple and its replacement by the community of faith. Jesus' action in the temple appears no more than a removal of wrong practices and the rending of the curtain, now placed before Jesus' death, a sign of divine grief or anger. Even when he does use some of the relevant material in the account of Stephen, he is careful to exonerate Stephen of the charge that he attacks the temple itself.

Within the gospel Luke mostly presents Jesus' teaching without specific relation to Torah. Yet it is always assumed that Jesus' teaching in no way contradicts Torah. Occasionally Luke emphasises that this is so and implies the same of the Church. The issues of potential departure from Torah come more to the fore in Acts, but Luke continues to assert faithfulness to Torah and its relevant demands among both Jewish Christians and Gentiles. There is a consistency, therefore, between the Gospel and Acts and within each, at least, an intended consistency. On the other hand, we detect that Luke's value system, his theology, operated with assumptions which inevitably put the priority on ethical rather than ritual and cultic demands, and then less on commands as command and more on attitude. He stops short of Mark's radical break, although not far short. We should probably attribute this in part to issues of his day: sensitivity to Jewish Christianity and perhaps also

---

tions instead of exegesis. When he writes of the temple purity system, "According to this system of economic and social stratification legitimated by purity classification, the rich were ranked above the poor, the clergy above the laity, urban dwellers (especially in Jerusalem) above the rural peasantry (especially in distant Galilee), men above women, married above unmarried, healthy above the ill, conformists above deviants" (pp. 221–222), he offers a fair generalisation. But what he says about the rich is not always true: rich toll collectors were despised. The economic model has failed to take sufficient note of the Law issues.

Elliott's apparent idealisation of the household leaves me with questions: for a slave (significantly Elliott uses the word, "servant"; p. 225), how wonderful was the household? In Luke's household Peter issues the death penalty to Ananias and Sapphira. Households were very much part of the economic system which sustained the regional economy and in that, slavery was essential. Luke's parables reflect the uncertain plight of life under the household. My plea is for more careful differentiation in use of the household model and, above all, consideration of what was central in the household: the authority issue, not least the authority of Torah. The playing off against each other of household and temple in Luke leaves too many questions unanswered. See also the criticism of van Aarde, "'The most high God does live in houses, but not houses built by men...'," who disagrees with Elliott that household replaces temple, and argues rather that Luke broadens the understanding of institution of the temple as a result of a changed symbolic universes, but without abandoning it (pp. 54, 61)

to the community's own sense of legitimacy and continuity as the true successors of the Old Testament religious heritage.

Luke has much in common with Matthew in affirming the place of the Law. This has a lot to do with their common heritage is using Q. Yet for both the issue is an alive one. But they appear to operate in very different settings. Matthew is in a Jewish setting, Luke in a primarily Gentile setting. Matthew is concerned to claim Jesus as the best Judaism. Luke claims a similar legitimacy but from a more distant perspective. From a Gentile perspective Luke claims legitimacy and continuity. Gentiles uphold all that Luke sees the Law asking of them. Luke employs the language used by Jews in cross cultural encounter to describe the Law as "the customs" of the Jews (eg. Acts 6:14; 15:1; 21:21; 28:17). These are God given to Israel; about this Luke shows no doubt. It allows him and his hearers however to accommodate the distance. The God-given customs of Israel are not to be imposed on Gentiles, not primarily because Gentiles are from different cultures, but because the Law itself does not require it. In this way Luke combines an assertion of total faithfulness to Torah on the part of both Gentiles and Jews with a sense of cultural difference which justifies the separation which has come about from those who continue to uphold their divinely sanctioned ways. Luke would thereby seek to appease both Gentile Christians anxious about the separation and Jewish Christians who continued full observance and to do so in a context in which the views of both would be increasingly seen as a departure from Israel's true faith. Luke is making a claim to heritage, continuity and Torah faithfulness on the part of Jesus and the Church. It will have convinced many within but few outside the Christian community.

Chapter 4

Jesus' Attitude towards the Law according to Q.

In turning to Q I am aware that there are a number of methodological issues which require clarification. These include, to begin with, acknowledgment that we are dealing with a hypothetical source, whose existence is still in dispute. I have chosen to work with the assumption that there was a Q source, largely because I believe it makes best sense of the data we have, though not without some remainder. But to assume a Q source raises questions of its extent and sequence. Here I shall generally depend on the findings of the International Q Project.[1]

In the other chapters I have deliberately begun with the writings which we have and sought to discover the approach each reveals as a whole. This is slightly more problematic with Q, since we are dealing with a hypothetical reconstruction, both with regard to its content and to its order. It is additionally complicated because so much Q research is focused on recovering stages of composition, including possible implications for understanding the historical Jesus. I am not concerned here with issues of stratification, but shall be discussing Jesus' attitude towards the Law as it is reflected in what the project sees as the Q text. This becomes important in the light of the fact that Kloppenborg, for instance, attributes key statements on the Law, Q 16:17, 11:42 and the temptation narrative to the latest stage of Q redaction.[2] This

---

[1] J. M. Robinson et al., "The International Q Project," *JBL* 109 (1990), pp. 499–501; 110 (1991), pp. 494–498; 111 (1992), pp. 500–508; 112 (1993), pp. 500–506; 113 (1994), pp. 495–500; 114 (1995), pp. 475–485. I have employed the following *sigla* which the group used: 1. "..." indicates probability that text existed here in Q, but no longer recoverable witch sufficient probability; 2. "[[ ]]" The reconstructed text has a probability of C on a scale from A to D. Readings with a probability of D are not included at all; 3. "< >" indicates conjectural emendation found neither in Matthew nor Luke; 4. "<< >>" indicates a train of thought, though the exact Greek text is irrecoverable.

[2] J. S. Kloppenborg, *The Formation of Q. Trajectories in Ancient Wisdom Collections*, Studies in Antiquity and Christianity, (Philadelphia: Fortress, 1987), pp. 246–248;

also means leaving to the side the complex issue of a possible pre-Matthean expansion of Q material, as might lie behind the Sermon on the Mount. It also means assuming that the reconstructed text has some integrity within itself.

In using the text of Q which emerges with some degree of consensus through the findings of the International Q Project, I shall assume that it makes some sense to analyse it sequentially. Inevitable this is a less secure operation where we cannot be sure how much Matthew and Luke have preserved of the text of Q. For instance, did Q narrate the baptism of Jesus? There is the additional perspective that much of the material is not narrative, although that does not mean compositional structures are not to be observed.[3] I shall follow the commonly accepted practice of referring to Q material by its versification in Luke, without implying thereby a priority for Luke's version.

4.1 Recent Research

As the first of his collection of "signal essays" on Q, Kloppenborg includes a brief article by Rudolf Bultmann.[4] With regard to the Law, Bultmann saw in Q the spirit of freedom. "The old Law no longer plays a role" (p. 29). There are no longer unbearable burdens. The simple, "those who did not comprehend the hairsplitting niceties of παράδοσις ([Pharisaic] tradition)", now comprehend (Matt 11:25–27; par. Luke 10:21–22). The woes are directed at those who focused on external rather than internal purity. Divorce should not be treated according to the Law. Even the sabbath can be broken if necessity demands. "The continued life of the Spirit that overrides the Law" is evident in the absence of references to the Law in Jesus' ethical

---

"Nomos and Ethos in Q," in *Gospel Origins and Christian Beginnings In Honor of James M. Robinson*, edited by J. E. Goehring et al., (Sonoma: Polebridge, 1990), pp. 35–48, here: 46.

[3] On this see the compositional discussion in J. M. Robinson, "The Sayings Gospel Q," in *The Four Gospels 1992. Festschrift Frans Neirynck*, edited by F. van Segbroeck et al., (Leuven: Leuven University Press, Peeters, 1992), pp. 361–388, who notes, for instance, the inclusio formed by the material about John the Baptist, Q 3:7–9,16–17 and 7:18–35 (pp. 361–362).

[4] R. Bultmann, "What the Saying Source Reveals about the Early Church," in *The Shape of Q. Signal Essays on the Sayings Gospel*, edited by J. S. Kloppenborg, (Minneapolis: Fortress, 1994), pp. 23–34, German original, "Was lässt die Spruchquelle über die Urgemeinde erkennen?" *Oldenburgische Kirchenblatt* 19 (1913), pp. 35–37, 41–44.

teaching, which surpasses the Law; yet the community also preserves a different spirit, reflected in "sayings buttressed by the motif of retaliation" (p. 30). "The saying that concerns the eternal validity of the Law (Matt 5:18 // Luke 16:17) displays crass disregard of the spirit of the new restructured view of the Law" (p. 30). However, "if one does not go beyond the material common to Matthew and Luke, antinomian sayings are as infrequent in Q as are sayings with a legal character" (p. 30). Luke 16:17 is positioned to mitigate Luke 16:18 (p. 31), reflecting the duality of the Spirit of freedom and "ecclesiality".

Bultmann's comments are interesting for the presuppositions they reveal, which were widely shared at the time: that the Law was burdensome; its interpreters were hairsplitting and focused on the external; Jesus' divorce and sabbath teaching effectively breached Torah; and, in contrast, Jesus offered freedom. He also discerns tension within Q between pro- and anti-Law statements, but observes that both were infrequent. Already Bultmann is identifying, thereby, some of the key issues.

Schulz[5] sees two levels in Q, a Palestinian and a Hellenistic Jewish, but, with regard to the Law, what he describes as the attitude of the early stage remains unchanged in the second level (pp. 94–141,485). It is a radicalising affirmation of Torah which even accepts Pharisaic interpretation, but accuses it of focus in the wrong place. Conflict with the Pharisees was on the basis of Q's radically strict interpretation of the Law on matters such as divorce and remarriage, retaliation, and love of enemies (pp. 172–173). Q implies no abrogation of purity or ceremonial laws (pp. 97–99). The concept of radicalisation of Torah, rather than abrogation draws on earlier work by Braun.[6] The radicalised understanding of Torah demanded of the disciples in this age is based on love. Q still largely reflects the theology of Jesus which was dominated by future eschatology; this is the setting for its approach to the Law. Only in its later stages did Q come to identify Jesus with Wisdom, but the eschatological orientation remained dominant (pp. 482–483).

Hübner[7] sees contradiction in Q, as in Luke, on the assumption that the divorce logion and the rejection of retaliation contradict Torah (p. 212). While Jesus is not portrayed as anti-Torah, Q 16:16 originally depicted the end of

---

[5] S. Schulz, *Q. – Die Spruchquelle der Evangelisten*, (Zurich: Theologischer Verlag, 1972).

[6] H. Braun, *Spätjüdisch-häretischer und frühchristlicher Radikalismus. Jesus von Nazareth und die essenische Qumransekte II: Synoptiker*, BHTh 24, (Tübingen: J. C. B. Mohr [Paul Siebeck], 2nd edn, 1969), p. 12.

[7] Hübner, *Gesetz*.

the Law; yet Q also contained 16:17 affirming its abiding validity (pp. 31). Schürmann[8] argues that Luke 16:16–18 was a Q tradition, which saw the kingdom as the place where the new understanding of the Torah applies (p. 126). He distinguishes a level deriving from Law observant Jewish Christians (Q 11:42,39–41), which was supplemented, first by a group which had broken with ritual law, but not yet with Judaism (Q 11:44,46), and later by an anti synagogue redaction which has broken with Judaism (Q 11:43,47, 49–51,52; pp. 130–131).

Dautzenberg,[9] argued that Q 16:17 reflects the need to address the irritations caused by discussion of the Law in Hellenistic Jewish Christianity and the Gentile mission (p. 64). Up until that point Q had been Torah observant and had not even needed to address the issue of Torah observance (p. 65). Q 11:39,42 assume not only written Law but also the validity of its Pharisaic interpretation (p. 65). Q directs its critique at one-sided concentration and draws on prophetic traditions. He dismisses Hübner's interpretation of the divorce logion as contrary to Torah. Rather it is "Toraverschärfung", but he says this term should not be applied to the wisdom teaching (pp. 66–67). The perspectives reflected in the divorce saying derive, as in Qumran, from the context of Jewish and priestly purification concerns (p. 67).

Tuckett[10] sees 16:17 affirming the Law in Q (p. 91). Originally 16:16a had implied the end of the era of the Law (p. 92). With 16:17, he writes, "It looks very much like the second saying is a reaction against the first" (p. 92). He agrees with Sanders[11] that 16:18, the prohibition of divorce and remarriage, is not an attack on the Law (p. 93). "With the arrival of John and Jesus a new era had dawned, but this is not one where the law loses any of its validity" (p. 93). With regard to the woe concerning tithing of minutiae, he sees the injunction not to neglect it (11:42c) as looking "very much

---

[8] H. Schürmann, "Das Zeugnis der Redenquelle für die Basileia-Verkündigung Jesu. Eine traditionsgechichtliche Untersuchung," in *Gottes Reich – Jesu Geschick. Jesu ureignener Tod im Lichte seiner Basileia-Verkündigung*, (Freiburg: Herder, 1983), pp. 65–152.

[9] Dautzenberg, "Gesetzeskritik," pp. 62–67.

[10] C. M. Tuckett, "Q, the law and Judaism," in *Law and Religion. Essays on the Place of the Law in Israel and Early Christianity*, edited by B. Lindars, (Cambridge: Clarke, 1988), pp. 90–101. See also his "The Temptation Narrative in Q," in F. van Segbroeck et al. (ed.), *The Four Gospels 1992. Festschrift Frans Neirynck* (Leuven: Leuven University Press, Peeters, 1992), pp. 479–508, where he strongly reiterates his view of Q's image of Jesus as Torah observant (pp. 487–489). See now also Tuckett's, *Q and the history of Early Christianity. Studies in Q*, (Edinburgh: T&T Clark, 1996), which reached me after conclusion of this manuscript, esp. ch. 12, "The Gentile Mission and the Law," pp. 393–424.

[11] *Jesus and Judaism*, p. 256.

like a secondary comment by a later hand to correct any 'misunderstand-ings' which the rest of the saying might imply" (p. 94). Tithing is not an optional extra. "It is not the case that for Q, some reassessment of the Jew-ish law is in mind here, as if the ceremonial law were being made subservi-ent to the ethical law" (p. 94). "The comment is not just about those who keep the law but about those who voluntarily do more than the law requires" (p. 95). Certainly it reaffirms "the practice of *pharisaic* law. The Q commu-nity is thus expected to continue the practice of tithing as practised by the Pharisees" (p. 95).

The same applies to the woe about purity (11:39-41): "The saying does not condemn the practice of purity rites in any way" (p. 96). Similarly the saying about the sabbath (14:5; cf. also 13:15) reflects current discussion (p. 97). It is the only appeal to a legitimate argument acceptable in Judaism (p. 97). "The Jesus of Q thus operates on the sabbath within the law as defined by later tradition to a far greater extent than the Jesus of Mark or the Jesus of Matthew" (p. 97).

Tuckett also assumes that Q probably had a version of the double com-mandment to love God and one's neighbour (behind Matt 22:34-40; Luke 10:25-28; p. 97). In Q 11:46 he does not see the burdens as such ques-tioned, but the lack of help (p. 98). Q material "appears to exhibit a strongly 'conservative' attitude towards the law. It shows a deep concern that the law should be maintained; it is aware that Jesus could be seen as antinomian, and appears to represent a strong movement to 'rejudaise' Jesus. Further there is some strong concern to uphold the pharisaic reinterpretation of the law. However coupled with this is an intense awareness of hostility from non-Christian Pharisees and/or non Christian scribes" (p. 98). Following a suggestion of Wild[12] about the proximity of early Christianity to Pharisaism, Tuckett proposes that Q preserves evidence of links with Pharisees and, in particular, with the Shammai strand (p. 100). Accordingly he suggests that this would fit a situation where Q was claiming to be truly Pharisaic, but facing hostility from within the movement.

Kosch[13] also agrees that Q assumes the validity of Torah. Thus on tithing and purity it criticises current attitudes, not the practices themselves. This is confirmed by 16:17 and by consideration of 14:5 (re: sabbath) and 10:7 (re: foods). These also show, however, that Q had no particular interest in

---

[12] R. A. Wild, "The Encounter between Pharisaic and Christian Judaism: some early Gospel Evidence," *Nov Test* 27 (1985), pp. 105–124.

[13] D. Kosch, *Die eschatologische Tora des Menschensohnes: Untersuchungen zur Rezeption der Stellung Jesu zur Tora in Q*, NovTest et OrbAnt 12, (Göttingen: Vandenhoeck und Ruprecht, 1989).

the issue of the Law itself (pp. 210, 359). For the issue of the Law comes up only where a word or action of Jesus appears to call it into question (p. 211). In the woes Q is not seeking to radicalise the Law. The Law is not part of Q's preaching, which is more concerned to portray Jesus' interpretation of God's will as encompassing the totality of life rather than being tied to detailed issues. Because Torah and Jesus are not set in contrast, Torah tends to be interpreted on the basis of Jesus' teaching, not the reverse (p. 211). This approach is therefore qualitatively rather than quantitatively different from that of the Pharisees.

Q shows no sign of reflection on the tension between continuing validity of the Torah and the critical potential which Kosch presumes was present in the Jesus tradition of Jesus' words (p. 212).[14] He rejects Schulz's notion of Q as radicalising the Law (p. 396). He sees the sermon rather as the "eschatological Torah of the Son of Man" (p. 415). The challenge from John and Jesus is not to return to the Law, but to acknowledge Jesus as Son of Man and Lord (p. 421). At the redactional level of Q, additions to sayings like 11:42 and 16:17, indicate that the whole Torah remains in force and that Jesus' demands should be fulfilled without disregarding those of Torah (p. 426). Jesus' message and person are the main point of reference for the self understanding and practice of the Q community, not the Law (p. 447). His is the supreme claim to authority (so Q 10:21–22; cf. also 10:16; 11:23; p. 448). To acknowledge Jesus, not just his teaching, is crucial for salvation (Q 12:8–9; pp. 448–449).

Effectively, Jesus and his message take the place of Torah for his followers (pp. 450–451). Kosch acknowledges that Torah obedience features in the temptation narrative, but dismisses its significance by attributing it to late redaction (p. 451). Nevertheless while acknowledging Jesus as Son of Man and following his teaching, Q also held to the validity of the Law which it saw as upheld in Jesus' teaching (pp. 451–452). The approach to the Law was not however nomistic (p. 452). For Q, not Jesus but "this generation" are the transgressors of the Law (p. 453). Q sensed neither the prohibition of divorce and remarriage (16:18) nor the rejection of retaliation (6:27–36) as in tension with Torah (though Kosch senses that they were: pp. 453–454). The relation between Jesus' teaching and the Law is not a significant concern for Q.[15] Hence the sparseness of references to "the Law", of quota-

---

[14] G. Dautzenberg, "Tora des Menschensohnes? Kritische Überlegungen zu Daniel Kosch," *BZ* 36 (1992), pp. 93–103, cautions about the notion of "critical potential" here, since he sees this really arising only from a standpoint outside the Torah, ie. as in Hellenistic Christianity (p. 97).

[15] Similarly R. Uro, *Sheep among the wolves: a study on the mission Instructions of*

tions from the Torah, aside from the temptation narrative, which like 11:42c and 16:17 reflect the later stages of redaction (pp. 454–455).

Kloppenborg,[16] noting that Q has little to say on Torah and its laws, points out that this could lead to two different conclusions: "Either Q takes for granted the validity of the Torah and therefore never engages such legal issues; or it ignores the issues with which Mark and Paul struggled, because the Torah does not figure importantly in the soteriology and paraenesis of the community" (p. 36). Instead of seeing in Q 11:39–41 an attack on purity abuses from an inner Pharisaic perspective, as Tuckett proposed, Kloppenborg believes that Q reduces the issue of purity to absurdity, shifting the focus to the ethical and demonstrating that the boundaries between clean and unclean are fluid (p. 39). "By subverting the boundaries between inside and outside and by diverting attention to ethical issues, Q is actually undermining the entire system of purity that depends for its existence on a well-defined taxonomy of the cosmos" (p. 37). The stance reflects Cynic rejection of ritual and resembles PsPhoc 228: "Purifications are for the purity of the soul, not (for the purity of) the body" (p. 40). He presses the significance of the composition of the woe section as a whole, which shows, he claims, that it is now addressed not to the Pharisees, but to all Israel (p. 38).

Similarly on tithing, Q is not showing interest in legal hermeneutics. The woe is directed at absurdities (p. 41). 11:42c is, therefore, not enjoining strict observance (p. 43). It is an intrusive gloss of an anxious redactor concerned with Torah observance in general (pp. 44–46). Generally "none of the extended compositions shows a tendency either to buttress admonitions by means of an appeal to Torah or to frame them in such a way as to contrast the admonitions with the Torah." (p. 43). He sees 16:17 also as an editor's attempt to obviate potential false understandings of 16:16 (p. 45). 16:18 is the new demand in new era 16:16. 16:17 intrudes (pp. 45–46). 16:18 now illustrates 16:17 (pp. 44–45).

Kloppenborg writes: "While it is usual to think that the further one traces the tradition back the more 'Jewish' it becomes and the greater the likelihood of nomocentric piety, this does not appear to be the case with Q" (p. 46). He cites Wernle[17] as having posited a "Judaizing form" of Q with sayings such as Mt 5:17–20; Q 10:5–6 and 23:3. But Kloppenborg believes,

---

Q, Academiae Scientiarum Fennicae Dissertationes Humanarum Litterarum 47, (Helsinki: Suomalainen Tiedeakatemia, 1987), pp. 189–190, who suggests that probably there was sympathy with the Gentile mission, perhaps because the group was not nationalistic.

[16] Kloppenborg, "Nomos and Ethos," pp. 35–48.

[17] P. Wernle, Die Synoptische Frage, (Freiburg, Leipzig, Tübingen: J. C. B. Mohr, 1899), pp. 229–231.

that, apart from the glosses Q 11:42c and 16:17, there is little evidence in the rest of Q for nomocentric piety. Torah became an issue only at the latter stages (p. 46), as in the temptation narrative (p. 46). Q belongs rather in a world of Judaism like that of the Wisdom of Solomon, Pseudo-Phocylides and Pseudo-Menander, not in the world of covenantal nomism (p. 47). "Salvation is better understood on the model of *paideia* provided by antique sapiential genres and chriae collections" (p. 47). Intuition of the divine is observable in families, and the world of nature.

In "The Saying Gospel Q",[18] Kloppenborg writes that Q "is far from unreflective, unsystematic oral tradition; it is the product of scribal activity" (p. 25). Here he is countering the view that Q represents the "little tradition" against the "great tradition". Thus he counters Horsley's position that Q represents a community setting itself in contrast to the scribal retainers, and promoting a vision of the kingdom as the vision of renewed village life based on egalitarian relations (p. 21).[19] Kloppenborg continues: the framers of Q, however, "do not, like their southern counterparts, appeal to Torah as the self-evident starting point for argumentation (the only exception is the late addition of the temptation story). Moses is not mentioned; purity distinctions are peripheral to Q's world, and the Temple is not a symbol of sanctification and redemption, but a place where the prophets are killed" (p. 25) He also notes the absence of "appeals to Torah, or to the ruling institutions of Israel (priesthood and temple). Instead, the argumentative appeals are to 'natural' processes (growth), familial transactions, and simple market processes (Q 12:6b)" (p. 27). Yet, he notes that Q is concerned to legitimate its ethos and does so by appeals to figures of the Old Testament epic tradition. In other words, it lays claim to an alternative base in tradition from that represented in the Jerusalem scribal authorities (p. 27). This contrast needs greater elaboration. Is it assuming the authority of Torah but expounding it in a different way? Or is it an alternative to Torah itself?

Sevenich-Bax[20] makes the point that for Q the authority of Jesus does not effectively replace the Law, but stands beside it (pp. 459–461). This is illustrated by the fact that the instruction of Jesus in the sermon is flanked, on the one side, by the temptation narrative which shows Jesus as Torah

---

[18] J. S. Kloppenborg, "The Sayings Gospel Q: Recent Opinion on the People behind the Document," *Currents in Research: Biblical Studies* 1, (1993), pp. 9–34.

[19] R. A. Horsley, *Sociology and the Jesus Movement*, (New York: Crossroad, 1989), p. 123.

[20] E. Sevenich-Bax, *Israels Konfrontation mit den letzten Boten der Weisheit. Form, Funktion und Interdependenz der Weisheitselemente in der Logienquelle*, Münsteraner Theol. Abhandlungen 21, (Altenberge: Oros, 1993).

faithful and, on the other, by the narrative of the healing of the centurion's servant, who is a model of faith. Jesus' teaching in Q is not a new or radicalised Torah, but reaffirms Law. The change is a new crisis situation. Wisdom teachings, with many Jewish parallels, have been set in an apocalyptic framework as teachings for this new situation. They are part of Jesus' teaching which also has Torah character beside the Torah itself.

Within this brief overview of some of the main contributors to research on Jesus' attitude towards the Law in Q we may note the following models. One, represented already in Bultmann, sees Q as not primarily interested in matters of Law, but rather in freedom. To some degree Kosch's approach stands in this line, although, contrary to Bultmann, it emphasises the assumption that the community upheld Torah. But Kosch agrees that the Law was not of interest for Q; rather the starting point for seeking God's will was Jesus and his radicalising of the commandments. Kosch, like Bultmann and Hübner, operates on the assumption that Jesus' teachings on divorce and retaliation were in breach of Torah, even though he believes Q did not sense this.

In a very different way Kloppenborg also maintains that the stance of Q is one of largely disinterest in matters of the Law. Q's origin and continuing ethos is in the wisdom tradition. It is not concerned to enjoin Torah obedience or to pit its own Torah observance against that of the Pharisees. Its approach is to ridicule the fastidiousness of Pharisaic observances. Kloppenborg acknowledges that at the redactional level a concern with the Law is evident (in the temptation narrative and the additions, 11:42c and 16:17). The question then becomes: does this redactional stage mean a reversal or simply a spelling out of assumptions already held?

The contrasting position is that of Dautzenberg who argues that we should assume Torah observance in Q. This is similar to the position of Sevenich-Bax. Tuckett, similarly, believes Q assumes Torah observance and suggests it may well reflect a stance which would put the community in close proximity to the movement of the Pharisees and closer to its Shammaite wing. This evaluation depends in particular on finding in Q allusions to what are believed to have been particular concerns of the Pharisaic movements of the time.

The difficulty in Kloppenborg's interpretation is that he has to explain key Torah passages as late redactional glosses. These additions certainly were of a kind to be accepted in the Matthean and, probably, the Lukan community. It will, therefore, be all the more important to see what sense we can make of the document as reconstructed in its 'final' form. We shall assume that such a version of Q was used and that the document had some

integrity. Kloppenborg certainly assumes such a formal integrity when he
proposes that the temptation narrative has been made to serve a role otherwise played by an ordeal scene in the prelude to bodies of wisdom teaching.[21] He also somewhat softens the transition to the final redaction when
he suggests that 11:42c is not enjoining observance of minutiae, but of Torah in general. But is this credible?

The issue at stake appears to be twofold: whether Torah observance may
be assumed for the community and what role Torah observance played in
Q's perception of what mattered. In particular what is Torah's relation to
other claims to authority in the community, not least the authority of Jesus,
himself, but also the authority of appeals to wisdom. This is the strength of
the positions taken by Kosch and Kloppenborg; they acknowledge the weight
of christology and the wisdom material, respectively, which is significantly
greater than any emphasis on the Law in Q. Appeals to wisdom in nature
and reason, such as Kloppenborg indicates by placing Q in the world of the
Wisdom of Solomon, Pseudo-Phocylides and Pseudo-Menander, may assume
Torah observance. This is certainly the case in the related, but much more
extensive, writings of Philo and, to some extent, in Josephus. Our focus is
the reconstructed Q in its final assumed form. The strength of a sequential
treatment is that it should enable us to detect the relative weightings of such
claims. To this we turn.

4.2 The Reconstructed Q Text

4.2.1 John, Jesus and the Temptations

The first clear evidence of Q lies in the material concerning John the Baptist, Q 3:7–10. Its introduction assumes reference to John's baptism. This
is, as we have noted elsewhere, indirectly a matter of Law, at least for those
who would be puzzled, if not unsettled and angry, at John's novel practice
and what it promised. But Q shows nothing of this; instead it has John
address those coming for his baptism, which implies acceptance of his baptism. Probably Q had the words of John addressed, therefore, to the crowds,
not just to religious leaders (Q 3:7; cf. "Pharisees and Sadducees" in Mt
3:7). This may appear rather strange at first: why attack the crowds? It
would appear to make better sense and cohere with other Q material if it had

---

[21] Kloppenborg, *Formation*, pp. 256–262, 325–327.

been religious leaders.[22]   Yet the focus is on the call to all coming for baptism to repent with genuine repentance before receiving the baptism; it is not about a particular group claiming they need no baptism or standing at a critical distance. The "fruits worthy of repentance" (Q 3:8) are attitudes and behaviours which indicate a commitment to change. Assumed is a value system which emphasises ethics; the text does not spell it out.

Q 3:8 confronts reliance on ethnic identity, "We have Abraham as our father", as ensuring escape from the coming wrath. Within a Jewish context this confrontation is most naturally understood as belonging within the prophetic tradition which contains similar warnings (cf. Amos 5:18–24; Zeph 1:14–18). It need not, in itself, be a revoking of the connection with Abraham;[23] nor an indication of universalism, although the challenge to dependence on national religious identity lays open that kind of possibility.[24]

Nothing indicates that John's statement challenges the Law, itself. On the contrary, within a context which still affirmed some continuity with Israel's religious heritage, we are probably correct to assume that the fruit is to be indicated and measurable by the Law and that the Law will, at least in some sense, be the measure for the final judgement. Law, as a guide to appropriate fruit, as an indicator of sin and as the measure of judgement, is a fundamental assumption. To put it another way, the theology of Q's John assumes a central place for law. The question is: law, understood in what sense? What follows in Q shows that it is law as in the Law.

---

[22] So R. Uro, "John the Baptist and the Jesus Movement: What Does Q Tell Us?" in *The Gospel behind the Gospels. Current Studies on Q*, edited by R. A. Piper, (Leiden: Brill, 1995), pp. 231–258, here: p. 234, who favours a reference to opponents as more likely, while recognising that "Pharisees and Sadducees" is Matthean and "the crowds" probably Lukan. See also the discussion in C. R. Kazmierski, "The Stones of Abraham: John the Baptist and the End of Torah (Matt 3,7–10 parr. Luke 3,7–9)," *Biblica* 68 (1987), pp. 22–40, here: 27–28, who leaves open the possibility that Sadducees and Pharisees were perceived to be among the crowd and concerned with John's new activity.

[23] So rightly A. D. Jacobson, *The First Gospel. An Introduction to Q*, (Sonoma: Polebridge, 1992), p. 83. Cf. F. W. Horn, "Christentum und Judentum in der Logienquelle," *EvTl* 51 (1991), pp. 344–364, here: 353, 364; Kazmierski, "Stones of Abraham," pp. 30–31, who understands it as a call to abandon election and the accepted channels of salvation. The problem here is that there is no hint in Q or elsewhere that John was ever understood in such a way. It would certainly have made the issue clearer for the temple authorities (cf. Mark 11:27–33), had the historical John the Baptist spoken thus.

[24] See Uro, *Sheep*, p. 221, who favours an allusion to Gentile mission here. Cf. Horn, "Logienquelle," p. 353, who sees a change of traditional expectations; now Israel, not the Gentiles, will be subject to judgement of fire. But this overlook the extensive prophetic tradition of threats against Israel.

The same issues emerge in John's prediction of the coming one (Q 3:16–17). The coming one will be God's agent on the day of wrath and judgement. To the image of the axe (Q 3:10) John adds the image of wind and fire, winnowing (hence: wind), gathering and burning (hence: fire).[25] There is an assumed coherence between the emphases of John and Jesus on attitude and behaviour and on judgement.[26] Jesus will also use the imagery of fruit (Q 6:43–44), but, beyond that, Q frequently presents Jesus as a teacher of moral integrity.

Q's introduction of Jesus strongly emphasises his role as judge. This implies that Jesus will be the interpreter of what is the criterion of judgement and the guide to what it means to live a life bearing good fruit. In some sense or other, that means he will be an interpreter of law. This beginning also implies a particular soteriology: salvation in the judgement will be for those who repent, in the sense of turning from evil to good, and do so on a permanent basis. The issue of law is fundamental for such a theology. Again, it is a question of how law is understood and its relation to the Law. The temptation narrative will show that it certainly includes Torah.

While we cannot recover a Q version of Jesus' baptism, a number of scholars assume that there was one.[27] We may assume that it would have, of necessity, raised for its hearers the connection between Jesus' baptism with Spirit, predicted by John, and his receiving the Spirit, assuming the baptismal account also referred to the Spirit coming upon Jesus. There was probably something like an identification of Jesus as God's Son. Both elements, Spirit and sonship, appear to be presupposed by the temptation narrative which follows (so Q 4:1,3,9). The baptism of Jesus would also have reinforced his identity as the one of whom John spoke, the coming agent of God's judgement.

---

[25] So Jacobson, *First Gospel*, p. 84.

[26] Uro, "John the Baptist," pp. 247–252, raises the possibility that the statement about the two baptisms is Christian in origin, reflecting not a word of John, but part of the move to subordinate John to Jesus in the tradition, and that Spirit referred from the beginning to Jesus' charismatic ministry. If an account of the baptism followed in Q at this point, this might be the meaning in Q. As it stands, the context is all focused on acts of judgement.

[27] J. S. Kloppenborg, *Q Parallels. Synopsis, Critical Notes and Concordance*, (Sonoma: Polebridge, 1988), p. 16. See also the recent discussion in Robinson, "Sayings Gospel," pp. 361–388, and the cautionary critique of Uro, "John the Baptist," pp. 237–239, 241, who makes the point that the link between the Baptist material and Jesus is not "Son of God", but "the coming one" and the issues raised by John's predictions and Jesus' behaviour. But this does not adequately take into account the temptation narrative. See also D. R. Catchpole, *The Quest for Q*, (Edinburgh: T&T Clark, 1993), pp. 62–63, who presses the point that the temptation narrative requires some reference to "Son of God" to precede it.

Q's account of John's prediction suggests Jesus will act primarily as judge. But this emphasis, so strong in Matthew, is not strong in the Q material. It is true, that Q preserves John's quandary about whether Jesus really was the one in the light of his activities (Q 7:19). But elsewhere Q has Jesus speak rather of God as the judge at the judgement (Q 12:8–9). The words of John do nevertheless portray Jesus as executing God's judgement.

We may also assume that Q would understand Jesus to be involved in a judgement based on God's Law and himself to be faithful to this Law during his life. The temptation story confirms this (Q 4:1–4,9–12,5–8). Being Son of God does not mean departing from divine Law.[28] The one who is to teach will do so as one who is faithful and obedient to the Law.[29] This makes it clear that the divine law which is fundamental in John the Baptist's theology and in his portrait of Jesus' future role is identified with Torah. Many see the temptation narrative as one of the most recent additions to Q.[30] Seeing it as such adds extra weight to its significance for understanding the way Q was understood at this stage of its redaction.[31]

The wilderness imagery evokes the image of Israel in the wilderness: the forty days, the forty years; the bread, the manna; the ascent of a mountain, Moses' viewing of the land of Canaan and perhaps also Sinai. All of Jesus' replies are drawn from Deut 6–8. The focus is primarily Jesus' obedience, but the typological allusions probably function in two different ways; they portray Jesus as obedient to the God of Israel and indirectly they recall Israel's disobedience.[32] This focus coheres with the attacks on the unbelief of Q's generation.

With regard to the particular temptations,[33] the temptation to eat is a temp-

---

[28] Tuckett, "Temptation," pp. 487–488, rightly emphasises that the temptation narrative plays a major role in emphasising Jesus' obedience to Torah. Kloppenborg, *Formation*, pp. 256–262, sees the temptation narrative as commending Jesus as the reliable, wise one who passes successfully through the ordeal of testing.

[29] On the links between the temptation narrative and the sermon, see Sevenich-Bax, *Konfrontation*, pp. 448–449.

[30] So Kloppenborg, *Q Parallels*, p. 20.

[31] So P. Pokorny, "The Temptation Stories and their Intention," *NTS* 20 (1974), pp. 115–127, here: 126, argues that the temptations summarise aspects of Q. Jacobson, *First Gospel*, p. 94, describes it as the work of scribal wisdom, which portrayed Jesus as the true wise "son of God" after the pattern of Wisdom 2, a precursor of Matthew where Jesus is directly identified with Wisdom as Torah. This may be so. Certainly, however, such an identification is not yet present here. In addition Jacobson suggests that Q may be countering apocalyptic enthusiasm within its community (p. 90). This assumes too harsh a contrast between the final redactor and the bulk of the Q material.

[32] So Jacobson, *First Gospel*, p. 88.

[33] On the wide range of interpretations of the temptations see Tuckett, "Temptation,"

tation to break a fast, which is assumed, though not explicitly stated as in Matthew (4:2). This probably assumes the practice of fasting in the Q community. It should be broken only when God wills it, even though, as Son of God, Jesus could have sated his hunger by divine magic.[34] Breaking fast is not evil, if God wills it. The second temptation is not an attack on miracles as such. Perhaps the Q community would hear it in the light of the eschatological hope for special miracles in the temple in Jerusalem.[35] Jesus rejects this particular one. He will not act as the devil's agent. Similarly, Q probably assumed that ruling the nations and their wealth should be Jesus' right, but not through worshipping the devil.[36]

The temptation narrative makes an important statement which sets the scene for what follows. Jesus is obedient to Torah. The Law was fundamental in the theology of John's preaching and in his understanding of Jesus' role at the judgement. In the light of the temptation narrative, that law must at least include the Mosaic Law. Given this beginning to Q, it is hardly possible to deny that the Mosaic Law is of fundamental significance for the Q community. The focus on judgement and right behaviour informs both its

---

Kloppenborg, *Formation*, pp. 248–256. He sees it providing in Jesus "an example of the absolutely dependent, non-defensive and apolitical stance of his followers" (p. 256).

[34] Tuckett, "Temptation," pp. 494–498, argues that we may be mistaken in reading "son of God" as a christological title; rather it amounts to "a son of God", thus making possible a paradigmatic reading of the temptations. Jesus sets an example for the community, who are also children of God. While acknowledging that Q does not use the title, "the Son of God", elsewhere, passages like Q 10:22 make it more likely that a christological sense is present. This is even more so the case if Q had a baptismal narrative which included the title. On the other hand, even with the christological understanding, the point is well taken that the story does function paradigmatically. This seems the best way to understand the temptation to break the fast.

[35] So P. Hoffmann, "Die Versuchungsgeschichte in der Logienquelle," *BZ* 13 (1969), pp. 207–223, here: 216–217. But see the critical discussion of this and other messianic interpretations in Tuckett, "Temptation," pp. 491–492. Other interpretations include: testing God manipulatively or presuming irresponsibly on God's care. Tuckett, "Temptation," pp. 498–501, favours taking it as teaching that miracles should not be sought as signs for their own sake. Cf. Kloppenborg, *Formation*, p. 256, who sees it providing in Jesus "an example of the absolutely dependent, non-defensive and apolitical stance of his followers." But surely the location is significant; this favours the notion that a particular kind of sign is in mind, which might be sought. It is sufficient to know that miraculous signs were sought in Jerusalem from time to time, without needing to find detailed correspondences. Perhaps the temptation is mocking them.

[36] Tuckett, "Temptation," pp. 501–506, makes the valid observation that there is a strong link between the theme of kingdoms here and the opening promise of the sermon which follows. I am less convinced by his attempt to explain the main point of the temptation as simply eschewing worship of the devil. This does not take the motifs of the temptation sufficiently into account (mountain, kingdoms of the world).

soteriology and its christology. Q portrays Jesus, the coming agent of God's judgement, as, himself, impeccable in doing God's will, in contrast both to Israel of old and probably to Israel of its time. This is especially the case if we should see allusions to political eschatology in the final two temptations. The first, however, reflects that the keeping of fasts when required is also part of bearing the true fruits which shall count at the final judgement.

To this point, therefore, doing God's will, God's Law in that sense, is fundamental for Q. But we have not had explicit references to the Law, as such. Within the sequence we are left wondering: what will this Jesus, who is judge to come, Son of God, and totally at God's command, do now? The temptations tell us what he will not do. Otherwise all we have is what John said: John preached judgement; will Jesus do that, too? John announced Jesus' role as judge; how will he go about this?

4.2.2 The "Sermon" to the Disciples

The first major teaching block of Q follows (Q 6:20–23,27–49). It is essential to bear in mind in what capacity Jesus speaks these words; he speaks them as the coming agent of God's judgement, the one who is God's obedient Son. In Q they are Jesus' words to his disciples. Thus the promises to the poor, hungry, and the weeping, are promises of reversal. The weeping will laugh, the hungry be filled and, by implication, those who have nothing and no power will have everything: the kingdom of God. The link with the disciples is more direct in Q 6:22–23, and the suffering more directly attributable to human agency and more clearly depicted as suffering because of Jesus, the Son of Man. This fourth blessing sets the focus for the instruction for the community of disciples which follows. It immediately addresses the issue of response to the persecutors, enjoining love for enemies and non resistance (Q 6:27–30). The focus becomes more generalised with the golden rule (Q 6:31) and with the teaching to be merciful as God is merciful (Q 6:32–36). But it returns to the concerns of the Christian community in applying this to being non judgemental (Q 6:37–38). Here the judgement theme returns. The same focus on the Christian community continues in the command that the disciples become like their teacher (Q 6:39–40) and that they refrain from being judgemental (with the saying about the mote and beam, Q 6:41–42). The teaching continues with the metaphors of good trees producing good fruit (Q 6:43–44), echoing John, and of good treasure being the resource of the good person (Q 6:45). Jesus appeals to the disciples to obey his commands and not just call him, "Lord" (Q 6:46). This recalls Jesus' example of obedience in the temptations. This immediately introduces the metaphor of right and wrong building with its implied theme of the last judgement (Q 6:47).

This teaching is presented as God's Law voiced by Jesus, but at no point is there evidence of concern to show its coherence with written Torah.[37] Direct concern with written Torah may well have shaped its tradition.[38] In the light of the passages considered above, we must assume that for Q such coherence and consistency is taken for granted and needs comment only when some might call it into question or when Pharisees interfere with claims of their own and need to be exposed for their own lawlessness or inappropriate use of Law.[39] Conflict is implied in the passage, but nothing indicates that it is conflict over the Law, although from the opposition's perspective it will have been. The sermon reflects the stance of those who claim Law observance; thus it can contrast its claims with the practices of sinners and toll collectors.[40]

It might be possible to see both in the comments about judging and in the exhortation to bear fruit an allusion to Pharisees and their handling of the Law,[41] but that would be at most secondary, since the context clearly presupposes that these words are addressed to the disciples (contrast Matthew

---

[37] So R. A. Piper, *Wisdom in the Q-tradition. The Aphoristic teaching of Jesus*, SNTSMS 61, (Cambridge: CUP, 1989), p. 74, who notes the same in Q 11:9–13; 12:2–9,22–31.

[38] On this see the strong case made by Catchpole, *Quest*, pp. 107–116, who, in describing the tradition behind 6:31,32–33,35c, argues that these reflect the three elements of Lev 19:18b: "You shall love | your neighbour | as yourself" (p. 115). He extends this to show that Lev 19:17 ("You shall not hate your brother in your heart, but you shall reason with your neighbour") also influences 6:36–45 (pp. 120–133), concluding that "the centre of the discourse is a spelling out of Lev. 19:17–18" (p. 133). "Structurally, vv. 36–38 are pivotal within vv. 27–45 as a whole. They gather together the themes of vv. 27–35, where Lev 19:18 dominates. They control vv. 36–45, where Lev 19:17 dominates. They are themselves controlled by v. 36, and thus the discourse is given its keynote, mercy" (pp. 133–134). The assumption is that these teachings are addressed to people who understand "neighbour" and "brother" as fellow Jew and the instruction as spelling out the Law. At the level of Q which we are considering, we cannot be sure that such an influence which shaped the tradition is still in mind; it may be. It is also very likely that this teaching continues to be seen as exposition of God's will, that is, God's law. R. A. Horsley, "Q and Jesus: Assumptions, Approaches, and Analysis," *Semeia* 55 (1991), pp. 175–209, here 184–185, argues that what is explicit in Matthew ("the giving of a renewed Mosaic covenant" p. 184) is implicit in Q. Referring to 6:27–28,32–33,35a and 29–31, he writes: "There are clear allusions in several of these sayings to traditional covenantal instructions such as those in Lev 19" (p. 185).

[39] So Kosch, *Tora*, p. 211.

[40] So Kosch, *Tora*, p. 388.

[41] Cf. Piper, *Wisdom*, pp. 49–50.

who applies the image of the blind guides directly to the Pharisees in 15:14). The focus, however, on the dangers of judgement presupposes that the community is concerned with right behaviour and therefore with God's will or law in the broader sense and certainly, therefore, with the Law, since Q affirms it elsewhere. The sermon is then, by implication, also giving instruction about how to treat the Law in the community. It is a false dichotomy to pose alternatives here between wisdom teaching and Law teaching, especially given the broader context of the sermon which is concerned with judgement, and of Q as a whole, with both its concern for the judgement (for which one needs law) and its affirmation of the Law.[42]

4.2.3 *Jesus' Ministry and John's Questions*

In Q 7:1–4,6–9 we have the first mention of Jesus' healing ministry. As such it is quite unmediated in the context. The focus is the centurion's faith as a Gentile in contrast to Israel's. The faith as portrayed acknowledges not only Jesus' ability to heal, but also his authority. As the centurion commands soldiers, Jesus can command that his servant or child be made well. He does so as one authorised by God, that is, with delegated authority. The centurion's statement is an important clue to Q's christology. In relation to the Law, this kind of christology portrays Jesus as another authority and inevitably poses the question of the relation between the two. But neither in this act nor in the sermon which preceded it is the issue addressed. Conflict here, as there, is with unbelief from within Israel. A Gentile's faith shames Israel.[43] Nothing indicates how Q viewed the story in relation to mission to Gentiles, let alone the Law issues which it would entail. Evidence elsewhere suggests that the Q community knew of the Gentile mission, so that we are probably right to see a possible allusion here.[44] It probably used also the

---

[42] Cf. Piper, *Wisdom*, pp. 43–44.

[43] So P. D. Meyer, "The Gentile Mission in Q," *JBL* 89 (1970), pp. 405–417, here: 410–411.

[44] So D. Lührmann, *Die Redaktion der Logienquelle*, (Neukirchen-Vluyn: Neukirchener, 1969), pp. 86–87; R. Laufen, *Die Doppelüberlieferung der Logienquelle und der Matthäusevangelium*, BBB 54, (Bonn: Hanstein, 1980), pp. 192–194, 237–243. Cf. Jacobson, *First Gospel*, pp. 110–111; Schulz, *Spruchquelle*, pp. 244–245; Wegner, *Hauptmann*, pp. 304–334, who argues that the point of the mention of Gentiles is not to talk about present inclusion, but to point up Israel's failure (p. 327). 10:2 does not envisage Gentile mission, but rather judgement against Israel (p. 328). The centurion believes for a particular act, but is not a believer (p. 329). No Law free Gentile mission can exist beside 16:17 and 11:42c (p. 332). Against any reference to the Gentile mission see also: Horsley, "Q and Jesus," p. 183.

influx of Gentiles into the church to shame Israel.[45] I shall return to the issue of Gentile mission in the concluding comments of this section.

There is the additional issue: does Jesus' response indicate a willingness to transgress the Law by entering the house of a Gentile (so, at least, on Luke's understanding of the Law in Acts 10:28; cf. also *mOhol* 18:7; John 18:28)?[46] Some have suggested that Jesus' response is in the form of a rhetorical question ("Am I to come and heal him?" QMatt 8:7), effectively refusing to heal the man.[47] This is not the punctuation suggested by the SBL Project Group (which therefore reads: "I will come and heal him"). At some stage, however, initial refusal may well have been the point of Jesus' response and may still be the meaning in Q. It makes good sense of the centurion's reply where he counters by acknowledging unworthiness to receive Jesus and by suggesting that Jesus' word, alone, would suffice. The effect is then similar to the Markan account of Jesus' encounter with the Syrophoenician woman (7:24–30). If this is the case, Q's Jesus would be reflecting a conservative attitude towards the Law.

John had identified Jesus as the coming one who would be God's agent of judgement. In Q 7:19,22 this has its inevitable sequel, since so far Jesus has exercised authority, but has not been doing what John had led us to expect: bringing judgement.[48] The patchwork of Old prophetic allusions which Q portrays as Jesus' answer (Isa 61:1–2; 42:6–7; 35:5; 29:18–19) is surprising in the context.[49] For the first time we hear of other healing: blind seeing, lame walking, lepers being cleansed, deaf hearing, the dead being raised.

---

[45] So Meyer, "Gentile mission," who suggests that Q knows and accepts Gentile mission, does not participate in it and struggles with the issue.

[46] Generally on the view that Gentiles are impure and rejecting this as erroneous, see E. P. Sanders, "Jewish Association with Gentiles and Galatians 2:11–14," in *The Conversation Continues. Studies in Paul and John. In Honor of J. Louis Martyn*, edited by R. T. Fortna and B. R. Gaventa, (Nashville: Abingdon, 1990), pp. 179–188, here: 172–180, arguing that statements made after the two revolts (like *mOhol* 18:7) should not be read into the earlier period. Unfortunately Sanders does not take into account Q 7:1–11 and does not directly discuss Acts 10:28, except to list it beside Jos *JW* 2.150 as both implying avoidance of close association (p. 187 n.11).

[47] So Wegner, *Hauptmann*, pp. 375–380, who cites T. Zahn, *Das Evangelium des Matthäus*, KNT 1, (Leipzig, 4th edn., 1922), pp. 338–339, on Matt 8:7 (p. 376). Similarly Schulz, *Spruchquelle*, pp. 241–243. See also the discussion above in the chapter on Matthew.

[48] See Robinson, "Sayings Gospel," pp. 362–372, who demonstrates that 7:22 also provides a clue to the compositional structure of the beginning of Q.

[49] Robinson, "Sayings Gospel," p.364, notes that these Isaianic motifs had already been spiritualised in Isaiah (eg. 42:18–20), but are intended literally within Q's narrative as 7:22 and the preceding miracle account suggest.

Only the last item, the poor receiving the good news, has a direct relation to what precedes, namely in the first beatitude. The assumption seems to be that Q can have Jesus say this because Q's hearers are aware of such deeds of Jesus. The assumption appears also to be that hearers would sense echoes of prophetic hope. Q 7:23 alerts the hearer to conflict again ("Blessed is the one who takes no offence at me"). In the immediate context it appears directed to John and any who might associate themselves with him.

None of this has a direct bearing on the issue of Jesus and the Law, except that it has the effect of raising anew the relation between Jesus' authority and the Law's authority. Jesus' predicted future activity was less problematic: judgement according to the Law. What about his present activity? Here were possible grounds for concern and offence. While the words of Q 7:22–23 form part of Jesus' response to John, they also indicate where the potential problem lay and form a transition to further material relating to John which will include the offence which both caused.

The narrative sequence continues in Q with mention of Jesus' words about John, after his envoys had departed (Q 7:24–28). Jesus' words have the effect of clarifying John's role and status. Again there is an appeal to the Old Testament (Q 7:27; Ex 23:30; Mal 3:1). Q 7:28 then sharply distinguishes the time of John from the kingdom of God ("[[ ]] I tell you among those born of women there has not arisen one greater than John; but the least in the kingdom of God is greater than he").[50] Q 7:31–35 turns the focus to "this generation". The very negative assertions about it recall John's words to the crowds, calling them a generation of vipers (Q 3:7). It also recalls the contrast in Q 7:9 between Israel's faith and that of the Gentile, and Jesus' comment in Q 7:23 about possible offence. Here Q juxtaposes John and Jesus as envoys of wisdom. They are different and this difference corresponds to what is outlined in Q 7:28. One prepares for the kingdom, is, therefore, preparatory and ascetic, neither eating nor drinking; he is accused of demon possession. The other is celebratory in the time of kingdom; he is accused of being a drunkard and a glutton and of befriending toll collectors and sinners. It is not clear why John's asceticism draws the accusation of demon possession. The accusation against Jesus relates implicitly to behaviour contrary to God's will: revelry and keeping bad company. Traditionally these two behaviours belonged together. The accusation, "glutton and drunkard" recalls the charge which Deut 21:18–21 advises should be brought

---

[50] At this point the SBL International Q Project has resolved that 7:29–30 do not form part of Q. So Robinson, "The International Q Project," 114 (1995), pp. 475–485, here: 479, although it remains included, surely an error, in the list on p. 485.

against a rebellious son before the elders of the people: "They shall say to the elders of the people, 'This our son is stubborn and rebellious; he will not obey our voice; he is a glutton and a drunkard'."

Q does not link these accusations to the Law, although we may assume that the grounds for the accusations would be based in an interpretation of the Law. They may be stereotypical, reflecting Deuteronomy, but the occurrence of the motif of eating and drinking throughout the anecdote and the direct mention of toll collectors and sinners suggest that the conflict relates to Jesus' participation in meals in bad company. Q's hearers know from the temptation narrative that Jesus was not disobedient to the Law. Here no defence is offered except the declaration that wisdom is vindicated by her children. The most natural reading is that something will appear wise when you see the fruits to which it leads. A general maxim[51] is being applied to the specific situation of John and Jesus. This amounts to the defence that the results of John's and Jesus' ministry will prove that they were not acting contrary to God's will. "Children" echoes the negative image of the "children" in the market place and, in contrast, may refer either to fruits as resultant deeds and behaviours (as Matthew appears to take it: 11:21) or to people in whose lives goodness will show (as Prov 8:32; Sir 4:11). The difference is not great.

Possible allusion to wisdom as a mythical figure (cf. Prov 1:20–33; 8:1–21; Wisd 7:27), widely assumed,[52] may be in the background, but the focus is not the vindication of the figure wisdom by John and Jesus, but the vindication of the wisdom of John and Jesus which is at stake. In addition there seems to be no link assumed between wisdom and Law.

4.2.4 The Mission of the Disciples and the Mission of Jesus

Q has rounded off a major section by returning to the beginning, namely, Jesus' association with John. Next comes a section dealing with discipleship. It begins with two anecdotes dealing with the call of disciples (Q 9:57–60). The first (Q 9:57–58) identifies homelessness as a characteristic of Jesus and to be expected of the disciple.[53] There is no sense here of this being in tension with the high place which the Law accords to home and a sense of place. Nor does Q indicate that the radical demand to abandon the

---

[51] So also Lührmann, *Redaktion*, p. 29.

[52] So Suggs, *Wisdom*, pp. 63–98; Christ, *Jesus Sophia*, pp. 63–80.

[53] Some see here an allusion to the wisdom myth according to which wisdom seeks a home on earth and finds none (1 En 42:1–2; cf. also Sir 24:7–12). Against this Kloppenborg, *Formation*, p. 192.

duty of burying a parent entails conflict with the Law (Q 9:59–60).[54] An
echo of Elijah's call of Elisha may be intended; here is something even more
demanding.[55] These incidents depict the demands of discipleship and so
belong closely with what follows.

In Q 10:2, Q has Jesus speak about the harvest. Harvest here doubtless
refers not to the harvest of judgement, but to the harvest of ingathering, in
other words, people.[56] Nothing indicates a mission to the Gentiles is in
view,[57] although Q may well have envisaged the harvest as also including

---

[54] So Kosch, *Tora*, pp. 350–351,359, who argues against seeing in Jesus' response a
fundamental statement of principle in relation to the fourth commandment; it reflects rather
a word in a particular situation of call to discipleship. On the importance of such burial
obligation see Hengel, *Charismatic Leader*, pp. 3–15. On the obligation see Gen 50:5;
Tob 4:3; *mBer* 3:1. Hengel points to similarities with God's demand of Ezekiel that he not
mourn his wife (Ezek 24:15–24) and to Jer 16:5–7 for the prophetic motif of leaving the
dead unburied (pp. 11–12). Sanders, *Jesus and Judaism*, pp. 252–255, who writes that in
this word "Jesus *consciously* requires disobedience of a commandment understood by all
Jews to have been given by God" (p. 254; original italics). Nothing in the context suggests this is so. See the discussion in Vermes, *Religion of Jesus*, pp. 28–29; also Kosch
(above) and Davies and Allison, *Matthew II*, pp. 53, 56–58; Hagner, *Matthew*, p. 217;
Salo, *Law*, pp. 101–102; Nolland, *Luke*, pp. 542, 544–545. On the suggestion of B. R.
McCane, "'Let the Dead Bury Their Own Dead': Secondary Burial and Matt 8:21–22,"
HarvTheolRev 83 (1990), pp. 31–43, that the reference may be secondary burial, see the
discussion in A. D. Jacobson, "Divided Families and Christian Origins," in *The Gospel
behind the Gospels . Current Studies on Q*, edited by R. A. Piper, (Leiden: Brill, 1995), pp.
361–380, here: 362–363, who notes that even abandoning secondary burial would be offensive to Jewish piety. In *First Gospel*, pp. 134–135, he emphasises that the saying has a
"comic nature" and should not be read as an indication of Jesus' attitude towards Torah.

[55] So H. Fleddermann, "Demands of Discipleship. Matt 8,19–22 par. Luke 9,57–62,"
in *The Four Gospels 1992. Festschrift Frans Neirynck*, edited by F. van Segbroeck et al.,
(Leuven: Leuven University Press, Peeters, 1992), pp. 541–562, here: 554, who notes that
prophetic tradition employs the motif of leaving the dead unburied (so Jer 16:5–7; Ezek
24:15–24). In Q the image of John as Elijah may well influence the Elijah imagery in the
stories of would-be disciples and Jesus' response to them, especially if originally in Q,
7:18–19,22–23,24–28,31–35 and 9:57–62 were juxtaposed. The command not to greet
people in the way (possibly Q 10:4) may reflect 2 Kgs 4:29. See also Horsley, "Q and
Jesus," p. 188.

[56] Cf. Jacobson, *First Gospel*, p. 147. While Piper, *Wisdom*, p. 134, is correct in
suggesting that the focus is on the enormity of the task, it is within the context of the task
to proclaim the kingdom in the hope of response. Catchpole, *Quest*, p. 164, rightly identifies 10:2 as providing the setting for understanding the mission instructions, and 10:3–16,
as concerned with "a reinforcement of an established small-scale mission led by the 'few'
and continuous with the missions of Jesus and (ultimately) John" (p. 164). As an isolated
saying, which it may have once been, Q 10:2 would be a graphic exhortation to the disciples to pray for the eschatological harvest, which also entailed judgement (as in Q3:17).
The harvesters would then be the angels (cf. Mark 13:27).

[57] Some see an allusion to the inclusion of Gentiles also in the image of harvest,
sometimes used negatively against Gentiles (Joel 4:1–21; Isa 24:13; Mic 4:11–13; Rev

Gentiles. The assumption in 10:2 is that Jesus addresses disciples, but in doing so asks them to pray that God will send harvesters into the harvest. Q apparently envisages that Jesus is addressing a group out of which, from among whom, God will send the harvesters, rather than addressing one group about people outside of it. Unmediated, the address now shifts to the disciples as those to be sent (ie. the disciples who are to be sent?). Accordingly in Q 10:3 Jesus sends them, itemising their limited equipment (Q 10:4).[58] Issues of the Law are not in view.[59] This is also the case in the greeting of peace (Q 10:5–6). Q 10:7–8 had some reference to eating food provided, but the rationale appears common place wisdom about wages, not a reflection on issues of food law.[60]

Q 10:9 is the first clue that the disciples are being commissioned to do what Jesus was doing: announcing the kingdom and healing. Q 10:10–12 is about judgement on those who refuse their ministry, not about issues of purity.[61] Q 10:13–15 returns to the context of Jesus' own rejection in Chorazim and Capernaum (where Jesus had contrasted a Gentile's faith with that of Israel). Again the reference to Tyre and Sidon may be a passing reference to

---

14:15). So Lührmann, *Redaktion*, p. 60; Uro, *Sheep*, p. 222. Cf. Horsley, "Q and Jesus," pp. 188–189 and see the critical discussion in Kloppenborg, *Formation*, p. 193, who points out that the image is also used of Israel (so Hos 6:11; 4 Ezra 9:1–25, 29–37).

[58] Uro, *Sheep*, p. 120, mentions the suggestion of T. W. Manson, *The Sayings of Jesus*, (London: SCM Press, 1964), p. 181, who pointed to *mBer* 9:5 which forbids entering the temple with staff, sandals or wallet, suggesting the tradition may envisage the whole land as holy. But the focus in Q is not issues of purity but rules for the road.

[59] Cf. Catchpole, *Quest*, pp. 165–171, who argues for the inclusion in Q of Matt. 10:5b, which excludes Gentiles and Samaritans from the mission activity. This is problematic, especially if we find evidence of acceptance of the Gentile mission elsewhere. Were it to be the case, it would strengthen the conservative Law observant tenor of Q.

[60] So Kosch, *Tora*, p. 198–199; Catchpole, *Quest*, pp. 176–178. Cf. Laufen, *Doppelüberlieferung*, pp. 288, 292, 524 n. 167; Uro, *Sheep*, pp. 68–83, who also sees it as coming from the time of the Gentile mission (p. 222). He suggests that the Q community was primarily Jewish and that Gentiles joining them adapted a Jewish way of life or perhaps a minimum as enjoined in Acts 15 (p. 223). Horn, "Logienquelle," pp. 350–351, 363, goes even further in arguing that for Q food laws are abolished as a result of the Gentile mission. Cf. Gosp Thom 14 which links it with a version of the logion found in Mark 7:15. It is significant that Q does not treat the instruction in this way.

[61] Shaking dust off the feet need not necessarily reflect a response to Gentile or unclean land; here the focus is not ritual impurity, but rejection of the message; cf. Acts 13:51; 18:6; Neh 5:13. See also Uro, *Sheep*, pp. 156–160; Davies and Allison, *Matthew II*, pp. 177–178; Luz, *Matthäus II*, p.101, who points out that the view of P. Billerbeck, P. (and H. J. Strack), *Kommentar zum Neuen Testament aus Talmud und Midrash*, 4 vols, (Munich: C. H. Beck, 1922-1928), *I*, p. 571, in favour of the former alternative, is not substantiated by the evidence.

the expansion of the mission to include Gentiles.[62] Q 10:16 links Jesus' rejection back again to the disciples and spells out their role, using envoy imagery: "Whoever receives you receives me, [[and]] whoever receives me receives the one who sent me." The effect is to restate the lines of authority: God sent Jesus; Jesus sent them. This, in turn, forms an inclusion with Q 10:2, which spoke of the sending of the harvesters.

Q 10:21 continues this summary character, but returns to the theme of conflict. It contrasts the simple disciples with the wise: "At <<that time>> he said, I thank you father, lord of heaven and earth, for you hid these things from the sages and learned, and disclosed them to babes. Yes, father, for such seemed fitting to you." Q would probably understand "the sages" as a reference to Jewish opponents claiming a better understanding of the Law.[63] "These things" entrusted to the disciples doubtless refer to knowledge of the kingdom. Q 10:22 remains within the model of the authorised envoy: "Everything has been handed over to me by my father; and nobody knows the son except the father, [[nor]] ... the father except the son and any one to whom the son wishes to reveal him." As such it echoes Q 10:16 (cited above). God has authorised Jesus. Jesus has authorised them. God and God's way, God's rule, is the message entrusted to them. Accordingly Q 10:23 hails them as blessed because of what they now know or see. Q 10:24 appeals again to the Old Testament to claim that in Jesus the hopes of prophets and kings are being fulfilled. In none of this is the Law directly a theme, except in so far as it establishes a new authority which must in some way be related to the existing authority of the Law.[64]

---

[62] So Uro, *Sheep*, p. 222.

[63] So Uro, *Sheep*, pp. 224–235.

[64] A number of scholars have argued that behind Luke 10:25–28 and Matthew 22:34–40 may lie a Q version. So Tuckett, "Temptation," p. 485; "Q, the law and Judaism," pp. 97–98; J. Lambrecht, "The Great Commandments Pericope and Q," in *The Gospel behind the Gospels . Current Studies on Q*, edited by R. A. Piper, (Leiden: Brill, 1995), pp. 73–96. He lists ten minor agreements (pp. 79–81): 1. omission of "Hear, O Israel: the Lord our God, the Lord is one". 2. Both are shorter having no parallel to Mark 12:32–33. 3. Both have Jesus initially addressed as "Teacher". 4. In both the questioner is identified as a νομικός. 5. Both portray the question as testing. 6. Both use the expression "in the law". 7. Both use the preposition ἐν rather than ἐξ with faculties. 8. Both end them with διανοία "mind", not ἰσχύς "strength", as in Mark. 9. Both introduce Jesus' response with ὁ δὲ, "but he", cf. Mark 12:29a ἀπεκρίθη ὁ Ἰησοῦς, "but Jesus answered". 10. Both have Jesus answer in direct not indirect speech. Kiilunen, *Doppelgebot*, had argued for dependence solely on Mark. Lambrecht believes the concentration of so much agreement is better explained by positing a Q version (pp. 81–82), but believes it is not possible to determine its place in the order of Q (pp. 87–88). My comment on the substance is that if it were part of Q, it would cohere well both with the respect for the Law and with the orientation Q demonstrates in determining God's will.

The instruction in prayer which follows in Q 11:2–4 echoes both the relationship Jesus has with the Father, just mentioned in Q 10:22, and the theme of the preaching of the disciples and of Jesus: the kingdom of God. The theme of prayer to God as a father continues in Q 11:9–13. Again issues of Law are not in focus. But, equally, the issue of the distinctive claim for Jesus and its significance for understanding the place of the Law remains and will reach a new crisis in what follows.

4.2.5 Jesus and "this generation"

Q 11:14 is a second brief miracle account: an exorcism frees a dumb man to speak. Q uses it to introduce controversy. In it Jesus defends the charge of collusion with Beelzebul at some length, measured comparatively within Q. Jesus rejects the allegation as absurd: it would mean evil attacking evil, civil war (Q 11:17–18). He also appeals to similar exorcisms done by others (Q 11:19). Then Q has Jesus return to the language of the kingdom of God and appeal again to the Old Testament. Moses performed miracles by "the finger of God" (Ex 8:15); Jesus casts out demons "by the finger of God" and this proves that it is God's reign which they are seeing in action: "But if by the finger of God I cast out demons, then upon you has come the kingdom of God" (Q 11:20). Another military metaphor follows: a stronger overthrows a weaker (Q 11:21–22). Q 11:23 poses the decisive issue about taking sides in relation to Jesus. Q 11:24–26 cites the danger of repossession by demons. In Q 11:29 Q appears to link Q 11:24–26 to "this generation", effectively countering the charge that Jesus uses Beelzebul by the charge that "this generation" is possessed.

Q then proceeds to reject the call for a sign. Instead, Jesus is himself a sign of judgement, like Jonah for Nineveh (Q 11:29–30,32). The judgement theme is strengthened with the appeal to the queen of the south (Q 11:31). This is effectively similar to the way in which Q uses the centurion and Tyre and Sidon. A non Israelite hails Solomon; Israel did not and Israel does not hail Jesus, even though he is greater than Solomon. Then Q returns to Jonah's role as a messenger of judgement (Q 11:32). Again the mention of Jonah's success with Gentile Nineveh and of the rising up of the Gentile queen may be passing allusions to the Gentile mission.[65] Q 11:33–35 uses the image of light and the eye to restate the plight of this generation; they are in darkness.

Altogether Q 11:17–35 is an extraordinary counter attack, but, again, no

---

[65] So Meyer, "Gentile Mission," pp. 405–410. He writes, "The condemnation predicted in the parallel judgements was understood as proleptically realized by the Gentiles' entrance into the church" (p. 409).

Law issues appear, except at the more obvious level that sorcery is contrary to the Law. The emphasis is on Jesus' authority and power as expressing God's authority and power. This is the manifestation of God's reign; hence also the abundance of political or kingdom metaphors in the passage. Q 11:23 marks a transition in the counterattack which effectively announces judgement on "this generation" as, itself, demon possessed. However, the effect of the section is to address the underlying seat of the conflict: Jesus' authority and God's authority, traditionally identified in God's Law. Jesus is placed squarely on the side of God and Moses (the Mosaic allusion to "the finger of God"), just as in the material which preceded this section Q's Jesus had expounded his unique relation of sonship with the Father. Q's focus is asserting Jesus' legitimacy against counter accusations. Thus the effect of the section is not dissimilar to that of the temptation narrative. Jesus emerges as indubitably on God's side. This sharpens the underlying issue still further. If Jesus is on God's side and, therefore, an upholder of the Law, how does his authority relate to its authority?

4.2.6 Jesus and the Pharisees

So far the impression given by Q is that "this generation" is evil because it does not believe in Jesus' claims about his authority (as did the centurion), but attributes Jesus' power to his being in league with Beelzebub. Earlier, in the application of the parable of the children in the market place, we heard a further hint concerning the substance of this rejection: the accusation that Jesus is revelrous and keeps bad company, more clearly related to observance of the Law. With what now immediately follows we receive more concrete indication about the substance of the conflict. It is concrete also in the sense that it portrays Jesus attacking not "this generation", but "the Pharisees" as its assumed leaders.[66] It brings us directly into the area of conflict over the Law and thus enables us to see Q's stance more clearly.

Following the order of the International Q Project, the first confrontation deals with tithing (Q 11:42, "But woe to you Pharisees, for you tithe mint and [[dill]] and [[cummin]] and neglect justice and the love of God"). There are historical issues here of whether Pharisees ever sought to tithe such things. Traditions reflected in the Mishnah suggest that tithing of minutiae was an issue in pre-Mishnah Judaism.[67] It is not possible to be certain what exactly

---

[66] So Schulz, *Spruchquelle*, pp. 94–114.

[67] Tuckett, "Q, the law and Judaism," pp. 94–95, notes that Matthew's version (23:23) gives a list of herbs tithed and this appears to cohere with practices reflected in Mishnaic tradition, whereas Luke's version speaks of "rue" and "every herb", the former explicitly

would have been the state of the discussion when Q was composed. We do not know enough. This makes it difficult to read Jesus' final injunction, "without neglecting the others," as anything other than acceptance of such practices.[68] It is not what we would expect if Q were intending to ridicule attention to such minutiae.[69] The point made is that attention to such should not lead to neglect of what, for Q, are much more important matters.

But while Q's Jesus accepts such observance, the contrast exposes an orientation. For could not the Pharisees retort that one of the ways to love God is do precisely this, to be meticulously obedient to God's Law? Q's Jesus does not see it this way. A different value system is operating which differentiates among laws, where others could not make sense of such differentiation, since all is commanded by God. This is an important indicator of an attitude towards the Law on the part of Q's Jesus.[70]

Q 11:39–40 deals with washing: "Woe to you Pharisees, for you cleanse the outside of the cup and the dish, but the inside is full from grasping and

---

exempted in such tradition (*mSheb* 9:1) and the latter far beyond what was required. Most favour Matthew's version, because it fits Jewish requirements of the time, assuming the Mishnaic traditions report requirements in force at the time. Tuckett raises the possibility that the version in Luke may be an example of deliberately going beyond what was required and that Matthew revised the list to bring it in line with current discussion.

[68] So Schulz, *Spruchquelle*, pp. 101–102; Kosch, *Tora*, pp. 144–145, who warns against overstating the significance of the likelihood that 11:42b is an addition. It secures what was already the presupposition of the original woe against misunderstanding. Catchpole, *Quest*, pp. 264–266, notes that it affirms Pharisaic practice, only not its preoccupation with one part to the neglect of the other.

[69] Cf. Kloppenborg, "Nomos and Ethos," pp. 41–43, who emphasises that Q is not showing interest in legal hermeneutics, here, but rather attacking absurdities. 11:42c is, therefore, not enjoining strict observance. It is an intrusive gloss of an anxious redactor concerned with Torah observance in general (pp. 44–46). But earlier in *Formation*, p. 140, Kloppenborg wrote of both this and the following woe concerned with washing: "In neither woe is the ceremonial law rejected. The dispute with the Pharisees is still *intra muros*." According to Kosch, *Tora*, p. 142, the minutiae are deliberately chosen for the contrast.

[70] L. E. Vaage, "Q and Cynicism: On Comparison and Social Identity," in *The Gospel behind the Gospels. Current Studies on Q*, edited by R. A. Piper, (Leiden: Brill, 1995), pp. 199–230, here: 225, cites parallels in Diogenes Laertius: Diogenes "was moved to anger that persons should sacrifice to the gods to ensure health, and in the midst of the sacrifice feast to the detriment of health" (6.28); and "Once he saw the officials of a temple leading someone away who had stolen a bowl belonging to the treasurers, and said, 'The great thieves are leading the little one away'" (6.45). The parallels are not close. Q seems better aligned with the stream of philosophical criticism which still participated in the cult though putting emphasis elsewhere, than in those who rejected it altogether. See the important review in Attridge, "The Philosophical Critique". It is also a differentiation with a strong prophetic tradition.

lack of self control. . . . Did not he who made the outside also make the inside?" It assumes that in the washing of cups these Pharisees make a distinction between the outside and the inside of cups. The distinction may well have been the subject of dispute between Hillel and Shammai factions of Pharisaism at the time.[71] Part of Jesus' response disputes the distinction: "Did not the one who made the outside also make the inside?" Literally it would be taking sides in the discussion by making the point that the inside and outside of a cup or plate are made by the same person, so that purity distinctions between washing the outer, the inner, or both, are meaningless. But this seems not to be the point at all.[72] Rather the saying cleverly addresses inner and outer in a broader sense: attitude and morality in contrast to concern with ritual cleansing of externals.[73] Thus the main point of Jesus' response shifts the focus from ritual cleansing to morality and, at the same time, from focus on externals altogether (whether the outside or the inside of vessels) to the inner person. In this sense the reply of Jesus, here, is similar in focus to the reply about tithing. Nothing implies an attack on ritual purification of vessels,[74] though, unlike in the response on tithing,

---

[71] So Neusner, "'First Cleanse the Inside'," pp. 486–495. See also the criticism by H. Maccoby, "The Washing of Cups," *JSNT* 14 (1982), pp. 3–15, who pointed out washing was by immersion and that the saying must be metaphorical. Against this Tuckett, "Q, the law and Judaism," pp. 96, 178–179 n. 31, argues that Neusner's view makes better sense of the saying.

[72] Cf. Kloppenborg, "Nomos and Ethos," p. 39, acknowledges that Q11:39–41 reflects knowledge of Pharisaic views dividing inner and outer, as Neusner had suggested, but disputes that Q is espousing an alternative Pharisaic standpoint. Rather he sees Q ridiculing such concerns. "By subverting the boundaries between inside and outside and by diverting attention to ethical issues, Q is actually undermining the entire system of purity that depends for its existence on a well-defined taxonomy of the cosmos" (p. 37). Thus Q reflects Cynic criticism of ritual and resembles PsPhoc 228: "Purifications are for the purity of the soul, not (for the purity) of the body" (p. 40). To my mind this conclusion exceeds the evidence, although it is fundamentally right in noting the element of ridicule. But what is being ridiculed is the concern with distinctions, not the general practice of washings.

[73] Cf. Catchpole, *Quest*, pp. 266–268, who argues that the issue is not between washing the inside or outside, but that what is in the vessels had made them unclean, in a broader sense, because it has been obtained by exploitation and greed. This suggestion, which attempts to retain a literal reference to the cups, does not satisfactorily account for Jesus' response about the maker.

[74] So Schulz, *Spruchquelle*, pp. 97–98, who argues that the woe recognises Pharisaic law, but says one cannot compensate for morality with ceremonial purity laws and reflects similar critique in Ass Mos 7:7–9 (p. 99). Similarly Tuckett, "Q, the law and Judaism," p. 96. Kosch, *Tora*, pp. 136–140, argues that the issue is not critique of concern with purity but only that it is not extensive enough. This slightly misses the point which is not expansiveness, but priority.

nothing is said to this effect. The contrast is between preoccupation with the external while neglecting the inner attitudinal stance. This is expressed negatively. Their attitudinal stance is characterised by rapaciousness and lack of self control.

A profile emerges of the ethical values of Q's Jesus: justice, love of God, and generosity, rather than greed; control, rather than lack of control. By implication, observing the Law should give these priority. These also matter more than laws governing externals.[75] Q's Jesus thus champions the Law, but with a distinctive basis for interpretation which, while inclusive, sets clear priorities on attitudinal and ethical values.

Q 11:43 affronts the Pharisees for seeking privilege and recognition (the best seats in the synagogues, greeting in the market places). The assumption is that such ambition is wrong; it reflects pride and desire for privilege at others' expense. It is not linked specifically with hypocrisy. Q 11:44 uses what Q assumes hearers would understand: the image of graves as unclean which render people unclean when they walk over them. It assumes a knowledge of the Law and probably also an acceptance of the laws of uncleanness pertaining to cemeteries, although it is used only as imagery. The ethos is clearly Jewish.

Q 11:46 returns directly to issues of Law. It acknowledges that Pharisees interpret the Law: "Woe to you [[<Pharisees>]], for [[you load]] people with burdens hard to bear, and you yourselves with [[ ]] your finger [[ ]] do not <move> them." It attacks two things: their interpretations as too hard to bear and their unwillingness to help people bear them.[76] From Q 11:42 and 39–41 we might be expected to think of burdening people with meticulous observances.[77] It does not assume abandonment of ceremonial law, nor accuse the Pharisees of evasion of their own rules or hypocrisy. As far as help is concerned, we are probably dealing with an aspect of the same thing: at least if you are asking people for meticulous observance, you need to interpret what is required in such a way that it is able to be fulfilled.[78] The issue

---

[75] Vaage, "Q and Cynicism," p. 225, draws attention to a parallel in Diogenes Laertius, that Diogenes said: "O unhappy one, don't you know that you can no more get rid of errors of conduct by sprinkling than you can mistakes of grammar."

[76] So Garland, *Matthew 23*, p. 51; Catchpole, *Quest*, p. 263, who notes that it assumes the validity of the body of Torah, but attacks the path of defining ever more detailed rules. These are burdens. A less likely alternative is to see Jesus accusing them of not keeping to such interpretations themselves. So Schulz, *Spruchquelle*, pp. 107–108.

[77] According to Horsley, "Q and Jesus," p. 193, "the focus is not on scribal interpretation of the Law, but on their religiously sanctioned political-economic function."

[78] Horsley, "Q and Jesus," p. 193, suggests that the saying "could conceivably be an ironical comment that they could if they would, in their authority as interpreters of the

in dispute is interpretation of the Law, not the Law itself, and coheres therefore with what precedes.

Q 11:47–48 returns to focus on rejection of Jesus. The effect is to recall the powerful attack on "this generation" (Q 11:23–26,29–35) and to associate the Pharisees with those attacked. Again Q's Jesus begins from one of their practices: adorning the tombs of prophets. Like Q 11:39–41, concerning ritual cleansing, its attack is not on the practice itself, but on their failure to see that they are behaving in a way which identifies them with the killers of the prophets.

Q 11:49–51 then portrays Jesus as bringing words of Wisdom. The link is the reference in Q 11:47–48 to the fathers who killed the prophets. That was in the past. Here Wisdom speaks of the future and takes into view the mission of Christian prophets and apostles. "This generation" will be held to account both for their persecution and death of apostles and prophets and for the killing of the prophets of former times. Q's Jesus speaks less of himself than of what came before and what will follow him. Here it is clearer that Q uses Wisdom as a personification than at Q 7:35.

Q 11:52 returns again to the Law theme: "Woe to you [[Pharisees]], for you have [[lifted]] the [[key of knowledge]] [[ ]]; [[ ]] you [[did]] not enter, [[nor permit to enter]] those who were entering". Q's Jesus acknowledges that the Pharisees have the "key of knowledge". Implicit in this is an acknowledgment of the Law and of the role the Pharisees should play.[79] Jesus disputes their use of the key. This doubtless refers to their interpretation of the Law. The assumption is that right use of the key would open doors; observing the Law according to appropriate interpretation leads to life.[80]

Law, alleviate the people's burden with a few strokes of their scribal pen". See also Limbeck, "'Nichts bewegen'," pp. 299–320.

[79] Cf. Catchpole, *Quest*, p, 262, who argues that this must be only in an ironic sense. The Pharisees' "convictions, promoted through their characteristic interpretation of torah, have gone beyond the will of God and thus have frustrated his purpose as authoritatively effected by Jesus."

[80] Tuckett, "Q, the law and Judaism," p. 100, noting the suggestion of Wild, "Pharisaic and Christian Judaism," that early Christianity and Pharisaism were closely related, argues that the woes indicate proximity between the Q community and Pharisaism and place it nearer the Shammaite strand. Accordingly he suggests that this would fit a situation where Q was claiming to be truly Pharisaic, but facing hostility from within the movement. A. Polag, *Die Christologie der Logienquelle*, WMANT 45, (Neukirchen-Vluyn: Neukirchener, 1977), pp. 82–83, argues that the woes are directed not at correctness or otherwise of Pharisaic interpretation, nor at actual observance, but at their failure to see the new, but this rests in turn on their failure to acknowledge God, their self righteousness, and therefore their failure to change their attitudes. Therefore they block the way for others to recognise the new. Schulz, *Spruchquelle*, pp. 110–112, says need to see 11:52 in

This woe forms a fitting climax for the woes section. It shows that for Q, Jesus is a champion of the Law as the way to life, does not dispute the right of Pharisees to interpret the Law, nor to apply it to the whole of life. The criticism is preoccupation with the minutiae and with externals in contrast to concern with attitudes and behaviours which flow from caring for people. It is, therefore, both against abuse and exploitation and against applications of the Law which create unnecessary hardship for people. A twofold value system emerges: internal, attitudinal, in contrast to external, ritual; and ethical, moral purity, in contrast to ceremonial, ritual purity.

4.2.7 Instructions for the Disciples

The saying about the covered being revealed and the hidden being made known (Q 12:2) continues the theme of judgement and, in some sense, provides the underlying rationale for what precedes: the true ways of the Pharisees will be exposed. The transition to Q 12:3 is less clear. The International Q Project version has Jesus speak about the disciples' future proclamation, rather than continue with the theme of judgement exposing what is hidden (cf. Luke 12:3). In its favour, Q 11:49–51 has introduced the disciples' work and Q 12:4–7 continues with it. Q 12:4–5 teaches them, too, to fear judgement, rather than death at the hands of the opponents and Q 12:6–7 reassures them of God's care using the images of sparrows and the numbered hairs of the head. The latter may reflect the legal practice of examining hair to determine cleanness from leprosy.[81] It would, then, reflect a Jewish ethos, as does Q 11:44 about tombs.

Q 12:8–9 enjoins fearless confession. The text in reconstruction is fragmentary ("Everyone who acknowledges me before men, . . . also will acknowledge before . . . ; but whoever denies me before men . . . will. . deny before . . . ."). It appears to allow that God will do the confessing or denying. Response to Jesus is central, but the focus in the context is on disciples testifying before others, rather than people in general responding to the Son of Man.[82] Q 12:10 appears to continue the theme, but focuses not on what

---

the context of the kingdom; obedience to the Law as interpreted by Jesus as essential for entering the eschatological kingdom.

[81] See 4QD^b f. 9. I owe this allusion to J. Charlesworth in his paper, "Jesus and the Dead Sea Scrolls," delivered at the SBL International Meeting, Budapest, July, 1995. Cf. also *mNeg* 4–10.

[82] E. Käsemann, "Sentences of Holy Law in the New Testament," in *New Testament Questions of Today*, (London: SCM Press, 1969), pp. 66–81, here: 77, identifies this passage as expressing a form of charismatic Christian law, but not related to Jewish Law as such. See the discussion in Piper, *Wisdom*, pp. 59–60.

the disciples do, but what others do in response to their mission. The mission context continues in Q 12:11–12, which presumes that disciples will be called to account before Jewish authorities. This implies conflict over Law, but the issues are not stated. Q 12:22–31 continues the theme of Q 12:6–7, focusing on God's care and the need for trust. Q does not relate the teaching to the Law. Q 12:30 reflects a Jewish perspective in citing Gentiles as negative examples. Q 12:31 returns to the language of the kingdom to describe the disciples' orientation. Q 12:33–34 also addresses earthly possessions, enjoining rather that the disciples seek treasure in heaven.

Q 12:39–40 introduces the image of the householder to exhort the disciples to be ready for Jesus' coming. Another household image follows in which Q's Jesus draws an analogy between the disciples and household slaves (Q 12:42–46). It amounts to a warning against abuse of other servants and against lax behaviour (eating and drinking). Focus remains on the disciples in Q 12:51,53, which speak generally of conflict (a sword, not peace) and highlight division within families in a form which echoes Micah 7:6. Nothing indicates that Q perceives an issue of Law here. Q 12:54–56 address the signs of the times. A particular reference is not clear. Q 12:58–59 are about the need for reconciliation, an echo of the warning in Q 12:45–46.

The section following the woes has thus very little reference to the Law. It addresses the challenges which will confront disciples, offering both encouragement and threat. Right behaviour is a central concern, but at no point is this expounded directly on the basis of the Law. Jewish ethos is reflected both in the assumption that the suffering will be at the hands of Jewish authorities and also in incidental detail. Law is doubtless at issue in such setting, but issues of Law are not the focus in the teaching, except in the underlying sense that the focus is on disciples' behaviour.

4.2.8 Inclusion and Exclusion

Q 13:18–19 and 20–21 bring the parables of the mustard seed and the leaven. It is unclear whether Q intends the imagery of birds nesting in the branches of the mustard tree to allude to the inclusion of Gentiles in the kingdom,[83] although both sets of images are about expansion and what follows focuses on who is included.[84] Behind Q 13:23–24 is some use of the metaphor of

---

[83] For an allusion to Gentiles: Jacobson, *First Gospel*, p. 204; Uro, *Sheep*, pp. 218–219.

[84] J. S. Kloppenborg, "Jesus and the Parables in Q," in *The Gospel behind the Gospels. Current Studies on Q*, edited by R. A. Piper, (Leiden: Brill, 1995), pp. 275–320, here: 308–311, reviews the various attempts to explain the parables in the Q setting. They lack

the narrow door. Q 13:25–27 focuses dramatically on the excluded who are shut out at the judgement. Q 13:28–29 continues the theme. It contrasts people who will come from east and west to dine with Abraham, Isaac and Jacob, with others who are excluded. This, too, probably has the Gentile mission in mind,[85] though not exclusively so. At least it assumes people other than "this generation" will come to the feast of the kingdom. But, again, no Law issues come to the fore. The claim, however, to belong to Israel and its patriarchs is strong. Q 13:30, the reversal of first and last, belongs to the same theme: first Israel, then? Probably, other less acceptable Jews, but possibly also an allusion to Gentiles, though this would be as elsewhere, secondary.

Q 13:34–35 brings the theme to its climax, focusing on Jerusalem's rejection and her judgement.[86] Matthew sensed the link with Q 11:49–51 and joined them. For here, too, Jerusalem's record of rejecting the prophets is in view. Q's Jesus speaks like Wisdom.[87] It probably has in mind both past history and more recent experiences (stoning). The statement that the house

---

the ominous tones of what precedes, but cohere with it in being concerned with the agents of the kingdom. "Q 12:2 states aphoristically what the two parables indicate metaphorically: that there is an ineluctable process at work that will bring to fruition what was originally small and hidden" (p. 311). He suggests that they may then form the conclusion for Q 12:2–12,13–14,16–21,33–34. I believe this does not give sufficient weight to the other aspect of the parable; there is not just the process, but also the effect: expansion. This links the parables far more with what follows, especially in the contrast between the new large group included and those excluded (so Q 13:25–27,28–29,30,34–35, and also 14:16–21,23 and 15:5,7).

85 So Lührmann, *Redaktion*, p. 86; Meyer, "Gentile Mission," pp. 411–412; Kloppenborg, *Formation*, p. 236; H. Koester, *Ancient Christian Gospels. Their History and Development*, (London: SCM Press; Philadelphia: Trinity Press International, 1990), p. 159; Uro, *Sheep*, pp. 214, 216–217, who notes that the only thing against it would be 10:5–6, if it had been part of Q (p. 215). Cf. Schulz, *Spruchquelle*, pp. 325–328, who sees here only a prediction of the coming of the Gentiles at the end of time, because, he believes, Q rejected the Law free mission under way in its time. For the view that it refers not to Gentiles, but a gathering of Israel, see Horsley, "Q and Jesus," p. 183; for the historical Jesus, see Sanders, *Jesus and Judaism*, pp. 218–220.

86 5 Ezra 1:30a, 33a offers a striking parallel: "'I gathered you as a hen gathered her chicks under her wings'....Thus says the Lord Almighty, 'Your house is desolate'." It may well be tradition independent of Q, whether Christian or Jewish. See Jacobson, *First Gospel*, p. 213; Stanton, *Gospel*, pp. 266–267.

87 For a recent discussion of the evidence for this association here see Piper, *Wisdom*, pp. 164–165. According to Uro, *Sheep*, p. 236, the saying assumes not only wisdom, but wisdom's place in Zion (cf. Sir 24). Meyer, "Gentile Mission," pp. 415–417, speaks of Wisdom giving up her special dwelling place in Jerusalem. Wisdom will now be heard by Jews and Gentiles. But in its conclusion it appears to me that 13:35 reasserts the Zion tradition.

is forsaken may refer to Jerusalem's leadership; more probably it refers to the temple and what will happen to it because of its leadership.[88] It amounts to a declaration that God has departed from the temple, as in the days of Jeremiah and Ezekiel (Jer 12:7; 22:5; Ezek 7:22; 8:6; 10:18–19).[89] It preserves an eschatology which still has a place for Jerusalem, for it assumes that in that day Jerusalem will be forced to acknowledge Jesus and welcome him.[90] Nothing in this suggests cult critique. It all belongs within a strongly Jewish ethos with a strongly Jewish eschatology,[91] and echoes John's prediction of Jesus as "the coming one".

The preceding section of material within Q 13 is remarkable for the way it focuses on the theme of inclusion and exclusion. Again issues of Law are not in focus. However Israel is. The sayings reflect the belief in a reversal which will see many excluded, in particular the Jewish leaders and those who follow them, in contrast to those who have accept Jesus, among whom, Q also assumes, will be Gentiles. Nevertheless the strongly Jewish flavour

---

[88] So Schulz, *Spruchquelle*, p. 356. Cf. P. Hoffmann, *Studien zur Theologie der Logienquelle*, (Münster: Aschendorff, 1972), p. 174, who thinks it means not the temple but the city. Horn, "Logienquelle," pp. 361, cites parallels supporting an allusion to the temple (2 Bar 8:2; Jer 33:6) and others which support the city (4QFlor 1:10; TLevi 10:4–5; 1 En 89:50ff). Tob 14:4 supports a link between the two as Lk 11:51 indicates. Horsley, "Q and Jesus," pp. 195–196, believes it means Jerusalem's ruling house, is directed against the wealthy and powerful in Jerusalem, not against Israel as a whole. He sees the tension very much in socio-economic religious terms. This may well be so, especially since the temple system and its leadership were seen as a whole.

[89] On God's abandonment of the temple see also 2 Bar 8:2; 44:7; Jos *JW* 2:539; 4:323; *Ant* 20:166.

[90] The transition in the saying from "I" as Sophia to Jesus as the one to come is not unmediated, if we understand Jesus as representative of Wisdom (so Piper, *Wisdom*, pp. 169–170; cf. Jacobson, *First Gospel*, p. 211); it is even less so, if we understand Jesus as the speaker throughout, who in poetic license or prophetic spirit, speaks initially as Wisdom. Horsley, "Q and Jesus," p. 196, sees here a sign of renewal, a similar role to that assigned to the Messiah in Ps Sol 17:26–32 and to the "Council of the Community" in 1QS 8:1–4. Cf. Horn, "Logienquelle," p. 362, who sees not hope, but only the acclamation of the condemned.

[91] P. Hoffmann, "The Redaction of Q and the Son of Man: A Preliminary Sketch," in *The Gospel behind the Gospels. Current Studies on Q*, edited by R. A. Piper, (Leiden: Brill, 1995), pp. 159–198, here: 190–198, drawing on O. H. Steck, *Israel und das gewaltsame Geschick der Propheten*, (Neukirchen-Vluyn: Neukirchener, 1967), pp. 228–229, suggests that the redaction of Q took place either immediately before, or, as he prefers, differently from Steck, shortly after the events of 70 CE. It reflects strong emergence at the time of the use of Daniel and the Son of Man image, a trend still alive at the time of Matthew, and reflects a Syrian rather than Palestinian environment; hence the positive attitude towards Gentiles, without direct espousal of a Gentile mission. Stanton, *Gospel*, p. 250, argues that a sin-exile-return pattern similar to Justin *Dial* 108 underlies the saying. See also Uro, *Sheep*, p. 237.

persists, especially in the oracle of judgement and hope concerning Jerusalem and its temple.

Q 14:5 preserves a response to sabbath law. The Project group assumes the original referred to rescuing an ox.[92] The saying does not call sabbath observance into question. It appears to be disputing some strict sabbath interpretation. The appeal of the saying is not to legal precedent or legal argument, but apparently to human pity for an animal. As such it is indicative of a 'practical' approach to Law which gives high priority to responding to need. Probably Luke and Matthew were right in seeing it as a response to objections to Jesus' healing practice on a sabbath. The presence and possible form of the saying within Q is very uncertain. It appears without particular link to its context.

Q 14:11 is a general statement about humility and exaltation set within an eschatological framework. There is considerable uncertainty about the next segment, as about the preceding verse. Q 14:16–21,23, the parable of the great feast, echoes the focus of the section on inclusion and exclusion and may well be making much the same point as Q 13:28–29,30. It probably includes allusion to the inclusion of Gentiles.[93] Q 14:26–27 shifts the focus again to the demands of discipleship: family conflict; taking up one's cross. Family conflict is expressed very sharply. Again there is no sense that Q saw here any conflict with the Law.[94] Q 14:34–35 uses the image of salt to continue the exhortation to committed discipleship. Q 15:4,7 brings the image of the shepherd rejoicing over finding the lost sheep. It is hard to find its relation to its Q context. Perhaps it is making the same point as the great feast and the Q 13:28–29,30, again. The point is the greater rejoicing over the sheep that is found, than over those who remain. This is somewhat more generous about the rest of the sheep (they remain in the fold; they are not excluded).[95]

Much of the material considered here continues the theme of inclusion and exclusion with, again, no direct reference to the Law. Only 14:5, standing on its own, reflects directly on an issue of Law and shows Jesus appeal-

---

92 Cf. Tuckett, "Q, the law and Judaism," pp. 96–97, who believes Q referred to rescuing a person and so would have Jesus arguing from a position acceptable in Law at the time.

93 So Lührmann, *Redaktion*, p. 87; Meyer, "Gentile Mission," pp. 413–415.; Kloppenborg, *Formation*, p. 230; Uro, *Sheep*, p. 220. See also Kloppenborg, "Parables," p. 292.

94 So Kosch, *Tora*, pp. 355–356, 359.

95 Similarly Jacobson, *First Gospel*, p. 226, who suggests "the parable represents material not yet adapted to the deuteronomistic perspective." Cf. Kloppenborg, "Parables," pp. 311–317, who sees it belonging primarily within the theme of reconciliation.

ing by analogy to human pity for an animal to the priority of care for people in need in determining sabbath law interpretation. With the material that follows the concerns of the Law return.

4.2.9 *Jesus and the Law*

16:13 addresses the issue of the need for single allegiance. It portrays the options as God or mammon. In part this relates to the call to discipleship and recalls the exhortation that they not seek wealth on earth, but treasures in heaven. It also recalls Jesus' attack on the greed of the Pharisees. They filled their vessels with greed (Q 11:39–40). The ultimate choice, God or mammon, also recalls the final temptation in the temptation narrative (Q 4:5–8). Addressing the ultimate call to obedience inevitably raises the issue of God's will and therefore God's Law.

It is not, therefore, unmediated when 16:16 addresses such fundamental issues. It makes two major statements within a twofold time framework. Up until John; and from John. The reconstructed text reads: "The law and [[]] the prophets...until John. From [[then]] the kingdom of God has suf-fered violence and the violent take it by force." In the light of Q 7:28, we should probably conclude that Q sees the period ending with John as a sin-gle period. The new period, the time of the kingdom, begins with Jesus. Nothing thus far suggests that this entails disparagement of either John or the Law and the Prophets. While relegating John to the previous period, Q takes John very seriously. This is an important clue. His preaching is cer-tainly still upheld as relevant. Therefore we should understand the Law and the Prophets similarly; they are to be taken seriously. Certainly this is the case, as far as the predictive function of the Law and prophets is concerned; but also with regard to the Law as God's will: nothing has indicated abroga-tion of its authority.[96] The issue is the relation between this authority and the authority of the kingdom in Jesus.

The imagery of violence in relation to the kingdom recalls Jesus words in response to the accusation that he cast out demons by Beelzebub (Q 11:17–35). There, too, military metaphors abounded (cf. Q 11:18,21–22). Finding a clear resolution of all the exegetical queries which 16:16b poses is not crucial for our theme. The context would lead one to expect an indication of conflict or opposition. After all, greed has been a focus of such conflict with the Pharisees. Just as the Law and the Prophets and John faced rejection, so

---

[96] So Catchpole, *Quest*, pp. 232–241.

now does the kingdom.[97] This sense of conflict and opposition also makes best sense of the negative language used.[98]

16:17 makes an assertion about the Law's abiding validity: "But it is easier for heaven and earth to pass away than for [[ ]] one stroke of the law to <<lose its force>>."[99] This reads as though one of the goals of the kingdom is to the press the claims of God's Law and that this is one of the reasons why conflict and opposition would arise. This is surely Q's intention. Luke understands this clearly, for he uses it as the basis to develop polemic against the Pharisees by inserting 16:14–15.[100] Q then understands 16:18 as applying this strictness to the matter of divorce for remarriage: "Everyone who divorces his wife [[ ]] commit[[s]] adultery, and the one who marries a divorcée [[ ]] commits adultery."[101] This, too, is related indirectly to the theme of greed (especially in the sense: divorcing in order to obtain another). It presses the strict claims of God's Law even beyond what the written Law requires, and certainly not with a view to undermining or abrogating its demands.

---

[97] So Kosch, *Tora*, pp. 438–439.

[98] So Jacobson, *First Gospel*, pp. 117–118.

[99] So Kosch, *Tora*, pp. 440–441; Koester, *Gospels*, pp. 162, 164; Tuckett, "Q, the law and Judaism," p. 91, who also discusses the relation between the Lukan and Matthean form of the tradition (pp. 91–92, 92 and 177, n. 10). For a critical discussion of attempts to deny that 16:17 ever belonged to Q, see Kosch, *Tora*, pp. 159–163. By contrast Horn, "Logienquelle," p. 347, sees Q 16:17 as belonging to the oldest Q material. Schulz, *Spruchquelle*, pp. 115–116, argues that the verse is implying that the Law is valid, but only until the end, not hereafter. But the focus in the context is validity, not limits of validity.

[100] Cf. Catchpole, *Quest*, p. 238, who writes: "Q 16:17 suggests that Q is aware of the conservative response to the Gentile mission, endorses it, but does not positively engage in the discussion of the issue". This would indicate a kind of two front sensitivity which many find in Matthew's use of the logion. This is not impossible. Certainly the focus should not be seen as confined to past history, nor just to Pharisees, since Q will go on to address what happens within the community where offences occur. These need have no relation, however, to issues raised by Gentile Christianity, unless, as Jacobson, "Divided Families," pp. 369–374, suggests 16:18 is addressing the issue of partners who might remarry after their conversion had led to the break up of their marriages.

[101] So Schulz, *Spruchquelle*, pp. 116–120; Kosch, *Tora*, pp. 441–442; Catchpole, *Quest*, pp. 237–238. See the discussion of this Q saying in Jacobson, "Divided Families." pp. 369–374, who also emphasises that the focus is remarriage, not divorce itself. He sees it referring in the community of Q to situations where marriages had broken up because of the call of the gospel (as Q 14:26 presupposes). Q then forbids them to form new families. This coheres, then, he argues, with Q's anti family stance. Kloppenborg, "Nomos and Ethos," pp. 44–45, understands 16:18 to have been sapiential, reflecting the new ethos, rather than an intensification of the Torah, but that with the addition of 16:17, it now illustrates the strictness of 16:17.

This is more convincing than taking 16:17 to indicate that the Law can be changed only with great difficulty and then seeing 16:18 as an example of such a change.[102] It is also more convincing than to see 16:17 as primarily corrective or at least cautionary, ie. to ward off possible misunderstandings of 16:16.[103] The battle for the kingdom – with the Pharisees – was over precisely the issue of having God's will done and declared. 16:16b is, therefore, to be read as a statement about Jesus' conflict with the Pharisees.[104] 16:17 reinforces Jesus' claim against Pharisaic modification of the Law. 16:18 was precisely one of the instances where this was likely to happen. 16:13 indicated another (or, perhaps, even the wider issue to which 16:18 belonged): greed. The focus of 16:18 continues in Q 17:1–4,6. The concern is such abuse in the community. Q 17:3–4 nevertheless enjoins forgiveness where people go astray.[105] Q 17:6 appears to identify the hope which underlies such faith in forgiveness.

It is important to note that 16:17 does not stand in isolation in Q, but coheres with the ethos of heightened demand which comes with God's kingdom and with the conflict which that brings. The same heightened demand applies to the community. The Law as demand retains authority within the context of the demand of the kingdom. It is interesting that 16:16–18 is only indirectly christological. What holds it together, and what holds the eras together, is God's authority. For Q, this is the clue to integrating the authority of the Law and the authority of Jesus. For Q, it seems, it is not possible to think of one replacing or abrogating the other.

4.2.10 The Last Things

Behind Q 17:20–23 may be warnings about false eschatological hopes. Q 17:24 speaks of the suddenness of the Son of Man's coming, like lightning. Q 17:37 uses the analogy of the corpse and eagles. Q 17:26–27,30 uses a

---

[102] Cf. Wilson, *Law*, pp. 44–45; Guelich, *Sermon*, p 165, who draws attention to the similar structure of the camel logion (Luke 18:25) about the difficulty with which the rich enter the kingdom of God. Against this, the focus of the context is not how to modify the Law, but the claims of the kingdom.

[103] Cf. Kloppenborg, "Nomos and Ethos," pp. 44–46, who sees 16:17 as a redactional attempt to obviate potential false understandings of 16:16. Originally 16:18 was the new demand in a new era announced by 16:16. With the intrusion of 16:17, he argues, 16:18 now illustrates 16:17.

[104] So also Catchpole, *Quest*, p. 235.

[105] Cf. Catchpole, *Quest*, pp. 135–150, who argues that elements of Matt 18:15–17 may well have formed part of Q, reflecting the concern with reproof and reconciliation reflected in 6:36–45 and 12:58–59 (p. 150).

biblical analogy: Noah. Q 17:34–35 speak of individuals being taken or left. None of this relates to Law issues. Q 19:12–13,15–24,26 contain the parable of the money. Q 22:28,30 conclude with the promise that the twelve will sit on thrones judging the twelve tribes of Israel. Judging here probably refers not to the final judgement, but rather to ruling, in which the judicial function is central. It also implies affirmation of law and probably, therefore, of the Law. In the rule of the kingdom Q doubtless envisages the centrality of Jesus' teaching on what is right; but that also includes a central place for the Law, as 16:16–17 indicates.[106] Q concludes as it began in John's preaching: with a vision of the judgement to come.

4.3 Jesus' Attitude towards the Law in Q – Conclusions

From the beginning Q puts the focus on the message of judgement. Jesus is to come as God's agent in judgement. Positively, it puts the focus on the kingdom, God's future reign. Already in exorcism God's reign is breaking into human affairs (Q 11:20). It promises reversal in the future (Q 6:20–21; 13:30). In Jesus' ministry of healing it is shown in advance (Q 7:22). People must believe Jesus, follow his teachings, and live righteous lives. God sent and authorised Jesus (Q 10:16,22; well reflected also in the centurion's affirmation: Q 7:8). Jesus, in turn, sent and authorised disciples (Q 10:2–3,10–12,16). He draws them into the relationship with the loving Father (Q 10:22; Q 11:2–4). As Jesus is totally obedient (Q 4:1–4,9–12,5–8), the disciples are to be totally obedient.

In this structure of thought, authority and instruction are central. They underlie christology, soteriology and ecclesiology. Where instruction is so central, Law plays a vital role. That was evident already in Q's portrait of John: the call for fruits worthy of repentance. For Q, John is not left behind; his message continues within the message of Jesus. In the same way the Law and the Prophets continue in the ministry of Jesus. This link is present conceptually in 16:16–17, and is evident throughout Q's presentation. Law which plays a vital role includes the Law of the scriptures.

With regard to the prophets and the prophetic role of scripture, Q's Jesus frequently relates his activity to Old Testament models (prophets and kings:

---

106 Horn, "Logienquelle," pp. 355–356, sees in it a reversal of traditional expectations: what Israel would do to the nations (judge them), is now turned against Israel. I think this misses the point, which is not judgement and condemnation of Israel, but rule within it in the fulfilment of the kingdom hope.

Q 10:23–24; Moses: Q 11:20; Jonah: Q 11:29–30,32; the queen of the south: Q 11:31; Abraham, Isaac and Jacob: Q 13:28–29; Noah: Q 17:26–27,30; Abel and Zechariah Q 11:51; possibly also an allusion to Ezekiel as well as Ps 118:26 in Q 13:35), and especially to Israel's rejection of the prophets (Q 11:47–48; Q 13:34–35). Jesus portrays John's (Q 7:27) and his own ministry (Q 7:19,22) as fulfilling prophetic prediction (cf. also the echo of Mic 7:6 in Q 12:51,53; Isa 14:13–15 in Q 10:13–15; Ps 6:9 in Q 13:26–27; Ps 118:26 in Q 13:34–35; Job 39:30 in Q 17:37; Dan 4:21 in Q 13:19). Q's narrative also reflects use of typology, especially in the temptation narrative and in the allusion to Elijah's call of Elisha (Q 9:57–58).

With regard to the Law as instruction, to respond appropriately to Jesus is to accept his authority and submit to his instruction. His instruction presupposes the validity of the Law. The message of the kingdom in Q is both future hope and something asserting itself in Jesus' ministry. This occurs not only through his activities, but also in his words. In his words he asserts God's Law over against disobedience and abuse. In this way John, the Law and the Prophets, are not left behind; they are taken up within the demands which the kingdom brings. Q 16:16–18 rules out possible alternatives. They would be that Q sees Jesus' teaching as replacing the Law or has no interest in the Law at all.

The structure of Q's theology, therefore, makes instruction in God's will for living fundamental; Q's statement in Q 16:16–17 indicates that the Law is assumed to have continuing validity within that instruction. It forms part of the struggle of the kingdom. Q's understanding of Jesus' approach to the Law becomes clearer when we consider detailed aspects of that struggle. The confrontation of the Pharisees in Q 11 sheds important light. No one Pharisaic practice, be it meticulous tithing, washing vessels, adorning tombs, interpreting the Law, or holding the keys, is attacked in itself. Q's Jesus even enjoins meticulous tithing, even if incidentally. He attacks neglect of justice and of the love of God and behaviours which manifest self grandeur, greed and lack of care in administering the Law. The attacks not only target abuse; they reflect Q's orientation with regard to Law. Q appears to accept ritual law, but to give far greater weight to ethical values. Associated with this is also a weighting of internal, attitudinal, and associated ethical behaviour over against external. In other words, Q views ritual law as treating matters at the level of the external and, as such, as of lesser importance.

Q knows of ritual and cultic law. It appears to value the practise of fasting; Jesus fasted (Q 4:2). It knows about purity law with regard to graves (Q 11:44). It is familiar with purity issues regarding vessels (Q 11:39–40). We have noted that it enjoins tithing practices (Q 11:42). It may reflect the procedures for discerning cleanness of lepers (examining hairs; Q 12:6–7). It may reflect sensitivity to purity issues in encounters with Gentiles, if we read Jesus' initial response to the centurion as an initial rebuff (Q 7:2–8). Its attack on Pharisees assumes the validity of the Law as knowledge and as providing the way to God; the problem is their use of the key (Q 11:52).

Q does not portray Jesus as living contrary to Law. Q has Jesus vigorously defend the charges of sorcery (Q 11:17–35), reject impropriety in dining with toll collectors and sinners (Q 7:31–35), and argue justification of "working" to help people on the sabbath (Q 14:5). The latter, disputed as part of Q, bears some similarity with halakic discussion, but rests on appeal to pity. Q gives no indication of seeing Jesus' radical demands in relation to family (Q 9:57–58; Q 12:51,53; Q 14:20–21) or, more striking still, burial obligation (Q 9:59–60) as setting Jesus in conflict with the Law. Q's Jesus appears to be predicting God's departure from the temple in Q 13:35 as punishment for Israel's sin, as had Jeremiah and Ezekiel in their time. But neither here nor elsewhere does Q portray Jesus as speaking against the Law or its institutions as such. This coheres with the introductory image of Jesus in the temptation narrative as obedient to God's Law.

Q's treatment of the Law belongs within a strongly Jewish ethos. This is reflected not only in the references to scripture and to Law practice, but also in its eschatology. It assumes that Jesus will return to Jerusalem (Q 13:35). It speaks of the disciples enthroned to rule the twelve tribes (Q 22:28,30). Future salvation is to dine with Abraham, Isaac and Jacob (Q 13:28–29).[107]

Yet at the same time Q reflects strong conflict with its own generation of Jews and, especially the Pharisees. In a number of ways it portrays both John and Jesus as challenging a false sense of security. Thus John assails those who rely on their descent from Abraham (Q 3:8). In a series of contrasts Q has Jesus portray the kingdom as resulting in a reversal of expectations: those who expect to be included are excluded; those who might expect to be excluded are included. This comes to expression, in particular, in Q 13:28–29 (the inclusion of people to be with Abraham, Isaac, and Jacob from both east and west), the great feast (Q 14:16–21,23); and possibly also

---

[107] Catchpole, *Quest*, pp. 277–278. Catchpole rightly observes: "The Q community thus inherited some traditions which expressed, on the one hand, a critical view of the Pharisees but a continuing commitment to the covenant, the law, and the temple, and on the other hand, the expectation that Jerusalem and the temple would be abandoned by God." (p. 279). The community was one whose "outlook was essentially Jerusalem-centred, whose theology was Torah-centred, whose worship was temple-centred, and which saw (with some justice) no incompatibility between all of that and commitment to Jesus" (p. 279).

in the parables of the mustard seed and leaven, which emphasise expansion and inclusion (Q 13:18–19,20–21), and in the parable of the lost sheep especially favoured above the rest (Q 15:4,7).

In a number of these references (3:8; 13:28–39; 14:16–21,23; 13:18–19,20–21; 15:4,7) Q may also have in mind the expansion of Christian mission to include Gentiles, despite reflecting a traditional stereotypical image of Gentiles in Q 12:30. Awareness of it may also be reflected in the anecdote about the healing of the centurion's servant (Q 7:1–4,6–9), and in the allusions to Tyre and Sidon (Q 10:13–15), Jonah and Nineveh (Q 11:30,32) and the Gentile queen of the south (Q 11:31). Q appears to use knowledge of Gentile response to the kingdom to shame unbelieving Jews. There is no indication that the community itself is engaged in such.mission or has grappled with issues which would have arisen from a Gentile mission.[108] If Jesus' response to the centurion is initially a rebuff, the story identifies one issue and shows Jesus' ultimate response as one which breaks no Law.

Q's interpretation of God's will, whether as expressed in interpreting the Law, or, in general, is primarily oriented towards loving attitudes and behaviour. This is evident in points made in Jesus' confrontation of the Pharisees. Q frequently grounds this approach in an understanding of God as loving and merciful. God's promise of the blessings of the kingdom is directed towards the poor and the needy (Q 6:20–21). God has thus given the kingdom to the simple (Q 11:21). God will reward the persecuted (Q 6:22–23), forgive their sins (Q 11:3), answer their needs and prayers like a caring father (Q 11:9–13), counts them like sparrows and the hairs of the head (12:6–7), cares for their needs (12:22–31). God's heaven is their reward and treasure (12:33–34). God raises the sun over good and bad (Q 6:35), provides the model of mercy (Q 6:36). Through Jesus and his envoys God brings good news and healing (Q 7:22; Q 10:9). Accordingly they are not to seek redress, but to love enemies (Q 6:27–33), be reconciled with one another (12:57–59) and be caring and forgiving leaders (12:45; Q 17:3–4,6).

Q sets Jesus' teaching in association with the Law in two main contexts: the confrontation of the Pharisees in Q 11 and the major statement about the Law in 16:16–18. In the latter, Q reinforces the prohibition of divorce and remarriage, and, in the wider context, the warnings about greed (Q 16:13)

---

[108] Meyer, "Gentile Mission," p. 417, "The Q-community accepted the Gentile mission as a *fait accompli*. They considered it God's activity and so acquiesced to it." I am less sure when he goes on to claim that according to Q the Jews have forfeited their privileges and must enter on the same terms as the Gentiles. It sounds too pauline. It may be the case, but probably in the sense that Gentiles would need to become proselytes.

and about abuses (Q 17:1), by affirming the Law's abiding validity (Q 16:17). Otherwise Q does not bring Jesus' instruction of the disciples into relation with the Law. The assumption is not that the Law is irrelevant, but that it is not to be taken for granted; it still applies. In that sense Jesus' instruction is instruction in the Law as God's will, but Q sees no need to legitimise Jesus' teaching from the Law. Jesus' authority is assumed, and assumed not to be in conflict with the authority of the Law. Even in linking Jesus with wisdom (Q 11:49–51; 7:35; cf. 13:34–35), Q gives no indication that a link with Law in intended. The issue of Jesus' attitude towards the Law is not a central concern. The assumption is one of a positive relationship, grounded in God as the common source of authority and in the assumption that God's kingdom is new, while not replacing the Law.

The conclusion is then that Q assumes the Law's validity, but within a theological perspective, that is, within the perspective of God's continuing activity. It is neither replaced nor surpassed nor modified, except by addition. Yet the addition is such that the Law can remain (in tact) in the background and does, through much of Q. Jesus gives eschatological Torah, but it includes also pressing the demands of those who have gone before, including John, but also Moses; for their demands remain valid. Q may reflect awareness of issues which concerned Pharisees of its time (concerning tithes, purification, perhaps also sabbath law), but its own stance is not Pharisaic by any model of Pharisaism known to us.[109] In apparently accepting Pharisaic application of Law, it resorts to ridicule when this leads to over preoccupation with detailed applications relating to externals.

Behind this is a value system which gives priority to human need (justice and love of God, rescuing the needy, loving the enemy, assisting the faithful in Law observance) and which makes a relative distinction between ritual and ceremonial, on the one hand, as concerned with externals, and attitudinal and ethical, on the other, as concerned with internals. But for Q the contrasts are inclusive, not exclusive. In the reconstructed text they belong within the commitment to Torah, and are not to be understood as anti religious or anti cultic. If, beside influence from the prophetic tradition, they reflect influence from non Jewish critique of cult and ritual, Q belongs with those movements of thought which still advocate cultic and ritual practices. This explains the fact that Q continues to uphold such practices as tithing, fasting, sabbath, and probably also caution about entering Gentile houses.

---

[109] Cf. Tuckett, "Q, the law and Judaism," p. 100, who speculates that Q may have "emanated from a Christian community in close touch with Pharisaism, experiencing some hostility or suspicion from non-Christian Pharisees, but also claiming to be a true part of the pharisaic movement."

Chapter 5

Jesus' Attitude towards the Law
according to John

The Gospel of John as we have received it is without doubt the product of a long process of composition. In this discussion I am concerned with the attitude of Jesus towards the Law reflected in the text as received. This raises the issue, as it did with Q, whether we can deal with the text as a whole if we assume its present form reflects subsequent redaction of what was already a gospel. Minor redactional modifications may reflect a mind-set opposed to the general orientation of the gospel itself and have made corrections only at some points, leaving the rest in tact. This would be potentially the case in early theories of a Church redaction such as Bultmann proposed. Without entering the detail of the debate, I shall assume rather that the present shape of the gospel has arisen within a community which stands in some continuity with users of earlier forms of the gospel, but reflects changing circumstances, in particular, concern with inner coherence and leadership within the community. This is reflected in the concerns of John 15–17 and 21, widely regarded as the most recent additions. The Johannine community looks back to a period of conflict with synagogue Judaism leading to its expulsion, and before that to a period of activity as part of the Jewish community. The present concerns with community and leadership presage a situation reflected in the epistles where the unity has been broken.

In focusing on the transmitted text I am aware that I shall probably be detecting what were the perceptions at only one stage of the history of the Johannine community. I write, "probably", because I assume the probability that what is in the text would have received the assent of both its readers and hearers. I also assume that because there is continuity within the community, allusions to Jewish scriptures and traditions would have been widely recognised. The break with Judaism does not imply a break in such awareness. It might even make the claiming of such heritage a matter of greater urgency, although this is not the only option. There is more than one strategy for dealing with separation and loss.

5.1 Recent Research

Without doubt the *magnum opus* in dealing with the Law in John's Gospel is that of Pancaro.[1] Most other treatments of the theme belong within some wider concern and are at most one hundredth of his in length, which is a massive 590 pages! Pancaro begins by showing how John treats the Law as a norm which the Jews vainly try to use against Jesus. He links this to the notion that the gospel is like a trial of Jesus. In the first direct confrontation John deliberately portrays Jesus as sanctioning a breach of sabbath law by commanding that the man carry his mat (5:8). In doing so, Pancaro argues, John wants to display Jesus' divine prerogative as Son of God (pp. 15–16). Jesus does break the Law, but only if you fail to see that his status gives him the right to do so. Similarly John shows Jesus also working on the sabbath in the second sabbath healing by making clay (9:6), and flags the fact by his use of "work" in 9:4 (pp. 18–19). These acts would count as breaches of sabbath law and are flagged as such, but they are not, because Jesus is the Son of God (p. 29). John portrays the Jews as accusing Jesus of being a "sinner", that is, a transgressor of the Law: he habitually violates the sabbath (pp. 45–47). Sabbath had come to assume great significance for Pharisaic Judaism, so that to reject the sabbath was to reject the Law. For John they are clearly wrong, for they fail to recognise who Jesus is. As Son of God he is above the Law and therefore has the right to set it aside, which he does.

On the charges of blasphemy (5:17–18; 8:58; 10:24–38; 19:7), Pancaro rightly observes that for John equality consisted in Jesus' being completely dependent on the Father (pp. 54–55,61–65,74). John has Jesus reject the accusation that he is a false teacher (7:45–49; 9:24–34; 18:19–21). Jesus' teaching is new revelation; it supersedes the Law, yet it is constantly presented in familiar biblical terms, so that John is implying that those who truly know the scriptures should follow Jesus (p. 116).

Accordingly, John presents Jesus as the one who is faithful to the Law and the Jews as failing to keep it. Pancaro goes on to show how John portrays the Law as testifying against the Jews and for Jesus. Their failure is shown by their failure to believe in Jesus (7:17–19; pp. 133–137). The Jews not

---

[1] S. Pancaro, *The Law in the Fourth Gospel The Torah and the Gospel, Moses and Jesus, Judaism and Christianity according to John*, SuppNovT 42, (Leiden: Brill, 1975).

only fail to understand; they act contrary to the Law in seeking to arrest Jesus, as Nicodemus points out (7:51; pp. 138–139). Failure to give him a hearing and to come to know what he does (7:51) effectively means that failure to acknowledge Jesus is failure to meet the demands of the Law (p. 156).

By contrast John portrays the Law as testifying in favour of Jesus. "In the Fourth Gospel, Jesus is not presented as one who violates the sabbath (although accused of doing so by the Jews), but as one who brings the sabbath to an end" (p. 160). In using the argument about circumcision on the sabbath (7:22–23), John appears to reflect a Jewish understanding which also sees circumcision as healing (*tShabb* 15,16/134; *bYoma* 85b; pp. 163–164). The practice is not mentioned to show they break the Law, but to show that Jesus' healing on the sabbath keeps the Law (p. 164).

John also has Jesus appeal to the Law to defend the charge of blasphemy (10:34–36; pp. 175, 179, 183–184) and of false teaching (5:31–47; p. 209). 5:37 does not deny revelation to Moses on Sinai, but denies only that the Jews have heard it rightly (pp. 230–231). John sees no opposition between Moses and Jesus, Torah and gospel. "Torah is absorbed into this higher reality represented by Christ" (p. 262). The appeal in 6:45 to Isa 54:13 ("They shall all be taught of God") and, by implication to the new covenant hope in Jer 31:31–34, refers not to renewal of the Law, but to teaching given by Jesus (p. 285). Because this is the case, when separation occurs and the community is cut off from the national religious community, its epistles can lack all reference to Torah, Jews, Israel, scriptures, Abraham, Moses, the prophets, the sabbath, circumcision, and fulfilment of the Old Testament (pp. 250–251). On the other hand, because Jews reject the Torah's witness to Christ, the Torah becomes the basis of their condemnation ((p. 262). John's Christians, like Nathanael, are the true Israel (pp. 288–289). They acknowledge the Messiah about whom Moses wrote.

In his treatment of the trial before Pilate, Pancaro shows how John portrays the Jewish leaders as Torah observant. They do not enter Pilate's house because they would contract ritual impurity (18:28);[2] they charge Jesus with contravening the Law by claiming to be God's Son (19:7); they ask that the body be removed (19:31; Deut 21:22–23; pp. 309–310). John finally has Jesus convicted on false charges that he is opposed to Caesar. Jesus' death occurs in fulfilment of scriptures (pp. 331–352). While John uses scripture and Law interchangeably, he is careful to portray Jesus' death as fulfilling the scriptures, not fulfilling the Law (pp. 327, 363).

---

[2] On the issue of purity see Brown, *Death of the Messiah*, pp. 744–745.

Pancaro also shows how John uses language associated with the Law to describe appropriate responses to Jesus. Thus traditional terminology like doing the will of God and doing the works of God now refer to Jesus' salvific work (pp. 368–397). Similarly keeping the word and keeping the commandments now describe response to Jesus (pp. 403–451). "The Law has fulfilled its function with the coming of Jesus; it has been neither destroyed nor preserved intact, but transformed by being transcended" (p. 450). Similarly symbols associated with Torah have been transferred to Jesus (pp. 453–487). This applies in particular to the symbols of bread (pp. 454–472); living water (pp. 473–485), light and life (pp. 485–487).

Pancaro notes that the sabbath is the only precept of Law discussed (pp. 499–500). John does not portray Jesus as abrogating sabbath or Torah, but rather as acting with a legitimacy which warrants his overriding the sabbath. "All the issues, the Sabbath violations, blasphemy, false teaching, going against the interest of the nation, are traced back to the one great issue: Jesus opposes Torah in the meaning and value given it by traditional Judaism" (p. 505). The issue of the Law is so central that Pancaro believes John must have a Jewish audience in mind (p. 510). Thus John's apologia is based on Law and his manner of argument is Jewish in a way unparalleled in the synoptic gospels (p. 510).

John assumes that Christians have the true understanding of the Law. It is the Jew's Law in the sense that they appeal to it and it is characteristic of Judaism and no longer applies to Christians (pp. 518–521). For John, Jesus does not oppose the Law, but claims to show its true meaning. John does not address the issue of the Law as a way to life before Christ's coming (pp. 525–526). Yet in John's community Christian Jews keep the Law. They are expelled from the synagogue not for transgression of Torah, but because they confess Christ (pp. 530, 531). They may have been lax in areas like the sabbath, but John indicates no interest in the issue of how they kept the sabbath. Pancaro sees John writing in a Jewish context, seeking to win over the secret believers among the Jews (pp. 532–533).

It is only at this stage of his work that Pancaro turns to the meaning of 1:17. He sees in it an expansion by the evangelist based on 1:14,16 (pp. 534–537). John accepts that Moses received revelation, but shows no interest in its relevance except as witnessing to Christ. Only in that sense did it contain grace and truth (p. 539). Otherwise the Word and the Law are antithetical. "John is opposing the law and Jesus on the basis of their claim to being the expression of divine revelation" (p. 542). Effectively John reduces the role of the Law to being part of the predictive scriptures and thus testifying to continuity (p. 543). 1:17 should not be seen as in tension with its context nor as relevant only within 1:14–18 with its Sinai imagery. For Pancaro, "Word" would have been associated for the evangelist both with Torah, based on Old Testament usage (cf. Isa 55:10–11), but also with the personification of Wisdom. Thus the prologue praises Jesus "in terms which recall not only divine Wisdom but also the Law" (pp. 546).

In short, according to Pancaro, John's Jesus effectively replaces the Law. In doing so he does not engage in critique of the Law; rather it testified to his coming and apart from that has ceased to apply since God's Son has appeared. Continuity is maintained not only through the Law's testimony, but also through the transformation of symbols and language associated with Torah so that they now apply to Christ. It is very much a case of a community claiming Jewish heritage, exclusively so, and doing so in a radically changed sense which includes leaving much that it demanded in the past as no longer applicable.

Pancaro's study is rich in detail and comprehensive in scope. I shall have occasion to address many of the detailed issues in the course of my sequential review of the gospel. If there is a lack in general, it is in not giving sufficient attention to issues which appear in John 2–4, especially related to purification and the temple. I also wonder whether we can assume that John's Jewish Christians were Law observant on the basis that John explains their expulsion only on grounds of their christological confession.

The only other major treatment has been that of Kotila[3] who offers an assessment of attitudes towards the Law at various stages of development of the composition of the gospel. For our purposes, his comments about attitudes of the Evangelist and Redactors are of concern, although Kotila tends to isolate redactional additions and the attitudes they represent rather than discuss the orientation of the redacted writing as a whole.

He sees 5:17 indicating that Jesus abolished the sabbath (pp. 20–21). The evangelist's focus in the conflict is only on using it as a means to assert his christology. Both Jesus' healing and his command that the man carry his mat break the sabbath (p. 22). 5:45 refers to the role not of Moses as a person, but of the Law as scripture in condemning Israel's unbelief, and not to the last judgement, but to the time since Jesus' exaltation (pp. 26–28). The kind of witness which John has in mind here is found in 3:14–15 (p. 28). Kotila notes that 7:19, "Did not Moses give you the law?", speaks in a distant way of the Law, in the sense that has Jesus contrast both God and

---

[3] M. Kotila, *Umstrittene Zeuge. Studien zur Stellung des Gesetzes in der johanneischen Theologiegeschichte*, Annales Academiae Scientiarum Fennicae Dissertationes Humanarum Litterarum 48, (Helsinki: Suomalainen Tiedeakatemia, 1988).

"Moses", and us and "you" (p. 41). Yet the author of 7:19–24 (a prejohannine tradition according to Kotila) also speaks as an insider in appealing to the Law (p. 42), a stance not consistent with that of the evangelist (p. 46). 7:22's comment about the command coming from the fathers not Moses is a later redactional insertion (p. 46).

8:17 presents the Law as belonging to the opponents, yet still uses the Law as an argument (p. 59); but the Law's function is solely to bear witness to Christ. The evangelist is not antinomist, but does not reflect on the status of the Law as revelation (p. 59). 9:29 shows that he believed that God spoke to Moses (p. 72). The theme of 5:31–47 and 9:18–39 is similar: anyone who believes Moses should believe Jesus (p. 74). Similarly the evangelist places Abraham on the side of Jesus, not that of the Jews (8:39–40; pp. 74–75). He notes that 8:30–59 begins with Jews who believe in Jesus and that the evangelist has these want to kill Jesus. This suggests that the evangelist's argument elsewhere may also be directed at Jewish Christians, because they reject his christology (eg. 5:18; pp. 75–76).

He raises the possibility that the disparaging of previous shepherds in 10:8 includes an attack by a redactor on Moses (pp. 76–77). 10:35b ("the scriptures cannot lie") is not about prophecy nor a blanket approval of all laws but a statement of principle, which the evangelist applies to the present context without comprehending its wider potential significance (pp. 92–93).

He sees 4:22 (salvation coming from the Jews) as tradition which predates the evangelist's signs source, but does not discuss its significance in John as it stands (pp. 103–104). 12:34 reflects the evangelist's belief that John's christology coheres with scripture (p. 109). Kotila argues that taken together 2:13–22 and 4:21–24 indicate that for the evangelist Jesus has abolished the cult (pp. 112–113). The basic thesis of the evangelist is as follows: because the Law, ie. the scripture, testifies to the envoy christology, the Jews have no reason to kill Jesus (p. 125). The evangelist assumes Jesus as the true passover lamb without directly linking it to the issue of the Law's status, since such conflict belonged in the past (pp. 126–127).

On 1:17, Kotila believes that, as part of the hymn before the evangelist made additions, it originally assumed the Law as God's gift (p. 141). Kotila claims that 1:18 derives from a redactor and has corrected the original reading of 1:17. The result is a theology of revelation which is extremely critical of the Law and which reads 1:17 antithetically, raising the question whether God was doing the giving at all (pp. 142–145). The evangelist, on the other hand, had valued 1:17 highly (pp. 145–146). Accordingly, God gave the Law, but as testimony to Christ and only for this purpose. Otherwise it belonged to the past. The evangelist assumes that Jesus has abolished both sabbath laws and the institution of the temple (p. 146).

In the bread speech Kotila sees the redactor disowning the Moses typology of the evangelist (p. 170). He argues that in 6:32–32 the redactor understood "bread" as meaning Mosaic Law. The effect, then, is to criticise the view that the Law came from heaven (pp. 170–171). For Kotila this is the redactor who also treats Moses as belonging to thieves and robbers (p. 172). 6:46, 5:37 and 1:18 express the same anti-Law view (pp. 172–173). Dying in the wilderness is used as proof against the Mosaic Law (p. 177). Only Jesus gives life, not the Law (p. 178). The redactor has an extremely critical approach to the Law (p. 179). Yet the redactor can still keep the positive prophetic function of the Law, reflected in 6:45 (p. 177).

Kotila discusses at length whether the "new" commandment, introduced by the redactor in 13:34–35, may be antithetical to the Law, but finally rejects it. The main reason is that the indication of conflict with the Jews belongs to material which entered the last discourses at a redactional stage (15:18 – 16:4a), prior to the addition of 13:34–35 and the final redactional composition of 13–17 (pp. 191–198). To interpret 1:17 one has to look at the whole gospel, because it is without comment (p. 204).

In summary, the focus of the evangelist is not orthopraxy in conflict with "Pharisees" as in the Signs Source, but orthodox christology in conflict with opponents, now designated "Jews" (pp. 205–206). The role of the Law and of scripture is to legitimise Jesus. Nevertheless tensions remain: Jews should believe in Jesus because of scripture, yet the true understanding of scripture is available only after Easter . A first redaction uses christology against the Law: Moses has not seen God (1:18; 5:26–37; 6:46; p. 209), but belongs to thieves and robbers (10:8; p. 210). The food of Moses (the Law) was not from heaven (6:32–33), yet the redactor still uses the Law for prophecy (adding 6:45 and 15:25). The redactor's community has experienced excommunication (9:22–23; 12:42; 15:18–16:4a). A secondary level of redaction speaks of a new commandment of love (13:34–35 and 15:12–17). This is not set in antithesis to the Mosaic Law, but reflects the type of the farewell speech (pp. 211–212).

Kotila is concerned to trace attitudes towards the Law at various redactional levels. This raises the question acutely, how, on any assessment of the development of the tradition, the final redactor held together the material which now forms part of the whole. For instance, in arguing that the reference in 13:34–35 to a new commandment has no hint of contrast with Mosaic commandments, Kotila excludes taking into account material in the last discourses which reflects conflict with the Jews because it came from an earlier redaction. This exposes a problem. Does the final redactor ignore the material he redacts? Kotila's proposal that the first redactor is extremely critical of the Law must be tested in the light of the gospel as a whole.

Both Pancaro and Kotila deal only with selected texts. As in other chapters I believe that there is great value in considering the document as a whole and sequentially. There is more about the Law in the gospel than either suggests. Already the sequence of episodes in 2:1 – 4:42 makes important statements, as we shall see, but neither author addresses them adequately. One misses also any adequate treatment of the festivals in John.

As already indicated, most other treatments of the Law in John are confined to a few pages. Nevertheless some deserve particular mention. Glasson[4] drew attention, as had Dodd[5] before him, to the use in rabbinic tradition of the images of life, light, bread and water for Torah (p. 86). He similarly noted the Torah associations of Wisdom or Word of God in some Jewish literature (p. 87). "We have thus in the Prologue a transference to Christ of what had been ascribed to Torah" (p. 88). The purifying jars represent purification under the Law "as contrasted with the festive wine brought by Jesus" (p. 88). He also proposed that Jacob's well suggests a contrast between the static and the new spiritual life Christ offers, just as Christ replaces the temple (p. 89). He mentions with some hesitation the suggestion of Augustine (*Exposition of Psalms* 70:20), that the five porches at the pool of Bethesda represent the Torah (p. 89). Searching the Law is only of use when it leads to Christ (5:39–40; p. 90). Jesus is the true bread, not Torah, as Jesus is the true vine, not Israel, and the true light, not John the Baptist, and the worshippers in spirit are the true worshippers in contrast to those who depend on special places (pp. 90–91).

Martyn[6] stands at the beginning of a significant new development in reconstructing Johannine history. He sees at the first stage a Torah observant Christian community unaware of the Gentile mission (pp. 100–101). Accusations against it later were christological, not because of breach of Torah (p. 100). Brown[7] speculates that the influx of Samaritan influenced

---

[4] T. F. Glasson, *Moses in the Fourth Gospel*, SBT 40, (London: SCM, 1963).

[5] C. H. Dodd, *The Interpretation of the Fourth Gospel*, (Cambridge: CUP, 1953), pp. 83–86.

[6] J. L. Martyn, *The Gospel of John in Christian History. Essays for Interpreters*, (New York: Paulist, 1978), cited here. See also his earlier work: J. L. Martyn, *History and Theology in the Fourth Gospel*, (New York: Harper and Row, 1968; rev'd edn, Nashville: Abingdon, 1979).

[7] R. E. Brown, *The Community of the Beloved Disciple. The Life, Loves, and Hates of an Individual Church in New Testament Times*, (New York: Paulist, 1979).

Christians brought both a higher christology and an anti-temple stance, but this depends to my mind on the doubtful methodology of seeing the first chapters of the gospel as an indication of the history of the community (pp. 34–47). Painter[8] suggests an anti-temple stance may have come from disciples of John the Baptist (p. 125). He suggests the signs also relate to the issue of Law in that they echo the signs done by Moses (Ex 3:12 – 13:16) and so form part of the legitimation of John's claim (p. 217 n. 15).

Neyrey[9] applies the grid of Douglas[10] to stages he perceives in Johannine christology. He also adopts the questionable methodology of seeing the history of the early Johannine community reflected in the early chapters. At the first stage, missionary propaganda, John's Jesus presents himself as a member of the covenant community, but challenging the way in which the scriptures, in particular, sabbath law, were interpreted (p. 127). At this stage he sees Jesus portrayed as challenging the ideology and structure of the Jewish purity system (temple and sabbath), and therefore hardly showing interest in rituals which reinforce it.

In the second stage, "replacement", he sees Jesus portrayed as supplanting Israel's central religious symbols: his body replaces the temple (2:19–22; 4:20–24); he replaces the old feasts (Passover, 6:4–14; 2:13, Tabernacles, 7:2, and Dedication, 10:22); he "is the authentic manna of the authentic Passover, as well as the true light (8:12) and water (7:37–39) of the true Tabernacles", and provides the new and superior basis for purification (2:6,10; p. 132; similarly, pp. 137–139). Jesus is also greater than Jacob (4:12), Abraham (8:53,56–58), and even Moses (1:17; 3:13–15; 5:36,46; 6:31–32; (p. 135).

A final stage, high christology, reflects the time of excommunication and apostasy, and is characterised by an "anti-" stance, revolt rather than reform (pp. 142–143). "The strong sense of an orderly system symbolized by the temple, its feasts, and cultic objects, which characterized stage two, collapses" (p. 143). The focus moves from ritual to spiritual and this includes an anti-sacramental stance.

It is not possible to discuss this proposal in detail here. I find the distinction between the christology of the second and third stage unconvincing and, more pertinent to our theme, the distinction at the level of purity. The "replacement" stage already, in my view, abandons "the strong sense of an

---

[8] J. Painter, *The Quest for the Messiah. The History, Literature and Theology of the Johannine Community*, (Edinburgh: T&T Clark, 2nd edn, 1993).

[9] J. H. Neyrey, *An Ideology of Revolt. John's Christology in Social-Science Perspective*, (Philadelphia: Fortress, 1988).

[10] Douglas, *Purity and Danger*.

orderly system". An anti-sacramental stance may have been one possible result of John's dualism, as already Bultmann suspected, but the transmitted text does not indicate such "logic" prevailed.

The difficulty with the preceding works is that treatment of the Law is incidental. Kotila's analysis is far to be preferred to this kind of analysis for it treats the theme directly. With regard to treatments of the gospel as a whole, the brief treatment by Luz[11] offers a compact analysis of the issues. "The Law" in John is the Old Testament in so far as it is used by unbelieving Jews as the basis for their action, in particular, of their attack on Jesus (p. 120). The term "Scripture" occurs almost exclusively in the words of Jesus and the evangelist (cf. 5:39); it is Scripture that is fulfilled in Jesus, not the Law. Luz begins by noting conflict over the sabbath. He sees the answer given in 7:22–24 as remaining at the level of rabbinic school discussion. But John's real focus is not the well being of the victim, but christological (p. 120). This is so both here and in ch. 9. There the narrative ends with the farce that the Jews condemn Jesus on the basis of the Law, where in reality they stand condemned by the Son of Man (p. 121). Conflicts over Law are a mere foil for exposing the Jews' failure to believe. The major charge against Jesus is blasphemy (10:23–39), against which Jesus even uses the Law, itself, citing Ps 82:6 in formal agreement with rabbinic interpretation (p. 121).

As scripture, the Law is part of the testimony for Jesus (5:31–47), whereas the Jews use it against him (pp. 121–122). They claim to be Moses' disciples (9:28), but he is their accuser (5:45–47). John assumes the content of the Old Testament witness is Christ. Christ is the sole basis for understanding the Old Testament. Nevertheless direct evidence for this is rare in John. It occurs when John has Jesus appeal to the Law concerning having two witnesses in a trial (Deut 17:6), but then in Johannine terms the two witnesses are the Father and the Son (8:17–18; p. 122). Otherwise John makes little attempt to prove or defend his claims about scripture. John develops the literary strategy of showing those who respond to Jesus positively, like Nathanael, as being true to Israel and the Law, and those who reject Jesus as failing the Law. Thus he has Nicodemus expose the illegality of the attempt to arrest Jesus (7:45–52; cf. also 7:19) and shows the Jewish leadership as concerned primarily with political realities (11:47–53). John assumes his hearers will note that the Jews lost their temple and their relative independence (p. 123). John drives this to a climax in the trial scene where he has Jews claim, "We have no king but Caesar," condemning themselves by their own Law (19:15; p. 124).

---

[11] Luz, *Gesetz*, pp. 58–156.

Accordingly, the Law plays no role in ethics in John. The only command cited is the command to love, but even then it is not set in relation to the Law, but introduced as a "new" law (13:34). It is "new" in that its rationale is Christ's love for the disciples. Yet the "new" also implies reference to the "old", Lev 19:18. This means, according to Luz, there is no longer a direct ethical continuity between the Old Testament Law and Christian ethics for John (p. 124). Luz raises the question whether the Law and the Scripture have not become superfluous for John, merely rhetorical source material (p. 125). In considering the issue, Luz notes that the Gospel derives from Jewish Christianity. This accounts for its familiarity with rabbinic exegetical traditions and for its consideration of Gentiles as being from another fold. Yet it is a group which has separated from Judaism, speaks of Jewish feasts from the perspective of outsiders, needs to explain the relations of Jews and Samaritans to its hearers, looks back on expulsions from the synagogues, and, above all, plays with misunderstanding in a way that shows dialogue is a thing of the past (p. 125). What appears as conflict with Judaism over the Law has now become, in reality, a medium for reassuring a community in its christological claims about Jesus as the revealer (p. 126). It is not just that "the Jews" have become simply a cipher for the world; the Christians now have the key to understanding their scripture; the Johannine community takes seriously the use of the Old Testament to witness to Christ (pp. 126–127). In that process it subordinates Old Testament figures like Abraham and Moses to the demands of christological exegesis (p. 127). The Law loses all significance as such and the cult is abolished. The Old Testament also effectively loses reference to its own story and becomes merely the mode of speech for expressing the words of the Revealer (p. 128).

In the context of discussing Jewish-Christian relations as reflected in John, Freyne[12] notes the striking absence of legal concerns in the fourth gospel, though it emphasises that the Jews are strictly Law observant (on the sabbath, 5:16; 9:10; blasphemy and stoning, 10:30–34; on exclusion from the synagogue, 9:22; 12:42; 16:2; in their attitude to non observers, 7:49; in their concern about what Law says about the Messiah, 12:34; and in their view that Jesus should die, 19:7; pp. 123–124). In contrast the command to love (sometimes the "commands") stands in John independent of the Law. The Law and the scriptures are not a source of life, but only a witness to

---

[12] S. Freyne, "Vilifying the Other and Defining the Self: Matthew's and John's Anti-Jewish Polemic in Focus," in *"To See Ourselves as Others See Us." Christians, Jews, "Others" in Late Antiquity*, Scholars Press Studies in the Humanities, edited by J. Neusner and E. S. Frerichs, (Chico: Scholars Press, 1985), pp. 117–144.

Christ (1:45; 5:39) and ultimately a witness against the Jews for not believing (5:45; 9:28–29; p. 125). The Jews never really comprehended the Sinai revelation (5:37). John's community is not claiming a place within Israel beside others; it is Israel (1:31,50; 3:10; 12:13),[13] though it still holds hope for the redemption of all Israel (11:52; p. 126). Johannine Christianity locates its self identity within, not outside Judaism and affirms that salvation is of the Jews (4:22; p. 128).

In their different ways Luz and Freyne raise major issues. To what extent does John's approach to the Law make both the Law, and the scriptures generally, little more than a repository of symbols? To what extent does John's vilification of "the Jews" also vilify Moses and Torah? We have already noted Kotila's response to the latter, when he sees John's Jesus (the Jesus of the redactor) counting Moses among the thieves and robbers.

In his study of the prologue and its relation to the rest of the gospel, Theobald[14] argues that 1:14–18 virtually puts the Torah in a vacuum, since all claims made for it now belong to Christ. He speaks of the "Entwirklichung der Tora" (loosely: "making Torah a virtual unreality"; p. 360; similarly pp. 258, 362). It does not bring life; only Christ does (5:39). Similarly 6:32 virtually robs the claim that manna came from heaven of its reality (p. 361). On the other hand, the Law does have a witness function in John which is taken seriously (so 1:45; 5:45). But, even then, John's argumentative use of scripture is confined to disputes with Judaism and the result is a relativising of scripture in John.[15] He finds 1:18 confirming the stance he sees taken in 1:17. There was no seeing of God at Sinai. The same point he identifies also in 5:37b, which, while couched in general terms, also includes a reference to Sinai and goes beyond 1:18 in denying that the Jews have even heard God's voice. This is meant polemically and refers to the Jews' failure to listen, to have God's word abide in them (so 5:38). It does not deny God's word entirely to the old covenant (cf. Deut 4:12, "You heard the sound of words, but saw no form, there was only a voice"), but it does include a denial of direct experience of God, whether visionary or auditory (pp. 363–364). It may also be directed at contemporary claims of mystical Judaism. While he sees the main point of 6:46 as clarifying that believers do not see God, but

---

[13] In contrast see J. Painter, "The Church and Israel in the Fourth Gospel: A Response," *NTS* 25 (1978), pp. 103–122, who denies such an ecclesiology is present in John.

[14] M. E. Theobald, *Die Fleischwerdung des Logos. Studien zum Verhältnis des Johannesprologs zum Corpus des Evangeliums und zu 1 Joh*, Neutestamentliche Abhandlungen NF 20, (Münster: Aschendorff, 1988).

[15] Theobald refers to E. Grässer, "Die antijüdische Polemik im Johannesevangelium," *NTS* 11 (1964/65), pp. 74–90, esp. p. 88.

that only Jesus does, he also notes its similarity to 1:18 and the possibility that it, too, wards off claims of Jewish mysticism (pp. 367–368).

In his study of Sophia, Scott[16] attributes to the evangelist a directly polemical intent in use of the motif of wisdom. He argues that John used it to develop the contrast between Jesus and the Law. This was in resistance to the Jewish tradition evident in Sirach 24 of confining Sophia to Torah (p. 159). It reflects a community which is coming to terms with its exclusion from the synagogue; it understands Jesus as "replacing, or even superseding what has been claimed for Torah" (p. 160). Scott's argument rests on his discussion of the use of Sophia not only in the Prologue (pp. 94–115), but also in the body of the gospel (pp. 115–159). The allusion to Jesus, especially as the bread of life (pp. 118–119), light (pp. 119–121), way (pp. 126–128), and vine (pp. 129–130), counters similar claims made for Torah in association with wisdom in Jewish tradition.

In contrast, Pryor[17] emphasises the positive attitude of John towards the Law. It witnesses to Christ (pp. 117–118). "On those occasions when John seems to distance Jesus (and his followers) from the Law, when it is spoken of as 'your Law' (10:34), 'our Law' (7:53), or 'their Law' (15:25), it is not the true witness of the Law which Jesus rejects, but that confidence in the Law which refuses to see fulfilment in Christ, so that the Law itself becomes self-sufficient and absolute, and thus a false substitute for the truth of Christ" (p. 118). Pryor sees John presenting Jesus as the fulfilment of the hope for a Mosaic prophet. He points to the echoes of Deut 10:4 in 17:8 and especially of Nu 16:8 in 7:16–17; 8:28 and 17:8 (p. 118–119). He sees also the motif of Jesus' sending, his doing signs and works, and his last discourses, as echoing Deuteronomy; they, therefore, reinforce this understanding (pp. 119–120).

Yet John shows Jesus as superior to Moses. He offers the true bread/Torah (p. 121), is himself the source of water (7:37–39) and healing (3:14–15), unlike Moses who is God's agent. Possibly in 3:13 John is also countering the view that Moses had ascended to see God (p. 121). 1:17 contains no denigration of Moses (p. 122). What came before was a foreshadowing and Moses a mediator; Jesus is the embodiment of truth (p. 122). John agrees with Sirach 24 that Torah, as God's wisdom and word, was present at creation, but identifies it as "but the type of the true Wisdom/Word who existed eternally and now has been made manifest" (p. 123). John

---

[16] M. Scott, *Sophia and the Johannine Jesus*, JSNTS 71, (Sheffield: JSOTPr., 1992).

[17] J. W. Pryor, *John: Evangelist of the Covenant People. The Narrative and Themes of the Fourth Gospel*, (Downers Grove: IVP, 1992).

also deliberately alludes to Sirach 24 (here 24:19–26) in the dialogue with the woman at the well in presenting Jesus as the source of the water of life (4:13–14). Covenant loyalty (Deut 6:1–9) is now to be directed no longer to the Law, but to Jesus. "When John takes up the Torah motif and applies it to Jesus, he does not want to present Jesus alongside Torah as a revelation of God, nor does he wish to replace one set of Torah regulations with another" (p. 123). Rather what Torah symbolised for Israel, life and hope, Jesus now is. "Thus all that Torah stood for both from God (as his revelatory word) and towards God (focus of commitment and obedience) was but a foreshadowing of the Word incarnate, Jesus. Revelation and covenant life now centre in him" (pp. 123–124).

It seems to me that here two approaches emerge. On one view John sees the Law as God's gift and claims that this gift, which manifests God's Word and Wisdom and is represented in symbols (light, life, bread, etc.), has been superseded by Christ; John affirms this without polemic against Moses and the Law. On the other view John argues directly against the status of the Law, denying that it could be associated with God's Word and Wisdom and be represented by the symbols.

Both positions claim 1:17 in evidence. In her article on the key phrase of this verse, χάριν ἀντὶ χάριτος, Edwards[18] argues, that it should be translated, in accord with common usage, "grace instead of grace", not "grace upon/in addition to grace". She shows that linguistic support for the latter is weak. In support of her translation she argues that for John, the Law, in contrast to the way John treats the Jews, is understood positively as something God-given, but now replaced. Thus she points to its positive use in 1:45 as prediction, to ch 6 where Jesus fulfils the prophecy of Deut 18 and to 5:45–47 and 7:19, where Jesus reproves the Jews for not believing Moses and the Law (pp. 8–9). She also draws attention to Jesus' use of the Law in 10:34 (as the word of God which cannot be broken) and in 8:17 (the two witnesses). She points also to the use of typology in 3:14 and in ch. 6 (the manna), and to the use of Old Testament imagery of light and living water. "These allusions do not deny that the Law was in its own way a light to those to whom its was given, a source of life and nourishment to God's people" (p. 9). "God's old methods of dealing with his people – the Temple, the sacrificial system, and all the rituals of Judaism – have now been replaced by the sending of the Son in love, in short by the good news of the gospel" (p. 9). John saw

---

[18] R. Edwards, "Χάριν ἀντὶ χάριτος, (John 1.16). Grace and the Law in the Johannine Prologue," *JSNT* 32 (1988), pp. 3–15.

the Law as God's gracious gift (p. 10). John has appropriated and christianised the Old Testament symbols (p. 11).

Within the context of highlighting the Jewishness of the fourth gospel, Deines,[19] in a study of the stone jars of 2:6, makes a strong case that John's gospel is fully acquainted with Palestinian Jewish purification practices.[20] He shows that stone jars were immune from becoming unclean and were in wide use before 70 CE in Palestine. He also discusses other material in John related to purification (3:23,25; 11:55; 13:1–11). In this context he notes that in John there is no implied criticism of the Jewish practices (p. 250). John never criticises the Jewish way of life, nor the tradition of the elders, but seeks to show the new in the old, so that no one any longer should want the old. Purification is now through the blood of the lamb.

There seems to be a broad consensus that John sees the primary role of the Law as bearing witness to Christ. Most would also agree that for John, Jesus has at least superseded the Law, and that that has rendered some, if not all, of its provisions obsolete (temple, probably also sabbath, purity laws). Some would extend this to every detail of the Law including ethics. But already here questions must be raised. What is being displaced? Does expulsion from synagogues on grounds of christology imply, as some assume, that these Christian Jews would have been seen as otherwise Torah faithful? Is there indication in John of change in the status of the Law or its laws? Is there indication of what in part provoked change elsewhere, namely the issues raised by the influx of Gentiles? Has the separation led to abandonment of Torah practices, to polemic not only against the synagogue Jews but also against Moses and the tradition? Are the signs of Jewish ethos indicators of continuing observance of some or all of Torah's demands or are they relics of earlier tradition? Does the use of imagery associated with Torah to apply to Jesus indicate a strong sense of continuity, a transcending, or a deliberate counterclaim, perhaps, even, a denial of such qualities to Torah? Is there any indication whether the gospel would contemplate Torah as a source of life before Christ? Or is it implying this was never the case? Finally, what other value systems are operating within the logic of the gospel in relation

---

[19] R. Deines, *Jüdische Steingefässe und pharisäische Frömmigkeit: eine archäologisch-historischer Beitrag zum Verständnis von Joh 2,6 und der jüdischen Reinheitshalacha zur Zeit Jesu*, WUNT 2.52, (Tübingen: J. C. B. Mohr [Paul Siebeck], 1993).

[20] See also J. C. Thomas, "The Fourth Gospel and Rabbinic Judaism," *ZNW* 82 (1991), pp. 159–182, who after surveying material relevant to 2:1–11; 4:9; the sabbath conflicts; laws concerning witnesses (5:31–47; 8:13); 13:8–9; and 18:28, concludes: "The Fourth Gospel exhibits an acquaintance with many of the issues which were of concern for pre-90 Pharisaism and/or emerging rabbinic Judaism" (p. 181).

to the Law, aside from christology? To what extent is dualism, cosmological or eschatological, a factor? What is the relation between what John claims about the Law in relation to Jesus and the actual effects of that claim? These and other questions will inform our survey.

5.2 John 1–4 in Review

In the prologue the evangelist describes Jesus as the Word, active at creation, shining (still) in the darkness, coming to his own, becoming flesh, and making the Father known. It has long been realised that one important background for the use of Word (λόγος) is Wisdom (so Prov 8:22–31), including its association with Torah (Sir 24).[21] We are probably right to assume that the evangelist and at least some of his hearers would have been aware of this association, given the extensive use of other related Torah imagery in the gospel. Even within the prologue, not only Word, but also light and life belong to a common stock of images which had been used with reference to Torah.

It is very likely that at some stage the hymn which forms the backbone of the prologue told first of the Word or Wisdom in creation, then of its appearance in Israel's history (1:11) and then climaxed in the coming of Jesus (1:14).[22] It would have reflected the myth of Wisdom seeking a dwelling place such as we find in Sir 24:8–12; Bar 3:37; and 1 Enoch 42. In its present form the allusions to John the Baptist and the present tense of "shines" in 1:5, suggest that throughout, the prologue refers to the coming of the Word in Jesus, or more correctly, the coming of Jesus, the Word. The prologue still includes reference to the Word in creation, but the salvation historical

---

[21] So Dodd, *Interpretation* , pp. 274–277. B. Lindars, *John*, NT Guides, (Sheffield: JSOT Pr., 1990), pp. 54–56, speaks of the link between Law and Wisdom in Sir 24:1–12 as "the greatest single literary influence behind." the prologue (p. 56). "John's christology is worked out against a spirituality in which the Law has cosmic status as the means of salvation." The Law is an important factor in nearly every discourse (p. 56). See also Theobald, *Fleischwerdung*, p. 255, who notes the allusion to Sir 24:3–12 which speaks of Wisdom seeking a dwelling place and which has structurally influenced the prologue. See also my discussion of the christology of the prologue in W. Loader, *The Christology of the Fourth Gospel: Structure and Issues*, BBET 23, (Frankfurt: Peter Lang, 2nd edn., 1992), pp. 154–160.

[22] Cf. Painter, *Quest*, p. 155, who suggests that prior to the evangelist's redaction of the hymn by introducing 6–9 everything before 1:14 referred to the eternal shining of Wisdom's light. See also R. E. Brown, *The Gospel according to John*, AncB 29, (New York: Doubleday; London: Chapman, 1966), pp. 28–29.

perspective which had been reflected in the Word's coming to Israel before Christ is no longer present. This appears to have happened primarily out of concern to highlight Jesus' identity with the Word and to set John the Baptist in his appropriate place. Now, for instance, "He came to his own" (1:11) refers to Jesus' coming to Israel in his ministry, not to the activity of the Word in Israel through the Law or the prophets. The effect of this change is not only to remove the link with salvation history, but also to leave open the question of the status of the Law and its relation to the Word. It is not, therefore, surprising that this issue surfaces in the final segment of the prologue, 1:14–18.

In 1:14–18 there are echoes of the account of Moses' presence at Sinai and his desire to see God's glory (Ex 33:7–23; 34:6).[23] There Moses pitched a tent, God promised his presence, Moses asked to see God's glory and God declared his grace. Here the Word became flesh and tented among us, we saw his glory and the Word was full of grace and truth (1:14).[24] The key to evaluating the typology comes in 1:16–17: "Because from his fullness we have all received, grace in place of grace; because the Law was given through Moses; grace and truth came through Jesus Christ." The typological allusions continue in 1:18: "No one has ever seen God; God the only Son who is in the bosom of the Father has made him known." Moses did not see God and therefore could not adequately make him known.[25]

The primary focus of this segment is to make a statement about Jesus the Word. It does so, however, by developing a correspondence with the Sinai event which is both positive and negative. The typology is complex. First

---

[23] On this see A. T. Hanson, *The Prophetic Gospel. A Study of John and Old Testament*, (Edinburgh: T&T Clark, 1991), pp. 21–32. However I do not find the evidence convincing that John means us to understand that Moses saw the pre-existent Christ (see pp. 21–22). The focus of the passage is not what Moses saw, but about what "we" have seen. It is true that the imagery reflects that of the Sinai epiphany and may well reflect tradition according to which Moses saw God's shekinah or glory. My argument is that, even if this is the case, this is not the point which the author is making. Hanson makes a similar claim concerning 5:37 (p. 81). See also Theobald, *Fleischwerdung*, p. 255., who notes the allusion to the revelation at Sinai (1:14d; cf. Ex 34:6; 33:18; 1:18a; cf. Ex 33:20,23). John's aim is not to show salvation historical fulfilment, but to claim the attributes of wisdom solely for Christ (p. 255). In the same way 1:17 leaves Torah now in a vacuum (pp. 257–258). 1:18 rejects all claims to mystical vision (p. 259). See also M.-E. Boismard, *Moses or Jesus. An Essay in Johannine Christology*, (Minneapolis: Fortress, 1993), pp. 94–98.

[24] Pryor, *Covenant*, p. 122, is hesitant about finding an allusion to Ex 34:6 in "grace and truth", but given the other associations of the passage, the balance is in favour of the recognising the allusion.

[25] For the view that John the Baptist is speaking these words, see Hanson, *Prophetic Gospel*, pp. 27–30.

"we" are implicitly compared with Moses, and the glory of the Son with the glory which Moses sought to see. It is not that Jesus and Moses are directly compared, initially. Rather we see the Son's glory; whereas Moses obtained only a back view of God's glory. The author is not concerned to suggest that Moses saw the back view of the Son's glory, although this might have been consistent with his approach. Rather, the author uses the Sinai scene in order, on the one hand, to associate the Son with the God whose glory Moses sought to see, and, on the other hand, to assert that "we" have seen what Moses did not see, at least, derivatively. It can be expressed in Pauline terms: we see the glory of God in the face of Jesus Christ (2 Cor 4:6). This is why 1:18 clearly excludes us from seeing God; what we see is the Son. We see God's glory only in the sense that, as John has Jesus put it elsewhere: "The one who has seen me has seen the Father" (14:9). This Moses could not see.

What does this tell us about John's view of Moses and the Law? It certainly sets Christians in contrast to Moses. They have seen what he could not see. This is a serious disqualification, but it is not a dismissal of Moses or the Law. This becomes clear in 1:17. Here the prologue juxtaposes the giving of the Law through Moses with what happened or came about in the Son. The Son who alone is in a position to see God therefore bears unique glory, acts as God and, like God's wisdom, came to dwell with humanity. He thus manifested the divine attributes of grace and truth. The Son is both the bearer of the glory, the light, the grace and truth, the message, and is, himself, the glory, the light, the grace and truth, the message.

Juxtaposed to this is the event whereby God gave the Law through Moses. The author appears to have in mind the occasion depicted in Ex 33 – 34. In response to Moses' request to see his glory God promises that he may see only his back parts. In Ex 34 he then invites him to ascend the mountain with new tablets to receive the Law and to see the promised vision. The contrast in 1:17 is positive in that it affirms that God gave the Law. The use of both the word "given"[26] in 1:17 and the word χάριτος ("grace" or "gift") in 1:16, suggests that the author saw the Law in fundamentally positive terms.[27] He is not a paulinist contrasting Law and grace.[28] Thus the exclusive

---

[26]. Cf. R. Schnackenburg, *The Gospel according to St John, Vol I*, (London: Burns & Oates, 1968), p. 277, who understands Moses as the giver.

[27] So F. J. Moloney, *Belief in the Word. Reading the Fourth Gospel: John 1–4*, (Minneapolis: Fortress, 1993), pp. 46–47.

[28] Cf. C. K. Barrett, *The Gospel according to St. John*, (2nd edn., London: SPCK, 1978), p. 168. So Schnackenburg, *John I*, p. 277, who argues that "the evangelist only dissociates himself from the Law in the same way that he finds the Jewish cult (4:21–24),

claim for Christ, expounded by the implicit contrast with what Moses could achieve, both in 1:14 and 1:18, nevertheless left room for acknowledgment of some interim positive value of the Law.

On the other hand the contrast has negative elements. For the gift of the Law was far less than what has come about in Christ. It was not a revelation of God's glory. In that sense the Law was a substitute for the real thing, a preliminary gift, now surpassed by the manifestation of the real glory of God in the Son. The author appears to be linking its lower status to the lower quality of the vision Moses received. Independently Paul had made a similar link between the status of the Law and the lesser glory of Moses in 2 Cor 3. For John, the Law could not be of the same quality, for no one has seen God (1:18), not even Moses. In this there is a sharp distinction between the Word and the Law. The Word is a person who saw God's glory. The Word is not to be identified with the Law. It would run contrary to the way the typology is used to suggest that John also saw the Law as "full of grace and truth".

At the same time, the passage seems also to suggest strongly that the Law no longer has relevance; it has been replaced,[29] since what Moses originally sought has now been made possible.[30] God's glory has become visible in Christ. The idea of replacement appears supported also by the most likely translation of χάριν ἀντὶ χάριτος, "grace instead of or in place of grace".[31] The same logic might also suggest that the allusion to the Word's "tenting" in 1:14 may imply that he is also now the place of God's glory, namely the replacement of the temple (cf. Rev 21:3).[32] This will find confirmation as we consider the rest of the gospel. The heavy qualification in 1:18 and, indirectly, in the use of the typology in 1:14, is not attacking the Law as gift.[33] At most it is warding off any claim that Moses or anyone else can be

---

purifications (2:6; 3:25; cf. 11:55; 19:40, 42) and feasts 'of the Jews' (2:13; 5:1; 56:4; 7:2; 11:55) obsolete and no longer important" (p. 277).

[29] Schnackenburg, *John I*, p. 277; Moloney, *Word*, pp. 47–48.

[30] Painter, *Quest*, pp. 147–148, suggests that a Hellenist Christian redaction using Pauline language introduced a contrast between law and grace which is now reflected in 1:14e,16–17.

[31] So Edwards, "Χάριν ἀντὶ χάριτος"; D. A. Carson, *The Gospel according to John*, (Leicester: IVP; Eerdmans: Grand Rapids, 1991), pp. 131–133.

[32] So Brown, *John*, pp. 32–34, referring to the hope expressed in Joel 3:17; Zech 2:10; Ezek 43:7. He points also to the use of the dwelling motif in association with wisdom (Sir 24:8) and with God's Shekinah. See also 1 En 42:1, according to which Wisdom found a resting place only in heaven.

[33] Cf. Kotila, *Zeuge*, pp. 142–145, who argues that 1:18 indicates an extremely critical reading of 1:17, which calls into question the divine origin of the Law.

in a position to have and pass on comparable revelation. This has the effect of also denying mystical claims of access to God, a concern present elsewhere in John (cf. 3:13; 5:37; 6:46). It means for the Law that it is recognised as God's gift, given in God's grace, but now replaced by the gift of the one in whom we have seen God's glory.

With regard to the possible link between Wisdom and Torah, I think it unmistakably clear that John has not identified the two. John does not espouse the view that the Word or Wisdom visited Israel through Moses and the prophets and then finally in Christ, even if this was once the message of the hymn. The gift of the Law was in a sense a replacement for what Moses sought. What Moses sought, to see God's glory, did not come to fulfilment in the reception of the Law, but only through Christ. Thus one major option of relating Christ, the Word, to salvation history appears to be ruled out. The Law was indeed God's gift through Moses; but it did not have the status of being the divine eternal wisdom, such as portrayed in Sir 24.[34] The Word has come in the Son who alone was with the Father and can make him known.

One may identify at least two secondary concerns in the prologue. The primary one is the claim about Christ. One secondary concern is John the Baptist. The evangelist portrays John as witness to the Word and wards off claims which would confuse his status with that of the Word. This is very direct. The other secondary concern is, as we have seen, with the Law and by association, the temple, the place of God's presence; but this is only indirectly addressed. It as though the evangelist is saying, as John was sent by God, so the Law was given through Moses. But beyond this, he is explicit in the case of John and allusive in the case of the giving of the Law at Sinai. The effect of this allusion is clearly to contrast the word then and the Word now, not just in content but also in substance: the Word is Jesus, bears the glory of the only Son and makes the Father known. Yet no role is ascribed to the Law at this point. The one role most acknowledge for the Law in the gospel as a whole is that of witness. This suggests a similarity in the way John treats both the Baptist and the Law. However this has not yet emerged in the prologue. The implications of the inferior position of both the Law and of the temple, which the prologue assumes, await further clarification in the text.

John's first concern is with John the Baptist (1:19–35). It is interesting

---

[34] Theobald, *Fleischwerdung*, p. 255., who notes that John's aim is not to show salvation historical fulfilment, but to claim the attributes of wisdom solely for Christ (p. 255). In the same way 1:17 leaves Torah now in a vacuum (pp. 257–258). 1:18 rejects all claims to mystical vision (p. 259).

that in the fourth gospel the encounters between the Baptist and the Jewish authorities (1:19–28) contain no direct polemic against the latter and are concerned solely with John's role. The biblical categories of hope ("the Messiah", "Elijah", "the prophet") and the prophecy of Isa 40:3 are all assumed to have validity. Already the role of the scriptures (and the Law) as prophetic testimony is evident. John is only the forerunner who announces Jesus; he is emphatically denied other roles (so especially 1:20!). The evangelist does not even record an account of the baptism: John has no independent knowledge of Jesus (1:31); he follows instructions, learns from what he is shown at the baptism and testifies accordingly (1:32–34). The focus is, in reality, on Jesus. The scriptures also testify to John the Baptist, who, in turn, testifies to Jesus.

John hails Jesus as "the lamb of God who takes away the sins of the world" (1:29,35). The evangelist does not set this in direct antithesis to the old system of sacrifices, although this may be a secondary implication, especially with regard to cultic sacrifice concerned with sin.[35] The evangelist would probably understand it in the context of the antithesis between the old and the new which we see in the chapters that follow, but this is not made explicit her. John knows traditions like this relating to vicarious atonement, but they are not as central as many assume.[36]

The reference in 1:31 to Israel as the recipient of John's revelation and in 1:47 to Nathanael as a true Israelite underlines a sense of continuity.[37] Philip announces to Nathanael that Jesus is the one "of whom Moses in the Law and the Prophets wrote" (1:45). For the first time we have explicit reference to the Law's role as witness to Jesus. The allusion to Nathanael's sitting under the fig tree has suggested to some, on the basis of later rabbinic texts, that Nathanael is pictured as studying Torah.[38] Dating makes this difficult to sustain. More secure are references to sitting under the fig tree as an ideal

---

[35] On the role of sacrificial imagery, passover typology, and generally the notion of vicarious atonement in John, see Loader, *Christology*, pp. 94–102.

[36] See my discussion in *Christology*, pp. 93–186.

[37] So Hanson, *Prophetic Gospel*, p. 37. J. Steiger, "Nathanael – ein Israelit, an dem kein Falsch ist. Das hermeneutische Phänomen der Intertestamentarizität aufgezeigt an Joh 1,45–51," *BerlinTheolZeit* 9 (1992), pp. 50–73, here: 52–55, points to the influence of Zeph 3:13–15, especially for the description of Nathanael as without guile and for his messianic acclamation. John has Nathanael represent the remnant of Israel of whom Zephaniah spoke.

[38] So Billerbeck, *Kommentar*, II, p. 371; Pancaro, *Law*, p. 304; Hanson, *Prophetic Gospel*, p. 39, who interprets John as implying that through believing in Christ Nathanael will see that Torah witnesses to Jesus. But see the discussion in Kotila, *Zeuge*, p. 100, who makes the point that there is no contemporary evidence for the association.

image of hope for Israel.[39] Significantly, the chapter ends with Jesus' promise that the disciples will be able to see what only Jacob saw (though he saw only the angels, Gen 28:12), when they behold his exaltation in heavenly glory.[40] This universalising of the privilege given to a special person of Israel's history coheres with the promise declared in 1:14–18 that what Moses alone glimpsed, or rather sought to glimpse, may now be seen by all, at least in the form of the glorified Son of Man. The allusion may also be implying that fulfilment of Israel's goal, seeing God, has negative implications for the former cult, especially if John intends an allusion to Bethel as symbolic of the house of God; however this, too, is not made explicit.[41]

The wedding feast at Cana (2:1–12) symbolically presents Jesus as fulfilling Israel's eschatological hope, often represented as a great feast. The words used to introduce it refer to "the third day". This may allude to Jesus' resurrection on the third day; it may also allude to Israel's receiving the gift of the Law on the third day, mentioned twice in Ex 19:10–19 (19:11,16).[42] Jesus performs the miracle by having the servants draw water from six stone jars used for Jewish purification requirements. The evangelist may well intend that we see this act as abolishing such requirements,[43] although this is not explicit. At most it may be implied by the fact that Jesus' act changes the water and leaves none remaining for purification. I think this is likely, especially if the author should intend an allusion to Sinai already in the reference to the dating in 2:1. The requirements would reflect Pharisaic

---

39 Steiger, "Nathanael," pp. 56–57), argues that the reference to Nathanael "under the fig tree" should be read in the context of Israel's hope of peace which envisioned people sitting both under the fig tree and under their grapevines (Mic 4:4; Zech 3:11; cf. also 1 Kgs 5:5; 1 Macc 14:11–12). Accordingly, the promise is only partly fulfilled when Nathanael sits there. The Cana episode, with its imagery of new wine, reveals the total fulfilment in Christ for the people of Israel (pp. 66–67).

40 On 1:50–51 as referring to Jesus' exaltation see W. R. G. Loader, "John 1:50–51 and the 'Greater Things' of Johannine Christology," in *Anfänge der Christologie. Festschrift für Ferdinand Hahn zum 65. Geburtstag*, edited by C. Breytenbach and H. Paulsen, (Göttingen: Vandenhoeck und Ruprecht, 1991), pp. 253–274, here: 257–260.

41 So Hanson, *Prophetic Gospel*, p. 37, who writes: "Jesus is now the place where God is permanently to be found" (p. 37). "The angels are there merely to identify the link with Genesis 28 and to prove that a permanent connection between heaven and earth has now been established in the risen Christ." J. T. Williams, "Cultic Elements in the Fourth Gospel," in *Studia Biblica 1978. II. Papers on the Gospels. Sixth International Congress on Biblical Studies*, edited by E. A. Livingstone, (Sheffield: JSOTPr., 1980), pp. 339–350, here: 344, says 1:51 implies replacement of the temple.

42 So Moloney, *Belief in the Word*, pp. 54–55.

43 So Glasson, *Moses*, p. 88; G. A. Yee, *Jewish Feasts and the Gospel of John*. Zacchaeus Studies: New Testament, (Wilmington: Glazier, 1989), p. 61; Neyrey, *Revolt*, pp. 132, 137–139; Carson, *John*. p. 173. The number, six, may also indicate inferiority.

hand washing scruples.[44] Alternatively, the detail is incidental. In any case it is interesting incidental information, reflective of a conservative Jewish ethos in the tradition. The allusion to the manifestation of Jesus' glory in the sign, 2:11, links back to the affirmation of 1:14d, which in turn, links with the Sinai event of the giving of the Law.[45] It also forms an inclusion with 2:1, another possible allusion to that event. The effect is to strengthen the sense that 2:1–11 is making a statement about Jesus' replacement of the Law. The language of "signs" in John may also allude typologically to the "signs" performed by Moses; they certainly function in John to legitimise Jesus' claims.[46]

The story of Jesus' action in the temple has been transferred from Jesus' last week in Jerusalem to a visit two years earlier (2:13–22). This seems, in part, so that it can function to support the antithetical claim being made for Jesus in relation to the Law, here in relation to the temple. The description of Jesus' action is surprisingly detailed and graphic. 2:16b articulates its meaning: "Do not make my father's house a house of merchandise". This probably alludes to Zech 14:21 and reflects similar concerns in Ezekiel (8:1–18; 9:1–2,6).[47] Jesus' action is directed not primarily against malpractice, but against commercial activity taking place in the temple court.[48] The supporting scripture quotation from Psalm 69:10 reinforces the impression that Jesus is acting out of zeal for the temple as God's house. Similarly the Jews' questioning of Jesus' authority seems to be related to his authority to enforce such a reformist stance.

---

[44] On the use of stone jars to store water for purification see Deines, *Steingefässe*, pp. 247–251, 263–275, who argues that the stone jars indicate a pre-70 tradition and that the purification must be that of hand washing before meals, evidence of a Pharisaic practice of applying priestly purity rules to everyday life.

[45] See Moloney, *Belief in the Word*, p. 57. I am much less certain about Moloney's use of rabbinic tradition about preparation for the gift of the Law in connection with feast of Pentecost. He suggests that John 1:19 – 2:12 reflects the tradition reflected in *Mekhilta* on Exodus, which, in expanding Ex 19:1–2,9–10, indicates the three days of preparation culminating in a fourth, then a further three days, in a way which interpreted the third day of Ex 19:10 as effectively the sixth day of the week. Thus he explains the pattern of three days in 1:19–42, with the fourth, 1:43–51, the day on which Jesus manifests his glory. The third day of 2:1 must then correspond to the final of the subsequent three days. We move in the realm of uncertainty in using the *Mekhilta*, even when we assume it is tannaitic. The explanation of the 2:1 third day, beyond the first three, is obscure.

[46] So Painter, *Quest*, p. 217 n. 15; Pryor, *Covenant*, pp. 119–120.

[47] So B. G. Schuchard, *Scripture within Scripture. The Interrelationship of Form and Function in the Explicit Old Testament Citations in the Gospel of John*, SBLDissSer 133, (Atlanta: Scholars, 1992), p. 25.

[48] Schuchard, *Scripture*, p.25, makes a link between Jesus' entering the temple. his

But from this point the narrative changes focus. The evangelist gives Jesus' prediction of the temple's destruction in the form: "Destroy this sanctuary and in three days I will raise it up" (2:19). This leads to a typically Johannine narrative use of misunderstanding on the part of the Jews. They think he is referring to the temple. Instead, the evangelist explains, he meant his own body. Either the evangelist is somewhat artificially leaving the temple scene to make use of temple imagery to have Jesus announce his coming death and resurrection without any real link between the two; or the evangelist wants the reader to see Jesus himself as God's sanctuary, and, by implication, as the replacement of the old temple. The latter is more likely and would echo the image of Jesus as the tent of the Word (1:14) and the true place of worship (if that lies behind 1:51).

Nevertheless 2:13–18 still reads as though Jesus had been primarily intent on reform and as though his attempts to do so would lead to his death. Perhaps the reference to their destroying the temple ("You destroy the temple..") alludes to the debacle of 70 CE. But it is not now the focus of the evangelist. The shift from the old temple to Jesus as God's sanctuary seems to imply replacement of the former by the latter and this, we shall see, finds confirmation elsewhere in the gospel. The other side of this is that, unless we see the evangelist simply making a traditional narrative the base for a more high flowing concept or conversation and leaving the original story incomplete or up in the air, we must assume that he could envisage Jesus as having had concern for the temple. This implies that John knows and respects the tradition about the temple,[49] but sees the temple replaced through the event of Jesus' death and resurrection, the "greater event" to which John has pointed forward already in 1:51 (see also 14:12).[50] Before that event he can have Jesus express concern about the Jerusalem temple. Significantly the "greater event" makes possible the understanding both of Jesus' words and of the scripture. The scripture is understood as testifying to Christ.

In John 3 the evangelist uses the encounter between Jesus and Nicodemus to contrast two approaches. One focuses on the material and physical; the other on the spiritual. The evangelist presses the contrast to the point of comedy or ridiculing irony. He has Nicodemus answer at the literal level

---

going to prepare places for his own (14:2) and his death as a passover sacrifice to end the sacrificial cultus (pp. 28–29). I am hesitant to read so much into the text.

[49] Cf. Yee, *Jewish Feasts*, p. 62, who suggests that attacking trade is attacking whole system, "fundamental opposition to the temple itself". The person of Jesus supersedes the old temple; the Father dwells not in the Holy of Holies but in Jesus (14:10; p. 62). But this does not adequately explain the reformist stance in the first part of the episode.

[50] On the significance of the cluster of events associated with Jesus' death as a major turning point in John, see Loader, *Christology*, pp. 93–134.

about being born a second time. Nicodemus, who is portrayed as representative of the teachers of the Jews (3:10), is hopelessly blind. He will not see the kingdom of God without being born from above (3:3). The evangelist understands the latter to include faith in Jesus and baptism (so 3:5). There is no meeting between the two, except in Nicodemus' recognition that Jesus must be from God; but even then Jesus is 'on another planet'. "That which is born of flesh is flesh; that which is born of the Spirit is Spirit" (3:6).

The passage is typically Johannine. It is a claim to represent what Nicodemus should know, that is, a claim to represent the interests and concerns of the Jewish religious tradition. Yet it makes this claim on the basis of a dualism which appears to deny any continuity. This dualism effectively disqualifies Nicodemus and his religious concerns as having to do only with the physical and temporal. While this is not spelled out specifically, it is implied in the contrast between the two realms: "above", "of the Spirit" and "below", "of the flesh".

3:13 develops a further dualism which contrasts Jesus' ascent and exaltation with all others who may claim to have ascended, but have not. The contrast is similar to 1:18 where it belonged to a contrast with the Sinai revelation. There it focused on Jesus' being as Son and his glory. Here, as there, it appears to counter not only the general claims of Jewish visionaries and ecstatics, but, in particular that Moses made such an ascent. By implication such a denial also undermines the status people would give to the Mosaic Law on the basis of this claim. Probably this is also in view here.

Here it focuses on what Jesus achieved through his ascent. The mention of Moses' lifting up a serpent in the wilderness (3:14–15) remains at the level of neutral analogy, affirming, at most, continuity between God's activity in Jesus and his activity in Israel's history. The author is concerned to highlight the gift of life which the Son of Man's exaltation will make possible. The implication is that the Law could not offer life, because this has been achieved only through Jesus. But this is only an indirect implication, for by 3:14–15 John has left behind the concern to diminish Judaism's claims and has moved on to make positive claims about Jesus.

Perhaps the evangelist also intends the reference in 3:25 about a dispute between a Jew and the disciples of John the Baptist about purification to contrast the new Christian purification and Jewish purification. Already 3:5 had indicated that John's Christianity still has room for a rite of purification, baptism; 4:1–3 reinforces this. 3:25 is important in providing such evidence. The verses which follow relate the dispute to Jesus' baptising activity. The author has not espoused a dualism of a kind that disparages all such symbolic or sacramental actions. This means that where such a dualism appears to operate, such as earlier in ch 3, it is with some qualification.

Jesus' meeting with the Samaritan woman (4:4–42) takes into account both Jewish scruples about sharing vessels in common with Samaritans and about conversing publicly with women, and the conflict between the Jews and the Samaritans over the claims of the latter for Mt Gerizim.[51] Jesus is prepared to override the Jewish scruples. His authority supersedes such concerns, though the question of their validity is not directly addressed. They are also not portrayed as practices which are divinely sanctioned, but as Jewish scruples. The explanation in 4:9 that Jews do not use the same vessels as Samaritans, or perhaps, do not have dealings with Samaritans, reflects a conservative Jewish stance and coheres with the conservatism of the purification practices behind 2:6.[52] The standpoint of the author is beyond such claims. In typically Johannine fashion what may well have begun as an anecdote displaying Jesus' willingness to sit lightly to such demands, now functions as a symbolic narrative where the real issue transcends the focus of the literal story, but is made to intersect with it. In the clever interplay between the two levels of meaning, the author has Jesus offer living water to a woman from whom he sought a drink, and who remains concerned with water only at that level.

The language used by John's Jesus, "the gift of God", "living water", is reminiscent of language used of Torah.[53] What Judaism claimed for Torah, John claims for Jesus, but there is no explicit hint that John is directly

---

[51] I do not see an allusion to the Pentateuch in the mention of the woman's five husbands. Cf. F. Wessel, "Die fünf Männer der Samaritanerin. Jesus und die Tora nach Joh 4,16–19," *BibNotiz* 68 (1993), pp. 26–34, here: 29–31, who argues that the five husbands are the five books of the Samaritan Pentateuch and that in 4:10 John is expressing the view that, had the Samaritans understood Torah, they would come to Jesus. This husband, the Torah, could have given her living water (p. 32). He then argues that the one who is not her husband is Jesus (p. 33). Jesus brings living water to those who do not have access to it because they are outside of Israel (p. 33). John is not concerned with Law observant Jews who already have the water in Torah (p. 34). The latter comment cannot be sustained, but also the claim that Jesus makes a self reference in the one who is not her husband (4:18).

[52] For the translation of συνχρῶνται as "use in common" or "have dealings with", see Daube, *Rabbinic Judaism*, pp. 373–382 (for the former) and Schnackenburg, *John I*, pp. 425 n. 19 (for the latter).

[53] For the Old Testament background to the image of the well see Gen 33:19 and 48:12, but also Nu 21:17–18, which is interpreted as Torah in CD 6:7. With regard to the imagery of living water associated with Torah, Hanson, *Prophetic Gospel*, pp. 60–62, speaks of an embarrassment of riches, but singles out three texts in particular: Ps 36:10a; Prov 18:4 and Isa 12. See also Barrett, *John*, pp. 233–234.

countering Torah or the status given to it. Rather the focus is positively on what Jesus offers. The stance is that of the prologue, where, similarly, language used of Torah is applied to Jesus. Yet there is a keen sense of linkage with Jewish heritage in the passage, not least in the ironic allusion to Jesus as greater than Jacob. Jesus is greater than Jacob and transcends Jewish religious tradition.[54]

The transcending of Jewish tradition, while at the same time retaining strong Jewish links, is most evident in the discussion on the matter of legitimate places of worship. The evangelist has Jesus predict that worship will be neither at Jerusalem nor at Gerizim (4:21). Both sites are obsolete, yet the author is careful not to treat both at the same level and, therefore, immediately has Jesus qualify his remarks. The effect is to uphold the legitimacy of worship at Jerusalem[55] and to imply that worship at Gerizim is based on ignorance and, therefore, error. In having Jesus add that salvation is of the Jews (4:22), the author makes it very clear that he intends his portrait of Jesus to be seen as fulfilling and transcending Jewish tradition. He will go on to spell this out in terms of messianic expectation and show that through Christ this salvation becomes available for all the world (4:42).[56] He is not interested in a similar link with Samaritan tradition, though its related hopes are also shown as finding their fulfilment in Jesus. The claim gives Jewish

---

[54] Cf. Glasson, *Moses*, p. 89, who saw a contrast between Jacob's well as static and the new spiritual life Christ offers, just as Christ replaces the temple (p. 89).

[55] So D. A. Lee, *The Symbolic Narratives of the Fourth Gospel. The Interplay of Form and Meaning*, JSNTSS 95, (Sheffield: JSOT Pr., 1994), p. 80. I am less happy with her claim that John offers not a spiritualising, but a symbolic alternative (p. 82), since this does not give sufficient weight to the underlying dualism which also determines the value system.

[56] E. Leidig, *Jesu Gespräch mit der Samaritanerin und weitere Gespräche im Johannesevangelium*, Theol. Diss. 15, (Basel: Reinhardt, 1979), pp. 103–133, argues that 4:22 should be understood christologically, as a reference to the messiah who comes from Judah and points to its echo in 19:3 and 19:19 (p. 121) and the immediate context where messiahship is in focus (4:25–26; p. 123). According to Leidig, the focus of 4:22 in its context is that the Jewish messiah is for all people (4:42; p. 125). The Jews are bearers of the promise (p. 126). Jesus represents the point in salvation history when all barriers are dropped (p. 129). Salvation ceases to be by joining the Jewish religion, but is accessible only through faith in Jesus (p. 129). Thus the christological also includes a salvation historical perspective (pp. 129–130). Torah promises but does not provide salvation (p. 130). John's christology transposes the most important salvation historical concepts. Jesus takes the place of the Law; it remains as testimony to him. Jesus stands above Abraham and allows the claim to election of the descendants of Abraham only for those who do the works of Abraham. Now disciples are the elect. Abraham, like Moses, is a witness for Jesus. Eternal life was never possible under the Law; it is possible only through Jesus. Sacrifice has been replaced by Jesus as Passover lamb. The temple is replaced by Jesus.

religious tradition the status it already assumes in the prologue: the Law was given by God.[57]

The following verse expounds the point made in the prediction of 4:21. It has Jesus announce fulfilment of what in Johannine theology becomes a reality after Jesus' death and return to the Father and his giving of the Spirit: "The time is coming and now is, when the true worshippers will worship the Father in spirit and in truth" (4:23). This is grounded not only by reference to a new time, but also, more substantially, by a theology: "God is spirit and they who worship him must do so in spirit and in truth" (4:24). The evangelist is having Jesus justify the abandonment of worship which is localised to particular sanctuary sites. It may be an argument for abandonment of such sites altogether and be anti-temple and anti-cult, though need not be. If it were anti-cult and anti-temple, it would stand in tension with Jesus' zeal for reforming the temple in 2:14–17. The use of "spirit" here refers clearly to spiritual as against material, but the frequency with which the evangelist associates the sphere of the spiritual with the activity of the Spirit suggests that the evangelist would primarily have the worship of the Christian community in mind here. The dualism implied is the same as what we found in 3:1–11 in the contrast between being born of the Spirit, from above, and being born of the flesh, from below. It is not absolute in the sense of totally disparaging what is "from below" or "of the flesh". It assumes that the Jerusalem temple has validity, though existing at the lower level of reality.

The healing of the official's son has no direct bearing on our theme. Unlike its equivalents in Matthew and Luke, it does not mention that the officer is a Gentile. At most it illustrates the life giving power of the one who has made such claims for himself and, like all miracles in John, serves to confirm that he is who he claims to be.

Thus far the effect of the prologue has been to make claims for Jesus which, at least, relativise all previous claims to revelation, "words of God". The evangelist's use of typology in 1:14–18 and the strong denial in 1:18 reinforce the claim. Accordingly, the Law has divine origin, but can have only a minimal role since the coming of the Word. While the prologue does not specify this role, the material which follows indicates that it includes a prophetic predictive role as testimony to Christ. John's use of typology in

---

[57] F. Hahn, "'Das Heil kommt von den Juden.' Erwägungen zu Joh 4,22b," in *Wort und Wirklichkeit. Festschrift für E. L. Rapp*, Band I, (Weisenheim, 1976), pp. 67–84, here: pp. 82–83, argues that 4:22b is genuinely Johannine and reflects the fact that John sees in the Jewish scriptures the witness to Jesus.

the allusions to Moses in the prologue and to Jacob in 1:51 (cf. also 4:12) show that he sees God as having been active in Israel's history. That includes also acknowledging the validity of the institution of the temple and Jerusalem (2:13–17; 4:22), in contrast to Gerizim of the Samaritans. Some other rather conservative practices are mentioned incidentally, but without indication that such validity applied also to them (so purification rites in 2:6 and laws governing relations with Samaritans in 4:9).

The superiority of the Word rests on a combination of factors: the being of the Son who alone is capable of giving the revelation which Moses and others had sought; the aspect of timing, the new replacing the old; and the dualism which implies that the old belonged to a lower category of reality, the sphere of "the flesh", "from below". Movement from one to the other, which in John is related to entering and seeing the kingdom, means being born at the new level of reality. In this new level of reality symbols once applied to Torah (word, light, life, water) have been transferred exclusively to Christ; they are denied to Torah. Thus, while John has some sense of salvation history, Torah is not an expression of the Logos, let alone identified with Logos or Wisdom. Nevertheless it was given by God and its institutions in that sense had interim validity; they offered a form of worship at the inferior level of reality.

There is therefore a heavily qualified sense of continuity which is at base theological: God gave the Law. But beyond that, the focus is the radical discontinuity implied in the dualism and centred in the nature of the Son. Therefore typology both establishes links with patterns of the past and transcends those patterns. In claiming the risen Christ as the new temple, the exalted Christ as the place of worship, the dying Christ as the lamb of God, the gift of Christ as the new wine and the living water, the event of Christ as the new Sinai, the contrast is not good and better, but one level of reality and another of a totally different order. The link between the two is that the Law and the scriptures predict the new reality. But even the predictions, which, as messianic, appear to presuppose the same level of reality, in fact, point beyond it.

Read in the context of these chapters, χάριν ἀντὶ χάριτος, "grace instead of grace" (1:16) appears to mean a new gift of God's grace replacing a previous one which was less adequate; "grace and truth", access to the divine reality, was not really accessible under the Law.

5.3 John 5–12 in Review

John 5 begins with the healing of a lame man (1–9), followed by controversy over the fact that the man carried his pallet on the sabbath as Jesus had instructed him (cf. Jer 17:21–22).[58] This finally becomes a confrontation of Jesus by the Jews because he did such things on the sabbath (9b–16). Jesus' response amounts to a claim to share God's work and therefore God's authority (5:17). The link with the sabbath derives from the contemporary understanding that God's work of sustaining the creation continues after his creation in six days and continues even on the sabbath (Gen 2:2–3; Ex 20:11; 31:17). The argument is christological: Jesus' association with his Father legitimises also his continuing work on the sabbath.

There is no attempt here to justify Jesus' activity in terms of sabbath law, but rather a claim that he is beyond sabbath law, as God is beyond sabbath law.[59] The Jews accuse Jesus of being in the habit of breaking sabbath law (5:18).[60] John implicitly rejects this as based on a misunderstanding about Jesus' person. This, then, leaves the question open, for the moment, whether mortals should continue to observe sabbath law.[61] John will return to the theme of sabbath law in 7:19–25. Here chapter 5 he is more concerned to make direct claims about Jesus[62] and to ward off the implication of blasphemy in Jesus' claims. For in 5:18 John shows that Jesus' claim in 5:17 to higher

---

[58] Glasson, *Moses*, p. 89, notes the suggestion of Augustine (*Exposition of Psalms* 70.20), that the five porches at the pool of Bethesda represent the Torah. As with the mention of the five husbands of the Samaritan woman it is difficult to verify or falsify.

[59] Lee, *Symbolic Narratives*, p. 124, argues that for John "the sabbath stands for Torah, as represented by Moses".

[60] So Pancaro, *Law*, pp. 45–47; Painter, *Quest*, p. 223. Cf. Kotila, *Zeuge*, pp. 20–21, who argues that ἔλυεν in 5:18 means not habitually break, but abolish. Both the context and the imperfect speak rather for a reference to the former.

[61] Lee, *Symbolic Narratives*, p. 112, makes the point that "Jesus' action in breaking the Sabbath challenges their religious understanding. For the evangelist, the Law in their hands has become life-denying, an obstacle in the way of life." "On the symbolic level, however, Jesus' breach of the Sabbath signifies that the work he is doing is the work of God, who goes on giving life and judging even on the Sabbath." She argues that John is showing "that the 'Jewish' understanding of the Law is distorted" (p. 124). "For the evangelist, the life-giving properties of the Torah belong in Jesus, to whom the Law points" (p. 124). "The Torah acts like a Johannine 'sign' or image, the meaning of which is to be found in symbolic relation to Jesus....Unless it is apprehended symbolically of Jesus as the giver of life, however, the Law itself is distorted and misunderstood, and ultimately rejected" (p. 120). "The Fourth Evangelist does not reject the Law, but rather reinterprets it as a symbol for 'grace and truth through Jesus Christ'" (p. 125).

[62] Pancaro, *Law*, pp. 15–16; J. Ashton, *Understanding the Fourth Gospel*, (Oxford: Clarendon, 1991), p. 139; Painter, *Quest*, pp. 225–226.

authority has been misunderstood as a claim to be equal with God. The following verses expound the claim, defending it against this misunderstanding by emphasising that the Son's unique relationship with the Father is one that involves his total subordination and obedience. That is the basis of the equality in word and deed.

Within Jesus' discourse, 5:19–47, the evangelist is making a number of claims which are of indirect relevance for assessing attitude towards Torah. 5:19–20 express in different terms the claims made in 1:14–18: the Son sees the Father and does what he sees the Father doing. This will find its echo in 5:37: the Jews have never heard God's voice or seen his form. According to 1:18 only the Son has seen the Father. This also sets his authority far above that of Moses and the Law given through him. The Son's authoritative acts extend to the day of judgement, when he will judge and raise the dead (5:21–22). John does not imply that judgement will be in accordance with Torah. According to 3:18–21 judgement will in accordance with response to Jesus; this should also be assumed here. 5:24–29 shows that this authority is to be exercised both in the present and at the eschaton.

5:36–37 contrasts the strength of evidence supporting Jesus and John. Both Jesus' works and God, himself, provide evidence for Jesus' claims. As the following verses show, the assumption is that, had the Jews heard God's word, heeded the scriptures, they would have understood that God legitimated Jesus. Instead, the Jews, "because they think that in them they have eternal life" (5:39), have all along missed the point of the scriptures. The point of the scriptures is, for John, to bear testimony to Jesus. This is an important statement also about the status of the Law, which is part of the scriptures. John denies it gives life; rather its role is to testify to Christ. The denial in 5:37b that the Jews had ever heard God's word or seen his form totally disqualifies them, but in two different ways. They should have heard God's word; they could never see God's form.[63]

In 5:41–44 John relates the failure to hear God's word, and so to hear God's endorsement of Jesus, to a failure to keep the first commandment: to love God. He also relates it to a failure to locate the right source of glory. Here glory is more than praise; it refers to something brought by other envoys who are preferred above Jesus and so must allude to divine revelation. Only Jesus manifests the glory of God. Quite possibly John has in mind the same 'competitors' as those against whom he has directed 1:18, 3:13 and 6:46.

---

[63] According to Hanson, *Prophetic Gospel*, pp. 81–83, the reference is to seeing the Word on Sinai. In this sense Moses and the scriptures testify to Jesus. This is doubtful. John seems rather to indicate a prophetic predictive role of the Law and the Prophets as in 1:45.

The image of glory again recalls 1:14. In alluding to "the only God", 5:44 strengthens the impression that in the words "the love of God" in 5:41 John has the first commandment in mind.[64]

5:45–47 returns to the point being made in 5:39. Moses, understood as author of the Law, is the Jews' accuser before the Father because they have failed to heed his endorsement of Jesus.[65] Again John acknowledges the Jews' positive regard for the Law ("in whom you have put your hope" 5:45), but declares that the Jews have failed to recognise that the hope which Moses promised has been fulfilled in Jesus. It also implies that to set one's hope in the Law apart from in its testimony to Jesus equates to the mistaken belief that the Law offers eternal life, a view John has rejected in 5:39.

It is important to recognise that many of the themes of 1:14–18 find their echo in 5:36–47. Both are concerned with Jesus' special status in relation to Moses and the Law and in relation to John the Baptist. Both define the role of the Law (the scriptures, Moses) and of John as testimony to Jesus. Both refuse to the Law and to John a life giving role.

In chapter 6 the Johannine accounts of the feeding of the five thousand and of Jesus' walking on the water echo Old Testament motifs, as do their synoptic counterparts. These echoes include typological allusions to the manna in the wilderness and to the crossing of the sea.[66] In John's account there seems also to be an allusion to Elisha's miraculous feeding, especially in the allusion to the lad with the barley loaves (6:9; cf. 2 Kgs 4:42–43). It is not my purpose to pursue the detail of such allusions here, since they are well documented. Like 1:51 and 3:14–15, they assume a status for the stories

---

[64] J. Beutler, "Das Hauptgebot im Johannesevangelium," in *Das Gesetz im Neuen Testament* QD 108, edited by K. Kertelge, (Freiburg: Herder, 1986), pp. 222–236, here: 227–228, shows that, when read in the light of reference to "God alone" in 5:44, "love of God" in 5:42 should be seen as an allusion to the great commandment of Deut 6:4 to love God. An allusion also lies behind 8:41–42 (pp. 229–231).

[65] Kotila, *Zeuge*, pp. 26–28, argues that 5:45 refers to the role not of Moses as a person, but of the Law as scripture in condemning Israel's unbelief, and not to the last judgement, but to the time since Jesus' exaltation. However the future perspective, expressed in, "Do not think that I shall accuse you", suggests rather that John is thinking of Moses as accuser in contrast to the common Jewish hope in Moses as intercessor (cf. Test Mos 11:17). So R. Schnackenburg, *Das Johannesevangelium. II. Teil. Kommentar zu Kap. 5-12*, HTKNT IV/2 (Freiburg: Herder, 2nd edn., 1977), pp. 180–182; Carson, *John*, pp. 265–266. The connection between Moses and the Law given through Moses is fundamental to the argument, as 5:46 shows.

[66] Yee, *Jewish Feasts*, p. 64, infers a polemical purpose already in the narratives themselves. Jesus replaces Moses: he ascends mountain (6:3; cf. Ex 19:3,20; 24:12–13); the disciples' question (6:5) echoes the question of Moses in Nu 11:13 (p. 64). I am hesitant to posit such polemic here.

and imply their symbolic use. In the case of the feeding, the symbolic use comes directly to expression in the discourse which follows. Here we find not only claims for Jesus, but also further clarification of the relation between these claims and the claims of Torah. The crossing does not receive such attention; but its action puts Jesus on the side of God; many also hear Jesus' self identification, ἐγώ εἰμι, ("It is I", "It's me", 6:20) as a deliberate echo of Yahweh's "I am".[67]

Jesus scolds the crowds because they fail to recognise Jesus' signs (6:26). Instead they remain at the level of satisfaction of their physical needs. The dual level recalls the conversation with Nicodemus in chapter 3 and with the Samaritan woman and later with the disciples in the same episode in chapter 4. There is the same element of absurdity. For in their blindness the crowds seek a sign, such as had occurred in the gift of the manna in the wilderness! What had Jesus just done, but give such a sign (6:30–31)! John has Jesus respond with the words, "Moses did not give you bread from heaven, but my Father gives the true bread from heaven" (6:32). The second half of the statement is a clear claim about Jesus and makes his miracle a sign of spiritual nourishment. The first half of the statement denies that Moses gave such nourishment. What is really being denied? Given the widespread use of the symbol of bread and nourishment for the Torah (cf. already Prov 9:5; Deut 8:3),[68] the statement seems to be denying that in giving the Law Moses provided the nourishment that brings life.[69] John appears to use the fact that the wilderness generation died in the wilderness as corroboratory evidence of this (6:49).[70] Assuming coherence with what has preceded, 6:32 should not be seen as an absolute denial of any value at all in what Moses gave.[71] The point is that it is not the nourishment which people have claimed it to be by associating it with the manna. Like the scriptures, it is not the source of eternal life except in so far as it points to Christ (as 7:39).[72] The imagery of

---

[67] See Schnackenburg, *Johannesevangelium II*, pp. 59–70; Brown, *John*, pp. 533–538. With Barrett, *John*, p. 281, and Carson, *John*, pp. 275–276, I do not see here a use of the self identification formula of Yahweh. See also my discussion in Loader, *Christology*, pp. 166–167, 45.

[68] See P. Borgen, *Bread from Heaven. An Exegetical Study of the Concept of Manna in the Gospel of John and the Writings of Philo*, SuppNovT X, (Leiden: Brill, 1965), pp. 148–158; Billerbeck, *Kommentar II*, p. 485; R. Schnackenburg, *Johannesevangelium, IV. Teil. Ergänzende Auslegungen und Exkurse*, HTKNT IV/4, (Freiburg: Herder, 1984), pp. 121–131, who argues for a background in mystical Judaism reflected in Joseph and Asenath.

[69] So Barrett, *John*, pp. 289–290; Carson, *John*, p. 286.

[70] So Kotila, *Zeuge*, p. 177.

[71] Cf. Kotila, *Zeuge*, pp. 170–171, who argues that in 6:32–32 the redactor is denying the heavenly origin of the Mosaic Law.

[72] Cf. Hanson, *Prophetic Gospel*, pp. 84–85, who suggests that John understood scripture

water and bread in 6:35 is imagery associated with Torah and the claim to be bread from God is a claim to be all that Torah had been claimed to be and more.

In 6:41 the typology extends to the echoes of Israel's grumbling in the wilderness. In the same way Jesus' hearers refuse to believe him. An allusion to divine instruction, such as Torah was understood to be, is present in the use of the Isaianic prophecy in 6:45. In the new age people will be themselves taught of God (cf. Isa 54:13; Jer 31:33–34). Here it refers primarily to people being drawn to Jesus on the basis of what they have learned from God. Probably John has in mind that this learning will be through the scriptures in their function as witness to Jesus. The reference is not to a new or renewed Torah. Significantly, in this context the evangelist has Jesus repeat the claim that only the Son has seen the Father (6:46). In other words Jesus is presented as alone the one to whom one should turn. The Torah merely points beyond itself to him.[73] We are not, therefore, dealing with internalised Torah.

The wider context, especially 6:47–50, shows that life comes through knowing the truth of who Jesus is and believing in him. This includes participating in the eucharistic representation of who he is (6:51–58). In this context John includes a reference to Jesus' vicarious death, but without setting it in relation to the Law and the cult. John 6:60–66 indicates that this was too much for some of his disciples to take. They, too, like the unbelieving Jews, echo the murmuring of unbelieving Israel in the wilderness (6:61; cf. 6:41). In the context "this word" (6:60) refers to what directly precedes and must include what Jesus claims for himself as the true nourishment which will bring life. 6:62 presages even greater offence which will be caused by Jesus' death and exaltation. 6:63 identifies what is at stake: two value systems. "The Spirit gives life; the flesh is of no profit. The words which I have spoken are spirit and life." We might expect also the other side of the contrast, but it is nevertheless implied: "The Law does not bring life".[74] The claim divides the community. The issue is a claim about words, about which is the word of life.[75] Accordingly Peter confesses: "Lord, to whom shall we go? You have the words of eternal life; and we have believed and come to know that you are the Holy One of God" (6:68–69).

---

to mean that the Word gave the manna. But the giver in the text is the Father, not the Word.

[73] On the allusion here to Sinai see Borgen, *Bread from Heaven*, pp. 153–154.

[74] On 6:63 Barrett, *John*, p. 305, writes: "Jesus supersedes Torah as the source of life." I think the contrast is even more exclusive than that.

[75] It misses the point of the following context to see the issue as concerned with sacramentalism. See the criticism in Brown, *John*, pp. 299–300.

Nothing suggests that with "Holy One of God" John means to portray
Jesus as a high priest, which would be very significant for our theme. But
even in general terms, the designation has the effect of identifying Jesus as
the centre of all worship of God. Perhaps not only the high christology but
also the exclusive claim to offer nourishment, with its implied demotion of
the Law's significance, had caused a split within the Johannine community.
If so, John's account reflects an aspect of his community's history. More
significant, chapter 6 confirms the findings from chapter 5. John is concerned
to underline that Jesus and only Jesus is the source of life. The Law does not
bring life; it bears witness to the life. In that sense only Jesus' words are
spirit and life. The Law belongs at a different level of reality. From that
level of reality it offers testimony and provides stories of God's involvement
in Israel's history which typologically point to the reality Jesus brings.

John 7 shows Jesus going secretly to Jerusalem for the Feast of the
Tabernacles.[76] This is contrast to the advice of his brothers who thought he
should go up to the festival to demonstrate his works and so promote his
cause (7:3–4). John disparages their approach and one of unbelievers. Jesus
adopts an alternative strategy. It is still not primarily to observe the festival.

---

[76] G. J. Brooke, "Christ and the Law in John 7–10," in *Law and Religion. Essays on
the Place of the Law in Israel and Early Christianity*, edited by B. Lindars, (Cambridge:
Clarke, 1988), pp. 102–112, here: 103, sees John 7–10 held together by its treatment of
Jesus in relation to the decalogue. He notes references to the decalogue in 7:19 and 9:16
(to the sabbath commandment, Ex 20:8; Deut 5:12), in 8:49 to honouring parents in Jesus'
words, "I honour my father" (Ex 20:12; Deut 5:16) and in 10:33 to the command not to
make an idol (the accusation that Jesus makes himself a god, Ex 20:4; Deut 5:8; pp. 103–
105). He also finds allusions to others: the command not to kill in 7:19 (see also 7:1,20,
25; 8:37,40), that John's defence of Jesus' behaviour on the sabbath in ch 5 and 9 is related
to God's work of creation. He also sees allusions in 10:1, 8 to the commandment prohibiting
theft and in 8:13 to bearing false witness (p. 106). In 8:41,44 he finds an allusion to the
prohibition of adultery (p. 107) and in 10:22–39 allusions to the first and third
commandments. He concludes: "It thus seems to be the case that the first three
commandments, those concerning God, are associated with the material concerning the
Feast of Dedication, whilst the last seven, those concerning humanity, are connected with
the feast of the Tabernacles. The structure of John 7–10 thus represents in reverse the
structure of the decalogue itself; this would seem to be deliberate" (p. 108).
As additional support Brooke cites the similar use of five commandments in ch. 5, the
use of Moses and Exodus material, and the use of septuagintal terms associated with the
giving of the Law. In addition he cites the use of the feasts in John, of "I am" as reflecting
the introduction of the decalogue, and the association of wisdom with Torah (pp. 108–
109). He also argues that Palestinian lectionary readings may have already included Deut
5–6 for the Feast of the Tabernacles (p. 109). Christian concern with the decalogue may
have led to its lack of use in rabbinic Judaism (p. 109). He also cites possible influence
from the Samaritan Pentateuch. He sees John 7–10 reflecting both Christian catachesis
and apologia. He concludes that interpretation of the decalogue played a significant role

Instead Jesus arrives half way through the festival in the temple and teaches (7:5–14). What follows in 7:16–18 seems to be an extension of the discourse of 5:18–47; the link with chapter 5 is even more striking in 7:19–24, which allude to the healing of the lame man during Jesus' previous visit. In the present state of the text we are to assume the issue is still alive in Jerusalem. It is important for our theme because it returns to the issue of the Law.

In 7:19 Jesus declares: "Did not Moses give you the Law? Yet none of you keeps the Law. Why are you trying to kill me?" The question implies acceptance of the premise that Moses gave the Law. In 7:19 general disobedience towards the Law may be in mind, although the lawlessness of wanting to kill Jesus may be the chief concern. For John, the decalogue command not to commit murder doubtless still has validity, at least as an ethical principle. The threat of death had already been Jesus' concern in 7:6–7 and recalls 5:17. There John had reported that the Jews sought to kill Jesus, in part, because he kept violating the sabbath. Thus, it is no surprise, when after the crowd's rebuff, suggesting Jesus was mad (had a demon, 7:20), Jesus returns to the sabbath issue.

Jesus seeks to expose the opposition by appeal to the practice of circumcision on the sabbath (7:22–24). He argues by analogy that making a person whole on the sabbath is justified since circumcision is justified on the sabbath on the ground that it makes part of a person whole. The argument is carried out on the basis of Jewish presuppositions (cf. *tShabb* 15,16; *bYoma* 85b; *mShabb* 18:3; 19:2–3; *mNed* 3:11).[77] Did John believe that Jesus shared such presuppositions or was he just using them to expose the injustice of their argument. The answer to that question is not clear from the immediate context. I suspect that the answer is that he did not share them. This would probably mean that the Johannine community did not practice circumcision, although it need not. The unproblematic character of the references in John to Gentile inclusion counts in favour of non observance.

The initial response of Jesus states: "Did not Moses give you the Law?" (7:19). The way the question is put may imply that Jesus does not include himself among the recipients of the Law; alternatively, the "you" may reflect

---

in the Johannine community. The issue should certainly be taken into account, but the allusions are scattered and frequently not central in their context, so that the argument as a whole is too forced.

[77] So Pancaro, *Law*, pp. 163–164; Kotila, *Zeuge*, p. 41; also Barrett, *John*, p. 320. See also J. D. M. Derrett, "Circumcision and Perfection: a Johannine Equation (John 7:22–23)," *EvangQuart* 63 (1991), pp. 211–224, here: 217–222, who argues that John is depending on a pun about perfecting a person, based on the Aramaic אשׁלם which "puts circumcision and the miracle into the same class, the perfecting of the man."

the fact that Jesus is confronting them as a group. The same issue arises with the use of "you" in 7:22, "Moses gave you circumcision – though it was not from Moses but from the fathers". In the light of the rest of the gospel I am inclined to the view that the debate over sabbath law reflects the stance of an outsider exposing inconsistencies, rather than a serious discussion of its application.[78]

In portraying Jesus' offer of thirst quenching water on the last day of the feast of Tabernacles (7:37–38), the evangelist shows himself well informed about festival rites. For on this day water plays a significant role in the ritual.[79] In 8:12 ("I am the light of the world") John again uses imagery of the feast. Jesus' offer of water recalls traditional imagery used of Torah. He also depicts his promise about water as fulfilment of prophecy.[80] John portrays Jesus as the source of the water of life in the way that Ezekiel had prophesied that from the temple streams of water would flow (Ezek 47). It is typically Johannine to apply symbols associated with Torah (and temple as part of Torah) to Jesus. As we have already seen, in doing so John makes an exclusive claim, not an inclusive one which would allow that the Law either now or in the past warranted such images. In addition, the passage appears to reinforce the claim that Jesus replaces the temple. He is the new temple.

In using the imagery of the feast (water and light), John is not attempting to reinterpret the feast in a way which retains its integrity, for instance, by offering a new way of celebrating it. Rather he has Jesus claim to offer in truth what the feast could only symbolise at a material level. Therefore just as the temple had its validity, so did its feasts; but it and they were not at the level of the Spirit. They could not bring life. Now that the true temple has been established, the feasts are obsolete; their function, to portray what was

---

[78] So Brown, *John*, p. 312.

[79] For links with the Feast of the Tabernacles see *mSukk* 4. Every morning water drawn from Siloam was taken in procession to the temple; every evening lamps were lit in the court of the women. On the last day the priests go through Water Gate and encircle altar seven times with waters from the pool Siloam for libation. See Yee, *Jewish Feasts*, pp. 79–80.

[80] On the scripture reference, see Hanson, *Prophetic Gospel*, pp. 109–112. He mentions Nu 20:11, the rock in the wilderness, as 1 Cor 10:4 (pp. 109–110). He suggests secondary influence also from Nu 21:16–18, the well dug by the princes of Israel, used in Qumran (p. 110). If the αὐτοῦ ("his") refers to the believer then there are other possibilities: Prov 18:4 and also Isa 48:21–22 and 58:11. If it refers to Christ, as Hanson believes, then the obvious background is Ezek 47 (p. 111). John is presenting Jesus as the new temple. See also: Zech 14:8 (living waters flowing from Jerusalem). Hanson also mentions Ps 40:9b: "you law within my heart" (pp. 111–112). See also Schnackenburg, *Johannesevangelium II*, pp. 211–217; Carson, *John*, pp. 321–328.

to come, has been fulfilled. The passage illustrates, therefore, two different ways in which scripture bears testimony: through its words and through the institutions it established.

In the Jewish leaders' debriefing of their attendants, the Pharisees deplore the failure to arrest Jesus and declare the crowd as ignorant of the Law and accursed (7:49). This provokes the response from Nicodemus that the Law does not condemn people without a hearing (7:51).[81] These comments are designed more to expose the Pharisees than to make a positive claim for the written Law. They also recall Jesus' claim in 7:19 that the Jews do not even keep the Law given them.[82]

As already noted, Jesus' claim to be the light of the world in 8:12 reflects a further aspect of the liturgy of the last day of the Feast of the Tabernacles.[83] It, too, is frequent Torah imagery, as is the language of walking in the light. The comments about the significance of the symbolic use of such imagery made above apply also here.

In the argument about Jesus' claims for himself which follows in 8:13–20, the evangelist has Jesus appeal to the Torah provision of having two witnesses before evidence is valid (8:18; cf. Deut 17:6). His appeal begins with the words, "In your Law" (8:17). But this is not really an argument from Torah. Jesus applies the provision without regard to its literal context. It is rather the use of a Torah motif to extend his own claim which lies beyond and above it. Yet in the discussion it is clear that both partners in the argument assume the validity of the decalogue command, not to bear false witness.

In 8:13–20 and in 8:21–29 John portrays Jesus and his opponents as belonging to two different worlds: Jesus is from above; they are from below (8:23), but it is a dualism that retains flexibility; faith enables one to cross the boundary. In 8:30 the evangelist reports that many Jews did believe. A sharp conflict then ensues when Jesus claims that his words are the way to freedom (8:31–36). The new believers take offence at the suggestion that they are not free. They appeal to their status as sons of Abraham. Jesus cites sin as the proof that nothing apart from what he brings can really set people free. The clear implication again is that the Law cannot set people free. The conflict sharpens further as Jesus denies their claims to be children of God, countering that their deeds show they are children of the devil (8:37–

---

[81] Kotila, *Zeuge*, pp. 53–54, notes that in 7:51 appeal is made to the Law, although the Law contains no such provision for the accused to be heard.

[82] Inserted into the fourth gospel in some manuscripts is a short episode illustrating Jesus' willingness to exercise mercy rather than follow the demands of the Law about adultery (7:53 – 8:11). It also exposes the hypocrisy of those wanting to carry out the Law in this way. On this see the following chapter.

47). They countercharge that he is a Samaritan and has a demon (8:48). The conversation reaches its climax with Jesus' claim that Abraham had rejoiced to see his day and that he had existed before Abraham (8:56–59).

This passage, 8:30–59, reflects shocking antipathy between John's Jesus and the Jews. With regard to what it tells us about the attitude of John's Jesus towards the Law, the passage at the very least implies that the Law does not benefit any child of Abraham who sins and who does not believe in Jesus. I suspect that John means more than this. He also means that the Law was not able to free people from sin. Yet John claims Abraham, a chief figure of the Law, as endorsing Jesus. This coheres with John's approach elsewhere of claiming that the Law, and the scriptures generally, bear witness to Christ. In this instance, John assumes a tradition according to which Abraham rejoiced at the coming of Jesus. John maintains a consistent balance: the Law is not the source of life, but it is nevertheless given by God. The issue is how to understand it. It is to be understood as testimony to Christ.

The healing of the man born blind in 9:1–7 includes washing in the pool of Siloam, from which water was drawn for the libation at the Feast of the Tabernacles. John was probably aware of the link. The imagery of light, associated with the feast, makes a further appearance (9:5; cf. 8:12). Washing in Siloam belongs to the healing procedure, rather than to fulfilment of a ritual purification. Like the reference to baptism in 3:5, its presence here should preserve us from assuming a rigidly exclusive dualism in John, which would exclude all external actions.

As in John 5, we learn after the event that the healing took place on the sabbath (9:14). But already in 9:4 the motif of "work" is introduced: "I must the do the work of him who sent me while it is day, because night is coming when no one can work." This recalls 5:17, "My Father has been working up until now and I am working."[84] An alert hearer might sense the

---

[83] Hanson, *Prophetic Gospel*, p. 117, argues that Zech 14:7, with its reference to light, influences "I am the light of the world", especially after it has just been referred to in 7:38, which immediately precedes. There is also an echo of Job 33:28a ("light of life", pp. 116–117) and of Ps 36:10 (pp. 117–118) and esp. Isa 43:8,9,10,26 behind John 8:12,25,18,28,26 (p. 119), used later of Torah in the Talmud (p. 120).

[84] Pancaro, *Law*, pp. 18–19. Cf. H. Weiss, "The Sabbath in the Fourth Gospel," *JBL* 110 (1991), pp. 311–321, here: 318–319, who argues that John is affirming that God and the Son are working during the day, on the sabbath. John has reinterpreted the sabbath so that now life is seen as lived in the sabbath. "Now they claim that for them every day is a sabbath in which they perform the works of the Son" (p. 320). Thus he argues John treats the sabbath the way he does the temple. I am not convinced. The crucially missing evidence is any indication that what applies to Father and Son also extends to the community.

connection and already have a pat answer when objections are raised: Jesus' works are the Father's works and as such above sabbath restrictions.

The Pharisees object to Jesus' healing action on the sabbath; it clearly constituted work (9:16). Jesus is a "sinner", a transgressor of the Law (cf. 9:24). The ensuing narrative paints the Pharisees as ridiculous for chasing the man and then his parents over such a worthy deed (9:17–41). Claiming to be disciples of Moses and being sure only that God spoke through Moses, they condemn themselves as blind. The butt of the evangelist's irony is not directly Moses and the Law, but the Pharisees' use of it. Nevertheless the implication is also present that to adhere to Mosaic Law, while refusing to acknowledge God's word through Jesus, leads to such absurd behaviour. Again, John is doubtless reflecting the community's own past experience of exclusion from the synagogue. He is mocking the synagogue faith and its leaders.

In 10:1–18 Jesus' exclusive claim to be the good shepherd and the gate of the sheep and his disparagement of rival shepherds who preceded him should not be seen as an attack on Israel's tradition, in particular, on Moses and the Law.[85] It is doubtless aimed, on one level, at Israel's teachers of the Law. The claim is absolute; there is no room for anyone who does not follow Jesus. John could not contemplate truly faithful Jewish leaders without faith in Christ, since the Law, according to John, would point them to Christ and former faithful interpreters of the Law would be people hoping for his coming. Incidentally the discourse also reflects that John continues to espouse decalogue values in relation to murder and theft, although this is probably at the level of ethical values rather than specific commandments of the Law.

As the good shepherd, Jesus will also lay down his life for the sheep (10:15,17–18). This reflects John's knowledge of the tradition of interpreting Jesus' death as vicarious, but it is not a central theme and not used by John here to express an attitude towards the cult. In this context John's Jesus gives us his first hint of the Gentile mission, when he speaks of sheep from outside the fold of Israel (10:16). There is no indication of present or past grappling with the issues which such a move would have raised concerning observance of the Law. Many, responding apparently to Jesus' claims, but also, in the present Johannine context, to the healing in John 9, declare him demon possessed (10:19–21), as they had in 8:48, certainly a Law issue and equally certainly false in John's eyes.

10:22 takes us to another festival: the Feast of Dedication. On this occasion the Jews accuse Jesus of blasphemy and, in accordance with Torah provisions,

---

[85] Cf. Kotila, *Zeuge*, pp. 76–77, 172.

make ready to stone him (10:22–39). The charge of blasphemy rests on their belief that Jesus is making himself God (or "a god"; 10:34). Jesus rebuffs the charge by appealing to their "Law", citing Ps 82:6, "Is it not written in your Law, 'I declare: You are gods'." Law here encompasses the psalms. The appeal here is not to the predictive function of "the Law", but its probative function. It furnishes evidence that it is acceptable for human beings to be addressed as "gods". Like 7:19–24, the argument rests on Jewish presuppositions. It may reflect exegetical tradition linking the statement with the occasion of the giving of the Law.[86] John has Jesus explain that the addressees are "those to whom the word of God came" (10:35). If it is allowed to have them addressed as "sons of god", it is surely allowed that the one directly sanctified and sent by God (10:36) should be called, "Son of God". In addition, John reinforces the argument by asserting the permanent validity of scripture (10:35, "scripture cannot be nullified").

In 10:22–39 there are important points in relation to our theme. First, it is further evidence that John believes that God gave the Law, as implied already in 1:17. Then it upholds the continuing validity of the scripture, which here doubtless encompasses the Law, the Prophets and, at least, the Psalms. However this validity must be understood in Johannine terms: the scriptures are valid as witness to Christ and as proofs in argument, such as here. The appeal to the immutability of the scriptures suggests that the presuppositions are taken seriously. In fact, however, John does not appear to adhere to the validity of scriptures except in a limited sense.[87] The use of Ps 82 is almost mocking and reflects exposure of inconsistency from an outsider rather than serious argument from within.

The intention of the Jews to stone Jesus colours the drama which follows (11:8). Jesus' raising Lazarus from the dead (11:1–46) will be the catalyst for Jesus' acclamation and arrest (12:9–11). Resuscitation becomes a symbol of resurrection and resurrection a symbol of eternal life in typically Johannine fashion. This symbol differs from the others in not having a strong association

---

[86] Hanson, *Prophetic Gospel*, pp. 145–149, notes that Ps 82 was later believed to have been addressed to Israel after receiving the Torah at Sinai. The possession of Torah gave them quasi-divine status which they would lose because of the golden calf (p. 145). He sees John understanding Ps 82 as judgement addressed by the pre-existent Word on the Jews contemporary with Jesus (p. 147). I do not find this convincing; the focus here is not judgement but christology. Cf. also Yee, *Jewish Feasts*, pp. 90–91, who argues that another link is the theme of idolatry reflected in the charge against Jesus.

[87] Kotila, *Zeuge*, pp. 92–93, suggests that 10:35b is neither about prophecy nor a blanket approval of all laws, but a statement of principle, which the evangelist applies to the present context without sensing its wider potential significance.

with Torah, except in the more general sense of life and eternal life. The episode is also without the conflictual allusions to the Law which characterise other such passages.

It is striking that the symbolic use of the passage almost leaves behind the literal meaning of the story. The claim, "I am the resurrection and life; the one who believes in me even though he die shall live. And all who live and believe in me shall never die" (11:25), cannot apply to Lazarus in a literal sense. In fact John is treating a miracle of Jesus in the same way that he treats Old Testament stories. They, too, are not denied their literal meaning, but their function is solely to bear testimony to Jesus as the bearer of eternal life. Not to see them in this light is to remain at the level of reality in company with Nicodemus. This comes most clearly to expression in the juxtaposition of 2:23–25 and 3:1–11, but occurs regularly throughout the gospel (eg. 4:48; 6:14–15; 7:2–5; cf. 12:37–40).

In 11:47–53 the evangelist offers a plausible report of the Sanhedrin's concern about Roman intervention, adding an unwitting prophecy from Caiaphas of Jesus' coming significance for both Israel and the Gentile world. Indirectly it attests to belief that the Jewish high priest did have status in the divine order and could thus become a vehicle of prophecy. This confirms what we have detected as John's attitude towards the temple.[88]

11:55 reflects the Jewish practice of purification one week before the Passover. 12:1 reflects that Jesus may have arrived in time for such purification, but John says nothing about it. At most we may observe Jesus coming to the Passover pilgrim festival, though he will die without eating it. In 12:1–8 Mary prepares Jesus for his burial by her loving act of anointing Jesus' feet. The evangelist portrays the crowd's messianic greeting of Jesus, noting, however, that it was not so apparent as to have been understood in this way by the disciples (12:12–19). The crowd's use of Ps 118:25–26 reflects scripture fulfilment, as does John's citation of Zech 9:9. For John this is the primary role of scripture. The clearing of the temple had been transferred to an earlier point by John.

12:20–33 reports the coming of the Greeks. Distance is assumed; Philip and Andrew act as intermediaries. Instead of telling us the result, the evangelist uses the occasion to have Jesus announce the significance of the event of his death, exaltation and glorification. He does so, because it will be the event which will signal new growth (12:24) and the beginning of the

---

[88] Freyne, "Vilifying," p. 126, believes that 11:52 indicates that John shares the eschatological hope that all Israel will saved. This is very uncertain. John probably has Gentile mission in mind. So Brown, *John*, p. 440; Barrett, *John*, pp. 407–408; Carson, *John*, p. 423.

Gentile mission (so 12:32). Again John gives no indication of issues of Law observance which might have arisen as a result. We must assume they have been long since resolved.

12:34 records the crowd's quandary that the Law states that the Christ is to remain forever, but it is again probably an allusion to the Psalms. Jesus bewails Israel's refusal to respond to his word, he whose glory already Isaiah (like Abraham) had extolled (12:35–43). Again John is claiming the endorsement of the saints of old. Here continuity is being reaffirmed. This is the clearest case of John indicating that Old Testament figures actually encountered the Logos in their own time (cf. 8:56; 1:51). But it is far from an identification between the Word or wisdom and Torah. The evangelist concludes Jesus' ministry with a summary of his challenge (12:44–50). Again he repeats his exclusive qualification to be the light for the world, the Father's envoy, speaking and acting according to his instructions and making acceptance or rejection of his message the criterion for judgement on the last day. Beside this there is effectively no room for the authority of the Law except as testimony to his status.

In John 5–12 the exclusive claims of the prologue continue to find expression. Not only is Jesus the one who alone has seen God, probably set against current claims being made for Moses (and the Law) and for visionaries (5:37; 6:46; cf. 1:18); he is also in more general terms the unique Son of the Father, who alone knows the Father, has seen and heard him and comes as his envoy to do his will. This fundamental structure of Johannine christology undergirds the claim to exclusivity, because no one else and nothing else carries such authority. This has implications for Torah. For John, it is not just that Torah is badly handled, as in the callous attitude of the Pharisees towards the people (7:49), their lawless intentions of the Jews against Jesus (7:20), and their stupidity in accusing him of blasphemy (5:18; 10:31–39) and in pursuing a healed blind man over a point of sabbath law (9:13–34; cf. 5:10–12). The Torah itself is called into question. Thus symbols traditionally associated with Torah (manna, nourishment, water, life and light) continue in John 5–12 to be applied to Jesus. And here, as in John 1–4, there is no indication of continuity between Torah and Jesus at this level. On the contrary, John has Jesus deny that Moses gave bread from heaven (6:32), that scriptures are a source of life (5:39; except in as much as they point to Jesus) or that the Law could make people free (8:32).

The Law and scriptures nevertheless play a significant role. As in 1:17, John acknowledges that God gave his word (10:35), probably referring in particular to the giving of the Law. In the same context he also speaks of scripture as inviolate (10:35). In terms of the role which John envisages for them, they are primarily predictive of Jesus, the Messiah. This is their chief function. Details of the predictions which John has in mind are few. They come to expression in the account of Jesus' entry into Jerusalem (12:13,15). John has Jesus assert that Moses' testimony will rebound in judgement on the Jews who fail to recognise it when they read the scriptures (5:45). Similarly 6:45 acclaims Jesus' fulfilment of the hope of the prophets that all the people will be taught of God. John understands the prediction as an indication that people will heed God (probably in the witness of the scriptures) and be drawn by God to come to Jesus. He also claims Old Testament figures like Abraham and Isaiah as directly witnesses of the Christ (8:56; 12:39–41). John also has Jesus allude to the great commandment to love God alone, but not directly as a command of Torah (5:42,44). Allusions to decalogue commandments indicate their validity is assumed, but not as enjoining cultic practices and not including the sabbath, and probably more at the level of shared values than specifically as biblical commandments.

There are three instances where John's Jesus appears to defend his stance on the basis of scriptural argument or on Jewish presuppositions. In 8:17 John's Jesus appeals to the Law requiring two witnesses in trials and claims to have testimony which accords with this requirement: he, himself, and God (Deut 17:6). It is almost a mockery of scriptural authority in its artificiality, demonstrating that, for John, authority lies elsewhere. The argument in 10:34–36 from Ps 82 as a proof that such recipients of God's word could be designated "sons of God" would also hardly convince. The analogy with Jesus' sonship is artificial; the Jews' objection lies at least as much in the substance of what is claimed as in the terminology. A better kind of argument appears in 7:20–24, where John has Jesus cite the practice of circumcising on the sabbath in defence of his healing on the sabbath. But even here John seems more concerned to expose inconsistency than to indicate a common commitment on the part of Jesus to the Law, sabbath and circumcision. In all three instances John has Jesus use the expression, "your Law". Cumulatively, this suggests that, for John, Jesus distances himself from that Law rather than that he seeks to justify his behaviour in its terms. This coheres with the fact that in the accounts of Jesus' healing on the sabbath, John uses his christology to have Jesus assert that he is beyond the application of sabbath law, since, as the Son, he belongs with the Father and his work, who continues the work of giving life and judgement on the sabbath (5:17; 9:4).

John appears to acknowledge the validity in the past of the feasts and the temple and also acknowledges the activity of God in Israel's history. These institutions and events belong, however, both to the past and to a lower order of reality. Thus John's use of typology based on them at the same time transcends them. Thus rites of water and light associated with the Feast of Tabernacles are the basis for portraying Jesus as the source of water and the light of the world (7:37–38; 8:12). While John had spoken in 2:19–21 of Jesus as the new temple, there is no attempt here to establish or argue continuity which might produce the notion of festivals or the sabbath existing in a transformed state. One might expect in the light of 1:29 that the few references to Jesus' vicarious death could reflect that kind of claim, but of this there is no sign.

It appears then from John 5–12 that John understands the Law as given by God. But its regulations and institutions belong to the world below. They are not as such evil, but they are as such discontinuous with the world above, the world of the Spirit. They belong both to the past and to an inferior order of reality and can therefore be left behind. John is not so rigid a dualist as to exclude all use of physical acts such as washing (9:7) and the eucharist, reflected in 6:51–58. This coheres with what we found in relation to baptism in John 3–4. But the discontinuity is striking. Only a predictive function remains for the Law and, more generally, the scriptures. Beside this, the institutions and events of the scriptures are nevertheless a rich supply of symbols. John never explicates a hermeneutical theory in this respect, but had he sat down with the author of Hebrews, we might have expected terms such as "earthly copies", "shadows", "foretastes" of heavenly reality to come to expression, since that seems to be the underlying philosophy.

5.4 John 13–21 in Review

John commences this final section of the gospel with a reference to the days before the Passover and to the coming event of Jesus' return to the Father (13:1–3). As an expression of his love for own, Jesus washes his disciples' feet. Again, as in 3:5,22,26; 4:1–2; 6:51–58 and 9:7, we note that John's Jesus does not disdain physical actions in themselves; John's dualism is not that rigid. Jesus' response to Peter is most naturally understood in its context (assuming the longer reading) as including an allusion to the purification required before Passover (13:9–10; Nu 9:6–14; cf. already 11:55).[89] It is typically Johannine playfulness in operating at two levels: what Jesus says

---

[89] See Deines, *Steingefässe*, pp. 254–257, 260–261, who points to the practice of purification by immersion which 13:10 assumes (alluded to also in 11:55; pp. 253–254).

is true of the Jew preparing for the Passover; it is also true of the believer, made clean by the word of Jesus, who now symbolises this by the act of washing.[90] Thus John treats the purification rite as he did the Feast of the Tabernacles. It is merely the source of imagery; the substance is left behind. In 13:10 John's Jesus declares the disciples (with the exception of Judas) "pure". Jesus now brings the purity which matters.

Some consider that Jesus' act of washing his disciples' feet symbolically represents the effects of his atoning death. I have argued elsewhere that John probably understood it more broadly than that.[91] A useful commentary on the passage may be found in Jesus' statement in 15:3, "You are pure through the word which I have spoken to you". I am therefore not inclined to see in the foot washing a statement about Jesus' death as a vicarious sacrifice nor an implied statement about sacrifices in the old order. The contrast is rather with the Jewish purification rites associated with preparation for the Passover. I shall return to his treatment of the Passover itself in discussing the crucifixion narrative.

Love for one another, washing one another's feet, follows the example of Jesus (13:12–17). The instructions concerning Judas and the narrative of his departure (13:18–30) include a scripture prediction to be fulfilled (13:18; Ps 41:10). The meal at which Jesus passes Judas the piece of dipped bread is not the Passover meal and within the narrative world at least some disciples think Judas is going to make preparations for the Passover (13:29). John's focus is elsewhere: the event which Judas' deed will unleash, Jesus' death and glorification on high (13:31–33). In John's account Jesus' first concern after announcing his departure is to offer new instruction to the disciples about mutual love. Thus 13:34–35 sets out mutual love, based on the model of Jesus' love for them; it is to be the trade mark of the true disciples: "I give you a new commandment, that you love one another, as I have loved you that you also love one another. In this shall all know that you are my disciples, is you have love one for another." The reference to the command as "new" reads most naturally in the context as reflecting the needs of the new situation which will arise through Jesus' absence.[92] Nothing in the context suggests

---

Altogether Deines makes a strong case that John's gospel is fully acquainted with Palestinian Jewish purification practices, but notes that John consistently portrays Jesus as now offering something new.

[90] Cf. R. Schnackenburg, *Johannesevangelium, III. Teil. Kommentar zu Kap. 13-21*, HTKNT IV/3, (Freiburg: Herder, 4th edn, 1982), p. 23, who argues that it is improbable that Jesus is only reminding Peter of the purification; but he leaves it at that. I agree, but I would add: he is doing so precisely in order to say more at the same time.

[91] Loader, *Christology*, pp. 94–102, esp. 100.

[92] Similarly F. F. Segovia, *The Farewell of the Word. The Johannine Call to Abide*,

that Jesus is setting it in relation to the commands of Torah, not even to its commands to love. In fact, in that sense the command would not be new, but simply a reiteration of Lev 19:18 with the additional qualification of Jesus' example. Nothing thus far has indicated that Jesus lays stress on Torah's commands, so that it appears unlikely that we have an allusion to them here.[93]

Jesus' final discourses with his disciples include his final instructions. Here we have, in a sense, the Law of Jesus, but at no point is it expounded as expansion of Torah or justified by reference to it. Motivation is primarily christological, though we should probably assume that basic ethical principles, such as those contained in the decalogue, are at no point abandoned.

The disciples are to follow Jesus' commandments (14:15,21,23–24). They will also receive instruction from the paraclete (14:26). Instruction takes place within the context of concern to comfort and encourage. The allusion to heavenly dwelling places in the house of the Father (14:2–3) may reflect temple imagery (cf. 2:17), but the focus is not contrast with the old. 14:6 again employs terms for Jesus used elsewhere of Torah: "the way, the truth, the life", and maintains the exclusive claim: "no one comes to the Father but by me." 14:7–11 reiterates the basis for the exclusive claim: the Father dwells in the Son, so that to see the Son is to see the Father. It is the claim of 1:18 in a different key. The exclusiveness is also reflected in the focus of what follows, which is entirely centred on loyalty to Jesus and keeping his commands. The language of covenant, of keeping the commandments, is now taken up and applied to the relation between Jesus and his own.[94] The

---

(Minneapolis: Fortress, 1991), p. 76 n. 37; Kotila, *Zeuge*, pp. 211–212. Cf. Beutler, "Hauptgebot," pp. 234, who argues that the "new" refers in particular to the new covenant. While covenant language is present when John portrays Jesus as teaching obedience to his commands, it is another step to suggest that the associations of new covenant are present, as does Beutler. John fails to indicate this connection, even when speaking of the promise of the Spirit where one might expect it. R. F. Collins, *"These Things have been Written."* *Studies on the Fourth Gospel*, Leuven Theological and Pastoral Monographs 2, (Leuven: Peeters Pr.; Grand Rapids: Eerdmans, 1990), pp. 238–243, argues that the command is "new" in the sense of belonging to the eschatological age. But while this may be implied, it is not the primary focus of the context. See also the discussion in Kotila, *Zeuge*, pp. 191–198, and my critical remarks on his argumentation in the review at the beginning of this chapter.

[93] So rightly Schnackenburg, *Johannesevangelium III*, pp. 59–60; Cf. Luz, *Gesetz*, p. 124; Carson, *John*, pp. 484–485.

[94] So Beutler, "Hauptgebot," pp. 224–225, who notes Pancaro's treatment of "keeping the commandments" or "keeping the word" which shows the Old Testament background of these terms (*Law*, pp. 368–397), but goes beyond Pancaro in exploring their significance in 14:15–21 as covenant language (so Deut 7:9; cf. also Ex 20:6; Deut 5:10). CD 19:1–2

silence about loyalty to Torah and its commands reflects the fact that Torah has ceased to have such a claim. For a new set of loyalties is being established, based on the community of disciples who are devoted to Jesus and who are to follow the Spirit which he shall send.

John 15 begins with the image of the true vine, a clear allusion to the image used of Israel, but now claimed by Jesus and his community.[95] This should not be understood as a claim to be Israel or the new Israel. John is not concerned with that kind of continuity. Rather he is saying that what was claimed of Israel is true only of Jesus and his community, just as he alone is the true bread from heaven. What Moses gave was not bread from heaven, but merely foreshadowed it. 15:9–17 returns to the command of mutual love (13:34–35). It expounds the example of Jesus' love for the disciples expressed through his laying down his life for them (15:13). As on most other occasions where John speaks in this way, he gives no indication that it should be seen in relation to cult (cf. 1:29). In 15:18 – 16:4a John has Jesus predict that the disciples, too, should expect a response of hatred from their fellow Jews. In 15:25 he adds that this fulfils the statement given in "their Law", and proceeds to cite Ps 35:19 (cf. also Ps 69:5). As elsewhere in John, scripture, here cited as the Law, is given a predictive function in relation to Jesus. 16:2, like 9:22 and 12:42, doubtless reflects past expulsions from the synagogue on which the author looks back.

16:4b–33 return to the tone of comfort and encouragement expressed in ch. 14. The Spirit will be the source of the disciples' instruction after Easter and will teach them Jesus' way (16:12–15). Sin and righteousness are now measured by the events surrounding Jesus' death (16:8–11). The final prayer of Jesus for his own in John 17 reflects a system of thought totally centred on Jesus as the authority and bearer of revelation and without any reference (or need to refer) to the former authority of the Law. He alone is the way to eternal life (17:3). He has made known the Father's name, expressed the Father's glory, spoken his words and done his works. Neither he nor his

---

also applies Deut 7:9 to the community of the covenant. Beutler suggests that John's reference to the Spirit is also to be seen in the context of covenant, the promise of the Spirit in a new covenant (14:16–17; pp. 234). This may be so, but John does not provide enough to confirm the association here. Beutler is certainly right that in any case the focus here is not renewal of Torah. The use of the language of Deuteronomy also influences christology directly as Pryor, *Covenant*, shows. He points to the echoes of Deut 10:4 in 17:8 and especially of Nu 16:8 in 7:16–17; 8:28 and 17:8 (pp. 118–119) and to the last discourses as echoing Deuteronomy as a whole.

[95] On the background of the image see Hanson, *Prophetic Gospel*, pp. 183–185, who points to Ps 80:9–20, but also Isa 5:1–7, Jer 2:21 LXX. and to the use of the image for the community in 1QH 8. See also 2 Bar 36:6–11; 37; 39:7–8; Ps Philo 12:8–9.

disciples belong to this world. The cultic language of sanctification appears, but it is now something achieved by the truth of God's word, just as in 15:3 Jesus had declared the disciples pure through his word. Jesus also uses the language of himself: he sanctifies himself for the sake of their sanctification by the truth. The focus is not sacrifice or priesthood, but an achievement of the word of truth. Nevertheless what it achieves makes all other measures for sanctification, by implication, obsolete.

The passion narrative proper begins with the arrest scene in which the forces seeking to seize Jesus are stunned by his divine aura (18:1–11). The interrogation portrays Jesus responding to questions about his disciples and his teaching by challenging his interrogators to speak to his hearers (18:19–24). No particular charge is laid. The first explicit reference to specific concerns of Jewish Law comes where the evangelist notes the Jewish authorities' decision not to enter the Roman praetorium lest they contract impurity (18:28).[96] John offers no evaluative comment. An alert hearer may recall the repeated assurances given the disciples that they have the purity which really matters. Before Pilate no charge is specified initially. By implication the narrative suggests it must have been of such a nature as to make sense of Pilate's question: "Are you the king of the Jews?" (18:33). Before that, Pilate had proposed the Jews deal with him according to Jewish Law and they had pointed out their legal incompetence to carry out a capital conviction (18:31).

It is not until 19:7 that the Jews specify a charge. Jesus ought to die, they claim: "We have a law and according to the law he ought to die, because he made himself Son of God" (19:7; cf. Lev 24:16). The narrative recalls the accusations in 5:17 and 10:31–39, already exposed as misunderstandings. Effectively Jesus' Jewish trial is portrayed by John as taking place in the course of his ministry,[97] so that 19:7 is a summary climax. In John's terms it is a false charge since it is based on a misunderstanding. Yet, understood correctly, Jesus is indeed Son of God and John has Pilate respond to its reality with fear. John's dramatic irony reaches a climax when Pilate presents Jesus to the Jews with the words, "Behold your king" (19:14). Pilate's act summarises what has been happening throughout the ministry of Jesus: the Jews have been presented with their king, their Messiah. The Jewish authorities give their allegiance instead to the Romans and betray their own

---

[96] On this see Brown, *Death of the Messiah*, pp. 744–746. He notes the likely irony: "Those who stand outside the praetorium are careful about ritual purity; yet they wish to put Jesus to death!" (p. 745).

[97] So Kotila, *Zeuge*, p. 123. See also A. E. Harvey, *Jesus on Trial. A Study in the Fourth Gospel*, (London: SPCK, 1976).

people, the messianic hopes of the scriptures, and God. By contrast, the disciples had believed the testimony of the scriptures and were alone faithful to God and to Israel's hopes. This motif of kingship dominates the crucifixion scene to follow.

John dates Pilate's declaration as noon on the day of preparation for the Passover (19:14). The implication is that, on John's reckoning, Jesus must have died during the period when the Passover lambs were being slaughtered, though he does not state this explicitly. Many consider that John is deliberately seeking to portray Jesus as Passover lamb and cite other evidence from the gospel. Thus John has John the Baptist hail Jesus as "the lamb of God who takes away the sin of the world" (1:29), which may well allude to Passover imagery. In 19:29 John speaks of hyssop being used in offering Jesus a drink. Hyssop is an element in the Passover meal. When John reports that soldiers did not break Jesus' legs to hasten his death, since he was already dead, he interprets this as fulfilling scripture, "None of his bones shall be broken" (19:32–37). The allusion may be to Ps 34:21 ("He keeps all his bones and not one of them is broken"), but if it (also) alludes to the provision that Passover lambs be without broken bones (Ex 12:10,46),[98] this might be a further indicator that John interprets Jesus as a passover lamb. I have expressed doubt about whether this is the intention of the author, although it may have been part of his tradition.[99] If Passover typology is intended, it would represent use of imagery from the festival much as occurs when John uses imagery drawn from the Feast of the Tabernacles. John does not indicate what might be the implications for the Passover celebration, itself, but we are probably right to assume that he would consider it obsolete.[100]

We have already mentioned the occurrence of scripture fulfilment of Ps 34:21 or Ex 12:10,46 in 19:36. A further fulfilment quotation follows in 19:37 (Zech 12:10). 19:38–42 reports the initiative of Joseph and Nicodemus to retrieve the body and give it an appropriate burial according to Jewish custom in a tomb that was nearby, because it was the day of preparation of the Passover. Both are clearly committed not only to Jesus, but also to observance of the Law. When John describes Joseph as a secret disciple, we are probably right to detect in that description a strongly negative statement, since in 12:42–43 John roundly condemns such people. Their meticulous observance of Jewish Law in this episode (burial rites, concerns about the

---

[98] So Hanson, *Prophetic Gospel*, pp. 218–222; Brown, *Death of the Messiah*, pp. 1185–1186.

[99] See my discussion in Loader, *Christology*, pp. 69–70, 96.

[100] Cf. Kotila, *Zeuge*, pp. 126–127, who believes the evangelist assumes Jesus is the true passover lamb, but makes no link to the Law, since the Law was no longer an issue.

day of preparation) may, for John, be characteristic of those who do not "come out" and believe. They should not therefore be seen as indications that John endorses such observance and the attitude towards Torah which it implies,[101] even though John reports their efforts in general in favourable terms. Mary Magdalene waits until the sabbath has passed before coming to the tomb (20:1), but, unlike with Nicodemus, John makes no explicit link between her behaviour and Law observance.

The accounts of Jesus' resurrection and the encounters which follow demonstrate fulfilment of Jesus' predictions during the last discourses. Issues of Law are not present, except in so far as the disciples must meet behind closed doors for fear of the Jews. John 21 includes further instruction, highlighting, above all, the distinctive leadership roles of Peter and of the enigmatic beloved disciple, and countering confusion which had arisen about the latter's death. The silence about matters of Law probably reflects the evangelist's sense that these are no longer relevant for his community.

In John 13–21 the focus has turned to Jesus' death. Issues of Law are secondary. The Law, and sometimes the scripture as Law ("their Law", 15:25), has a predictive function referring to Jesus (Ps 41:10 in 13:18; Ps 35:19 in 15:25; Ps 34:21 or Ex 12:10,46 in 19:36; Zech 12:10 in 19:37). John appears to use the purification requirement before Passover as a symbolic starting point for portraying Jesus as the true source of purification and sanctification. Jesus purifies by his word of truth. John's Jesus proceeds to the Father's heavenly house, the heavenly temple, where places will be prepared for his own (14:2–3). John does not develop the death of Jesus as the event which achieves purification. This is consistent with his usage elsewhere. The exception may be Passover typology, through which John may be alluding to Jesus as the lamb who takes away the world's sin. But even so, John does not develop the argument about Jesus' death as a sacrifice to replace all sacrifices and open the way to the heavenly temple as we find in Hebrews.

The discourses continue the theme developed in the rest of the gospel: Jesus is the unique source of knowledge of God, who effectively renders all

---

[101] So Weiss, "Sabbath in the Fourth Gospel," pp. 319–320, who argues that the sabbath concerns reflected in removing Jesus' body from the cross and the concerns about burial are seen by John not as acts of true disciples, but as Jewish concerns of half-believers. But see the discussion in Brown, *Death of the Messiah*, pp. 1265–1268, who points out that in contrast to the condemnation of secret disciples in 12:42–43, here both are no longer making an secret of the fact of their concern for Jesus. He also notes that it is unlikely John would intend such a "dead end" to the narrative.

other revelation obsolete. Passover rites, vine imagery, Law and scripture, are of value only in as much as they point to Christ. He alone is the way, the truth and the life, images associated elsewhere with the Law. The instructions of Jesus are set so centrally within the concerns of Jesus and his community, that the reference to a "new" commandment (13:34–35) probably carries no allusion to commands of the Law, but only to the instructions as relating to the new situation after Jesus' departure.

John has Pilate present the Jews with their Messiah and the Jews instead choose Caesar. John shows their trial of Jesus, which extended through his ministry, coming to a climax in the charge before Pilate that Jesus claimed to be the Son of God, a claim which John has shown they misunderstood. Jewish enmity is reflected in allusions to synagogue expulsions. Jewish scruples about remaining pure for Passover (18:28) contrast with the purity Jesus offers. John also depicts believers who remain within Judaism negatively and may see the activities of Joseph and Nicodemus at the burial in the same light. For John Jewish customs may have their place, but they have no authority as divine law. At the same time we noted that for all the commitment to the world of the Spirit and the spiritual, John's Jesus is not a thoroughgoing dualist who might despise all physical actions as irrelevant to faith: he washes his disciples' feet.

5.5 Jesus' Attitude towards the Law in John – Conclusions

Our analysis confirms the view that John's Jesus sees the chief role of the Law as that of bearing testimony to himself. As such it functions as part of scripture and sometimes as a designation of scripture as a whole.[102] In this function the Law and the scriptures function as does John the Baptist. The Law's testimony is worth hearing because the Law and the scriptures have divine authority. That is an underlying presupposition. Thus John has Jesus assert the immutability of scripture, though this must be understood within the context of johannine thought. The gospel assumes that God gave the Law. This is implied in the passive, "was given", in 1:17 and through the

---

[102] So Pancaro, *Law*, p. 515, who points out that by the term, "Law", John always has the Law as a whole in mind, as the body of teachings revealed to Moses which constitute the foundation of the whole social and religious life and thought of Israel (so especially 1:17; 7:19,23,49). This is so, even though he can sometimes use it exclusively of the Pentateuch in contrast to the Prophets (1:45) or of the whole Old Testament (eg. of the Psalms: 10:34; 12:34; 15:25) or of particular precepts and principles (8:17 cf. Deut 17:6; 7:51; 19:7; 18:31).

allusions in the context to Sinai. It is also implied in the use the word χάριτος in the expression χάριν ἀντὶ χάριτος where χάρις carries in it both the sense of gift and of God's goodness.

The divine origin of the Law and the scriptures is the necessary presupposition for their authority as witness and is assumed throughout. It coheres with this assumption that the gospel treats biblical events and biblically sanctioned institutions and practices as worth citing in order to expound the significance of Christ. They are not just any set of religious traditions, such as those of the Samaritans, but are those of the Jews. In this line of tradition salvation is to be found, not elsewhere (4:22). This makes sense of the fourth gospel's complex use of typological symbolism and explains why it is so extensive within the gospel. It also explains why the evangelist has Jesus call on Old Testament figures, such as Abraham and Isaiah, for direct endorsement. Concern with the scriptures also explains the familiarity with a number of Jewish exegetical traditions.

The list of typological allusions to events narrated in scripture is extensive and includes Sinai (1:14–18; 5:37b; 6:46), Jacob's vision at Bethel (1:51), Moses' lifting up the snake (3:14–15), Jacob's well and well side encounters (4:4–26), and the supply of manna in the wilderness (6:5–15,26–58). The pattern in each case is not: just as then, so now, only more or greater; but: like the first event, so another has taken place which formally corresponds to it, but achieves something not achieved by the first. The point of recalling the first event is not to show how the second improves on it, but to establish a correspondence which appropriates the authoritative quality and ethos claimed for the first, but then, and also partly on that basis, claims that the second event is qualitatively quite different. What joins the two events is theology. God was involved in the first. Its formal structure almost functions in such a way that we are to see traces of God's action then which should enable us to recognise that it is God who is acting in the second event. But the events are otherwise incomparable. In terms of the Sinai event: through Moses God gave the Law, though Moses never saw God's glory, but only a minimally significant back view. To this John juxtaposes Jesus, who alone has seen the Father, is the Father's Son, bearing his glory, has tabernacled with us and made God known. In colloquial terms, there is no comparison! Yet for John it has been worth the effort, because he assumes some divine authority for the Law and so some advantage in using it to point to the event of Christ.

The list of typological allusions to institutions and practices includes the following: the lamb which takes away sin (1:29,35), the sitting under the fig tree (1:48,50), the six stones jars with water for purification (2:6), the temple

(2:13–22), purification/baptism (3:25), purity scruples in relation to Samaritans (4:9), the temple mount (4:20–24), the sabbath (5:1–30; 9:1–41), the laws of testimony (5:31–37a; esp. 8:17–18), the water and light of the Feast of Tabernacles (7:37–39; 8:12; 9:5); the shepherd (10:1–21), purification for the Passover (13:1–11; cf. 11:55), and possibly also the Passover lamb (19:29,36). Here we note that in a similar way the author has exploited the given to point beyond it. The assumption is that all of these institutions have had validity. John does not call a single one of them into question in an absolute sense. This is striking.[103] Yet his aim is to claim their validity as God given in order to help legitimise his claim for Christ.

We have also found no evidence that the author is seeking in some way to reproduce Israel's institutions at a higher level or even to reproduce Israel. It is not a typology of good and better; but of one gift replacing another. John wants his hearers to recognise from the indicators (the matching patterns) that the new gift comes from the same person, the same God. What Christ brings, or, in Johannine terms, what Christ is, is not supplementary, let alone, complementary; it replaces. Yet to help validate this claim the author uses the authority already associated with these institutions and practices as given by God in the Law.

We have been concerned to explore the basis of this approach to the Law. In part, one could point to an eschatological perspective. With Jesus the new has come which must affect the status of the old. To some degree we see this perspective reflected in the images of eschatological hope which John employs: the wedding feast (2:1–12), the image of water flowing from the temple (7:37–38), the statements in relation to the temple that the hour is coming and now is (4:21,23). By far the most common form is where John indicates that Jesus fulfils messianic hope (eg. 1:41,45; 4:25–26; 12:15). The argument that the scriptures, including the Law, testify to Christ in this sense carries great weight. It is a regular charge against the Jews that they refuse to believe Moses and the Law or the scriptures (5:39,46–47; 6:44–46). Eschatological fulfilment need not imply a diminishing of the authority of the Law or the scriptures; yet in John clearly it does. For in John the scriptures and the Law only have authority in as much as they testify to Christ.

Christology is a vital clue. For John's Jesus is more than the fulfilment of eschatological hope. He is at another level entirely in his origin and being. As Son of God, he alone has seen and known the Father. He alone has come

---

103 So Deines, *Steingefässe*, p. 250, who notes that John does not engage in criticism of Jewish practices, nor Jewish way of life, nor the tradition of the elders.

as the Father's heavenly envoy, authorised to make him known. He alone has ascended, returning to the Father's glory in exaltation. In John the claim is absolute. He alone offers the true bread. He alone is the way to the Father. He alone is the source of eternal life. He alone is the vine. Such absolute claims raise the question acutely whether they leave any room for anyone or anything else. At points it certainly appears to be negating claims to visions of God (1:18; 5:37; 6:46) and it makes a special point of reducing John the Baptist's significance to that of witness (1:6–8, esp. 1:20,31), though at least it is acknowledged that he is sent by God. The author's approach seems similar with regard to the Law and the scriptures. They also have authority. God also gave the Law. Even if their only continuing valid function is to testify to Christ and provide a hermeneutical springboard for christological assertions, they have this function in John because he upholds their authority. It is not the case that the gospel in its present form denies the divine origin of the Law, as Kotila suggests for its redaction.[104] This can only be maintained by assuming the redactor is blind to the major role which the Law and scriptures play and to the theological reason why they do so.

We gain confirmation of the author's stance when we turn to another major phenomenon of the gospel: the application to Jesus of images associated in tradition with Torah, usually identified with Wisdom. This is not the place to rehearse the detail since it has been identified in the review of the gospel. From that review it is clear that the author makes extensive use of such imagery, which includes the logos of the prologue, but also associated images there and elsewhere in the gospel: light, life, water, bread, the gate, the way, the truth. As the prologue does not identify the Law or the prophets as a work of the Logos, so in the rest of the gospel, the images belong exclusively to Jesus. What Moses gave, the Law, was not the food of eternal life (6:32). Eternal life is not to be found in the scriptures (except indirectly as they testify to Christ its source; 7:39). Freedom is not possible apart from Christ (8:30–36). Such claims, John tells us, caused many Jewish believers such offence that they abandoned their faith and became Jesus' enemies (8:33–59; cf. also 6:60–71). The use of Wisdom/Torah imagery exclusively for Christ may be a deliberate ploy on John's part to counter its use for Torah, as Scott suggests,[105] but I consider such a specific strategy on John's part unlikely. Its first occurrence, in the prologue, is not polemical and elsewhere the focus is not so much against use of a motif as against what that use would imply.

---

[104] Kotila, *Zeuge*, pp. 209–210.
[105] Scott, *Sophia*, pp. 159–160.

John's christology is, therefore, the ultimate basis for understanding the way John has Jesus approach the Law. But beside this, or perhaps, better, within this, is a further important aspect frequently overlooked. John's Jesus is from above; the Jews are from below (8:23). Nicodemus stays at the earthly level and fails to comprehend what it means to be born from above or born of the Spirit. He is at the level of the flesh (3:1–11). Similarly John has Jesus answer the complaints of the Jews about Jesus' claims which exclude the Mosaic Law as a source of life: "The Spirit is life-giving; the flesh is of no use; the words I speak are Spirit and life" (6:63). In the age that is coming and now is, people will not worship on temple mounts, legitimate or illegitimate: the true worshippers will worship in spirit and in truth, because God is spirit (4:19–24).

These texts are not atomistically juxtaposed; they belong together because they give expression to a common stance present throughout the gospel and important for our theme. They reveal a particular dualistic value system which contrasts the realm of the Spirit and the realm of the flesh, but one which requires careful definition.[106] It does not imply the flesh is evil. The flesh is a legitimate sphere of human activity. John portrays Jesus as engaging in this sphere. He can be tired and thirsty; he suffers and dies. He performs miracles in this sphere. He engages in symbolic acts of washing and enjoins that others do the same, whether baptism or immersion for healing. John does not espouse an anti sacramental dualism.[107] He does, however, build his entire theology on the distinction between the realm of the Spirit and the realm of the flesh.

I believe that this also helps explain his understanding of the Law and his portrait of Jesus' attitude towards the Law. In treating typological events and Jewish institutions and practices enjoined by the Law, John, as we noted, assumes two levels. By identifying the pattern of God's actions at one level, you can come to recognise it at another. The events, institutions and practices belong to one level, Jesus to another. They are at the level of this world.

---

[106] On Johannine dualism see the studies by J. Becker, "Beobachtungen zum Dualismus im Johannesevangelium," *ZNW* 65 (1975), pp. 71–87; L. Schottroff, *Der Glaubende und die feindliche Welt*, WMANT 37, (Neukirchen-Vluyn: Neukirchener, 1970); R. Bergmeier, *Glaube als Gabe nach Johannes*, BWANT 12, (Stuttgart: Kohlhammer, 1980); Ashton, *Understanding the Fourth Gospel* pp. 205–237; see also Loader, *Christology*, pp. 141, 151–153. I am focusing on one aspect of that dualism only which belongs to a wider use which is rightly characterised as dualism of decision. This term can, however, be misleading. John's dualism includes spheres of reality which are contrasted and also assumes that part of the higher reality is the heavenly world from which the Son comes and to which he returns.

[107] Cf. Neyrey, *Revolt*, pp. 142–143.

Jesus is from above. By seeing reality in this way John is able to uphold that God gave the Law and that God was active in Israel's past and gave the scriptures as a whole. Because all of that belongs at the lower level of reality, it is incomparable with Christ, yet it can function as a foretaste or pattern of his reality. In this sense John's approach has similarities with that espoused by the author of the epistle to the Hebrews, only there the contrast is employed almost exclusively in relation to the cult and sacrifice. The latter is not John's focus. Only 1:29 indicates a step in that direction. Unlike in Hebrews, we do not have the conceptual language of type and antitype, shadow and reality. The dualism is more directly theological, which results at times in difficulty in knowing whether or not to capitalise "spirit" (eg. 3:6,8; 4:23–24).

As already noted, John's dualism leaves room for some value to be given to the lower level. The lower level is not evil. However to remain at the lower level is disparaged. This forms the basis for some of John's most cutting irony. John's narrative of Jesus' encounter with Nicodemus ridicules the representative Jewish teacher for staying at the level of the flesh. The same sense of ridicule is entailed in the way John depicts the Jews/Pharisees in the sabbath controversies, especially in John 9. It appears also where John reports the accusations of blasphemy: the Jews fail to understand. To remain at that level is to be condemned. John is not appealing for a wider view of reality in general which looks beyond the lower level; he is too christologically focused for that. He appeals for faith in Christ as the one who has come from above, which means believing this is so and responding appropriately by submission to his authority to receive the life he offers.

The treatment of the Law as God's gift to the Jews at the level of the lower order of reality, explains why John sees no need to attack it as such. It explains why he reports its practices without criticism. Occasionally he has Jesus argue at the level of the Jews, such as in citing the precedent of circumcision on the sabbath to counter their attack on him for healing on the sabbath (7:22–24), but this does not portray a Jesus intent on keeping that Law. It shows him to be one who is above it, but who is engaging in an act of exposure.[108] John has Jesus claim the Jewish heritage, but as something both preliminary and inferior to what he brings. It has authority as God's gift and as reporting divine activity. Only once does John place Jesus within that history: Isaiah sees him in a vision (12:39–41). Abraham also recognised him, when his day came (8:56). John assumes others were inspired to foretell

---

[108] Similarly Luz, *Gesetz*, p. 121.

that day. He also has the high priest inspired in Jesus' day to predict Jesus' death on behalf of the people (11:51–52).

Other apparent uses of the Law by Jesus are scarcely serious (eg. 8:16; 10:32–34; even 7:22–24). They are superficial to a degree which indicates that the scriptures have in effect ceased to have probative worth except in as much as they serve to testify to Christ. Thus even the wording of scripture is used in a manner similar to the way John uses its institutions and events: they offer a form of words now transferred to a new context with a new meaning. It is appropriate in this context to note that John's Jesus refers to the Law as the Jews' Law ("your Law"; "their Law"; 8:17; 10:34; 15:25; cf. 7:19,22), since it has ceased to be the Law of Jesus and the community, except in its christological function.

Now that the Son has come, the logic of John's theology demands that the validity of the Law, the scriptures, the institutions and practices of Israel, cease. For those for whom they once had authority and significance, the validity of the Law and the scriptures should exist now only as a pointer to Christ. This is also the reality in John's account. Occasionally this effective replacement of Torah by Jesus is expressed by having Jesus assume the identity of the institution in a symbolic way. This occurs most notably when John portrays Jesus as the temple (2:18–22) and fulfilling temple hopes (7:37–39; also 1:51). We have noted other such typological correspondences in relation to the Feast of the Tabernacles (water and light) and the Passover (purification, the lamb). John does not appear bent on working out a full catalogue of correspondences. The implication however is that he has made all such institutions and practices obsolete. This means that, in John's view, such practices cease to have validity for Christian Jews.[109] John disapproves of secret believers who remain practising Jews, but do not confess Christ openly (12:42–43).

There is a certain tension in the gospel between statements which indicate that the turning point is the event of Jesus' death and resurrection and others which suggests it has come in Jesus' person.[110] 2:13–22 is a good example. It portrays Jesus still caring about the temple as something which has validity,

---

[109] Cf. Pancaro, *Law*, pp. 530–531, who argues that in John's community Christian Jews continue to keep the Law. They are expelled from the synagogue not for transgression of Torah, but because they confess Christ. They may have been lax in areas like the sabbath, but John indicates no interest in the issue of how they kept the sabbath. But John's interest is christological and since the expulsion lies some way in the past we should not press the detail for information about current practice in John's community or his own view.

[110] So Kotila, *Zeuge*, p. 206. On this tension in John's christology, see Loader, *Christology*, pp. 125–134.

while at the same time announcing its coming replacement through his resurrection (the same perspective is in 1:50–51 and reinforced in 7:37–39). Certainly after Jesus' return and the coming of the Spirit the turning point has passed and the Law and its institutions have become a thing of the past.

John sees the community of disciples, whom Jesus addresses in language drawn from the accounts of Israel's covenant with God in Deuteronomy, as a self contained group. He looks back on their expulsion from the synagogues. This was inevitable because in John's view the Jews remain at the level of unbelief and blindness; they are of the world. In the last discourses, but even more so, in the epistles, we see how the logic of John's theology leaves no place for a continuing role of Israel's religious heritage, except as foretaste and testimony.[111] Even at the level of ethics, instruction is not Torah based, but derived from Jesus and the example he set. Some of the values enshrined in the decalogue, whose commands find their echo occasionally within the gospel (prohibition of murder, adultery, false witness, theft, the command to honour parents), continue to have validity, but without recourse to the Law as authority. The same is true of the command to love God. Its value is assumed, but quite without the implications assumed in its context in the Law. The command of mutual love, urged on the disciples as Jesus prepares his disciples for his departure, is based on the example of Christ's love and is new solely because of the new situation they are to face.

The new ethical base will have been tempered by the fact that members were still within a community which shared the Law's ethical heritage. The danger would be when this heritage receded further into history. Probably we see signs of the dangers of this development behind 1 John, which addresses both a collapse in moral awareness among believers, those who had abandoned the community, and an incipient docetism which appears to have developed John's dualism to the point of detaching Christ from history and his humanity.

John's account of Jesus' attitude towards the Law assumes the Law as God's gift to Israel through Moses. It is appropriate to a level of reality which is both inferior and preliminary to the realm of the Spirit opened by Jesus. It nevertheless pointed towards it and through its institutions to some degree prefigured it. Beyond that, John gives no indication of how he really dealt with the theological issues which such a stance must raise. But in this he has the company in different ways already of Paul and also of the writer to the epistle to the Hebrews. The judgement on unbelieving Jews for failing to heed their scriptures as pointing to Christ is problematic in the light of

---

[111] So Pancaro, *Law*, pp. 250–251, 518–521. See also Luz, *Gesetz*, p. 128

John's statements that even the disciples only grasped their meaning after the gift of the Spirit. But at least it enables John to maintain a consistent position for the time after Easter.

The key to John's understanding of Jesus' attitude towards the Law is his high christology with its absolute claims and the dualistic framework within which it is set. Through this dualistic framework he can hold together both the divine origin of scripture and Law and its inferior status. Within this framework he can pass judgement on those who persist at that inferior level. It also enables him to distinguish Jewish from all other religious heritage, such as those of the Samaritans and of Gentiles. With the abandonment of Jewish Law and its institutions, John's community can include Gentiles without controversy, even though it is still so heavily dominated by Jewish ethos. Hence the paradox of the fourth gospel, which at one and the same time reflects the strongest Jewish ethos of all the gospels and the sharpest break from Judaism.

Chapter 6

Jesus' Attitude towards the Law according to Thomas and Other Non Canonical Gospels

6.1 The Gospel of Thomas

6.1.1 The Gospel of Thomas in Review

Much discussion concerning Thomas is concerned with identifying its place within early Christianity, in particular its relation to the canonical gospels and their traditions and to the historical Jesus. This is bound up, in turn, with the issue of the relation of Thomas to gnosticism. In this section I want to continue my practice thus far of discussing the received text. This is already a matter of some complexity, since we have both the Coptic version and variant Greek versions of some parts.[1] There is also the question whether one can really assume a structural coherence in Thomas sufficient to add weight to inform exegetical observations. I shall dispense with a review of literature on Jesus' attitude towards the Law in Thomas, because no such study is known to me, apart from incidental discussions related to particular texts.

There are no sayings in Thomas dealing directly with the status of Torah as such, but a surprisingly large number dealing with attitudes to Jewish and Jewish Christian practices based on Torah.

Saying 6 has the disciples ask about fasting, almsgiving, prayer and diet.

---

[1] Unless otherwise indicated, the English translation is the one edited by R. McL Wilson of Beate Blatz, "The Coptic Gospel of Thomas," in *New Testament Apocrypha. Volume One: Gospels and Related Writings*, edited by W. Schneemelcher, (Cambridge: James Clarke; Louisville: Westminster/John Knox Press, 2nd edn, 1991), pp. 117–133. It sets side by side the Coptic (*NHC* II 2,32.10 – 51.28) and the relevant parallels in the Greek Oxyrhynchus Papyri 1, 654 and 655.

His disciples asked him (and) said to him: Do you want us to fast? And how shall we pray (and) give alms? What diet should we observe? Jesus said: Do not lie, and what you abhor, do not do; for all things are manifest in the sight of heaven; for there is nothing hidden which will not be revealed, and there is nothing covered which will remain without being covered.

In it Jesus makes no direct response to these questions. Instead he enjoins the disciples not to lie and not to do what they abhor, perhaps a variant of the golden rule. We are left wondering what Jesus' attitude is. The saying may indicate that Thomas' Jesus is setting a higher priority on honesty and ethical behaviour than on such things. In the attitude displayed elsewhere in Thomas (not least in Saying 14), we can assume that Thomas' Jesus places no value on fasting, almsgiving, prayer (in contrast to Matthew's Jesus in 6:1–18!), nor on food laws. Avoiding falsehood is probably also more than an appeal to straightforward honesty; it will include a polemical reference to false teaching (of Jews and Jewish Christians).[2]

The first part of Saying 14 returns, in effect, to the question asked in Saying 6.

Jesus said to them: If you fast, you will put a sin to your charge;[3] and if you pray, you will be condemned; and if you give alms, you will do harm to your spirits.

Apparently fasting gives rise to sin – by facing people with the temptation to break the fast? The words, "If you pray, you will be condemned", are astonishing; perhaps they are countering a particular discipline of prayer, for instance, praying at the hours of prayer. Equally astonishing is the statement which follows: "If you give alms, you do harm to your spirits." It is not clear how such harm would come. Does it, perhaps, reflect the mission situation which is about to be addressed in the remainder of the saying? For in that situation the disciples would be in no position to give alms. Alternatively, all three sayings reflect condemnation of the practices characteristic of Jews and Jewish Christians and mean little more than that to follow their practices is evil.[4] This is probably correct, although part of the reason for rejection may well include the mission setting and an aspect of the rejection of prayer may be hours of prayer, as I have suggested. It is significant that the preceding Sayings 12 and 13 have set Thomas in contrast to representatives of Jewish Christianity. In Saying 14, then, Thomas' Jesus

---

[2] So M. Fieger, *Das Thomasevangelium. Einleitung, Kommentar und Systematik*, Neutestamentliche Abh. NF 22, (Münster: Aschendorff, 1991), p. 40.

[3] Or "bring sin upon yourselves". So M. W. Meyer, *The Gospel of Thomas: the Hidden Sayings of Jesus*, (San Francisco: Harper, 1992), p. 29.

[4] So Fieger, *Thomasevanglium*, p. 75.

attacks central features of Jewish Christian (and Jewish) piety and lays down central concerns of its mission.[5] The spirituality of Thomas is such that it spurns outwards practices, espouses a different kind of asceticism and claims immediacy which renders prayer problematic. With Saying 6, Saying 14 portrays Jesus as rejecting the traditional Jewish piety triad of fasting, prayer and almsgiving.

Prayer and fasting feature in two further sayings. In Saying 104 Jesus rejects the disciples' suggestion that he join them in prayer and fasting.

> They said [to him]: Come, let us pray today and fast. Jesus said: What then is the sin that I have done, or in what have I been overcome? But when the bridegroom comes out from the bridal chamber, then let them fast and pray.

Jesus' response reflects the assumption that prayer and fasting are designed to deal with sin and failure.[6] Jesus' response represents a claim not to have sinned, but also assumes a similar status for the disciples. The explanation about fasting and praying when the bridegroom leaves the bridal chamber may appear to sanction prayer and fasting for that occasion. The parallel in Mark 2:18–20 sanctions fasting when the bridegroom goes away, ie. in the post Easter period. The Thomas saying may reflect a similar awareness, although the Gospel of Thomas introduces the sayings as already those of the "living Jesus" (Saying 1). Some have suggested that Thomas may consider that prayer and fasting is only for the initiated.[7] It is better, however, to read the saying in the light of bridal chamber imagery elsewhere (Saying 75; cf. Gosp Philip 60–96). The image of the bridegroom in the bridal chamber is an image of the oneness or wholeness which is the goal for the believer. Saying 104 implies, therefore, that prayer and fasting would only be necessary when that state breaks down, were the bridegroom (the light) to depart from the bridal chamber (cf. also Saying 75). It confirms what we observed concerning the rejection of prayer in Saying 14: immediacy renders prayer unnecessary. Therefore, Saying 104 constitutes further evidence of the denial of prayer and fasting as appropriate for the disciple.[8] Thus these

---

[5] So Fieger, *Thomasevangelium*, p. 73.

[6] A similar response is found in the Gospel of the Nazareans 2: "Behold, the mother of the Lord and his brethren said to him: John the Baptist baptises unto the remission of sins, let us go and be baptised by him. But he said to them: Wherein have I sinned I should go and be baptised by him? Unless what I have said is ignorance (a sin of ignorance)."

[7] So R. A. Funk, R. W. Hoover, et al. *The Five Gospels. The Search for the Authentic Words of Jesus*, (New York: Macmillan, 1993), p. 528.

[8] So Fieger, *Thomasevangelium*, p. 262. On the bridal chamber imagery, see M. W. Meyer, "Making Mary Male: The Categories of 'Male' and 'Female' in the Gospel of Thomas," *NTS* 31 (1985), pp. 554-570, here: 557–558.

sayings appear to rule out standard aspects of Pharisaic piety, prayer and fasting, and probably also almsgiving. In doing so, they show no sign of sensing issues about what this might mean for the Law and its authority; such authority appears not to matter.

The only other saying to mention fasting is Saying 27.

> <Jesus> said: If you do not fast to the world, you will not find the kingdom; if you do not keep the Sabbath as Sabbath, you will not see the Father.

Fasting is used metaphorically to describe an attitude of self discipline towards the world, a metaphor used also by Clement of Alexandria (*Strom* III.15.99.4; cf. also Justin *Dial.* 12.3).[9] Here it reflects strong asceticism over against the world. As in Sayings 14 and 104, Thomas is mocking Jewish asceticism as inadequate and demands celibate asceticism which then negates sexual differentiation (so Saying 22; cf. also 21, 37).[10]

Saying 27 also uses the image of the sabbath metaphorically. This is more likely than that the first half of the saying uses a Jewish practice metaphorically and the second literally enjoins the sabbath in some way.[11] Sabbath probably alludes to spiritual rest, rest from the world, which is a state in which the believer lives rather than a day to be observed.[12] The two different spellings employed in the Coptic, *sambaton* and *sabbatton,* may indicate that the Saying means: "Observe the whole week as the sabbath".[13] Given the meaning of sabbath as rest from the world, the effect is the same. The motif of rest appears also in Sayings 2 (in the P.Ox. 654 version only), 50, 51, 60, 90.

---

[9] So Meyer, *Thomas*, p. 81; earlier B. Gärtner, *The Theology of the Gospel of Thomas*, (London: Collins, 1961), pp. 239–240.

[10] So J. D. Crossan, *The Historical Jesus. The Life of a Mediterranean Jewish Peasant*, (San Francisco: Harper, 1991), p. 267.

[11] Cf. R. J. Bauckham, "Sabbath and Sunday in the Post–Apostolic Church," in *From Sabbath to Lord's Day. A Biblical, Historical and Theological Investigation*, edited by D. Carson, (Grand Rapids: Zondervan, 1982), pp. 251–298, here: 265, who argues that the saying derives originally from a strict Jewish Christian saying which enjoined literal observance.

[12] So Fieger, *Thomasevangelium*, p. 110; Bauckham, "Sabbath and Sunday", pp. 265–266; Meyer, "Making Mary Male", p. 555: "The true sabbath is rest from the cosmos."

[13] See Meyer, *Thomas*, p. 82, who cites the same thought in Tertullian, *Against the Jewish People* 4: "We ought to keep a sabbath from all servile work always, and not only every seventh day, but all the time." He also mentions the alternative that the expression, "observe the sabbath as the sabbath" could derive from the LXX idiom, "Keep the sabbath (with reference to) the sabbath". He also notes the parallel in Ps–Macarius which speaks of keeping the sabbath in terms of abstention from the shameful (p. 81). See also Fieger, *Thomasevangelium.* pp. 108–109.

As we have seen, Saying 6 contains a question about diet ("What diet should we observe?"). We should probably see Jesus' response (or lack of response) as placing no value on the issue. As we have seen, however, Saying 14 does appear to respond to the issues raised in Sayings 6. We have considered the responses which relate to the triad: fasting, prayer and almsgiving. In response to the question on diet Saying 14 has the following:

> And if you go into any land and walk about in the regions,[14] if they receive you, eat what is set before you; heal the sick among them. For what goes into your mouth will not defile you; but what comes out of your mouth, that is what will defile you.

The saying appears to belong to mission instruction to the disciples.[15] The command in 14a to eat whatever their hosts place in front of them (similarly Luke 10:8) would mean in a Jewish context not having scruples about the extent to which their Jewish hosts observe tithing laws and possibly purity laws in food preparation; in a Gentile context, as probably envisaged here, it effectively means ignoring Torah food laws altogether. This coheres with the approach in Saying 6, but also with what immediately follows in 14b: "For what goes into your mouth will not defile you; but what comes out of your mouth, that is what will defile you." As Mark in Mark 7:15, Thomas understands the antithesis exclusively, even though unlike Mark, and more like Matthew (15:11), it uses the image to contrast what enters or proceeds from the mouth. Unlike either, it offers no explanation of what proceeds from the mouth or the person, but obviously considers attitudes and behaviour as the chief concern.

In Saying 53 the disciples raise the value of circumcision.

> His disciples said to him: Is circumcision useful or not? He said to them: If it were useful, their father would beget them from their mother (already) circumcised. But the true circumcision in the Spirit has proved useful in every way.

Already the Old Testament had used circumcision metaphorically and Paul makes great use of the tradition (Rom 2:25–28; Deut 30:6; Jer 4:4). Thomas doubtless uses the image of true circumcision to describe the state of oneness which constitutes salvation. This coheres with the spiritualising interpretation of fasting and the sabbath. The argument here against

---

[14] Or "When you go into any region and walk through the countryside" – so Meyer, *Thomas*, p. 119.

[15] Cf. Funk et al., *Five Gospels*, p. 481, who deny a link with mission and suggest it concerns "the question of social and religious practice more generally". But surely the instruction about healing points in a more specific direction, even if, it, too, has been spiritualised to represent those without the light, as in *Pistis Sophia* and elsewhere. See Fieger, *Thomasevangelium*, p. 74 n. 141, for references.

circumcision is different from Paul's and reflects a rationalising argument which appeals to what is allegedly natural.[16]

Saying 89 criticises purification of vessels.

> Jesus said: Why do you wash the outside of the cup? Do you not understand that he who made the inside is also he who made the outside?

In the ethos of Thomas we are probably right to recognise here an interpretation that draws the implication, that since the inside needs no ritual cleaning neither does the outside. Saying 22 also uses the antithesis, inside-outside, as part of a set of antitheses which include, upper-lower, male-female. To enter the kingdom, oneness must be achieved, singleness, which obliterates such distinctions. Doubtless the same thought is also present here, rather than a debate with Pharisees about whether to separate inside and outside in determining purifications requirements.[17] On the other hand, the saying reflects awareness of that debate and, effectively, dismisses it as irrelevant.[18] Thomas' Jesus has no place for the distinctions of Jewish purity Law, but has developed its own ascetic scheme of purity.

Saying 39 mentions the Pharisees and scribes directly.

> Jesus said: The Pharisees and the scribes have taken the keys of knowledge (and) have hidden them. They did not go in, and those who wished to go in they did not allow. But you, be wise as serpents and innocent as doves.

The saying assumes Pharisees have power and that they have, at least, the repository of knowledge. Perhaps "they have taken the keys", could indicate that Thomas' Jesus implies they have no right to the power. An alternative translation is: "They have received the keys". The knowledge for which they have hidden the keys doubtless refers to Jewish religious heritage, probably the scriptures in general, rather than just the Law. The complaint is that they have failed to use the scriptures in the way Thomas' Jesus approves. That is, they have not used them as a way to true salvation, for themselves, and therefore they have prevented others from doing so. Saying

---

[16] Meyer, *Thomas*, pp. 90–91, notes the tradition according to which a Judean governor made similar response about being born circumcised to Akiba. Similarly Fieger, *Thomasevangelium*, p. 162 n. 276, citing Billerbeck, *Kommentar* IV, 1, p. 35.

[17] See the discussion and notes on Q 11:39–41; Matt 23:25–26.

[18] Cf. Fieger, *Thomasevangelium*, p. 234, who prefers to interpret the saying on the basis of the similar contrast between inner and outer in Saying 22 and to see not a reference to Jewish practices, but to the need for inner unity. Koester, *Gospels*, pp. 91–92, also sees no polemical intent. The main focus may be on unity within, but, to my mind, the initial question in all probability alludes to Jewish practices and contrasts their concerns with this inner concern.

102 makes a similar point, adapting material from Aesop's fables about the dog in the manger, a widespread proverbial image.[19]

This raises the status of the scripture and of the Law in particular, for Saying 39, just considered, appears to assume their value. Saying 52 makes comment about the prophets.

> His disciples said to him: Twenty-four prophets spoke in Israel, and they all spoke of you. He said to them: You have abandoned the living one before your eyes, and spoken about the dead.

The saying rebukes the disciples for their attention to the words of the prophets, while not necessarily denying the substance of what the disciples report. The saying is probably not anti-Old Testament, but rather treats the Old Testament as no longer relevant, since Christ, the living one, is with them. Some negativity is probably implied by the association of Saying 52 and 53 which declares physical circumcision of no value.[20] Saying 65, the parable of the wicked tenants, assumes some recognition of previous emissaries. Saying 31 also assumes some status for the prophets; they exemplify those who are not received in their own country. Saying 88 appears to assume that prophets still function as itinerants within the area of the community. There is no comment, however, in relation to the Law as a part of scripture.

Saying 43 attacks "the Jews"[21] in the context of chiding the disciples.

> His disciples said to him: Who are you that you say these things to us? <Jesus said to them:> From what I say to you, do you not know who I am? But you have become like the Jews; for they love the tree (and) hate its fruit, and they love the fruit (and) hate the tree.

Loving the tree and hating the fruit, or loving the fruit and hating the tree is a striking metaphor for lack of integrity between being and doing. The point of the analogy is not immediately clear. Perhaps knowledge of the Jews' question about Jesus' authority lies in the background (Mark 11:28; cf. John 2:18). Jesus' initial response is Johannine in tone (cf. John 14:8–9). The fruit and tree imagery echoes Matt 7:17–20; 12:33; par. Luke 6:43–44. The argument may be that the Jews allegedly love God, but do not accept Jesus

---

[19] Cf. Lucian, *Timon* 14; *Adv. Indoctum* 30. So Fieger, *Thomasevangelium*, p. 258.

[20] Cf. Gärtner, *Thomas*, pp. 156–157, who argues that the juxtaposition of Saying 52 (treating the 24 prophets as "dead") and 53 reflects an anti Old Testament stance reminiscent of Marcion, yet he also notes that gnosticism did not necessarily abandon the Old Testament, but saw Christ active in the prophets (*Pistis Sophia* 7,18,135; p. 158). This may also be assumed in Thomas.

[21] Cf. Funk et el. *Five Gospels*, p. 496, "the Judeans".

who may be represented by the fruit in the first half of the saying. The second half then means: they love (what they consider to be the fruit), but fail to love God. If this be so, the second half would summarily dismiss Jewish practices. But this is far from certain. The following Saying 44, in speaking of blaspheming the Spirit, may well be linked with Saying 43 by the motif of "fruit". The motif of fruit bearing had already appeared in Saying 40 which spoke of a vine to be uprooted which had not established itself, probably another allusion to the Jews. This is made all the more probable by the fact that it is preceded by Jesus' warning about the Pharisees and scribes in Saying 39. Saying 45 continues the metaphor of fruit.

> Jesus said: Grapes are not harvested from thorn bushes, nor are figs gathered from hawthorns [f]or they yield no fruit. [A go]od man brings forth good from his treasure; a bad man brings forth evil things from his evil treasure, which is in his heart, and he says evil things, for out of the abundance of his heart he brings forth evil things.

While the focus here is not directly the Torah, it does confirm the basis of Thomas' ethics. Only fruit bearing plants can bear fruit; this is the nature of the true believer. The inner person is the key to what is produced in attitude and behaviour. While the imagery echoes Matt 7:16; 12:34–35; Luke 6:44b–45, the heart within as a source for ethics also reflects Mark 7:21–22. In the world of Thomas' thought, what matters is wholeness of being, oneness, purity within.

Perhaps the contrast between old and new wine, and the image of the old patch on the new garment in Saying 47 also reflect the conflict with the Pharisees, as they do in Mark. However in the saying about the wine the old is preferred, so that the focus is incompatibility and incomparability[22] rather than a salvation historical scheme which would entail the new being superior. Saying 47 confronts the hearer with choices: one cannot ride two horses, stretch two bows, serve two masters, mix new wine and old wineskins or use old patches on new garments. Read in the light of the preceding context from Saying 39 on, it must include the choice against Judaism (probably including Jewish Christianity).[23]

Some other sayings may reflect on Jesus and the Law. Saying 90 has Jesus call people to take upon themselves his easy yoke and find rest, an echo of Matt 11:28–30, where Jesus speaks as Torah does in Sirach 51. The juxtaposition with Saying 89, which dismisses purity concerns about washing cups, may indicate that, as in Matthew and Sirach, the yoke image alludes to

---

[22] Similarly, Fieger, *Thomasevangelium*, p. 153.
[23] Another possible allusion to the rejection of Judaism may be found in Saying 107 which contrasts love for the one lost sheep more than for the ninety–nine

Torah. If so, it is to the Law of Jesus as alternative to Jewish Torah and as
not derived from it. Saying 30, "Where there are three gods, they are gods;
where there are two or one, I am with him", is similar to Matt 18:20 and
similarly echoes Jewish ideas about the presence of God's shekinah where
people gather to study Torah; but the Saying appears to highlight the
individual as against the group, a characteristic emphasis in the collection,
and not to relate to the Law. This is more clearly evident in the apparently
earlier parallel to Saying 30 in P Ox 1, Recto lines 23–26. Funk et al. suggest
it is anti-institutional, since it gives preference to the individual or the couple
over against the group.[24]

In Saying 71 Jesus appears to allude to the destruction of the temple.[25]

Jesus said: I will des[troy] this house and none shall be able to build it [again].

An allusion to the destruction of the temple may also be present in the
reference to the plucking out of the vine in Saying 40. Saying 71 is striking
in preserving the form, "I will", as authentic, and in not having a comment
about Jesus raising it up or rebuilding it. The reference to the cornerstone
rejected by the builders (Saying 66), in association with the parable of the
wicked tenants (Saying 65), is probably not an allusion to the idea of a new
temple.

It is interesting that Saying 48 also refers to a "house":

If two make peace with one another in this one house, they will say to the mountain,
"Be removed, and it will be removed."

In Mark the community of faith is the new temple. Mark reports this promise
of the power of prayer to move mountains (Mark 11:23) in the context of the
account of the cursing of the fig tree and its demise, which encloses the
episode describing Jesus' action in the temple. Thomas may also associate
"house" with community and with its power to move mountains (cf. also
Saying 106). Alternatively, the translation could read, "in a single house",[26]
in which case no such allusion is present. In that case the "house" would
refer to the single individual who has overcome division and found wholeness.
This would find some support in Saying 106, which speaks of those who
"make the two one", who will be able to move mountains, and in what follows

---

[24] Funk et el. *Five Gospels*, p. 490.

[25] Cf. Fieger, *Thomasevangelium*, p. 202, who argues that it refers to the material
world. Crossan, *Historical Jesus*, p. 355, considers that it did originally refer to the temple,
but may not do so now in Thomas.

[26] So Meyer, *Thomas*, p. 43. Fieger, *Thomasevangelium*, pp. 153–155, sees "im selben
Haus" as referring to the gnostic person.

in Saying 49, which also highlights the solitary and elect who will find the kingdom as the place whence they came and to which they return.

The conclusion of the parable of the great supper in Saying 64 seems also to echo what elsewhere is the message of Jesus' clearing of the temple: "Traders and merchants shall not enter the places of my Father" (cf. John 2:16; Luke 19:45–46). It seems that the saying has made a connection between the temple and "the places of the Father", but identifies these with the heavenly realm. It appears then that Thomas knows of the demise of the temple and considers it a deed of Jesus, because the true temple is the place of the Father to which the true believer returns. There is no place for earthly temples.

Saying 100 about tribute to Caesar gives no indication of relating to Torah issues. The same is true of sayings enjoining loyalty to Christ above loyalty to family (Sayings 16, 55, 99, 101).[27] Saying 93 about not giving what is holy to dogs also gives no indication of possible connections with Jewish thought. Saying 60 speaks of a Samaritan carrying a lamb to Judea which he will consume and may allude to sacrifice or even Passover, but serves the metaphor of consuming rather than becoming a corpse and being consumed (cf. also Sayings 7, 11).

It is interesting that Saying 12 acknowledges James the Just as the leader of the Christian community. Saying 13 mentions also Simon Peter and Matthew, but the focus is on Thomas. The Saying sets him above all three. The identification of James as leader may indicate close contact and conflict with conservative Jewish Christianity of the kind that looked primarily to James. Many of the attacks on Jewish practices would apply equally to such Jewish Christianity.[28] It is also interesting to note that Matthew and Simon Peter feature together here, perhaps also reflecting the same general Jewish Christian ethos. Thomas' approach to the Law is certainly furthest from theirs.

6.1.2 Jesus' Attitude towards the Law in Thomas – Conclusions

The Gospel of Thomas touches on a range of Jewish issues. It consistently rejects Jewish practices. These include fasting, prayer (perhaps particular forms of prayer, but usually associated with fasting) and almsgiving. It rejects dietary laws and also, by implication: sabbath, circumcision, purification

---

[27] On the negative attitude towards family and sexuality as belonging to the world, see Meyer, "Making Mary Male", pp. 555–556.

[28] Cf. Crossan, *Historical Jesus*, pp. 410–411, who argues the transition is peaceful, not polemical.

laws, and the temple. Many of these it spiritualises. Fasting becomes a term for strict asceticism over against the world; sabbath, a symbol of permanent rest; circumcision, the life of the Spirit; and the temple, an image of the places of the Father, the heavenly kingdom. It rejects Pharisees and scribes and Jews in general. It appears to allude to the destruction of the temple and the demise of Israel as the true vine.

The Gospel of Thomas portrays Jesus as coming from beyond this world to address those who come from the world of light and who, if restored to wholeness, will return there. This dualism doubtless informs its rejection of the relevance of all Jewish observances. They would be considered as belonging to the world. In this Thomas is similar to John. But, unlike John, Thomas shows no concern about the status of the Law and of scripture. It appears that these had no authority for Thomas, although they have had an acknowledged role at the level of prophecy and of having been a key to true knowledge. In contrast to John, Thomas even denies the validity of this role for the believer. Thus while there are occasional neutral allusions to Old Testament figures (eg. "Adam" in Saying 46, "prophet" in Saying 31), Thomas condemns continuing concern with the prophets.

A comparatively large number of sayings reflect contact with Judaism and Jewish themes. The references to James as the leader of the disciples, but also to Matthew and Simon Peter, indicates that the encounter with Judaism has taken place in association with Jewish Christianity, perhaps, even within some conservative form of Jewish Christianity.[29] The Christianity reflected in the Thomas sayings understands Jesus to give no place to the Law. Instead he speaks as in Judaism the Law spoke, offering its yoke. Ethics flow from within and belong to a system of thought which calls for separation from the world, including sexuality, on the basis of belonging to a higher order.

---

[29] Peter's negative attitude towards women may reflect conflict over the place of women in the community of Thomas, but Saying 114 counters Peter's desire to exclude women with its understanding of salvation as necessarily obliterating such distinctions.

6.2 Other Gospels and alleged Sayings of Jesus[30]

Very little relevant material is present in other gospels or fragments of gospels claimed to be early.

6.2.1 POx 840 gives an account of Jesus assailed for entering the Court of Israel of the Temple in an unpurified state: "A Pharisaic chief priest" asks: "Who gave thee leave to <trea>d this place of purification and to look upon <the>se holy utensils without having bathed thyself and even without thy disciples having <wa>shed their f<eet>."[31] The Pharisee goes on to explain the requirement either to bathe or to change one's clothes and, when asked by Jesus, assures him that he has bathed and put on clean clothes. Jesus then responds:

> Woe unto you blind that see not! Thou hast bathed thyself in water that is poured out, in which dogs and swine lie night and day and thou hast washed thyself and hast chafed thy outer skin, which prostitutes also and flute-girls anoint, bathe, chafe, and rouge, in order to arouse desire in men, but within they are full of scorpions and of <bad>ness <of every kind>. But I and <my disciples>, of whom thou sayest that we have not im<mersed> ourselves, <have been im<mersed in the liv<ing . . .> water which comes down from < . . . B>ut woe unto them that . . .

This portrays Jesus as rejecting the purification requirement. It does so by implicitly rejecting the value of immersion in literal water and by ridicule. The note of ridicule is contained in the reference to dogs and especially pigs, who symbolise the unclean. In ridicule this Jesus is turning Jewish scruples against the Jews themselves. The fragment continues with the common religious polemic of alleging sexual immorality. It echoes, but goes beyond, Matt 23:27–28. The author of the saying assumes not only such immorality, but also the presence of pigs in Jerusalem. At least the latter underlines the unreal quality of the encounter. The claim to have been immersed in living water represents justification for abandoning (and disparaging) Jewish purification practices.[32]

---

[30] The English translations of the following material are those edited by R. McL Wilson in *New Testament Apocrypha. Volume One: Gospels and Related Writings*, edited by W. Schneemelcher, (Cambridge: James Clarke; Louisville: Westminster/John Knox Press, 2nd ed., 1991).

[31] Deines, *Steingefässe*, p. 257 n. 528, draws attention to the possibility that there existed a provision that after the their immersion for purification people passing through the Gentile court wash their feet before proceeding further to remove potential uncleanness.

[32] See also the discussion in Booth, *Purity*, pp. 211–213, who, in discussing issues of

On the other hand, as Deines points out,[33] some aspects of the story do reflect knowledge of purity requirements, reflected also in John 11:55. Archaeology has confirmed the presence of baths for immersion. The Pharisee's explanation that he entered by one step and left by another corresponds to practice in the Second Temple period. It appears that priests or Levites supervised bathing for the various purposes for which it was required and gave those who had immersed some kind of note which they then had to show as evidence at the entry, in order, for example, to take part in a sacrificial meal. The account assumes that Jesus and the disciples do not have such evidence. There may also have been an additional requirement that feet be washed.

The rejection of the purification requirement has been formulated by someone apparently familiar with the procedures. The polemic employs Jewish presuppositions about pigs to ridicule the practice and to symbolise the hypocrisy, which it attacks otherwise with reference to sexual immorality. Behind the rejection is a dualism which pits what comes from above against mere physical water. It is the kind of conflict one would have expected in Jerusalem had Jesus not observed the immersion requirement. The author assumes this would have been so.

6.2.2 *The D text of Luke 6:5* recounts an exchange concerning the sabbath.

On the same day he [Jesus] saw a man working on the sabbath. He said to him, "Man, if you know what you are doing, you are blessed; but if you do not know, you are accursed and a transgressor of the law!"

Jeremias argues that the saying is directed against frivolous neglect of the sabbath and is all the more remarkable for occurring in Codex D which does not otherwise exhibit Jewish Christian tendencies.[34] He rightly emphasises the sternness of the warning. Unless this is merely rhetorical, it probably reflects a stance which is concerned to uphold sabbath law, but as interpreted by Jesus. This assumes that the first half of the saying is not sanctioning

---

historicity, rejects the account as "the product of a Hellenistic, strongly anti–Jewish church" (p. 213).

[33] Deines, *Steingefässe*, pp. 257–260. See *mHag* 2:6; Jos *Ant* 12:145; *Ap* 2:103–104; Philo *Spec Leg* 1:156. See also D. R. Schwartz, "Viewing the Holy Utensils (P. Ox. V, 840)," *NTS* 32 (1986), pp. 153–159, who explains the viewing of holy utensils as something which reflects not entry into the sanctuary, but a concern of the Pharisees to enable lay people to see such utensils against the more restrictive views of the Sadducees. In fact, he argues, this fragment confuses the facts by having Jesus attack a stance as Pharisaic, whereas tannaitic traditions indicate that the Pharisees themselves attacked the stance as Sadducean.

[34] Jeremias, J. *Unknown Sayings of Jesus*, (London: SPCK, 2nd edn, 1963), p. 63.

just any kind of work, but the kind of work which according to Jesus' interpretation of sabbath law overrides the sabbath.

Alternatively, the saying is along the same lines as Paul's argument in Romans 14:23 about the integrity of conscience and assumes that Jesus no longer binds people to the Law (at least, the sabbath law).[35] This would be especially so if "knowing" here implies belonging to the elect who are above such concerns as the sabbath and Jewish Law, as we might understand it, were it found in the Thomas collection. But even then the second half seems too stern.

6.2.3 Papyrus Egerton 2 has material pertaining to Jesus' attitude towards the Law. Fragment 1 has strongly Johannine echoes. It begins with the statement: ". . . <to> the lawyer<s: Punish e>very one who act<s contrary to the l>aw, but not me!" The assumption is that Jesus is not acting contrary to the Law. The material which follows echoes the Johannine sabbath controversies (John 5:39,45; 9:29; 5:46), expounding the view that the scriptures and Moses testified to Christ and therefore threatening the Jews that Moses is their accuser, much in line with Johannine thought concerning the role of Moses and the scriptures.

The reverse side of the fragment contains reference to the outcome of the trial: the attempt to stone Jesus and his escape. It then continues with an account of the healing of a leper, related to Mark 1:40–45 and parr. The leper hails Jesus as one who is "wandering with lepers and eating with them." Table fellowship of Jesus with lepers is without parallel, but reflects an understanding of Jesus' dining habits as not only in conflict with the Law at a general level because he was mixing with the wicked, but also because some were ritually impure, as here the lepers. The account tells how Jesus "cleansed" the leper, which is understood, as in Mark, not as a priestly act, but as a healing, which still requires that the man show himself to the priests and make the purification offering.[36] The document assumes some validity for the cult, but beyond that it is not possible to determine what that might have been. It is certainly not dismissive of priests, temple or sacrifice.

Fragment 2 has an echo of John 3:2 in acknowledging Jesus on the basis of his works as having come from God. In addition it identifies Jesus' works

---

[35] Bauckham, "Sabbath and Sunday in the Post–Apostolic Church," p. 256, writes: "Only the basis of a right understanding of his relation to the Law might he work on the sabbath. The closest New Testament parallel is Romans 14:23."

[36] See Crossan, *Historical Jesus*, pp. 321–323, for the view that PapEgerton 2 preserves an account of the story independent of the gospels.

as giving the evidence which the prophets had given for themselves. The question is about tax, but what is preserved of Jesus' answer is a rebuke of the questioners, rather than a response to the substance of the question.

6.2.4 P. Ox. 1224 reports the anger of the scribes and Pharisees and priests that Jesus reclined at table with sinners. Jesus responds, as in Mark 2:17, by pointing out that the sick need a doctor.

6.2.5 The Gospel of the Nazareans includes a version of the rich man coming to Jesus (fragment 16). There is no initial exchange about the manner with which the man addresses Jesus as in Mark 10:17–18 and parr. Instead Jesus responds directly: "Man, fulfil the law and the prophets." There is no elaboration about commandments. The man affirms he has done so, but Jesus responds: "Go and sell all that thou possessest and distribute it among the poor, and then come and follow me." To the man's consternation, Jesus then responds as follows:

> How canst thou say, I have fulfilled the law and the prophets? For it stands written in the law: Love thy neighbour as thyself; and behold, many of thy brethren, sons of Abraham, are begrimed with dirt and die of hunger – and thy house is full of many good things and nothing at all comes forth from it to them!

The episode concludes with Jesus turning to Simon and uttering the famous camel logion.

This story reveals an attitude which affirms the Law. The focus is ethical and, in particular, related to the use of wealth, as in the Synoptic accounts. It reveals an understanding of the story according to which the command to give to the poor is not an extra, associated with following Jesus, but something which the Law demands. This, in turn, associates following Jesus closely with keeping the Law. Jesus' demand is to keep the Law and the prophets.[37]

On the other hand, there is some ambiguity concerning the extent to which it affirms the Law. The only command cited is the one added to Matthew's version of the story: love of neighbour. It is possible that the author had only the love command or ethical commandments in mind in affirming the Law. Yet the fact that this is the Gospel of the Nazareans, identified as the Jewish gospel, makes it likely that more is intended. The Jewish narrative world is reflected in the reference to "neighbours" as fellow descendants of Abraham; this reference may also reflect the author's world.

The Nazarean gospel also differs from the Synoptic passion narratives in

---

[37] So also Berger, *Gesetzesauslegung*, pp. 457–458.

having not the curtain of the temple torn, but its lintel capsized (fragment 21 and 36), but without indication of the meaning of the event.

6.2.6 The Gospel of the Ebionites has Jesus declare: "I am come to do away with sacrifices, and if you do not cease from sacrificing, the wrath of God will not cease from you" (fragment 6). This is a clear rejection of the temple cult and may well have originated at a time when the temple still stood, but need not have.[38]

6.2.7 The Gospel of Philip reflects acquaintance with Judaism. Its opening verse speaks of Hebrews and proselytes. 8 reflects sabbath observance. In 14 archons are exposed as the powers demanding animal sacrifices. This makes the Jewish cult a servant of such powers. 76 uses details of the temple building as symbols of the gnostic mysteries; it rejects actual temple worship in Jerusalem on the same grounds as in John 4: it is not worship in spirit and truth. The rending of its curtain represents its insufficiency to contain the deep mysteries of gnostic oneness. Believers are a third race which has left Judaism and Gentile paganism behind (102). But in none of these instances are we dealing with reports of alleged words of Jesus.

6.2.8 The fragment of the passion narrative in the Gospel of Peter mentions the ritual of washing hands (1:1; cf. Deut 21:6–8 LXX; Matt 27:24–25), concern of Herod about having Jesus buried before the sabbath (2:5), concern of the Jews about Jesus' not being left dead after sunset in contravention of Torah (5:15), but little else of particular relevance to our theme.

6.2.9 John 7:53 – 8:11, the woman taken in adultery, is one of the best known episodes long considered part of John but doubtless secondary. It is found in some manuscripts after Luke 21:38 and in some Georgian manuscripts after John 7:44 or after John 21:25.

It concerns an occasion in the temple where scribes and Pharisees bring to Jesus a woman caught in the act of adultery. We may assume that it is not about a bride to be, but a married woman, even though stoning is prescribed only for the former (and the man involved; so Deut 22:23–24). While the Mishnah later prescribed strangulation for the latter, the practice in earlier times appears to have been stoning. The sentence of death, but not its manner, is set out in Lev 20:10; Deut 22:22. Jesus' question, "Has no one condemned

---

[38] See Betz, *Sermon*, p. 175.

you?" (8:10) may suggest that no formal court hearing had taken place and that we have to do with "spontaneous justice".

Some see the issue as Jesus' adherence to the Law and even as his willingness, thereby, to transgress Roman law by supporting her execution (cf. 18:31).[39] It would then place Jesus at the point of dilemma between two systems of Law as did the question about paying tax. Possibly the action of Jesus in writing in the dust is meant to recall God's judgement on all, set out with similar imagery in Jer 17:13.[40]

Jesus then cleverly appeals to human compassion by asking those without sin to be the first the cast a stone. On the surface the argument appears to be that only totally innocent people may carry out the sentence of the Law. No society can afford such restriction. Jesus' statement is less an argument than an action which puts the accusers on the spot. It does not entail contravention of Torah, except in the sense of carrying out the sentence of death. But it is, in any case, clear that not all Torah provisions were carried out to the letter, not least sentences of death which were illegal under the Romans. Therefore the account need not imply Jesus contravenes Torah. His response indeed leaves it open for Torah to be fulfilled. It shames the accusers by appealing to their own sinfulness, so that it is they who do not carry out the prescribed sentence. The shaming paralyses them. It also contains an element of appeal to human solidarity and compassion on the basis that "we are all human". At the same time it makes clear that Jesus condemns the action and tells the woman not to sin further. The account, therefore, portrays Jesus as Torah observant, at least in relation to the laws concerning adultery, but as interpreting that Law in a compassionate manner which both upheld the Law and granted the woman a new beginning.

---

[39] So Schnackenburg, *Johannesevangelium II*, p. 227.

[40] For this and other alternatives see Schnackenburg, *Johannesevangelium II*, pp. 228–229.

Chapter 7

Conclusion

The aim of this final chapter is not to repeat the detailed conclusions found at the end of each chapter, but to compare and contrast them. I shall then append some comments of a preliminary nature about the issue of Jesus' attitude towards the Law behind the gospels.

7.1 Jesus' Attitude towards the Law in the Gospels

No two gospels are identical in their approach to Jesus' attitude towards the Law. This is very evident in comparing Mark and Q. In Mark the focus is on Jesus' authority in deed and word. Jesus is the ultimate authority under God. By this authority he not only declares God's will in relation to issues of Law such as the sabbath, and so declares the authority of Jesus' interpretations; he also rejects much of the Law: food laws, purity laws (or at least the principles underlying them), and the sacrificial cult of the temple. In doing so, Mark's Jesus still has a place for temple functions in relation to the leper, but probably now understood as largely a social function related to reintegration. Mark can also portray Jesus' initial reluctance on occasion to cross such boundaries, but then makes much of the crossing. In fact, Mark has composed large blocks of his material around the theme of rejecting previous barriers based in the Law and replacing the temple with a community of faith.

The attitude of Mark's Jesus towards food laws, purity laws, and the sacrificial cult, is not as in Matthew that they are of lesser importance or as in John that they were interim provisions enjoined by God. Rather they are irrelevant, on the basis that 'everyone knows' that such things have only to do with externals. For Mark operates with a value system which disparages such concerns. His attack is therefore not just on abuses and hypocrisy, nor just interpretation, oral or otherwise, but against having such laws at all. It is not a salvation historical perspective which might see them as God's gift in the interim.

Mark's Jesus has such authority that he can be selective with regard to the Law. The values that matter are not ritual and cultic, but ethical and, in a Markan sense, spiritual. Thus the command to love God and one's neighbour, the ethical commandments of the decalogue, remain in force. Mark's Jesus interprets them less as a series of demands and more as enjoining behaviours and attitudes which need to be internalised. This coheres with the way Mark's Jesus approaches interpretation of sabbath law: compassion for people is the basis for such interpretation for it reflects God's intention. God's intention, and perhaps, compassion, features in Mark's version of Jesus' teaching about divorce. Mark's Jesus is the ultimate authority. Correspondingly, while he asserts the continuing validity of the greater commandments refocused in line with his concern with love and human relationships, much of the rest of Jesus' teaching in Mark has nothing to do with the Law. It focuses on the mission of Jesus and his disciples and people's response to it.

By contrast, Q's Jesus upholds Torah in its entirety. Already its introduction of John the Baptist and judgement gives the concept of law a more central role and for Q this law is unmistakably *the* Law. Seen in this context Q's sermon, while lacking the direct references to the Law found in Matthew's version, nevertheless assumes Torah's validity throughout. For Q, the breaking in of the kingdom entails not only miracle and exorcism, but also the confrontation of the Pharisees over abuses of the Law. That is also part of the kingdom's battle. In this context and against abuses, Q's Jesus makes his most unambiguous declaration about the Law's continuing validity. Just as John's preaching remains valid for Q, so does Torah (16:16–17). Q's Jesus does not play off written against oral Law. He shows respect and acceptance of various applications of Torah in his time. The criticism is twofold: abuse, which manifests itself in hypocrisy and greed; and preoccupation with unnecessary distinctions. In this context Q's Jesus sets a higher priority on justice and love of God. In one sense this corresponds to Mark's focus on the great commandments, but there is a significant difference. Mark employs the contrast exclusively. Q employs the contrast inclusively: tithing of minor foodstuffs, for instance, remains a requirement. The same tenor of inclusiveness of Torah's demands is reflected elsewhere in Q. To excerpt 11:42c, 16:17 and the temptation narrative from Q as the work of a final redaction does not substantially alter this perspective, since it is enshrined already in the law structure of the message of John and Jesus. On the other hand, Q's claims for Jesus and the way it gave emphasis to ethics and the spiritual would have to lead to tensions. We see these emerging in different ways in Matthew and Luke.

It is therefore fascinating to see the way these two evangelists bring Q and Mark together. Matthew clearly opts for the approach represented in Q. This is reflected not only in the prominence he gives Q16:17 in 5:18 and its introduction in 5:17, but also in the way Matthew strengthens both the continuity between John the Baptist and Jesus and the image of Jesus as judge to come. Matthew extrapolates the motif of authorisation so that it supplies the main grid both for his christology and his understanding of the church. As in Q, law assumes central significance in such a grid and Matthew leaves us in no doubt that law is *the* Law. It is the Law as interpreted by Jesus and, under delegated authority, by the disciples and the community of faith. Like Q, Matthew assumes the validity of many Pharisaic applications of the Law, but criticises hypocrisy and over pre-occupation with detailed compliance. The focus is on applying and interpreting the Law on the basis of compassion. Matthew's twice repeated use of Hosea 6:6, "I desire mercy, not sacrifice", enunciates the stance. But it is one which understands such contrasts inclusively. Matthew still has a place for ritual and cultic law, even if he strongly emphasises "justice and mercy and peace" as being weightier.

This does not prevent Matthew from using Mark. Obviously Matthew views Mark's overall emphasis on Jesus and his authority positively. Yet it is striking that he reworks Mark in a way that removes all statements disparaging the Law and the cult. He employs the great Markan composition 6:7 – 8:26 with its centrepiece, 7:1–23, but has so revised it, that it now no longer celebrates the inclusion of Gentiles, but focuses on fulfilment for Israel. Gone is Mark's conclusion that Jesus rejected food laws and gone is the supporting material in the context which disparages them and associated concerns with purification of externals. The target is now extreme Pharisaic demands about handwashing. Similarly Matthew undoes Mark's theme of the community of faith as the new temple. Only abuses are attacked, for which God's judgement will come in the form of the destruction of the temple.

Yet while Matthew asserts the continuing validity of the Law, it is noticeable that, where Jesus expounds it for his own, the focus is not on the extent of detailed compliance quantitatively across all Torah provisions, but largely on ethics and Christian versions of Jewish acts of piety: almsgiving, prayer and fasting. The antitheses contrast restrictive interpretation with radical interpretation which focuses on both behaviour and attitude. The approach is typical throughout Matthew and corresponds essentially to the kind of ethical focus found also in Mark and Q. Within a salvation historical perspective Matthew places the mission to the Gentiles after Easter, but is silent about the implications for issues of Law. It may even be that Matthew would still hold to circumcision of Gentiles as a continuing requirement. His radical revision of Mark's composition to remove the solutions preserved in Mark indicates that he views such issues from a much more conservative, Jewish perspective.

Compared with Mark, Matthew has not diminished Jesus' authority. On the contrary, through the story of Jesus' miraculous birth, his expanded use of typology and of Old Testament prophecies, he has enhanced it. But it is an authority which stands in much closer continuity with Torah's authority, expanding the line already found in Q, that the message of the Law and of John the Baptist are taken up within the larger authority. Matthew is convinced of the coherence. Recent assessment by Judaists of individual antitheses would concur. Nevertheless Matthew's strongly christological orientation and emphasis on ethics and the spiritual would create severe tensions. These are already reflected in the community's alienation from the synagogue in his time.

Luke also opts in favour of Q's approach, though apparently writing from a less Jewish setting than Matthew. The striking thing about Luke in relation to the Law is that he gives so much attention to ritual and cultic Law. Luke will have us believe that faithful Jews continued to be faithful Jews (even as Christians) and remained observant of Torah, from Zechariah to Paul. He even appears to be claiming that Gentiles live in conformity with the Law's demands by keeping to the inspired decree of the apostles about food and marriage law. It is extraordinary that Luke not only includes material which indicates such observance incidentally, but often draws the hearers' attention to it. Luke's position seems to be consistent throughout. On the surface there is only one clear exception: declaring Gentiles clean and dropping the requirement of circumcision. Even then Luke does not appear to see it as a serious breach of Torah, but rather as a divine modification which otherwise leaves Torah in tact. It is an exception which proves the rule.

Yet beneath the surface, in the Acts material, there are contrary currents. Peter's vision portrays clean and unclean animals; in it God declares all clean and edible. It is difficult to weigh this within Luke's theology. He makes no use of the insight at a literal level with regard to food laws. On the contrary, he still appears to assume categories of purity in relation to foods when reporting the apostolic decree and to assume that Christian Jews still observe Torah to the full. This suggests that Luke has not taken the insight 'on board'. Luke strains to assert and imply consistency with Torah. He sees neither Stephen's speech nor the remarks of Paul or Peter about the Law as Law critical.

While Luke has not used the Q account of John the Baptist's preaching to develop the image of Jesus as judge as much as has Matthew, nevertheless the grid is not dissimilar. John, Jesus and the early church call for repentance and that repentance means turning from bad ways to good ways. This implies a central role for law and such obedience entails for Luke obedience to *the* Law. In particular, Luke makes it clear that this is the only way to salvation: believing what God has said and doing it. Under that rubric he gathers the commandments and the demands of discipleship together as one. The parable of the good Samaritan is paradigmatic of Luke's approach, both towards the Law and towards its interpreters. He attacks their distraction with purity issues which ought not to override compassion and friendship. In the same spirit he repeats the attacks on the Pharisees taken from Q and directs them with greater differentiation to their targets, Pharisees and lawyers. While Luke avoids explicit contrasts among commandments, a differentiation is implied. The focus is on compassion for people. Luke also appeals to 'common sense' values such as rescuing a child or an ox from a pit on the sabbath. The sabbath controversies show Jesus holding the concerns of his opponents up to ridicule rather than entering into dialogue with them. Luke assumes his hearers will share such common sense values, just as they will naturally sympathise with attacks on greed and wealth and will warm to the action of the Samaritan in the parable and judge those of the priest and Levite.

Luke's stance seems to be one of a Gentile claiming legitimation for a Christian community of Jews and Gentiles, believing he can show Torah faithfulness throughout the story of Jesus and the church. The issues would doubtless have been real in his time, but Luke's grasp of detail sometimes appears shaky (esp. 2:21–24). Luke appears to want to put a Torah observant face upon the Church, but in doing so scarcely disguises contrary currents. I think the indications are that Luke genuinely believes he is right. His concern is unity and continuity. He has submerged indications to the contrary. The great omission, which happens to delete Mark's careful composition celebrating inclusion of Gentiles and reporting Jesus' rejection of significant parts of Torah, I consider to have been deliberate. The material did not suit Matthew, either, so he rewrote it. Luke's solution was simpler. He retains allusion to the dispute about washing by introducing it elsewhere (11:38) and even echoes Mark's conclusion of 7:19c, but in a much modified sense that no longer implies rejection of food laws (11:41). Luke does not want to espouse Mark's radical option. Although effectively christology has long since held centre stage for Luke and Gentiles have filled the church, he continues to claim Torah faithfulness and continues to have a strong sense of identity with Israel, not only through the past, but also in the future. Looking for the redemption of Israel, hoping for the restoration of Jerusalem, remains part of Luke's hope. Accordingly, upholding Torah and identity with Israel remains a continuing concern.

When we move to John's gospel, we find a solution closer to Mark's, yet with its own distinctiveness. Unlike in Q, Matthew and Luke, John has reduced the role of the Baptist to being a witness to Christ. John has done the same to the scriptures and the Law. The Baptist was sent from God; the Law was given by God; that is not denied. The only abiding function is to point to Christ. The events which the Law reports and the institutions and practices for which the Law provides also function only as witnesses to Christ. John treats the events typologically; they show God in action. They therefore provide a pattern for recognising God's action in Christ. That is now the only value which they have. Similarly with the institutions and practices. God gave them. Their features therefore provide a pattern for recognising God's action in Christ. That is now the only value which they have. In that sense John assumes continuity; God was involved then; God is involved now. But apart from that, there is radical discontinuity. The events and institutions belong to the realm of the flesh, the world below. That does not make them evil. Rather it means that they are not able to provide what belongs to the realm of the spirit, the world above. 'Everyone knows' that God is spirit and is not to be worshipped on this or that mountain, but in spirit and in truth. Yet during Jesus' ministry the institution of the temple stood and Jesus even concerned himself to clear it of merchandise. With the "hour" of Jesus, the earthly temple is replaced by Jesus himself.

John, therefore, allows divine legitimacy to the old and acknowledges its validity up until the time of the new. But at the same time he emphatically denies that it mediates the truth from above; only the Son can do that. The old never mediated that kind of life; its Law was never manna from heaven in that sense. Its Law was given as an interim replacement to Moses, who wanted to see God's glory. The Law is not God's glory. Similarly, John denies that the Logos came in the Law. The Law is not light and life and truth and bread. Only the Logos is light and life and truth and bread. What streams of Judaism claimed for Torah through identification with Wisdom John claims for Jesus, and, unlike the allusive use in Q, Matthew and Luke, exclusively for Jesus.

The effect is to reduce the role of scripture and the Law to that of prediction and of providing divinely inspired patterns through the events it reports and the institutions it established. Even then, John shows no concern to develop detailed correspondence. John continues to use the scripture and the Law for this purpose, but, outside a context where appropriation of Jewish heritage is an issue, John and his community can largely ignore it, as in the farewell discourses and the epistles. Identity is established by identity with Jesus not with Israel. Ethics consists in following his command, not by following commands of Torah, even though in broad ethical terms there was considerable overlap.

John's approach effectively cuts off the authority of Torah, reflecting a complex history in which John's community had been cut off from the synagogue and no longer acknowledged its authority. John's Jesus does not really engage in interpretation of Torah; his appeal to the analogy of circumcision is an attempt to expose inconsistency in the opposition not to argue on common ground. Yet it is striking that John never attacks the institutions or practices themselves. This is different from Mark's approach who has Jesus declare that such things as food and external washing are by their nature irrelevant for the spiritual life. Mark tends to discredit and disparage, much as on occasion Hebrews could declare the old system useless because it dealt only with such things as blood of animals and food and drink (7:18; cf. 9:13). Mark's Jesus seems not to abrogate or revise, but to reject laws because of their inherent irrelevance. John's Jesus comes close to this in the discussion about places of worship, but it is still strongly tied to a sense of salvation history. God had commanded that worship be on Mt Zion. The Jewish heritage is not any old cultural baggage; it is God given, in contrast to that of the Samaritans (4:22). In fact, this is also the position represented most frequently in Hebrews (eg. 9:9–10). John's dualism operates with two spheres which are opposite and yet not opposite. With the coming of Christ the antithesis between the two sharpens, so that to reject Christ and to remain at the level of the flesh is now to choose enmity against God, to follow the way of darkness. This raised the possibility of deleting the proviso about time and generalising the dualism to the point where the Law's provisions always belonged to the world of enmity with God, a position to be espoused later by the Gospel of Philip, as we have seen.

In Thomas we are at a point much further removed, yet Thomas is rich in allusions to Jewish practices. It also alludes to Jewish Christians: James at their head, but also Peter and Matthew. In the name of Thomas it directly disparages a wide range of Jewish practices: fasting, prayer (perhaps particular forms of prayer, but usually associated with fasting), almsgiving, dietary laws, and indirectly: the sabbath, circumcision, purification laws, and the temple. Some it spiritualises, but it shows no respect for these as given by God, unlike John, even if in John the gift is only for an interim and is at a lower level. For Thomas rejects the Law outright and dismisses as irrelevant the kind of concern which John shows in pointing to the role of the scriptures and the Law as testimony to Christ. Thomas' Jesus and Thomas' community are beyond such need.

Of the fragments of gospels considered, the Gospel of the Ebionites attacks sacrifices, claiming Christ came to put an end to them. Unfortunately we do not have the wider context to show whether the author sees Jesus condemning sacrifices as being no longer valid or as never having been valid. The motif of Jesus' sacrifice replacing other sacrifices finds classic expression in Hebrews. It is noteworthy that it nowhere features in treatment of Jesus' attitude towards the Law in the canonical gospels.

POx840 (the controversy over immersion) reflects a Law critical stance, but one that is probably well informed about temple practice of the time. In its appeal to "living water from heaven" it sounds strongly Johannine, but its disparagement of the Jewish practice has more in common with the stance reflected in Mark 7. The D text of Luke 6:5 appears to reflect a liberal stance on sabbath law similar to that reflected in Rom 14:23. On the other hand, the accounts of Jesus' encounter with the leper in P Egerton 2 and of his encounter with the rich man in the Gospel of the Nazareans reflect a more positive stance towards Torah. The former, like Mark 1:40–45, shows Jesus respecting temple procedure, the latter depicts strong commitment on the part of Jesus to, at least, the ethical commandments. The anecdote, traditionally designated as John 7:53 – 8:11, recalls the anecdotes in Mark 2:1 – 3:6 and elsewhere, where Jesus, challenged about application of the Law, stuns his questioners with a clever aphorism. The issue is application of Torah. Jesus champions the compassionate mode of interpretation.

Of the gospels considered, all reflect some grappling with the issue, even Thomas, whose solution is rejection of Jewish practices, though without bedevilling the scriptures or the Law as such. John's is thoroughgoing, reflecting a reduction of the Law's authority. John achieves this by a combination of dualism and salvation history, which has the effect of retaining the scriptures and the Law as a source of symbolic witness beyond themselves and bedevils all who from now on remain at the literal level of observance and do not espouse Christ. He would probably see no further role for Law observance among Christian Jews. In the broadest sense John's stance may be described as reflecting a Platonic model, in the sense that it turns the Law and its institutions into a pattern only for higher reality. In this regard it is also like Colossians which can describe Jewish practices as shadows of what was to come (2:17). However, unlike Hebrews, John does not employ the philosophical terminology.

Mark's dualism informs the way he has Jesus effectively deny that ritual and cultic law can ever have validity. He does not use the notion of the old being a pattern or shadow of the new, although it may play a role in his view of the temple. Rather, especially in Mark 7, Mark's Jesus employs common rationalising critique of religion against aspects of the Law. In doing so, Mark raises different theological issues. At least in John cultic and ritual laws served a purpose; Mark seems to deny their value altogether. Mark, therefore, differentiates within the Law; John does not, nor does Hebrews. On the divorce provision Mark has Jesus offer a reason: it was either to harden or to provoke sin; but this does not fit the issue about food and cultic law. Berger argued that Mark was espousing a belief that distinguished between commandments given before the golden calf and the cultic law given after it, as similarly a provocation to sin, but the evidence is too late. However Mark's approach does cohere with critique of religion known to be present at the time and doubtless stands in some sense under its influence. The same kind of 'practical common sense' values about religion is present in Luke's traditions, but he submerges it beneath his claim about Torah faithfulness.

What distinguishes Mark from Matthew and Luke, in this regard, is that he employs antitheses exclusively. It is one thing to spiritualise ritual and cultic aspects of religion so that as well as practising them one sees them as symbolic of deeper meaning. This was a practice already evident in Aristeas and Philo and also in Deuteronomy and the prophets. It is another to pit the metaphorical against the literal meaning. Philo rails against Jews who did so (*Migr Abr* 89–93). Paul does so when he uses the inclusive biblical contrast between physical and spiritual circumcision to support abandonment of the former. Similarly Mark 7:15, with its explanation in 7:17–23, turns a contrast which gave higher priority to ethical over ritual purity into one which denies the validity of the latter altogether. He similarly appears to use the inclusive contrast between the love commandments and burnt offerings and sacrifices to serve an exclusive antithesis in his wider context which disparaged the latter. This is clearly part of Mark's redactional agenda, although there are signs, at least, in 7:15–23, that it was already present in Mark's tradition.

Matthew will have none of it; nor will Luke, though it was alive and well in his traditions. Matthew comes through as trying to gain the high ground over against Pharisaic interpretation of the Law and doing so in a strongly Jewish context. The Q material comes to his aid and, at points, has probably already been reworked before Matthew to emphasise the point. Luke's claim seems more defensively motivated. He is not in a struggle with a dominant Pharisaic movement trying to claim the high ground, but rather wants to prove something against the allegation that his Christianity represents abandonment of the Law. The issue is not just continuity with the past, but doubtless the continuing basis for unity in the present among Gentiles and Jews, and perhaps, also, political defence of the church against charges of the synagogue.

7.2 Jesus' Attitude towards the Law behind the Gospels – an Approach

The material we have considered represents the distillation of complex movements and processes behind which, in some form, is the event of Jesus of Nazareth, but also a number of other influences. It is compelling, for faith, or just for curiosity, to ask what lay behind these gospels and, in particular, what connection the attitudes they represent have to what may been the attitude of the historical Jesus towards the Law. To address such a task is well beyond the scope of the closing pages of this book and demands at least another! I want, however, to make some preliminary observations.

The divergence between Q (Matthew and Luke), on the one hand, and Mark, on the other, is the result, in part, of Markan interpretation of the tradition. I believe it is possible to detect an overlay of Markan radicalism. It is most apparent in Mark's creative composition of the material in 6:7 – 8:26 and in his treatment of the temple theme. 7:15–23, to which Mark added 7:19c, shows that his dualism was also developing in the tradition. The shift seems to have been from inclusive antithesis to exclusive antithesis. Behind Mark are traditions according to which Jesus gave priority to ethical behaviour and attitude over cultic and ritual law, but without surrendering the latter. Behind the saying about food in 7:15 is an inclusive antithesis which implies: this is more important than that, rather than: that is irrelevant. The inclusive understanding explains why the early Christian communities still had to grapple with food law issues. Similarly, Mark had obviously developed his own contrast between the temple and the new community. His tradition appears to preserve a Jesus concerned at temple abuses and predicting God's judgement on the system.

Mark's controversy stories seem based on earlier forms in which the 'punch line' was a clever aphorism of Jesus. To this has been added scriptural argument (in the controversy about plucking grain, 2:23–38, and in the discussion of divorce, 10:2–9) and directly christological reflection, which imply an appeal to Jesus' authority (so 2:10; 2:17b, 2:28). The earlier forms of the anecdotes portray a Jesus arguing not on the basis of his own authority or of scripture, but by riddles or brief clever replies which challenge people's way of thinking. They all indicate an attitude towards the Law which upholds it, but changes the emphasis in interpreting it. Sometimes they have the effect of juxtaposing response to human need and an approach concerned with compliance with commandments (2:9: "Which is easier, to say to the lame man, Your sins are forgiven, or to say, Rise, take up your pallet and walk"; 2:17a: "The well need no doctor, the sick do"; 2:27: "The sabbath was made for people, not people for the sabbath"; 3:4a: "Is it lawful on the sabbath to do good or do harm?"). Sometimes in doing so they assert God's intention (10:9: "What God has joined, let no human being set apart"; cf. also 11:17: "Give to Caesar what is Caesar's and to God what is God's"). To these belongs 7:15 which playfully and provocatively asserted the priority of inner purity ("Nothing which enters a person from outside can defile them, but the things which come out of a person, they defile them"). One of the aphorisms appears to justify Jesus' lifestyle on the basis of the coming of the new age (2:19a: "The children of the bridal chamber cannot fast while the bridegroom is with them").

Mark's tradition seems to have preserved a body of material with a strong coherence in thought and form, which portrayed Jesus' responses to issues of Law. In addressing application of the Law they emphasise: the priority of compassion for human need, of following God's original intention, of ethical behaviour and attitude above ritual and cultic. When we look at this kind of pre-Markan tradition, we see that it has much in common with emphases in Q and also in the special material of Matthew and Luke. While Mark lacks any indication that Jesus enjoined Pharisaic practices such as we find in Q 11:42 about tithing, his tradition shares with the others the emphasis on human compassion and on human need as taking a higher priority than ritual and cultic law. Matthew and Luke are very comfortable with Mark's stories which emphasise the centrality of the love commandments and the ethical commands of the decalogue.

In his special material, Matthew has traditions which depict a Jesus limiting his own mission and that of his disciples to Israel (10:5–6; 15:24; cf. also 10:23). Both Matthew and Luke portray the expansion of the mission to the Gentiles as occurring after Easter and limit Jesus' connections with Gentiles during his ministry accordingly, or, especially in the case of Luke, limit the nature of those encounters. In this they are doubtless reflecting tradition and, probably, reality. Jesus and his movement were initially Jewish. The indications are particularly strong in John, even though the equally strong sense of alienation created by expulsion from the synagogue colours the material. This is even more so the case with Thomas, which nevertheless is remarkable for its preoccupation with Jewish practices. There are strong indicators of Jesus' Jewishness in Matthew and Luke. Luke makes a point of emphasising it, but it is also traditional. Jesus' Jewishness is also reflected in John, where a special point is made of bringing him into contact with "Greeks" (12:20), the assumption being that this was not the norm.

In this regard Mark also preserves some striking traditions. Some, like the encounter with the Gerasene demoniac (5:1–20) are laced with Jewish values: triumph over the unclean land, demons, cemeteries, pigs, the seas. That is at the level of story telling. Others depict Jesus initially reluctant when faced with traditional Jewish boundaries. These include: his angry response to the leper flouted the boundaries to approach Jesus(1:40–45); his angry response to the woman with the flow of blood who crossed the limits and touched him (5:25–34); his initial refusal to help the Syrophoenician woman as a Gentile "dog" (7:24–30). Thus Mark also allows us to glimpse an image of a conservative Jewish Jesus. Q's account of the healing of the Gentile centurion's servant or child should probably be read in this light: Jesus initially refuses to come and in his response the centurion addresses the purity issue directly (Q7:1–11; Matt 5:8–13; cf. Luke 7:1–11). These stories were doubtless retold because their Jesus did cross the boundaries. The initial conservatism may then be important incidental evidence; or it may be the creation of a stereotype created to set off the more liberal image of Jesus.

One has to ask how such conservatism coheres with the humane focus of Jesus' application of Torah which is reflected in the aphorisms of Mark and in the emphasis elsewhere in the tradition on the importance of responding to human need. If both reflect historical material, what emerges may well be credible and realistic; Jesus had his own struggle on the issues, just as did his disciples, later. Any historical reconstruction must give full weight to the strength of the cultural and religious setting, which was strongly Jewish. It has been all too easy for Christian scholars, in particular, to imagine a Jesus without taking into account the Jewish practices which would have formed part of his daily life. The silence of the gospel materials about such things as tithing, purification after body emissions or the like, should not be interpreted as implying non observance. Rather they will have formed part of Jesus' life as a Jew. Had he repudiated them, there would have been a clear case against him. Jesus was never charged with such non compliance. The account in POx840 about Jesus' refusing purification by immersion before entering the temple is someone's deduction from a later perspective. Had it really happened, we should expect to find evidence among the charges against Jesus. It is striking that, despite the links which Mark is careful to forge between the controversies and the Jewish trial, none of the passion narratives reports allegations of this sort.

Some would take the matter further and argue that some of Jesus' attitudes reflect Pharisaic options. A conservative context appears to be assumed in the Johannine anecdote of the wedding at Cana (2:1–10). Water in stone jars is probably for hand washing. This tells us nothing of Jesus' own stance, which as Mark's tradition suggests, was critical of the practice (7:1–2,5, 15). More problematic is Jesus' logion about divorce and remarriage. Is it stemming from moral concern or from purity concerns? If from the latter, is it concerned about actions which force the woman to become unclean or is it extending laws applying to the high priest to ordinary people? Moderns are inclined to interpret the logion along the lines of the compassion found elsewhere in the tradition. That could explain the prohibition of divorce which would cast a woman into a desperate plight, but it does little to explain the prohibition of remarriage, which effectively closes off one major solution. 10:9 ("What God has joined, let no human being set apart") probably confronts preoccupation of Pharisaic interpreters with defining a ruling, rather than laying down a ruling itself. I am inclined to think that Jesus' concern is primarily moral, reflected also in a range of teachings which enjoin right moral attitude and behaviour. Nevertheless Jesus' sexual ethics seem to be a special case; his choice to be single would have stood out in his day. Sexual asceticism was commonly espoused by Jewish and non Jewish teachers of the period.

One of the problems in approaching the traditions is that they do not portray Jesus as a formal interpreter of the Law, despite what the Matthean antitheses suggest. Much of Jesus' instruction in Mark, and doubtless, therefore, in Markan tradition was about mission, his own and that of his disciples, and about responses to it. Apart from that Mark's Jesus teaches about humility in leadership. By contrast, Q has Jesus rove widely over a range of concerns, some ethical, some to do with trust. Matthew's and Luke's special material also includes such teaching. Broadly, much of it is at the level of popular wisdom which uses examples from nature and from human relationships in the process of teaching about God and God's will. Its orientation is of a piece with the approach found in Mark's aphorisms, though this needs to be argued in detail. It has a number of parallels also with non Jewish preacher philosophers. Treated in isolation from other traditions, equally ancient, such teaching could easily give the impression that Jesus stands under their influence, or, at least, shares a common influence.

More broadly, Jesus belongs in a period where Jews had been grappling with the validity of their own religious heritage in the face of the many other religious heritages to which Hellenistic culture exposed them. Reactions were diverse, from radical separation to full blown syncretism. In such a context the values which have the best chance of survival are the ethical and transcendent, rather than rites and practices peculiar to a single culture. Is Jesus' emphasis on the universal values over particularist ones of his culture to be seen as part of this response? These are important avenues of research to follow and have become associated in particular with the reconstruction of an earliest sapiential layer of Q. They need also to be linked to the Markan aphorism tradition, which both in form and content reflects a similar ethos.

The so called wisdom also has strong parallels with bodies of Jewish teaching, such as is preserved in the Testaments of the Twelve Patriarchs, but also in free summaries of the Law in Philo, Josephus and in writings like Pseudo Phocylides, and earlier Sirach. These saw themselves expounding Torah in the broadest sense. Probably much of Jesus' teaching is to be seen in the same light. The boundaries are fluid. Exposition of God's will is exposition of God's Law, whether or not one can find chapter and verse in the Pentateuch. Jesus the sage is doubtless to be seen in this light and the parallels to be explained as they are in other wisdom teachers, as early as in the material in Proverbs, by common insights shared across cultures. Concretely, we have to imagine a Jesus from a relatively conservative Jewish context in Galilee also having access to such traditions, through local Jewish traditions and teachers and perhaps also through some knowledge of non Jewish Hellenistic teaching or preaching. I would imagine that of the latter the most compatible for a staunch Jew would be those attacking paganism and idolatry. It is, after all, here that Jesus' teachings are closest to those of the popular preachers of the time, who attacked excessive preoccupation with cult and ritual and promoted individual ethics of love, friendship, self control and trust.

All of the gospels, with the exception of Thomas, indicate a strong link between Jesus and John the Baptist. We have seen that in Q and its successors, Matthew and Luke, John's emphasis on repentance implies a significant role for Torah. Matthew exploits this to the greatest effect, but all uphold the validity of John's challenge. Mark also links them strongly, though not through the motif of judgement. The relationship between John and Jesus in the tradition is of major importance for assessing Jesus' attitude towards the Law. A common feature is a shared sense of facing the climax of history, although this is also an area of controversy. John's behaviour, his asceticism, reflects an attitude of preparation for the climax. Jesus' behaviour, participation in feasts, reflects an attitude of celebration that the joy has come. Mark's anecdote, 2:18–19a (possibly 2:21–22), reflects the differences as does Q's account in 7:31–35, contrasting John and Jesus.

The implications for dealing with Jesus' attitude towards the Law are complex. None of the synoptic writers takes from Mark's anecdote the implication that John's demands for repentance (in its full sense of turning to a changed lifestyle) no longer apply. We have to differentiate temporary preparatory behaviours from permanent demands. While the latter is an emphasis in the Q stream, Mark still has Jesus uphold John's authority, with which Jesus associates his own. The contrast between John and Jesus also does not imply that Jesus is claiming total fulfilment of the hope which John espoused. In the Q stream this is even directly addressed by having John raise the issue. Future eschatology remains a component of Jesus' teaching. Partly for the same reason the early community retains its version of John's baptism.

The eschatological teaching of Jesus entails both a claim to fulfilment in the present and a focus on final future reversal in the time when God's reign is fully established. It forms an important context for understanding his attitude towards the Law. Luke presents Jesus' eating with toll collectors and sinners as an evangelistic strategy: to lead them to repentance. Tradition, both in Luke and elsewhere, suggests a different orientation. In part, it belongs to Jesus' celebratory activity; he sees no need to be ascetic. In part, it indicates an inclusiveness which coheres with the stance represented in his teaching that God offers all a place in his coming reign. In part, it may reflect a common strategy of popular moral preachers of the period to become the invited or uninvited guest at dinners of the rich. Such activity would raise Law issues about keeping the company of people who were wicked or unclean or both. Jesus' teaching about compassion, modelled on God's compassion, also informs his understanding of eschatology and so determines his inclusive behaviour in the present, which extends also beyond meals and includes his attitudes towards the poor, to women, to lepers and those with disabilities. There is a coherence here. It also coheres with his conservative Jewishness, since these are Jews whom he includes. Luke's special tradition has him justify an inclusive response to Zacchaeus on grounds that he, too, was a child of Abraham. Doubtless Jesus' appointment of twelve disciples and the traditions which promise them a role in the rule of Israel and which envisage his return to Jerusalem reflect the same kind of orientation. There is no question yet of eating with Gentiles.

A reconstruction of Jesus' attitude towards the Law needs then to take into account diverse strands of tradition: the radically humane Jesus; the culturally conservative Jesus; the theologically strict Jesus in issues of morality; the Jesus who is like popular Hellenistic preachers, Jewish and non-Jewish; the Jesus who give priority to ethical behaviours and attitudes above ritual and cultic Law; the Jesus who shares John's eschatology, but claims its partial fulfilment. Any treatment of Jesus' attitude towards the Law needs to weigh each carefully and examine the way they interrelate. In my view each is an aspect of the whole. The interrelationship between these aspects is important. This is an exercise in critical historical research and also in historical imagination.

Bibliography of Works Cited

Aarde, A. G. van, "'The most high God does live in houses, but not houses built by men...':
The relativity of the metaphor 'temple' in Luke–Acts," *Neotestamentica* 25 (1991), pp.
51–64

Alexander, P. S. "Jewish Law in the Time of Jesus: Towards a Clarification of the Problem,"
in *Law and Religion. Essays on the Place of the Law in Israel and Early Christianity*,
edited by B. Lindars, (Cambridge: Clarke, 1988), pp. 44–58

Allison, D. C. "A New Approach to the Sermon on the Mount," *EphTheolLov* 64 (1988),
pp. 405–414

Allison, D. C. "Matt. 23:39 = Luke 13:35b as a Conditional Prophecy," *JSNT* 18 (1983),
pp. 75–84

Allison, D. C. "Two notes on a Key Text: Matthew 11:25–30," *JTS* 39 (1988), pp. 477–
485

Allison, D. C. *The New Moses. A Matthean Typology*, (Minneapolis: Fortress, 1993)

Anderson, H. *The Gospel of Mark*, (London:Oliphants, 1976)

Arai, S. "Zum 'Tempelwort' Jesu in Apostelgeschichte 6.14," *NTS* 34 (1988), pp. 397–410

Ashton, J. *Understanding the Fourth Gospel* (Oxford: Clarendon, 1991)

Attridge, H. W. "The Philosophical Critique of Religion under the Early Empire," in *ANRW*
II.16.1, (Berlin: de Gruyter, 1978), pp. 45–78

Attridge, H. W. *First Century Cynicism in the Epistles of Heraclitus*, HarvTheolSt 29,
(Scholars: Missoula, 1976)

Bacchiocchi, S. *From Sabbath to Sunday. A Historical Investigation of the Rise of Sunday
Observance in Early Christianity*, (Rome: Pont. Greg. Univ., 1977)

Bachmann, M. *Jerusalem und der Tempel. Die geographisch–theologischen Elemente in
der lukanischen Sicht des jüdischen Kultzentrums*, BWANT 9, (Stuttgart: Kohlhammer,
1980)

Bacon, B. W. "Jesus and the Law. A Study of the First 'Book' of Matthew (Mt 3–7)," *JBL*
47 (1928), pp. 203–231

Bailey, K. E. *Through Peasant Eyes*, (Grand Rapids: Eerdmans, 1980)

Balch, D. "The Greek Political Topos Περὶ νόμων and Matthew 5:17,19 and 16:19," in
Social History of the Matthean Community, edited by D. Balch, (Minneapolis: Fortress,
1991), pp. 68–84

Balch, D. L. (ed.), *The Social History of the Matthean Community. Cross–Disciplinary
Approaches*, (Minneapolis: Fortress, 1991)

Banks, R. "Matthew's Understanding of the Law: Authenticity and Interpretation in Matthew
5:17–20," *JBL* 93 (1974), pp. 226–242

Banks, R. *Jesus and the Law in the Synoptic Tradition*, SNTSMS 28, (Cambridge: CUP,
1975)

Barrett, C. K. *A Critical and Exegetical Commentary on the Acts of the Apostle s, Vol 1*,
ICC, (Edinburgh: T&T Clark, 1994)

Barrett, C. K. *The Gospel according to St. John*, (London: SPCK, 2nd edn, 1978)

Barth, G. "Das Gesetzesverständnis des Evangelisten Matthäus," in *Überlieferung und
Auslegung im Matthäusevangelium*, WMANT 1, edited by G. Bornkamm, G. Barth, H.
J. Held, (Neukirchen–Vluyn: Neukirchener, 1960, 2nd edn, 1970), pp. 54–154; English:

G. Barth, "Matthew's Understanding of the Law," in *Tradition and Interpretation in Matthew*, edited by G. Bornkamm, G. Barth, H. J. Held, (London: SCM, 1963, 2nd edn, 1982), pp. 58–164

Bauckham, R. J. "Jesus' demonstration in the temple," in *Law and Religion. Essays on the Place of the Law in Israel and Early Christianity*, edited by B. Lindars, (Cambridge: Clarke, 1988), pp. 72–89

Bauckham, R. J. "Sabbath and Sunday in the Post–Apostolic Church," in *From Sabbath to Lord's Day. A Biblical, Historical and Theological Investigation*, edited by D. A. Carson, (Grand Rapids: Zondervan, 1982), pp. 251–298

Beare, F. W. "The sabbath was made for man?" *JBL* 79 (1960), pp. 130–136

Beavis, M. A. "Women as Models of Faith in Mark," *BibTheolBull* 18 (1988), pp. 3–9;

Becker, H. J. *Auf der Kathedra Mose. Rabbinisch–theologisches Denken und antirabbinische Polemik in Matthäus 23,1–12*, ANTZ, (Berlin: Institut Kirche und Judentum, 1990)

Becker, J. "Beobachtungen zum Dualismus im Johannesevangelium," *ZNW* 65 (1975), pp. 71–87

Berger, K. "Hartherzigkeit und Gottes Gesetz. Die Vorgeschichte des antijüdischen Vorwurfs in Mc 10:5," *ZNW* 61 (1970), pp. 1–47

Berger, K. *Die Gesetzesauslegung Jesu. Ihr historischer Hintergrund im Judentum und im Alten Testament. Teil I: Markus und Parallelen*, WMANT 40, (Neukirchen–Vluyn: Neukirchener, 1972)

Bergmeier, R. *Glaube als Gabe nach Johannes*, BWANT 12, (Stuttgart: Kohlhammer, 1980)

Betz, H. D. "The Logion of the Easy Yoke and of Rest (Mt. 11.28–30)," *JBL* 86 (1967), pp. 10–24

Betz, H. D. *The Sermon on the Mount*, Hermeneia, (Minneapolis: Fortress, 1995)

Beutler, J. "Das Hauptgebot im Johannesevangelium," in *Das Gesetz im Neuen Testament*, QD 108, edited by K. Kertlege, (Freiburg: Herder, 1986), pp. 226–236

Bihler, J. *Die Stephanusgeschichte im Zusammenhang der Apostelgeschichte* (Münster: Huber, 1963)

Billerbeck, P. (and Strack, H. J.)*Kommentar zum Neuen Testament aus Talmud und Midrash*, 4 vols, (Munich: C. H. Beck, 1922–1928)

Bishop, E. F. F. *Jesus of Palestine*, (London: Lutterworth, 1955)

Blenkinsopp, J. "Interpretation and the Tendency to Sectarianism: an Aspect of Second Temple History," in *Jewish and Christian Self–Definition*, edited by E. P. Sanders et al., Vol 2, (London: SCM, 1980), pp. 1–26

Blomberg, C. L. "Marriage, Divorce, Remarriage, and Celibacy: an Exegesis of Matthew 19:3–12," *TrinJourn* 11 (1990), pp. 161–196

Blomberg, C. L. "The Law in Luke–Acts," *JSNT* 22 (1984), pp. 53–80

Bock, D. *Luke 1:1 – 9:50*, (Grand Rapids: Baker, 1994)

Bockmuehl, M. N. A. "Matthew 5:32; 19:9 in the light of Pre–rabbinic Halakhah," *NTS* 35 (1989), pp. 291–295

Boismard, M.–E. *Moses or Jesus. An Essay in Johannine Christology*, (Minneapolis: Fortress, 1993)

Booth, R. P. *Jesus and the Laws of Purity. Tradition History and Legal History in Mark 7*, JSNTS 13, (Sheffield: JSOTPr., 1986)

Borg, M. J. *Conflict, Holiness and Politics in the Teachings of Jesus*, Studies in the Bible · and Early Christianity 5, (New York: Edwin Mellen, 1984)

Borgen, P. *Bread from Heaven. An Exegetical Study of the Concept of Manna in the Gospel of John and the Writings of Philo*, SuppNovT X, (Leiden: Brill, 1965)

Bornkamm, G. "Enderwartung und Kirche im Matthäusevangelium," in *Überlieferung und Auslegung im Matthäusevangelium*, WMANT 1, edited by G. Bornkamm, G. Barth, H. J. Held, (Neukirchen–Vluyn: Neukirchener, 1960, 2nd edn, 1970), pp. 13–47

Bovon, F. *Das Evangelium nach Lukas (Lk 1,1 – 9,50)*, EKK III/1, (Zurich: Benziger; Neukirchen–Vluyn: Neukirchener, 1989)

Brandon, S. G. F. *Jesus and the Zealots*, (Manchester: Manchester Univ. Pr., 1967)

Branscomb, B. H. *Jesus and the Law of Moses*, (New York: R. R. Smith, 1930)

Branscomb, B. H. *The Gospel of Mark*, Moffat NT Comm., (London: Hodder & Stoughton, 1941)

Braun, H. *Spätjüdisch–häretischer und frühchristlicher Radikalismus. Jesus von Nazareth und die essenische Qumransekte II: Synoptiker*, BHTh 24, (Tübingen: J. C. B. Mohr [Paul Siebeck], 2nd edn., 1969)

Brawley, R. L. *Luke–Acts and the Jews. Conflict, Apology, and Conciliation*, SBLMS 33, (Atlanta: Scholars, 1987)

Broadhead, E. K. "Christology as Polemic and Apologetic: the Priestly Portrait of Jesus in the Gospel of Mark," *JSNT* 47, (1992), pp. 21–34

Broadhead, E. K. "Jesus the Nazarene: Narrative Strategy and Christological Imagery in the Gospel of Mark," *JSNT* 52 (1993), pp. 3–18

Broadhead, E. K. "Mark 1,44: The Witness of the Leper," *ZNW* 83 (1992), pp. 257–265

Broadhead, E. K. *Teaching with Authority. Miracles and Christology in the Gospel of Mark*, JSNTS 74, (Sheffield: JSOTPr., 1992)

Broer, I. "Anmerkungen zum Gesetzesverständnis des Matthäus," in *Das Gesetz im Neuen Testament*, QD108, edited by K. Kertelge, (Freiburg: Herder, 1986), pp. 128–145

Broer, I. "Das *Ius Talionis* im Neuen Testament," *NTS* 40 (1994), pp. 1–21

Broer, I. "Die Antithesen der Bergpredigt. Ihre Bedeutung und Funktion für die Gemeinde des Matthäus," *BibKirch* 48 (1993), pp. 128–133

Broer, I. "Jesus und das Gesetz. Anmerkungen zur Geschichte des Problems und zur Frage der Sündenvergebung durch den historischen Jesus," in *Jesus und das jüdische Gesetz*, edited by I. Broer, (Stuttgart: Kohlhammer, 1992), pp. 61–104

Broer, I. (ed.), *Jesus und das jüdische Gesetz*, (Stuttgart: Kohlhammer, 1992)

Broer, I. *Freiheit vom Gesetz und Radikalisierung des Gesetzes*, SBS 98, (Stuttgart: KBW, 1980)

Brooke, G. J. "Christ and the Law in John 7–10," in *Law and Religion. Essays on the Place of the Law in Israel and Early Christianity*, edited by B. Lindars (Cambridge: Clarke, 1988), pp. 102–112

Brooks, S. H. *Matthew's Community. The evidence of his special sayings material*, JSNTS 16, (Sheffield: JSOTPr, 1987)

Brown, R. E. *The Birth of the Messiah. A Commentary on the Infancy Narratives in the Gospels of Matthew and Luke*, (New York: Doubleday, 2nd edn, 1993)

Brown, R. E. *The Death of the Messiah. From Gethsemane to the Grave. A Commentary on the Passion Narratives of the Four Gospels*, 2 Vols, (New York: Doubleday, 1994)

Brown, R. E. *The Gospel according to John*, AncB 29/29A, (New York: Doubleday; London: Chapman, 1966/1970)

Brown, R. E., *The Community of the Beloved Disciple. The Life, Loves, and Hates of an Individual Church in New Testament Times*, (New York: Paulist, 1979)

Bryan, C. *A Preface to Mark. Notes on the Gospel in its Literary and Cultural* Setting,s (Oxford: OUP, 1993)

Bultmann, R. "What the Saying Source Reveals about the Early Church," in *The Shape of Q. Signal Essays on the Sayings Gospel*, edited by J. S. Kloppenborg (Minneapolis: Fortress, 1994), pp. 23–34

Bultmann, R. *The History of the Synoptic Tradition*, (Oxford: Blackwell, 1963)

Burkill, T. A. "Historical Development of the Story of the Syro–phoenician Woman," *NovT* 9 (1967), pp. 161–177

Campbell, K. M. "The New Jerusalem in Matthew 5.14," *SJT* 31 (1978), pp. 335–363

Carlston, C. E. "Betz on the Sermon on the Mount – A Critique," *CBQ* 50 (1988), pp. 47–57

Carlston, C. E. "The Things that defile (Mark vii. 14) and the Law in Matthew and Mark," *NTS* 15 (1968), pp. 75–96

Carson, D. A. "Jesus and the Sabbath in the Four Gospels," in *From Sabbath to Lord's Day: A Biblical, Historical, and Theological Investigation*, edited by D. A. Carson, (Grand Rapids: Zondervan, 1982), pp. 57–97

Carson, D. A. "Matthew," in *The Expositor's Bible Commentary*, edited by F. E. Gaebelin, Vol 8, (Grand Rapids: Zondervan, 1984), pp. 1–599

Carson, D. A. *The Gospel according to John*, (Leicester: IVP; Eerdmans: Grand Rapids, 1991)

Catchpole, D. R. *The Quest for Q*, (Edinburgh: T&T Clark, 1993)

Cave, H. C. "The Leper: Mark 1.40–45," *NTS* 25 (1978–79), pp. 245–250

Chance, J. B. *Jesus, the Temple and the New Age in Luke–Acts*, (MercerUP, 1988)

Charette, B. "'To proclaim liberty to the captives.' Matthew 11.28–30 in the Light of OT Prophetic Expectation," *NTS* 38 (1992), pp. 290–297

Chilton, B. D. *The Temple of Jesus. His Sacrificial Program within a Cultural History of Sacrifice*, (University Park, Penn: Penn State Univ. Pr., 1993)

Christ, F. *Jesus Sophia: Die Sophia–Christology bei den Synoptikern*, ATANT 57, (Zurich: Zwingli, 1970)

Collins, J. J. "A Symbol of Otherness: Circumcision and Salvation in the First Century," in *To See Ourselves as Others See Us*, edited by J. Neusner and E. S. Frerichs, (Chico: Scholars, 1985), pp. 163–186

Collins, J. J. *Between Athens and Jerusalem. Jewish Identity in the Hellenistic Diaspora*, (New York: Crossroad, 1984)

Collins, J. J. *The Sceptre and the Star. The Messiahs of the Dead Sea Scrolls and Other Ancient Literature*, (New York: Doubleday, 1995)

Collins, R. F. *"These Things have been Written." Studies on the Fourth Gospel*, Leuven Theological and Pastoral Monographs 2, (Leuven: Peeters Pr; Grand Rapids: Eerdmans, 1990)

Conzelmann, H. *The Theology of St Luke*, (London: Faber and Faber, 1960), first published as *Die Mitte der Zeit* (Tübingen: J. C. B. Mohr [Paul Siebeck], 1953, 2nd edn, 1956)

Coser, L. *The Functions of Social Conflict*, (London: Routledge and Kegan Paul, 1956).

Cranfield, C. E. B. *The Gospel according to Saint Mark*, (Cambridge: CUP, 1963)

Crossan, J. D. *The Historical Jesus. The Life of a Mediterranean Jewish Peasant*, (San Francisco: Harper, 1991)

Dahl, N. A. "The Story of Abraham in Luke–Acts" in *Jesus in the Memory of the Early Church*, (Minneapolis: Augsburg, 1976), pp. 66–86

Dalman, G. *Jesus–Joshua. Studies in the Gospels*, (London: SPCK, 1929)

Daube, D. "Responsibilities of Master and Disciples in the Gospels," *NTS* 19 (1972–73), pp. 1–16

Daube, D. "Temple Tax" in *Jesus, the Gospels, and the Church. In Honor of W. R. Farmer*, edited by E. P. Sanders, (Macon: Mercer UP, 1989), pp. 121–134

Daube, D. *The New Testament and Rabbinic Judaism*, (London: Athlone, 1956)

Dautzenberg, G. "Frühes Christentum – Gilt die Tora weiterhin? Hellenistische Mission, Paulus und das Markusevangelium," *Orientierung* 55 (1991), pp. 243–246

Dautzenberg, G. "Gesetzeskritik und Gesetzesgehorsam in der Jesustradition," in *Das Gesetz im Neuen Testament*, QD108, edited by K. Kertelge, (Freiburg: Herder, 1986), pp. 46–70

Dautzenberg, G. "Jesus und der Tempel. Beobachtungen zur Exegese der Perikope von der Tempelsteuer (Mt 17,24–27)," in *Salz der Erde – Licht der Welt: Exegetische Studien zum Matthäusevangelium, FS für Anton Vögtle zum 80. Geburtstag*, edited by I. Oberlinner, and P. Fiedler, (Stuttgart: KBW, 1991), pp. 223–238

Dautzenberg, G. "Tora des Menschensohnes? Kritische Überlegungen zu Daniel Kosch," *BZ* 36 (1992), pp. 93–103

Dautzenberg, G. "Über die Eigenart des Konfliktes, der von jüdischer Seite im Prozess Jesu ausgetragen wurde," in *Jesus und das jüdische Gesetz*, edited by I. Broer, (Stuttgart: Kohlhammer, 1992), pp. 147–172

Davies, W. D. and Allison, D. C. *A Critical and Exegetical Commentary on the Gospel according to Saint Matthew*, Vol I. I–VII, Vol II. VIII–XVIII, ICC, (Edinburgh: T&T Clark, 1988/1991)

Davies, W. D. *The Setting of the Sermon on the Mount*, (Cambridge: CUP, 1966)

Davies, W. D. *Torah in the Messianic Age and/or Age to Come*, JBLMonSer. 8, (Philadelphia: SBL, 1952)

Deines, R. *Jüdische Steingefässe und pharisäische Frömmigkeit: eine archäologisch-historischer Beitrag zum Verständnis von Joh 2,6 und der jüdischen Reinheitshalacha zur Zeit Jesu*, WUNT 2.52, (Tübingen: J. C. B. Mohr [Paul Siebeck], 1993)

Delling, G. *Die Bewältigung der Diasporasituation durch das hellenistische Judentum*, (Göttingen: Vandenhoeck und Ruprecht, 1987)

Derrett, J. D. M. "Circumcision and Perfection: A Johannine Equation (John 7:22–23)," *EvangQuart* 63 (1991), pp. 211–224

Derrett, J. D. M. "Law in the New Testament: The Syro–Phoenician Woman and the Centurion of Capernaum," *NovT* 15(1973), pp. 161–186

Derrett, J. D. M. *Law in the New Testament*, (London: DLT, 1970)

Deutsch, C. "Wisdom in Matthew: Transformation of a Symbol," *NovT* 32 (1990), pp. 13–47

Deutsch, C. *Hidden Wisdom and the Easy Yoke. Wisdom, Torah and Discipleship in Matthew 11:25–30*, JSNTSS 18, (Sheffield: JSOTPr., 1987)

Dewey, Joanna, *Markan Public Debate: Literary Technique, Concentric Structure, and Theology in Mark 2:1 – 3:6*, (Chico: Scholars, 1980)

Dodd, C. H. *The Interpretation of the Fourth Gospel*, (Cambridge: CUP, 1953)

Donaldson, T. L. *Jesus on the Mountain: a Study in Matthean Theology*, JSNTS 8, (Sheffield: JSOT Pr., 1985)

Douglas, M. *Natural Symbols*, (New York: Vintage Books, 1973)

Douglas, M. *Purity and Danger*, (London: Routledge and Kegan Paul, 1966)

Downing, F. G. "Law and custom: Luke–Acts and late Hellenism," in *Law and Religion. Essays on the Place of the Law in Israel and Early Christianity*, edited by B. Lindars, (Cambridge: Clarke, 1988), pp. 148–158

Downing, F. G. "The Social Contexts of Jesus the teacher: Construction or Reconstruction," *NTS* 33 (1987), pp. 439–451

Dumbrell, J. "The Logic of the Role of the Law in Matthew 5:1–20," *NovTest* 23(1981), pp. 1–23

Dunn, J. D. G. "Jesus and Ritual Purity: A Study of the Tradition–History of Mark 7:15," in *Jesus, Paul and the Law. Studies in Mark and Galatians*, (London: SPCK, 1990), pp. 37–60

Dunn, J. D. G. "Mark 2:1 – 3:6: A Bridge between Jesus and Paul on the Question of the Law," in *Jesus, Paul and the Law. Studies in Mark and Galatians*, (London: SPCK, 1990), pp. 10–36

Dunn, J. D. G. *Jesus, Paul and the Law. Studies in Mark and Galatians*, (London: SPCK, 1990)

Dunn, J. D. G. *The Partings of the Ways. Between Christianity and Judaism and their Significance for the Character of Christianity*, (London: SCM, 1991)

Ebersohn, M. *Das Nächstenliebegebot in der Synoptischen Tradition*, MarbTheolStud 37, (Marburg: Elwert, 1993)

Edwards, R. "Χάριν ἀντὶ χάριτος (John 1.16). Grace and the Law in the Johannine Prologue," *JSNT* 32 (1988), pp. 3–15

Elliott, J. H. "Temple versus Household in Luke–Acts: A Contrast in Social Institutions," in *The Social World of Luke–Acts*, edited by J. H. Neyrey, (Peabody: Hendrickson, 1991), pp. 211–240

Eppstein, V. "The Historicity of the Cleansing of the Temple," *ZNW* 55 (1964)

Ernst, J. *Das Evangelium nach Markus*, RNT, (Regensburg: Pustet, 1981)

Esler, P. *Community and Gospel in Luke–Acts. The Social and Political Motivations of Lucan Theology*, SNTSMS 57, (Cambridge: CUP, 1987)

Evans, C. A. "Jesus' action in the temple and evidence of corruption in the first century temple," *SBLSemPapers* 1989, pp. 522–538.

Evans, C. A. "Jesus' action in the temple: Cleansing or Portent of destruction?" *CBQ* 51 (1989), pp. 237–270

Evans, C. A. "Predictions of the Destruction of the Herodian Temple in the Pseudepigrapha, Qumran Scrolls, and Related Texts," *JournStudPseud* 10 (1992), pp. 89–147

Evans, C. F. "The Central Section of Luke's Gospel," in *Studies in the Gospels. Essays in Memory of R. H. Lightfoot*, edited by D. E. Nineham, (Oxford: Blackwell, 1955), pp. 37–53

Evans, C. F. *Saint Luke*, (London: SCM, Philadelphia: Trinity, 1990)

Fander, M. *Die Stellung der Frau im Markusevangelium : unter besonderer Berücksichtigung kultur– und religionsgeschichtlicher Hintergründe*, (Altenberge: Telos, 1990)

Fieger, M. *Das Thomasevangelium. Einleitung, Kommentar und Systematik*, Neutestamentliche Abh. NF 22, (Münster: Aschendorff, 1991)

Filson, F. V. *The Gospel according to Saint Matthew*, Black's NT Comm., (London: A&C Black, 1960)

Fitzmyer, J. A. "The Jewish People and the Mosaic Law in Luke–Acts," in *Luke the Theologian. Aspects of his Teaching*, (London: Chapman, 1989)

Fitzmyer, J. A. "The Matthean Divorce–Texts and Some New Palestinian Evidence," in *To Advance the Gospel*, (New York: Crossroad, 1981)

Fitzmyer, J. A. *The Gospel according to Luke*, AncB 28/28A, (New York: Doubleday, 1981/1985)

Fleddermann, H. "Demands of Discipleship. Matt 8,19–22 par. Luke 9,57–62," in *The Four Gospels 1992. Festschrift Frans Neirynck*, BETL 100, edited by F. van Segbroeck et al., (Leuven: Leuven University Press, Peeters, 1992), pp. 541–562

Fowler, R. M. *Loaves and Fishes. The Function of the Feeding Stories in the Gospel of Mark*, SBLDS 54, (Chico: Scholars, 1981)

France, R. T. *Matthew. Evangelist and Theologian*, (Exeter: Paternoster, 1989)

Frankemölle, H. *Jahwebund und Kirche Christi: Studien zur Form- und Traditionsgeschichte des "Evangelium" nach Matthäus*, NTAbh 10, (Münster: Aschendorff, 1974)

Franklin, E. *Christ the Lord. A Study in thew Purpose and Theology of Luke–Acts*, (London: SPCK, 1975)

Freyne, S. "Vilifying the Other and Defining the Self: Matthew's and John's Anti–Jewish Polemic in Focus," in *"To See Ourselves as Others See Us." Christians, Jews, "Others" in Late Antiquity*, Scholars Press Studies in the Humanities, edited by J. Neusner and E. S. Frerichs, (Chico: Scholars Press, 1985), pp. 117–144

Freyne, S. *Galilee, Jesus, and the Gospels: Literary Approaches and Historical Investigations*, (Philadelphia: Fortress, 1988)

Funk, R. A. Hoover, R. W. et al. *The Five Gospels. The Search for the Authentic Words of Jesus*, (New York: Macmillan, 1993)

Garland, D. *The Intention of Matthew 23*, SuppNovT 52, (Leiden: Brill, 1979)

Gärtner, B. *The Theology of the Gospel of Thomas*, (London: Collins, 1961)

Giblin, C. H. *The destruction of Jerusalem according to Luke's Gospel: A Historical–Typological Moral*, AnBib 107, (Rome: BIP, 1985)

Giesen, H. "Der verdorrte Feigenbaum – Eine symbolische Aussage? Zu Mk 11,12–14.20f.," *BZ* 20 (1976), pp. 95–111

Giesen, H. *Christliches Handeln : eine redaktionskritische Untersuchungen zum* δικαιοσύνη *Begriff im Matthäusevangelium*, Eur. Hochschulschriften 181, (Frankfurt: Peter Lang, 1981)

Glasson, T. F. *Moses in the Fourth Gospel*, SBT 40, (London: SCM, 1963)

Gnilka, J. *Das Evangelium nach Markus*, II/1.2, (Zurich: Benziger; Neukirchen–Vluyn: Neukirchener, 1978/79)

Gnilka, J. *Das Matthäusevangelium*, HTKNT I/1.2, (Freiburg: Herder, 1986)

Gowler, D. B. *Host, Guest, Enemy, and Friend. Portraits of the Pharisees in Luke and Acts*, Emory Studies in Early Christianity 2, (Frankfurt: Peter Lang, 1991)

Graham, S. L. "Silent Voices. Women in the Gospel of Mark," *Semeia* 54 (1992), pp. 145–158

Grams, R. "The Temple Conflict Scene: a Rhetorical Analysis of Matthew 21–23," in *Persuasive Artistry*, FS. G. A. Kennedy, JSNTS 50, edited by D. F. Watson, (Sheffield: JSOTPr, 1991), pp. 41–65

Grässer, E. "Die antijüdische Polemik im Johannesevangelium," *NTS* 11 (1964/65), pp. 74–90

Grassi, J. A. "Matthew as a Second Testament Deuteronomy," *BibTheolBull* 19 (1989), pp. 23–29

Green, J. B. "The Death of Jesus and the Rending of the Temple Veil (Luke 23:44–49). A Window into Luke's Understanding of Jesus and the Temple," in *SBL Seminar Papers 1991*, edited by E. H. Lovering, (SBL: Scholars, 1991), pp. 543–575

Grundmann, W. *Das Evangelium nach Lukas*, THNT 3, (Berlin: Ev. Verlagsanstalt, 1971)

Grundmann, W. *Das Evangelium nach Markus*, THNT 2, (Berlin: Ev. Verlagsanstalt, 1977)

Guelich, R. A. *Mark 1–8:26*, WordBibComm 34A, (Waco: Word, 1989)

Guelich, R. A. *The Sermon on the Mount* (Waco: Word, 1982)

Gundry, R. H. *Mark. A Commentary on His Apology for the Cross*, (Grand Rapids: Eerdmans, 1993)

Gundry, R. H. *Matthew. A Commentary on his Literary and Theological Art*, (Grand Rapids: Eerdmans, 2nd edn, 1994)

Haenchen, E. *Der Weg Jesu. Eine Erklärung des Markusevangeliums und der kanonischen Parallelen*, STÖ II,6, (Berlin: 2nd edn, 1968)

Haenchen, E. *Die Apostelgeschichte*, KEKNT III, (Göttingen: Vandenhoeck und Ruprecht, 1968, 1st edn, 1956

Hagner, D. "Righteousness in Matthew's Theology," in *Worship, Theology and Ministry in the Early Church. Essays in Honor of Ralph P. Martin*, edited by M. J. Wilkins et al., (Sheffield: JSOTPr., 1992), pp. 101–120

Hagner, D. A. *Matthew 1–13*, WordBibComm 33A, (Dallas: Word, 1993)

Hahn, F. "'Das Heil kommt von den Juden.' Erwägungen zu Joh 4,22b," In *Wort und Wirklichkeit. Festschrift für E. L. Rapp*, Band I, (Weisenheim, 1976), pp. 67–84

Hahn, F. *Der urchristliche Gottesdienst*, SBS 41, (Stuttgart: KBW, 1970)

Hamm, D. "Zacchaeus Revisited Once More: A Story of Vindication or Conversion?" *Biblica* 72 (1991), pp. 249–252

Hanson, A. T. *The Prophetic Gospel. A Study of John and the Old Testament*, (Edinburgh: T&T Clark, 1991)

Hare, D. R. A. – Harrington, D. J. "'Make Disciples of All the Gentiles' (Mt 28:19)," *CBQ* 37 (1975), pp. 359–369; also in Harrington, D. J. *Light of All Nations. Essays on the church in New Testament Research*, Good News St. 3, (Wilmington: Glazier, 1982), pp. 110–123 (cited according to the latter)

Hare, D. R. A. *The Theme of Jewish Persecution of Christians according the Gospel of St. Matthew*, SNTMS 6, (Cambridge: CUP, 1967)

Harrington, D. J. "Sabbath Tensions: Matthew 12:1–14 and Other New Testament Texts," in *The Sabbath in Jewish and Christian Traditions*, edited by T. Eskenazi, D. Harrington, W. S. Shea, (New York: Crossroads, 1991), pp. 45–56

Harrington, D. J. *Gospel of Matthew*, Sacra Pagina 1, (Collegeville: Liturgical, 1991)

Harvey, A. E. *Jesus on Trial. A Study in the Fourth Gospel*, (London: SPCK, 1976)

Hauck, F. Art. "ἀκάθαρτος, ἀκαθαρσία" *TWNT* 3 (1938), pp. 430–432

Hengel, M. "Mc 7,3 πυγμῇ: Die Geschichte einer exegetischen Aporie und der Versuch ihrer Lösung," *ZNW* 60 (1969), pp. 182–198

Hengel, M. and Deines, R. "E. P. Sanders' 'Common Judaism', Jesus, and the Pharisees," *JTS* 46 (1995), pp. 1–70

Hengel, M. *Judaism and Hellenism*, 2 vols, (London: SCM; Philadelphia: Fortress, 1974)

Hengel, M. *The "Hellenization" of Judaea in the First Century after Christ*, (London: SCM; Philadelphia: Trinity, 1990)

Hengel, M. *The Charismatic Leader and his Followers*, (Edinburgh: T&T Clark; New York: Crossroad, 1981)

Hengel, M. "Jesus und die Tora," *Theol. Beitr* 9 (1978), pp. 152–172

Hengel, M. "Jesus, der Messias Israels. Zum Streit über das 'messianische Sendungsbewusstsein' Jesu," in *Messiah and Christos: studies in the Jewish Origins of Christianity presented to David Flusser on the occasion of his seventy-fifth birthday*, Texte und Studien zum antiken Judentum 32, edited by I. Gruenwald, (Tübingen: J. C. B. Mohr [Paul Siebeck], 1992), pp. 155–176

Hill, C. C. *Hellenists and Hebrews. Reappraising Division within the Earliest Church*, (Minneapolis: Fortress, 1992)

Hill, D. "False Prophets and Charismatics: Structure and Interpretation in Matthew 7,15–23," *Biblica* 57 (1976), pp. 341–348

Hill, D. "On the Use and Meaning of Hosea VI.6 in Matthew's Gospel," *NTS* 24 (1978), pp. 107–119

Hoffmann, P. "Die Versuchungsgeschichte in der Logienquelle," *BZ* 13 (1969), pp. 207–223

Hoffmann, P. "The Redaction of Q and the Son of Man: A Preliminary Sketch," in *The Gospel behind the Gospels . Current Studies on Q*, edited by R. A. Piper, (Leiden: Brill, 1995), pp. 159–198

Hoffmann, P. *Studien zur Theologie der Logienquelle*, (Münster: Aschendorff, 1972)

Hofius, O. "Vergebungszuspruch und Vollmachtsfrage. Mk 2,1–12 und das Problem priesterlicher Absolution im antiken Judentum," in *"Wenn nicht jetzt, wann dann?": Aufsätze für Hans-Joachim Kraus zum 65. Geburtstag*, edited by H.-G. Geyer, (Neukirchen–Vluyn: Neukirchener, 1983), pp. 115–127

Holtzmann, H. J. *Die Synoptiker*, HCNT 1/1, (Tübingen: J. C. B. Mohr [Paul Siebeck], 3rd edn, 1901)

Hooker, M. D. "Traditions about the Temple in the Sayings of Jesus," *BJRL* 70 (1988), pp. 7–19

Hooker, M. D. *A Commentary on the Gospel according to St Mark,* Blacks NTComm (London: A&C Black, 1990)

Hoppe, R. "Vollkommenheit bei Matthäus als theologische Aussage," in *Salz der Erde – Licht der Welt: Exegetische Studien zum Matthäusevangelium. FS für Anton Vögtle zum 80. Geburtstag*, edited by I. Oberlinner and P. Fiedler, (Stuttgart: KBW, 1991), pp. 141–164

Horbury, W. "The Benediction of the *Minim* and Early Jewish–Christian Controversy," *JTS* 33 (1982), pp. 19–61

Horn, F. W. "Christentum und Judentum in der Logienquelle," *Evang Theol* 51 (1991), pp. 344–364

Horn, F. W. *Glaube und Handeln in der Theologie des Lukas*, (Göttingen: Vandenhoeck und Ruprecht, 1983)

Horsley, R. A. "Q and Jesus: Assumptions, Approaches, and Analysis," *Semeia* 55 (1991), pp. 175–209

Hübner, H. *Das Gesetz in der synoptischen Tradition* , (Witten: Luther–Verlag, 1973; 2nd edn, Göttingen: Vandenhoeck und Ruprecht, 1986)

Hultgren, A. *Jesus and his Adversaries. The Form and Function of the Conflict Stories in the Synoptic Gospels* (Minneapolis: Augsburg, 1979)

Hultgren. A. J. "Things New and Old in Matthew 13:52" in *All Things New. Essays in Honor of Roy A. Harrisville*, edited by A. J. Hultgren et al., (St Paul: Luther Northwestern Theological Seminary, 1992), pp. 109–118

Hummel, R. *Die Auseinandersetzung zwischen Kirche und Judentum im Matthäusevangelium*, BETh. 33, (Munich: Kaiser, 1966)

Hurtado, L. W. *Mark*, New International Biblical Commentary, (Peabody: Hendricksen, 1989)

Iersel, B. van, *Reading Mark*, (Edinburgh: T&T Clark, 1989)

Jackson, H. M. "The Death of Jesus in Mark and the Miracle from the Cross," *NTS* 33 (1987), pp. 16–37

Jacobson, A. D. "Divided Families and Christian Origins," in *The Gospel behind the Gospels. Current Studies on Q*, edited by R. A. Piper, (Leiden: Brill, 1995), pp. 361–380

Jacobson, A. D. *The First Gospel. An Introduction to Q*, (Sonoma: Polebridge, 1992)

Jeremias, J. *Neutestamentliche Theologie. Die Verkündigung Jesu*, (Gütersloh: Mohn, 1971)

Jeremias, J. *Unknown Sayings of Jesus*, (London: SPCK, 2nd edn, 1963)

Jervell, J. "The Law in Luke–Acts," in *Luke and the People of God. A New Look at Luke–Acts*, (Minneapolis: Augsburg, 1972), pp. 133–152

Jervell, J. "The Twelve on Israel's Thrones. Luke's Understanding of the Apostolate," in *Luke and the People of God. A New Look at Luke–Acts*, (Minneapolis: Augsburg, 1972), pp. 75–112.

Jervell, J. *Luke and the People of God. A New Look at Luke–Acts*, (Minneapolis: Augsburg, 1972)

Johnson, M. D. "Reflections on a Wisdom Approach to Matthew's Christology," *CBQ* 36 (1974), pp. 44–64

Jones, F. S. *An Ancient Jewish Christian Source on the History of Christianity. Pseudo–Clementine Recognitions 1.27–71*, Texts and Translations 37, Christian Apocrypha Series 2, (Atlanta: Scholars, 1995)

Juel, D. *Luke–Acts. The Promise of History*, (Atlanta: Jn Knox, 1983)

Juel, D. *Messiah and Temple. The Trial of Jesus in the Gospel of Mark*, SBLDS 31, (Missoula: Scholars, 1977)

Käsemann, E. "Sentences of Holy Law in the New Testament," in *New Testament Questions of Today*, (London: SCM Press, 1969), pp. 66–81

Kato, Z. *Die Völkermission im Markusevangelium. Eine redaktionsgeschichtliche Untersuchung*, EHS.T 252, (Frankfurt: Peter Lang, 1986)

Kazmierski, C. R. "Evangelist and Leper: A Socio–Cultural Study of Mark 1.40–45," *NTS* 38 (1992), pp. 37–50

Kazmierski, C. R. "The Stones of Abraham: John the Baptist and the End of Torah (Matt 3,7–10 parr. Luke 3,7–9)," *Biblica* 68 (1987), pp. 22–40

Kee, H. C. "Aretalogy and the Gospel," *JBL* 92 (1973), pp. 402–22

Kertelge, K. "Das Doppelgebot der Liebe im Markusevangelium," *TrierTheolZeit* 103 (1994), pp. 38–55

Kertelge, K. (ed.), *Das Gesetz im Neuen Testament*, QD 108, (Freiburg: Herder, 1986)

Kertelge, K. *Die Wunder Jesu im Markusevangelium. Eine redaktionsgeschichtliche Untersuchung*, (Munich: Kösel, 1970)

Kienle, B. von, "Markus 11,12–14.20–25. Der verdorrte Feigenbaum," *BibNotiz* 57 (1991), pp. 17–25

Kiilunen, J. "Der nachfolgewillige Schriftgelehrte. Matthäus 8.19–20 im Verständnis des Evangelisten," *NTS* 37 (1991), pp. 268–279

Kiilunen, J. *Das Doppelgebot der Liebe in synoptischer Sicht. Ein redaktionskritischer Versuch über Mk 12,28–34 und die Parallelen,* Annales Academiae Scientiarum Fennicae Dissertationes Humanarum Litterarum 250, (Helsinki: Suomalainen Tiedeakatemia, 1989)

Kiilunen, J. *Die Vollmacht im Widerstreit. Untersuchungen zum Werdegang von Mk 2,1–3,6*, Annales Academiae Scientiarum Fennicae Dissertationes Humanarum Litterarum 40, (Helsinki: Suomalainen Tiedeakatemia, 1985)

Kilpatrick, G. D. *The Origins of the Gospel According to St. Matthew*, (Oxford: Clarendon, 1946).

Kimelman, R. "*Birkat Ha–Minim* and the Lack of Evidence for an Anti–Christian Jewish Prayer in Late Antiquity," in *Jewish and Christian Self–Definition*, edited by E. P. Sanders et al., Vol 2, (Philadelphia: Fortress, 1981), pp. 226–244, 391–403

Kingsbury, J. D. "On Following Jesus. Matt 8:18–22," *NTS* 34 (1988), pp. 45–59

Kingsbury, J. D. *Conflict in Luke. Jesus, Authorities, Disciples*, (Minneapolis: Fortress, 1991)

Klinghardt, M. *Gesetz und Volk Gottes. Das lukanische Verständnis des Gesetzes*, WUNT 32, (Tübingen: J. C. B. Mohr [Paul Siebeck], 1988)

Kloppenborg, J. S. "Nomos and Ethos in Q," in *Christian Origins and Christian Beginnings. In Honor of James M. Robinson*, edited by J. E. Goehring et al., (Sonoma: Polebridge, 1990), pp. 35–48

Kloppenborg, J. S. "The Sayings Gospel Q: Recent Opinion on the People behind the Document," *Currents in Research: Biblical Studies* 1 (1993), pp. 9–34

Kloppenborg, J. S. et al. *Q–Thomas Reader*, (Sonoma: Polebridge, 1990)

Kloppenborg, J. S. *Q Parallels. Synopsis, Critical Notes and Concordance*, (Sonoma: Polebridge, 1988)

Kloppenborg, J. S. *The Formation of Q. Trajectories in Ancient Wisdom Collections*, Studies in Antiquity and Christianity, (Philadelphia: Fortress, 1987)

Kloppenborg, J. S.(ed.), *The Shape of Q. Signal essays on the Sayings Gospel*, (Minneapolis: Fortress, 1994)

Klostermann, E. *Das Markusevangelium*, HNT 3, (Tübingen: J. C. B. Mohr [Paul Siebeck], 1950)

Klumbies, P.-G. "Die Sabbatheilungen Jesu nach Markus und Lukas," in *Jesu Rede von Gott und ihre Nachgeschichte im frühen Christentum. Beiträge zur Verkündigung Jesu und zum Kerygma der Kirche. FS für Willi Marxsen*, edited by D.-A. Koch et al., (Gütersloh: Mohn, 1989), pp. 165-178

Koch, D.-A. "Inhaltliche Gliederung und geographischer Aufriss im Markusevangelium," *NTS* 29 (1983), pp. 145-166

Koch, D.-A. "Jesu Tischgemeinschaft mit Zöllnern und Sündern. Erwägungen zur Entstehung von Mk 2.13-17," in *Jesu Rede von Gott und ihre Nachgeschichte im frühen Christentum. Beiträge zur Verkündigung Jesu und zum Kerygma der Kirche. FS für Willi Marxsen n*, edited by D.-A. Koch et al., (Gütersloh: Mohn, 1989), pp. 57-73

Koch, D.-A. *Die Bedeutung der Wundererzählungen für die Christologie des Markusevangeliums*, BZNW 42, (Berlin: de Gruyter, 1975)

Koester, H. "Q and its relations," in *Christian Origins and Christian Beginnings. In Honor of James M. Robinson*, edited by J. E. Goehring et al., (Sonoma: Polebridge, 1990), pp. 49-63

Koester, H. *Ancient Christian Gospels. Their History and Development*, (London: SCM Press; Philadelphia: Trinity Press International, 1990)

Kosch, D. *Die eschatologische Tora des Menschensohnes. Untersuchungen zur Rezeption der Stellung Jesu zur Tora in Q*, NovTest et OrbAnt 12, (Göttingen: Vandenhoeck und Ruprecht, 1989)

Kosch, D. *Die Gottesherrschaft im Zeichen des Widerspruchs. Traditions- und redaktionsgeschichtliche Untersuchung von Lk 16,16 par. Mt 11,12f. bei Jesus, Q und Lukas*, EHS.T 257, (Frankfurt: Peter Lang, 1985)

Kotila, M. *Umstrittene Zeuge. Studien zur Stellung des Gesetzes in der johanneischen Theologiegeschichte*, Annales Academiae Scientiarum Fennicae. Dissertationes Humanarum Litterarum 48, (Helsinki: Suomalainen Tiedeakatemia, 1988)

Kraft, R. A. and Nickelsburg, G. W. E. *Early Judaism and its Modern Interpreters*, (Atlanta: Scholars, 1986).

Kümmel, W. G. "Ein Jahrzehnt Jesusforschung (1965-1975). III. Die Lehre Jesu (einschliesslich der Arbeiten über Einzeltexte)," *ThR NF* 41 (1976), pp. 295-263

Kuhn, H.-W. "Das Liebesgebot Jesu als Tora und als Evangelium. Zur Feindesliebe und zur christlichen und jüdischen Auslegung der Bergpredigt," in *Vom Urchristentum zu Jesus. Für Joachim Gnilka*, edited by H. Frankemölle and K. Kertelge, (Freiburg: Herder, 1989), pp. 194-230

Kuhn, H.-W. *Ältere Sammlungen in Markusevangelium*, SUNT 8, (Göttingen: Vandenhoeck und Ruprecht, 1971)

Lambrecht, J. "Jesus and the Law. An Investigation of Mk 7,1-23," *EThL* 53 (1977), pp. 24-82

Lambrecht, J. "The Great Commandments Pericope and Q," in *The Gospel behind the Gospels. Current Studies on Q*, edited by R. A. Piper, (Leiden: Brill, 1995), pp. 73-96

Lambrecht, J. *The Sermon on the Mount*, (Wilmington: Glazier, 1985)

Lane, W. L. *The Gospel according to Mark*, (Grand Rapids: Eerdmans, 1974)

Laufen, R, *Die Doppelüberlieferung der Logienquelle und der Matthäusevangelium*, BBB 54, (Bonn: Hanstein, 1980)

Lee, D. A. *The Symbolic Narratives of the Fourth Gospel. The Interplay of Form and Meaning*, JSNTS 95, (Sheffield: JSOT Pr., 1994)

Leidig, E. *Jesu Gespräch mit der Samaritanerin und weitere Gespräche im Johannesevangelium*, Theol. Diss. 15, (Basel: Reinhardt, 1979)

Levine, Amy–Jill, *The social and ethnic dimensions of Matthean Salvation History. "Go nowhere among the Gentiles..." (Matt 10:5b)*, Studies in the Bible and Early Christianity 14, (Lewiston: Mellen, 1988)

Levine, E. "The Sabbath Controversy according to Matthew," *NTS* 22 (1976), pp. 480–483

Limbeck, M. "Die nichts bewegen wollen! Zum Gesetzesverständnis des Evangelisten Matthäus," *TheolQuart* 168 (1988), pp. 299–320

Lindars, B. "'All foods clean': thoughts on Jesus and the law," in *Law and Religion. Essays on the Place of the Law in Israel and Early Christianity*, edited by B. Lindars, (Cambridge: Clarke, 1988), pp. 61–71

Lindars, B. (ed.), *Law and Religion. Essays on the Place of the Law in Israel and Early Christianity*, (Cambridge: Clarke, 1988)

Lindars, B. *John*, NT Guides, (Sheffield: JSOT Pr., 1990).

Lips, H. von "Schweine füttert man, Hunde nicht – ein Versuch, das Rätsel von Matthäus 7:6 zu lösen," *ZNW* 79 (1988), pp. 165–186

Loader, W. R. G. "Challenged at the Boundaries: A Conservative Jesus in Mark's Tradition," *JSNT* 63 (1996), pp. 45-61

Loader, W. R. G. "Christ at the Right Hand – Ps. cx.1 in the New Testament," *NTS* 24 (1978/79), pp. 199–217

Loader, W. R. G. "Hellenism and the Abandonment of Particularism in Jesus and Paul," *Pacifica* 4 (1991), pp. 245–256

Loader, W. R. G. "John 1:50–51 and the 'Greater Things' of Johannine Christology," in *Anfänge der Christologie. Festschrift für Ferdinand Hahn zum 65. Geburtstag*, edited by C. Breytenbach and H. Paulsen, (Göttingen: Vandenhoeck und Ruprecht, 1991), pp. 253–274

Loader, W. R. G. "Son of David, Blindness, Possession, and Duality in Matthew," *CBQ* 44 (1982), pp. 570–585.

Loader, W. R. G. *Sohn und Hoherpriester. Eine traditionsgeschichtliche Untersuchung zur Christologie des Hebräerbriefes*, WMANT 53, (Neukirchen–Vluyn: Neukirchener, 1981)

Loader, W. R. G. *The Christology of the Fourth Gospel: Structure and Issues*, BBET 23, (Frankfurt: Peter Lang, 2nd edn, 1992)

Lohmeyer, E. *Das Evangelium des Matthäus. Nachgelassene Ausarbeitungen und Entwürfe zu Übersetzung und Erklärung, für den Druck erarbeitet und herausgegeben von W. Schmauch*, KEK Sonderband, (Göttingen: Vandenhoeck und Ruprecht, 4. Aufllage, 1967)

Lohse, E. "'Vollkommen sein.' Zur Ethik des Matthäusevangeliums," in *Salz der Erde – Licht der Welt: Exegetische Studien zum Matthäusevangelium. FS für Anton Vögtle zum 80. Geburtstag*, edited by I. Oberlinner, and P. Fiedler, (Stuttgart: KBW, 1991), pp. 131–140

Luck, U. "Was wiegt leichter? Zu Mk 2,8," in *Vom Urchristentum zu Jesus. Für Joachim Gnilka*, edited by H. Frankemölle and K. Kertelge, (Freiburg: Herder, 1989), pp. 103–108

Lührmann, D. *Das Markusevangelium*, HNT 3, (Tübingen: J. C. B. Mohr [Paul Siebeck], 1987)

Lührmann, D. *Die Redaktion der Logienquelle*, (Neukirchen–Vluyn: Neukirchener, 1969)

Luz, U. *Das Evangelium nach Matthaus (Mt 1–7)*, EKK I/1, (Zurich: Benziger; Neukirchen–Vluyn: Neukirchener, 1985). English: *A Commentary on Matthew. Vol I. 1–7*, (Minneapolis: Augsburg, 1990)

Luz, U. in R. Smend and U. Luz, Gesetz, Kohlhammer Taschenbücher - Biblische Konfrontationen 1015, (Stuttgart: Kohlhammer, 1981), pp. 58–156

Mack, B. L. *A Myth of Innocence. Mark and Christian Origins*, (Philadelphia: Fortress, 1988)

Mack, B. L. and Robbins, V. K. *Patterns of Persuasion in the Gospels*, (Sonoma: Polebridge, 1989)

Mack, B. L. *The Lost Gospel: the Book of Q and Christian Origins*, (San Francisco: Harper, 1993)

Maddox, R. J. *The Purpose of Luke–Acts*, SNTW, (Edinburgh: T&T Clark, 1982)

Malbon, E. S. "Fallible Followers: Women and Men in the Gospel of Mark," *Semeia* 28 (1983), pp. 29–48;

Malbon, E. S. *Narrative Space and Mythic Meaning in Mark*, The Biblical Seminar 13, (Sheffield: JSOTPr., 1991)

Malina, B. J. "A Conflict Approach to Mark 7," *Forum* 4 (1988), pp. 3–30

Malina, B. J. *The New Testament World. Insights from Cultural Anthropology* (Atlanta: jn Knox, 1981)

Mann, C. S. *Mark*, AncB 27, (New York: Doubleday, 1986)

Manson, T. W. *The Sayings of Jesus*, (London: SCM Press, 1964)

Manson, T. W. *The Teaching of Jesus*, (Cambridge: CUP, 2nd edn, 1955)

Marcus, J. *The Way of the Lord. Christological Exegesis of the Old Testament in the Gospel of Mark*, (Louisville: Jn Knox/Westminster, 1992)

Marshall, C. *Faith as a Theme in Mark's Narrative*, SNTSMS 64, (Cambridge: CUP, 1989)

Marshall, I. H. *The Gospel of Luke. A Commentary on the Greek Text*, NIGNT, (Exeter: Paternoster, 1978)

Martyn, J. L. *History and Theology in the Fourth Gospel*, (New York: Harper and Row, 1968; rev'd edn, Nashville: Abingdon, 1979)

Martyn, J. L. *The Gospel of John in Christian History. Essays for Interpreters*, (New York: Paulist, 1978)

Mattill, A, J, *Luke and the Last Things. A Perspective for the Understanding of Lukan Thought*, (Dillsboro: Western North Carolina Pr., 1979)

McCane, B. R. "'Let the Dead Bury Their Own Dead': Secondary Burial and Matt 8:21–22," *HarvTheolRev* 83 (1990), pp. 31–43

McNeile, A. H. *The Gospel according to St. Matthew*, (London: Macmillan, 1915)

Meier, J, P, "Nations or Gentiles in Matthew 28:19?" *CBQ* 39 (1977), pp. 94–102

Meier, J. P. *Law and History in Matthew's Gospel. A Redactional Study of Mt 5:17–48*, AnBib 71, (Rome: PBIPr., 1976)

Menninger, R. E. *Israel and the Church in the Gospel of Matthew*, Am. Univ. St. VII 162, (New York: Peter Lang, 1994)

Merkel, H. "Israel im lukanischen Werk," *NTS* 40 (1994), pp. 371–398

Metzger, B. *A Textual Commentary on the Greek New Testament*, (London/New York: United Bible Societies, 2nd edn, 1994)

Meyer, M. W. "Making Mary Male: The Categories of 'Male' and 'Female' in the Gospel of Thomas," *NTS* 31 (1985), pp. 554–570

Meyer, M. W. *The Gospel of Thomas: the Hidden Sayings of Jesus*, (San Francisco: Harper, 1992)

Meyer, P. D. "The Gentile Mission in Q," *JBL* 89 (1970), pp. 405–417

Mitchell, A. C. "Zacchaeus Revisited: Luke 19,8 as a Defence," *Biblica* 71 (1990), pp. 153–176

Mohrlang, R. *Matthew and Paul . A Comparison of Ethical Perspectives*, SNTSMS 48, (Cambridge: CUP, 1984)

Moloney, F. J. *Belief in the Word. Reading the Fourth Gospel: John 1–4*, (Minneapolis: Fortress, 1993)

Motyer, S. "The Rending of the Veil: a Markan Pentecost," *NTS* 33 (1987), pp. 155–157

Moxnes, H. *The Economy of the Kingdom: Social Conflict and Economic Relations in Luke's Gospel*, (Philadelphia: Fortress, 1988)

Müller, K. "Beobachtungen zum Verhältnis von Tora und Halacha in frühjüdischen Quellen," in *Jesus und das jüdische Gesetz*, edited by I. Broer, (Stuttgart: Kohlhammer, 1992), pp. 105–134

Müller, K. "Gesetz und Gesetzeserfüllung im Frühjudentum," in *Das Gesetz im Neuen Testament*, QD108, edited by K. Kertelge, (Freiburg: Herder, 1986), pp. 11–27

Müller, K. "Möglichkeit und Vollzug jüdischer Kapitalgerichtsbarkeit im Prozess gegen Jesus von Nazaret," in *Der Prozess gegen Jesus. Historische Rückfrage und theologische Deutung,* QD 112, edited by K. Kertelge (Freiburg: Herder, 1988), pp. 84–110

Munro, W. "Women Disciples in Mark?" *CBQ* 44 (1982), pp. 225–241

Myers, C. *Binding the strong man: a political reading of Mark's story of Jesus*, (Maryknoll, NY: Orbis Books, 1988)

Nebe, G. *Prophetische Züge im Bilde Jesu bei Lukas*, BWANT 127, (Stuttgart: Kohlhammer, 1989)

Neirynck, F. "Jesus and the Sabbath. Some observations on Mk II,27," in *Jésus aux origines de la christologie*, BEThL 40, edited by J. Dupont, (Leuven, 1975), pp. 227–270

Neusner, J. "'First Cleanse the Inside'," *NTS* 22 (1976), pp. 486–495

Neusner, J. *Judaic Law from Jesus to the Mishnah. A Systematic Reply to Professor E. P. Sanders*, South Florida Studies in the History of Judaism 84, (Atlanta: Scholars, 1993)

Neusner, J. *Judaism in the Beginning of Christianity*, (London: SPCK, 1984).

Neusner, J. *Judaism: The Evidence of the Mishnah*, (Chicago: Univ. of Chicago Pr., 1981)

Neyrey, J. H. "A symbolic Approach to Mark 7," *Forum* 4 (1988), pp. 63–91

Neyrey, J. H. "The Idea of Purity in Mark's Gospel," *Semeia* 35 (1986), pp. 91–128

Neyrey, J. H. "The Symbolic universe of Luke–Acts: 'They Turn the World Upside Down'," in *The Social World of Luke–Acts. Models for Interpretation* , edited by J. H. Neyrey, (Peabody: Hendrickson, 1991), pp. 271–304

Neyrey, J. H. (ed.), *The Social World of Luke–Acts. Models for Interpretation*, (Peabody: Hendrickson, 1991)

Neyrey, J. H., *An Ideology of Revolt. John's Christology in Social–Science Perspective*, (Philadelphia: Fortress, 1988)

Nineham, D. E. *The Gospel of St Mark*, (Harmondsworth: Penguin, 1963)

Nolland, J. "The Gospel Prohibition of Divorce: Tradition History and Meaning," *JSNT* 58 (1995), pp. 19–35

Nolland, J. L. "A Fresh Look at Acts 15:10," *NTS* 27 (1980), pp. 105–115.

Nolland, J. L. "Uncircumcised Proselytes? *JSJ* 12 (1981), pp. 173–194.

Nolland, J. L. *Luke,* Word Bibl Comm 35ABC, (Dallas: Word, 1989/1993/1993)

Oakman, D. E. "Cursing Fig Trees and Robbers' Dens: Pronouncement Stories Within Social–Systemic Perspective. Mark 11:12–25 and Parallels," *Semeia* 64 (1993), pp. 253–274

Overbeck, F. "Über das Verhältnis Justins des Märtyrers zur Apostelgeschichte," *ZWT* 15 (1872), pp. 321–330

Overman, J. A. *Matthew's Gospel and Formative Judaism. The Social World of the Matthean Community*, (Minneapolis: Fortress, 1990)

Painter, J. *The Quest for the Messiah. The History, Literature and Theology of the Johannine Community*, (Edinburgh: T&T Clark, 2nd edn, 1993)

Painter, J. "The Church and Israel in the Fourth Gospel: A Response." *NTS* 25 (1978), pp. 103–122

Pancaro, S. *The Law in the Fourth Gospel. The Torah and the Gospel, Moses and Jesus, Judaism and Christianity according to John*, SuppNovT 42, (Leiden: Brill, 1975)

Pantle–Schieber, K. "Anmerkungen zur Auseinandersetzung von ἐκκλησία und Judentum im Matthäusevangelium," *ZNW* 80 (1989), pp. 145–162

Parrott, R. "Conflict and Rhetoric in Mark 2:23–28," *Semeia* 64 (1993), pp. 117–138

Paschen, W. *Rein und Unrein. Untersuchungen zur biblischen Wortgeschichte*, StANT 24, (Munich: Kösel, 1970)

Pedersen, S. Art. "κύων", *EWNT II*, pp. 821–823

Pesch, R. *Das Markusevangelium*, HTKNT II/1.2, (Freiburg: Herder, 1977)

Pesch, R. *Die Apostelgeschichte*, EKK V1/2, (Zurich: Benziger; Neukirchen–Vluyn: Neukirchener, 1986)

Pettem, M. "Luke's Great Omission and his View of the Law," *NTS* 42 (1996), pp. 35–54

Pilch, J. J. "Biblical Leprosy and Body Symbolism," *BTB* 11 (1981), pp. 108–113

Piper, R. A. (ed.), *The Gospel behind the Gospels. Current Studies on Q*, (Leiden: Brill, 1995)

Piper, R. A. *Wisdom in the Q–tradition. The Aphoristic teaching of Jesus*, SNTSMS 61, (Cambridge: CUP, 1989)

Pokorny, P. "From a Puppy to a Child: Problems of Contemporary Biblical Exegesis Demonstrated from Mark 7.24–30/Matt 15.21–28," *NTS* 41 (1995), pp. 321–337

Pokorny, P. "The Temptation Stories and their Intention," *NTS* 20 (1974), pp. 115–127.

Polag, A. *Die Christologie der Logienquelle*, WMANT 45, (Neukirchen–Vluyn: Neukirchener, 1977)

Powell, M. A. "Do and Keep what Moses Says (Matthew 23:2–7)," *JBL* 114 (1995), pp. 419–435

Pryor, J. W. *John: Evangelist of the Covenant People. The Narrative and Themes of the Fourth Gospel*, (Downers Grove: IVP, 1992)

Rad, G. von *The Problem of the Hexateuch and Other Essays*, (Edinburgh: Oliver & Boyd, 1966)

Radl, W. "Das Gesetz in Apg 15," in *Das Gesetz im Neuen Testament*, QD108, edited by K. Kertelge, (Freiburg: Herder, 1986), pp. 169–174

Räisänen, H. *The "Messianic Secret" in Mark's Gospel*, (Edinburgh: T&T Clark, 1990)

Räisänen, H. *The Torah and Christ. Essays in German and English on the Problem of the Law in Early Christianity*, SESJ 45, (Helsinki, 1986)

Rhoads, D. "Social Criticism: Crossing Boundaries," in *Mark and Method. New Approaches in Biblical Studies*, edited by J. C. Anderson, and S. D. Moore, (Minneapolis: Fortress, 1992), pp. 135–161

Richardson, P. and Westerholm, S. *Law in religious Communities in the Roman Period. The debate over Torah and Nomos in Post-Biblical Judaism and Early Christianity*, Studies in Christianity and Judaism 4, (Waterloo: Wilred Laurier Univ. Pr., 1991)

Riches, J. K. *Jesus and the Transformation of Judaism*, (New York: Seabury, 1980)

Robbins, V. K. and Mack, B. L. *Rhetoric in the Gospels: Argumentation in Narrative Elaboration*, (Philadelphia: Fortress, 1987)

Robinson, J. M. "The International Q Project," *JBL* 109 (1990), pp. 499–501; 110 (1991), pp. 494–498; 111 (1992), pp. 500–508; 112 (1993), pp. 500–506; 113 (1994), pp. 495–500; 114 (1995), pp. 475–485

Robinson, J. M. "The Q Trajectory between John and Matthew via Jesus," in *The Future of Early Christianity. Essays in Honor of Helmut Koester*, edited by B. Pearson, (Minneapolis: Fortress, 1991), pp. 173–194

Robinson, J. M. "The Sayings Gospel Q," in *The Four Gospels 1992. Festschrift Frans Neirynck*, BETL 100, edited by F. van Segbroeck et al., (Leuven: Leuven University Press, Peeters, 1992), pp. 361–388

Robinson, J. M. *The Problem of History in Mark*, SBT 21, (London: SCM, 1957)

Roloff, J. *Das Kerygma und der irdische Jesus. Historische Motive in den Jesus–Erzählungen der Evangelien*, (Göttingen: Vandenhoeck und Ruprecht, 1970)

Rordorf, W. *Sunday: The History of the Day of Rest and Worship in the Earliest Centuries of the Christian Church*, (London: SCM, 1968)

Russell, E. A. "The Image of the Jew in Matthew's Gospel," *ProcIrBibAssoc* 12 (1989), pp. 37–57

Saldarini, A. J. *Matthew's Christian–Jewish Community*, (Chicago: Univ. of Chicago Pr., 1994)

Salo, K. *Luke's Treatment of the Law. A Redaction–Critical Investigation*, Annales Academiae Scientiarum Fennicae Dissertationes Humanarum Litterarum 57, (Helsinki: Suomalainen Tiedeakatemia, 1991)

Salyer, G. "Rhetoric, Purity, and Play: Aspects of Mark 7:1–23," *Semeia* 64 (1993), pp. 139–170

Sand, A. *Das Gesetz und die Propheten. Untersuchung zur Theologie des Evangeliums nach Matthäus*, BU 11, (Regensburg: Pustet, 1974)

Sanders, E. P. *Jesus and Judaism*, (London: SCM, 1985)

Sanders, E. P. "Jewish Association with Gentiles and Galatians 2:11–14," in *The Conversation Continues. Studies in Paul and John. In Honor of J. Louis Martyn*, edited by R. T. Fortna and B. R. Gaventa, (Nashville: Abingdon, 1990), pp. 179–188

Sanders, E. P. *Jewish Law from Jesus to the Mishnah*, (London: SCM; Philadelphia: Trinity, 1990)

Sanders, E. P. *Judaism: Practice and Belief 63 BCE – 66CE*, (London: SCM; Philadelphia: Trinity, 1992).

Sanders, E. P. *Paul and Palestinian Judaism*, (London: SCM, 1977)

Sanders, J. T. *The Jews in Luke–Acts*, (London: SCM, 1987)

Sariola, H. *Markus und das Gesetz. Eine redaktionsgeschichtliche Untersuchung*, Annales Academiae Scientiarum Fennicae Dissertationes Humanarum Litterarum 56, (Helsinki: Suomalainen Tiedeakatemia, 1990)

Sauer, J. "Traditionsgeschichtliche Überlegungen zu Mk 3:1–6," *ZNW* 73 (1982), pp. 183–203

Schäfer, P. "Die Torah der messianischen Zeit," in *Studien zur Geschichte und Theologie des rabbinischen Judentums*, AGJU 15, (Leiden: Brill, 1978), pp. 198–213

Schmeller, T. R. "Jesus im Umland Galiläas. Zu den markinischen Berichten vom Aufenthalt Jesu in den Gebieten von Tyros, Caesarea Philippi und der Dekapolis," *BibZ* 38 (1994), pp. 44–66

Schmithals, W. *Das Evangelium nach Markus, 2 Bde.* OekTNT 2/1, 2, (Gütersloh: Mohn, 1979)

Schnackenburg, R. *Das Johannesevangelium. I. Teil. Einleitung und Kommentar zu Kap. 1–4*, (HTKNT IV/1, 5th edn, Freiburg: Herder, 1981); *II. Teil. Kommentar zu Kap. 5–12*, (HTKNT IV/ 2, 2nd edn, Freiburg: Herder, 1977); *III. Teil. Kommentar zu Kap.*

13–21, (HTKNT IV/ 3, 4th edn, Freiburg: Herder, 1982); *IV. Teil. Ergänzende Auslegungen und Exkurse*, (HTKNT IV/ 4, Freiburg: Herder, 1984); ET (Vols 1–3): *The Gospel according to John*, 3 vols, (London: Burns & Oates, 1968/1980/1982)

Schneemelcher, W. (ed.), *New Testament Apocrypha. Volume One: Gospels and Related Writings*, (Cambridge: James Clarke; Louisville: Westminster/John Knox Press, 2nd edn, 1991)

Schneider, G. *Die Apostelgeschichte*, HTKNT V1/2, (Freiburg: Herder, 1980/1982)

Schniewind, J. *Das Evangelium nach Matthäus*, (Göttingen: Vandenhoeck und Ruprecht, 1964)

Scholtissek, K. *Die Vollmacht Jesu. traditions und redaktionsgechichtliche Analyse zu einem Leitmortiv markinischer Christologie*, NTAbh NF 25, (Münster: Aschendorff, 1992)

Schottroff, L. *Der Glaubende und die feindliche Welt* , WMANT 37, (Neukirchen–Vluyn: Neukirchener, 1970)

Schuchard, B. G. *Scripture within Scripture. The Interrelationship of Form and Function in the Explicit Old Testament Citations in the Gospel of John*, SBLDissSer 133, (Atlanta: Scholars, 1992)

Schulz, S. *Q. – Die Spruchquelle der Evangelisten*, (Zurich: Theologischer Verlag, 1972)

Schürmann, H. "Das Zeugnis der Redenquelle für die Basileia–Verkündigung Jesu. Eine traditionsgechichtliche Untersuchung," in *Gottes Reich – Jesu Geschick. Jesu ureignener Tod im Lichte seiner Basileia–Verkündigung*, (Freiburg: Herder, 1983), pp. 65–152

Schürmann, H. *Das Lukasevangelium. 1. Teil*, HKNT III/1, (Freiburg: Herder, 4. Auflage, 1990)

Schwartz, D. R. "Viewing the Holy Utensils (P. Ox. V,840)," *NTS* 32 (1986), pp. 153–159

Schweizer, E, "Observance of the Law and Charismatic Activity in Matthew," *NTS* 16 (1969–1970), pp. 213–230

Schweizer, E. "Matthäus 5, 17–20 – Anmerkungen zum Gesetzesverständnis des Matthäus," *TheolLitZ* 77 (1952), 479–484.

Schweizer, E. *Das Evangelium nach Markus*, NTD 1, (Göttingen: Vandenhoeck und Ruprecht, 1968); English: *The Good News according to Mark*, (London: SPCK, 1970)

Schweizer, E. *Das Evangelium nach* Matthäus, NTD 2, (Göttingen: Vandenhoeck und Ruprecht, 1973); English: *The Good News According to Matthew*, (London: SPCK, 1976)

Scott, B. B. *Hear Then the Parable*, (Minneapolis: Fortress, 1989)

Scott, M. *Sophia and the Johannine Jesus*, JSNTS 71, (Sheffield: JSOT Pr., 1992)

Segal, A. F. "Matthew's Jewish Voice," in *The Social History of the Matthean Community. Cross–Disciplinary Approaches*, edited by D. L. Balch, (Minneapolis: Fortress, 1991), pp. 3–37

Segovia, F. F. *The Farewell of the Word. The Johannine Call to Abide*, (Minneapolis: Fortress, 1991)

Sellew, P. "Aphorisms in Mark: A Stratigraphic Analysis," *Forum* 8: 1–2 (1992), pp. 141–160

Sellin, G. "Einige symbolische und esoterische Züge im Markus–Evangelium," in *Jesu Rede von Gott und ihre Nachgeschichte im frühen Christentum. Beiträge zur Verkündigung Jesu und zum Kerygma der Kirche. FS für Willi Marxsen*, edited by D.-A. Koch, et al., (Gütersloh: Mohn, 1989), pp. 74–90

Selvidge, M. J. "Mark 5:25–34 and Leviticus 15:19–20," *JBL* 103 (1984), pp. 619–623

Selvidge, M. J. *Woman, Cult, and Miracle Recital: A Redactional Critical Investigation on Mark 5:24–34*, (Lewisburg: Bucknell Univ Pr./London/Toronto: Associated Univ. Pr., 1990)

Sevenich–Bax, E. *Israels Konfrontation mit den letzten Boten der Weisheit. Form, Funktion und Interdependenz der Weisheitselemente in der Logienquelle*, Münsteraner Theol Abhandlungen 21, (Altenberge: Oros, 1993)

Shepherd, T. *Markan Sandwich Stories. Narration, Definition, and Function*, Andrews Univ. Sem Doct Diss Ser 18, (Berrien Springs: Andrews Univ. Pr., 1993)

Sigal, P. *The Halakah of Jesus of Nazareth according to the Gospel of Matthew*, (Lanham: Univ. of America Pr., 1986).

Smith, S. H. "Mark 3,1–6: Form, Redaction and Community Function," *Biblica* 75 (1994), pp. 153–174.

Snodgrass, K. R. "Matthew's Understanding of the Law," *Interpretation* 46 (1992), pp. 368–378

Stanton, G. N. *A Gospel for a New People. Studies in* Matthew, (Edinburgh: T&T Clark, 1992)

Steck, O. H. *Israel und das gewaltsame Geschick der Propheten: Untersuchungen zur Überlieferung des Deuteronomistischen Geschichtsbildes im Alten Testament, Spätjudentum und Urchristentum*, WMANT 23, (Neukirchen–Vluyn: Neukirchener, 1967)

Stegemann, W. *Zwischen Synagoge und Obrigkeit. Zur historischen Situation der lukanischen Christen*, FRLANT 152, (Göttingen: Vandenhoeck und Ruprecht, 1991

Steiger, J. "Nathanael – ein Israelit, an dem kein Falsch ist. Das hermeneutische Phänomen der Intertestamentarizität aufgezeigt an Joh 1,45–51," *BerlinTheolZeit* 9 (1992), pp. 50–73

Strack, H. J. and Billerbeck, P. *Kommentar zum Neuen Testament aus Talmud und Midrash*, 4 vols, (Munich: C. H. Beck, 1922–1928)

Strecker, G. "The Law in the Sermon on the Mount," in *The Promise and Practice of Biblical Theology*, edited by J. Reumann, (Minneapolis: Fortress, 1991), pp. 35–49

Strecker, G. *Der Weg der Gerechtigkeit. Untersuchungen zur Theologie des Matthäus*, FRLANT 82, (Göttingen: Vandenhoeck und Ruprecht, 3rd edn, 1971)

Strecker, G. *Die Bergpredigt. Ein exegetischer Kommentar*, (Göttingen: Vandenhoeck und Ruprecht, 1984); English: *Sermon on the Mount. An Exegetical Commentary*, (Edinburgh; T&T Clark, 1988)

Suggs, M. J. *Wisdom, Christology, and Law in Matthew's Gospel*, (Cambridge, MA, 1970)

Sylva, D. "The Temple Curtain and Jesus' Death in the Gospel of Luke," *JBL* 105 (1986), pp. 239–250

Syreeni, K. "Matthew, Luke, and the Law. A Study in Hermeneutical Exegesis," in *The Law in the Bible and its Environment*, Publications of the Finnish Exegetical Society 51, edited by T. Veijola, (Helsinki: Finn. Exeg. Society; Göttingen: Vandenhoeck und Ruprecht, 1990), pp. 126–157

Syreeni, K. "Separation and Identity: Aspects of the Symbolic World of Matt 6.1–18," *NTS* 40 (1994), pp. 522–541

Syreeni, K. *The Making of the Sermon on the Mount. A procedural analysis of Matthew;s redactoral activity*, Vol 1, Annales Academiae Scientiarum Fennicae Dissertationes Humanarum Litterarum 44, (Helsinki: Suomalainen Tiedeakatemia, 1987)

Taeger, J. W. "Der grundsätzliche oder ungrundsätzliche Unterschied. Anmerkungen zur gegenwärtigen Debatte um das Gesetzesverständnis Jesu," in *Jesus und das jüdische Gesetz*, edited by I. Broer, (Stuttgart: Kohlhammer, 1992), pp. 13–36

Tannehill, R. "Types and Functions of Apophthegms in the Synoptic Gospels," *ANRW* II.25.2 (1994), pp. 1792–1829

Telford, W. R. *The Barren Temple and the Withered Tree. A redaction–critical analysis of the Cursing of the Fig–Tree pericope in Mark's Gospel and its relation to the Cleansing of the Temple tradition*, JSNTS 1,(Sheffield: JSOT Pr., 1980)

Theissen, G. *Lokalkolorit und Zeitgeschichte in den Evangelien*, NTOA 8, (Freiburg, Schweiz: Universitätsverlag; Göttingen: Vandenhoeck und Ruprecht, 1989)

Theissen, G. *The Miracle Stories of the Early Christian Tradition*, (Edinburgh: T&T Clark, 1983)

Theobald, M. E. *Die Fleischwerdung des Logos. Studien zum Verhältnis des Johannesprologs zum Corpus des Evangeliums und zu 1 Joh*, Neutestamentliche Abhandlungen NF 20, (Münster: Aschendorff, 1988)

Thomas, J. C. "The Fourth Gospel and Rabbinic Judaism," *ZNW* 82 (1991), pp. 159–182

Tiede, D. L. *Prophecy and History in Luke–Acts*, (Philadelphia: Fortress, 1980)

Tisera, G. *Universalism according to the Gospel of Matthew*, Eur. Univ. StudiesXXIII 482, (Frankfurt: Peter Lang, 1993)

Tolbert, M. A. *Sowing the Gospel. Mark's World in Literary Historical Perspective*, (Minneapolis: Fortress, 1989)

Trilling, W. *Das wahre Israel. Studien zur Theologie des Matthäus–Evangeliums*, SANT 10, (Munich: Kösel, 3rd edn, 1964)

Trummer, P. "Zwischen Gesetz und Freiheit. Überlegungen zu einer Antinomie bei Jesus und Paulus," in *Jesus und das jüdische Gesetz*, edited by I. Broer, (Stuttgart: Kohlhammer, 1992), pp. 37–60

Trunk, D. *Der messianische Helfer. Eine redaktions– und religionsgeschichtliche Studie zu den Exorzismen im Matthäusevangelium*, Herd. Bib. St. 3, (Herder: Freiburg, 1994).

Tuckett, C. M. "Q, the law and Judaism," in *Law and Religion. Essays on the Place of the Law in Israel and Early Christianity*, edited by B. Lindars, (Cambridge: Clarke, 1988), pp. 90–101

Tuckett, C. M. "The Temptation Narrative in Q," in *The Four Gospels 1992. Festschrift Frans Neirynck*, BETL 100, edited by F. van Segbroeck et al., (Leuven: Leuven University Press, Peeters, 1992) pp. 479–508

Tuckett, C. M. *Q and the History of Early Christianity. Studies on Q*, (Edinburgh: T&T Clark; Peabody: Hendrickson, 1996)

Turner, M. M. B. "The Sabbath, Sunday, and the Law in Luke/Acts," in *From Sabbath to Lord's Day. A Biblical, Historical and Theological Investigation*, edited by D. A. Carson, (Grand Rapids: Zondervan, 1982), pp. 99–157

Tyson, J. B. "Acts 1:6–7 and dietary regulations in early Christianity," *Perspectives in Religious Studies* 10 (1983), pp. 145–161

Tyson, J. B. *Images of Judaism in Luke–Acts*, (Columbia: Univ. of Sth Carolina Pr., 1992)

Ulansey, D. "The Heavenly Veil Torn: Mark's Cosmic *Inclusio*," *JBL* 110 (1991), pp. 123–125

Uro, R. "John the Baptist and the Jesus Movement: What Does Q Tell Us?" in *The Gospel behind the Gospels. Current Studies on Q*, edited by R. A. Piper, (Leiden: Brill, 1995), pp. 231–258

Uro, R. *Sheep among the wolves: a study on the mission Instructions of Q*, Annales Academiae Scientiarum Fennicae Dissertationes Humanarum Litterarum 47, (Helsinki: Suomalainen Tiedeakatemia, 1987)

Vaage, L. E. "Q and Cynicism: On Comparison and Social Identity," in *The Gospel behind the Gospels. Current Studies on Q*, edited by R. A. Piper, (Leiden: Brill, 1995), pp. 199–230

Vermes, G. *Jesus the Jew: A Historian's Reading of the Gospels*, (London: Collins, 1973)

Vermes, G. *The Religion of Jesus the Jew*, (Minneapolis: Fortress, 1993)

Via, D. O. *The Ethics of Mark's Gospel in the Middle of Time*, (Philadelphia: Fortress, 1985)

Viviano, B. T. "Social World and Community Leadership: The Case of Matthew 23:1–12,34," *JSNT* 39 (1990), pp. 3–21

Vögtle, A, "Das markinische Verständnis der Tempelworte," in *Die Mitte des Neuen Testaments. Einheit und Vielfalt neutestamentlicher Theologie. FS für E. Schweizer*, edited by U. Luz, and H. Weder, (Göttingen: Vandenhoeck und Ruprecht, 1983), pp. 362–383

Vouga, F. "Die Entwicklungsgeschichte der jesuanischen Chrien und didaktischen Dialoge des Markusevangeliums," in: (ed.), *Jesu Rede von Gott und ihre Nachgeschichte im frühen Christentum. Beiträge zur Verkündigung Jesu und zum Kerygma der Kirche. FS für Willi Marxsen*, edited by D.-A. Koch, et al., (Gütersloh: Mohn, 1989), pp. 45–56

Vouga, F. *Jésus et la Loi selon la Tradition synoptique*, Le Monde de la Bible, (Genève: Labor et Fides, 1988)

Waetjen, H. *A Reordering of Power. A Socio–political Reading of Mark*, (Philadelphia: Fortress, 1989)

Waibel, M. "Die Auseinandersetzung mit der Fasten und Sabbatpraxis Jesu in urchristlichen Gemeinden," in *Zur Geschichte des Urchristentums*, QD 87, edited by G. Dautzenberg, H. Merklein, K. Müller, (Freiburg: Herder, 1979)

Wainwright, E. *Towards a Feminist Critical Reading of the Gospel according to Matthew*, BZNW 60, (Berlin: de Gruyter, 1991)

Walker, R. *Die Heilsgeschichte im ersten Evangelium*, FRLANT 91, (Göttingen: Vandenhoeck und Ruprecht, 1967)

Wander, B. *Trennungsprozesse zwischen Frühem Christentum und Judentum im 1. Jh. n. Chr*, Texte u. Arbeiten z. Neutestamentlichen Zeitalter 16, (Tübingen: Francke Verlag, 1994)

Weder, H. "'But I say to you...' Concerning the Foundations of Jesus' interpretation of the Law in the 'Sermon on the Mount'," in *Text and Logos. The Humanistic Interpretation of the New Testament*, SPHomSer, edited by T. W. Jennings, (Atlanta: Scholars, 1990), pp. 211–228

Weder, H. "Die 'Rede der Rede'. Beobachtungen zum Verständnis de Bergpredigt Jesu," *EvangTheol* 45 (1985), pp. 45–60

Wegner, U. *Der Hauptmann von Kafarnaum (Mt 7,28a; 8,5–10.13 par Lk 7,1–10). Ein Beitrag zur Q–Forschung*, WUNT 2.14, (Tübingen: J. C. B. Mohr [Paul Siebeck], 1985)

Weiss, H. "The Sabbath in the Fourth Gospel," *JBL* 110 (1991), pp. 311–321

Weiss, H. "The Sabbath in the Synoptic Gospels," *JSNT* 38 (1990), pp. 13–27

Weiss, J. *Die drei ältesten Evangelien*, SNT 2, (Göttingen, 1906)

Weiss, J. *The History of Primitive Christianity*, 2 vols, (New York: Wilson and Ericksson, 1957)

Weiss, W. *"Eine neue Lehre mit Vollmacht." Die Streit- und Schulgespräche des Markusevangeliums*, BZNW 52, (Berlin: de Gruyter, 1989)

Wenham, G. J. "Matthew and Divorce," *JSNT* 22 (1984), pp. 95–107.

Wernle, P. *Die Synoptische Frage*, (Freiburg, Leipzig, Tübingen: J. C. B. Mohr, 1899)

Wessel, F. "Die fünf Männer der Samaritanerin. Jesus und die Tora nach Joh 4,16–19," *BibNotiz* 68 (1993), pp. 26–34

Westerholm, S. "The Law in the Sermon on the Mount: Matt 5:17–48," *CriswellTheolRev* 6 (1992), pp. 43–56

Westerholm, S. *Jesus and Scribal Authority*, Coniectanea Biblica NT Ser 10, (Lund: Gleerup, 1978)

White. L. M. "Shifting Sectarian Boundaries in Early Christianity," *BJRL* 70 (1988), pp. 7–24

Wiefel, W. *Das Evangelium nach Lukas*, THNT 3, (Berlin: Ev. Verlagsanstalt, 1988)

Wild, R. A. "The Encounter between Pharisaic and Christian Judaism: Some Early Gospel Evidence," *NovT* 27 (1985), pp. 105–124

Williams, J. T. "Cultic Elements in the Fourth Gospel," In *Studia Biblica 1978. II. Papers on the Gospels. Sixth International Congress on Biblical Studies*, edited by E. A. Livingstone, (Sheffield: JSOT Pr., 1980), pp. 339–350

Wilson, S. G. *Luke and the Law*, SNTSMS 50, (Cambridge: CUP, 1983)

Wink, W. *John the Baptist in the Gospel Tradition*, SNTSMS 7, (Cambridge: CUP, 1968)

Witherington, B. "Matthew 5.32 and 19.9 – Exception or Exceptional Situation," *NTS* 31 (1985), pp. 571–576.

Wojciechowski, M. "The Touching of the Leper (Mark 1,40–45) as a Historical and Symbolic Act of Jesus," *BZ* 33 (1989), pp. 114–119

Wong, Kun–Chun, "The Matthean Understanding of the Sabbath: A Response to G. N. Stanton," *JSNT* 44 (1991), pp. 3–18

Wong, Kun–Chun, *Interkulturelle Theologie und multikulturelle Gemeinde im Matthäusevangelium: zum Verhältnis von Juden– und Heidenchristen im Matthäusevangelium* ,(Freiburg, Switzerland: Universitätsverlag; Göttingen: Vandenhoeck und Ruprecht, 1992)

Wouters, A. *"...wer den Willen meines Vaters tut". Eine Untersuchung zum Verständnis vom Handeln im Matthäusevangelium*, BU23, (Regensburg: Pustet, 1992)

Yee, G. A., *Jewish Feasts and the Gospel of John*, Zacchaeus Studies: New Testament, (Wilmington: Glazier, 1989)

Zahn, T. *Das Evangelium des Matthäus*, KNT 1, (Leipzig, 4th edn, 1922)

Zeller, D. "Jesus als vollmächtiger Lehrer (Mt 5–7) und der hellenistische Gesetzgeber," in *Studien zum Matthäusevangelium, FS W. Pesch*, SBS, edited by L. Schenke, (Stuttgart: KBW, 1988), pp. 299–317

Index of References

Old Testament

Apocrypha and Pseudepigrapha

Josephus and Philo

Qumran Writings

New Testament

The canonical gospels and Acts are discussed following the order within each writing.

Other Christian Writings

Rabbinic Literature

Greco-Roman Literature

Index of Authors

Index of Subjects

Wissenschaftliche Untersuchungen zum Neuen Testament

Alphabetical Index of the First and Second Series

Fletcher-Louis, Crispin H.T.: Luke-Acts: Angels, Christology and Soteriology. 1997. *Volume II/94.*
Forbes, Christopher Brian: Prophecy and Inspired Speech in Early Christianity and its Hellenistic Environment. 1995. *Volume II/75.*
Fornberg, Tord: see *Fridrichsen, Anton.*
Fossum, Jarl E.: The Name of God and the Angel of the Lord. 1985. *Volume 36.*
Frenschkowski, Marco: Offenbarung und Epiphanie. Volume 1 1995. *Volume II/79* – Volume 2 1997. *Volume II/80.*
Frey, Jörg: Eugen Drewermann und die biblische Exegese. 1995. *Volume II/71.*
– Die johanneische Eschatologie. Volume I. 1997. *Volume 96.*
Fridrichsen, Anton: Exegetical Writings. Ed. by C.C. Caragounis and T. Fornberg. 1994. *Volume 76.*
Garlington, Don B.: 'The Obedience of Faith'. 1991. *Volume II/38.*
– Faith, Obedience, and Perseverance. 1994. *Volume 79.*
Garnet, Paul: Salvation and Atonement in the Qumran Scrolls. 1977. *Volume II/3.*
Gräßer, Erich: Der Alte Bund im Neuen. 1985. *Volume 35.*
Green, Joel B.: The Death of Jesus. 1988. *Volume II/33.*
Gundry Volf, Judith M.: Paul and Perseverance. 1990. *Volume II/37.*
Hafemann, Scott J.: Suffering and the Spirit. 1986. *Volume II/19.*
– Paul, Moses, and the History of Israel. 1995. *Volume 81.*
Heckel, Theo K.: Der Innere Mensch. 1993. *Volume II/53.*
Heckel, Ulrich: Kraft in Schwachheit. 1993. *Volume II/56.*
– see *Feldmeier, Reinhard.*
– see *Hengel, Martin.*
Heiligenthal, Roman: Werke als Zeichen. 1983. *Volume II/9.*
Hemer, Colin J.: The Book of Acts in the Setting of Hellenistic History. 1989. *Volume 49.*
Hengel, Martin: Judentum und Hellenismus. 1969, ³1988. *Volume 10.*
– Die johanneische Frage. 1993. *Volume 67.*
– Judaica et Hellenistica. Volume 1. 1996. *Volume 90.*
Hengel, Martin and *Ulrich Heckel* (Ed.): Paulus und das antike Judentum. 1991. *Volume 58.*
Hengel, Martin and *Hermut Löhr* (Ed.): Schriftauslegung im antiken Judentum und im Urchristentum. 1994. *Volume 73.*
Hengel, Martin and *Anna Maria Schwemer* (Ed.): Königsherrschaft Gottes und himmlischer Kult. 1991. *Volume 55.*
– Die Septuaginta. 1994. *Volume 72.*
Herrenbrück, Fritz: Jesus und die Zöllner. 1990. *Volume II/41.*
Hoegen-Rohls, Christina: Der nachösterliche Johannes. 1996. *Volume II/84.*
Hofius, Otfried: Katapausis. 1970. *Volume 11.*
– Der Vorhang vor dem Thron Gottes. 1972. *Volume 14.*
– Der Christushymnus Philipper 2,6-11. 1976, ²1991. *Volume 17.*
– Paulusstudien. 1989, ²1994. *Volume 51.*
Hofius, Otfried und *Hans-Christian Kammler:* Johannesstudien. 1996. *Volume 88.*
Holtz, Traugott: Geschichte und Theologie des Urchristentums. 1991. *Volume 57.*
Hommel, Hildebrecht: Sebasmata. Volume 1 1983. *Volume 31* – Volume 2 1984. *Volume 32.*
Hvalvik, Reidar: The Struggle for Scripture and Covenant. 1996. *Volume II/82.*
Kähler, Christoph: Jesu Gleichnisse als Poesie und Therapie. 1995. *Volume 78.*
Kammler, Hans-Christian: see *Hofius, Otfried.*
Kamlah, Ehrhard: Die Form der katalogischen Paränese im Neuen Testament. 1964. *Volume 7.*
Kieffer, René und *Jan Bergman (Ed.):* La Main de Dieu / Die Hand Gottes. 1997. *Volume 94.*
Kim, Seyoon: The Origin of Paul's Gospel. 1981, ²1984. *Volume II/4.*
– „The 'Son of Man'" as the Son of God. 1983. *Volume 30.*
Kleinknecht, Karl Th.: Der leidende Gerechtfertigte. 1984, ²1988. *Volume II/13.*
Klinghardt, Matthias: Gesetz und Volk Gottes. 1988. *Volume II/32.*
Köhler, Wolf-Dietrich: Rezeption des Matthäusevangeliums in der Zeit vor Irenäus. 1987. *Volume II/24.*
Korn, Manfred: Die Geschichte Jesu in veränderter Zeit. 1993. *Volume II/51.*
Koskenniemi, Erkki: Apollonios von Tyana in der neutestamentlichen Exegese. 1994. *Volume II/61.*
Kraus, Wolfgang: Das Volk Gottes. 1996. *Volume 85.*
– see *Walter, Nikolaus.*

Kuhn, Karl G.: Achtzehngebet und Vaterunser und der Reim. 1950. *Volume 1.*

Laansma, Jon: 'I Will Give You Rest'. 1997. *Volume II/98.*

Lampe, Peter: Die stadtrömischen Christen in den ersten beiden Jahrhunderten. 1987, [2]1989. *Volume II/18.*

Lau, Andrew: Manifest in Flesh. 1996. *Volume II/86.*

Lichtenberger, Hermann: see *Avemarie, Friedrich.*

Lieu, Samuel N.C.: Manichaeism in the Later Roman Empire and Medieval China. [2]1992. *Volume 63.*

Loader, William R.G.: Jesus' Attitude Towards the Law. 1997. *Volume II/97.*

Löhr, Gebhard: Verherrlichung Gottes durch Philosophie. 1997. *Volume 97.*

Löhr, Hermut: see *Hengel, Martin.*

Löhr, Winrich Alfried: Basilides und seine Schule. 1995. *Volume 83.*

Maier, Gerhard: Mensch und freier Wille. 1971. *Volume 12.*

– Die Johannesoffenbarung und die Kirche. 1981. *Volume 25.*

Markschies, Christoph: Valentinus Gnosticus? 1992. *Volume 65.*

Marshall, Peter: Enmity in Corinth: Social Conventions in Paul's Relations with the Corinthians. 1987. *Volume II/23.*

Meade, David G.: Pseudonymity and Canon. 1986. *Volume 39.*

Meadors, Edward P.: Jesus the Messianic Herald of Salvation. 1995. *Volume II/72.*

Meißner, Stefan: Die Heimholung des Ketzers. 1996. *Volume II/87.*

Mell, Ulrich: Die „anderen" Winzer. 1994. *Volume 77.*

Mengel, Berthold: Studien zum Philipperbrief. 1982. *Volume II/8.*

Merkel, Helmut: Die Widersprüche zwischen den Evangelien. 1971. *Volume 13.*

Merklein, Helmut: Studien zu Jesus und Paulus. 1987. *Volume 43.*

Metzler, Karin: Der griechische Begriff des Verzeihens. 1991. *Volume II/44.*

Metzner, Rainer: Die Rezeption des Matthäusevangeliums im 1. Petrusbrief. 1995. *Volume II/74.*

Mittmann-Richert, Ulrike: Magnifikat und Benediktus. *1996. Volume II/90.*

Niebuhr, Karl-Wilhelm: Gesetz und Paränese. 1987. *Volume II/28.*

– Heidenapostel aus Israel. 1992. *Volume 62.*

Nissen, Andreas: Gott und der Nächste im antiken Judentum. 1974. *Volume 15.*

Noormann, Rolf: Irenäus als Paulusinterpret. 1994. *Volume II/66.*

Obermann, Andreas: Die christologische Erfüllung der Schrift im Johannesevangelium. 1996. *Volume II/83.*

Okure, Teresa: The Johannine Approach to Mission. 1988. *Volume II/31.*

Park, Eung Chun: The Mission Discourse in Matthew's Interpretation. 1995. *Volume II/81.*

Philonenko, Marc (Ed.): Le Trône de Dieu. 1993. *Volume 69.*

Pilhofer, Peter: Presbyteron Kreitton. 1990. *Volume II/39.*

– Philippi. Volume 1 1995. *Volume 87.*

Pöhlmann, Wolfgang: Der Verlorene Sohn und das Haus. 1993. *Volume 68.*

Pokorný, Petr und *Josef B. Souček:* Bibelauslegung als Theologie. 1997. *Volume 100.*

Prieur, Alexander: Die Verkündigung der Gottesherrschaft. 1996. *Volume II/89.*

Probst, Hermann: Paulus und der Brief. 1991. *Volume II/45.*

Räisänen, Heikki: Paul and the Law. 1983, [2]1987. *Volume 29.*

Rehkopf, Friedrich: Die lukanische Sonderquelle. 1959. *Volume 5.*

Rein, Matthias: Die Heilung des Blindgeborenen (Joh 9). 1995. *Volume II/73.*

Reinmuth, Eckart: Pseudo-Philo und Lukas. 1994. *Volume 74.*

Reiser, Marius: Syntax und Stil des Markusevangeliums. 1984. *Volume II/11.*

Richards, E. Randolph: The Secretary in the Letters of Paul. 1991. *Volume II/42.*

Riesner, Rainer: Jesus als Lehrer. 1981, [3]1988. *Volume II/7.*

– Die Frühzeit des Apostels Paulus. 1994. *Volume 71.*

Rissi, Mathias: Die Theologie des Hebräerbriefs. 1987. *Volume 41.*

Röhser, Günter: Metaphorik und Personifikation der Sünde. 1987. *Volume II/25.*

Rose, Christian: Die Wolke der Zeugen. 1994. *Volume II/60.*

Rüger, Hans Peter: Die Weisheitsschrift aus der Kairoer Geniza. 1991. *Volume 53.*

Sänger, Dieter: Antikes Judentum und die Mysterien. 1980. *Volume II/5.*

– Die Verkündigung des Gekreuzigten und Israel. 1994. *Volume 75.*

Salzmann, Jorg Christian: Lehren und Ermahnen. 1994. *Volume II/59.*

Sandnes, Karl Olav: Paul – One of the Prophets? 1991. *Volume II/43.*
Sato, Migaku: Q und Prophetie. 1988. *Volume II/29.*
Schaper, Joachim: Eschatology in the Greek Psalter. 1995. *Volume II/76.*
Schimanowski, Gottfried: Weisheit und Messias. 1985. *Volume II/17.*
Schlichting, Günter: Ein jüdisches Leben Jesu. 1982. *Volume 24.*
Schnabel, Eckhard J.: Law and Wisdom from Ben Sira to Paul. 1985. *Volume II/16.*
Schutter, William L.: Hermeneutic and Composition in I Peter. 1989. *Volume II/30.*
Schwartz, Daniel R.: Studies in the Jewish Background of Christianity. 1992. *Volume 60.*
Schwemer, Anna Maria: see Hengel, Martin
Scott, James M.: Adoption as Sons of God. 1992. *Volume II/48.*
– Paul and the Nations. 1995. *Volume 84.*
Siegert, Folker: Drei hellenistisch-jüdische Predigten. Teil I 1980. *Volume 20* – Teil II 1992. *Volume 61.*
– Nag-Hammadi-Register. 1982. *Volume 26.*
– Argumentation bei Paulus. 1985. *Volume 34.*
– Philon von Alexandrien. 1988. *Volume 46.*
Simon, Marcel: Le christianisme antique et son contexte religieux I/II. 1981. *Volume 23.*
Snodgrass, Klyne: The Parable of the Wicked Tenants. 1983. *Volume 27.*
Söding, Thomas: Das Wort vom Kreuz. 1997. *Volume 93.*
– see Thüsing, Wilhelm.
Sommer, Urs: Die Passionsgeschichte des Markusevangeliums. 1993. *Volume II/58.*
Souček, Josef B.: see Pokorný, Petr.
Spangenberg, Volker: Herrlichkeit des Neuen Bundes. 1993. *Volume II/55.*
Speyer, Wolfgang: Frühes Christentum im antiken Strahlungsfeld. 1989. *Volume 50.*
Stadelmann, Helge: Ben Sira als Schriftgelehrter. 1980. *Volume II/6.*
Strobel, August: Die Stunde der Wahrheit. 1980. *Volume 21.*
Stuckenbruck, Loren T.: Angel Veneration and Christology. 1995. *Volume II/70.*
Stuhlmacher, Peter (Ed.): Das Evangelium und die Evangelien. 1983. *Volume 28.*
Sung, Chong-Hyon: Vergebung der Sünden. 1993. *Volume II/57.*
Tajra, Harry W.: The Trial of St. Paul. 1989. *Volume II/35.*
– The Martyrdom of St.Paul. 1994. *Volume II/67.*
Theißen, Gerd: Studien zur Soziologie des Urchristentums. 1979, ³1989. *Volume 19.*
Thornton, Claus-Jürgen: Der Zeuge des Zeugen. 1991. *Volume 56.*
Thüsing, Wilhelm: Studien zur neutestamentlichen Theologie. Ed. by Thomas Söding. 1995. *Volume 82.*
Tsuji, Manabu: Glaube zwischen Vollkommenheit und Verweltlichung. 1997. *Volume II/93*
Twelftree, Graham H.: Jesus the Exorcist. 1993. *Volume II/54.*
Visotzky, Burton L.: Fathers of the World. 1995. *Volume 80.*
Wagener, Ulrike: Die Ordnung des „Hauses Gottes". 1994. *Volume II/65.*
Walter, Nikolaus: Praeparatio Evangelica. Ed. by Wolfgang Kraus and Florian Wilk. 1997. *Volume 98.*
Watts, Rikki: Isaiah's New Exodus and Mark. 1997. *Volume II/88.*
Wedderburn, A.J.M.: Baptism and Resurrection. 1987. *Volume 44.*
Wegner, Uwe: Der Hauptmann von Kafarnaum. 1985. *Volume II/14.*
Welck, Christian: Erzählte 'Zeichen'. 1994. *Volume II/69.*
Wilk, Florian: see Walter, Nikolaus.
Wilson, Walter T.: Love without Pretense. 1991. *Volume II/46.*
Zimmermann, Alfred E.: Die urchristlichen Lehrer. 1984, ²1988. *Volume II/12.*

For a complete catalogue please write to the publisher
Mohr Siebeck, P.O. Box 2040, D–72010 Tübingen.